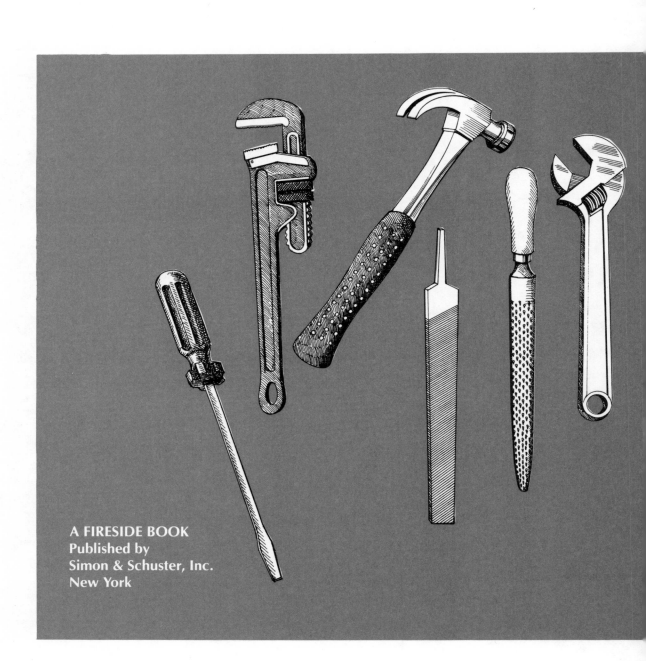

A FIRESIDE BOOK
Published by
Simon & Schuster, Inc.
New York

The SIMON AND SCHUSTER COMPLETE GUIDE to HOME REPAIR AND MAINTENANCE

BY Bernard Gladstone

Home Improvement Editor of *The New York Times*

First Fireside Edition, 1987

Published by Simon & Schuster, Inc.
Simon & Schuster Building
Rockefeller Center
1230 Avenue of the Americas
New York, New York 10020

FIRESIDE and colophon are registered trademarks of Simon & Schuster, Inc.

Designed by Irving Perkins Associates

Manufactured in the United States of America

10 9 8 7 6 5 4 3   Pbk.

Library of Congress Cataloging in Publication Data

Gladstone, Bernard.
  The Simon and Schuster complete guide to home repair
and maintenance.

  Includes index.
  1. Dwellings—Maintenance and repair—Amateurs'
manuals. I. Title. II. Title: Simon and Schuster
complete guide to home repair and maintenance. III.
Title: Complete guide to home repair and maintenance
TH4817.3.G56   1984   643.7   83-20409

ISBN 0-671-63940-4 Pbk.

Acknowledgments

I would like to thank all those at Simon and Schuster who worked so hard with me to complete this comprehensive homeowner's manual, including Fred Hills, the editor who first met with me to start this project and helped with the original planning to crystallize the concept; Don Hutter, who took over as editor and worked so diligently with me on the manuscript during the many months it took to edit and organize the contents for maximum effectiveness; Barbara Berson, who worked with Don during all this time, spending long hours in reading and helping to polish up the final manuscript; and Ted Johnson, who painstakingly copy-edited and corrected all the typographical errors that inevitably creep into such a lengthy volume.

I would also like to acknowledge the invaluable contribution made by Bob Strimban, the artist, who worked so many long hours, often under the stress of almost impossible deadlines, to complete all the drawings that were needed to make this book a truly useful and easy-to-understand guide.

INTRODUCTION   8

——— 1
TOOLS AND TECHNIQUES   11

——— 2
HARDWARE, FASTENERS, AND ADHESIVES   41

——— 3
BASIC CARPENTRY AND WOODWORKING TECHNIQUES   59

——— 4
SOLVING COMMON DOOR PROBLEMS   79

——— 5
REPAIRING WINDOWS   97

——— 6
INTERIOR WALLS AND CEILINGS   117

——— 7
REPAIRING FLOORS AND STAIRS   141

——— 8
PAINTING AND FINISHING   159

——— 9
ELECTRICAL REPAIRS   195

Contents

―――― 10
PLUMBING REPAIRS   223

―――― 11
HEATING AND COOLING   263

―――― 12
WORKING WITH CONCRETE AND MASONRY   283

―――― 13
ROOF REPAIRS   305

―――― 14
EXTERIOR REPAIRS AND MAINTENANCE   317

―――― 15
ENERGY-SAVING TECHNIQUES   335

―――― 16
HOME SECURITY   359

―――― 17
**DEALING WITH CONTRACTORS—FOR LARGE JOBS AND
MAJOR REMODELING**   375

―――― Appendix
FURNITURE FINISHING AND REFINISHING   381

INDEX   425

REGARDLESS OF whether you live in a house or in an apartment—and regardless of whether you own or rent your quarters—you will find this book a valuable reference guide that can save time, money, and frustration in the day-to-day maintenance and care of your home. You don't have to be a dyed-in-the-wool do-it-yourselfer, or even a very handy person: The answers you need to solve hundreds of home repair and maintenance problems are described and illustrated in this book.

Written to be understood even by the neophyte with no previous knowledge of tools, materials or techniques, *The Simon and Schuster Complete Guide to Home Maintenance and Repair* will also prove valuable to those who have had considerable experience doing their own work. For beyond those problems that continually crop up in day-to-day living, this book also describes how to tackle many repairs that the average homeowner or apartment dweller does not encounter often.

All of this information has been accumulated in the course of my thirty-five years in the home maintenance and improvement field—as a contractor and consultant, as well as a writer. In addition to serving as Home Improvement Editor of *The New York Times* for more than twenty-five of those years—a job that involves writing a nationally syndicated weekly column on home repair and improvement, as well as a weekly column on home repair for the Sunday regional sections of the *Times*—I have published hundreds of magazine articles and over a dozen books, all on various aspects of home repair and improvement.

While many other home repair books have come out over recent years, I know of no other as all-encompassing, or as complete and up-to-date. In this book I have tried to include not only everything you will need to know about maintaining your home or apartment, but also how to save money by doing nearly all repairs yourself.

Years of answering homeowners' letters from every part of the nation, as well as questions from audiences at lectures or on live radio and television shows, have taught me how to diagnose commonly encountered home repair and maintenance problems and to supply a clear answer in each case. Out of this background of experience I have tried to put this book together in such a way that every reader can easily locate whatever he or she needs to know—from a simple problem such as how to repair a squeaky floorboard to a major project such as putting up a new ceiling in a bedroom or kitchen.

Having discovered long ago that in trying to show how to make home repairs one good picture is often worth *more* than a thousand words, over six hundred detailed, easy-to-understand drawings and clear photographs supplement the text throughout. Unlike some volumes of this type, this one takes nothing for granted about how much knowledge or previous experience you may have. The text and illustrations are designed to give *all* the facts relating to each problem, not just an outline of the work that has to be done.

You learn what tools are required, the techniques involved, and the materials needed to get the job done right. Repair problems are presented as encountered in almost every type of house or apartment, regardless of design and structure.

There are no sections of technical information and data that you don't really need to know and that you would seldom, if ever, find use for. For

Introduction

example, the chapter on electrical repairs tells you all the practical basics of electricity and wiring. There are no paragraphs of complicated theory or detailed data that would be of little if any use to you when all you want to do is fix a broken lamp. In the same way, the chapter on concrete and masonry tells you everything you need to know about the repairs you are likely to tackle yourself; it doesn't attempt to provide a detailed description of how to pour your own concrete foundation when building a new house or addition. That would be a once-in-a-lifetime project that few homeowners would tackle themselves.

For neophytes, there are no technical terms in this book that cannot be understood, or that aren't immediately explained. This eliminates the need for a separate glossary, customary for books in this field yet inevitably an inconvenience requiring continual cross-reference. Also, the instructions for each job leave no gaps where it is assumed you already have some experience: Everything is fully and simply explained, or you are referred to another part of the book where the information you need can be found.

Those who are more experienced will still find a tremendous amount of valuable information, including unusual problems that even a veteran home handyman is not likely to have faced. And there are many shortcuts, time-savers, and other "tricks of the trade" that will save even the most experienced do-it-yourselfers time or money—sometimes both. Dozens of these are presented in the form of separate "sidebar" features—widely or generally applicable information that handily enables you to perform a common kind of repair or maintenance procedure.

Some things in the home service field have remained basically the same for many years, but there are many others that are constantly changing. New and improved tools and materials are continually being introduced, as well as products to do a better job, or techniques that will make a job quicker and easier to complete. Updating of such information is always needed in the columns, magazine articles, and books that I write. And this is why some books that were long considered "old standbys" are no longer valid as current guides.

Times have also changed in other ways. For example, nowadays it is not just homeowners who are interested in how-to information about repairs and maintenance—many of today's apartment-dwellers are just as eager for this kind of guidance. Why? Because not too many years ago all apartment dwellers were tenants who rented their living quarters; when something needed fixing they called the superintendent or building maintenance man in to take care of the problem. But these days an increasingly large percentage of apartment dwellers own their own apartments, or they own a share of the building they live in, so repairs are no longer free for the asking. Even for those who do rent, getting the building superintendent or building maintenance man to come in to take care of a minor breakdown is becoming exceedingly difficult; in many buildings if tenants want something fixed they will have to do it themselves, or else hire an outsider to get the job done.

Unfortunately, local handymen who are willing to come in and do small jobs for a modest hourly wage are a vanishing breed rarely found in most communities. Traditional "specialists," on the other hand (plumbers, electricians, etc.), often don't want to be bothered with small apartment jobs. As a result, apartment dwellers are also becoming do-it-yourselfers as they find it necessary—and often gratifying—to be able to take care of their own home repair problems.

Another sign of the changing times: Only a few short years ago few homeowners were seriously concerned with energy costs—homes were built with only a minimum amount of insulation, often with little or no caulking, and sometimes without weatherstripping around the windows. Nowadays the high cost of fuel and electricity, coupled with inflationary pressures in general, have made it essential—even patriotic—to cut down on energy waste. That is why this book includes a chapter devoted entirely to the subject of saving energy, explaining what you can do to make your house more energy-efficient and less expensive to heat and cool.

Although the book is a comprehensive how-to manual, it is not just for how-to enthusiasts. The hundreds of detailed illustrations, their fully explanatory captions, and the clearly written text work together to constitute a kind of education for those who want to hire a contractor for all or part of any job. Reading the chapter on plumbing repairs, for example, will enable you to become familiar with the various parts of the plumbing system so that you can understand what the plumber means when he speaks of the "drain and waste" system, or when he suggests doing something to improve your heating system. You will be better able to answer him intelligently, and thus to discuss and decide what needs to be done.

This ability to understand and then communicate with the contractor will not only make things easier for both of you, it will often save you money, inasmuch as an unscrupulous contractor is less likely to try to pull the wool over your eyes if he immediately sees that you know what he is talking about. Nor are you as likely to be taken in by a fast-talking high-pressure salesman, or duped by misleading claims. For this reason a separate, comprehensive chapter is included on dealing with contractors. It will tell you how to protect yourself against dishonest or unethical contractors and servicemen, and it will give you all the guidance needed to avoid misunderstandings—before you sign on the dotted line or agree to a price for the job.

And finally, there is an unusually long appendix, on furniture finishing and repair. This amounts to another complete book within the book. In itself, it can save you more than the cost of this volume with just one of the many quick and easy furniture fix-ups it describes. For with prices for new furniture higher than ever before, more and more people are fixing up traditional older pieces to give them a new lease on life—for sentimental reasons as well as for financial saving.

The information included in this appendix tells you everything you need to know about repairing and refinishing furniture—including how to strip off old finishes down to the bare wood; how to touch up and repair minor blemishes without refinishing; how to work with varnishes, enamels, and other finishes (even how to do old-world French polish finishing); how to repair chairs and tables that are shaky; and how to apply "novelty" finishes such as antique and gilded finishes.

In every case the techniques described require only those commonly available materials to be found in local stores everywhere, nothing esoteric or hard to find. The emphasis is on modern, easy-to-use products that will still give you old-fashioned quality—but without all of the hard and tedious work that our ancestors had to go through to get the same results.

There is even a special "bonus" section in this appendix devoted to unfinished furniture—an economical alternative that many people find worthwhile when additional furniture is needed. This section includes pointers on what to look for when buying unpainted furniture, and it tells you how you can finish "furniture in the raw" to make it look as if professionally finished at the factory.

To sum up, then, this book is an attempt to supply a simple but complete answer to every question readers have asked me over the years about their home repair and maintenance problems. It was conceived to combine all those answers in one volume—in addition to supplying a wealth of additional background information. This, combined with the organization of the book into usable, easy-to-find sections devoted to specific subjects, will allow any reader to find the answers to his or her particular home repair and maintenance problems.

Bernard Gladstone

Chapter **1**

Tools and Techniques

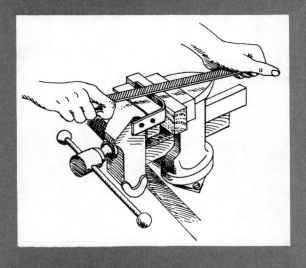

A typical small home workshop with plywood workbench

THE FIRST time you try to tackle even the simplest of repair jobs around the house you will discover that you need a basic assortment of hand tools—with perhaps one or two power tools added. As you gain more experience and acquire more confidence, you will become more ambitious and take on larger jobs around the house, and your collection of tools will start to grow and become more diversified.

Especially for those who have had little or no experience working with tools, selecting the right ones can be a problem at first. There are some people who advocate that the neophyte buy tools only as the need for each one arises. It is true that in this way one avoids spending money needlessly, but there are certain tools that almost everyone will need fairly frequently, and without which you may find yourself stuck if an emergency develops at night or on a weekend when the stores are closed.

This does not mean that you have to go into your local hardware store and stock up on all the tools you see on display—there actually are many tools that you can forget about until they are needed. But you should start out with a reasonably complete assortment of basic tools. This assortment may, of course, vary with how much experience you have had and with the kind of projects or repair jobs you plan to tackle.

When shopping for any tool—regardless of whether you are looking for a simple pair of pliers or a complete assortment of specialized plumbing and electrical tools—there is one rule you should always follow: Buy only good-quality tools that are made by reputable manufacturers and stay away from "bargain" tools that are priced well below recognized name brands.

There are good reasons for this caution. Not only will a good tool last longer—and thus actually cost you less in the long run—it will also make jobs faster, easier, and less frustrating to complete. In addition, a good-quality tool that is properly maintained is also safer, being less likely to slip or break down while in use.

HAND TOOLS

Here is a discussion of the tools most often needed in a basic tool kit, along with some pointers on how to use them and some information about what each tool is most often used for:

Hammers

The most popular type of hammer, and probably the only one most beginners will need, is a conventional carpenter's claw hammer. Designed both for driving nails and for pulling them out, claw hammers come in various sizes, with heads that weigh from about 8 to 20 ounces. Generally speaking, a medium-weight hammer with a 12-ounce or 16-ounce head will be right for most home jobs. The claws on the hammer may be either straight or curved, but you'll probably find curved claws more useful for pulling nails (straight-claw hammers are preferred by professional carpenters for ripping joints apart).

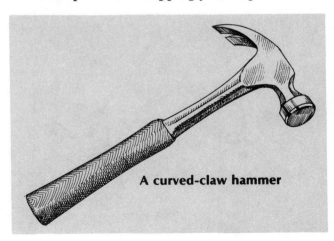

A curved-claw hammer

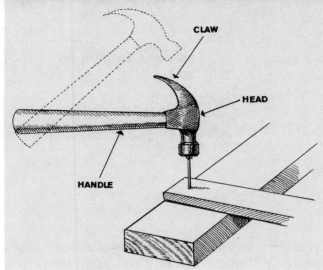

CLAW

HEAD

HANDLE

Regardless of weight, the hammer should be well balanced, with a nice "feel" when you lift it. The hammer head should be made of polished steel and have a slightly crowned or bell-shaped face. The handle should be securely fastened to the head with wedges to keep it from slipping off, and it should provide a firm but comfortable grip.

When using a hammer for driving nails you should hold it near the end (not up near the head) and swing the hammer with your forearm, not just by flexing your wrist. Try to aim your blows so that the face of the hammer always comes down squarely on the head of the nail, and concentrate on driving the nail in with a number of medium to light blows, rather than one or two very hard blows.

When using a claw hammer to pull nails, it's often advisable to put a small block of wood under the head of the hammer after you have pulled the nail partway out—especially if it is a long nail. The block of wood provides extra leverage so that the claws will continue to pull straight up instead of sideways. The nail will then come out more easily, without bending, and

there will be less chance that the hammer head will mar the surface of the wood.

Although a medium-size claw hammer will probably take care of 95 percent of your needs, another type of hammer that often comes in handy is a mallet. Its head may be made of wood or plastic (or have plastic facing on a wooden head), which makes it better than a metal hammer for pounding on the handle of a wood chisel, forcing pieces of wood together when assembling tight-fitting wood joints, bending or shaping sheet metal, driving wood dowels into holes without splitting or mashing, and similar chores; it minimizes the chance of damaging the surface of the material you are working on.

If you decide to do any metalwork that calls for heavy pounding on a cold chisel (a chisel that cuts through metal or masonry), or for shaping metal parts, then you'll probably want a heavier hammer with a specially hardened head, one not as likely to chip as a claw hammer. A machinist's ball-peen hammer is used for pounding on cold chisels or masonry-cutting chisels and to work sheet metal, while a small sledgehammer may be needed for driving in masonry fasteners or for other heavy-duty pounding jobs.

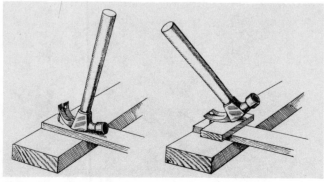

Extracting a long nail with a claw hammer. To avoid bending nail use block of wood as at right.

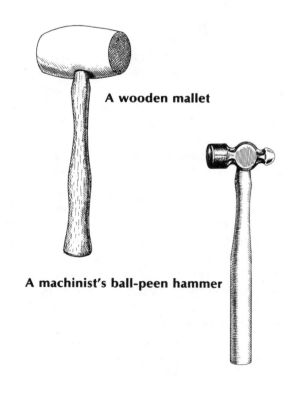

A wooden mallet

A machinist's ball-peen hammer

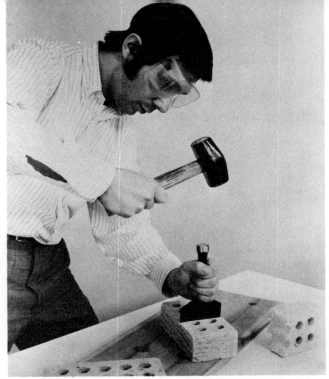

A small sledgehammer is useful for masonry work

Screwdrivers

Screwdrivers can be bought with various types of blades, depending on the types of screw head they are designed to fit. There are specialized variations that are widely used in industry, but for home use you are likely to need only two basic blade types—the conventional flat-blade or straight-blade screwdriver that fits ordinary slotted screws, and the Phillips-type screwdriver that has an X-shaped blade to fit into Phillips-head screws (cross-slotted screws that are widely used in furniture, appliances, and other such manufactured equipment).

Screwdrivers also come in a wide range of sizes that vary both in the length of the blade and in the width of the blade's tip. You don't have to

start out with one of every size and style, but you should begin with at least the following:

1. Two flat-blade screwdrivers of medium length, one with a blade about ¼ inch wide, and another with a blade about ³⁄₁₆ inch wide.

2. A very small "jeweler's-type" screwdriver with a small flat blade to loosen or tighten the very small screws that are often found on instrument panels, electrical appliances, and similar items. These screwdrivers can be purchased individually or in small compact sets in a handy plastic pouch.

3. Two Phillips-type screwdrivers, one with a medium-size blade and one with a smaller blade.

4. Two "stubby" screwdrivers with very short handles and blades—one with a flat blade of medium width and the other with a Phillips-type blade of medium size. No more than 2 or 3 inches long overall, these screwdrivers are often essential for reaching into narrow spaces or tight corners where no ordinary-size screwdriver will fit. You won't need them every day, or necessarily on every project, but when you do need them nothing else will do.

After you have acquired and used this basic assortment of screwdrivers, you will want other more specialized variations for certain jobs.

For reaching into places that are so cramped or narrow that even a stubby screwdriver won't fit, you will need an offset screwdriver. This type has a short blade that projects out at right angles to the handle or body of the screwdriver. Offset screwdrivers come in two basic styles: a solid L-shaped steel bar with a fixed blade at each end, and a ratcheting type that has two blades at the same end projecting in opposite directions. The ratcheting feature makes it easy to swing the

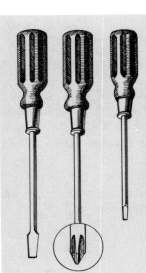

Three basic screwdrivers (left to right): **medium flat-blade screwdriver, Phillips-type screwdriver, and small flat-blade screwdriver**

Two "stubby" screwdrivers, flat-blade and Phillips-head

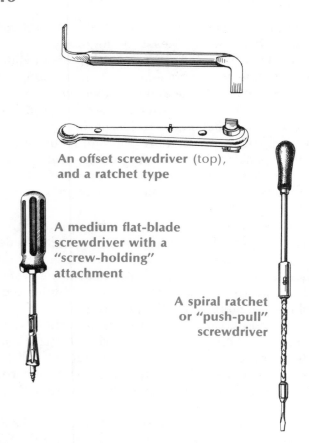

An offset screwdriver (top), and a ratchet type

A medium flat-blade screwdriver with a "screw-holding" attachment

A spiral ratchet or "push-pull" screwdriver

Some Tips on Using Screwdrivers

Screwdrivers come in many different sizes to fit the many sizes of screw heads. For maximum driving power the blade should fill the slot in the head of the screws as snugly as possible—especially with conventional, flat-blade screwdrivers. (Phillips-type drivers have a bit more room for error.)

The blade should fill the slot of the screw in width as well as in thickness. If you select a blade that is wider than the head of the screw, it is likely to gouge or scratch the surface of the wood when the screw is driven home. If, on the other hand, you use a blade that is too narrow, you won't be able to apply the leverage needed to drive the screw down tight (or to free it up if you are trying to loosen it). You are also very likely to damage the screwdriver blade or the screw head, even both.

It is important to remember that screwdrivers are designed only for removing screws or driving them home. They should not be used as pry bars, chisels, scrapers, or punches. Such use will invariably damage the blade, and could render it almost useless for turning screws. When a blade does get nicked or worn, touching it up with a file will often restore its square edge.

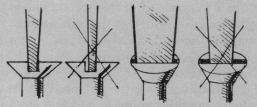

Proper and improper fits for a flat-blade screwdriver in the slot of a screw

handle in short arcs when you are working in really cramped quarters.

Another handy special-purpose screwdriver is the "screw-holding" type. Its most popular version has spring jaws that snap over the head of the screw when the blade of the screwdriver fits into the slot. This simplifies the job of starting screws in tight places where you cannot reach in with your other hand to hold the screw. It can also be used to thread bolts into holes when you cannot hold the fastener in position.

On tackling projects that require driving a great many screws home, a spiral ratchet or "push" screwdriver can be a real worksaver. With these you merely push the handle down to rotate the blade, and a spring in the handle brings it back up. Adjusting a lever changes the blade's direction from forward (for driving screws) to reverse (for taking them out). The ratchet can also be disengaged to lock the blade so you can use the screwdriver like an ordinary one.

Pliers

Like screwdrivers, pliers come in a great many sizes and styles. You won't need all of them, but you cannot get by for long with just a single pair of all-purpose pliers. Every toolbox will need at least two or three pairs for a variety of different purposes. Here are the most widely used versions around the home, as well as some pointers on when and where each will be most handy.

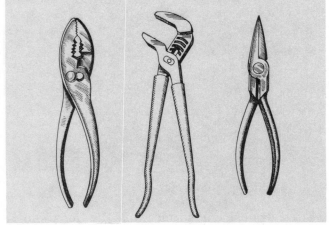

Slip-joint pliers. Channel-type pliers. Needle-nose pliers.

Slip-joint pliers are probably the most useful, and are the first ones most people acquire. The jaws are serrated and are curved, with the tips slightly rounded. The pivot bolt is of slip-joint construction so that you can set the handles in two positions: a standard position for gripping average-size objects, and another that allows the jaws to open much wider so they can grip wider objects. The handles in this position are much closer together, so you cannot apply as much pressure and the grip won't be quite as strong as in the "normal" position.

Channel-type pliers are sometimes referred to as water-pump pliers or mechanic's pliers. These versatile models have angled jaws and are equipped with a series of grooves at the pivot point which permit the jaws to be set for a range of different-size openings. Available in various sizes from 6 to 18 inches in length, they are most generally useful in the 8-inch or 10-inch lengths. The angled jaws make them especially handy in plumbing work, to reach in to grab pipes and packing nuts where ordinary pliers would not fit. The handles are designed to apply greater leverage and turning power than is possible with an ordinary pair of straight slip-joint pliers.

Needle-nose pliers, as the name implies, have long tapered jaws that are ideal for reaching into tight corners or for handling small-diameter objects and tiny parts. Some models also have built-in wire cutters in the jaws—a handy feature for electrical jobs (and indeed needle-nose pliers are often required when working with wires, to bend loops at the ends and to pull wires around terminals). They come in various sizes or lengths, but as a rule you will find a pair 5 to 6 inches in length most useful, especially with built-in wire cutters.

Diagonal cutting pliers are often referred to simply as "dikes." These are strictly cutting tools for snipping wires or for neatly clipping off small brads, nails, and staples. Their very sharp jaws cut right out to the tip, so you can clip wires or brads flush with the surface and can reach into places where the cutting jaws on the side of regular pliers would not fit. With practice, these pliers can also be used for stripping insulation off electrical cables, though care is required to avoid nicking the wire.

Lineman's pliers, also called electrician's pliers (when the handles are insulated) or engineer's pliers, have straight jaws that are lightly serrated, have blunt, bevel-nosed ends, and have built-in wire cutters on one side. They provide a firmer and stronger grip than conventional slip-joint pliers on flat surfaces and are widely used for working with sheet metal, as well as in electrical work.

Locking pliers. Often referred to as a plier-wrench because it can perform many of the functions of a wrench as well as those of pliers, a pair of locking pliers is an extremely versatile tool. Its uses overlap those of an adjustable wrench, slip-joint pliers, and heavy-duty cutting pliers, although unlike ordinary pliers the jaws on this tool can be locked or clamped firmly onto the work to grip securely until manually released. The amount of tension applied to the jaws can be adjusted by turning a knurled screw or knob in the end of the handle.

Diagonal cutting pliers. Lineman's (or electrician's) pliers. Locking pliers.

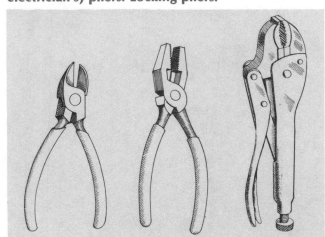

The compound lever action used for clamping pressure permits you to apply tremendous force to the jaws—for cutting as well as for gripping—and the locking action makes it practical to use this tool as a small portable vise, as well as an efficient clamp. The type with curved serrated jaws can also be used as a pipe wrench or for grasping round objects that an ordinary wrench could not grasp tightly.

Locking pliers come with either straight or curved jaws, and with or without built-in wire cutters near the pivot joint. They also come in various lengths and sizes, as well as in a wide range of specialized models for unusual commercial or industrial uses.

MEASURING AND LEVELING TOOLS

There are very few repair or improvement projects that don't require some kind of measuring, leveling, or squaring up in order to align parts correctly.

Rulers. For measuring, you will need some type of fairly accurate ruler. The most convenient for the average do-it-yourselfer is a flexible steel tape that rolls in and out of a case. Such tapes come in sizes that extend anywhere from 6 to 50 feet, but an 8-foot or 10-foot tape should prove adequate for most projects. The best ones have extra-wide blades which make it easy to keep them extended, vertically or horizontally, when working alone. Any such tape can be used for inside measurements between surfaces by adding the case's width (usually 2 inches) to the measured reading when the back of the case is

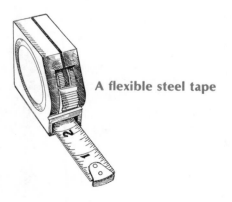
A flexible steel tape

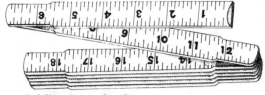
A folding wood ruler

butted against one surface and the hook end is pressed against the other surface.

Folding wood rulers are preferred by many carpenters because they can be extended across open spaces and wide openings, but they are generally limited to 6 feet in length and, unless carefully handled, can be easily damaged or broken. The better-quality models have a short extendable brass leg that slides out from one end for accurate inside measurements; also, their hinges or joints work more smoothly, without excess play or wobble, than those of cheaper models.

Squares

Squares are used to assemble pieces with proper right angles, as well as to mark pieces of lumber for an accurate square cut. At least one square will be needed for most construction projects. Squares usually have inches marked along the blade, so that they can also be used as rulers for small measurements, and they often have miter gauge marks for 45- and 90-degree angles.

The try square is the most popular square for ordinary woodworking. It consists of a metal

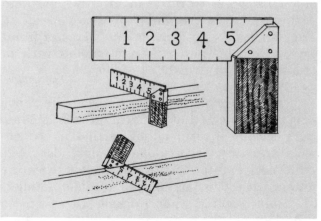
A try square, used to measure 90-degree right angles and 45-degree angles

blade with a wooden or plastic handle securely riveted to it at right angles. The handle, being thicker than the blade, can be butted against the edge of the lumber while the blade lies flat on the surface, as illustrated. Most try squares have a 45-degree bevel at the end of the handle next to the blade, and with this beveled edge pressed against the work the blade can also be used to draw a 45-degree angle—especially useful for marking miter cuts.

A combination square is a much more versatile square for all-round use on many different types of projects. Its blade is an accurate steel rule (usually 10 to 12 inches long) with a movable sliding head that can be locked anywhere along its length. The tool is used in basically the same way as a try square, but its longer, more adjustable blade, coupled with its ability to measure 45- and 90-degree angles, makes it possible also to use the tool as an accurate depth gauge for measuring mortised holes or other recesses.

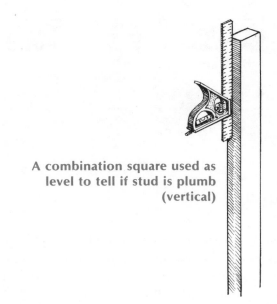

A combination square used as level to tell if stud is plumb (vertical)

In addition, combination squares have a built-in bubble level on the handle for leveling horizontal surfaces, or making sure vertical surfaces are absolutely plumb (you hold the blade against the vertical surface and read the level on the handle). Most combination squares also have a built-in metal scriber for scratching accurate lines on wood, metal, or plastic surfaces.

A carpenter's steel square is very useful for large construction projects, particularly when cutting up large sheets of plywood. It is also called a rafter or framing square. It is usually 24 inches long on one leg and 16 inches on the other, with inch markings on both the inner and outer edges of each blade. These squares are handy not only for drawing square lines on larger pieces of lumber and paneling; professional carpenters use them also for marking angles on roof rafters when constructing hip roofs or dormers.

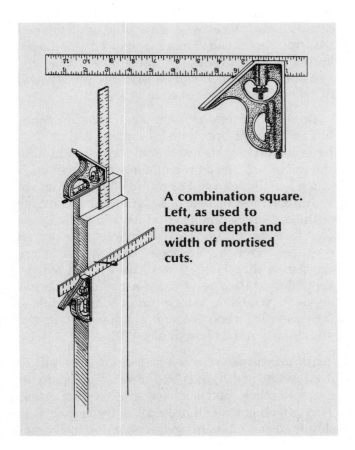

A combination square. Left, as used to measure depth and width of mortised cuts.

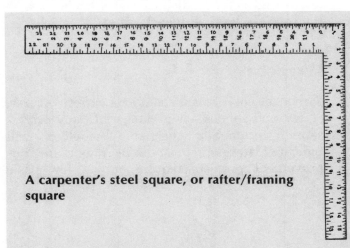

A carpenter's steel square, or rafter/framing square

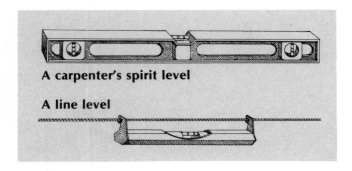

A carpenter's spirit level

A line level

Levels

Spirit levels (also called bubble levels) may be made of wood, metal, or plastic and come in various lengths—from pocket-size models only a few inches long to professional models that may be 4 to 6 feet in length. As a rule, a 24-inch carpenter's level, equipped with two or three sets of bubbles, will be adequate for most home jobs. One set of bubbles is used for checking the level of horizontal surfaces, while another set at right angles to the first checks vertical edges to make certain they are plumb. Some models have a third set of bubble vials for measuring 45-degree angles.

A line level is a miniature version of a carpenter's spirit level. Usually made of metal and only about 3 inches long, it has a single vial or bubble in the center and small hooks at either end which permit hanging it from a tightly stretched line. Since the level then reads whether or not the string is level, and since the string can be almost any length that can be stretched tight without sagging, the line level is used in place of a regular level when a long span is involved. For example, a line level is ideal for checking the slope of a long driveway or a length of rain gutter, as well as for lining up a row of fence posts so the tops are level with each other.

Wrenches

Wrenches come in a tremendous variety of sizes, styles, and shapes—as a glance into any professional automobile mechanic's toolbox will indicate. However, most home repair and improvement projects require only a few basic types for tightening and loosening common-size nuts and bolts, and for gripping pipes and other round objects.

The adjustable open-end wrench is usually the first wrench most people acquire. It has one movable jaw and one fixed jaw and comes in various sizes—from as short as 6 inches to as long as 18 to 24 inches. The most useful sizes for home use would be one small model, 6 to 8 inches long, and a larger one, 10 to 12 inches long. These have worm-screw adjustments that enable you to set the size of the opening between the jaws. When setting the opening it is best to place the wrench over the nut or bolt head, then turn the screw until a snug fit is obtained. Adjustable wrenches do not grip as firmly as fixed wrenches, so you have to be more careful to avoid slipping. Make sure you check the adjustment periodically to see if it has loosened.

Open-end wrenches, which are nonadjustable, are a good investment for those who plan to do even a moderate amount of mechanical work. These provide a stronger grip than adjustable wrenches, and since they are less bulky they will fit into tight places where an adjustable wrench will not. Open-end wrenches can be purchased individually or in sets, and they have a different-size opening at each end so that one wrench will fit two different sizes of nuts or bolts.

Box-end wrenches are also nonadjustable, but differ from open-end wrenches in that they have completely enclosed jaws that wrap around the nut or bolt head for a much firmer grip that is much less likely to slip or round off the corners of a stubborn nut or bolt head. Another advantage of the box-end wrench is that its thin-walled jaws enable it to fit into places inaccessible to an open-end wrench. However, box wrenches are limited to those jobs where the wrench can be slipped over the top of the nut or bolt (whereas open-end wrenches can be slid in from the side—for example, when loosening a hex nut in the middle of a rod or length of pipe).

Combination wrenches consist of a single fixed wrench with open-end jaws at one end and a box wrench of the same size at the other. Though a box wrench provides a firmer grip, it is slower to use than an open-end wrench. So me-

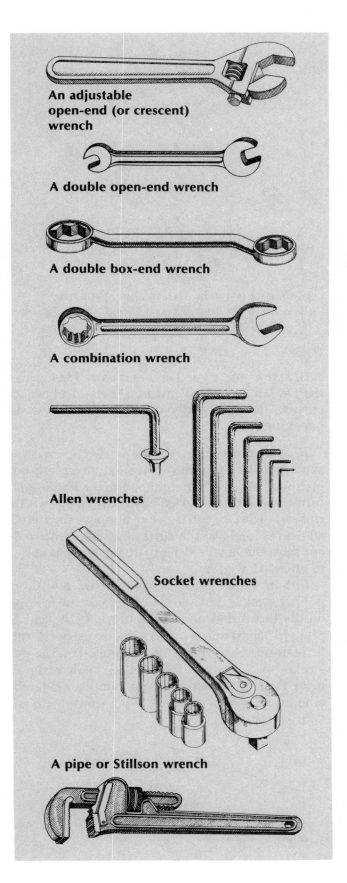

An adjustable
open-end (or crescent)
wrench

A double open-end wrench

A double box-end wrench

A combination wrench

Allen wrenches

Socket wrenches

A pipe or Stillson wrench

chanics like these combination wrenches—they can start tightening with the open-end wrench, then flip the tool over for final tightening with the box wrench.

Allen wrenches should be in almost every home tool kit. Unlike conventional wrenches, these do not have jaws that lock onto the outside of the fastener—they fit inside a hollow in the head of the screw or bolt. An Allen wrench is actually a hexagonal length of steel rod bent into an L shape so that you can use either end while the other end serves as a handle to provide leverage for turning. They come in various sizes or diameters to fit hex-shaped recesses in setscrews and locking screws on tools, appliances, toys, and other household items. You probably won't need these wrenches very often, but they're indispensable when you're making repairs or adjustments on appliances or tools, because manufacturers make wide use of Allen-head setscrews in assembling their equipment.

Socket wrenches are usually purchased in sets of one or two handles with an assortment of individual sockets, each designed to fit over a single size of nut or bolt head. Widely preferred by professional mechanics for their speed of action and versatility, socket wrenches are most often used with a ratchet-type handle that makes fast work of loosening or tightening nuts and bolts. A wide range of extension holders and angled handles are also available for reaching into awkward corners where no other type of wrench will fit.

Pipe wrenches (also called Stillson wrenches) are adjustable wrenches with serrated, slightly curved jaws, one movable and one fixed. They come in various lengths or sizes, and are designed so that the more force you apply on the handle, the more pressure the jaws will apply. For most plumbing jobs, especially when dealing with threaded pipe and fittings, you'll need two pipe wrenches. The reason for two wrenches is that you'll almost always need one to turn the pipe and another to hold the fitting or coupling into which it fits. As a rule, one 10-inch and one 12-inch model will be adequate for most work, but for large-diameter galvanized pipes you may want a 15- to 18-inch wrench.

Some Pointers on Using Wrenches

With any type of wrench—fixed or adjustable—always make sure the head of the bolt or nut is clean and dry and that there is no grease or oil on the jaws of the wrench. The jaws should fit snugly with a minimum amount of play.

Always position the wrench so that you will be pushing the handle in the direction of the open jaws, as shown in the drawing. Try not to push or pull the wrench handle in the opposite direction, since this will often result in the jaws slipping off the work or sliding open when a great deal of pressure must be applied. Repeated slipping will not only round off and eventually ruin the nut or bolt head (thus making it almost impossible to get a firm grip), it can also cause skinned knuckles or other injuries.

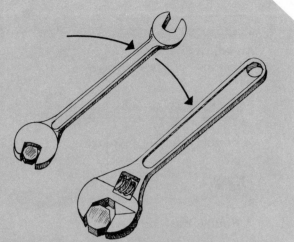

Using a wrench. Always apply pressure in the direction the jaws face.

Handsaws

The first handsaw most people will buy is a conventional carpenter's crosscut saw 24 to 26 inches in length. These vary in coarseness depending on the number of teeth (points) per inch. Most have from 7 to 12 teeth per inch. A 7-point saw (7 teeth per inch) will cut faster than a 10- or 12-point saw, but it will also leave a rougher edge; 10- or 12-point saws give a finer cut, but are slower-working. Generally speaking, blades with 8 to 10 points per inch are about right for most home jobs.

Crosscut saws, as the name implies, are primarily designed for cutting across the grain, although they can also be used for ripping (cutting parallel to the grain) if you don't mind working a little harder. Professional carpenters and serious woodworkers usually keep both a crosscut and a ripsaw in their boxes, but most people can get by

easily with just a good crosscut saw. This is also the saw to use when cutting sheets of plywood, particle board, hardboard, and similar wood panel materials.

Ripsaws are about the same size as crosscut saws, but they generally have only 5½ teeth per inch and the teeth are shaped more like miniature chisels. The most efficient way to cut with a ripsaw is with its cutting edge at approximately a 60-degree angle to the surface, while with crosscut saws the most efficient cutting angle is closer to about 45 degrees.

In both cases, start the cut with a few short pulling strokes, but thereafter all cutting is done on the forward stroke of the blade. If the saw is properly sharpened and the teeth properly set, little or no pressure should be applied on the upstroke—use your arm to guide the blade and pull it up. On the downstroke, apply only a moderate amount of pressure; don't bear down with all your strength.

A carpenter's hand saw

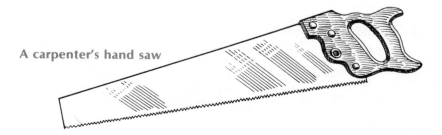

Starting a cut with a crosscut saw; note use of thumb knuckle to guide initial strokes.

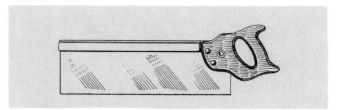

A backsaw, usually used with a miter box

A keyhole saw (also called a compass saw) is often used for cutting in tight places where an ordinary crosscut saw will not fit, or for cutting openings in the middle of a panel. Its narrow, tapered blade can fit through a small starting hole drilled beforehand, and it can also cut curves. Some models come with only one blade, but others, often referred to as a utility saw set, come with three or four interchangeable blades in different sizes and types, one of which is usually a metal cutting blade.

A coping saw is the hand tool you will want for cutting intricate curves and patterns in thin wood, plastic, or soft metal. It's named for its use in "coping," or trimming, moldings to fit them into corners instead of mitering them (see page 77).

The backsaw is another handy tool most often used for accurate cutting of moldings in conjunction with a miter box. This saw has a rigid steel back to keep it from flexing and usually has 12 or 13 teeth per inch for a smooth, splinter-free cut. It is used to cut moldings and trim pieces to length, as well as for mitering and making joints. Most models are shorter than a conventional saw.

A hacksaw cuts metal, and in addition to saws for cutting wood, every tool kit will need at least one metal-cutting saw. The hacksaw has a steel frame that accepts replaceable blades which are available in a range of coarse and fine teeth. Equipped with the right blade, a hacksaw can cut almost any of the metals normally encountered around the house. It is also handy for cutting pipe and tubing when doing plumbing work. A

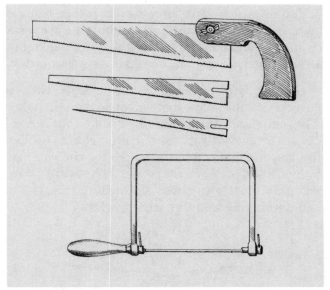

A utility saw set, with interchangeable blades. A coping saw, for cutting fine curves.

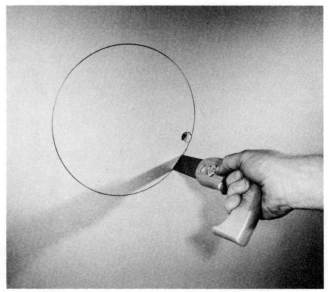

Cutting a circle with a keyhole saw, starting from a predrilled hole

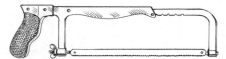

A hacksaw, for cutting metal

Cutting out a dado or notch with a wood chisel

blade with fine teeth is used for cutting light-gauge, thin stock such as sheet metal or thin-wall tubing. A blade with coarser teeth is better for cutting thicker metal, including rods, bolts, and angle iron. Like the woodworking saws, hacksaws do their cutting on the forward stroke, so you should get in the habit of lifting up slightly on the backward stroke. Otherwise the teeth will dull very rapidly. For maximum efficiency and accuracy, a hacksaw should be operated with two hands—one holding the handle, the other gripping the front end of the frame. Make sure the blade is fully tensioned by tightening the wing nut as much as you can by hand (using pliers on this wing nut can exert too much pressure, for the blades break easily).

Chisels

Most wood chisels nowadays come with tough plastic handles that no longer split or "mushroom" when struck with a hammer or mallet, but it's still a good idea to use a plastic-, wood-, or rubber-faced mallet instead of a conventional steel hammer to pound on the chisel handle.

For fine trimming, a well-sharpened wood chisel can serve without a hammer—one hand guides the front end of the blade while the other pushes on the handle to force the blade along.

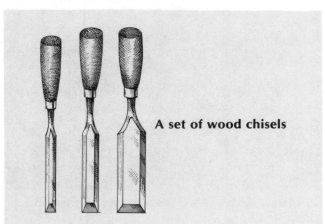

A set of wood chisels

The chisel should cut with a paring action, rather than the chopping or splitting action imparted by a hammer or mallet. On most jobs, such as when cutting mortises (recesses in the wood) for snug-fitting joints, you will use both methods—first hammering on the chisel handle for the preliminary roughing out, then switching to hand chiseling for the final trimming.

Most wood chisels are from 8 to 10 inches in length and have a blade that is beveled along the sides as well as on the cutting edge. For use in tight places, butt chisels are a couple of inches shorter, but only the larger hardware stores that cater to professional carpenters normally stock them.

You'll want two or three wood chisels, from ½ inch to 1 inch in width. You can buy these in sets (½ inch, ¾ inch, and 1 inch) which are packed in a handy plastic pouch, or separately as needed.

Gouges are basically wood chisels with a curved cutting edge instead of a straight edge. They are used for trimming inside concave recesses or curved pieces, but are seldom needed for the ordinary repairs made by the average homeowner or do-it-yourselfer. They will prove valuable mostly to those seriously interested in cabinetmaking and fine woodworking.

A popular style of wood gouge

Sharpening Chisels, Plane Blades, and Knives

Chisels and similar blades with sharp, knifelike cutting edges can be sharpened on a grinding wheel or whetstone (also called an oilstone). As a rule, use a grinding wheel only if the cutting edge is very dull or nicked; otherwise most of your blade sharpening should be done with a whetstone or oilstone.

You can buy grinding wheels in various grades of coarseness for use in a conventional bench grinder, but for sharpening you will need only the finest grade of abrasive wheel. A tool rest supports the blade at a uniform angle against the face of the wheel. You should wear goggles to protect your eyes.

You must adjust the tool rest so that the blade's beveled edge meets the wheel's edge at the proper angle. The adjustment is simpler to make while the wheel is not rotating—looking at it from the side, you can tell when you have the correct angle. Wait till the wheel is turning at full speed before bringing the edge of the blade in contact, and move the chisel or plane blade steadily from side to side while you press lightly against the wheel. Inspect the edge frequently to avoid overgrinding or "burning" the edge.

When you are using an oilstone or whetstone, the blade's beveled cutting edge must be flat against the surface of the stone—if anything, the angle should be just slightly steeper than the bevel in order to ensure good contact between the stone and the cutting edge. Spread some light machine oil over the surface of the stone before starting, then hold the blade so your fingertips are close to its edge. Move it back and forth in a slightly oval or elliptical pattern while keeping the blade angle constant.

Final sharpening with an oilstone, using a back-and-forth motion

Many stones have a medium grit on one side and a fine grit on the other. These are ideal for chisel and plane blades; you start on the rougher side, then hone on the very fine side. After the beveled edge has been sharpened, turn the blade over and hone its flat side lightly to remove burrs, again rubbing in an elliptical or oval motion over the face of the stone.

Knife blades are sharpened in much the same way, except that you hold them at about a 25-degree angle to the surface and move them across the stone with an angular slicing motion. Unlike chisel and plane blades, knife blades are sharpened equally on both sides. Alternate your strokes, making five or six passes over the stone on one side of the blade, then flipping the blade over and making an equal number of passes on the other side. Old-timers prefer to finish off by stropping on a heavy leather belt or strip of thick leather in order to remove any fine wire edges that remain. This gives the blade an ultrafine, razor-sharp edge.

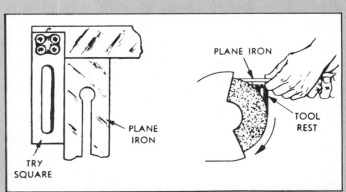

(Left) **A try square is a quick and convenient way to test if the edge of a plane blade is square.** (Right) **Use a grinder to sharpen plane blade when it isn't square.**

Pointers on Using Wood Chisels

Generally speaking, a chisel is used with the beveled side of the blade up (facing the part to be trimmed off or removed), but it can also be used with the beveled side down, for thin paring cuts or fine trimming where you don't want the blade to dig in too deep.

Whether you're working the chisel with your hands or tapping on the handle with a hammer, try to remove wood in small amounts and not dig too deep.

When cutting parallel to the grain, be careful that the blade doesn't try to follow the grain if it slopes away from you—this can cause it to dig in much deeper than you want it to, and leads to splitting. When cutting recesses or mortises, always do the job in stages, making a series of shallow cuts rather than trying to cut the full depth at one time.

Cold chisels are made of a single piece of specially hardened steel and are primarily used for cutting away metal that can't be removed in any other manner—chopping off a nut, or the head of a rusty bolt or rivet. They come in many sizes with various-width blades, with some of the wider models used primarily for cutting bricks, cement blocks, and other forms of masonry. These chisels should be struck with a small sledgehammer or special impact-type hammer, rather than with a conventional carpenter's hammer. (An impact hammer is a special type that is designed to eliminate rebound or "bounce-back.") The hard steel of the chisel handle is likely to chip or deform the polished head of a conventional hammer.

A cold chisel

Wood Planes

A plane shapes or trims wood, and gives it a smooth finish when fitting to precise dimensions. It consists basically of a sharp, chisel-like blade that is held firmly at about a 45-degree angle to the base of the tool, with its cutting edge sticking down through a slot in the base. How deeply the blade projects determines how much wood it will shave off with each stroke, and this can be controlled precisely with a depth-adjustment knob.

Although wood planes come in a wide range of sizes and types, most do-it-yourselfers will need only two types: a small block plane and a bench plane or jack plane. Block planes vary from about 4 to 6 inches in length and can be easily worked with one hand. Bench planes or jack planes run from 7 to 10 inches in length and require two hands to work properly—one on the handle at the rear, and the other on the extra knob on or near the front end.

Block planes are small, one-hand planes that are handy for trimming moldings, shelf edges, and other pieces of wood where only small surfaces are involved. The one-handed operation can be an advantage, particularly when you have to hold the wood with your other hand. The blade on this type of plane is mounted at a much lower angle—usually 15 to 20 degrees, instead of 45 degrees—so it is less likely to dig in when trimming end grain and narrow strips. It is particularly useful for planing end grain, because it is less likely to cause splintering.

Jack planes and **bench planes** have a longer base that allows for more accurate work, since the longer the base of the plane, the less likely it is to follow dips or hollows on the surface. For really accurate work on long boards, still longer planes that measure up to 24 inches are also available. Called jointer planes, these models

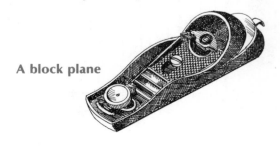

A block plane

Pointers on Using Wood Planes

When using any wood plane, it is important that you adjust the depth of cut carefully before starting, preferably by experimenting on some scrap pieces of wood to see if the blade digs in. Also, make sure the blade is sharp and free of nicks. With a properly sharpened blade the shavings should come out in long continuous spirals (except when trimming end grain) and should be of relatively uniform thickness.

Hold the plane at a slight angle to the direction of travel, and try to work with the grain—that is, with any angle in the grain running up and away from you. There will be less likelihood then of the blade digging in or snagging as it tries to follow the grain down into the wood—you'll feel the difference quickly if you merely reverse the direction of travel and plane from the other end.

As you begin each stroke, apply more pressure to the knob at the front end of the plane to keep the back end from dipping. As the back end comes onto the surface, gradually shift pressure so that you are bearing down harder on the handle at the back end. Be careful to avoid dipping the front end of the plane as it goes out past the edge of the board. If you are planing end grain, work from either side toward the middle to avoid splitting off or splintering the edge of the wood. If you must plane past an edge, clamp a piece of scrap wood snug against that edge; splintering will then occur on the scrap piece, rather than on the piece you are working on.

When using a plane on end grain, clamp scrap piece against end to avoid splintering.

A bench plane

provide maximum accuracy when trimming doors and long boards, but most homeowners will get by easily with a 10-inch bench plane (technically classified as a smoothing plane).

Files and Rasps

Files come in an almost unlimited range of sizes, shapes, and styles, with many of highly specialized design that will be of little or no concern to the home handyman who does not get involved in modelmaking or some similar craft.

Broadly speaking, files are classified by their shape or cross section—flat, half-round, round, triangular, square, or diamond-shaped. The most useful metal files are flat, round, or triangular. In wood rasps, the half-round style is most practical.

A good selection of files and rasps

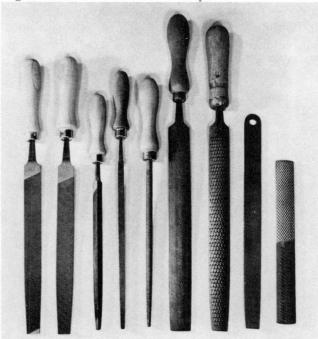

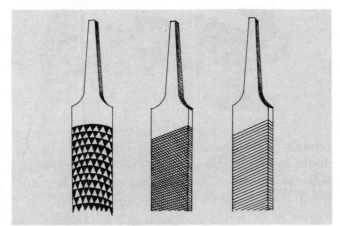

File "cuts": single, double, and rasp

Files also vary as to the coarseness or "cut" of the teeth. The most common are the single-, double-, and rasp-cut.

Single-cut files give the smoothest finish, but they are also the slowest-cutting. Double-cut files are faster, but do not leave quite as smooth a surface as a single-cut file will. Rasps (mainly used on wood) have coarse, widely separated teeth that dig into soft materials (such as wood or plastic) to remove stock rapidly, but they leave a fairly rough surface. As a rule, wood rasps are used for rough shaping; you finish off the surface with sandpaper.

Most people need just two or three general-purpose files—an 8- or 10-inch flat combination file which has single-cut teeth on one side and double-cut teeth on the other, a small triangular file, and a medium-sized round file for reaming

To file the edge of thin metal, clamp the piece in a vise and back up with a block of wood.

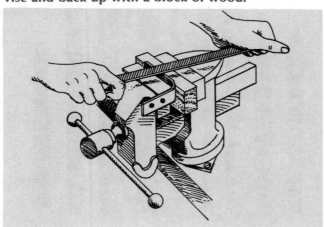

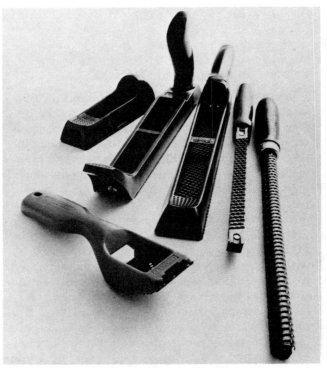

Some popular styles of Surform hand tools

out holes or trimming inside curves. Specialized files, such as those for sharpening power-mower blades or chain saws, can be added individually as needed.

In wood rasps, a single half-round model with teeth on both the curved and flat sides will probably handle most chores. Instead of a conventional rasp you can also use one of the various trimming and shaping tools. The Surform tools (made by Stanley Tools) work well on wood, plastic, and soft metals, and come in a variety of shapes and sizes. They have steel blades which resemble the face of a wood rasp, with multiple teeth like those on an old-fashioned potato grater. Often they can be used in place of a plane and file.

Hand Drills

Portable electric drills have become so popular and moderate in price that few people still use hand drills for boring holes. A hand drill will prove useful, though, when working at some distance from the nearest electrical outlet, or when you merely want to make one or two small pilot holes before driving screws and don't want to go to the trouble of unreeling a long extension cord for the electric drill.

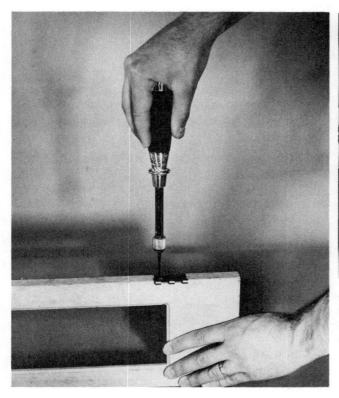

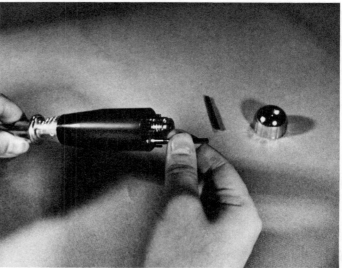

A ratcheting hand drill, which can be used to drill pilot holes for screws with a continuous push-pull action. The handle stores a selection of bits.

For making pilot holes for screws, the most convenient hand drill is a push drill or ratcheting model that takes special fluted bits that are stored inside the handle when not in use. As you pump the handle, built-in ratcheting action causes the bit to spin rapidly. When pressure is released the handle springs back up, ready for the next stroke.

Crank-operated hand drills use conventional twist drill bits that clamp in a regular three-jaw chuck. As you crank the handle a large gear wheel drives one or two smaller gears, which pass the needed torque and speed to the drill chuck. Most models have a handle that you hold with one hand while the other hand cranks the gear wheel, but there are also heavy-duty models with a breast plate at the handle so you can lean against them for extra pressure.

The carpenter's brace is a hand drill that uses long auger bits with corkscrew-like tips. Specifically designed for drilling holes in wood, they range from ¼ to 1 inch in diameter. For larger holes there are also special expansion bits with cutters adjustable up to 3 inches in diameter. By sliding the cutter in or out, then tightening an adjusting screw in the center, the diameter of the cut can be altered.

A crank-operated or "eggbeater" hand drill

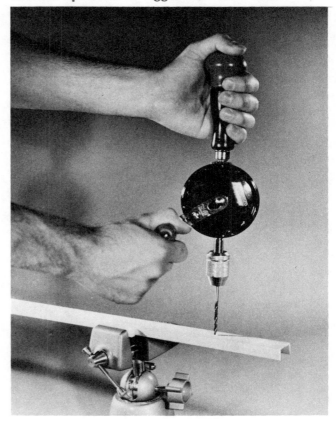

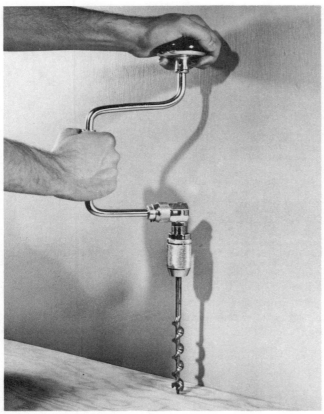

A carpenter's brace

Carpenter's braces usually have a built-in ratchet mechanism in the handle. When there is no room for spinning the handle in a full circle, it can be swept back and forth while the bit will continue turning in one direction. Extension bits are available for drilling extra-deep holes through thick beams, or for boring through walls when fishing through wires or pipes.

Expansion bit has adjustable cutter for boring large holes.

Wood Clamps

At least three or four assorted clamps will be needed to complete almost every home tool kit. You will use these for many jobs—applying pressure to joints while gluing wood together, for holding pieces in alignment for precision drilling, soldering, or brazing, and for applying pressure when straightening bent metal or bending metal and plastic.

The most popular type of all-purpose clamp for most home projects is the *C-clamp*. Made of metal, it has a threaded shaft, turned by means of a T-shaped handle, that applies pressure to anything between the end of the shaft and the other jaw of the C. These clamps come in sizes that range from a 1-inch to 12-inch opening. You will want at least one pair that will open to about 4 inches, with perhaps another pair that will open to about 6 inches.

Another useful type of all-purpose clamp is the *spring clamp*. This looks like an oversize clothespin and comes in handy for many gluing jobs, particularly where several clamps have to be positioned or removed in a hurry. It cannot apply as much pressure as a C-clamp, but there's also much less chance of damaging delicate surfaces.

In woodworking projects there will be many times when you will need clamps with greater capacity than can be provided by most C-clamps, and for these jobs a couple of fast-acting small *bar clamps* are ideal. As shown in the drawing on page 31, these clamps have one fixed jaw and one sliding jaw with a threaded rod that is turned by a handle. Since the sliding jaw can be moved farther out along the bar, capacity is limited only by the bar's length. You retract the screw as much as possible, then open the sliding jaw for a loose fit over the work. Final tightening is accomplished by turning the handle attached to the threaded screw.

When still greater jaw capacity is needed—for example, when clamping large pieces of furniture or picture frames—you can use long bar clamps that have a length of ordinary black iron pipe as the bar. As illustrated in the drawing on page 31, one fixed jaw is threaded onto one end of the pipe (you buy the pipes separately and in any length

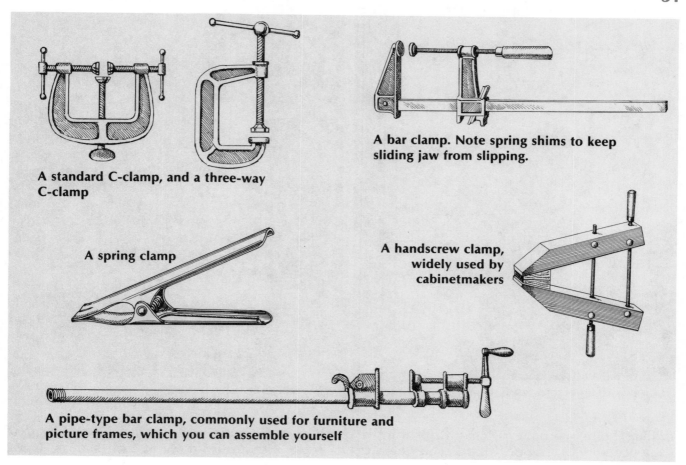

A standard C-clamp, and a three-way C-clamp

A bar clamp. Note spring shims to keep sliding jaw from slipping.

A spring clamp

A handscrew clamp, widely used by cabinetmakers

A pipe-type bar clamp, commonly used for furniture and picture frames, which you can assemble yourself

you desire) and a second movable jaw slips on over the other end. This movable jaw has a threaded clamping screw equipped with a crank-type handle for final tightening.

Hand screws are the traditional woodworking clamps preferred by most cabinetworkers and professional carpenters because they have large hardwood jaws that apply pressure evenly and thus eliminate the need for pads of scrap wood to protect the work. They are easily adjusted for uneven or irregular shapes simply by tightening one screw more than the other, and they have a much deeper "reach" than most C-clamps or bar clamps.

When using any clamps with metal jaws on wood, cushion the jaws with pads of scrap wood or thick cardboard; otherwise, they'll put dents in the wood. Align work carefully before applying pressure, and remember that too much pressure with any clamp can be almost as bad as not having enough pressure—it can distort joints or indi-

vidual pieces, and it can squeeze so much glue out of the joint that there will no longer be a satisfactory bond.

PORTABLE POWER TOOLS

Although it is possible to use only hand tools on most home repair and maintenance projects, these days the majority of do-it-yourselfers own at least two or three portable power tools. Today's portable power tools are not only lighter and more versatile than ever, they also save time, effort, and annoyance, making it possible to complete jobs that would otherwise never get done. You can probably get by without them if you must, but they can sure make life a lot easier for you—and make your work more fun—once you learn how to handle them.

Electric Drills

A portable electric drill is probably the first power tool most people will acquire—and with good reason. In addition to their basic function of

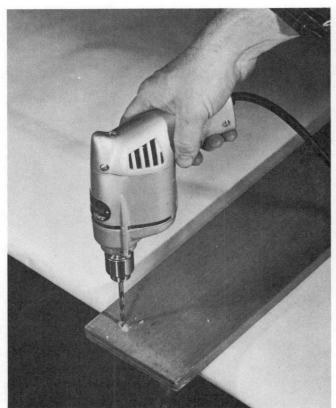

Drilling with an electric drill. Heavy-duty ½-inch drill (right) has handle on its side.

drilling holes, portable electric drills can be equipped with accessories that enable them to sand, grind, sharpen, and buff. They can even mix paint. Remember, however, that a drill is still basically a tool for making holes—and this is the job it does best. Its adaptability for sanding or buffing can be a valuable side benefit, but such tasks can shorten the life of the tool as you apply loads and stresses for which it was not designed—and a drill used as a sander will still not be as efficient as an electric sander.

The size of an electric drill is determined by the size of the largest-diameter drill bit that the chuck will accept. Generally speaking, electric drills designed for home use come in three basic sizes: ¼ inch, ⅜ inch, and ½ inch. As a rule, a ½-inch drill will have a more powerful motor than a ¼-inch drill, and the larger-size drills will have a lower maximum speed (revolutions per minute) and greater torque. Their lower speed often makes these larger and heavier-duty drills less suitable for use with sanding and buffing attachments (which work better at the higher speeds).

A ¼-inch drill can be used to bore holes larger than ¼ inch, for you can buy larger bits that come with turned-down ¼-inch shanks. However, since many ¼-inch drills do not have the power to handle these oversize bits without strain, and since there is usually only a slight difference in price between a ¼-inch drill and a ⅜-inch drill of similar quality, it's wise to pay the difference and buy a ⅜-inch model.

An assortment of electric drill bits, spade bits, and hole saws. Drill extension is along bottom.

Electric drills also vary in their features. Many models are now double-insulated to minimize the likelihood of shock, particularly for work outdoors or in damp locations. And many drills now offer variable speed control: The less you press on the trigger switch the slower it runs—all without a loss of torque. This feature is quite handy when you're working with large-diameter bits that need a slower speed, or when starting a hole on smooth surfaces on which you want to avoid skittering or sliding.

In addition, variable-speed drills can be equipped with screwdriver blades for use at low speeds. Many also include a reversing switch which enables them to be used for removing screws as well as for driving them in. The reversing switch also comes in handy for backing drill bits out when they bind or stick.

The most popular type of drill bit is the twist drill. It can drill holes in both wood and metal, but those intended for metal should be made of high-speed steel. They are generally available in sizes up to ½ inch in diameter, but for drilling larger-diameter holes there are other types of bits and hole saws (some of which are shown on page 32).

Electric Saws

Portable power saws for home use generally fall into two categories: circular saws and saber saws or jigsaws (the names are used interchangeably these days). As its name implies, a portable electric circular saw has a circular blade, while the saber saw or jigsaw has a reciprocating straight blade that works with an up-and-down motion (or in-and-out).

Portable circular saws are powerful fast-cutting tools primarily designed for cutting straight lines. They can be equipped with different types of blades for cutting metal, masonry, plastics, and other materials—and there is a wide variety of specialized wood-cutting blades available, so you can choose the one most suitable to the job at hand. The most popular type of blade is a combination blade, which can crosscut or rip, as well as saw plywood and hardboard panels. When you have a lot of straight ripping to do on regular lumber, you may want one of the special ripping blades. These leave a much smoother edge that needs little or no sanding, but they do cut slower than a combination blade. For ultra-smooth cuts in plywood and paneling, there are also special hollow-ground blades that practically eliminate splintering. And for cutting through old lumber that may contain nails, there are special blades that will not be ruined when they cut through the metal. Abrasive-type cutoff wheels are also available for cutting masonry and metal, in addition to carbide-tipped blades that will withstand long use in cutting particle board, asbestos board, and similar abrasive materials that tend to dull ordinary blades quickly. The designated size of a portable circular saw is determined by the size of the blade it uses. The most popular-sized saw for home use is one which takes a 6½-inch to 7½-inch blade; with it you can cut through a 2×4 at a 45-degree angle in a single pass. All portable circular saws can be adjusted for depth of cut, as well as for vertical angle. When the blade is straight up and down it cuts at a precise 90-degree angle, but when the blade housing is tilted it will cut at any beveled angle between 45 and 90 degrees.

Cutting plywood with a portable circular saw is fast and easy.

Standard and special blades for a circular saw

Hollow-ground planer blade, for precision crosscutting, mitering, and ripping on all woods, plywood, and laminates where the smoothest of cuts are desired

Master combination blade, for use on all woods, plywood, and wood-base materials, such as fiberboard, chipboard, etc. This type of blade is better for crosscut and mitering than for ripping in solid woods. The teeth are set, and deep gullets are provided for cool and free sawing.

Rip blade, primarily intended for rip cuts in solid woods. The teeth are set and deep gullets are provided for cool and free cutting.

Plywood blade, a fine-tooth crosscut-type blade intended for crosscutting of all woods, plywood, veneers, chipboard, etc. It is especially recommended for cutting plywood where minimum of splintering is desired. The teeth are set and sharpened to give a smooth but free-cutting blade.

Cabinet combination blade, for general cabinet and trim work in solid wood. It will crosscut, rip, and miter hard and soft wood, making good accurate cuts for moldings, trim, and cabinet work.

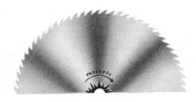

Standard combination blade, used for all hard and soft wood for crosscut, rip, or miter cuts. It is especially recommended for use on power miter boxes and for accurate molding and framing work.

Thin-rim satin-cut veneer blade, the best blade for the cutting of fine veneers, plywood, and other sensitive material where the minimum of splintering and excellent glue line smoothness of cut is required. Cuts require little sanding before finishing. Depth of cut is limited to 1¼ inches. This blade is good for cutting thin plastics.

Pointers on Working with a Portable Power Saw

Portable power saws cut either on the upstroke of the blade (in the case of a saber saw) or from the bottom up (in the case of a circular saw), so any splintering that does occur will take place on the top side, the side you are working from. This means that you should place the panel or piece of lumber with the good side *down*, so that you cut from the back side, the side that won't show when the job is done.

In the interests of safe and accurate cutting, the work should be solidly supported for minimal vibration. If the cutoff piece is sizable, it too should be supported to prevent binding as it begins to fall free. The idea is to support the work on both sides of the cut—or have a helper hold one half for you—so that the saw will not tend to bind as the wood sags or twists.

When cutting with a circular saw, adjust the depth of cut so that the blade protrudes only slightly through the wood.

With any saw make sure you cut on the waste side of the penciled line if accuracy is important. Start the machine with the foot or base of the tool just resting on the work, with the blade not yet in contact with it. Advance slowly, watching carefully to see where the cut will actually be made. That way, you can still correct a slight misalignment before much damage is done.

Portable power saws can make "blind" pocket cuts (openings in the middle of a panel or board), as well as crosscuts from one edge to the other. Rest the toe (front end) of the base plate on the work, with the saw tilted forward enough so the blade is not in contact with the surface. Start the saw, and gradually lower the blade into the work until the base is flat against the surface—then continue to cut in the usual manner.

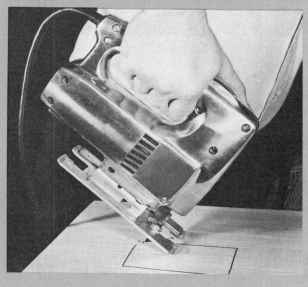

Making pocket cuts with a circular saw and a saber saw

The saber saw or **jigsaw** is an extremely versatile cutting tool, much lighter in weight than the circular saw and therefore much easier to handle on vertical surfaces or overhead. It can cut straight lines when a suitable guide or straightedge is clamped to the work surface, but it will not cut anywhere near as fast as a portable circular saw. However, the saber saw is much better suited to cutting curves and making pocket cuts—for example, when cutting small openings for electric switches or other fixtures in the center of a plywood panel or board. Like the portable circular saw, the saber saw has a built-in adjustment that permits tilting the blade for

A saber saw is ideal for scrollwork. Some models allow cuts flush to a vertical surface with special blade.

bevel cutting or angle cutting, and a wide choice of blades is available for cutting wood, metal, plastic, and other materials. There are also special blades for cutting flush against a vertical surface, as well as variations in blade coarseness for a choice of fine or coarse cut (the fine will cut slower than the coarse cutting blade). Most portable saber saws can be equipped with blades long enough to cut through a 2×4 at a 45-degree angle, but this will be slow going and is only suitable for occasional use and when few such cuts have to be made.

Portable Electric Sanding Machines

Electric sanders come in three basic types: disk sanders, orbital sanders (also called finishing sanders), and belt sanders.

The disk sander, in its most common form, is actually an accessory to an electric drill—a flexible rubber or plastic pad with an abrasive disk attached or cemented to the face. The whole attachment is mounted on an arbor that can be chucked in an electric drill. Commercial disk sanders, such as those used by auto body finishing shops and other commercial finishers, have larger disks and are built to withstand considerable pressure of disk against surface. However,

while pros can do fairly fine sanding, in the hands of the do-it-yourselfer the typical home-type disk sander is really only for rough work such as removing paint or cleaning rust off metal. A disk sander should never be used on furniture or paneling, and it should be handled with care even working around the outside because of its tendency to dig in and leave gouges or swirl marks on the surface.

A disk sander is useful for rough work around the outside.

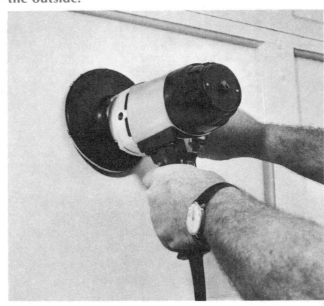

Orbital sanders, also called finishing sanders, have a flat pad that moves in an oval or orbital path to give a finish as smooth as that achieved when hand sanding with a block or sanding pad. Some finishing sanders offer a dual-action movement—a straight-line action for ultrasmooth finishing, and an oval or orbiting action for normal sanding and finishing. Orbital sanders accept ordinary sheets of abrasive paper, cut into halves or thirds depending on the size of the machine. However, ordinary flint paper (the least expensive type) won't last very long and will tear apart very quickly. Use instead aluminum oxide paper (also called production paper) or silicon carbide abrasive paper, the kind usually referred to as wet-or-dry sandpaper. (See pages 397–98 for more information about abrasive papers.) The orbital sander is primarily designed for finish sanding—it is not very effective at removing paint or sizable amounts of wood. The machines come in various sizes and styles, but the very inexpensive models that have a simple vibrator instead of a regular motor are scarcely worth the trouble and expense. If you're going to buy an orbital sander, buy a good-quality, motor-driven model. The size of the sanding pad will vary from 3 to 4 inches in width, and anywhere from 5 to 9 inches in length. To choose the one that best fits your needs, try handling it to determine weight and balance. Many models have an auxiliary handle on the front for two-hand control, but some are strictly one-hand models (often easier to use on cabinets and paneling).

Belt sanders are the fastest-working of all portable electric sanding machines. They can remove multiple coats of paint and smooth very rough surfaces. They even do fine finishing—but this must be done carefully by someone fairly experienced in handling these machines. They take wide belts or loops of abrasive paper which travel endlessly around two wide wheels—one at the front of the machine and one at the rear under the handle. Because belt sanders cut much faster than other sanders, they must be used with greater caution. Hold one in one place for too long, and it will dig in or remove more stock than intended. It must be kept moving at all times while the belt is running and in contact with the surface to avoid such accidents. This type of sander costs more than most others, but for those who do a great deal of sanding on large surfaces the extra cost is well worth it. Sanding belts may be either 2½, 3, or 4 inches in width, and either 21 or 24 inches in length (circumference), so you have to buy the size that fits your

An orbital or finishing sander is best for furniture and cabinets.

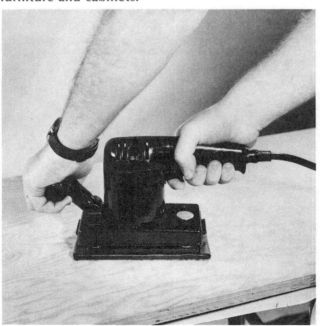

A belt sander with dust-bag attachment simplifies cleanup.

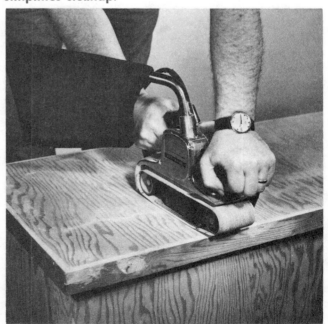

machine. Belts cost much more than an equivalent amount of sheet sandpaper for an orbital sander, but unless you're removing paint or trimming sappy wood, which clogs the belt, they do last quite a while, and the extra cost is more than repaid in time saved. One valuable extra feature on many belt sanders is a built-in dust bag or vacuum attachment that catches most of the sanding dust as you work—thus minimizing the mess that has to be cleaned up afterward. In its most popular form, this consists of a dust bag attached to a swiveling nozzle, situated at the top or back of the machine, that swings the bag to either side.

CHOOSING AND USING LADDERS

Most homeowners will need two types of ladders for working around the house: a stepladder for indoor work and low-level jobs outside; and an extension ladder tall enough for the highest reaches outside the house.

Both types of ladders, as well as a number of specialized varieties, are available in wood or metal (usually an aluminum alloy) and in different qualities. Since a good-quality ladder will last almost a lifetime, and since a poor-quality ladder can result in accidents and personal injury, this is one tool not to economize on.

Most reputable companies grade ladders according to the load they are supposed to carry and the kind of abuse they can normally be expected to withstand. Ladders graded as Type III are considered household-grade. Those graded as Type II are commercial-grade, and Type I are industrial-grade.

In spite of its grade, it is best *not* to buy a Type III ladder—even if you will just be using it indoors. Stick to either Type II or Type I ladders. They will cost slightly more, but will last longer and provide extra safety and serviceability.

As a rule, a 6-foot stepladder will be adequate for reaching ceilings in most homes and apartments. It can also be used outside for reaching the first-floor-level windows in most cases. If the ladder is for indoor use only, and if the ceilings are normal in height, then a 5-foot stepladder will be even more convenient.

Regardless of size, a stepladder should not flex or wobble excessively when you climb it, and it should have a good sturdy bucket stand that folds down in the back to support a paint bucket, roller tray, or other tools. This fold-down bucket shelf, incidentally, is only for supporting tools or other equipment—*never* for standing on.

Extension Ladders

As the name implies, an extension ladder is one that can be extended vertically to the desired height. It consists of two straight sections joined together by special hardware, or interconnected so that one slides inside the rails of the other (the case with many metal ladders).

One half of the ladder stands on the ground while the other half is raised or extended upward. The halves are the same length, but you can never actually raise an extension ladder to its full height, because when the ladder is fully extended, there must be a section where the two pieces overlap in the center—usually at least 2 feet. For example, a 24-foot extension ladder, which consists of two 12-foot sections, will only reach up to about 22 feet, and for maximum safety most experts agree you should extend it no more than 21 feet, thus allowing for a 3-foot overlap.

To raise or extend the ladder, pull down on a rope attached to the bottom rung of the lower

The spring-actuated hook on the movable section engages the rung on the stationary half of an extension ladder.

Pointers on Using Ladders

When using a stepladder, make certain the legs are fully opened and the side braces are firmly locked in position to keep it from accidentally collapsing or slipping. Do not climb up higher than one step below the top, and *never* stand on the top itself. Always make sure that the ladder stands on solid ground and on a level surface where it will not slip or tip when you climb up.

Whenever possible, avoid setting up a ladder directly in front of a closed door that could be swung open and knock into you. If you must set your ladder up in a doorway, make sure the door is locked, or tie it all the way open so that people coming through can see the ladder and won't close the door out of habit.

To erect a tall extension ladder against the house wall, lay it on the ground at right angles to the wall as illustrated, with its feet against the base of the wall. Raise the top end of the ladder over your head, then start toward the house while you walk your hands down the ladder from rung to rung. When the ladder is vertical and against the wall, pull the bottom end out a few feet so that the ladder leans easily against the house.

To raise or extend it to another height, stand the ladder vertical again, bracing one foot against the bottom end to keep it from slipping. Pull down on the free end of the rope to raise the

Raising and extending an extension ladder

LOCK THE DOOR

NEVER STAND HERE

Safety pointers on setting up a stepladder

upper half of the ladder to the height desired. Make sure the hooks are firmly engaged on the rung before you completely release all tension on the rope, then let the ladder fall gently back against the house wall (be certain it's not falling against a window).

For the safest climbing angle, the distance between the bottom end of the ladder and the wall should equal approximately one-fourth of the ladder's extended height. Before climbing, be sure the ladder is standing on solid ground and is set up so that it cannot slip. If the ground is soft, place a wide board or scrap piece of plywood under the feet, and if the surface is paved, make sure the ladder is equipped with nonskid feet. When working outside on a windy day, tie the top end of the ladder to something solid on the house to keep it from being blown sideways, or throw a long rope over the house's peak and tie it to a window frame on the other side.

An extension ladder properly positioned for safest climbing angle

section. This rope goes up between the ladder sections, over a pulley attached to the top of the bottom section, then down on the outside behind the ladder. Pulling on the free end of the rope pulls up on the bottom end of the sliding section.

Once you have it at the proper height, there are special latches that hold the ladder in place. Spring-actuated hooks engage the rungs of the bottom (stationary) section when you release

tension on the rope. When you want to lower the ladder, pull the rope down for a few inches until the hooks are disengaged. A metal pivot then swings down to close the hook's opening temporarily so that the ladder can continue to slide down past each of the rungs. When you want it to stop, raise it back up a few inches until the metal pivot swings out of the way. The hook will grab onto the next rung when you lower it a little.

Chapter 2

Hardware, Fasteners, and Adhesives

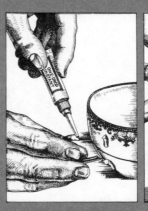

BEING FAMILIAR with the various types of nails, screws, bolts, adhesives, and other frequently used hardware and fastening materials is essential to the success of almost every home repair and improvement project. So is knowing when and how each can be used. While it would be impossible to list or describe all of the hardware and materials you will use in the maintenance and care of your house, this chapter will describe the most frequently required materials you will be likely to need for most jobs.

CHOOSING AND USING NAILS

Nails come in hundreds of different sizes and styles and may be made of steel (plain or galvanized), aluminum, copper, or brass. Few hardware stores or lumberyards stock more than a handful of basic types, each in a normal range of sizes, but you are likely to need only a few types to do practically any job around the house. These will generally include the following: common nails, box nails, finishing nails, roofing nails, and spiral threaded or ring-shank nails.

Although most nails nowadays are sized by their length in inches, many still carry the old-fashioned "penny" designation (6-penny, 10-penny, etc.). This goes back to the days when nails were priced in pennies per hundred (the larger and heavier the nail, the more pennies it cost per hundred); nowadays nails are sold by the pound, but the old designation has persisted to some extent.

Common nails have regular-size heads and a shank with slight grooves directly under the head to increase holding power. They are used in ordinary construction when framing or building homes, and in general wherever you don't mind seeing nail heads.

Box nails are similar to common nails in that they also have a large head with grooves on the shank, but they are usually of lighter gauge for an equivalent length and thus are more suitable for use with thin, easily-split lumber or when holding power is not as important.

Finishing nails have very small, scarcely noticeable heads which can be easily countersunk (recessed below the surface) to leave a small hole that is then easy to fill in. A very similar type of nail, called a casing nail, is of slightly heavier

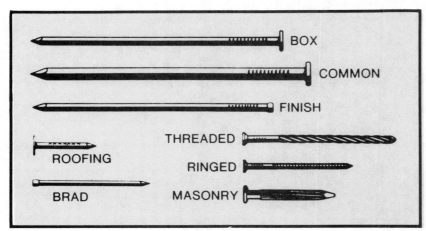

The most frequently used nail types for home repair

gauge (for the same length) in order to provide increased holding power when securing moldings and narrow strips that might be split if too many ordinary finishing nails were used.

Brads are very small finishing nails, 1 inch or less in length. They often have a slightly rounded finishing head instead of the usual blunt head of a regular finishing nail. When these small, light-gauge nails have a conventional head (like a common nail), they are referred to as wire nails.

Roofing nails are used for fastening down composition roofing or shingles. They generally have larger heads than common nails, and are heavily galvanized or made of aluminum to resist rusting. They are also of heavier gauge than common nails of comparable length, with the most popular sizes running from 1 to 2 inches in length. There are also specially designed versions, available for use with metal and fiberglass corrugated roofing, that have rubber gaskets under the heads to ensure a watertight seal.

Ringed or **"threaded" nails** are used where extra holding power is required—some have almost as much holding power as a wood screw, even though you drive them in with a hammer in the usual way. Ringed nails have rings around the shank, and "threaded" nails have spiral-threaded shanks, but because of their great holding power both types should be used only where you want a really permanent joint—they are extremely difficult to pull out once you have driven them home.

Coated nails also provide better-than-average holding power, though they don't grip quite as strongly as ringed nails. They are coated with a special type of resin that softens and melts from the friction created when the nail is driven in, and that then acts like an adhesive to increase the nail's holding power and minimize the likelihood of its pulling out. It is important when using these nails that you don't stop hammering before the nail is all the way in—once you start, keep going, for with any real pause the glue on the part that's already in the wood will set, with a good chance that further hammering will then cause the nail to bend.

Masonry nails are made of specially hardened steel and often have flutes or spiral grooves in the shank to increase holding power. As their name implies, they are used for fastening to masonry and brick—for example, when nailing furring strips or other lumber to concrete walls or floors. Masonry nails must be driven straight home with heavy blows from a large hammer or small sledgehammer, and you have to hit them square on the head with each blow. Striking them even slightly off-center will cause them to break or snap. So it is very important when using masonry nails to wear safety goggles to protect your eyes—flying chips could be dangerous.

Driving a masonry nail through lumber into concrete. Safety goggles protect eyes from flying chips.

Masonry Fastening Tools

If you have a job that involves driving in many masonry nails, then it may pay to buy one of the special hammer-in masonry anchoring tools. These consist of a rubber- or plastic-covered cylindrical tool that accepts specially hardened masonry fasteners (nails or threaded studs) in its hollow center with the point of the nail sticking out through the bottom end. An anvil, or driving head, slides down on top of the nail head and protrudes from the top of the tool for easy striking with a hammer. You position the point of the nail over the masonry at the spot where you want it to go, then pound on the anvil to drive in the nail. The tool's hollow center keeps the nail from bending, and the anvil makes sure that all blows are concentrated squarely on the head of the nail-like fastener.

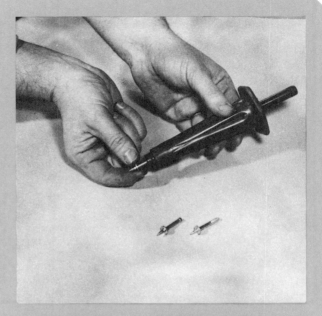

Masonry fastening tool has hollow center for holding nails (top) **and protruding anvil for accurate hammering** (bottom) **without bending nail.**

CHOOSING AND USING WOOD SCREWS

Screws have much more holding power than nails, and when you use them properly they are also less likely to cause damage such as splitting or denting of the surface. They may be made of steel (plain, cadmium-plated, or galvanized), brass, bronze, aluminum, or stainless steel, and can be anywhere from ⅜ inch to as much as 6 inches long. Each length also comes in different diameters or gauges, the smallest being #2 and the largest generally being #24.

Wood screws vary as well in one other important respect: the shape of the head. As shown in the accompanying illustration, screw heads may be either half-round, flat, or half-oval. Most have conventional slotted heads that take an ordinary straight-blade screwdriver, but all are also available with cross-slotted or Phillips-type heads (for use with Phillips screwdrivers). The latter are preferred by professional cabinetmakers, since they reduce the risk that the screwdriver will slip, especially when using power equipment, and they work better with electric screwdrivers or screw-driving drill attachments. However, they

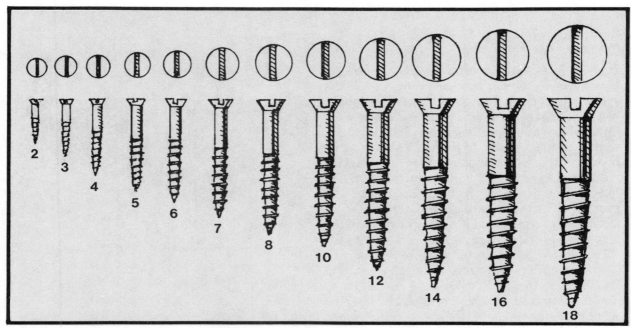

A sample of the various lengths and diameters (actual size) of slotted wood screws

are generally not as easy to find in local hardware stores.

The shape of the screw head is normally decided by where and how the screw will be used.

Flat-head screws are used when the head will be either flush with the surface or countersunk below the surface and then covered over with some kind of wood plastic. This is desirable when you want to conceal the screw completely or at least have the head flush with the surface.

Oval-head screws are designed to be partially countersunk with only the lower portion of the head recessed below the surface—the half-oval top sticks up or projects above the surface.

Not only is the screw easier to remove, it also makes a neat-looking joint, short of having the screw head covered over.

Round-head screws are not countersunk at all—the underside of the head is flat rather than tapered, and the entire half-round top of the head sits on top of the surface. These are generally used when appearance is not important, or when you may want to take the joint apart in the future. Round-head screws are also used for joining very thin materials to wood, when countersinking or recessing is not possible, and when a flat washer is required under the head to reinforce thin materials or to protect soft materials against crushing when the screw is tightened.

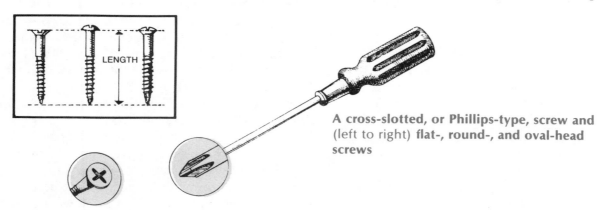

A cross-slotted, or Phillips-type, screw and (left to right) **flat-, round-, and oval-head screws**

Pointers on Driving Wood Screws

A wood screw should be long enough to provide a proper grip. Ideally, the unthreaded shank of the screw should go through the top layer of material, with the threaded part long enough so that at least two-thirds of its length is buried in the wood to which you are fastening. If the wood is not thick enough for this, then select a screw that is long enough to go almost, but not quite, through the wood.

Before you drive a wood screw home, you should drill a pilot hole in the base material, and sometimes a larger clearance hole is needed through the material that is being fastened to it. For example, if you're screwing a thick piece of plywood to a heavier frame of thick lumber, then the clearance hole that goes through the plywood should be large enough to accept the unthreaded shank of the screw easily.

The pilot hole in the piece of wood to which the top piece is being fastened should be approximately the same diameter as the solid core in the threaded part of the screw. In softer woods such as pine the pilot hole should be slightly less than this core diameter; in harder woods such as oak it should be the same as the core diameter. This pilot hole should be deep enough to equal about two-thirds the length of the threaded portion of the screw when going into softer woods, and almost equal to the full length of the threaded portion when screwing into harder woods.

You can lubricate the threads of the screw with soap—an old trick—thus making it easier to drive, especially into the harder or denser woods.

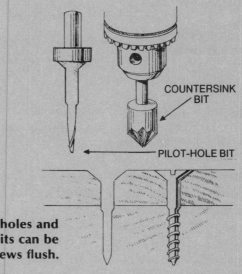

COUNTERSINK BIT

PILOT-HOLE BIT

A pilot hole bit drills both holes and countersinks. Countersink bits can be used to set flat-head screws flush.

HOLLOW-WALL ANCHORS

When you want to fasten something to a hollow inside wall of plaster or gypsum board, there are two possibilities:

1. You can position the object you are hanging so that it is directly over one of the 2×4 studs in the wall and then use nails or wood screws to secure it, driving them into the studs.

2. Or you can use one of the various types of widely available hollow-wall anchors. They can be found in almost any hardware store or lumberyard. Some are made of metal and some of plastic, but all work on the same basic principle—the anchor or fastening device goes through a small hole in the plaster or gypsum board, and a screw or bolt goes through the device so that when tightened it causes the fastener to expand or spread open inside the wall and lock firmly against the back side of the plaster or gypsum board.

Although there are many different brands and variations of wall anchors on the market, most fall into one of three overall categories: plastic anchors, expansion anchors, and toggle bolts.

Plastic anchors are the least expensive of all and are the easiest to use—but they can be used only for comparatively light loads. They consist of tapered plastic sleeves that are serrated along the outside and accept wood screws or special threaded nails in the center. After pushing a plastic anchor into a hole drilled in the plaster,

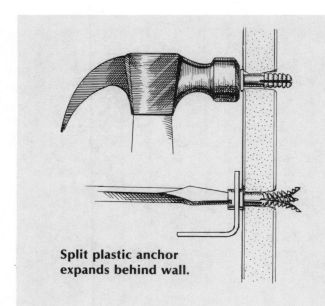

Split plastic anchor expands behind wall.

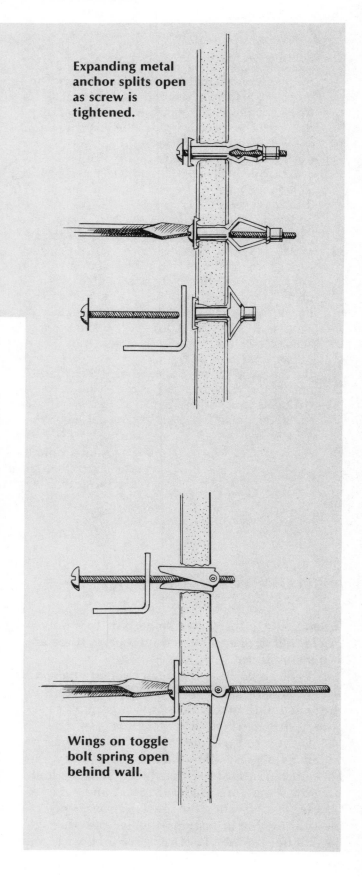

Expanding metal anchor splits open as screw is tightened.

Wings on toggle bolt spring open behind wall.

you drive a screw into the center. The anchor then splits or expands to lock itself tightly and permanently in place, as shown.

Expansion anchors usually consist of a hollow metal sleeve or shield that is slotted so that it will split open and mushroom out when a threaded bolt is inserted in the center and then tightened (the end of the bolt goes through a threaded nut on the inside end of the sleeve).

These metal anchors will hold heavier loads than the plastic ones, depending on the strength and condition of the wall material. Like the plastic anchor, the expansion anchor is inserted through a hole of the right size drilled in the wall beforehand. The bolt that will hold the fixture in place is then inserted and tightened, causing the anchor to spread out and lock into place. Molly is the best-known brand of this type.

With either a plastic anchor or a metal expansion anchor, after you drill the hole in the wall, insert the anchor, and then tighten the screw or bolt that goes in the center, you will be able to remove the screw or bolt and the anchor will stay in place in the wall. This allows you to position and secure the anchor in the wall without having to hold up the fixture or appliance being installed. You simply remove the bolt or screw and, after securing the anchor, use it to mount the fixture or appliance.

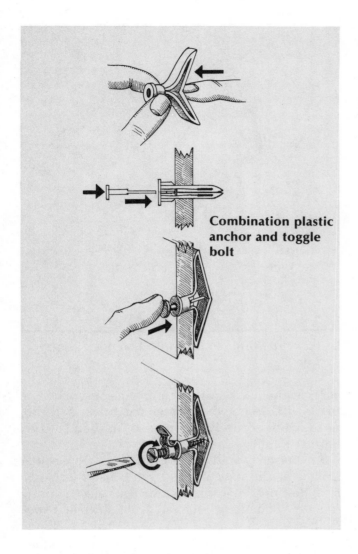

Combination plastic anchor and toggle bolt

Toggle bolts generally hold heavier loads than metal or plastic expansion anchors, but they require larger holes. They consist of a long threaded bolt whose front end goes through a nut attached to folding metal wings, and the hole drilled has to be large enough to accept the folded wings and the nut. You insert them by holding the wings folded tightly against the shank of the bolt and pushing them through the hole until they protrude into the hollow space inside the wall. Built-in springs then cause the wings to snap open. As you tighten the bolt, the wings are drawn up tightly against the back side of the wall.

This creates an exceptionally strong support, but once a toggle bolt is installed the screw cannot be removed without losing the wings inside the wall. This means that when you are installing a shelf bracket or cabinet, for example, the fixture being installed must be held up and positioned at the same time that you press the toggle through the hole in the wall. You then have to hold the whole thing in place while you tighten the toggle. The procedure is more demanding than for expansion anchors, which can be installed in the wall ahead of time, then the bolt removed for putting up the fixture or bracket.

Combination toggle bolt/expansion anchors that are made of plastic, rather than metal, eliminate this handicap. As shown in the drawing, these work like a toggle bolt in that they have wings that spring open behind the wall surface. But they also have a collar or neck on the inside end that serves to lock them in place once installed. After you push the folded toggle/anchor through the hole in the wall, the wings are popped open on the inside by pushing a small plastic pin in through the center as shown (a nail could also be used).

The pin is then removed, leaving the fastener permanently locked in place without the wings dropping down into the wall (as happens with an ordinary metal toggle bolt). You can then drive a screw through the center to secure the fixture or bracket you want to fasten in place. This means you can install this type of toggle ahead of time, just as you would an expansion anchor, and you can remove the fixture or bracket at any time without losing the anchor inside the wall. In addition, the anchor can be used in solid walls of masonry or brick—in this case the wings do not get fully opened, they merely expand to lock the anchor firmly in place when a regular screw is driven in through the center.

ANCHORS FOR SOLID MASONRY WALLS

Although you can use masonry nails (see page 44) to fasten wood strips and 2×4 studs to a concrete wall or floor, such nails are really not designed to take much of a load or resist a great deal of stress. Nor are they suitable for use in brick or cement block. For such jobs, and indeed for any occasion when maximum holding strength is required for fastening to a solid masonry wall—for example, when hanging heavy objects or securing fixtures and appliances that are subject to vibration—there are various types of masonry anchors specifically designed for use in solid walls. Such anchors enable you to bolt down large appliances, metal railings, and similar fixtures, as well as hang heavy signs, lighting fixtures, shelves, and other heavy loads.

All anchors designed for use in solid masonry walls work on the same principle—a plug, shield, or hollow insert is tapped into a hole previously drilled in the masonry, then a screw or bolt of suitable size is threaded into the hollow center of the insert. The screw or bolt splits or expands the anchor so that it locks firmly against the sides of the hole inside the masonry, gripping with tremendous strength.

The most common types of wall anchors for use in solid concrete or masonry are illustrated. Some are made of plastic, some of a reinforced fiber, and some of lead or other soft metal. They range from small plastic anchors measuring only about ⅛ inch in diameter (very similar to those designed for use in hollow walls) to heavy lead-and-steel anchors into which large-diameter steel bolts can be inserted. When you are installing such anchors in a brick wall, it is better to locate the plugs or anchors in the mortar joint rather

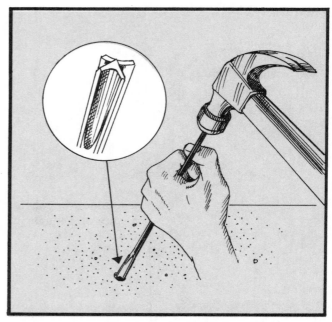

Using a "star drill" to prepare a hole for a masonry anchor

The three most common types of masonry anchors for solid walls

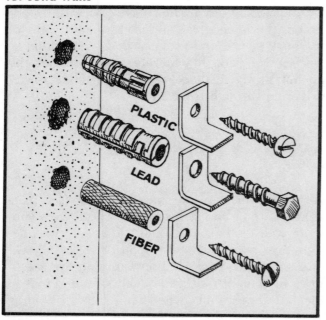

than in the brick itself—an expansion anchor in brick will often split or crack the brick, and will not hold as securely as when set into one of the mortar joints.

All masonry-wall anchors require a hole predrilled in the masonry, so you'll need either a carbide-tipped masonry bit for your electric drill, or a type of hammer-in hand drill known as a star drill.

Carbide-tipped masonry drill bits are available in sizes up to ½ inch in diameter. They can be used with almost any electric drill, but a variable-speed drill is best. You want to run the carbide bit at a slower speed than you would use to drill into wood or soft metal. Make sure you maintain a steady pressure on the drill while it is turning so that the bit doesn't slip inside the hole; otherwise it will dull rapidly.

A star drill is more like a cold chisel that you hammer in manually. To make a hole of a particular size you will want a star drill of the same size, plus a small sledge or heavy hammer. Made of one piece of steel, and resembling a cold chisel, a star drill has two cutting edges at the tip at right angles to each other (forming a starlike pattern), rather than the single cutting edge of an ordinary cold chisel.

To use one of these, position the tip against

the masonry and hit the head of the star drill repeatedly with a heavy hammer while rotating the drill about a quarter turn after each blow. Periodically pull the drill out and blow out the dust, then continue hammering and rotating until the hole is as deep as required. After blowing out the last of the dust, insert the metal or plastic anchor, then pass the bolt or screw through the fixture or bracket and thread it into the center of the anchor. Tighten securely, being careful not to overtighten to a point where you could actually pull the plug back out of the wall.

RIVET GUNS

One of the quickest, easiest, and neatest methods for joining sheet metal, leather, plastic, and other thin materials is by riveting—especially when you use "pop-type" rivets inserted and clinched with an inexpensive tool often referred to as a "pop" rivet gun (POP rivets are actually the brand name of the USM corporation, one of the original manufacturers of these tools and rivets).

Specifically designed for the do-it-yourselfer, these rivet guns are ideal for "blind" riveting—that is, when you can reach only one side of the material. Unlike conventional rivets, which call for a hammer on one side and an anvil or backup hammer on the other side, these rivets can be inserted and secured while working from one side.

Joining sheet metal with handy rivet gun. These tools are great for blind riveting.

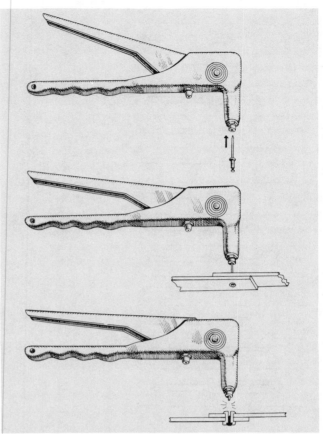

Technique for using a rivet gun, top to bottom (see text)

You do this by inserting the rivet into the jaws of an inexpensive rivet "gun," then pushing one end of the rivet into a hole that has been punched or drilled through the materials to be joined. Press down until the flange of the rivet is against the surface, then squeeze the handles of the tool together. This pulls up on the nail-like pin that goes through the center of the rivet and compresses it (as shown in the illustration) until it fits tightly. The pin then snaps off, leaving the rivet firmly locked in place inside the hole.

Riveting tools are made in various models, ranging from light-duty home units for occasional use to large models designed for heavy continuous use. Most are for rivets of more than one diameter, and in all lengths.

The rivets themselves are available in steel or aluminum and come in three different lengths: short, for materials up to 1/8 inch thick; medium, for work up to 1/4 inch thick; and long, for work up to 3/8 or 1/2 inch thick. They also come in three diameters—1/8 inch, 5/32 inch, and 3/16 inch. The thin-

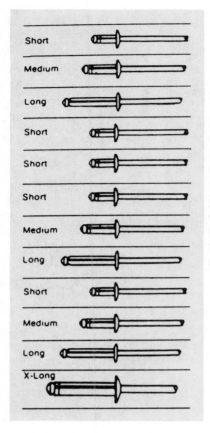

Rivets come in various lengths (depending on thickness of material to be joined) and diameters (depending on the strength needed).

ner ones are used for lighter materials that will be under minimum stress, and the thicker ones are used for heavier materials or when more holding power is needed.

To keep the rivets from pulling through when working with rubber, leather, canvas, or similar soft materials, or to join pieces together when the hole is slightly oversize, special backup plates resembling small metal washers are available. These fit under the rivet head or flange at one or both ends, and provide extra gripping power to join thin metals or soft materials that are easily distorted. Steel rivets are the strongest, but when corrosion is likely, use rivets made of aluminum.

CHOOSING AND USING ADHESIVES

Visit any well-stocked local hardware store and you'll find literally dozens of different kinds of glues and adhesives in bottles, cans, tubes, and cartridges, each making special claims of being the answer to all of your gluing and bonding problems.

Unfortunately, it's just not so. True, many of these "miracle" adhesives can be used to join many different materials together, but there is still no such thing as a universal adhesive to be used for every purpose or every job. For any long-lasting, truly permanent results you still have to match the adhesive to the job at hand—you have to consider not only the types of materials to be bonded, but also the conditions under which you will be working (temperature, accessibility, bonding time, whether or not clamping is needed, etc.).

That is why you will have to know something about the various types of glue or adhesive available (the terms are used almost interchangeably nowadays). Distinctions are not always clear-cut, for new brands and new formulations are being introduced constantly, making it difficult in some cases to tell from the label just what type of adhesive you are buying. Some are special-purpose adhesives that are designed for specific products—such as the special mastic adhesives that are sold for use with a particular brand of floor tile—but these will be described in the manufacturer's literature for that particular product, leaving no question about which one you should use.

Most of the multipurpose glues and adhesives to be found in your local hardware store or home center fall into one of the following broad categories, and will have the general characteristics described.

White Glues

These are probably the most widely sold of all adhesives. They usually have a polyvinyl acetate emulsion base and are almost always packaged in plastic squeeze bottles. They look white and milky in the container and are most suitable for use on porous materials such as wood, paper, cork, fabric, and foamed plastic. They are very widely used in woodworking projects when only moderate strength is required and when little or no resistance to moisture is needed. They dry clear and thus do not leave ugly stains or glue lines in the finished joint.

For extra strength on woodworking projects, the newer aliphatic brands of white glue have become increasingly popular. Like regular white glues, these dry almost clear, but they are usually a bit darker in color, ranging in the bottle from a pale yellow to a light tan. In addition to providing increased strength for any and all woodworking, these glues also have more "grab" than conventional white glue, making it easier to join large pieces that have multiple joints.

All wood glues or adhesives of this type require clamping pressure while the joints are drying. Clamping time may vary from one to twelve hours, depending on the manufacturer's recommendations, but full strength generally requires at least 24 to 48 hours.

Plastic Resin Glue

Specifically designed for jobs that require extra-strong woodworking joints, plastic resin glue comes in powdered form and generally has a urea formaldehyde base. It is very water-resistant, though not always completely waterproof if the joint is to be frequently immersed in water or continuously exposed to dampness. When properly used, however, plastic resin glue will form a joint that is stronger than the wood itself.

Plastic resin glues work well only on snug-fitting joints that leave practically no gaps to fill. They should not be used when temperatures are lower than about 68 degrees, and overnight clamping is required for a strong bond. A word of warning: Be sure you clean off promptly any excess that oozes out. Once the glue dries it turns quite dark and becomes very hard to remove.

Resorcinol Glue

This is a two-part adhesive consisting of a powder and a liquid that you mix together just before use. Specifically designed for use with wood, it forms an exceptionally strong bond that is also completely waterproof and thus is suitable for outdoors and even when the joint will be constantly immersed in water. It can fill moderate-size gaps and requires clamping for at least 8 to 10 hours to ensure a strong joint.

Epoxy Adhesive

This is also a two-part adhesive that must be mixed together before use. Once mixed, it leaves

Some epoxys come in cans, so you can mix exactly as much as you'll need.

you only a limited amount of working time—from a couple of minutes up to several hours. Epoxies are more expensive than most other adhesives, but they are also probably the strongest of all. They cure by chemical action, so they don't have to be exposed to air, and they are excellent for filling gaps and voids in poorly fitted joints. All are sensitive to heat and cold when curing—the chemical action is slowed up by cold—and work best at room temperature.

Epoxies will bond wood, metal, masonry, ceramics, glass, and most plastics, and they can be used indoors or outdoors—the cured adhesive is completely weatherproof. Some epoxies are packaged in tubes, while others come in cans, jars, and other containers designed to simplify measuring and mixing when only part of the package is used. Epoxies vary from a thick liquid to a puttylike paste, and generally require no clamping pressure while drying—you simply keep the parts in contact and in proper alignment while the adhesive cures.

Silicone Rubber Adhesive

Both an adhesive and a sealant, silicone rubber is probably best known as a caulking material. It is used around bathtubs and sinks, as well as for many hard-to-seal joints around the outside of the house. As an adhesive it remains rubbery almost indefinitely, and under a tremendous range of temperature extremes—from 60 degrees below zero to 450 degrees above. Excellent for bonding glass, china, and ceramic materials, silicone adhesives cure slowly, taking anywhere from 12 to 24 hours to dry. Though flexible, the joint is usually not as strong as those formed by the epoxies and some of the other new multipurpose adhesives.

Plastic Household Adhesive

Usually packaged in metal squeeze tubes, these are the comparatively inexpensive clear adhesives that have been around for years and usually have the word "cement" on the label or as part of the brand name. They are solvent-base adhesives that dry clear and very quickly without need for clamping. Extremely versatile in that they can be used on both porous and nonporous materials, they form a quick bond adequate for light-duty use when only moderate strength is required. They dry in a matter of minutes in most cases, though full strength doesn't develop for about 24 hours. Most are moderately resistant to moisture.

Contact Cement

Made with a synthetic rubber or neoprene base, and available in both solvent-thinned and water-thinned varieties, contact cements do just what their name implies—bond almost instantly on contact, with no need for clamping or applying pressure. They are most widely used for bonding plastic laminates to table tops, counter tops, furniture, and cabinets, but they can also bond metal, rubber, plastic, or leather to wood, or any of these materials to each other. The bond formed is of moderate strength, fine if very little stress will be encountered.

Contact cement differs from most other adhesives in that you apply a coat to both surfaces, then allow each coat to dry before bringing the pieces in contact with each other. A surface coated with contact cement will stick only to another surface coated with the same cement—but then once the two parts are brought together they bond instantly, so there's no room for error. Surfaces must be properly aligned the first time.

In actual practice, a "slip sheet" of brown wrapping paper is often put between the two coated surfaces while you line them up, one on top of the other. Then, while holding the pieces in place, you slide the sheet of paper out from between the two. As the cement-coated surfaces come in contact with each other an instant bond is formed.

Instant or "One-Drop" Adhesives

Best suited for use on nonporous materials such as metal, glass, ceramics, and some plastics,

Using a "slip sheet" when bonding with contact cement. The sheet prevents the surfaces from bonding together until you've lined them up; then (right) you slide the sheet out. Surfaces will bond instantly.

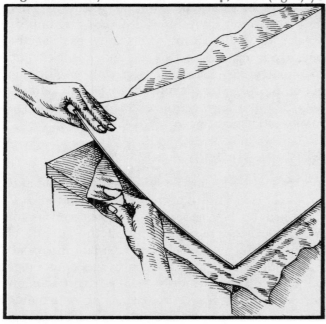 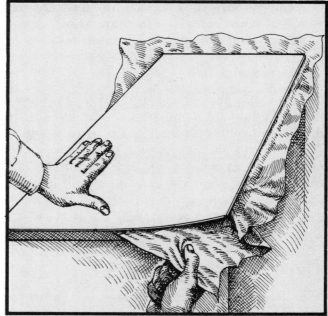

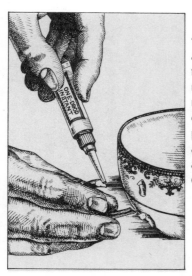

"One-drop" adhesives are best for nonporous materials such as metal, glass, ceramics and plastics. Very little adhesive is needed, and it bonds quickly.

these are the cyanoacrylates. They come in very small tubes (from 1 to 3 ounces). Only a very thin film is required (one drop, according to most ads) in order to achieve a proper bond. In fact, a thick film will not cure properly.

These adhesives set very rapidly—in less than a minute in most cases—and no clamping is required other than a minute or so of finger pressure to bring the parts in firm contact. But you do have to get everything ready and work fast in order to achieve the right contact before the glue starts to set. These "instant" glues do not permit shifting things around.

Cyanoacrylates form a bond that is almost as strong as an epoxy, but they are not quite as resistant to moisture. Also, they must be used with extreme caution, since the glue will stick to skin as readily as to most other materials, and there have been cases where carelessness has resulted in eyelids being glued shut or fingers getting glued together. When this happens, acetone will dissolve the adhesive—but don't try it if the adhesive is on or near your eye; go to a doctor or hospital instead.

CABINET HARDWARE

Although a description of all the various types of hardware that might be used in building, improving, or repairing a house would require a separate volume, there are certain basic types of hardware that you will be using repeatedly and should be familiar with so that you'll know what to ask for when the need arises.

Hinges

When you're choosing hinges for a cabinet—regardless of whether you are building a new unit or simply renovating an old one—the first factor that you will have to consider is the type of door the hinges will support and the way in which the door is hung or fitted. Some doors are flush-mounted—that is, they are recessed in their frames so the outside face of the door is flush with the framework of the cabinet.

Other doors are lipped or inset. They have a piece extending over the edge to overlap the framework of the cabinet while the rest of the door's thickness is recessed into its opening on the front of the cabinet.

A third type is the overlay door, also called a flush overlay door, which is mounted completely on the outside of the cabinet so that its full thickness is outside the frame, overlapping and covering the opening when the door is closed.

Here are the types of hinges used with each of these cabinet door styles:

Flush-mounted doors can be hung with conventional butt hinges that are a miniature version of the hinges used on most full-size doors. They are installed by mortising (recessing) one leaf into the edge of the door and the other into the edge of the frame in which the door fits. With the door closed, only the barrel of the hinge is visible from the outside. A problem arises with cabinet doors made of plywood, for screws that are driven into plywood edges (to hold the leaf of the butt hinge) really do not hold very well. Since plywood doors are quite common, flush cabinet doors are more often hung with full-surface hinges instead of butt hinges. Mounted on the outside face of the door, they are the simplest of all to install. They come in a wide range of decorative styles and finishes, including strap hinges that are H-shaped, L-shaped, or T-shaped. The semiconcealed effect of a butt hinge, showing only the barrel of the hinge when the door is closed, can also be achieved on a flush door with a special type of hinge that wraps around the edge of the door. One leaf is fastened to the inside face of the door, where the screws do not show, and the other, shorter leaf screws to the edge of the frame in the same way as does a butt leaf hinge. Often referred to as a semiconcealed or "bent-leaf" hinge, this type provides a much stronger mounting than is possible with a butt hinge mortised into the edge, and the final installation is just as neat-looking. For a truly elegant concealed effect, flush doors can also be mounted with "invisible" hinges, which are mortised into the edge of the door and into the edge of the frame. As shown in the accompanying drawing, these hinges are completely hidden from sight when the door is closed. They come in various sizes to fit doors of different thicknesses and weights, though nothing less than ¾ inch in thickness. These hinges require more skill to install because exact alignment is necessary to ensure a neat-looking fit when the job is done.

Lipped doors are probably the most widely used type of door on kitchen cabinets and cupboards. They require specially formed hinges made so that the leaf that is attached to the door is bent to fit around the lip. The bend matches the depth on the lip of the door (usually ⅜ inch), allowing the leaf to be secured to the back or inner side of the door. The other half of the hinge

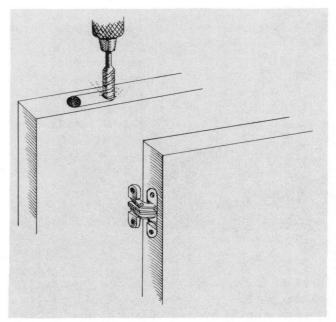

Fully concealed hinge for flush doors is mortised into door edge and frame.

is fastened to the frame; in some cases it goes flat against the outside face, and in others it has a double bend that fits around the inside edge of the frame so it won't show when the door is closed.

Overlay doors are the easiest type of cabinet door to make or install, since exact dimensions are not critical. The door is most often mounted with semiconcealed hinges that are similar to those used on lipped doors. One leaf is fastened to the frame and has a bend that accommodates the thickness of the door. The half that is fastened to the door also has a right-angle bend, so

Butt hinges (top) or surface hinges (bottom) can be used on flush doors.

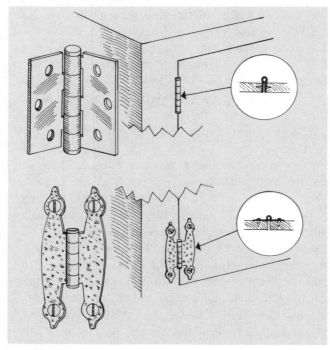

A semiconcealed hinge for a lipped door: The bend in the hinge fits around the lip, and the leaf is secured to the door's inner side.

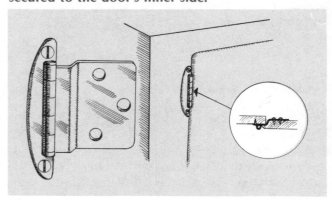

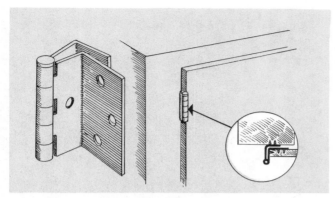

Overlay doors are mounted with semiconcealed bent hinges similar to those for a lipped door.

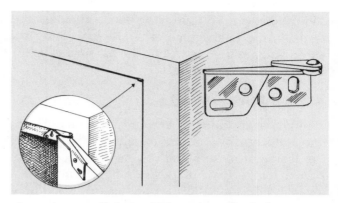

A semiconcealed pivot hinge for a flush door

that the hinge leaf curls around the edges of the door and is fastened to the back or inner side. For those who want only a minimum amount of hardware showing, overlay doors can also be hung with a special type of hinge known as a pivot hinge. Unlike conventional hinges, a pivot hinge is designed to be mounted at the top and bottom of the door, instead of along the vertical edge. When it is installed, only two thin metal edges are visible. Pivot hinges can also be installed on flush doors if one leaf of each hinge is recessed into the top and bottom edges of the door. Most cabinet hinges do not have removable hinge pins—that is, the pins cannot fall out and the hinges do not come apart. There are some hinges with loose pins, however. They come in right-hand or left-hand styles, and it should be remembered when installing them that they cannot be reversed, because if a left-hand hinge is turned over to be used on the other side the pin will fall out.

Cabinet Door Catches

Unless spring-activated or self-closing hinges are used, every cabinet door will require some type of catch to hold the door closed. Most of them fall into one of three general categories—friction catches, roller catches, and magnetic catches.

All of these catches consist of two parts: one piece that mounts on the door, and another that mounts on the frame of the cabinet or on one of the shelves inside. As the door closes, the two parts lock together and are held closed by either friction, spring tension, or magnetism. The drawings below illustrate some typical catches and show how they are installed on various types of doors.

When shopping for cabinet catches, remember that most come with instructions and auxiliary strikes that enable you to mount them under or above an inside shelf, as well as on either side of the frame. Not all catches are universally adapt-

Cabinet door catches (left to right): roller catch, spring catch, and magnet catch

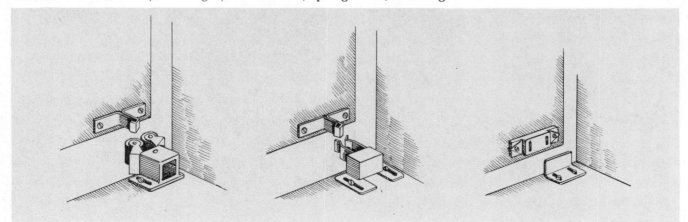

able, however, so study the illustrated instructions on the package carefully to make sure the catch you are buying will fit the particular installation you have in mind.

SHELF HARDWARE

There are all kinds of special-purpose brackets and supports for mounting shelves on walls or on the inside of closets and cabinets. Some are designed for permanent positioning of each shelf, while others permit rearranging or adjustment when the need arises.

For nonadjustable shelving, utility-type painted steel angle brackets are popular, especially in basements, attics, garages, and closets, where appearance is of secondary consideration. If appearance is important, there are more decorative types made of ornamental wrought iron, brass, and other attractive metals.

For adjustable shelving, which permits you to vary the height or spacing between shelves as your needs change, you can use shelving standards or pilasters that screw into the wall (or into the sides of a closet or cabinet). The most popular type, shown in the accompanying drawing, has slots to accept metal brackets or shelf supports, which simply slip in and out when you want to raise or lower one of the shelves. The standards are screwed into the studs of the wall, or are fastened with hollow-wall anchors such as toggle bolts or expansion anchors (see page 47). For average loads they should be spaced no more than about 32 to 36 inches apart; for heavy loads of books and similar equipment they should be closer together (24 to 30 inches).

Another kind of slotted standard for adjustable shelving inside cabinets and closets. Small metal clips snap into slots or holes.

This same type of slotted shelf standard can be used inside cabinets and closets for adjustable shelves, but as a rule another type of slotted standard is preferred. This is the kind that accepts small metal clips that snap into the slots or holes in the standard. You need four standards for each set of shelves, two at each end, although if the shelves are longer than 36 inches, you will probably need an extra standard in the center to keep the shelf from dipping or buckling under a heavy load.

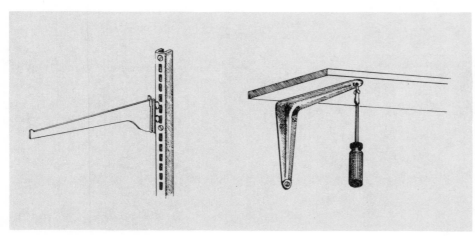

Two commonly used shelf brackets: (left) slotted standards allow for adjustment of shelf height; (right) utility-type metal brackets are nonadjustable.

Chapter 3

Basic Carpentry and Woodworking Techniques

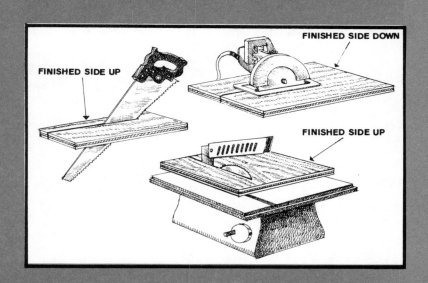

FINISHED SIDE UP

FINISHED SIDE DOWN

FINISHED SIDE UP

ALTHOUGH MANY kinds of materials are used to build a house, wood is still the most popular structural material—especially for framing out walls and partitions, and for constructing shelves, cabinets, and other built-ins. That's why every homeowner planning to do any of his own work should become familiar with basic carpentry and woodworking techniques, and with buying and working with lumber, plywood, hardboard, and other types of wood products.

WHAT YOU NEED TO KNOW ABOUT BUYING LUMBER

To make sure you'll be getting what you want and need when shopping for lumber, you have to know how lumber is sized: For example, a 2×4 never actually measures 2 inches by 4 inches. And you should know something about how it is graded.

Much of the confusion about how lumber is sized stems from the fact that these days solid lumber is milled or dressed before you get it. This means that a certain amount has been planed off the width and thickness of the original piece—yet prices are based on those original (nominal) dimensions. In addition, green or wet lumber has moisture in it, and as this moisture dries out the lumber tends to shrink still further. For this reason most of the lumber you buy will actually be either ¼ inch or ½ inch less than its nominal size in thickness (see chart). A 1-inch-thick board, for example, will actually be only ¾ inch in thickness.

The same thing goes for board width—a board that is nominally 2, 4, or 6 inches in width will actually be ½ inch narrower. Boards 8 inches or more in nominal width will actually be a full ¾ inch narrower. The chart shows some of the common board sizes in both nominal and actual dimensions, so you'll have some idea of what you will be buying when you order a few lengths of 2×4, 1×6, etc.

When renovating an old house you may have trouble matching lumber sizes because years ago a 2×4 actually measured 2 inches by 4 inches, so a modern 2×4 will be smaller. This means you may have to add strips to build up the thickness, or have lumber milled to size.

What You Should Know About Lumber Grades

Lumber is graded according to its appearance, its ability to withstand stress, and its knots, sap streaks, splits, and other blemishes. Needless to

ACTUAL DIMENSIONS OF LUMBER WHEN PURCHASED

Nominal Size as Ordered	Actual Size You Will Receive
1″ x 2″	¾″ x 1½″
1″ x 3″	¾″ x 2½″
1″ x 4″	¾″ x 3½″
1″ x 5″	¾″ x 4½″
1″ x 6″	¾″ x 5½″
1″ x 8″	¾″ x 7½″
1″ x 10″	¾″ x 9½″
1″ x 12″	¾″ x 11½″
2″ x 2″	1½″ x 1½″
2″ x 3″	1½″ x 2½″
2″ x 4″	1½″ x 3½″
2″ x 6″	1½″ x 5½″
2″ x 8″	1½″ x 7¼″
2″ x 10″	1½″ x 9¼″
2″ x 12″	1½″ x 11¼″
4″ x 4″	3½″ x 3½″
4″ x 6″	3½″ x 5½″

say, the better the grade, the better the lumber's appearance (important when you're going to apply a "natural" finish) and strength (less likely to warp or crack under load).

Most of the lumber you will buy for around the home will fall into one of two broad categories: Select and Common.

Select is the top-of-the-line quality you'll want when appearance is important and a fine finish will be applied. In the Select category three grades are sold: Clear, also called B and Better; C Select, and D Select.

B and Better grade provides the ultimate in appearance, with few if any knots, and a clear straight grain that is ideal for natural finishes. The C Select grade has some very minor defects, such as a few small knots, but it is often very close to B and Better in appearance. In the D Select grade the imperfections will be slightly larger (knots, etc.) but they will always be minor enough to be easily covered by paint—and often barely noticeable even when a clear finish is applied.

Common grades of lumber cost much less than the Select grades, and very often you'll have to settle for one of these—not only because of the difference in price, but also because some lumberyards do not carry Select grades in many sizes (of those that do carry Select, very few will carry them in B and Better).

There are five grades of Common lumber, numbered 1 through 5, 1 being the highest and 5 the lowest grade. The No. 1 grade contains very tight knots and few if any blemishes, but you'll seldom see this stocked locally because boards this close to a Select grade usually wind up in the D Select category.

No. 2 Common has slightly larger knots and blemishes and is usually adequate for most projects, including wood paneling if you do a bit of careful selection when choosing the boards.

No. 3 Common may have some loose knots and actual knotholes, as well as other noticeable flaws. It is the grade most often used for shelving, fencing and similar structural purposes where appearance is not an important consideration.

No. 4 Common is a utility grade of fairly low quality and is quite a bit cheaper than the other grades. It is most popular for general construc-

tion such as sheathing, subflooring, and building concrete forms.

The No. 5 grade is not really suitable for many jobs around the home, and not all lumberyards even stock it. It is primarily for industrial and commercial use, where strength and appearance are minor considerations—for example, for building crates and packing boxes.

All of these grades refer to board lumber—that is, boards less than 2 inches thick and anywhere from 4 to 12 inches wide (nominal sizes). However, lumber for framing, such as 2×4s, 2×6s and 2×8s, is generally divided into one of three grades: Construction, Standard, and Utility.

These grades are determined more by the strength of the lumber—its ability to withstand stress and distortion—than by its appearance. Construction is the best grade and includes the strongest, best-looking, and straightest pieces. Standard is not quite as good; Utility is definitely lower in cost and in overall strength.

WORKING WITH PLYWOOD

Plywood is a dimensionally stable form of wood paneling made up of several thin layers of wood veneer (plies) glued together under pressure. The ply grains are alternated in each layer, so they run at right angles to each other. This makes plywood much stronger and less susceptible to warping than conventional wood of equivalent thickness.

Most common forms of plywood have an odd number of layers so that the grain in the two outside layers of veneers runs in the same direction—for uniformity of appearance, as well as for increased stability. Plywood is usually made from fir, pine, or similar softwood, but there are also hardwood-faced plywoods which have softwood on the inner plies. These are most practical for wall paneling, as well as for building furniture and cabinets.

Most local lumberyards stock plywood in 4×8-foot sheets, although longer sheets are sometimes available on special order. Local yards will often cut sheets when you need only part of one, though there may be an extra cutting charge. The most commonly available thicknesses are ¼ inch, ⅜ inch, ½ inch, ⅝ inch, and ¾ inch.

Choosing Plywood

Plywood is usually available in two types—interior and exterior. The primary difference between the two is that exterior plywoods are supposedly made with a more waterproof glue, and the quality of the inner plies is higher—fewer knots and other defects—thus creating a stronger panel.

Interior and exterior grades of plywood are classified according to the quality of the outside plies or layers of veneer on each side of the panel—qualities that affect appearance more than anything else. They are graded from A through D, with A the best quality and D the worst. (There is also an N quality, which is the smoothest and finest grade of all. It consists of all hardwood or sapwood without any knots or other defects. It is seldom stocked by local lumberyards, however; it is mostly sold through industrial channels to cabinetmakers and furniture producers.)

Grade A plywood has only minor blemishes that have been neatly repaired, and a smooth surface that takes paint better than any of the other grades. Grade B may have a few tight knots up to 1 inch in diameter and may also have repair plugs in places, although the overall surface is solid and fairly smooth.

Grade C allows for tight knots up to 1½ inches in diameter, as well as a few splits of limited size. Grade D permits knotholes up to 2½ inches across, plus other defects that may be slightly larger than those allowed in Grade C.

When you buy a full sheet of plywood you should find the grade stamped on each sheet. Two large capital letters will indicate the grade for the two sides. A sheet stamped A-A has a smooth attractive Grade A outside ply on both sides. If the appearance on one side is not as important as that on the other, then you will probably select a sheet stamped A-B or A-C. Few, if any, lumberyards stock all combinations.

There is also a type of plywood known as MDO (stands for Medium Density Overlaid) that has an exceptionally smooth resin-impregnated finish ideal for painting. It needs no sanding and almost eliminates the later problems of checking and splitting that often plague conventional plywood.

MDO plywood comes in exterior type only and costs more than interior types—but it is well worth the extra cost for indoor projects when you want a really smooth painted finish that won't show cracks or checks after a few years.

Pointers on Working with Plywood

Cut plywood with a fine-tooth saw to minimize splintering and to give the cleanest possible edge. Make sure the panel is firmly supported on both sides of the cut. If you are cutting with a handsaw, place the panels with the face—the good side—up. A handsaw cuts on the downstroke, so any splintering will occur on the bottom side.

On the other hand, if you're using a portable power saw, then cut with the face down. Power saws (circular saws as well as saber saws) cut on the upstroke, so any splintering will occur on the top side. When cutting panels on a table saw or radial-arm saw, however, you'll want to cut with the face up, because these saws cut down through the wood.

There will be occasions when it is important to avoid splintering either face—for example, when both sides will be visible and smoothly finished. You can do this best with a portable circular or table saw equipped with a special hollow-ground blade made for cutting plywood. The best of these give a smooth, splinter-free cut that looks and feels sanded. Special fine-tooth blades for cutting plywood are also available for most saber saws, but these cut much slower and are less likely to give you a really straight cut unless you clamp a straightedge to the plywood for a guide.

When you're cutting with a handsaw, there are a few tricks to help minimize splintering: (1) Make sure the saw has sharp, fine teeth; (2) score the plywood along the cutting line on both faces with a sharp knife and a metal straightedge; (3) lay a strip of masking tape along the line on the back side, and saw right through it. These steps will minimize splintering, though they may not prevent it completely in every case.

Splintering can also be a problem when drilling holes through plywood, so always try to drill from the good side so that any splinters will be on the back side. And when the back side is accessible, you can avoid splintering entirely. Clamp a scrap piece of lumber to the back side of

Finishing Plywood Edges

If the plywood is to be painted, the simplest way to smooth off exposed raw edges is to fill in their end grain with a wood putty or ready-mixed latex (acrylic or vinyl) spackling compound. Smooth this on with a flexible putty knife, or with your finger, rubbing it well into the grain, then sand smooth after it has dried hard.

Another method for concealing exposed plywood edges is to cover them with a piece of solid wood molding. If the plywood will be stained and varnished, then the molding should be of the same species as the plywood so that the color will match. It can be half-round, flat, or grooved and fluted, but it should ideally be the same width as the plywood's thickness. After sanding the plywood edges reasonably smooth, fasten the molding with glue and small brads.

You can also cover plywood edges with thin strips of wood tape (actually wood veneer) that you can buy in rolls. It comes in widths of ¾ inch and wider, and in various species of wood (pine, mahogany, etc.) and is sold in many lumberyards and hardware stores. It is fastened to the edges with contact cement. It forms a clean edge that makes the plywood look like solid lumber and can be matched to most plywoods on which a clear finish is being applied.

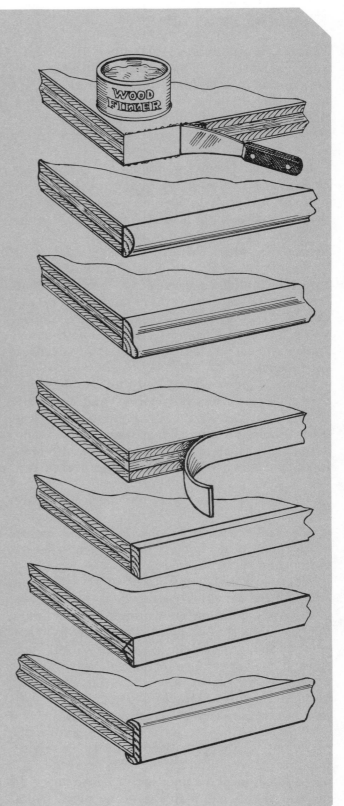

Finishing plywood edges (top to bottom): **with different kinds of wood molding, spackling compound and wood tape**

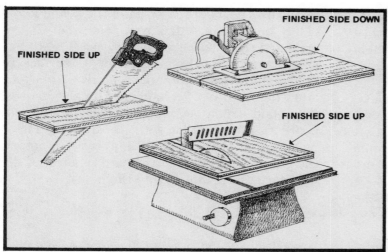

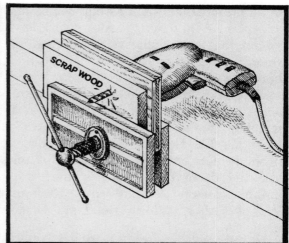

Cutting and drilling through plywood to avoid splintering

the plywood before you start, then drill through both pieces at once; if any splintering does occur it will be on the back of the scrap piece of wood, not on the plywood.

Another way to prevent splintering, especially when boring large-diameter holes, is to stop drilling when the tip or point of the drill bit just barely breaks through on the back side. Pull the bit out and finish drilling the hole from the other side.

Plywood Joints

When joining plywood with nails or screws, remember that these fasteners do not hold very well when driven into the edges of the plywood. Make sure the fasteners are longer than normal, and use glue along with the nails and screws. Better yet, try to arrange joints so that nails or screws will go into one of the faces instead, and be kept as far away from the edges as possible. When nailing, drive nails in at oblique angles to each other, rather than straight in.

Like joints in conventional lumber, joints in plywood are the strongest and neatest when formed by rabbeting or dadoing, rather than by merely butting one piece on top of the other (see page 74). Always reinforce with glue and screws or dowels. If appearance on the inside of the joint is no problem, triangular or square blocks of wood can be glued into the inside corner.

WORKING WITH HARDBOARD AND PARTICLE BOARD

Like plywood, hardboard and particle board (sometimes referred to as flakeboard) are both made of real wood. But instead of being built up in layers or plies of thin veneer, hardboard panels are made by compressing softwood pulp into sheets under high heat and pressure after mixing it with special binders and resins. Particle board is made by compressing wood flakes or chips with binders, again under heat and high pressure. In both cases the result is a dimensionally stable and exceptionally strong panel that has no grain, thus is less likely than plywood to crack or check on the surface.

Hardboard is also very abrasion-resistant and is much easier than plywood to bend when curved frameworks or surfaces must be covered. It is most widely available in ⅛-inch and ¼-inch thicknesses, and usually comes in 4-foot-wide panels that are either 8 or 10 feet long. There are also special sheets sold for floor underlayment which come in either 4×3-foot or 4×4-foot sheets.

Hardboard is made in two grades: standard and tempered. Standard is for general interior use where moisture is not a problem, while tempered is much harder and denser and has been treated with special resins that make it much more resistant to dampness and moisture. Tempered hardboard is used on outdoor projects, or in damp locations such as bathrooms and laundry rooms. While most hardboard sold is smooth on only one side (called S1S), it is also available smooth on both sides (S2S), though most lumberyards will have to order this for you.

Hardboard panels are also made with baked-on or laminated specialty finishes ideal for wall paneling. Some have a wood-grain finish that looks just like the real thing, while others come in solid colors, in tile or marbleized patterns, and in other decorative finishes. There are also a number of embossed patterns that simulate the look of leather, textured wood, and basketweave materials.

Hardboard siding for outdoors is now quite popular. It is made in a variety of patterns and finishes, some fully prefinished so that no further painting is needed, and some coated with factory-applied primer that you can paint over yourself. The most popular style is the horizontal siding designed to resemble conventional clapboard. Vertical panel hardboard siding is also available, finished and unfinished, either with a smooth face or embossed with a wood grain or similar texture.

One type of hardboard popular for indoor use is perforated hardboard, commonly referred to as Pegboard (Pegboard is actually the brand name of the original manufacturer, Masonite). It can create storage space on walls, because it has evenly spaced holes punched in its surface to hold a variety of metal hooks, holders, brackets, and other fixtures for hanging kitchen utensils, tools, and similar equipment. Perforated hardboard must be installed with spacers behind it, or mounted on strips so that there is room behind the panel to permit insertion and removal of the holding fixtures that fit into the holes.

FRAMING OUT WALLS

A partition wall is one that does not carry a load. It divides one room into two smaller rooms, or frames out a new closet in an unused corner of a room. Most partition walls are framed out with vertical 2×4s, called studs, which are spaced 16 inches on center—16 inches from the center of one stud to the center of the next one. Where local building codes permit, studs may be spaced 24 inches apart, center to center. With some types of structural designs, this is often adequate for partitions, particularly when plywood or hardboard panels will be installed to finish the wall. The drawing on page 68 shows how a typi-

Backed by a frame of 1-inch or 2-inch lumber, sheet or perforated board can be mounted on any wall. Right, some of the fixtures available to fit standard perforated board.

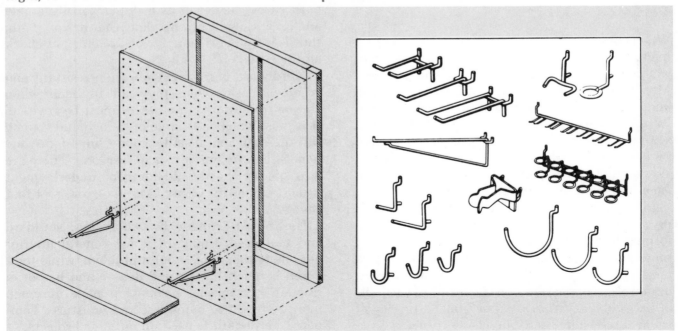

Working with Hardboard and Particle Board

Although hardboard panels are very strong, their edges can be easily damaged, so be careful when handling to avoid splintering or cracking. Avoid sanding the edges whenever possible, but if you must—to take out irregularities or trim off excess—seal them first with a thin coat of shellac (diluted half and half with alcohol) to stiffen the fibers. Wait till this dries before you actually sand it.

Hardboard is cut and drilled with ordinary woodworking tools, using the same techniques as for working with plywood (see page 63). However, though it's possible to join plywood edges if you use the right techniques, you cannot join the edges of hardboard together at all. It must be installed over some kind of framework or backing into which you fasten the individual panels, rather than fastening them to each other.

Also, hardboard does not hold nails or screws very well, so never try to fasten things to it directly—instead, drive nails or screws *through* the board and into the backing or framework behind it.

Like hardboard, particle board is sold in standard 4×8-foot panels, although longer panels are available on special order. It is made in various thicknesses that range from ¼ inch to 1 inch, and is most effective for building counters, cabinets, drawers, doors, and other built-ins that will have their surface covered with some type of plastic laminate.

Particle boards vary in finish; some types are smoother than others. Choose a smoother finish if you will not be covering the panel with anything more than paint. These boards are more brittle and less flexible than hardboard, so they are not suitable for application around curves, and most types are not practical for shelving—they will sag or crack under load if supported only at the ends.

Generally, working with particle board is exactly the same as working with hardboard in that it can be cut or drilled with ordinary woodworking tools. It holds screws and nails better than hardboard does, but the end grain won't hold fasteners at all. So wherever possible, reinforce corners with rabbet joints, glued-in reinforcing blocks, or brackets. As with plywood, the thicker panels can be joined together with rabbeted or dadoed joints (see pages 74–75).

cal partition wall is framed out when an opening for a door is to be included.

Although some carpenters advocate preassembling the framework for a partition wall while it is lying flat on the floor, then tipping up the partition in one assembled piece, most home carpenters will find it easier—and less conducive to errors—to frame out the wall by building it right in place in the traditional manner. Each piece can then be cut to an exact fit before being nailed into position. This may take a little longer, but it greatly minimizes the likelihood of mistakes and the subsequent waste of materials this can lead to. It also eliminates the extra help needed to tip the framed-out wall into place.

You can start building a partition wall in an existing room either by nailing the sole plate to the floor or by nailing the top plate to the ceiling or overhead beams. As a rule, most do-it-yourselfers will find the latter an easier way to begin. The sole plate (on the floor) can then be positioned directly underneath by hanging a plumb line from each end of the top plate.

If the partition is being put up in an unfinished basement, then you will be able to nail your top plate directly against the exposed overhead floor beams. If you are putting a wall up in a room with a finished ceiling, however, you will have to determine which way the overhead joists or beams run to locate nailing points for the 2×4 top plate—you want to drive nails into the beams, not just into the plaster or gypsum-board ceiling.

If the new wall will run at right angles to the overhead beams, you can simply nail the top plate directly to each beam it crosses. But if the new wall will run parallel to the overhead beams, try to position the top plate directly under and parallel with a beam so you can nail the 2×4 directly into it.

If you must position the wall between two overhead beams (but parallel to them), you will first have to nail short 2×4 header pieces between the beams so that the bottom edge of each 2×4 header is flush with the bottom edge of the beams between which it fits. Then nail your top plate to the underside of these header pieces.

After the top plate has been securely nailed in place, locate the position of the sole plate on the floor with a plumb bob. Make sure the plate will

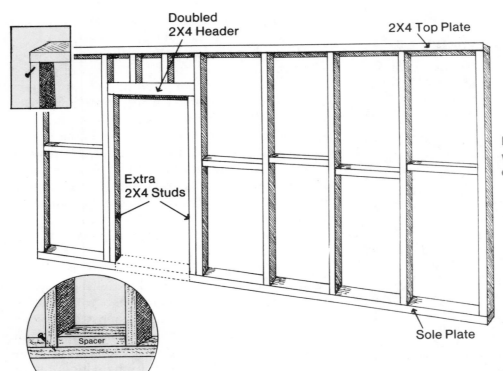

Doubled 2X4 Header

2X4 Top Plate

Extra 2X4 Studs

Sole Plate

Framework for a typical wall partition with door opening

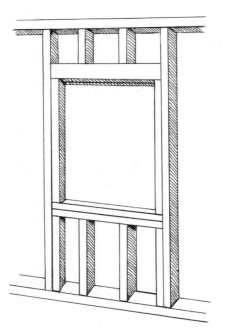

Spacer

Framing wall that is perpendicular to overhead floor beams (see also photo on page 69, top left)

Framing out a window opening

Short crosspieces are installed between beams to support top plate when wall is parallel to overhead floor beams.

be directly under, and in line with, the top plate. Make a pencil mark on the floor at each end, then lay the 2×4 sole plate along this line. You can put it down in one long piece, even carrying it across openings where a doorway will be located later on. You will find it best to cut out the section for the door opening after this piece is nailed down, because it is much easier to accurately align one piece in a straight line than to align several shorter pieces.

If you are building your new wall on a wood floor, fastening the sole plate down is simple—all you have to do is drive nails in every 12 inches or so. If you're building the wall in a basement with a concrete floor, however, you'll have to use specially hardened masonry nails or a hammer-in type of masonry nail fastener (see page 45). Another method of fastening to a concrete floor is to use lead or plastic anchors (see Chapter 2) set into holes in the concrete first, then bore holes through the 2×4 to insert lag screws into the anchors. (Lag screws are very heavy screws with square or hex heads on them so they can be tightened with a wrench instead of a screwdriver.)

After the top and bottom plates have been nailed into position, you're ready to start erecting the vertical 2×4 studs. Cut each one to fit firmly between the bottom and the top plates. Each stud should fit snugly enough to require

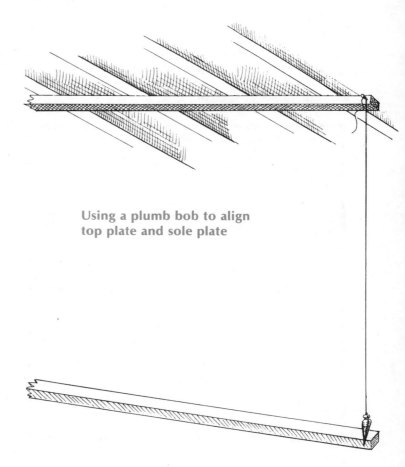

Using a plumb bob to align top plate and sole plate

that you tap it lightly in place with a block of wood, but not so snugly that you must bang away at it to wedge it into position. Measure each one separately, because in many cases the vertical distances will vary slightly, because of irregularities in the floor or variations in the overhead beams. Fasten the studs in place by toenailing at the top and bottom as shown, driving the nails in at an angle from each side so they pass through the stud and penetrate the top or bottom plate by at least an inch.

One trick to keep the stud from slipping sideways while being nailed is to brace your shoe against the opposite side of the stud while nailing. An even better method that will also save measuring is to cut a 14½–inch-long piece of 2×4 to be used as a spacer between the studs. After the first stud has been nailed into place, lay this spacer down on top of the sole plate (or push it up against the top plate when nailing the top end). It will serve as a temporary brace for toenailing, as well as a spacer between studs. A sideways blow with your hammer will dislodge it easily so you can use it again for lining up and nailing the next stud.

As mentioned previously, studs are normally spaced 16 inches apart, center to center. When you are putting up a non-load-bearing wall with a

Two methods of toenailing a stud so that it doesn't slip

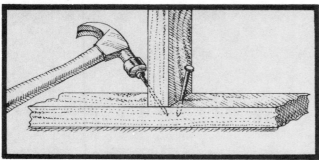

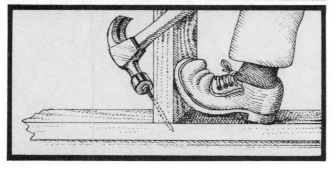

fairly rigid wall panel, however, it is practical to put studs up at 24-inch intervals instead—as long as you remember that you will always need a stud centered every 48 inches to provide a nailing edge for the wall panels to be put up later on.

After you have nailed studs uniformly along the whole length of the wall you will usually find that the last stud will be less than 16 inches from the corner or end of the wall. The same thing will often happen with door openings. Just make sure the space is less than the required 16 inches, not more. That way you will be sure of adequate nailing supports for the wall panels, particularly along the edges.

When framing out a door, first fit extra studs, called jack studs, on each side under the header that forms the top of the door opening. These are nailed flat against the full-height studs on each side of the door opening. The header—consisting of a doubled 2×4 nailed together and then set edgewise across the top of the opening—is then nailed across so it rests on top of these short jack studs.

Short lengths of vertical 2×4, called cripple studs, are installed above this to fit between it and the top plate. After all studs are in place, short horizontal lengths of 2×4 (called fire stops) are installed between the vertical studs as shown. These are located approximately halfway up from the floor, although height is not critical. You can stagger heights as shown to simplify the job of driving nails in through the ends, thus eliminating the need for toenailing.

To form inside and outside corners, extra studs will be required to create a corner post with a nailing surface for the wall paneling on each side. The drawings show the most common methods for forming outside and inside corners, as well as T-shaped joints where two walls intersect.

Framing out partition walls in an attic is not very different from working in a basement or garage, except that an attic often has a sloping roof that leaves you with short "knee" walls along the sides. Also, you may have to put up collar beams to form the ceiling. You don't want to carry the finished ceiling right up to the peak, because you will have to put insulation above the ceiling and there should be space for ventilation above this insulation.

In many cases the attic will already have collar

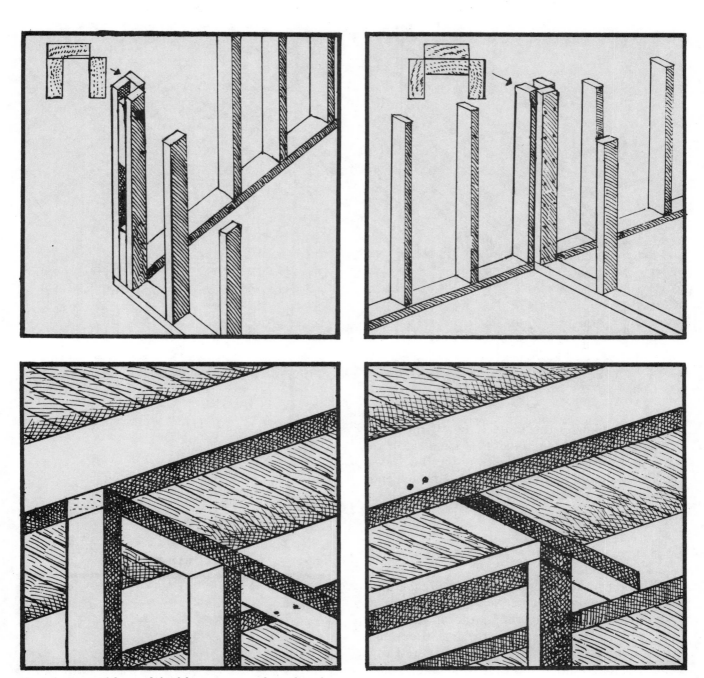

Forming outside and inside corners when framing

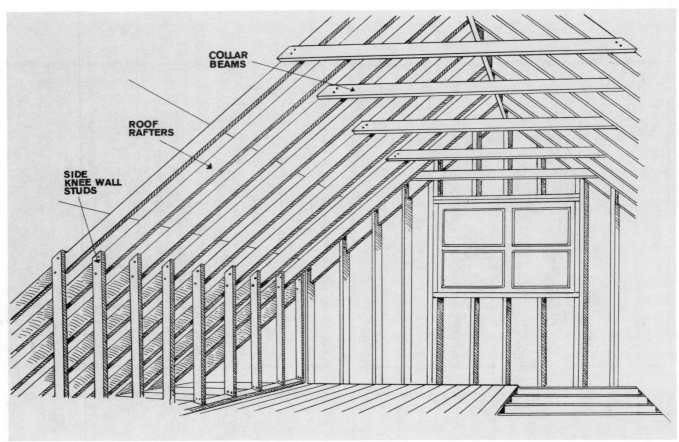

Framing out typical attic room

beams installed by the builder, but if not, you can nail horizontal lengths of 2×4 from rafter to rafter up near the top, as illustrated in the drawing. There should be vents above this in each end of the peak to permit air to circulate.

COMMONLY USED WOODWORKING JOINTS

Of all woodworking joints, the butt joint is the simplest to make. Its pieces fit together in a T-shaped or L-shaped configuration. Usually, this joint is assembled by driving the nails through one piece and into the end grain of the other. Although quick and easy, this joint is also one of the weakest. One way to make it stronger is to drive the nails in at opposing angles, so they slant in opposite directions. This will greatly increase the holding power. You can make an even stronger joint by using serrated or "threaded" nails (see pages 43–44 for more about nails). Screws will hold even better, and combined with glue will add still more strength to the joint.

When joining boards with nails, drive them in at opposing angles for better grip.

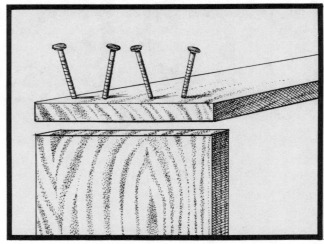

Metal Braces for Joints

When appearance is not important, butt joints and T-joints can be strengthened with an assortment of metal braces or angle irons. As shown in the drawings, these are attached to the wood with screws on the edges or faces of the pieces being assembled. Inside corner braces generally make a neater installation than flat T-braces screwed to the surface. With either type of brace you can improve appearance by chiseling a shallow dado or recess in the wood so that the brace is recessed flush with the surface.

A faster way to assemble simple joints is with corrugated fasteners or Skotch fasteners that have sharp spurs along one side and are simply hammered into place. Designed to pull parts tightly together as you hammer them in, they are generally not as strong as mending plates or T-plates, and they are more likely to cause splitting in soft woods. But for light-duty joints they are fine.

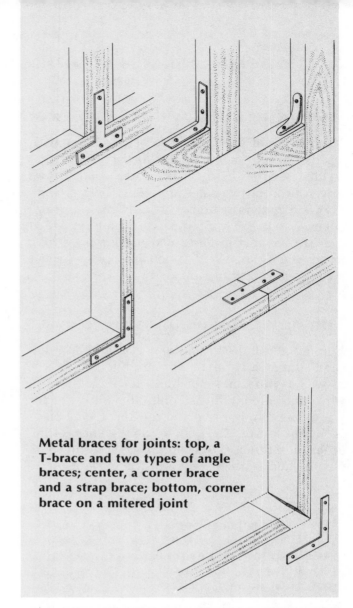

Metal braces for joints: top, a T-brace and two types of angle braces; center, a corner brace and a strap brace; bottom, corner brace on a mitered joint

Both corrugated (right) **and Skotch** (left) **fasteners are good for reinforcing the joints of storm sash and screen frames.**

Reinforcing Joints with Wood Blocks

Many types of joints can also be reinforced with wooden blocks or braces, as illustrated. For best results, secure these blocks with wood screws driven in from two sides, and glue them as well. Plywood gussets or braces, usually cut in a triangular shape, and widely used in building wood roof trusses and girders, also make very strong joints when glued and nailed into place—especially with ringed or threaded nails.

Other Useful Woodworking Joints

Full-lap and half-lap joints, neater and stronger than simple butt joints, are often used in fences as well as in framing for built-in cabinets, furniture, and similar units. Full-lap joints are for pieces that are not of equal thickness. One piece is cut out to a depth equal to the thickness of the other piece, then the second piece is set in so its face is flush with the edge of the cut-out piece.

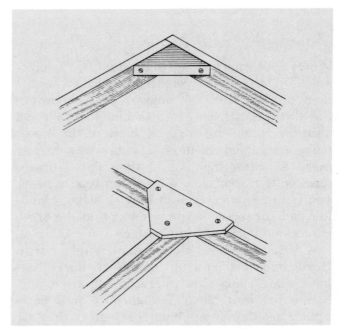

Reinforcing a corner with plywood gusset, and a perpendicular joint with a triangular brace

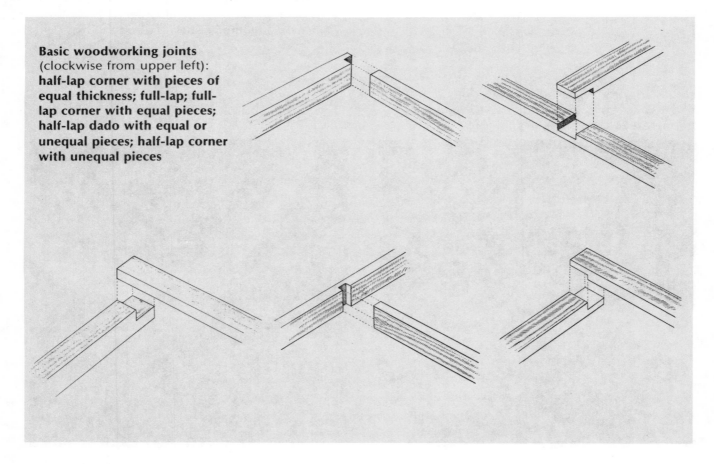

Basic woodworking joints (clockwise from upper left): **half-lap corner with pieces of equal thickness; full-lap; full-lap corner with equal pieces; half-lap dado with equal or unequal pieces; half-lap corner with unequal pieces**

Both pieces of a half-lap joint have half their thickness cut away, so that when fit together they still equal one thickness at the joint. Half-lap joints are for joining pieces end to end, and for creating L-shaped or T-shaped joints.

A small backsaw (see pages 77–78) is the best tool for cutting out the notches or recesses for a lap joint. Clamp the work firmly in a vise or similar support. You'll want the notch or recess to match the exact width of the piece to fit into it, so lay the crosspiece in the actual position in which it's to fit. Then mark the wood for cutting with a knife or very sharp pencil.

For supporting the ends of bookcase and cabinet shelves, stair treads, and the bottoms of drawers, a popular woodworking joint is the dado joint. A dado is simply a groove or recess into which the edge of another board fits. Dado joints are most easily made with a power-driven table saw or other power tools, but a backsaw can make the two lengthwise cuts, and a narrow chisel can then remove the waste stock.

Generally, a dado should not be deeper than about one-third the thickness of the wood, and its width should be such that it forms a snug, almost forced fit for the edge of the board that will go into it. Dado joints are usually secured with glue, and sometimes with screws driven in through the edge.

A dado joint is often used for bookshelves.

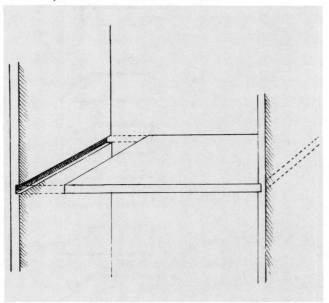

A rabbet joint is actually another version of the dado joint, or a partial dado, as some describe it. The rabbet joint is often used to form corners of drawers and cabinets where moderate strength is required. They make neat-looking joints, and since glue can be applied to two edges on the crosspiece, they are stronger than simple butt joints. In addition, nails or screws can be driven in from different directions if desired.

There are a wide variety of other, more complicated woodworking joints for furniture building and cabinetmaking, but many of these require considerable skill and experience to make, and will seldom if ever be needed by the do-it-yourselfer who is primarily interested in home repairs and improvements.

WORKING WITH MOLDINGS

Wood moldings are widely used around the house for finishing trim around windows and doors, ceiling-to-wall corner joints, covering cabinet joints, and finishing off all kinds of built-ins. Since neat-looking, snug-fitting joints are obviously important, moldings should be cut only with a sharp, fine-tooth saw to minimize splintering and leave a clean edge. When possible, a miter box should be used to ensure square, accurate cuts.

To join moldings at rights angles for a corner joint, there are two techniques you can use. In one you create a mitered joint by cutting the end of each piece off at a 45-degree angle so that when the two pieces are brought together they will form an accurate 90-degree angle. The other technique is called coping. As illustrated in the drawings on pages 77–78, it is often handy where two pieces of molding meet to form an inside corner. It is faster than mitering, and in most cases will enable you to make a neater-looking joint with less chance of a noticeable gap in the corner. It is particularly effective when applying moldings to a wall or along the baseboard where two walls meet. Mitering such joints is often tricky, because the walls do not form an exact 90-degree angle—but coping takes care of this nicely.

A coped joint can be formed in one of two ways. If the back of the molding is flat or square, trace the outline or contour of a scrap piece of

Common varieties of decorative molding

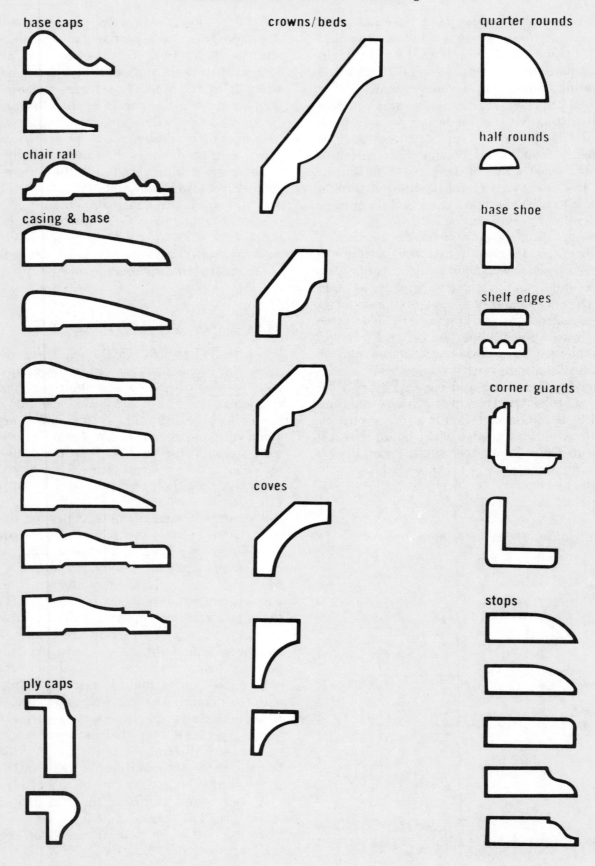

base caps

chair rail

casing & base

ply caps

crowns/beds

coves

quarter rounds

half rounds

base shoe

shelf edges

corner guards

stops

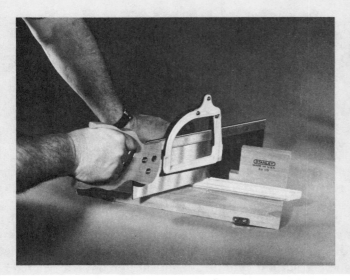

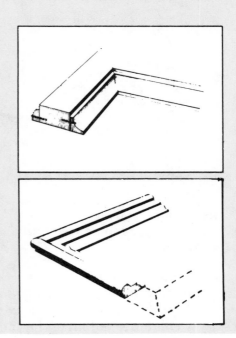

Cutting a mitered joint with a backsaw and miter box. Right, mitered joints for the corner of a frame, or for decorative molding.

molding onto the back side of the piece to be fitted. Then with a coping saw, trim the end of the molding along this outline as shown, so that its end butts up against the piece already in place and fits neatly against its contoured face to form an almost invisible joint. (A file or folded piece of sandpaper cleans off any splinters or ragged edges left after sawing.)

The other way to form a coped joint is to first cut an inside miter as shown. Then, with the

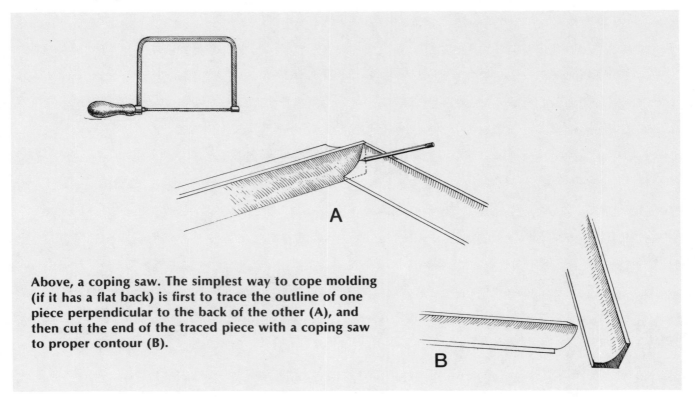

Above, a coping saw. The simplest way to cope molding (if it has a flat back) is first to trace the outline of one piece perpendicular to the back of the other (A), and then cut the end of the traced piece with a coping saw to proper contour (B).

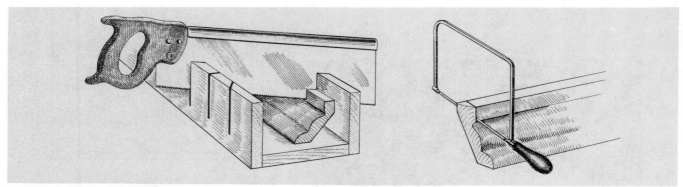

With crown or other more complex moldings, after cutting the end to form an inside miter (left), **use coping saw to trim off end by following contour of joining piece (see also illustration on page 77) along mitered end.**

coping saw held at 90 degrees to the face of the molding, trim off the mitered portion, following the molding's profile or contour. The result will be an exactly contoured cutout of the end. When butted up against the piece to which it must be joined, it will fit neatly. This all sounds a bit trickier than it actually is—especially to the in-experienced home carpenter. You will find it not at all hard to master, and it's actually the only technique that works well on crown moldings or similar moldings that do not have a flat back or that are normally installed at an angle to one or both surfaces.

Chapter 4

Solving Common Door Problems

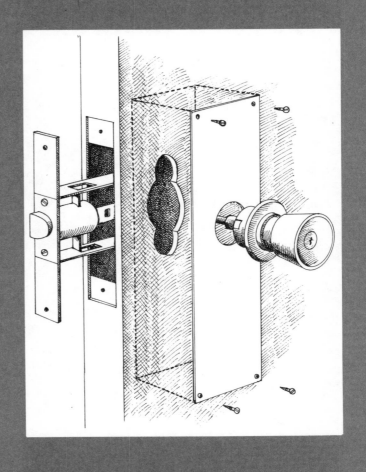

WHEN a hinged door fails to open and close smoothly, or when the lock or latch fails to snap shut after the door is closed, muttering under your breath and kicking the bottom of the door will seldom solve the problem—nine times out of ten it will only make matters worse.

DOORS THAT STICK OR BIND

Most people think the only real cure for a door that sticks or binds is to get out a plane or sanding machine and trim off the edges. While this may be necessary if the edges of the door have swollen from excessive humidity, or if the door-frame has "settled" or buckled out of alignment, more often than not these conditions are not what is causing the trouble. In a high percentage of cases the problem is caused by hinge screws that have worked loose, or by hinges that were not properly installed in the first place (a leaf is recessed either too deep into the wood or not deep enough).

Loose Hinge Screws

Since this is probably the most frequent reason why a door suddenly starts to stick and bind—and since it is probably the easiest problem to solve—it makes sense to check the hinge screws first. Swing the door wide open and test each screw with a large screwdriver whose blade fits snugly into the slot of each screw so you can apply the degree of torque required. If the screws' slots are clogged with paint, use the point of a knife or the edge of a putty knife to clean the slots out first.

Sometimes you will find that no amount of turning tightens the screw because the wood is so chewed up that the screw no longer holds. The solution to this problem is to remove the screw

When a door sticks or rubs, the first thing to check is the hinge screws. See if any are loose by trying each one with a large-bladed screwdriver.

and then fill the hole with slivers of wood (wooden toothpicks work fine). Keep packing wood in until no more pieces will fit, then break each one off flush with the surface.

If the hole seems to go all the way through so that the slivers fall through on the inside, use wood plugs or small pieces of dowel instead. Provide a snug fit inside the hole (whittle a piece to fit if necessary), then dip the plug or dowel in glue and tap it in. Allow the glue to harden before you trim off the plug flush at the surface.

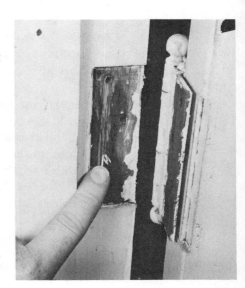

If the wood is so badly chewed up that the screws can no longer be tightened properly, remove the screws and pack the holes with wooden toothpicks, then reinsert the screws.

After the hole has been packed with wood slivers or a small plug as described above, reinsert the screw and tighten securely. (Make sure first that the old screw head is not badly chewed up; if it is, don't try to reuse it—throw the screw away and replace it with a new one of the same size.)

Improperly Mounted Hinges

If loose hinge screws are not the cause of the door's sticking or rubbing, then the next most frequent possibility is the way the hinges are mounted. The first step in checking for this is to find out exactly where the rubbing or sticking occurs. Look for signs of abrasion along the edges or close the door over a sheet of paper, then slide the paper along and note where it sticks or won't pull out easily.

When this happens along the closing edge near the top or bottom of the door, or along the top and bottom edges near the outside corners, chances are that the problem is being caused by one of the hinges—it is set either too deep in the wood or not deep enough.

As you can see from studying the drawings, if a leaf on the top hinge has not been mortised sufficiently into the edge of the door or the doorjamb, the top corner of the door will project slightly farther from the jamb than it should, causing the door to rub at point A or B in the drawing.

Rubbing may also occur in these places if the lower hinge is set too deep into the wood, in which case the door is pulled in toward the hinge along the bottom when it closes.

If the reverse is true—that is, if the bottom hinge is not set into the wood as deep as it should be—then the door may rub at point C or D. Rubbing may also occur at C or D if the top hinge is set too deep.

In all of these cases you'll notice that you have a choice, an alternative method for solving the problem. You can either set one hinge deeper (the one that is not deep enough) or you can shim out the other hinge, the one that is set too deep. You do the latter by placing pieces of cardboard behind the hinge leaf, thus bringing it out slightly to straighten the door's vertical alignment. Shimming out one hinge will have much the same effect as recessing the other hinge slightly—the end result is that the door hangs straight without rubbing along the top or the bottom. To determine which method you should use, swing the door wide open and examine the two hinges. You should be able to tell if one hinge leaf is not set deep enough: It will not be quite flush with the surface. In a majority of cases this will not be the problem—the problem will be that one of the hinge leaves has been set too deep. To correct for this, prop the door open by wedging a magazine under the outside corner, then remove the hinge screws that hold that

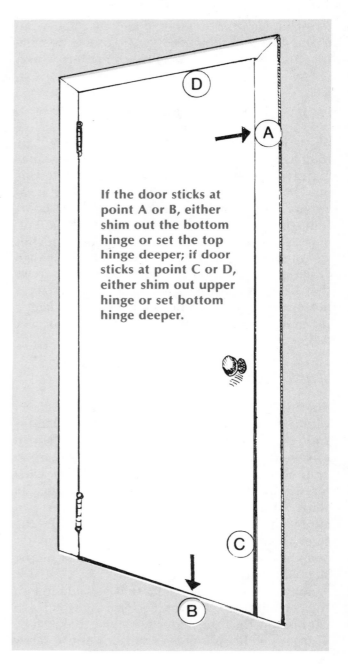

If the door sticks at point A or B, either shim out the bottom hinge or set the top hinge deeper; if door sticks at point C or D, either shim out upper hinge or set bottom hinge deeper.

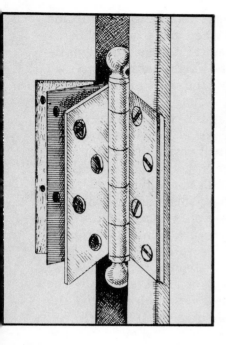

Cardboard shim behind hinge leaf compensates for leaf that was set too deep into wood.

hinge leaf against the doorframe or doorjamb. Cut a piece of cardboard the same size as the hinge leaf and slip it behind the hinge, then replace the screws and tighten securely. Now try the door again. You may find that a single thickness of cardboard is not quite enough—the door closes better but still sticks or binds slightly. If so, add a second or even a third piece if necessary to build up the required thickness.

Shimming can be impractical when there is not enough clearance between the lock edge of the door and the doorframe to allow for the added thickness of a cardboard shim behind the hinge. You will be better off in that case if you set the other hinge slightly deeper. This is only feasible, however, if the hinge is not already recessed below the surface of the wood—that is, if it actually sits above the surface of the wood.

To recess a hinge more deeply on the edge of a door, you will have to remove the door from its hinges so that you can prop it up on its other edge while you work on the hinge mortises. Removing the door is not very difficult. With the door closed and latched, use a large screwdriver and a hammer to drive each of the hinge pins upward as shown. Remove the bottom hinge pin first, then the top one (if there are three hinges, leave the middle one for last).

With all the hinge pins out you can grasp the door by the knob, unlatch it, and swing it open while lifting slightly. The hinges will come apart quite easily, allowing you to lift the door and lay it over on its edge. To support the door in this working position, you can either clamp it against the side of another door or wedge it into a corner of the room where two walls meet.

Of course, you do not have to remove the door if the leaf you want to work on is the one that is fastened to the doorframe—just prop the door wide open by wedging something under the free edge, then unscrew the hinge leaf on the frame and swing it out of the way so that you can use a chisel to deepen the mortise (recess) in which it fits.

DOORS THAT BIND, OR SPRING OPEN

Up till now we have been talking about doors that swing closed easily until the edge of the door comes in contact with the doorframe and starts to rub or stick. There is another problem that

Remove hinge pins by tapping lightly with a hammer and large-bladed screwdriver.

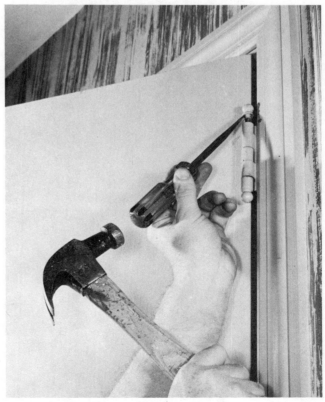

Deepening a Mortise

Cutting the existing mortise slightly deeper calls for careful work with a very sharp chisel. Since the hinge outline is already cut out, all you have to do is cut within it. Start by tapping the chisel around the perimeter while holding the blade at right angles to the surface, then make a series of light cuts across the recessed surface by tapping the chisel.

To actually remove the excess wood you push the chisel in with your hand, along the grain, shaving off only a little at a time until the mortise is deep enough. Push with a sideways shaving or slicing action, using the thumb of one hand and the forefinger of your other to guide the cutting edge. Use a hammer or mallet if you must, but if possible avoid it. You'll be running the risk of taking off too much wood or splitting the edge of the door.

Cutting a hinge recess with chisel. Hand pressure is best; use hammer or mallet only if necessary.

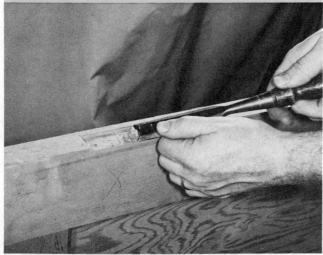

occurs almost as often: A door resists closing and seems to spring open when you swing it shut.

Nine times out of ten this is also a hinge problem—at least one of the hinges has been recessed too deeply, either into the edge of the door or into the doorframe.

You can check this out by watching the hinges carefully while someone else swings the door closed. Probably you will notice that as the edge of the door starts to make contact with the doorframe the hinges are still not fully closed. Then, in the effort to close the door the rest of the way, the hinges seem to spring or bend slightly (the hinge leaves cannot meet). This condition is usually caused by the hinges having been improperly set. Either they were recessed too deeply, or they were not recessed uniformly (the pin edge of the hinge leaf was set deeper than the inside edge of the same hinge leaf).

In the first case—when the whole hinge has been set too deep—it's simply a question of the door meeting the frame before the hinge closes fully. In the second case—when only the pin side of the hinge is deeper than the rest of the hinge leaf—the metal leaves of the hinge come together before the door is fully closed. In both cases the door will tend to spring open before it latches.

Either problem is solved by installing shims behind the hinges. If the full hinge has been recessed too deep, you install one or more card-

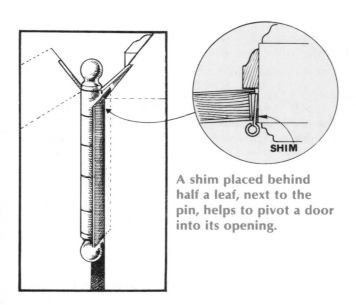

A shim placed behind half a leaf, next to the pin, helps to pivot a door into its opening.

board shims as described on page 83. If only the pin edge of the hinge leaf has been set too deep, you still install shims behind the hinge leaf, but in this case you use narrow pieces of cardboard that are only about one-third the width of the hinge leaf. These go behind the pin edge of the hinge as illustrated in the drawing so that they cause the hinge to swing around slightly (more into the door opening). This should eliminate the springy, last-minute resistance to closing that can cause binding when the hinge edge is set too deep near the pin.

To install full-size shims you'll have to remove all the hinge screws so you can swing the leaf out of the way, as previously described on pages 82–83. However, for narrow shims that only have to fit behind the pin edge of the hinge, you need only loosen the screws, then slide the strip of cardboard into place as shown.

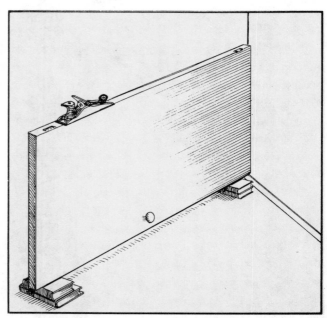

Supporting a door by jamming its end into a corner simplifies planing its long edge.

WHEN ALL ELSE FAILS—GET OUT THE PLANE

There are, of course, cases where shimming alone simply will not solve the problem—for example, if the door sticks along its entire length, or if it is rubbing or sticking in several different places along the top and bottom. Chances then are that some planing or sanding will be required to trim off extra wood along those edges where the rubbing occurs.

If only a slight amount of trimming is required you may be able to do it without actually taking the door down, particularly if the rubbing occurs along the lock edge (as long as it is not right near the lock itself) or along the top edge. Prop the door open by wedging a book or magazine under the bottom, then use a small block plane or wood rasp to trim the edge where the rubbing occurs. Take off only a little at a time and keep testing by swinging the door shut to make sure that you're not taking off more than is necessary. When finished, sand the edge smooth, then touch up with paint, shellac, or varnish to seal out moisture.

Working on the door within its frame is impractical when wood must be trimmed away along the full length of the door, and it won't work when wood must be removed next to the lock itself. Obviously you cannot plane past the lock without removing the lock and then resetting it—a tricky job even for an experienced carpenter.

Under these circumstances it is best to take the door down and trim the needed amount off the *hinge* edge, rather than along the lock edge. The hinge leaves are easy to remove, and after the necessary planing has been completed they can easily be reset by chiseling out the mortise slightly deeper (as described on page 84), until the hinge leaves are once again flush with the edge of the door. Since you will be working on the edge opposite the lock (where the rubbing actually occurs), you'll have to approximate the amount that has to be trimmed off, then hang the door back on its hinges temporarily to see if you have removed enough.

If trimming is required on the top or bottom edge of the door, make sure you plane from the corners in toward the center, never out toward the corners. Running the plane past the edge on a corner is almost certain to cause splintering. With the door lying on one of its long edges, this will mean planing downward for about half the width of the door, then turning the door over so that it rests on the opposite long edge and plan-

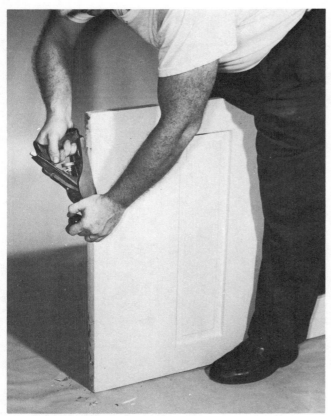

When trimming bottom or top edges, work toward the center to avoid splitting the corners; with door propped on edge and, if possible, straddled between the legs, work halfway down, then turn door over and do the other half.

ing the other half of the door's width, again in a downward motion.

After you have removed the required amount of wood, replace the hinge leaves in the mortise to see how much deeper the mortises will have to be in order for the face of the hinge leaf to once again sit flush with the edge of the door, then trim the mortise to the required depth as previously described (page 84).

WHEN THE LOCK WON'T LATCH

This is another annoying door problem—the door closes easily without sticking or binding, but it won't stay closed or snap shut because the latch bolt on the door lock is not quite in line with the opening in the strike plate on the doorframe.

You can almost always correct a condition of this kind by moving the strike plate slightly in order to line up its opening with the latch bolt

when the door is fully closed. The trick is in finding which way to move it.

You start by closing the door slowly while your eye is level with the strike plate. Have someone else stand on the other side of the door, shining a bright light on the latch bolt so you can watch the action of the bolt as it slides across the curved part of the strike plate and tries to slip into the opening. In this way you should be able to tell whether the opening in the plate is too high or too low to line up with the latch bolt.

Depending on exactly how much out of line it is, you have two options: (1) You can remove the strike plate and reinstall it slightly higher or lower to compensate for the misalignment; or (2) having removed the plate, you can use a metal file to elongate the opening slightly at the top or bottom (depending on whether the strike plate was sitting too low or too high) and reinstall it in the same position.

Generally, if the distance the plate must be moved is ⅛ inch or less, it is easier to file the opening to compensate for the misalignment. If the plate is more than ⅛ inch out of line, however, it is better to remount the plate in a higher or lower position.

You remove the plate by taking out the two screws that hold it in place. Then fill the old screw holes by jamming in as many wood slivers

Cutting a higher recess to move the strike plate up

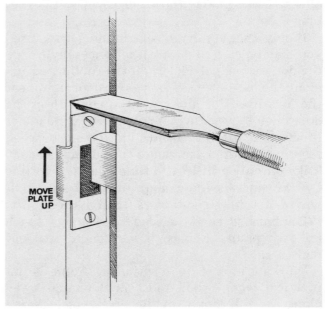

MOVE PLATE UP

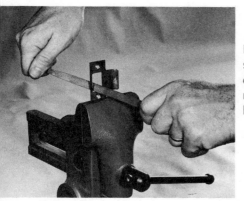

Elongating the strike plate's opening with a metal file so latch bolt will fit

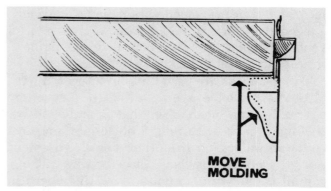

Stop molding can be moved for a snugger door fit to eliminate rattling.

(pieces of wood toothpick work fine) as you can. Break each piece off flush at the surface. Hold the plate in its new position, then drill pilot holes for the screws and mount the plate in its new location. You may have to chisel away a little extra wood to permit recessing the strike plate flush with the wood, and you may have to enlarge the opening in the wood slightly so the latch bolt can slide all the way in.

Sometimes the problem is horizontal rather than vertical alignment. The strike plate may be too close to the stop molding (against which the door closes) so that the door hits the stop molding before the latch bolt can slip into the strike plate's opening.

To cure a condition of this kind you again have two choices: (1) You can remount the strike plate slightly farther away from the stop molding; or (2) you can pull the stop molding off and move it slightly farther away from the strike plate (so the door can swing a little more into its opening when fully closed).

Sometimes a door will close easily enough, and then will rattle to show that it isn't really snug, even when closed all the way. In this case the stop molding is too far away from the door when the door is fully closed—or, to put it another way, the strike plate is too far away from the stop molding. Again, two options: (1) You can remount the strike plate slightly closer to the molding; or (2) you can pry off the stop molding and renail it slightly closer to the door (with the door closed and the latch bolt engaged in the strike plate, you renail the molding so that its edge just makes contact with the face of the door).

There is also another simple solution that will work when only a slight amount of "play" needs to be taken up: Place a strip of foam-type self-adhesive weatherstripping (described in Chapter

15) on the inside of the stop molding to take up the slack. This will not only eliminate the rattle, it will also cut down on sound transmission.

SOLVING DOOR LOCK PROBLEMS

An interior keyless door lock is normally referred to as a knob set or knob-and-latch set. The most popular type is the cylindrical or tubular set, which is installed by boring two holes in the door—a large one through the door and a smaller one into the edge of the door. The small one intersects the larger hole so that the latch bolt assembly (which fits into this hole) can engage the main lock mechanism.

In older homes, there may be mortised locksets or knob sets that have the whole mechanism recessed into the edge of the door. This is done by drilling a series of vertically aligned holes in the door edge and then using a chisel to hollow out a rectangular-shaped mortise or recess in which to fit the lock.

From the description above you can see that there are several different types of locks used on residential doors, so this would be a good time to explain the principal types and how they differ.

Broadly speaking, all home door locks fall into one of four categories: tubular locks, cylindrical locks, mortise locks, and rim locks (often called night latches or auxiliary locks).

Tubular locks and cylindrical locks are similar in that both are easily installed merely by boring two holes through the door as described above. Cylindrical locks are generally more rugged and are designed for use on exterior doors for which security is a prime consideration, and when a key is needed to lock the door from the outside (a knob or pushbutton is used on the inside in most cases to lock and unlock without a key).

Tubular locks are used only on interior doors. Most do not have a key, although they often have a locking mechanism that is activated by pushing a knob or turning a button on one side (you can unlock on the other side in an emergency by pushing a heavy piece of wire or long nail into a hole in the knob or directly under it).

All door locks have moving parts, so occasional lubrication is required to keep them operating smoothly. Often this is the only thing wrong with a balky lock, or a knob set that isn't working smoothly. Powdered graphite is the best lubricant to correct such a condition. It comes in plastic squeeze tubes with a narrow nozzle that enables you to puff the powdered lubricant into a lock, through the latch bolt opening. Never use ordinary oil, which can cake up and gum the mechanism (there are some lubricating liquids that contain graphite and, used like oil, also work well on locks).

Squirt the graphite in around the latch bolt while turning the knob back and forth, then remove the knob and squirt some more alongside the knob stem while turning the knob on the other side back and forth. It may also help to rub a little paste wax on the face of the strike plate,

or spray a small amount of silicone lubricant onto the plate and the sloping face of the latch bolt, which should then slide in more easily when the door is slammed shut.

Lubrication is especially important on outside door locks—not only because they are exposed to the weather, possibly causing oxidation or corrosion of the metal parts, but also because lubrication is your best protection against the lock freezing up when wind-driven rain or snow gets inside.

(When a lock does freeze up, the easiest way to thaw it out is to heat the key with a match or cigarette lighter, then work the heated key gradually into the cylinder until the ice on the inside melts. You may find at first that the key only goes partway in; keep heating the key and reinserting it until it goes all the way in and the lock turns smoothly. Never force the key in, and never use a pair of pliers or similar tool to turn the key when you can't turn it with your fingers.)

As a rule, when a tubular or cylindrical lockset (sometimes referred to as a bored lockset because it is installed by just boring two holes) starts to act up, the simplest solution is to replace it with a new one. Replacement locks are widely available in all hardware stores and home centers, and they come complete with installation instructions and templates for boring the necessary holes (for installation in a new door).

Most of these locks are designed to fit holes of the same size spaced the same distance from the edge, but some do vary. So to play safe when buying a new lock, either bring your old one with you or measure the size of the holes and the distance in from the edge for the larger hole. That way you will be sure the new lock will fit the original holes in the door.

To take the old lock off, you first have to remove the knobs. In cylindrical locks, and some of the better tubular ones, these knobs are usually threaded onto the shaft and will have a setscrew to lock them on. After this screw is loosened, the whole knob can be unscrewed. In tubular locks the knob is usually attached to the decorative escutcheon plate—or rose, as it is sometimes called—so that loosening the two screws or bolts that go through it will enable you to pull the whole thing out of the door, the knob with the spindle attached.

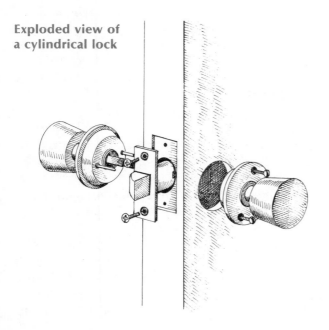

Exploded view of a cylindrical lock

In a cylindrical lock, the rose is a separate plate fastened to the door with two screws; once the knob is removed, the plate can be slid off. You then take out the two screws that hold the latch bolt mechanism in place against the edge of the door and pull out the latch bolt and faceplate. This frees up the lock mechanism so that you can pull the whole assembly out.

In the case of a tubular-type lock, you cannot pull out the latch bolt mechanism until you have pulled out the knob with stem attached, since the stem goes through a square hole inside the latch bolt assembly, as shown in the accompanying drawings.

Mortise locks are long, rectangular-shaped units that have to be mortised or recessed into the edge of the door. Mortise locks are not widely used on interior doors nowadays, but they are excellent for entrance doors for which maximum security is desired, since they are especially hard to force.

Many older houses still have mortise locks on interior doors, and when one of these acts up your best bet is to replace the lock entirely with one of the newer tubular or cylindrical types. To cover up the holes left by the old knobs on the

A mortise lock

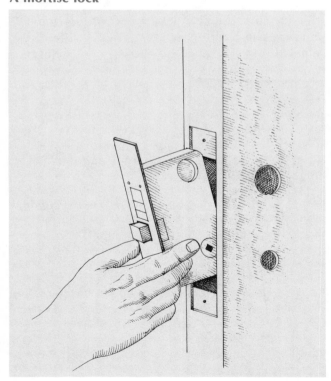

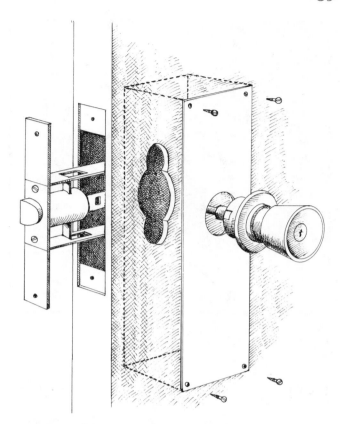

When an old mortise lock is replaced with a cylindrical lock, long escutcheon plate covers the old lock's holes and provides hole needed for the new door handle.

mortise lock, you can buy special modernization kits that include oversize escutcheon plates. These will not only cover the old holes in the door, they also allow for holes to be bored that accept the knob handles and latch bolt mechanisms of the new lockset.

CURING A WARPED DOOR

A door that is warped or twisted will be difficult to close, or will tend to rattle and vibrate when it is closed. If the door is bowed or warped along the hinged edge, then the best method for curing may be to install a third hinge in the middle. Attach the hinge to the edge of the door first, then have someone press as hard as possible on the curved side of the door to force it straight while you mark the location for that hinge on the doorframe. Now mount that hinge leaf against the doorframe or jamb in the position marked,

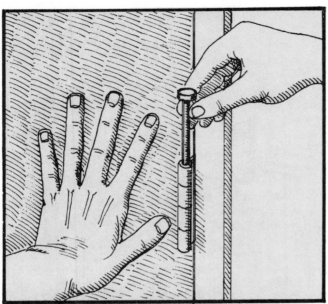

Pushing a warped door flat to force hinge leaves together and slide pin home

then push the door straight to force the hinge leaves together and slide the pin home.

If the door is bowed or too warped for this correction, your best bet is to remove the door and try to straighten it with weights. Place the door flat across two sawhorses or similar rigid supports, with the bowed side facing up. Place heavy weights over the highest point of the bulge or warp, using bricks, large rocks, or pails filled with water or sand. You may not be able to place enough weight on the door to straighten it immediately, but the idea is to leave the door with the weights on it for at least 24 to 48 hours. The continuous pressure should gradually straighten the warp.

For best results, leave the weights on long enough (and make sure they are heavy enough) to give the door a slight reverse bend. This "overcorrection" should result in a straight door when the pressure is removed. If the edges of the door, including the top and bottom, are not painted, make sure they are painted as soon as the door has been straightened. This will prevent further absorption of moisture.

If the door is twisted or warped diagonally, you can use the same method of applying weights, but you'll have to put extra blocks or bricks under the corners to correct for the propellerlike twist in the door.

When a door is only slightly warped, so that the top or bottom corner of the door touches the stop molding before the rest of the door, it is sometimes simpler to leave the door alone and simply renail the stop molding so it matches the slight curve in the door. You'll have to pry it off along the lock edge and then renail it, starting from the top so that its inside face just touches the door along its full length—even if this means curving the molding slightly as you nail it into place.

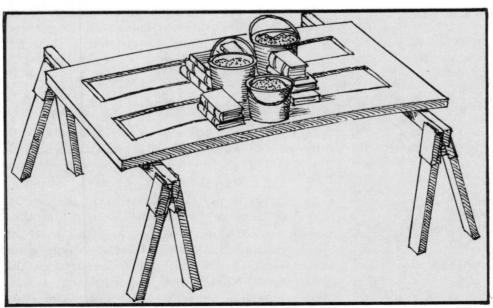

Straightening a warped door with weights

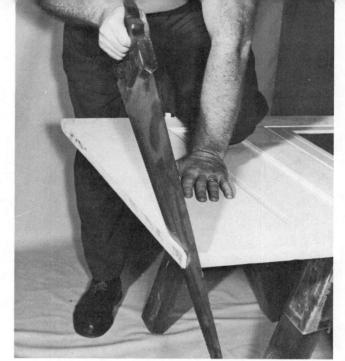

Use a combination saw to trim bottom and/or top edge of door.

If at least ¼ inch of wood is to be taken off the top or bottom, use a saw. If less than ¼ inch is to be removed, use a bench plane or jack plane. Make sure you plane from the edge in toward the center from each side, and never allow the plane to run off past the end of the door, as this will almost certainly result in splintering.

For doors that swing into a carpeted room, remember to allow for the thickness of the carpet. Usually an additional clearance of ¾ inch to 1 inch at the bottom will suffice.

The next step is trimming the edges, usually by planing, to ensure approximately ⅛ inch of clearance on each side—in other words, the total width of the new door should be approximately ¼ inch less than the width of the opening into which it must fit.

To install the hinges, prop the door in place in

Trim long edge of door with bench plane.

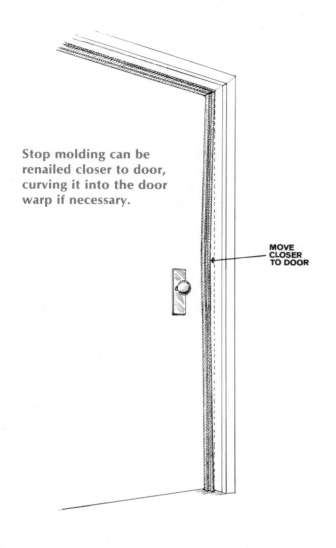

Stop molding can be renailed closer to door, curving it into the door warp if necessary.

MOVE CLOSER TO DOOR

HANGING A NEW DOOR

Replacing an old interior door with a new one is a carpentry job any home handyman can tackle with ease and assurance. You can find a door in the style and size you want at most any local lumberyard, or your local dealer can order whatever you want (some yards also make them to order).

After you get the door home, your first step is to trim it to the proper height. If the door has projecting ends on the vertical stiles at each side, saw these off to make the ends flush with the top and bottom rails, then trim the door to height. There should be about ⅛-inch clearance at the top and about ¼-inch clearance at the bottom when the door is in place inside the frame.

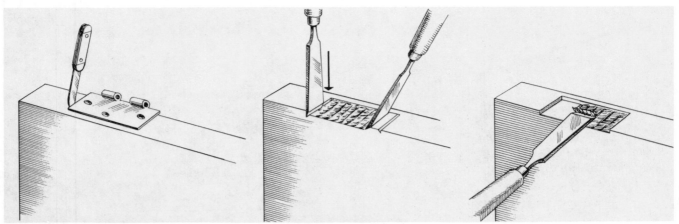

Cutting out a hinge leaf mortise. Left, score outline; center, deepen score line with chisel tapped vertically, then make shallow cuts across the grain; right, remove excess wood by tapping chisel from the side.

its opening, using ¼-inch wedges (scrap pieces of plywood or hardboard work well) along the bottom to raise the door to the height at which it will actually hang. Wedge additional pieces along each side to center the door in its opening, then use a sharp knife or chisel to mark the location of the hinges on both the door and its frame. If the door is being hung in an opening where originally there was a door of the same size, then the hinge mortises will have already been cut in the doorframe; use these as a guide to mark the top and bottom of each mortise to be cut in the edge of the door. If, on the other hand, you are hanging a new door where there was none before, locate the hinges so the upper one is about 7 inches down from the top and the lower one about 10 inches up from the bottom.

After marking the location for each hinge, take the door down and prop it on its lock edge so you can chisel out the mortises. Use the hinge leaf as a pattern to mark the outline of the new mortise, then score around this outline by tapping lightly with a sharp chisel held as illustrated. To chisel out the mortise, start by making a series of shallow cuts across the surface, along the grain, then remove the excess wood by tapping the chisel in from the side while holding the blade horizontal. Remove a little bit of wood at a time to avoid digging too deep; cut the mortise just deep enough so the face of the hinge leaf will be flush with the surrounding wood. Now hang the door by interlocking the hinge leaves and tap the hinge pins into place.

The final step is to install the door lock or knobset. Use one of the tubular or cylindrical models described on pages 87–88. These locks come with special templates that help you locate the holes that must be bored through the door, along with other detailed installation instructions. Your dealer may also have a jig for rent which can make the job even easier. These are metal guides that clamp to the edge of the door and have openings to guide you in drilling holes exactly where needed.

Installing the door lock. Left, outline the cuts and holes to be drilled using template that comes with lock kit; center, drill holes in door and make latch recess cut; right, install latch first, then knob assembly.

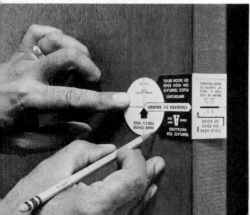

SLIDING DOORS

Sliding closet doors are generally suspended from an overhead track by means of small wheeled hangers or roller brackets that ride on channels fastened across the top of the door opening. In some cases the doors are bypassing—that is, there are two doors that bypass each other and can slide full-length in either direction. Each door rides on a separate track on the overhead channel, so they can pass each other easily. A single sliding door (used between rooms, for example) will slide into a hollow pocket or cavity inside the wall, and the overhead track will have only a single channel or track for the roller brackets. In either case there are guides on the floor (little plastic clips) that serve to keep the doors from swinging in or out as they move.

In some installations the sliding doors also fold (these are usually called bifolding doors). They are suspended like regular sliding doors from

Hardware and components of a bifolding, sliding door

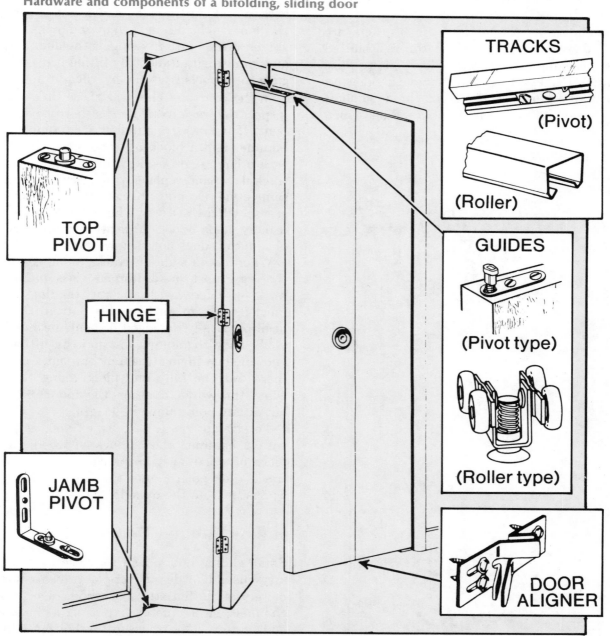

TOP
PIVOT

HINGE

JAMB
PIVOT

TRACKS

(Pivot)

(Roller)

GUIDES

(Pivot type)

(Roller type)

DOOR
ALIGNER

overhead tracks with pivot guides or roller guides fastened to the top of each door or section. These guides may be attached either to the inner face of the door or to the top edge, and they move inside a track or channel attached to the top of the doorframe or doorjamb.

All sliding or bifolding doors that ride on overhead tracks have some type of adjustment that permits slightly raising or lowering the individual hangers, in order to compensate for minor misalignments of the door or its frame, and for the fact that many doorframes and floors are not exactly level.

In some cases the hangers or brackets are mounted with screws that run through slotted holes; loosening these screws allows one to raise the bracket or lower it, even to move it sideways slightly. In other cases there is a threaded shaft with a nut on it that permits similar adjustments.

Overhead tracks and floor guides used on most large sliding doors

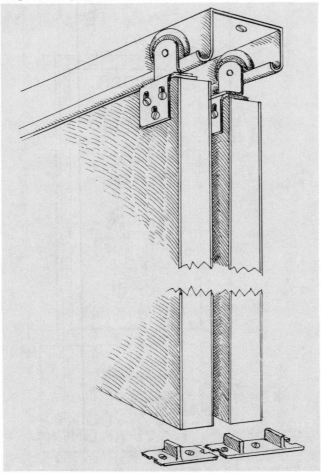

Directions furnished with the hardware, or close study of one of the brackets, should indicate how it can be adjusted, in either case.

When a sliding door tends to jump its track, or seems to bind at some point, the first thing you should check is the condition of the hangers or brackets at the top of the door. Should they be bent out of alignment or otherwise damaged, they may need replacing, though in most cases it is simply a matter of readjusting them to correct for a slight misalignment.

Such a readjustment can usually be made without taking the door down, but if necessary the door can be disengaged by removing the floor guides at the bottom, swinging the door outward, and almost simultaneously lifting it up to disengage the wheels from the overhead track.

In the course of checking these brackets, also inspect the track to see if it has become dented or bent. If it has, straighten it by tapping with a hammer and a block of wood, or by bending it with a large pair of pliers. If necessary, take the track down and replace with a new length of the same style. Do not lubricate these tracks; oil or grease will attract dirt. The rollers or wheels are usually made of self-lubricating nylon or similar plastic that does not require further lubrication.

When doors slide on tracks along the floor—the way most metal-framed glass patio doors work—problems with sticking, binding, or jamming usually mean that this bottom track has been physically damaged or bent. In most cases you'll have to remove the door by lifting it up and then swinging the bottom out, but often there may be only one place along the track where this works. In others the door can be lifted out at any point along its length.

To straighten the bent track you simply tap with a hammer and a block of wood. Cut the piece of wood so it forms a snug fit inside the track, then push it into the track and hammer against it from the outside.

Sliding Cabinet Doors

Small sliding doors such as those used on cabinets usually ride on simple tracks consisting merely of slotted strips of wood, or of grooved channels, either metal or plastic, along the top and bottom. The track on the bottom is not as

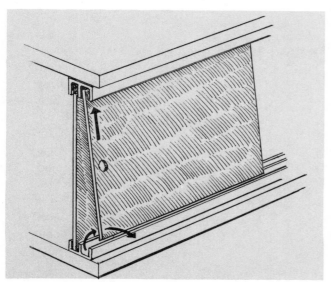

Removing a typical sliding cabinet door

deep as the track along the top, so each door can be lifted enough to clear the bottom track. To remove a door, you first raise it as high as it will go, then swing the bottom edge out and pull free.

This type of arrangement is almost always trouble-free, unless the door warps or swells, or dirt or some other foreign matter gets into the track. Use a stiff brush or a vacuum cleaner to remove any such obstruction, and spray with a silicone-type lubricant (never use oil) to ease up a set of doors that is otherwise difficult to move.

If a door persistently jumps out of its track when slid back and forth, chances are that something is stuck inside the track, or that the track is bent. The problem can also occur when the doors are a little too short, or when the framework of the cabinet has warped slightly so that the tracks are now a little farther apart than they were originally. Any of these defects will result in the door's not extending far enough into the upper track, so that the top pops out when you slide the door. To correct this condition, remove one of the tracks (the upper or the lower) and insert a thin strip of cardboard or plastic under it to shim the track up and bring the two slightly closer together. The door should then project far enough into the upper track to keep it from jumping out.

Chapter 5

Repairing Windows

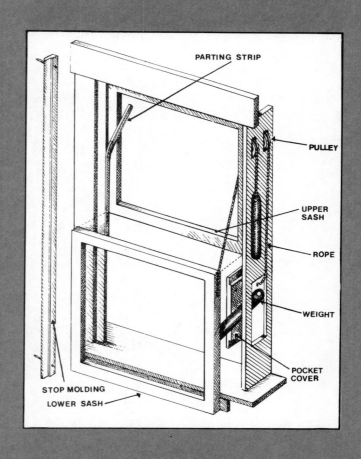

PARTING STRIP

PULLEY

UPPER SASH

ROPE

WEIGHT

POCKET COVER

STOP MOLDING

LOWER SASH

WINDOWS ARE not only a means of allowing daylight to enter the house and people to see out during the day, they are also essential for ventilation in most homes. For this reason most windows are constructed so that they can be opened or closed when desired—and this is exactly what causes most window problems. A fixed pane of glass is fairly easy to seal, and there is nothing movable to get out of order. But windows that open and close are movable, so mechanical breakdowns can occur, and there is always the problem of maintaining a watertight, airtight seal that will not interfere with easy opening and closing.

With modern improvements in design, including the development of more efficient weatherstripping materials (these are more thoroughly described in Chapter 15), a surprisingly good seal can be created around any hinged or sliding window. And because a single pane of glass is an extremely poor insulating material, adding storm windows, or using double-pane glass, is essential for those who want to minimize energy losses all year round (in the winter to keep heat in, and in the summer to keep it out).

Windows for the home will generally fall into one of four categories: double-hung windows that slide up and down in separate channels in the window frame; sliding windows that operate from side to side so that one panel slides behind the other; casement windows that swing open on hinges like a door; and awning windows that have sashes that are hinged along the top so that they swing out from the bottom, like an awning. (Jalousie windows might be described as another version of the awning window, except that they consist of many narrow panes of glass that swing out together when the operating mechanism—either a crank or a lever—is activated. There is no standardization of parts for these specialized windows, so repairs usually must be made by a professional dealer/installer.)

REPAIRING DOUBLE-HUNG WINDOWS

Double-hung windows are far and away the most popular type of residential window in common use. Offering a choice of lowering the upper sash or raising the lower sash, they provide maximum flexibility for ventilation. They may be made of wood, metal, or vinyl plastic, or a combination of these materials, with wood still the most popular (some newer wood windows are vinyl-clad on the outside to eliminate the need for painting).

When a double-hung window starts to stick or bind, nine times out of ten the trouble is caused by dirt or paint clogging the channel in which the window sashes slide.

Opening a Stuck Window

In most cases when a window is stuck shut—either because paint is caked around the edges or because the wood has swelled—unless the condition is really severe you should be able to free the sash by prying carefully around the edges with a stiff putty knife, as shown on p. 100, top left.

Force the blade in between the sash and the molding, using a hammer if necessary, then wiggle or twist it back and forth as illustrated to break the "seal" formed between the two. Work your way slowly up one side and then down the other side, twisting and wiggling the blade repeatedly in each spot before moving on to the next position. Then try opening the window again.

If it is still stuck, there is an additional step that sometimes works. Get a small block of wood,

Freeing a stuck sash with a stiff
putty knife

Tapping a wooden block into a window frame
will sometimes free a stuck sash.

slightly narrower than the width of the window channel, and place it in position inside the channel just above the frozen sash frame (see drawing). Rap this block sharply with a hammer two or three times. This will serve to spread the frame momentarily—just enough to break the sash loose so you can move it.

Prying loose the stop molding to remove sash frame that won't open

STOP
MOULDING

SASH
FRAME

If you still cannot get the window open, your best bet is to pry the stop moldings off on each side of the window frame and remove the sash completely, then follow the directions on the pages that follow.

Assuming the window sash can be removed, even if it is with great difficulty, the first thing you should do is clean out the channel by scraping with a narrow putty knife, then scrubbing with a stiff brush. If paint has caked inside the channel or along the edges, use a small hook-type scraper to remove it, along with any dirt or other foreign matter that may have accumulated.

Pay particular attention to the edges of the stop moldings where they come up against the face of the sash. This edge often becomes so caked with paint that moving the sash up or down becomes extremely difficult (sometimes impossible). Use a brush or vacuum to clean out dust and chips, then lubricate the channels by spraying with a silicone lubricant, or by rubbing a piece of paraffin or candle wax along the inside of each channel.

If none of these measures makes the window work any easier, it is possible that the wood has swollen. The way to cure this condition is to remove the stop moldings on each side (see drawing at left) so that you can take the bottom sash

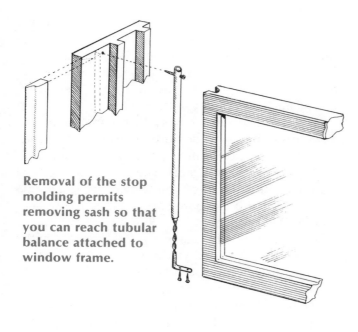

Removal of the stop molding permits removing sash so that you can reach tubular balance attached to window frame.

out and trim off the edges by sanding or planing.

Use a wide chisel or stiff putty knife to pry the stop moldings off, then use a scraper to clean excess hardened paint off the face of the sash. Once the stop moldings have been pried off, the lower sash will be easy to remove—just lift up slightly, then pull it toward you and up out of the window frame. The cords or chains that are attached to each side (and connected to the sash weights at the other end) can then be detached to let you get in with a small block plane or a wood rasp to trim the edges.

If your window does not have sash weights but instead has spiral-type spring balances, you'll find that you won't have cords or chains to contend with, but you will have to unscrew the tubular balance from the window frame in order to get the sash out. You will then have to detach it from the sash at the bottom, so that you can get at the edge of the sash with a plane or rasp.

Although taking off the stop moldings on the inside will make it easy for you to remove the lower sash, it still will not enable you to remove the upper sash. This sash rides in a separate, outer channel which is separated from the inner channel by a strip of wood molding known as a parting strip (see drawing on page 102). To get the upper sash frame out you will have to remove

this parting strip, having first removed the lower sash and the stop moldings as described above.

Start by lowering the upper sash as far as it will go. Then grasp the square parting strip near the top with a pair of heavy pliers. Pull straight out with a firm grip until the upper end comes free. Chances are that it won't come out easily, having over the years become virtually glued into place with layers of paint. But if you work carefully, prying along the edges with a sharp chisel or knife and pulling steadily with the pliers, you should be able to get it out in one piece (don't worry if you don't—a new parting strip can be bought readily at any lumberyard). As soon as the top of the parting strip starts to come loose, move your pliers down a few inches and start pulling again till you gradually get more of it loose.

There are two precautions to remember when you are trying to remove this parting strip: (1) Sometimes there are small nails or screws that hold it in place, so look carefully for any of these and pry around them rather than between them. (2) In many instances you will find that the bottom rail of the lowered upper sash will overlap the parting strip; in that case you cannot pull it straight out along its full length, but will have to bend the top end out past the side of the window frame, then pull up and out while gripping hard in order to get the whole length out.

Repairing Broken or Jammed Sash Cords

Older windows have sash cords and weights, and these frequently present problems. When the upper sash keeps falling down, or when the lower one won't stay up after you raise it, chances are that the ropes connected to the sash weights are broken. These sash weights are on the inside of the window frame, riding up and down in concealed pockets on each side as shown in the drawings on pages 102 and 103.

Sometimes a window sash will jam or stick because the rope that goes over the pulley is jammed—the rope has "jumped the track" and come out of the pulley groove. When this happens the rope often gets caught between the edge

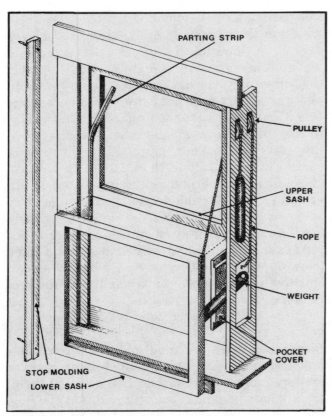

Double-hung window sash and frame structure, showing "old-fashioned" sash weights and interior view of rope-and-pulley arrangement

of the pulley and the wood frame in which it is mounted, and the harder you pull, the tighter the rope gets jammed in. To correct this, raise the sash enough to give you some slack, then use a blunt screwdriver or the side of a dull putty knife to work the rope free by pushing it upward. If necessary, tap the tool with a hammer. When the rope is clear of the pulley's side, guide it over the top of the pulley and back into the groove where it belongs.

In most cases, however, the problem is not that simple. You will probably find that the rope going up and over the pulley is slack—or it will be missing entirely, because it has broken and the weighted end has fallen back down inside the window frame's pocket. To repair this properly, you will have to replace the broken rope with sash chain (sold in all hardware stores and lumberyards).

Start by removing the stop moldings on each side, as described on page 100, then lift the sash

frame completely out of the window and disconnect the cords from both edges of the sash. After the bottom sash has been removed, examine the window frame inside the channel on both sides. Along each, you should be able to discern the barest outline of a cut-out panel.

Called the pocket cover, this panel may be hard to see at first if the outline has been covered over by many layers of paint. If you cannot find it, try tapping hard against the lower part of the channel with a hammer; this may cause the paint to crack around the panel and enable you to see its outline more easily.

In some cases the panel is held in place with two small screws, one at the top and one at the bottom of the panel, but in others it will just be a force fit. In still others the pocket cover may never have been completely cut out around the edge, so you may have to use a keyhole saw to complete the rest of the cut. If the panel is partially covered by the parting strip, then you will have to take this strip out first (see drawing at left). After you have located the cut-out or panel, either unscrew it or work a chisel carefully around the edges to pry it out. This will reveal an opening through which you can reach inside the pocket and find the sash weight.

If your window has no pocket cover or removable panel inside the channel—or if you just cannot find it on your window—then the only way to get at the sash weights inside the frame is to pry off the window trim around the inside. This will expose the hollow space where the sash weights are suspended.

After the pocket cover (or the inside window trim) has been removed, reach in and lift the sash weight—it will be sitting on the bottom if the cord is broken. Untie the old cord, then cut a new piece of sash chain the same length as the old cord. If you are not sure of the correct length, start with an extra-long piece of chain so that you can trim it off afterward.

Feed the new chain over the top of the pulley, starting at the outside. Let it fall down inside the pocket until you can reach through and grab the end as it comes down. Attach this end to the sash weight, using the small hooks or clips sold for this purpose, then set the sash weight back inside the pocket; make sure the free end of the chain (the end that will be attached to the sash) can't

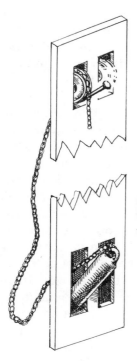

Installing a new chain. Nail temporarily keeps chain from pulling through.

pull through by pushing a nail or large paper clip through one of the chain links on the other side of the pulley. Now install chain on the other side of the window frame in the same way.

Set the sash frame back into the window so that it rests on the sill, then pull down the free end of one chain until you have raised the weight up high enough (inside the pocket) so that it almost touches the pulley. Slide a small nail through one of the links in the chain to keep the weight from dropping (the nail will get caught in the pulley opening), then fasten the other end of the chain to the side of the sash frame in the same place where the old rope was fastened; use one or two small nails, or the clips provided on some windows.

Repeat this on the other side of the sash frame, then test by raising the sash as high as it will go—the weight should clear the bottom by at least a couple of inches.

Replacing the cords for the upper sash frame is done in much the same manner, except that you have to take the lower sash out first (even if only one cord is broken it's a good idea to renew all four cords while you are at it and have the window apart). You can then remove the parting strip on each side (see page 102) in order to get the upper sash out. Since this is harder than just replacing the cords on the lower sash, there is a temptation to do only the lower ones when the upper cords are not broken—but this is only delaying the day when you will have to do the whole job over again.

Replacing Sash Cords with Spring Tape Balances

Instead of replacing broken sash cords with chain, you can get rid of sash weights altogether—as well as the need for rope or chain—by taking out the pulleys at the top of the window frame on each side and replacing them with a half-round, drum-shaped device that has a spring-wound tape on the inside. Its outside dimensions are such that the housing will fit into the opening left when the old pulley is removed, using two small screws at the top and bottom to hold it in place as shown.

Installing a spring-tape balance to the side of a sash frame

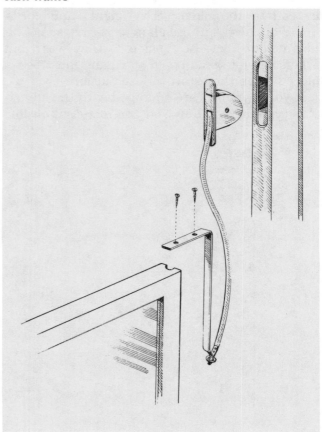

Designed so that the unwinding metal tape builds up spring tension (to counterbalance the weight of the sash frame) as it is pulled downward, these spring balances come in various sizes to match sash frames of different weights and sizes, so you have to be sure of your window measurements when buying them.

To install them you start by removing the stop moldings and sash frames as described on page 102. Then disconnect and remove the old cords and weights. Pry out and remove the pulleys at the top on each side, then install the spring balances in the old pulley openings. A special metal bracket supplied with each balance is then attached to the side of the sash frame in the groove where the old rope originally fitted, and the free end of the spring-loaded tape is pulled down and clipped onto this bracket.

Repairing Windows with Tube-Type Spring Balances

Many windows installed over the past two or three decades have tubular-type spring balances, instead of the older sash weights and cords. Some of these spring balances permit some adjustment to increase tension as they wear, but others cannot be adjusted at all and must be replaced when they start to lose tension.

If your windows are equipped with the adjustable type, here is how you can increase tension:

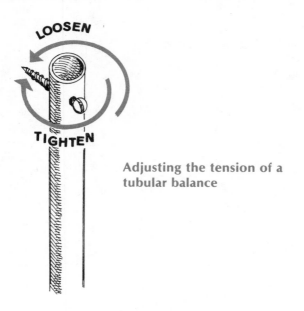

Adjusting the tension of a tubular balance

Hold the tube firmly with one hand and remove the screw holding it in place at the top. When the screw is out (keep holding the tube firmly because it will try to spin away from you!) you can adjust the tension by turning the tube clockwise two or three turns.

If the spring is too tight (the window creeps up), then you want to decrease tension, and you do this by letting the spring unwind slowly after the screw at the top has been removed.

If the balance doesn't work at all, or is not the adjusting type, or if adjusting the tension doesn't solve the problem, you will have to replace the balance entirely. To do this you first raise the sash as high as it will go, then unscrew the brackets on the bottom of the sash frame which attach the spring balance to the sash (see drawing on page 101). Now remove the stop moldings and lift the sash out of the window frame.

The new spring balances are installed simply by reversing the order—screw the upper end of the tube in place against the window channel, then replace the sash and attach the brackets that fasten the end of the spiral rod to the bottom of the sash. When buying a replacement unit, bring the old one along to make sure the new one will fit.

REPAIRING CASEMENT WINDOWS

Unlike sliding double-hung windows, casement windows are attached by hinges so that they can swing open and be closed much like an ordinary door. Made of wood or metal, they usually operate with a lever-type mechanism that is activated by a crank on the inside. Some older models do not have cranks, but rather a rod or lever that you merely push to open or pull to close. The rod slides through a pivot bearing that in turn slides in a track on the sill.

When a casement window starts to stick and bind, the trouble almost always has one of four causes: (1) The hinges that support the window need lubrication. (2) The window frame's edges are caked with paint and/or dirt. (3) The opening and closing mechanism—crank, rod, or tracks in which the guides slide—needs lubrication. (4) The rod or pivot lever that actually pushes the window open and pulls it closed has been bent.

Installing New Window Channels

One way to rejuvenate an old double-hung window with broken sash cords, or with poor weatherstripping and hard-to-move sash, is to install replacement channels that eliminate the need for weights and cords—or balances of any kind.

Sold in home centers and lumberyards, these replacement channels come with permanent weatherstripping, as well as a friction-type channel that holds the sash in position regardless of where you leave it. They are available in various lengths to fit most standard-height windows.

You install them by first removing the stop moldings on either side, then taking out the lower sash and the upper sash, disconnecting the cords or chains attached to the sides of each. Taking out the upper sash will usually require removing the parting strip first (see page 102). With both sashes out, the cord pulleys at the top of each channel are removed next, either by prying them out or simply by driving them into the hollow space behind the frame with a hammer. Don't worry about the holes that remain—these will be covered by the new channels.

Now use sandpaper to clean the edges of each sash and scrape off any ridges of paint that remain. Then, as shown in the illustrations, stand the two sashes up behind each other and place one channel on each side. Press everything firmly together and lift the whole assembly up and set it in place inside the window. Set the bottom ends of the channels in place first, then tip the upper ends into position. The channels are then fastened in place against the sides of the window frame with screws—first at the top, then at the bottom. The job is finished when you replace the stop moldings on each side (they are no longer needed to hold the sash in place, just to give the frame a finished look).

Installing friction-type replacement channels. Left, channels are held against sides of sash and entire assembly is slid into place; right, upper end of channel on each side is then nailed securely.

Lubricating the lower pivot joint often helps to free up a sticking casement window.

The crank mechanism of a casement window may have to be removed for greasing.

Start by lubricating the hinges or pivoting supports on which the window swings, using a few drops of lightweight oil and working it in by opening and closing the window a few times. Next, lubricate the crank mechanism that activates the rod or lever that opens and closes the window. To do this you will have to take off the handle assembly (it is held in place by two screws), then clean out the gears and the inside of the case and repack with fresh grease.

If the window still doesn't work right, swing it all the way open and inspect the track along the bottom edge of the sash (on some wood casement windows this track will be on the inside face of the sash, not under the bottom). Use a wire brush to clean out dirt, paint, or encrusted grease, then rub a little fresh white grease (Vaseline works fine) along the track.

When a casement window swings open easily until the last inch or so, but then "gets stubborn," the first thing you should suspect is an accumulation of dirt and hardened paint along the edges of the sash frame, or inside the window frame itself where the sash contacts the casing. Use steel wool and a wire brush to clean off any such accumulation on metal frames, and a scraper and sandpaper for wooden frames.

If none of these steps makes the window work

easily, the trouble is most likely either inside the crank mechanism, or in the actuating rod slide (where the end of the rod slides along the track on the bottom of the sash frame). If the rod or lever is bent, or if the part that slides along the track is sticking, you can try, in the first case, to straighten the rod, or, in the second, to unstick the sliding track and guide by cleaning and lubricating.

One sure way to make certain whether or not the problem lies with the crank mechanism,

A wire brush is used to clean sliding track under a casement window.

rather than with the slide or the rod as described above, is to disconnect the rod from the sash frame. You can usually do this by swinging the window open as far as it will go, then slipping the sliding guide out of one end of the track (depending on its style, and on which way the window swings, the guide will come out of either the left or right end of the track).

After the rod or arm is disconnected, turn the crank handle to see if it works easily. If it does, you know the problem lies with the track or guide. If it doesn't, then you know the crank mechanism is the trouble. Take the whole thing off (it is held in place by two screws), then examine the gears on the inside (wiping off any excess grease to help you see). Note whether any of the gears or other moving parts are bent, or if the teeth are chipped and broken.

If everything looks okay, flush out the mechanism with kerosene or paint thinner, then squirt some fresh oil inside and try again. If the handle still does not work easily, your best bet is simply to replace the entire mechanism with a new unit. You can buy it at many large building supply outlets and home centers, or your local dealer should be able to tell you where you can order one. Bring the old one along to be certain you get a new one that will match.

Casement windows are often plagued with one other type of problem—drafts caused by the fact

Inserting a shim or spacer behind a casement window handle assembly provides firmer closing pressure.

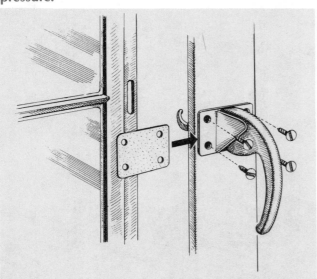

that the window doesn't shut tight enough. This is particularly true of metal casements, which have a lever-action handle with a hook-shaped lock on the outside that swings up through a slot to engage the sash frame. The mechanism is supposed to pull the sash up against the window frame and create a tight seal, but in some cases it does not pull in tight enough. To correct this condition, remove the handle from the inside, then slide a shim or spacer made of cardboard or plastic behind it, as shown in the drawing. The effect will be to move the handle slightly farther inward, and thereby apply greater closing pressure as the hook part swings inward.

REPAIRING SLIDING WINDOWS

The most common cause of trouble with a horizontal sliding window—wood or metal—is dirt or paint inside the track, or on the edge of the sash frame. This is especially true in older houses with wood windows on which multiple layers of paint have built up over the years.

Sometimes you can correct the problem simply by cleaning out the track with a wire brush, or by scraping the edges of the movable sash frames with a narrow putty knife. In most cases, however, you will have to take the window sash out, then use a scraper and some sandpaper to remove the hardened paint from both the window frame and the sash frame. (Horizontal sliding windows can be removed by lifting up and swinging the bottom end out of the track, then pulling the top out.) Spray the track and the edges of the sash with silicone lubricant, then replace the sash.

Lubrication is also the answer on metal sliding windows—after tracks and sash edges have been thoroughly cleaned with fine steel wool and a wire brush. Use a silicone spray or rub with paraffin, but don't use oil in this case—it will only attract and hold dirt that will then cake up and cause more trouble.

If lubrication doesn't solve the problem, then the track is probably damaged or bent. Examine the inside of the track carefully to find the damaged section. If it is just bent in one place, you should be able to straighten it with a hammer and a small block of wood, or by using a pair of heavy pliers. If it is bent in many places, or is cracked and broken, you should replace the entire window frame.

REPAIRING AWNING WINDOWS

These windows are practically the same as casement windows, except that they are hinged along the top and thus swing out from the bottom, instead of from one side or the other. Most of the cleaning and lubricating techniques described above for casement windows will also apply to awning windows.

While most awning windows have crank mechanisms similar to the ones used on casement windows, some have a scissors-type lever-arm action that helps support the opened window sash. Like the operating levers or rods that are used on a casement window, the pivot points on the operating mechanism should be lubricated regularly with a lightweight penetrating oil. Don't forget the pivoting arm at the side that rides up and down in a track as the window frame swings up and down. Very often when a window is hard to work, cleaning and lubricating the track in which the end of this arm rides is all you need to do.

REPLACING BROKEN PANES OF GLASS

The hardest part of replacing a windowpane is, more often than not, getting the broken pieces of the old glass out and then removing the old hardened putty. For safety's sake, you should wear heavy work gloves to protect your hands, and when pulling the broken pieces of glass out of the frame, play safe and grab with an extra piece of cloth (in addition to the gloves) or with a pair of pliers before you start twisting or pulling.

After the broken pieces of glass have been removed, scrape out all of the old, hardened putty or glazing compound, using a narrow chisel or a stiff putty knife. If you find the putty to be exceptionally hard and stubborn, you can make things easier by first applying heat to soften it, using either an electric heat lamp or a portable propane torch. An electric heat lamp will take longer, but it is safer and less likely to scorch the wood or the surrounding paint. Either way, it is a good idea to keep a bucket of water or a small fire extinguisher handy—just in case.

After the glazing compound has been removed, clean out the rabbet thoroughly (the rabbet is the groove or recess into which the glass fits), either scraping or rubbing with steel wool. Then coat the exposed wood inside the rabbet with boiled linseed oil, or with a thin coat of exterior primer. This seals the wood and helps to ensure a better bond (otherwise the wood will absorb the oil in the glazing compound, which then, in time, dries out excessively). If the window is metal, make sure you clean off all rust and corrosion and apply a coat of metal primer before glazing.

When measuring for the new pane of glass, make sure you allow for a slight amount of clearance on all sides—usually about ⅛ inch less around all four sides. Bring these measurements to your local dealer (be sure you tell him you have already made the needed allowance for extra clearance), and have him cut a new piece to size.

A word of caution here about the kind of glass to buy: If the window or door is in a location where it can be easily broken (by children throwing balls, for example, or by accidental en-

Using a propane torch to soften old glazing compound

Cutting Glass

Although all hardware stores and lumberyards will cut glass to size, there are times when you may want to cut your own—for example, when trimming down a large piece for a small pane, or when using scrap pieces for a picture frame. Fortunately, there are only two tools you'll need: a glass cutter and a straightedge. A pair of square-jaw pliers may also come in handy if you have to break off small strips, though this is not always necessary.

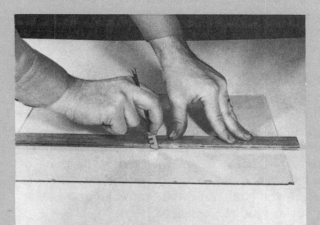

Lay the piece of glass on a flat surface that you have covered with several layers of newspaper (to serve as padding). Then place the straightedge along the line of cut and hold it down firmly with one hand. Now grip the glass cutter with your thumb and index finger, as shown, and dip the cutting wheel into a little kerosene or very light machine oil.

You make the cut by scoring the glass *only once* with a single stroke, bearing down with firm, steady pressure during the entire length of the stroke. *Do not bear down hard*—just press with moderate pressure and move the cutter along steadily. The idea is to score the surface of the glass with a single smooth stroke so that the cutter makes a crisp, crackling sound and leaves a uniform score mark without skipping and with no tiny chips flying off the surface. Going over the stroke almost always results in breaking or chipping the glass at some point.

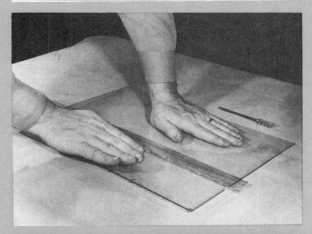

Now place a pencil, dowel, or strip of wood under the glass so it is positioned directly under the score mark you've just made. Then press down on both sides of the glass, more smartly on the smaller piece. It should snap off neatly along the line of cut. If any narrow slivers remain, grasp these with a pair of pliers and snap off by twisting up or down.

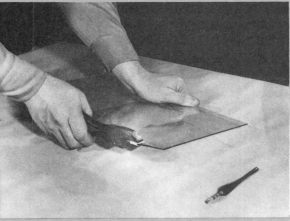

Using a glass cutter: scoring, breaking the cut, and snapping off any remaining pieces

counters with large packages or big dogs) you should buy safety glass or tempered glass, or instead of a glass get a clear plastic such as one of the break-resistant acrylics. In many communities there are laws or building codes that require such materials for hazardous locations.

Before installing a new pane of glass you should first apply a layer of glazing compound behind it to ensure a waterproof seal. Roll a wad of glazing compound into a long thin strip (about ⅛ inch in diameter), place it along the rabbet where the glass will go, then press the pane of glass into place, shoving it in hard enough to squeeze the compound flat, with the excess oozing out around the edges.

Glazier's points—triangular-shaped bits of metal—are what actually hold the glass in place, not the glazing compound. Use about two points on each vertical side in smaller windowpanes, more on the larger ones. You install glazier points by pushing them in with the blade of a screwdriver or stiff putty knife, or you can buy the kind that has a slight flange at one side and, very carefully, tap them in with a tack hammer.

The last and final step of window replacement is applying the glazing compound around all four sides to seal the edges of the glass with an airtight and watertight fit. The easiest way to do

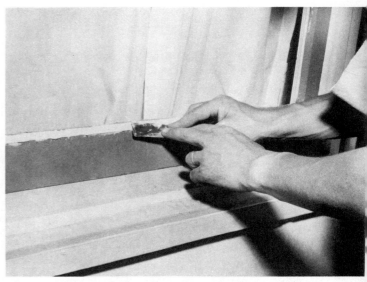

Holding putty knife at proper angle when applying glazing compound will ensure smooth bevel.

this is to roll the glazing compound into a long strip—a "bead" slightly thicker than a pencil—then press it firmly into place with your fingers. Knead it down so that it makes firm contact with both glass and frame. You are then ready to form a neat bevel with your putty knife, smoothing off any excess in the process.

Holding the blade at such an angle to the surface that only a corner of the blade contacts the glass (see illustration), press down firmly while dragging the blade smoothly along the surface. This will shave off excess compound so that it can be peeled away with your other hand. The idea is to form a neat beveled surface that will be both flush with the wood on the outside and tight against the glass on the inner side. If you have trouble getting the compound smooth because the knife tends to "drag" or crumple the surface, try heating the knife slightly—the warm blade will make the glazing compound easier to finish smoothly.

The glazing compound should come up just high enough on the glass to cover the wood that is visible through the glass, but not high enough so that you see the edge of the glazing compound from the inside.

Metal-frame windows are glazed in much the same manner as wood windows except that you don't use glazier's points to hold the glass in place. Instead, there are special clips that snap into the channel in the window where the glass fits. Some windows have plastic splines that hold the glass in place instead.

Using a putty knife and hammer to insert metal glazier points

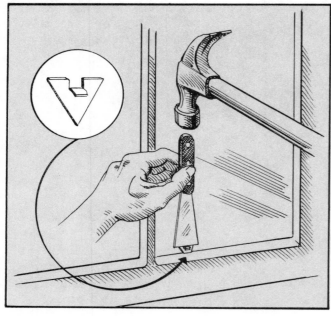

REPAIRING WINDOW SHADES

Window shades are wound on rollers that have an internal spring which supplies the tension or power required to pull the shade up and to keep it up when released. This spring is attached to the inside of the roller at one end, and to a flat metal pin that projects out the other end. This flat pin can turn without the whole roller turning, and when the shade is in place the pin fits into a slot in the shade mounting bracket so that it cannot turn when the shade rolls up and down—in other words, when the shade roller is turning (as you pull the shade up or down), the flat pin is held fixed in one position.

So here is what happens: When you pull the shade down, the spring on the inside gets wound tighter and tighter, thus building up tension and energy that will serve to raise the shade. The spring is kept from unwinding by a ratchet mechanism. You disengage the ratchet by giving the shade a short downward pull, and the shade goes up as the spring unwinds. If it were not for the ratchet mechanism on the end of the roller, the shade would simply fly up with a bang every time you let it go—and this is exactly what happens when there is something wrong with the ratchet mechanism, or when the shade is wound too tight.

The ratchet mechanism consists of a pivoted pawl that drops down naturally (by gravity) to engage a notch on the side of the flat pin's collar when you stop pulling. When you then pull down with a little tug, the roller rotates slightly, allowing the pawl to drop out of the way so the shade

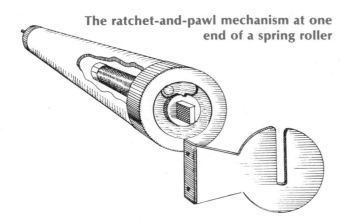

The ratchet-and-pawl mechanism at one end of a spring roller

can roll itself back up (until you stop it with another little tug).

The two most common problems encountered with a window shade are: (1) not enough tension in the spring, so the shade keeps unrolling when you let it go; and (2) the spring is wound so tight that every time you release the shade it goes flying all the way up to the top with a loud bang.

To cure the first condition—a shade that keeps falling—you only need to wind the spring a little tighter. Pull the shade down as far as it will go, then reach up and lift the roller out of the brackets that support it at the top of the window. Holding the roller in both hands, roll the shade up as shown in the accompanying drawing. When you have rolled it up completely, replace the shade in its brackets and try again. This time the tension should be much stronger, probably adequate for making the shade work properly. If not, repeat the process, only this time roll the shade up by hand just about halfway—rolling it all the way up once again would probably build up too much tension and cause it to fly up out of control when released.

If winding the spring in this manner has no effect at all on increasing tension, then the spring is broken and you need a new shade roller. Replacement rollers are available from stores that sell window shades, as well as from many hardware stores.

To cure the second condition—a shade that is wound so tight that it has too much tension and flies up out of control when released—you do just the opposite. Raise the shade carefully as high as it will go on the window, then reach up and lift it out of its brackets while it is still fully rolled up. Holding the roller in your hands, unroll about half to three-quarters of the length of the shade by hand, then, holding the shade in the same position, replace it in its brackets. Now check the tension again. If it is still too tight, repeat the process, but this time unroll it only about half as much as you did the first time.

Sometimes a shade roller will have the right amount of tension in its spring, yet still won't stay in position when you release it. This usually means that the ratchet mechanism at the end of the roller is not working properly—or, more exactly, that the metal pawl is not swinging into place when it should to engage the notch next to

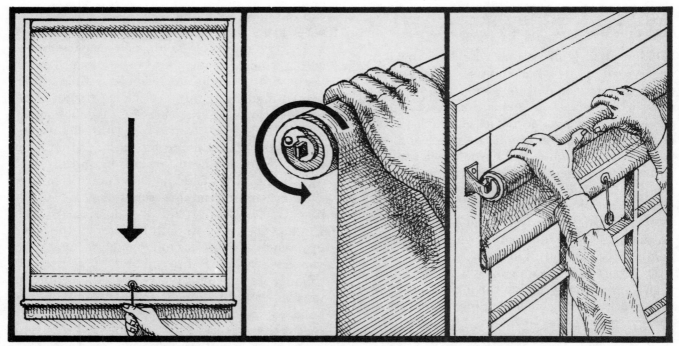

Tightening a loose roller blind. Pull it all the way down and remove it from brackets; roll it firmly by hand; replace it in its brackets and pull down.

the flat pin. The most common cause of this malfunction is dust or lint in the mechanism, so use a small brush to clean out any foreign matter. In some cases it also helps to lubricate with a little silicone spray or graphite powder, but don't use oil—it will eventually cake up and clog the works.

If cleaning and lubricating don't solve the problem, and if a visual examination of the ratchet and pawl mechanism seems to indicate that these parts are working properly (the pawl swings back and forth easily when you turn the shade roller in your hands), then the next thing you should suspect is the mounting brackets on the window frame. The slotted bracket is supposed to hold the flat pin vertical when the shade is in position on the window; the pawl then falls into place when the shade stops. If the bracket is bent or worn, however, the flat pin can turn sideways and the ratchet will not engage when it should. The cure for this is to replace the bent or distorted bracket with a new one.

There are also times when the trouble is due to the fact that the shade was never mounted properly in the first place. If, for example, the shade keeps falling out of its brackets, you know that the brackets are too far apart for the length of

the shade roller. Moving one of them slightly closer to the other will solve the problem. If the brackets are mounted inside the window frame, so that moving them closer together is not practical, the solution lies in lengthening the roller. Usually only a small fraction of an inch is involved, so all you have to do is pull the round pin out slightly (it is like a nail that has been driven into the end of the roller). If this is still not enough, you will simply have to buy a longer roller and remount the shade.

The opposite condition—brackets that are too close together—causes the shade to stick so it won't roll easily, up or down. If the brackets are mounted outside the window frame, the condition can usually be cured simply by bending the brackets slightly away from each other. If they are mounted inside the window frame, then hammering them to flatten them a little will often do the trick.

If this slight amount of additional clearance is not enough, it may pay to shorten the shade roller slightly. Pull out the round metal pin, then pry off the metal cap that covers that end of the wood roller. Now use a fine-tooth saw to trim off a small amount on the end, then replace the metal cap and tap the round pin back into its original hole. This will leave the shade cloth slightly off-center on the roller, but if only a slight amount of wood has been removed the difference should scarcely be noticeable.

Replacing a Window Shade Roller

To replace the wooden roller, you will have to buy a new one that is as long as the old one or, if the frame opening is not standard width, a longer one that will then have to be cut to the exact length is needed. To do this you have to pull out the round pin at one end, then pry off the metal cap that covers that end. Use a fine-tooth saw to cut the wood roller to the length you need (some stores will do this for you). Remember when measuring the length of the roller to allow for the added length of the metal cap and pin when they are replaced.

With the roller cut to length, replace the metal cap and the pin that goes into the center (you just tap them into place with a hammer), then unroll the old shade on the floor and pry out the staples that hold the fabric to the roller. Restaple the top of the fabric to the new roller, being sure to line up the top edge of the fabric with the line drawn on the roller—if you don't get this aligned the shade will roll up at an angle and will bind. Also make certain the shade cloth is centered on the roller so that the same amount of roller projects at each side (as measured from the tip of each pin).

You can shorten a roller by trimming off one end with a saw after removing metal cap and pin.

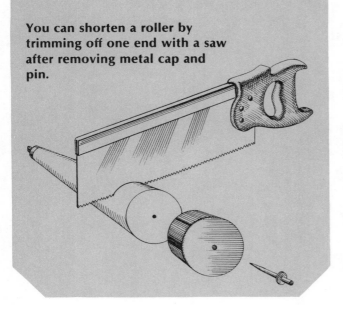

REPAIRING VENETIAN BLINDS

There are really only two components that can wear out on a venetian blind—the ladder tapes that support the individual slats, and the control cords that raise, lower, and tilt the slats.

Tapes and cords for conventional blinds with 2-inch-wide slats are available in hardware and houseware stores, and replacing them on your old blinds is a fairly simple task that requires more patience than actual skill.

Regardless of whether they are made of wood or metal, all venetian blinds work in basically the same manner and are assembled in much the same way. As the illustration on page 114 shows, the slats on a conventional blind are supported by short strips of cloth tape (string is used instead of cloth for the "ladder strips" on most of the newer models with narrow 1-inch slats). These strips are attached to the vertical bands of tape (or string on the narrow models) on each side, thus forming a ladder effect.

Each slat has a slot or hole at each end through which the cord that raises and lowers the blind can pass. This same cord also keeps the slats from slipping sideways between the tapes, thus getting out of alignment with the other slats.

The vertical tapes are attached to the underside of the bottom slat or bar, either by special clips (in the case of metal blinds) or with staples (in the case of wooden blinds). At their upper ends these same tapes are attached to the tilt tube at the top of the blind. When this tube is rotated the tapes on one side are lowered while the tapes on the other side are raised, thus tilting the slats. The tilt tube is rotated by pulling down on the tilt cord, which runs over a pulley that activates a worm gear, which in turn rotates the tilt tube.

Generally speaking, the lift cord—the one that raises and lowers the blind—is the one that seems to wear out first. As you can see in the diagram on page 114, this cord starts at the bottom at one end of the blind, then continues up and across until it finally ends up at the other end of the same bottom slat.

To replace the lift cord you lower the blind all the way, then cut or untie the knots that secure the ends of the cord and remove it. The new cord

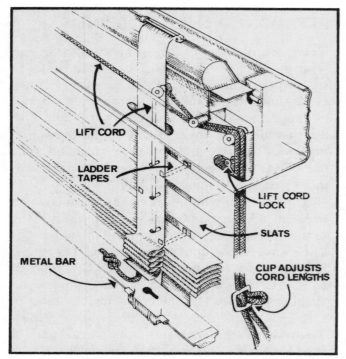

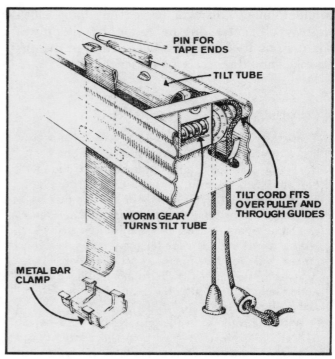

Headbox and other parts of typical venetian blind

is then threaded through the holes in each slat, starting at the right side of the bottom slat and carrying it across the top and out over the lift cord's pulley, then bringing it down to form a loop of approximately the same length as the original cord. Don't forget to thread it through the lift cord's lock clip as you come down to form the loop, and again as you come back up to the pulley. Finish by threading the cord down through the slats along the left side, then secure the cord to the bottom at each end.

To replace damaged or torn ladder tapes (the cloth strips that support the slats), you first lower the blind as far as it will go, then remove the lift cord as described above. Detach the tapes from the bottom slat at each side and put this

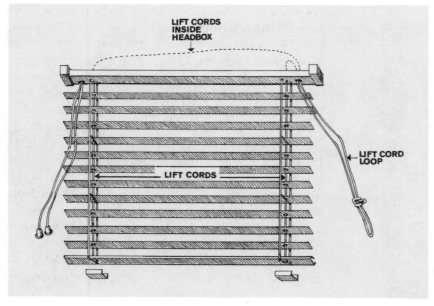

How lift cords and lift cord loop work on venetian blind

bottom piece aside for the moment. Now slide out all the other slats from between the old tapes, leaving only the ladder tapes hanging from the top assembly.

The next step is disconnecting the tapes from the tilt tube mechanism at the top. Metal clips or plastic snaps attach these tapes to the tilt tube in most cases, so it is a relatively simple matter to remove the old ones and to attach the new ones in the same way. Now slide all of the slats back into place on top of each ladder strip, then thread a new length of lift cord back in the manner previously described (you might as well install a new length of cord while you have the blind apart). Bear in mind as you thread this cord into place that since the ladder strips are alternately offset, the cord should pass successive strips on alternate sides.

REPAIRING WINDOW SCREENS

Window screens with wood frames will need regular painting, in addition to occasional repairs to the framework as it starts to age or crack. Metal-frame screens generally need little or no maintenance other than cleaning, and possibly waxing or painting for aesthetic reasons. With both types, however, the wire or plastic screening can get torn or otherwise damaged, and will need occasional repair or replacement.

To replace wire screening on a wood screen you can use either metal mesh (copper or aluminum) or a plastic mesh such as fiberglass. Generally speaking, metal is a bit more resistant to tearing and to damage from burns, but it costs more and is also a lot harder to work with and stretch neatly. In addition, metal tends to oxidize, and the buildup can in time partially obstruct vision through the screen.

Fiberglass and other forms of plastic mesh are easier to cut and stretch tight, and are generally easier to work with. In addition, plastic screening is more broadly available, especially in wider widths.

Lay the screen flat on a suitable working surface and use a stiff putty knife or chisel to pry off the moldings that hold the old screening in place. Try to avoid splitting the moldings—you can then reuse them, though new molding can be purchased in most lumberyards. Now strip off the old wire and take out any staples or tacks that are left in the wood, then use a small scraper to clean out the rabbet (the recess or groove) into which the mesh fits.

Your new piece of mesh should be at least 12 inches longer than the screen frame and at least 4 to 6 inches wider. Position it on top of the frame and fold a small hem at one end (about ½ inch wide) before stapling this across the screen frame. To avoid wrinkles, start at the midpoint or center of the hemmed end and staple out toward each corner.

With one end stapled, move to the opposite end of the frame and pull the mesh tight with your hands (that is why you wanted the extra foot of material—it gives you something to grab). Now staple this end down, again working from the center out to each of the corners. Then do the two long sides, starting in the midpoint of each side and working both ways out to the corners. In this way, any slight wrinkling or bunching of excess will take place in the corners where it can more easily be hidden or trimmed off. Replace all moldings with rustproof brads, including those on the center crossbar. Trim off excess mesh that sticks out from under the moldings with a sharp utility knife or a single-edge razor blade.

Replacing the wire mesh on a metal-screen frame is usually easier, because the mesh is held in place by a plastic or metal spline that eliminates the need for stapling or tacking. The spline fits into a groove on the face of the screen and serves to wedge the edges of the screening in place, avoiding the need for separate moldings to pry off or renail.

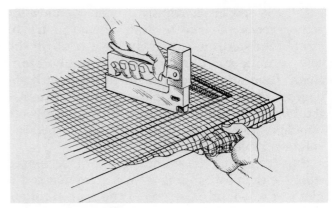

Stapling window mesh to wood frame

Repairing Wooden Screens

The most frequent problem encountered with old wooden screens is corner joints starting to work loose. The whole frame then becomes wobbly and loose, and if not repaired promptly will soon need total replacing.

The simplest way to reinforce the corners of a wobbly screen is to use metal corner brackets or mending plates. These come in various shapes and sizes, and are available with zinc plating to resist rusting (the plating won't last long, however, so such hardware should be painted soon after installation). For reinforcing the center crossbar, you can use T-shaped mending plates in the same way. Corrugated fasteners, which are simply hammered in, can also be used in both corner joints and end joints, but these are generally not as strong as mending plates.

To keep wood screens from deteriorating, the frames should be painted as soon as bare spots start to show, or when peeling is evident. Make sure to fill in any cracks or open joints with putty or wood plastic, and make certain that badly split or rotted pieces are cut out and replaced. Fit any new piece in with an overlapping or scarfed joint, if possible, rather than with a simple butt joint, and use glue as well as screws and mending plates to reinforce the repair. If the screen is badly split or shows signs or rotting in several places, then the smartest thing to do is replace the entire screen with a new one.

To remove the old screen wire you simply pry out one end of the plastic or metal spline on each side, then pull the whole length of spline out of its groove and peel the screen wire off.

Cut the new mesh slightly oversize to allow for some excess material to grab when you try to stretch the screening, then lay the mesh over the screen frame and align it evenly around all four sides. Trim off each corner of the mesh at a 45-degree angle so that the material just cuts across the corner of the screen groove. This prevents bunching up or jamming in the corners when the spline is replaced.

Start replacing the splines on one of the longer sides—either by tapping with a hammer and a block of wood, or using one of the special rollers that are sold for this purpose. (This inexpensive tool makes the job faster and easier to complete.) Begin at one end and force the spline snugly down into its groove, then do the other side in the same manner. Be sure you pull the mesh tight across the surface of the screen frame as you proceed (one hand pulling outside of the spline, the other rolling or tapping the spline down on top of the mesh). When all four sides are secure, use a sharp knife or razor blade to trim off any excess material sticking out beyond the spline.

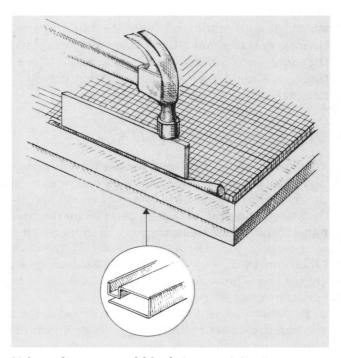

Using a hammer and block (or special roller) to force plastic spline into its groove. Trim off excess mesh with razor knife.

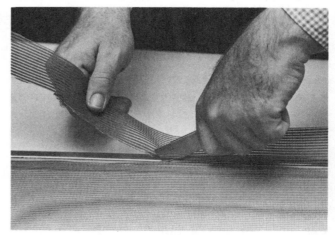

Chapter 6

Interior Walls and Ceilings

ALTHOUGH YOU may not be planning to build a major addition to your house or make any major alterations, you should still be at least generally familiar with how interior walls are framed out and constructed. Why? Because there are times when you may have to break into a wall (for plumbing or electrical repairs, for example), or when you will want to make changes that involve fastening things through a wall. And as you gain experience, you may want to build in an extra closet, or even divide one large room into two smaller ones.

All of these projects, as well as such home improvements as finishing an unused basement or attic or creating a new room out of a garage, will call for some knowledge of how a wall or partition is framed out and finished.

As described in Chapter 3, a wall is normally framed out with vertical 2×4s, called studs, which run from floor to ceiling. These are generally spaced 16 inches apart center to center—in other words, it is 16 inches from the *center* of one stud to the *center* of the next stud; it does not mean that it is 16 inches *between* studs.

This rule can vary in places—for example, in or near the corners of a room where there may not be 16 inches between the last stud and the one in the corner, or near windows, doors, and other openings, where again there may not be 16 inches between the last wall stud and the first to frame out the opening. Also, some walls, especially interior partitions that were added after the original structure, may have studs spaced 24 inches apart instead of the usual 16 inches.

Remember too that doors and windows usually have additional framing in the form of doubled 2×4s alongside each opening, as well as doubled headers across the top of each opening. A header usually consists of two 2×4s nailed together after they have been placed on edge. The sill that crosses under the window opening is also formed by using doubled 2×4s in most cases, and there may be short vertical lengths of 2×4, called cripple studs, nailed between the header and the top plate, as well as between the bottom plate and the underside of the window sill. (See Chapter 3 for more information on wall framing.)

WORKING WITH GYPSUM WALLBOARD (DRYWALL)

Gypsum wallboard is probably one of the most widely used wall-surfacing materials, having almost entirely replaced plaster in homes built over the last thirty or forty years (although it is often called Sheetrock, that is actually the brand name of one manufacturer). Gypsum board is strong and easy to work with, and much simpler than plaster to install. It is one of the easiest ways for the homeowner to finish off a newly erected partition wall (or to make a sizable patch on a plaster wall).

Gypsum-board panels are normally sold in 4×8-foot sheets, although larger sheets 10, 12, or 16 feet long can be specially ordered. They come in three standard thicknesses: ⅜, ½, and ⅝ inch, with the ½-inch thickness being by far the most popular. Each panel has a slight recess along its long edges, designed to make a smooth, flush joint when the joint is to be covered with the special perforated paper tape and compound sold for this purpose.

The sheets are secured with special large-headed nails. For maximum holding power there are nails that are also ringed or "threaded" and are much more effective in preventing eventual loosening or "popping." Nails should be spaced no more than 6 inches apart along the seams, and no more than about 12 inches apart along studs at the center of the sheet.

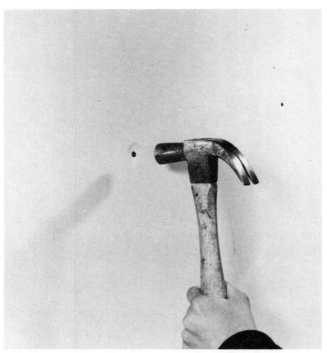

Large-headed nails for gypsum board should be driven in just below surface, creating dimpled hollow.

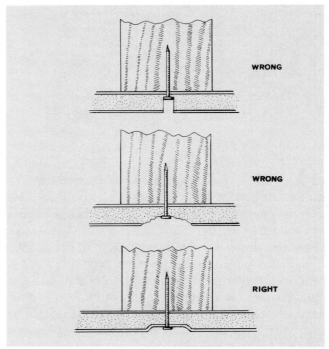

Wrong and right ways to recess nail into gypsum board

As each nail is driven home, its head should be recessed slightly below the surface with the face of the hammer to create a "dimpled" hollow (not so deep as to tear or break the surface of the paper facing on the wallboard, but just deep enough to set the nail head slightly below the surface). This cavity will then be filled with compound later on to cover the nail head and smooth over the depression.

It is important to allow space for expansion between panels. There should be a gap of about ¼ inch at top and bottom, and about 1/16 to 1/8 inch between the edges of all adjoining panels. This gap not only allows for expansion, it also permits the joint compound to work its way in between sheets and thus bond to the edge of each board as well as to its face.

These panels are heavy, so to make sure that they butt up against the ceiling (most ceilings are more than 8 feet high), it is usually helpful to rig up some way to keep them raised when nailing, so that they are not standing on the floor. The easiest method is to wedge each sheet up with a scrap piece of wood and a block, as shown in the illustration at left. You step on the piece of wood to raise the sheet, leaving both hands free to press the sheet against the studs and start nailing.

Using scrap wood to keep wallboard pushed up against ceiling, leaving hands free to hammer

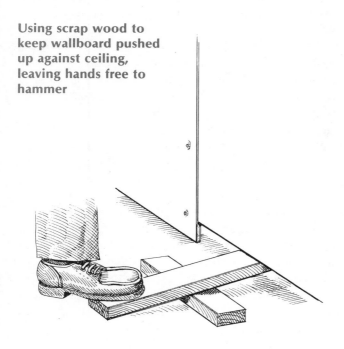

Cutting panels to size is simple. All you need is a sharp utility knife and a straightedge. Use the knife to cut through the paper facing on one side

Cutting panels to size. Score through paper on one side, then fold panel and cut through paper on other side. Snap off.

and score the gypsum core. Then fold the panel away from that side to break the gypsum core. Finish by using the knife to cut through the paper on the other side, then snap the sheet back in the opposite direction to break it off neatly.

To make curved cuts or pocket cuts—as for an opening for an electrical outlet box—the simplest method is to use a small keyhole-type saw. Drill a hole wide enough to start the tip of the saw blade, then cut the opening to the shape desired.

Using keyhole-type saw to make a pocket cut

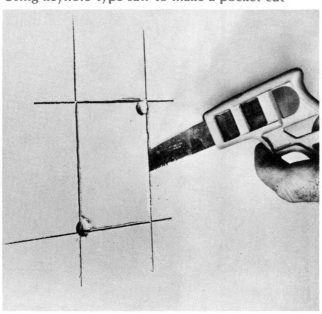

Taping Wallboard Seams

After all seams and joints have been filled and all nail-head depressions have been covered, a gypsum-board wall will have a smooth, unbroken, monolithic surface that can then be painted or wallpapered just like plaster. To achieve this surface you use a special joint cement (also called joint compound) combined with a specially treated paper tape made expressly for the purpose (the tape has very fine perforations in it to let trapped air and moisture escape).

Joint compound is available in two forms: in a powder which you mix with water, or in a ready-mixed paste. The powdered form is a little cheaper, but since you cannot save any once it is mixed you often waste a lot. Moreover, when you mix your own you will sometimes make it too thick (it will be hard to work and will dry too fast) or too thin (it will sag and run, or shrink excessively). With the ready-mixed paste you use only what you need, without waste, and the compound is always the right consistency.

To apply the compound you will need a putty knife or taping knife at least 6 to 8 inches wide. Start by spreading a layer of joint cement over the seam, filling the recess formed where the boards meet (where there is no recess, as on the end seams, you just spread the compound over the seam in a wide band). The paper tape is then pressed down on top of this, using the blade of the knife to smooth it down and partially embed it in the compound. If you do the job right, the tape should be almost—but not completely—covered. Excess cement or compound is smoothed off with the blade of the knife as you work it down along the seam.

Allow this first coat to dry hard (usually overnight), then apply a second coat of the compound alone, again using the wide knife. This time you want to cover the tape completely and fill the seam to bring it up level with the surrounding surface. To accomplish this you will have to "feather out" the compound on each side, forming a still-wider seam anywhere from 8 to 10 inches across. This second coat is not a thick layer—it is just heavy enough to cover the tape and fill in all the low spots in the first coat.

If the joint to be filled does not have the usual recess formed when two sheets are installed alongside each other, you still use the same technique, except that a bit more effort is required to feather out the compound, even more to avoid a bulge or ridge along the seam.

Although it is not always required, walls that are to be painted will usually look better if a third coat of the joint cement is troweled on over the seams (again without tape) for a final smoothing. This coat can be applied with the same wide joint knife previously used, but you will get better results if you use one of the special extra-wide drywall tools made for this purpose (some have a flexible edge that makes it much easier to feather out to a smooth finish). Done right, the surface of the seam should be smooth enough so that little or no sanding will be required to get it ready for painting.

Nail heads are covered with two or three applications of the same joint cement—only without any paper tape. You can do this with the wide joint knife, or with an ordinary 4-inch spackling knife. Again, try to apply the last coat so smoothly that no sanding will be required. If you do have to sand, use a fine grade of paper, and avoid sanding the paper facing surrounding the plastered area—sanding will make the paper fuzzy.

Inside corner joints are taped and filled in much the same manner, except that here you have to fold or crease the tape lengthwise down the center. You spread compound over one side of the joint at a time and give the first side a

Sealing wallboard seams (left to right)**: spreading compound over seam; pressing tape on and partially into compound; applying second coat to cover tape and level it with surface**

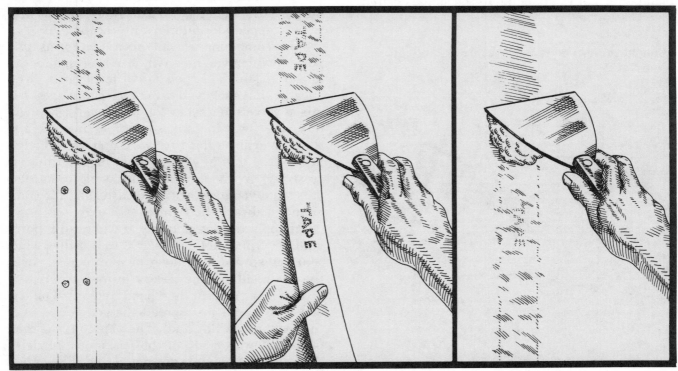

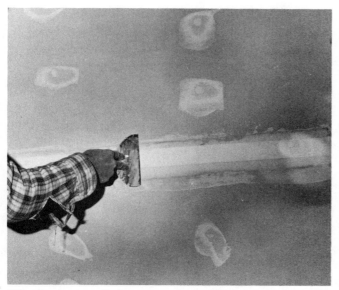

"Feathering out" the second coat of compound. Right, a flexible-edge, extra-wide drywall tool for smooth feathering out.

chance to stiffen before you start spreading compound on the other side. If you don't follow this procedure you may find the edge of the putty knife marking up the wet compound on the adjoining wall.

Outside corners are another matter. They really need reinforcing to keep them from getting banged up and dented, so there is a special type of rigid metal bead to be used on corners. It has a flange attached to each side of the rigid metal

To tape corner joints, crease tape and apply compound to one side of joint at a time.

corner, and you cover these flanges with layers of joint cement on each side after nailing the strip in place against the outside of the corner joint. Allow the first coat of joint cement to dry hard, then apply a second coat to bury the flanges completely, along with the heads of the nails that hold the bead in place. Some of the rigid metal along the corner may still be slightly exposed, but you won't see this at all after the wall is painted or papered.

Often called drywall, gypsum-board walls and ceilings are much less likely to crack than plaster, but this does not mean that they are maintenance-free. Occasionally they will develop cracks along the joints or seams, and there is the fairly common problem of nails "popping" or working loose in various places.

Gypsum board is also more easily damaged by accidental bumping or banging—for example, when moving furniture, or when somebody swings a door open so hard that the knob comes in violent contact with the wall behind it. Fortunately, gypsum board is easy to repair, even when a sizable hole must be patched (a situation you also face when you have to cut a wall open to make plumbing or electrical repairs).

Repairing Popped Nails in Drywall

Popping or working loose of nails can be due to warping or shrinking of the wall studs, or to the fact that the wrong type of nail was used. In

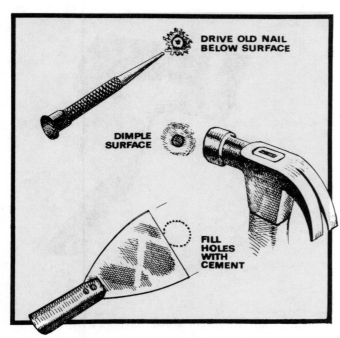

Securing nails that have worked loose in drywall

Patching Cracks in Drywall

Cracks along seams or joints are not as common as popped nails, but they do sometimes show up. If it is only a hairline crack with no sign of the tape's actually pulling loose, and is no more than a few inches long, you can repair it with ordinary spackling compound, similar to the way you would repair a crack in plaster (see page 127). But if the crack is larger and there are definite signs that the tape is pulling loose, you will have to do a more thorough job of patching. Start by pulling off any cracked or loose tape and any cracked or flaking cement. Then use joint cement and fresh tape to redo the joint from scratch, as described on page 122.

Repairing Holes in Drywall

To patch a small hole—for example, one left by a crashing doorknob, or by the removal of an electrical fixture or outlet—you can use several methods. One that works particularly well on

When patching a large crack in drywall, remove old tape and compound, then retape seam from scratch.

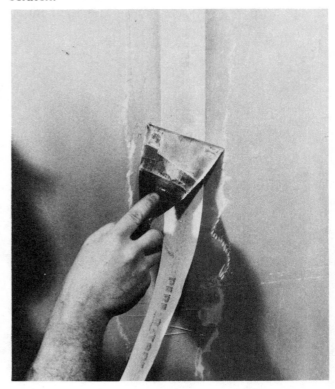

either case, the problem is cured by removing the loose nail or, if you can't remove it easily, driving it deep enough so that the head is well below the surface of the wallboard, then driving in another nail an inch or two away from the original one—only this time using a ringed or threaded nail with a common head (not a finishing nail).

Before you drive this new nail all the way in, push hard against the wallboard to press it against the studs, and hold it in until you are finished driving the nail. Drive the nail head just slightly below the surface of the wallboard—deep enough to create the slight dimple required, but not so deep as to tear the paper facing of the panel.

After the new nails are in, use a ready-mixed vinyl or acrylic spackling compound, or regular joint cement, to fill in and smooth over the depression, and to cover up the nail heads and holes. Apply one coat to fill in and bring the surface almost smooth, let it dry, then apply a second coat for final smoothing. Crisscross your strokes to avoid score marks and give an extra-smooth finish that should need no sanding. If you must sand, use fine paper and a sanding block, and avoid sanding the paper facing around the patch.

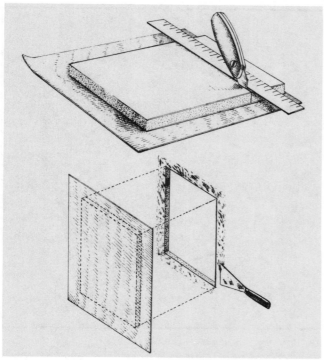

Repairing hole in drywall. Trim gypsum board and backing paper to size, leaving border of facing paper intact; then apply compound to paper border and hole edges, and push in patch.

openings that are no more than a few inches across is the technique illustrated by the drawings here.

1. Start by cutting out the damaged section of wallboard with a keyhole saw, using a straight-edge to guide you in making the cuts. Shape the cutout so it forms a neat square or rectangle.

2. Cut a patch out of a scrap piece of gypsum board, about 2 inches larger on all sides than the cutout (for a total of 4 inches wider and 4 inches longer).

3. Place this piece face down on a flat surface and with a sharp utility knife cut away the excess 2 inches of gypsum core and the paper backing on all four sides as shown in the drawing. *Do not* cut away the paper on the face side of the wallboard. You will be left with a 2-inch-wide paper flap around all four sides, and with the solid core (including backing paper) sized to make a neat fit inside the rectangular hole cut in the wall.

4. Smear a layer of joint cement over the back of the paper flaps, as well as around the edges of the hole in the wall, then push the cut-out patch into place so that it fits into the opening with the

flaps on all four sides overlapping the face of the wall. Use a wide putty knife to smooth flaps onto the surface and to squeegee out excess compound from around the edges.

5. Allow the patch to dry hard, then apply a second coat of compound on top of and around the flaps to feather out the patch neatly so that it will blend in smoothly with the surrounding surface. A third coat of cement may or may not be required for the final smoothing, depending on how careful you have been with the first two.

Another technique that works well on small holes—and is preferable for patching holes more than about 2 or 3 inches across—involves gluing a backing strip of plywood or hardboard across the hole on the inside of the wall, as illustrated in the drawing on page 126. Here are the steps to follow:

1. Cut out the damaged section of wallboard in the form of a neat square or diamond-shaped opening, or it can even be circular in shape.

2. Out of scrap wallboard of the same thickness cut a patch the same size and shape as the opening in the wall, but about 1/16 inch smaller all around.

3. Cut a wide strip of 1/4-inch plywood or hardboard about 2 to 3 inches longer than the width of the opening, then drill a hole in its center large enough for you to insert your finger through it, as shown in the illustration, page 126.

4. Coat the ends of this strip of wood with a fast-setting glue or adhesive (the kind that sets up in a few minutes), then feed the piece of wood through the opening at an angle and use the finger hole to position the strip across the middle of the opening as shown. Pull it toward you so as to bring the glue-coated ends in firm contact with the back of the wallboard on each side of the hole.

5. Hold the strip in place until the adhesive is tacky enough to keep it from slipping, then pull your finger out and wait till the adhesive hardens completely.

6. Spread joint cement over the face of this plywood or hardboard backing and over the edges of the opening, then press the previously cut-out patch into place.

7. Wait till the cement hardens, then use joint cement and tape around the patch, to fill in the seams between patch and wallboard, feathering

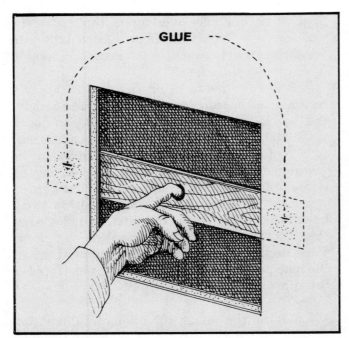

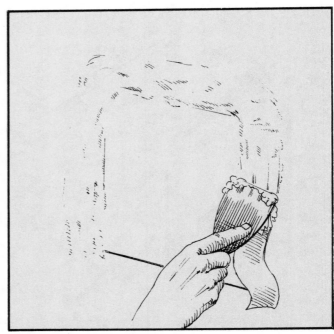

Another method for patching drywall, using wood strip as backing. Glue strip across on inside of opening and let dry; then coat strip with compound, press patch into place, and tape seams.

the compound out neatly so the patch blends in smoothly. (See pages 121–22 for more information on using the joint cement and drywall tape.)

For extra-large holes and extensively damaged sections for which even this technique is not practical, there is a third patching method you can use. Cut out the section of damaged wallboard, extending the cutout to expose half the thickness of the studs on each side (leaving the old wallboard backed by the other half) to allow for wood against which the new patch can be nailed. Then all you have to do is cut a new piece of the same size and shape and nail it to the studs to fill the opening.

Cut out the damaged section with a keyhole-type saw or by making repeated cuts with a sharp utility knife. The cutout should be at least 10 inches high so that the new patch, itself 10 inches high, will be strong enough to resist bending. Since you cannot use a saw for the side cuts (which will be directly over the center of each stud), you will have to employ a hammer and chisel, or score repeatedly with a sharp utility knife until the piece comes off neatly.

The new piece of gypsum board should make a reasonably snug fit inside the opening, and should be nailed against the studs on each side

Replacing damaged drywall. Cut out section to reveal half of studs, preparatory to nailing in new drywall.

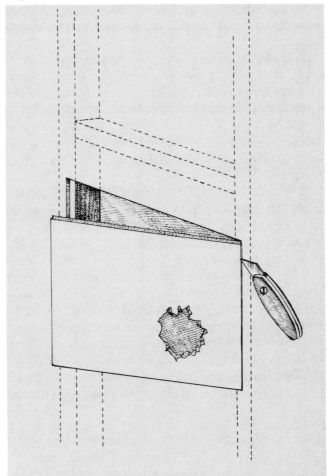

with ringed or threaded nails. Space the nails no more than 4 to 6 inches apart, and angle them slightly to make sure they go into solid wood.

Complete the job by applying joint tape and cement around all four sides of the patch, feathering the compound out neatly on all sides. The technique for applying the joint cement and tape is exactly the same as when finishing new wallboard seams (see page 122).

PATCHING PLASTER WALLS AND CEILINGS

Small holes and cracks in plaster walls and ceilings are normally patched and filled with spackling compound—a material you can buy ready-mixed in paste form, or as a powder that must be mixed with water. The paste type costs slightly more, but it is much easier to work with and forms a stronger bond because it contains a vinyl or acrylic latex base. And since you use only what you need, there is less waste. If you mix too much of the powdered material, the excess hardens up in a comparatively short while and cannot be saved.

The best tool for patching cracks and holes in plaster is a flexible putty knife with a blade made of springy, polished steel. It should be at least 3 inches wide—narrower blades won't bridge the crack or hole as well, making it harder to "feather" the patch out neatly.

The first step is to widen and undercut the crack, using a chisel or a V-shaped tool such as a "church key" can opener. The idea is to make the crack wider on the inside or bottom than along the surface (see drawing below left) in order to ensure a good bond with the old plaster. Brush out dust and loose particles, then wet the crack thoroughly with water before starting to apply the spackling compound.

Scoop up a wad of the compound with a corner of the spackling knife, then spread it into the crack by wiping it across with the full width of the blade, pressing hard enough to flex it slightly, while at the same time forcing the patching material down to the bottom of the crack or hole. Draw the knife back and forth until the whole length of the crack is filled, then remove the excess and smooth off the surface by wiping with strokes almost parallel to the length of the crack, as illustrated. Done with reasonable care, this should leave you with a surface that is smooth enough to need little or no sanding when the patch is dry.

Small holes are filled in much the same manner, except that undercutting is seldom required.

Filling Holes and Larger Cracks in Plaster

Holes and larger cracks (more than about ⅛ inch wide) are generally filled with patching plaster, although spackling compound is often used for the final smoothing. Patching plaster does not set up as fast as regular plaster (which the amateur

Widen and undercut plaster crack with chisel (left) in preparation for spackling, then press compound across crack (center) and smooth surface (right). Inset: Knife should be flexed slightly as you work.

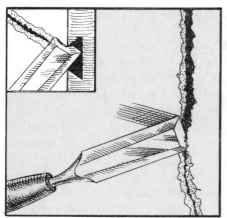
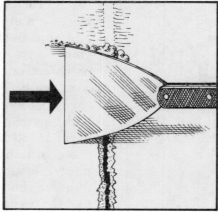
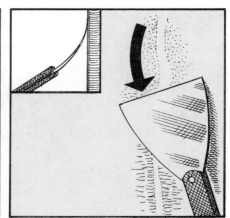

can find hard to work with), but it does set up faster than spackling compound and will not sag or shrink as much as spackling compound (which is why spackling compound is not used on large patches).

Begin by removing loose, crumbling, and flaking material, either scraping or chipping it out. Be ruthless—any part of the plaster that seems soft or crumbly should be scraped out or chipped away until only solid material is left, or unless you are down to the lath.

Next, wet the surface of the exposed lath and the edges of the old plaster with a sponge or brush. Mix a batch of patching plaster, using only enough water to form a plastic, workable mass, then trowel onto the area to be patched. Press firmly into all crevices to make sure of solid contact with the exposed metal or wood lath, as well as with the edges of the surrounding plaster. You can use a wide putty knife for this, but if the area to be covered is more than just a few inches across you are better off using a metal plasterer's trowel.

The first coat of plaster should fill the depression about halfway to the surface, and it should be left relatively rough at the surface to help ensure a good mechanical bond when the second coat is applied. If necessary, use a piece of wire lath or mesh, or even the corner of the

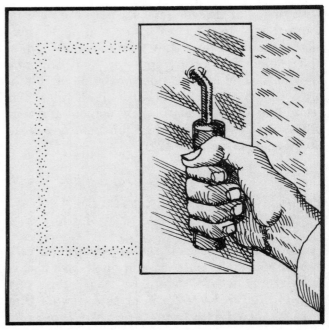

Applying a second plaster coat with metal plasterer's trowel

trowel, to scratch or score the surface of the first coat while it is still soft.

Allow this first coat to dry hard, then wet the surface again and spread on a second coat of plaster—this time bringing it up just about flush with the surrounding surface. This part of the job definitely requires a metal plasterer's trowel, rather than a putty knife; you will be able to bridge the area more easily with less chance of score marks. In addition, you can bear down harder with a trowel—and this pressure is essential for a smooth finish and elimination of air pockets.

There is another method for filling in a large patch, whereby you eliminate the need for troweling on multiple coats of plaster, which in turn makes it much easier to get a smooth finish on your patch. You fill in the depression with a patch cut out of a piece of plasterboard or gypsum board. This is nailed into place inside the cavity as illustrated on page 130 top left, after which patching plaster is troweled in around the edges to fill in the spaces that remain between the board and the edges of the old plaster. The plaster should be applied in two layers, the first filling in the joints about halfway to the surface, and the second filling them in flush with the sur-

Chip away any crumbly plaster before you repair hole or crack.

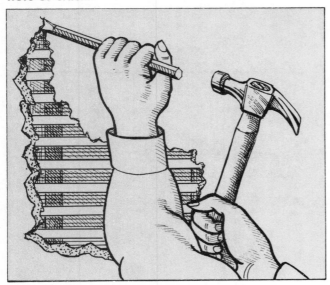

Repairing Plaster When a Hole Has No Backing

Sometimes you have to patch a hole that goes clear through the plaster—for example, when a light fixture or electrical outlet is removed. You will then have to create some sort of backing for the first coat of plaster. One way to do this is to stuff enough wads of newspaper or folded cardboard into the hole to fill it in to the back side, with the wads tight enough to stay in place. This paper or cardboard can then be dampened and covered with a base coat of patching plaster, which is packed in around the edges and spread lightly over the surface of the paper. As this coat hardens it forms enough of a backing so that additional coats of plaster can be troweled on until the hole is filled flush with the surface.

A better way to create a backing that will also be more stable and less likely to shrink or crack is to use a piece of wire lath or coarse wire mesh of some kind. Cut this patch a little larger than the hole, then tie a string to the middle of the mesh. Push the mesh through the hole in the wall and use the string to pull it tight against the back of the plaster, as shown. Tie the string to a stick that is longer than the hole is wide, and twist it tight to hold the mesh firmly in place against the back of the plaster or lath.

Apply the first coat of patching plaster by buttering it in around the edges of the hole and over the face of the wire mesh. You don't want to cover or fill the hole completely—just get a layer over the mesh to form a complete bond with the edges of the old plaster. Allow this to harden, then cut the string, wet the surface, and apply a second coat of patching plaster, this time filling in about two-thirds the way to the surface. Allow the surface to remain rough.

Let this second coat dry hard, then apply your third and final coat to finish the job, using the smoothing techniques described on page 130. As mentioned previously, you can use a wide flexible putty knife if the patch is small; for sizable patches a steel plasterer's trowel is much easier to use and will do a better job.

Wadded newspaper stuffed into hole and lightly covered with plaster forms backing for plaster when filling "bottomless" hole in plaster ceiling or wall.

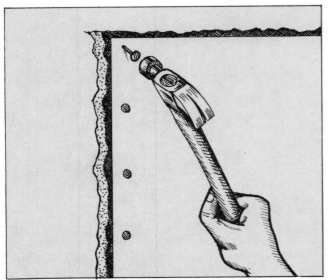

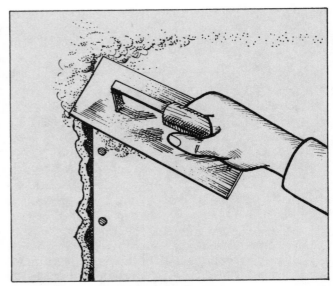

Another method of repairing large plaster hole. Nail piece of gypsum board into cavity, then trowel patching plaster into joints.

face. Spackling compound can then be used for the final smoothing, if necessary.

Regardless of whether you are using a steel plasterer's trowel or a putty knife, there is one professional trick that will help ensure a smooth finish on the final coat of plaster or spackling compound. Wait till this coat starts to stiffen slightly (about 3 minutes), then use a clean paint brush to spread a film of water over the patch.

For a smooth finish, wet second coat with brush when slightly stiff, then drag trowel across surface.

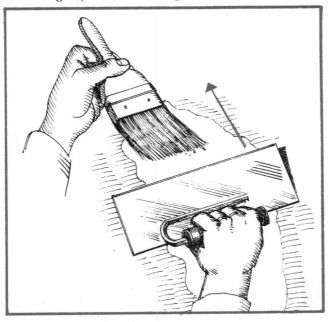

Immediately drag the trowel over the surface of the patch while bearing down hard with the front edge slightly raised. Keep wetting the plaster in front of the trowel or putty knife with your brush, or keep dipping the tool into water to keep the surface wet as you work. You'll wind up with a super-smooth, glazed finish that would be impossible to match otherwise.

After this final coat has hardened, spackling compound can be used as necessary to fill in any visible defects or low spots. No sanding should be required, but if it is, use a fine-grit paper.

PUTTING UP WOOD PANELS

Wood panels come in many different styles and types, but the most widely sold varieties fall into four broad categories: solid lumber paneling, plywood, hardboard, and those variations of composition board formed of compressed wood shavings or other wood by-products.

Solid lumber usually comes in boards or planks that are ½ or ¾ inch thick and anywhere from 6 to 16 inches wide. The boards generally have beveled or tongue-and-groove edges that form neat-fitting joints between boards, and they may be installed by nailing directly to the studs. When put up over an existing wall, wood furring strips (1×2-inch strips) are usually nailed up first to provide a level surface. The paneling is then nailed to this furring.

Plywood, hardboard, and composition board are most often available in 8-foot-long, 48-inch-wide sheets, and some types of wood paneling also come in 16-inch-wide "planks" that are easier to handle (some of these can be put up with clips so that no nails are visible). Most wood panels are ¼ inch thick and can be installed horizontally as well as vertically.

Almost all hardboard and composition wall panels are factory-finished—though in most cases this is more of a coating than a true wood finish. A "finish" may be an embossed or printed-on simulated wood grain, or it may be a plastic coating that is baked on to withstand lots of hard wear and abuse. Unfortunately, even the toughest of these can get damaged, and on many of such finishes scratches and dents are almost impossible to touch up.

Plywood panels come either unfinished or factory-finished. The ones that are prefinished at the factory far outsell the ones that are unfinished, for once they are put up there is nothing else to do. Keep in mind, however, that the quality of the different finishes available can vary considerably from one brand to another—some of the cheaper brands apply no more than just a light coating of hot wax.

When possible, try to buy your wood paneling from a dealer who actually has the material in stock and will let you look at it before it is delivered; ordering from a small manufacturer's sample is never a guarantee that the material you get will really match that sample. It is also a good idea to order all the panels you will need for the whole job; buying piecemeal could result in your winding up with batches that don't match accurately.

Have the material delivered several days before you expect to start installing it, then keep it stored in the room where it will actually be put up for 36 hours before you start the installation. This allows the wood to adjust to the humidity and temperature of that room, so panels will remain dimensionally stable when installed. And with plywood or solid lumber, it gives you a chance to move the panels around for the best possible blend of tones—natural wood does vary from piece to piece (this is seldom a problem with hardboard and other paneling that has a printed or overlaid finish).

Most ¼-inch-thick wall panels can be put up in one of two ways: by nailing, or by cementing with a panel adhesive. If you are going to use nails, you can buy them with colored heads that will blend in with the panels, and you can furthermore drive them into the V-grooves of most

Installing panels with adhesive (left) **or nails** (above). **Hammer nails into panel grooves.**

panels so they will be scarcely noticeable when the wall is up. Construction adhesive (also called panel adhesive) for putting up wood panels (and gypsum-board panels) is packaged in cartridges that fit into a standard caulking gun, so you can dispense the adhesive quickly in a series of ribbons spaced according to the manufacturer's instructions. A few nails will still be required along the top to get started and to hold the panels in place while the adhesive sets.

If the panels are being installed over bare studs, the only precaution required is to make certain that the spacing of the studs allows for one stud or other nailing member located behind the edge of each panel, as well as at the required intervals across the center of the panel (usually every 24 inches). This also holds true if the panels are to be put up with adhesive, since solid support is still needed around every edge of each panel.

When the panels are to be put up over an existing plaster or gypsum-board wall you can either apply the panels directly over the wall with a panel adhesive or you can nail them up. In the latter case you will first have to nail up horizontal 1×2-inch furring strips. Use nails that are long enough to go through the plaster, and thin wedges of wood or similar material to shim out those places where the wall surface dips or waves. If necessary, chop away a little of the plaster, using a hammer and wide cold chisel, to remove high spots.

You must keep in mind that installing new panels over an existing wall is only feasible if the existing surface is relatively flat and smooth. If you try to put panels up over a wavy or bumpy wall, not only will the panels take on the same irregularities, but it may also be impossible to get neat-fitting joints between panels—or even to get them to fit together at all. Since most old walls are anything but flat and smooth, furring strips will often be required.

When used for this purpose, furring strips must be spaced so there is one under the edge of every panel and behind each seam between panels, and they must be installed in straight lines. Use a level to help line them up vertically and horizontally, and a tightly stretched string or long, straight piece of lumber to determine where shimming or blocking out will be needed. To en-sure a flat surface for the panels, furring strips should be uniformly spaced according to the recommendations of the manufacturer of that particular panel.

When installing wall panels, you should always allow for expansion and contraction. You do *not* want a snug fit for the panels between the floor and the ceiling. The panels should end an inch or two below the ceiling and a couple of inches above the floor. Small blocks of scrap wood placed under the bottom of each panel as it is being installed will raise it by the required amount. The gaps will be covered by baseboard moldings later on.

When butting panels together you want them touching, but not forced tightly together. This is especially important in the corner—don't force that last piece into place; it should be an easy fit. Since corners are seldom exactly straight and plumb, you will usually have to scribe the last piece with a compass or dividers, then trim it to fit along the scribed line.

Moldings Can Help

When you install wood panels over existing walls you usually first have to take off all the old baseboards, window trim, and other moldings. So when the job is done you will want to put up all new moldings—not just to replace the old trim, but also to cover up rough or unsightly edges, corner joints, and gaps along the top and bottom of the new wall. Moldings come in plastic composition as well as in wood, and are available with a factory finish already applied to match most of the more popular wood finishes. The plastic moldings have wood-grain finishes that make them look—and feel—just like real wood.

REPAIRING DAMAGED CERAMIC TILE

Although ceramic tile is probably as durable as any wall surfacing material made, there are times when repairs or replacement of individual tiles becomes necessary. In most cases there has been a breakdown of the backing material (the surface on which the tile is mounted)—for example,

Installing new moldings gives paneling job a neat, finished look.

when a leak causes the plaster or lath behind the tile to crumble. In other cases repairs may be required because you had to cut an opening in the wall in order to get at some pipes or electrical wiring, or because one or more fixtures are being replaced.

Joints between individual tiles are filled with grout—a cementlike compound that is applied after the tile has been installed. As grout ages, it not only gets dirty and stained-looking, it may also start to crumble and crack. When this condition develops, repairs should be made promptly—otherwise water will enter and speed the deterioration of the backing or lath behind the tiles.

Grout comes in two forms: as a ready-mixed paste, and as a powder that you mix with water. You can use either type when replacing defective grout—it's just a matter of cost and convenience. There is also a silicone rubber grout, but this is primarily used for caulking the joints where the tile meets the top of a bathtub or sink (it is also used on sheets of tile that come already grouted). Although regular grout can serve in the joint between the tub and the tile, if the problem recurs you are probably better off using silicone rubber or an acrylic caulking compound. Usually when grout cracks around the edge of a tub or sink, the cause is a slight movement of the structure members, or twisting of beams. Ordinary cement-base grout is brittle, so it is more likely to crack out again. Silicone rubber and acrylic caulking com-

pounds remain flexible—they will "give" with the movement, and thus will last longer. You will find these more elastic compounds packaged in easy-to-use squeeze tubes, as well as in regular cartridges that fit into a caulking gun.

To replace the grout in regular tile joints, you first have to rake or scrape out most of the old grout, using the edge of an old chisel or screwdriver, or the point of a "church key" can opener.

Tips on Caulking

Here are some pointers that will help you do a neater and longer-lasting job when applying caulking around tubs or sinks:

Before you start, make sure to clean out all of the old grout or cement, then wash the joint with a detergent to which you have added a little household laundry bleach (one part bleach to three parts water). This will clean the surfaces and kill any mildew in the joint.

Cut the plastic tip of the cartridge nozzle off at approximately a 45-degree angle, then hold the tube at this same angle to the joint as you move it along.

Apply the compound by moving the nozzle of the tube *away* from you, as shown in the photo. *Don't* pull it toward you as most people do, even though the latter seems more "natural." The reason for this is that as you squeeze and push away from you the compound will be forced into the joint in a more tightly packed bead; pulling toward you causes the bead to "stretch" and get stringy as it comes out of the nozzle.

Caulking with squeeze tube. Push nozzle *away* from you to force caulking into joint.

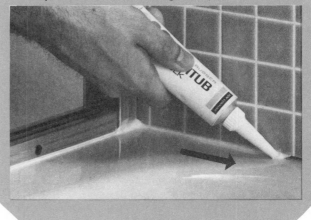

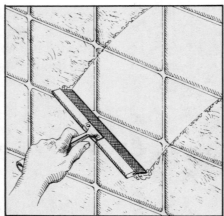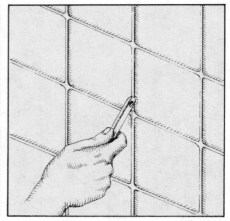

Regrouting tiles. Left, scrape out old grout with chisel or putty knife; center, apply new grout to damp tiles with squeegee; right, compact grout in joints with old toothbrush handle.

You don't have to get out all of the old grout, only what is loose and crumbling, down to a depth of at least ¼ inch. Next, scrub the joints clean and wash out all dust and dirt. Then while the tiles are still damp apply the new grout by rubbing it into and over the joints with a squeegee or stiff piece of cardboard held on edge (if you have only a few joints to do, you can use your fingertip).

It is important that the grout be thoroughly compacted in each joint. If you have many joints to do, a small stick rounded at one end—or the handle of an old toothbrush—will help in this part of the job.

Use a damp sponge to rub the grout in and to remove all excess from the face of the tiles. Keep dipping the sponge in water and wringing it out to get rid of the cement it picks up, and try to remove all of the excess before it hardens—otherwise you will wind up with a very messy-looking tile wall when the job is done. Finish by polishing with a dry cloth, rubbing hard on the face of each tile to remove any slight haze (indicating excess grout) that may remain.

Smear grout into joint with finger, then use damp sponge to clean excess off tile face.

Replacing a Loose or Broken Tile

To replace a damaged or cracked tile, you first have to remove what is left of the old one without damaging the tiles next to it. Start by scraping out all of the grout around the damaged tile, then see if the pieces that remain will come out easily with a little gentle prying or tapping. If not, use a small cold chisel and hammer to break up the tile, starting in the center. Hit the chisel with light blows only—strong enough to crack or break that tile, but not heavy enough to loosen up the tiles around it.

When you have broken through, start chipping and prying until you have removed all pieces of the old tile, then scrape away any of the old grout still sticking around it. If the surface behind has some cement still on it, try scraping most of this off, but without damaging the backing or wall behind the tiles. This may be difficult if a mastic adhesive was originally used, so just remove what you can. If the surface underneath is wood or metal-mesh lath, pry off any of the old cement left on the lath that comes off easily.

If quite a few loose tiles are involved, take them all off at once and inspect the surface behind the tiles. Chances are you will find this area also badly deteriorated. If you put tile up over crumbly plaster, softened drywall, or rotted lath, you will find the tiles working loose again in a short while, so replace the defective backing material where necessary before you start. You do this by covering the area with moisture-resistant gypsum board (make sure you use *only* the moisture-resistant variety).

Special mastic adhesives for putting up ceramic tile or replacing loose tiles are sold in most hardware stores and home centers. If you have only one or two tiles to replace, or if the old mortar cement is still in place so that you don't have much of a recess for the new cement, you will probably be better off using a silicone rubber adhesive. This will bond firmly even in comparatively thin layers, and it is completely waterproof.

Apply the cement or mastic to the back of the tile, keeping it at least ½ inch away from the edges, then push the tile firmly into place. Use toothpicks or small slivers of wood as spacers around the edges if necessary to make certain it is uniformly spaced around all four sides, and tap carefully with a rubber mallet or wood block to seat the tile firmly.

After the tile is in place, use a small stick or

Silicone rubber adhesive can be used to bond loose tiles back into place.

Removing damaged tile with chisel

similar tool to scrape out any of the adhesive that has oozed up into the joints. You want the joints left open so they can be filled with grout—though not until the adhesive is fully cured. See pages 133–34 for information on filling joints with grout after the adhesive is dry.

Repairing or Replacing a Broken Tile Fixture

When a soap dish, toothbrush holder, or similar fixture comes loose from a tile wall, replacing it is in most respects the same as replacing a loose

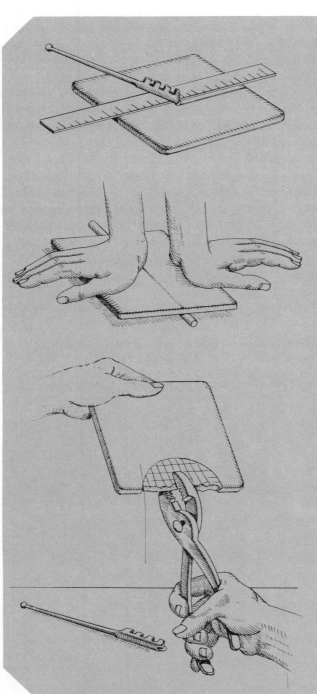

Cutting a tile. Score tile face with glass cutter (above), **place face up over pencil aligned with score mark, and snap in two** (below).

Cutting Ceramic Tile

The simplest way to cut a tile to fit is with an ordinary glass cutter. Score the glazed face with a single smooth stroke along the line to be cut, then place the tile face up directly over a pencil centered under the score mark. Press down hard on both sides of the cut as shown to snap the tile neatly in two. Use a piece of medium-grade abrasive paper to smooth off any rough edges.

If you have to make a curved cut—for example, to fit around a pipe or faucet—score the curved line with the glass cutter, then make a series of radial cuts from this curve out to the edge. Now use a pair of end-cutting pliers or nippers to "nibble" away at the waste areas, splitting off one small piece after another until you have the shape you need.

To make curved cut in tile, score line and make radial cuts, then use pliers to split off pieces.

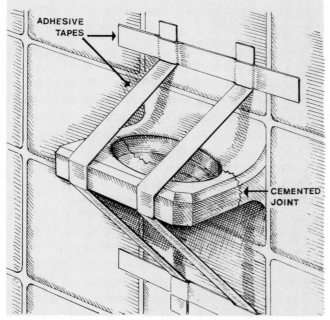

Adhesive strips hold cemented soap dish in position while adhesive hardens.

tile. As described on page 135, you start by scraping out all of the grout on each side, then removing the damaged unit by chipping away with chisel and hammer.

If the old fixture is cleanly broken off with no missing pieces, your best bet may be to repair it rather than replace it. If the base is still solidly stuck in place in the wall you can use a clear, two-part epoxy adhesive to glue the broken part back in its original position. You will have to rig up some way to hold the pieces in position while the epoxy sets; the simplest is to use strips of adhesive tape as shown in the drawing.

If you have to replace the entire fixture, your biggest problem may be finding one that matches—in color and in size or shape. Assuming you can find a suitable unit, install it by following the techniques outlined in the previous pages on replacing a damaged tile, and use adhesive tape to hold the fixture in place while the mastic sets. Because of the weight of a new fixture, you may be better off using a two-part epoxy adhesive instead of a silicone rubber adhesive.

CEILING PROBLEMS

Since most ceilings are made of plaster or gypsum board (drywall), repairing them is exactly the same as repairing a wall of the same material—except, of course, that you will be working

overhead. Many old ceilings are so badly cracked, flaking, and bumpy that a few simple patches will not do much except add to the overall messy appearance. When things are that bad, the best cure is to recover the ceiling entirely with a new surface or paneling of some kind. There are a number of easy-to-apply materials you can use.

Putting Up Ceiling Tiles

The most popular way to remodel an old ceiling, as well as to erect a new ceiling when finishing a basement, attic, or new addition, is to put up some type of acoustical ceiling tile.

Ceiling tiles may be made of wood fiber, mineral fiber, or fiberglass, and depending on what they are made of and what type of surface was applied by the manufacturer, they vary in their ability to withstand fire and wash-cleaning. They also vary in acoustical qualities. Most can be put up in one of two ways: by cementing them directly to the surface of the old ceiling with a mastic adhesive, or by stapling them to furring strips. Cementing the tiles up is practical only if the old ceiling is reasonably straight and solid, and if all peeling or flaking paint has been scraped off first.

Since almost any old ceiling is in pretty bad shape by the time a homeowner decides to tile it

Ceiling tiles should be stapled to ceiling when adhesive is used to hold them in place.

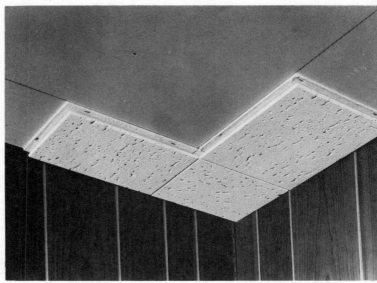

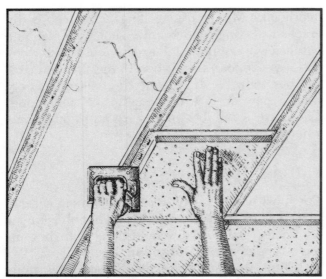

Furring strips, spaced according to tile size, serve to provide level fastening surface for tile.

over, installations will usually call for nailing up 1×2-inch furring strips first. These strips will have to be spaced according to the size of the tiles so that one strip is located under the edge of each tile row. Make sure the strips are firmly nailed to overhead joists or beams—if necessary, drill pilot holes to locate these beams—and use thin strips of wood as needed to shim out the strips where the ceiling dips or waves.

For stapling the tiles to the furring strips you will need a heavy-duty staple gun that can take

Nailing strips at right angles to exposed overhead beams

staples up to 9/16 inch in length. Most ceiling tiles are 12 inches square and have flanges or tongue-and-groove edges that interlock. The staples are driven through the flange into the furring strip under that edge, then the overlapping edge of the next tile covers the flange, thus hiding the staples.

Furring strips will also be needed when putting up ceiling tiles directly against exposed beams or rafters. This is because beams are seldom if ever spaced properly for the size of the tiles, and the rough beams or joists are themselves never truly level and straight enough to provide the properly aligned fastening surfaces needed for individual tiles.

The furring strips should be nailed up at right angles to the direction of the overhead beams—in other words, running across the beams. If you are resurfacing a finished ceiling and are not sure which way the beams run, you can usually assume that they run across the shortest dimension of the room. This can be checked by drilling small holes in the ceiling where you think the beams are (the holes will eventually be covered by the new ceiling), then probing the holes with a short length of bent wire, working it from side to side until you strike solid wood.

Before nailing up the strips, you will have to plan the layout for the whole ceiling so that you wind up along any one side of the room with border tiles of a reasonable width, rather than with very narrow strips of tile. Each border piece should be at least 6 inches wide (half a tile). Your best method is to draw a small-scale plan on graph paper, penciling in the furring strips to see how the layout works out, then erasing and moving as necessary until you get borders of uniform width on each side of the ceiling.

Putting Up a Suspended Ceiling

Wherever you have enough headroom so you can afford to lose a few inches of height in the room, one of the best ways to cover up a problem ceiling—or put up a new one—is with a suspended ceiling.

The framework for such a ceiling consists of an aluminum grid suspended by wires fastened to screw eyes driven into the existing ceiling, or, where there is no existing ceiling, into the overhead beams. This system eliminates the need for nailing up furring strips or installing individual small tiles. It is also an easy way to hide unsightly pipes, wires, and other overhead eyesores.

The aluminum strips that form the supporting grid for this type of ceiling are designed to snap together with special clips, making it easy to assemble the suspended frame in place. There are holes or slots at regular intervals for tying the wires that suspend the framework, and the strips are usually designed to form a grid that accepts 24×48-inch acoustical ceiling panels.

The panels rest on the flanges of the T-shaped moldings and are easily dropped into place when the suspended framework is finished. They can be just as easily lifted out when it becomes necessary to gain access to the space above the ceiling. For some systems you need at least 6 inches of clearance between the original ceiling and the suspended framework in order to tip the panels into place, but for some of the newer ones, which have semiflexible panels that can be bent slightly for installation, this space can be as little as 2 or 3 inches.

The first step in installing a suspended ceiling is to measure the area. Then take these measurements to your local lumberyard or home center to compute the materials you will need: main runners (the long pieces that serve as the main support for the ceiling), crosspieces (which clip to the main runners), angle-shaped border moldings (which are fastened to the wall around the perimeter), and the actual ceiling panels.

The companies that make these ceiling systems supply detailed instructions on how to assemble the main runners and crosspieces and how to join them to the angle pieces around the walls of the room. You start by nailing the angle-shaped pieces to the walls, using a tightly stretched string and a line level to mark the height at which each strip will be fastened. *Don't* depend on measuring down from the ceiling or up from the floor to achieve a level line—few ceilings or floors are themselves that level.

The T-shaped main runners are installed next by suspending each one with a length of wire from screw eyes or hooks driven into the overhead beams. Space these according to the directions recommended by the manufacturer, and take time to make sure that each runner is hanging straight with its ends resting on the angles previously fastened in place against the walls. A

A suspended ceiling is often the best cover-up for overhead eyesores.

Aluminum grid strips clip together with special clips.

Installing border moldings for suspended ceiling

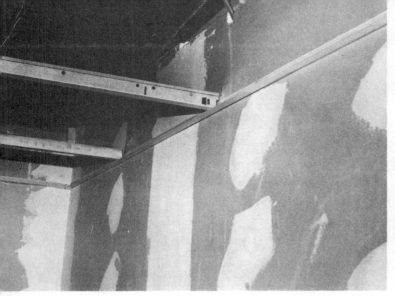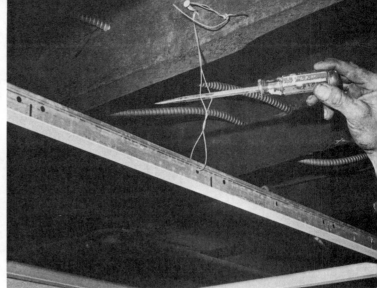

Ends of main runners should rest on border molding. Wire can be bent to adjust length and keep runners level.

stretched length of string is the best way to align each row of hooks. The individual lengths of the wire are adjusted by bending them to keep the runners level and thus ensure a level ceiling.

The final step is installing the actual panels. Push each one up through its opening, then tilt it forward and allow it to drop into place on the flanges of the T-shaped runners. Being acoustical, the panels will also help absorb or muffle noise in that room. Some are also plastic-coated to resist soiling, a feature useful in kitchens, laundry rooms, and similar locations.

One big advantage of this type of ceiling is that with it you can install modular fluorescent lighting fixtures, fitted into the same framework as one of the ceiling panels. In other words, the lighting fixture will rest on, and become part of, the ceiling, providing recessed lighting where needed. Translucent panels fit under and conceal each lighting fixture—all you see is the light-producing panel. This panel is usually hinged to let you reach into the fixture to change bulbs or for routine cleaning and service without the need to take down the whole fixture.

The final step: putting up panels

Chapter 7

Repairing Floors And Stairs

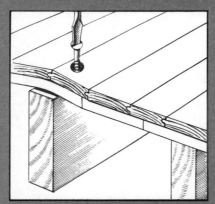

ASQUEAKING wood floor or a creaky set of stairs is not only annoying, in some cases it may indicate a sore need for repairs—to the flooring or stairs, or to the beams and columns that support them. Fortunately, most floor problems are not difficult to solve, and most repairs are not difficult for the home handyman to complete. But first you have to locate the source of the trouble.

FIXING A SQUEAKY WOOD FLOOR

This is probably the most commonly encountered problem. It can happen in a new house as well as in an old one. Sometimes it happens every time you step on a certain board, in other cases it is random. Some days (or nights) the squeaking or creaking noises can be very loud, other times they are scarcely noticeable.

In order to locate and correct the source of the trouble, you have to know something about how a typical wood floor is built. As shown in the drawing on page 144, most of them are built with two layers of flooring—a subfloor and a finished floor. The subflooring may consist of wide boards that run across the supporting joists, usually at a 45-degree angle, or it may consist of large sheets of plywood. The finished flooring is made of narrower strips of wood that fit together with tongue-and-groove joints. In most cases the strips run at right angles to the joists, but in some they will run almost parallel (they should never run parallel to the subflooring).

Nine times out of ten, squeaking or creaking noises are caused by loose boards in the floor—that is, boards that move up and down when someone steps on them. This can be the result of buckling or warping of the joists on which the floor rests, or of warping of the floorboards themselves—either because they were not nailed

down properly in the first place, or because the boards were jammed so tightly together that no room was allowed for expansion and contraction.

Regardless of the specific cause, as the boards move up and down when stepped on, the edge of one board rubs against the edge of an adjacent board, creating the squeaking or creaking noises you hear. The loose boards may be in the finished flooring or the subflooring, but in most cases it is the finished flooring that is the cause of the trouble.

To locate the loose boards, have someone walk around on the floor while you listen, trying to pinpoint the trouble spot, then mark this section with tape or chalk. If you haven't got time to do a permanent job of repair (as described on the pages that follow), you can silence the squeaking temporarily by squirting some powdered lubri-

Powdered lubricant will silence squeaky floorboards temporarily.

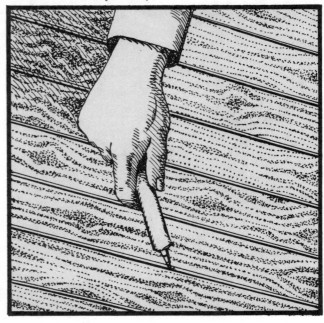

cant into the cracks between the offending boards. You can use powdered graphite, or any of the white powdered lubricants sold in hardware stores. In a pinch, you can even use talcum powder, though it won't last as long. Puff the powder into the joint between the boards, then step on and off them a few times to work it in. This will lubricate the edges enough to keep them quiet for a while, though the problem will almost certainly return.

If the floor is over an unfinished basement so that the joists are exposed from below, it is often best to have someone walk around upstairs while you listen and watch from below. Having pinpointed the location, your next step is to watch closely while the person above steps off and on the boards in that spot—you want to see whether it is the finished flooring that is moving, or if the problem comes from the subflooring under it.

If the finished flooring is loose and you cannot get at it from below, you can simply drive a couple of long nails in at an angle, as shown in the drawing. Use finishing nails that are 2½ to 3 inches long to reach through the subflooring and go into the joist by at least one inch, and drive them in next to the joint between the two boards so that they catch the tongue edge of one board and the grooved edge of the other. They should be angled in opposite directions, as shown, in order to ensure maximum holding power; you can also use ringed or "threaded" nails that grip much better than regular nails. And if possible, have someone stand on the boards to hold them down while you nail—don't depend on the nails to tighten the boards by themselves.

To avoid damaging the surface of the flooring with your hammer, drive the nails in till the heads are within approximately ½ inch of the surface, then drive them the rest of the way with a nail set.

When the floor is over an unfinished basement, you can do a neater and even better job in many cases by working from below. This is also much more convenient if the floor is covered with tile or wall-to-wall carpet that you don't want to disturb. And it is sometimes the only way you can determine whether the trouble is in the finished flooring or the subflooring.

You begin by shining a bright light up onto the underside of the floor to see if the subfloor moves when someone steps on that spot upstairs. If so, then the simplest way to prevent further movement is to drive a thin glue-coated wedge between the top of the joist and the subflooring above.

Another method that can accomplish the same

Driving nails through loose boards at an angle will eliminate squeaking (left). **To avoid damaging board with hammer, finish nailing with nail set** (right).

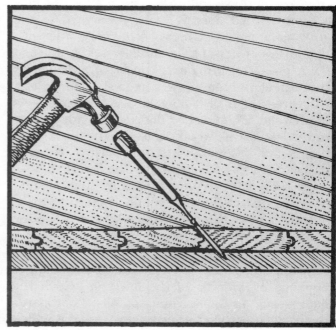

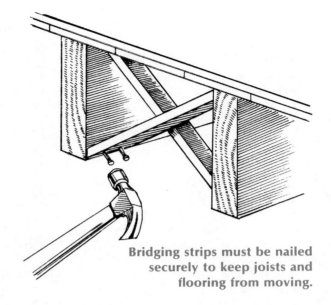

Bridging strips must be nailed securely to keep joists and flooring from moving.

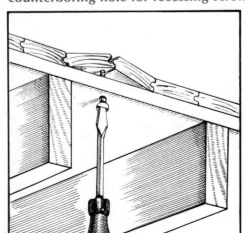

One way to support a warped floor: screw wood block to joist with upper edge firm against subfloor's underside.

thing is to screw a 2-inch-thick block of wood to the side of the joist so that its upper edge comes in firm contact with the underside of the flooring, as shown in the drawing above. Before placing it in position, coat glue over its top edge where it comes in contact with the bottom of the flooring.

While working from underneath, it is also a good idea to check the diagonal bridging strips that cross at an angle between the joists as shown. These are supposed to brace the joists

and keep them from warping, but if the nails holding them in place work loose, the joists can twist, which tends to leave a gap on top of the joist that permits the flooring to move.

When it seems that the loose boards are in the finished flooring, then the neatest way to secure them—still assuming you can work from below—is to drive long wood screws up from the bottom as shown below left. The screws will draw the boards together, thus preventing any future up-and-down movement of the finished flooring. However, the screws must be long enough to go clear through the subflooring and penetrate ap-

Driving wood screws into loose floorboards from below (left) **and from above** (center), **after counterboring hole for recessing screw head** (right)

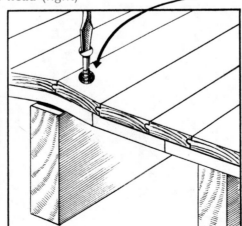

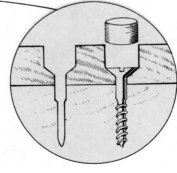

Replacing a Damaged Board

When a floorboard is badly warped and/or split, simply fastening it back down is probably not enough. The only way to do a proper repair is to replace the damaged section of board entirely. But most flooring is joined together with tongue-and-groove edges that interlock, and removing the damaged section of flooring without ripping up an entire section of floor (from that board to the nearest wall) requires careful carpentry. It can be done, and here's how:

1. Draw a line across the board at each end of the damaged section, then drill a series of holes across the board as shown in the drawing, keeping the holes just inside (on the waste side) of the line. Use a bit about ¾ inch in diameter, and overlap each hole slightly. Drill through the finished flooring only, not into the subflooring.

2. Use a hammer and sharp chisel to split the damaged piece lengthwise, from one end to the other—that is, from one line of holes to the other—then pry the split pieces of board up and lift them out.

3. Use the chisel and hammer to trim off the remaining ends and "inside" bits of the board still on the floor; each cut-off end should be straight and square across, necessary if you want to fit in a new piece neatly.

4. Cut a new strip of matching flooring so that it is an exact fit between the trimmed-off ends—it should be snug enough to require pressing into place, but not so tight that you have to hammer it in. Because of the tongue-and-groove edges, you won't be able to just drop it in. Turn the board over and trim off the lower part of the grooved edge, as shown in the drawing. Now, with the trimmed-off edge on the bottom, you will be able to tip the board slightly as shown to engage the tongue edge of the insert piece with the grooved edge of the board on the floor. Tap down the other edge for a snug fit, with its remaining lip overlapping the tongue edge of the board on the other side.

5. Finish securing the board by driving two nails in at each end, using cement-coated or ringed nails for maximum holding power. Countersink each nail head slightly, then fill the holes with a colored wood plastic or filler.

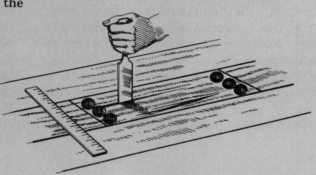

Replacing damaged piece of flooring. Split section out with chisel; trim off lower grooved edge of replacement board as shown in detail so board can be dropped in from above.

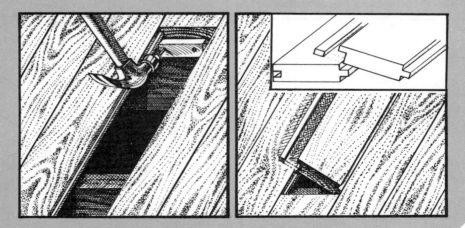

proximately two-thirds the way (about ½ inch) into the finished flooring. Assuming the subflooring and the finished flooring are both ¾ inch thick, then the screws should be 1¼ inches long.

Even when the floor is over an unfinished basement, you may find in some cases that the place where the screws are needed is inaccessible from below because of pipes or other structural members. The solution in that case is to drive the screws in from above. But then you will want to cover up or hide the screw head after the job is done. The neatest way to do this is to counterbore the screw hole slightly so that its head will be recessed below the surface of the wood. You can then fill the remaining hole with a colored wood plastic, or with a wood plug that can then be stained and finished to match. If you can't buy a suitable wood plug, cut off a short length of dowel, coat it with glue, and drive it into the hole. After the glue dries, use a sharp chisel to trim the top off flush with the surrounding wood.

Although in most cases the problem is solved if the screws go only into the subflooring, you can be surer of the job if you locate the screws where they will also go into the joists and then secure both layers of flooring. In this case you will want to use screws at least 1½ inches longer than the combined thickness of the two layers of flooring.

Anytime screws are to be driven into or through an oak floor, regardless of screw length and regardless of whether you are driving from above or below, make sure you drill pilot holes first. Otherwise you may wind up with split floorboards, or you may break the screws, or both. (Even when driving nails into oak, very small pilot holes are a good idea.)

CORRECTING A SAGGING FLOOR

When a floor starts to sag or dip, the problem may be an exceptionally heavy load that has been sitting on that part of the floor for some time, causing the joists to buckle or sag; or it can be the result of partially rotted or badly cracked supporting columns or posts, or even inadequate supporting beams when the house was originally built.

All of this not only leads to flooring problems, it can also cause cracks to develop in the walls and make doors and windows harder to open as their frames become distorted or twisted out of shape.

Even if the sagging or dipping is only slight, it's a good idea to take steps promptly to prevent it from going any further—and the easiest way to do this in most cases is to install telescoping jack posts in the basement under the low spots. These adjustable steel posts can be raised or lowered by turning a handle that fits through a hole in the top of a large vertical screw (much like the way an old-fashioned automobile jack works). Composed of two pieces of heavy-gauge steel pipe, one that slides inside the other, the top section is raised to the height you want it to be, where it is then supported by heavy steel pins running through both sections. A steel plate is welded to the bottom to act as a base and another is welded to the top of the adjustable screw to provide uniform pressure under the overhead beams as the post is jacked up.

The first step is to decide just where the new supporting post is to go. In most cases this is easy to determine simply by visual inspection along the beams in the basement to find the low spot,

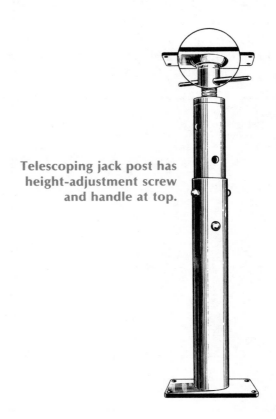

Telescoping jack post has height-adjustment screw and handle at top.

but if in doubt, stretch a string across the top of the floor from one side of the room to the other. You will then be able to see where the floor dips down (away from the string).

In some cases you will be able to get by with just one post located under the low spot, but most times—either because the depression is too extensive or because there is something permanently in the way where a single post would go—you will need two posts and a short length of heavy timber or piece of steel beam with which to bridge the part of the floor that needs jacking up. Using two posts and a beam across the top will also be necessary when you want to brace up a section of the floor that has to support an exceptional weight (a large piano or a new fireplace, for example).

After deciding on the location for the posts, you may find that you have to reinforce the basement floor—especially if the concrete in that spot is cracked or crumbling. Keep in mind that the basement support has to be strong enough to take the pressure of the floor above—the post will exert the same amount of pressure downward on the base on which it rests. The metal base plate furnished with each post helps to spread the load, but it could crack the concrete floor if that floor is less than 4 inches thick.

If in doubt, it is always best to pour a new footing or foundation for each post to stand on—even if this means chopping a hole in the existing floor or slab. As shown in the drawing below, the footing should be 18 to 24 inches square, and at least 12 inches deep. This means digging a hole to the required size and depth first, then pouring concrete in to fill. Use the kind of gravel mix you can buy in most lumberyards (all you have to do is add water), or mix your own out of one part portland cement, two parts sand, and four parts gravel. Fill each hole, then trowel the concrete level at the surface. Allow it to cure for at least a week before setting the post in place on top.

To install the post, place the base plate in position first, then set up the two steel tubes with the wider section at the bottom, the narrower one sliding in from the top. Raise the upper section till it almost touches the overhead beam against which it must exert pressure, then insert the cross pins that go through the holes provided to keep it in this position (you will have to raise or lower the inner section slightly to line up the holes). Set the top plate in place and turn the adjusting screw until the plate makes firm contact with the bottom of the overhead beam.

Now use a spirit level to check that the post is standing absolutely plumb and vertical—from side to side, as well as from front to back. Then give the screw one more full turn. *Don't* give it any more turns just yet.

From here on out you have to raise the floor

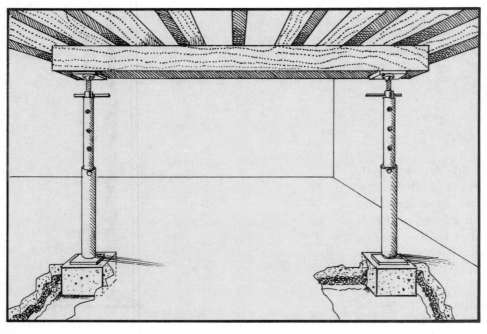

Two jack posts with timber bridge, the most common arrangement for supporting a sagging floor

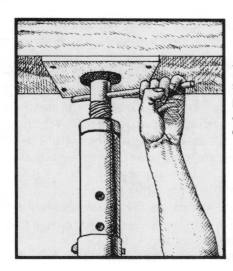

Turn adjusting screw until top plate presses against overhead beam.

very *slowly* if you want to avoid causing more serious problems above, such as cracking of walls and ceilings, or possible damage to plumbing lines, floor beams, and other structural members. Generally speaking, this means raising the screw plate by only about one-fourth of a turn every three or four days—or about half a turn each week. Jacking up that slowly gives everything a good chance to settle without causing serious disruptions or sudden stresses.

SANDING AND REFINISHING WOOD FLOORS

Sanding a wood floor down to the raw wood and then applying a new finish is the only way to really rejuvenate an old floor that has been so

badly neglected as to show severe wear and ugly discolorations. The job is best done with a heavy-duty floor-sanding machine, which can be rented from many hardware stores, as well as from tool-rental agencies and lumberyards or home centers.

Your first step is to remove all the furnishings from that room—not only the furniture, but also any pictures hanging on the wall, as well as curtains or draperies. This is necessary because the fine dust created by the sander will coat everything, so the more you remove the less tedious the cleanup job will be.

It is also a good idea to pry off all the floor moldings before you start, although this is not absolutely necessary. As you sand near the walls you will tend to scratch these moldings if they are left in place, so they will have to be repainted anyway. And if you do take them off, sanding around the edges will be that much easier because you won't have to worry about getting so close to the baseboard (with the moldings off, you can count on the last ½ inch of flooring being covered by the moldings when they are eventually replaced).

Next, examine the floor to see if there are any nails sticking up that might damage the sanding machine, and replace any damaged sections of flooring that are badly split or warped. Also, nail down any boards that are loose or show signs of squeaking (see page 144).

You will actually have to rent two different machines from your dealer: a large drum-type sander to be used on most of the floor, and a smaller disk-type sander (called an edger) for

A large sander for open floor areas (left), **and a smaller disk-type sander for edges and corners** (right)

sanding around the edges and in places where the large machine will not fit. The edger is also useful on stairs or steps.

If the floorboards are at all cupped or warped in places, three sandings will usually be required—the first with coarse paper while moving the machine at about a 45-degree angle to the length of the boards in order to level the surfaces off; the second straight and parallel to the grain with a medium-grade paper to remove the scratches left by the coarse paper; and the third with a fine paper that smooths off the scratches left by the medium-grit paper. You can buy the abrasive papers you need from the same dealer who rents you the machine.

Sometimes when a floor is really not that bad you can get by with only two sandings, both parallel to the grain. In this case the first sanding is done with a medium-grit paper and serves to remove all of the finish. The second sanding is done with a fine-grit paper that will remove the scratches left by the first sanding and give the wood its final smoothing. Parquet flooring usually requires three sandings—the first at a 45-degree angle to the length of the room, the second at a 45-degree angle in the opposite direction, and the final one along the long dimension of the room.

Before starting, close all doors leading into the room (to confine the dust) and open all the windows. Begin sanding at one end of the room and work your way down to the other end. When you press the switch to start the motor, always have the machine tipped back so the drum is *not* in contact with the floor. After it starts, lower the drum gradually till it touches the floor while beginning to move forward even before contact. The idea is never to start the machine while it is in contact with the floor—instead, start it and bring the drum down as you slowly move ahead—and to be moving as soon as and whenever the machine is sanding.

You don't have to really push the machine forward, because when the drum comes in contact with the floor it will "grab" and try to pull you forward. So be prepared—you just have to maintain a firm grip on the handles to keep the machine from "running away." And always keep moving while sanding to prevent gouging or digging in. As you approach the end of the room, raise the drum so that it loses contact with the floor just before you come to a complete stop, and never allow the drum to remain in contact with the floor while it is turning.

After you have completed one pass by walking forward, make the next pass by moving the ma-

A warped floor needs two sandings, with different grades of paper at various angles to wood grain.

Belting yourself to sander to keep it from running away and ease strain on back

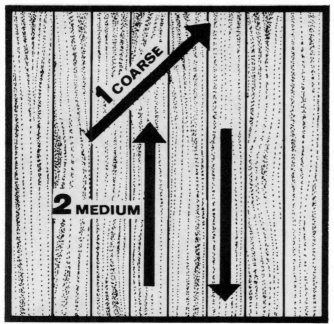

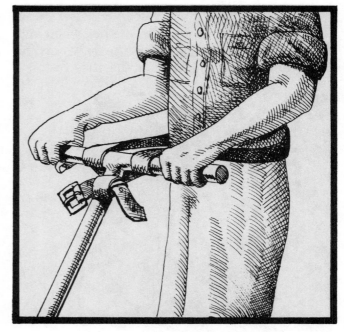

A hook-type wood scraper for hard-to-reach corners

chine over a couple of inches, then walking backward and pulling the machine after you. For the third pass you move over a couple of inches again, then start walking forward again. And so on. Work your way back and forth across the room in this manner, overlapping each pass by a couple of inches to make certain none of the boards are missed. Sand to within a couple of inches from the baseboard on all sides.

After you have sanded the entire floor with the coarse paper, switch to the smaller disk sander to do all the edges next to the walls. You won't be able to reach into all the corners even with this machine; just leave those spots until all the machine sanding is done. For these spots you will have to get down on your hands and knees with a small hook-type wood scraper, followed by some hand sanding.

Reload your sanding machine with the next-finer grit of paper, then repeat the process. Remember to remove the dust bag on the machine and empty it (*outside*) as soon as it is half full (and won't be so heavy to handle).

Selecting and Applying the New Finish

Although you may find it confusing trying to differentiate between the many different brands of finishing materials available for wood floors, all of them can be roughly classified as falling into one of two broad categories: penetrating sealers and surface coatings.

Penetrating sealers soak into the pores of the wood and bond with the fibers to seal and protect the wood without leaving any appreciable surface coating, and therefore little or no gloss on the surface. And since there is no surface film to scratch, they do not show scratch marks (although you can scratch the wood itself). All such sealers require at least two coats on freshly sanded floors, and any of them will give you a beautiful finish that is easy to maintain or touch up when necessary (worn or damaged areas can be touched up by rubbing a little of the same sealer into the wood with a pad of fine steel wool, then buffing with a cloth). They can be applied with a brush, roller, or lamb's-wool pad; of the three methods, mopping it on with a long-handled lamb's-wool applicator is by far the easiest and most foolproof. Directions furnished with the various brands of sealer vary to some extent, but as a rule you simply wipe the sealer on and allow it to soak in, then wipe off the excess with a dry cloth. Once it is thoroughly dry, the floor should be given a light coat of wax and buffed to bring up the luster. Penetrating sealers come in clear, as well as in various wood-tone colors (walnut, dark oak, etc.). If you cannot find the shade you want, colors can be intermixed, or you can mix your own by adding regular tinting colors (the kind sold for tinting paints) to the clear or to any of the ready-mixed shades. Be sure to test the color first before you start applying it to the entire floor, and avoid adding too much color, since this can interfere with proper drying. If you want a dark shade, start with a ready-mixed tone that is close to what you want, then add your own colors to darken it. If it is too dark, you can lighten it by thinning, or by buffing with steel wool after the stain is dry.

Surface coatings differ from penetrating sealers in that they build up a decided surface coating on the wood. The best finishes in this category are both hard and tough, and they build up to a beautiful shine, but they will also show scratches more readily than a penetrating sealer. Also, surface coatings can be much more difficult

to touch up (when only one part of the floor shows signs of wear). Most of the surface coatings sold for use on floors fall into one of three broad classifications: shellac, varnish, and lacquer or synthetic-type finishes.

Shellac is probably the oldest of clear floor finishes, and it is still used frequently. It dries very clear, so it does not darken the wood, and it dries very quickly—45 to 60 minutes in most cases. Thus, two or three coats can usually be applied on the same day, and the room can be used that same night. However, shellac does stain easily if water or other liquids are not mopped up promptly (it turns white in most cases). On the other hand, it is easier than varnish and most other surface coatings to touch up, because each new coat of shellac tends to dissolve the old coat, so patches blend together more easily.

Varnish comes in dozens of variations sold under many brand names, but you will want one that is made specifically for use on floors. It will dry to a hard, abrasion-resistant finish that is also highly resistant to staining and discoloration when liquids are spilled on it. Most varnishes tend to darken with age, and almost all take at least 6 to 8 hours to dry hard, so you can seldom put more than one coat on in a single day. In most cases this means you can't use that room for a couple of days.

Probably the toughest and longest-lasting floor varnish you can use is a polyurethane varnish. A clear synthetic finish that is radically different from most conventional varnishes, it still falls into the varnish category. Available with either a high-gloss or semigloss finish (also called satin-gloss), polyurethanes dry to a much harder finish than most of the other surface coatings—hence their exceptional resistance to scratching.

Contrary to what some polyurethane manufacturers claim about waxing being unnecessary, even these tough finishes will start to show scratch marks in time, and waxing will help prevent or at least minimize this. On the other hand, waxing may also make the floor more slippery, so if this is a serious consideration for the room you may prefer to skip the waxing and accept the fact that the finish will wear a bit more rapidly than it would with a coating of wax.

Lacquers and similar fast-drying synthetic finishes are not as popular as they once were. They dry so fast that they are often difficult to apply, and they are not as durable or long-lasting as the polyurethane varnishes. However, they don't darken a floor as much as varnish does, and their quick-drying characteristics make them useful for floors that cannot be kept out of use for days at a time, so many people still prefer them.

All surface coatings can be applied with a brush or roller, or with a flat painting pad. The coating should be applied liberally but uniformly, and without leaving pools or puddles on the surface. You must allow adequate drying time between coats, and if you plan to use a wood stain on the floor, make sure the stain you choose is compatible with the type of finish you intend to apply over it. Read the specifications on the label, and if still in doubt, ask your dealer. Wait at least three days after the last coat has dried hard before applying the first coat of wax.

Caring for Wood Floors

There are a few important rules to be observed in maintaining any type of finished wood floor:

1. Keep the surface as clean as possible—cleaning every day in heavily trafficked areas and at least once a week in other areas, using a vacuum to pick up dust, and wiping up spills as soon as possible after they occur. If dirt gets ground in it shortens the life of the finish and also darkens and discolors the wood.

2. Never scrub the floor with water, and do not use water-based cleaners or waxes to clean it. Water is the natural enemy of a wood floor, and of most of the finishes used on wood floors.

3. Keep the surface waxed, and renew this wax coating as soon as it shows signs of wearing off, usually when the surface starts to look dull.

4. When simple sweeping or vacuuming won't get the floor clean, use a solvent-based cleaner-wax to get up the dirt. The solvents will dissolve the old wax on the surface so that it comes off on the applicator as the new coat is applied, with the dirt imbedded in the old wax as it comes up. The applicator cloth should be changed frequently as you work—otherwise you will be merely spreading the same dirt around.

5. Waxes, liquid or paste, should be applied sparingly, for a thin film dries harder and thus is less likely to absorb and hold dirt. A light film of wax is also less slippery than a heavy one. Most waxes stand up better if each new coat is vigorously buffed after application, not only to bring up the luster but also to make the wax harder and remove any excess.

As a rule, waxing should not be required more than once or twice a year, even in frequently used rooms. An exception might be an entrance hall or similar area where people walk in from the outside. Here waxing may be needed more often, if only for the cleaning action rewaxing provides.

Solvent-based cleaner-wax strips old wax coat as it applies new coat.

REPAIRING STAIRS

A squeaking or creaking set of stairs may be only a slight nuisance if you don't mind the noise, but it can also be an indication of loose treads or risers that need fastening down if they are not to deteriorate into a potentially hazardous condition.

Most stair noises are caused by loose or warped treads (the tread is the part you step on), but the problem can also be caused by a loose or warped riser (the vertical piece on which the tread rests). Either one may be rubbing against the stringer along the side of the staircase, or it can be rubbing against one of the other treads or risers when stepped upon.

As can be seen from the drawing on page 154 right, treads usually have grooves on the bottom that fit over the top of the riser. If such a groove is not down tight, its edges will rub on the top of the tread when you step on it, and this creates a squeaking or rubbing noise. To check for this, shine a light under the bottom edge of the tread where it projects out over the top of the riser to see if there is a slight gap. (In some cases there will be a small molding under the nose of the tread, so you will have to pry this off first in order to see if the top of the riser goes inside a groove on the bottom of the tread.) Another way to check this joint is to have someone step on and off the suspected tread to see if you notice any slight up-and-down movement. If the back of the staircase is open so that you can get at the steps and risers from underneath (for example, on steps that go down to the basement), it is neater and easier to make repairs from underneath. A

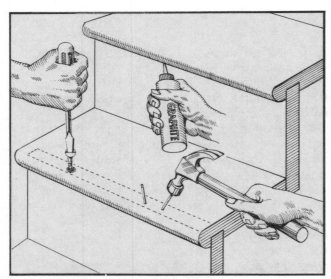

Two ways to cure squeaky stairs. Drive screws or nails down through loose tread into riser, or apply graphite under bullnose.

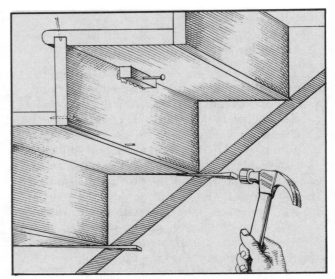

Two ways to repair loose tread from beneath. Drive thin wood wedge into tread groove, or brace wood block against tread and riser.

loose tread notched to fit over the riser can be secured from below by driving thin wood wedges up into the groove, as shown above right. Pieces of wood shingle are ideal for this, but any piece of wood that is planed to a taper will work just as well. Trim for a snug fit, then coat with glue and drive the piece upward as shown.

If driving wedges is impractical because the space left is too small or because the tread is not grooved on the underside, you can secure the tread by bracing wood blocks against tread and riser as shown. Use screws and glue to secure them snug up against the bottom of the tread and the back of the riser. If the problem seems to be a matter of the bottom edge of the riser pulling away from the back edge of the tread it helps to support, then the solution lies in driving long screws in from the back, as shown. These should be at least 2 inches long, and pilot holes should be drilled first to avoid splitting the wood.

Sometimes rubbing occurs where the side of a tread or riser meets the stringer at the side; if this joint is loose, the tread will move slightly each time it is stepped on, and there may be enough play to permit it to warp slightly. If you are able to get at the joint from underneath, you can fix it in the same way as you would a loose tread—either by driving glue-coated wedges into the gap, or by installing wood blocks against the back of the tread or riser.

When the back of a staircase is finished or closed off, and therefore is inaccessible, you will have to work from the top. Loose treads can usually be fastened down by driving nails or screws in at an angle as pictured above left. Be sure you drill small pilot holes for the nails or screws first, especially if the treads are oak—nails will bend otherwise—and have someone stand on the tread to hold it down while you are driving or nailing the screws down. Screws will do a better job of pulling the tread down, but their heads will be more noticeable unless you countersink them (predrilling the top of the pilot hole with a countersink bit, then screwing the head below the surface of the wood) and fill the depression with wood putty or a wood plug. If you use finishing nails, the heads can be neatly countersunk, and the small holes that remain can then be easily concealed by filling with a putty stick (sold for use on paneling), or with a wood plastic of the right color.

One problem that should be attended to promptly is a cracked or split front edge or "bullnose" on a tread. This makes the tread unsafe, as well as unsightly. A neat-looking permanent repair can be made in most cases by working some glue into the split with a thin spatula or blade of some kind, then driving a few small brads in to hold the split together (drill small pilot holes for the brads first to avoid splitting the wood). If the front of the tread has split off completely, you may be able to shape a new piece of hardwood to fit, using a rasp and some sandpaper, then glue this onto the front of the tread with epoxy glue. Make the filler piece slightly oversize, then trim it to a neat fit after the adhesive hardens, using a plane or rasp, and finish with sandpaper.

If a tread is so badly split or warped that repairs are impractical, it should be replaced entirely. Getting the old tread off can be a tricky job if it fits into mortises (grooves) in the stringers at each side of the stairway. You will have to pry the tread up carefully by working from the center along the front edge, then reach underneath with a hacksaw blade or pair of metal cutters to cut off any screws or nails that hold it in place. In some cases you may also have to cut an opening in the riser to enable you to reach in with a keyhole saw and cut the riser off (you will then have to replace both the riser and the tread).

If, on the other hand, the tread merely butts against the stringer and is attached to it by nails or screws, the job is a lot easier—you should be able to pry the tread up and out without having also to ruin the riser on which it rests.

Because there are many variations in how stairs are assembled, and unless you are really sure of yourself, you will probably be better off calling in a professional carpenter when altogether new treads or risers are required on a finished staircase.

REPAIRING DAMAGED RESILIENT TILE FLOORS

Small scratches, dents, and other minor imperfections in vinyl, vinyl–asbestos, or asphalt floor tiles can sometimes be repaired without replacing the entire tile, if you have a few scrap pieces of the same or a closely matching tile on hand. You can use these scrap pieces to make your own matching-color patching compound with which to fill in and hide defects, the same way you use a wood filler for dents and scratches in wood. Use a coarse piece of sandpaper or a rasp to shave off or shred some of the scrap material, then save the powder that you scrape off (you can also pulverize or powder the tile by working its edge against a rotary rasp chucked in an electric drill). The powder or shavings can then be mixed with a little clear varnish or shellac to form a pastelike putty, which you then apply with a small trowel or putty knife. Fill the scratch or dent flush with the surface and allow the compound to dry hard. Buff with steel wool to smooth it off, then rub wax on to restore the luster.

Replacing a Damaged Tile

Of course, the best cure for a damaged tile is to replace it with a new one. To simplify removal of the old tile it often helps to apply mild heat to the tile, which softens it and makes it more pliable. The heat also helps to soften the old cement or adhesive that holds it down, making it easier to lift the tile off the floor. Heat can be applied with a small propane torch or heat lamp, or with a hot clothes iron. The torch or heat lamp will be faster than the iron, but be careful not to scorch nearby tiles, and always keep a pail of water or fire extinguisher handy—just in case.

After heating, lift the damaged tile out by inserting a sharp knife or thin putty knife near one of the corners and prying up carefully. Sometimes the tile will come up easily, but other times

Predrill pilot hole before driving screw into loose tread.

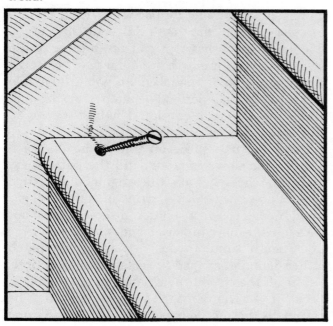

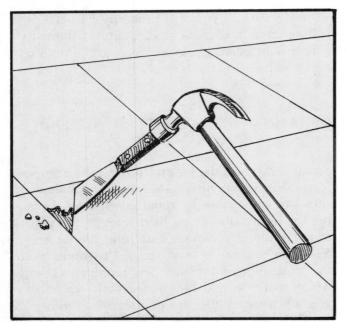 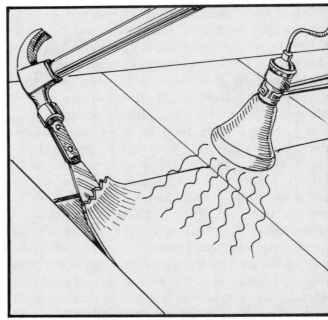

Use chisel or sharp putty knife to cut away one corner of damaged tile (left), then use heat lamp to soften tile so you can pry it up, starting from cut-off corner (right).

it won't come up without damaging the tiles next to it—something you definitely want to avoid. The safest procedure is to cut away one corner of the damaged tile first, using a knife or small chisel. Pry this corner piece out, working from the center of the tile, and you should then be able to slide a putty knife or chisel under the rest of the tile to get it up.

After the entire tile is up, any cement left on the floor should be scraped away. Make sure no lumps remain, and clean out all dirt and debris. Test-fit your new tile to see how it matches (sometimes it helps to turn it 90 degrees in one direction), then set it aside and spread a thin layer of adhesive over the area. Use the type of adhesive recommended for the kind of tile involved, and put it down sparingly. Most adhesives are applied with a finely notched spreader, but some can also be applied with a brush. Either way, keep the adhesive about ¼ inch away from the edges to avoid excess oozing up through the seams after the tile is pressed down.

If the new tile feels stiff and brittle, warm it first in order to make it more pliable. Set it into place by bringing one edge down first, snug against the adjoining tile, then flex it slightly and lower the rest of it down onto the adhesive-coated area. Pat down hard with both hands,

then place a few heavy books or other weights on top. Leave the weights in place for a couple of hours to keep the tile from curling or raising.

Patching Sheet Flooring

Patching a damaged section on a sheet vinyl floor covering is usually done by cutting out the damaged section and replacing it with a matching piece of the same material—but this can be done only if you have, or can get, a piece of the same material (or one that matches very closely). And in order to do the job right, you will have to cut a patch that perfectly matches in size and shape the piece you cut out. The best way to do this is to cut both pieces out at once.

Place the new piece on top of the damaged section and move it around till the pattern exactly matches that on the original floor, then tape it down with a few strips of tape. Using a straightedge and a sharp utility knife, cut through the new material and the old flooring underneath simultaneously, making the patch either diamond-shaped or rectangular in outline.

Lift off the cut-out new patch and lay it aside, then lift out the damaged section under it. The cutout in the old floor will be exactly the same size and shape as the patch that was just laid aside. Next, scrape off as much of the old adhesive from the floor as you can, then clean the area thoroughly to remove all dust and specks of dirt or old adhesive (a vacuum cleaner is best for this job).

You can now spread new adhesive (sparingly) over the exposed floor inside the cutout, then fit the newly cut-out patch into place by bringing one edge or one corner in contact with the edge or corner of the old material, then gradually lowering the patch into place. Try to avoid sliding it by positioning the first edge properly the first time (just as if you were installing a tile), and if the flooring material seems a bit stiff or brittle, warm it first by placing it in a warm oven for a few minutes, or by heating it carefully with a heat lamp. Place weights on top of the patch to hold it down around all edges.

CARPET REPAIRS

A burn or scorch mark caused by a hot ash or match dropped on the carpet is often only on the surface—that is, only the tips of the individual fibers have been scorched. A simple way to get rid of such damage is simply to snip the burned tips off with a sharp pair of scissors, holding the blades almost flat against the carpet as shown on page 158. If slight scorch marks still are noticeable, rub the spot lightly with a pad of fine steel wool, then vacuum up the residue before it can soak in and cause more staining.

When cosmetic surgery of this kind won't do the job, you can operate more drastically by trimming the burned fibers off completely. This will leave a slight "hole" in the carpet, but one you can fill in neatly in the following manner:

Snip some extra fibers or tufts from a scrap piece of the same carpeting—if you have an extra piece. If you don't, then snip the tufts from under a large piece of furniture where a similar "hole" will never be noticeable. Bundle this in your fingers, then cover the bottom end of the tuft with some white glue (the kind that dries clear). Push the glue-coated end down into the place where you clipped off the burned fibers and wait till the glue dries. Then snip off the tops of the newly inserted tuft to make the new fibers the same height as the rest of the fibers around it.

When there is a burn or bad stain too large to be repaired by the technique above, you can often make a neat patch by cutting out the damaged section and then inserting another piece of the same material. If you do not have a spare piece of the same carpet, and cannot buy any, there is yet another possibility, similar to the method of repairing a "hole," that can save the day:

Cut a patch out of the existing carpet in a place where it will not show—for example, under a couch, breakfront, or similar large piece of furniture that is seldom if ever moved. After you have cut out the damaged piece you can install this

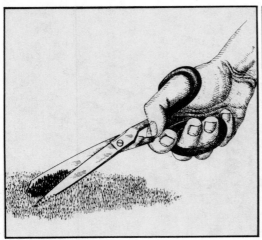

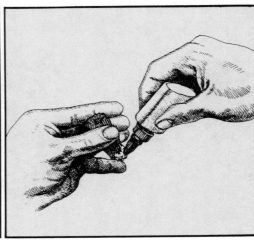

When only tips of carpet fiber are damaged, snip top ends off. Fill in any carpet holes with clumps of glued fibers.

piece in the hole where you cut out the patch, thus "moving" the damage from a conspicuous spot to a place where it will probably never be seen.

Use a metal square and a sharp utility knife to guide you in cutting out the patch you will need (again, make it rectangular or diamond-shaped), then lift this piece out and lay it in place over the damaged section of carpet, making certain you have positioned it to cover all of the damaged section. Hold this piece firmly in place with one hand and cut around it with the other, bearing down hard enough to cut through the carpet completely. The idea is to cut out a section of the carpet on the floor that will exactly match the outline of the patch you are holding on top. The two pieces will be exactly the same size and shape, so the patch will match perfectly when

the cut-out piece is lifted out and the patch is inserted in its place.

If the carpet is a type that tends to unravel around the edges, brush a light coat of clear-drying white glue around the edges of the cutout after the damaged section has been removed, then brush more glue around the edges of the piece that will be inserted as a patch. Don't get any glue up near the tips of the fibers, only down near the base (gluing the tips will make them stiff).

Your best bet to hold the new patch in place is a double-faced carpet tape (sticky on both sides). Apply strips of tape to the floor around the perimeter of the cutout, then press the piece of fresh carpet down on top to secure it. The damaged piece that you remove can then be put back into the place from which you cut out the patch.

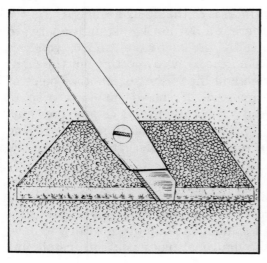

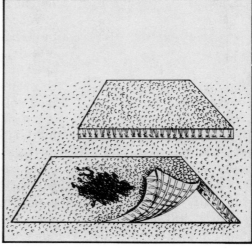

To replace damaged carpet section, place patch over damaged section and cut out; patch will fit perfectly when laid in place of damaged piece.

Chapter 8

Painting and Finishing

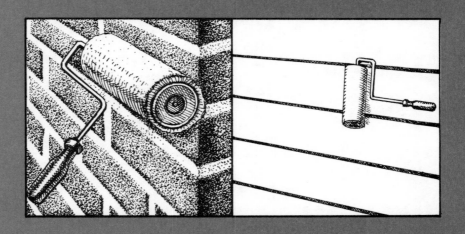

ASIDE FROM the decorative or aesthetic value, painting and finishing are essential to the maintenance of every house—at least around the outside—because they are the homeowner's best means for protecting wood, metal, masonry, and other materials against the elements. Fortunately, most do-it-yourselfers can easily handle these periodic maintenance chores, and the results are instantly gratifying—and economical (in most painting and paperhanging jobs, labor accounts for anywhere from half to two-thirds of the total cost).

Today's paints are easier to work with and more foolproof than ever before, but while some paints serve more than one purpose, there is still no such thing as a truly universal paint for all surfaces and all conditions. Always read the label carefully to make sure you are getting the product you need, and follow the manufacturer's directions as to priming or other preparation required. A knowledgeable dealer can be a big help, but unfortunately not all dealers—or the clerks who work for them—are really familiar with all the products they sell, so they cannot always be depended on for proper advice.

The choice of applicator—brush, roller, or flat painting pad—will generally depend on personal preferences, as well as on the type of surface being coated. More often than not you will probably combine two or more of these painting tools—for example, you might use a roller on walls and ceilings, but use a brush for painting in the corners and "cutting in" next to the trim. Or you could use a special doughnut-shaped roller for the corners and a painting pad with a protective flange on it for cutting in next to the woodwork (these wipe the paint onto the wall while the flange keeps the paint from getting onto the woodwork).

CHOOSING AND CARING FOR PAINTBRUSHES

Brushes are still probably the most versatile and useful applicators for home painting. Rollers, pads, and spray cans are faster and easier in many cases, but a brush is still the only painting tool for every surface and almost every kind of house paint (there are some fast-drying commercial and industrial finishes that cannot be applied by brush; they must be sprayed).

As with most other tools, a poor-quality brush will make a good job almost impossible—regardless of the quality of the paint or finish applied. On the other hand, a good-quality brush not only will do a much better job, it will last longer and enable you to finish the job faster. So it is really foolish economy to buy cheap "throwaway" brushes simply to save you the job of cleaning the brush afterward—you won't have to clean the brush, but you may very well have to do the whole job over.

All good-quality paintbrushes contain a high percentage of bristles with "flagged" or split ends—the more the better. Good-quality Chinese hog bristle is naturally tapered and split at the ends—which is why these bristles were for years considered the best for top-quality paint and varnish brushes. However, these days most brushes are made of synthetic or man-made bristles, and manufacturers have developed techniques to imitate the flagged and split ends characteristic of natural bristle.

Although top-quality Chinese hog bristle works well with most oil-base and synthetic coatings, it is not as suited to water-thinned (latex) paints and finishes. The bristles are porous and absorb water readily, so latex finishes make them swell. This distorts the shape of the

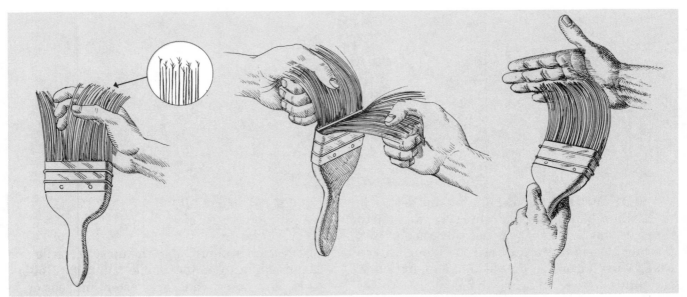

Qualities to look for when buying a paintbrush (left to right): **Flagged bristles that vary in length ensure smooth paint application; block's thickness shows how much brush you're really getting; when pressed, bristles should be springy, and fan out to a sharp straight edge.**

brush and ruins its sharp "cutting" edge, and the brush becomes so soft and floppy that smooth application becomes almost impossible. Also, hog bristles tend to wear rapidly on rough surfaces.

Nylon bristles, first introduced after World War II when Chinese bristle disappeared from the market, do not lose their springiness in water-thinned paints, and they stand up well on rough surfaces. The better-quality nylon bristles are tapered and flagged for smooth coverage, but nylon tends to soften after a while in hot weather or direct sun. Also, nylon loses much of its springiness in shellac, lacquer, and other quick-drying "synthetic" finishes.

The newest type of synthetic bristle is polyester filament—an extremely versatile material that does not lose its resiliency with the water-thinned (latex) or solvent-thinned (oil, shellac, or lacquer) coatings normally used around the house—including the quick-drying synthetic finishes. In addition, it retains its springiness even in the hottest weather.

Like nylon, polyester is made with flagged or split ends to ensure even application of any paint or finish, but it does not quite have nylon's durability on rough, coarse surfaces. To compensate for this, some manufacturers make brushes with a blend of nylon and polyester bristles—nylon

around the outside to take the hard wear, and polyester on the inside to provide smooth application and the best working qualities.

Here are some other points to check when shopping for a good-quality paintbrush:

1. Hold the brush up to a bright light to see how much of the bristle is flagged or split, and if the bristles are tapered and varied in length.

2. All brushes need some sort of block in the center to provide a "pocket" for holding paint, but some manufacturers use the block as a way of padding out the brush to make it look thicker. Separate the bristles and look down the center to make certain that the block in the middle is not so thick as to deceive you into thinking you are getting a lot more bristles than you actually are.

3. Holding the brush by the handle, press the tips of the bristles against your hand to see if this creates a clean, sharp edge for easy trimming or "cutting." Also, test the bristles for a springy feel and a natural tendency to fan out to a straight edge.

4. Select a brush wide enough to minimize the back-and-forth brushing you will have to do, but not so wide and heavy that you can't handle it easily. A 1½-inch or 2-inch brush is generally right for windows and similar narrow trim; a 2-inch or 2½-inch brush is better for baseboards, doorframes, and similar woodwork; a 3-inch

brush is about right for doors, cabinets, shelves, and most furniture.

5. Handle sizes and shapes vary, but don't let anyone tell you that one is definitely better than another. When you have a choice, select the handle that feels most comfortable when held in a normal working position.

Cleaning Brushes

The job that people seem to dread most when painting is cleaning the paintbrush out afterward—yet this does not have to be a particularly messy or time-consuming job if you tackle it immediately after you finish working for the day. And, contrary to popular opinion, thorough cleaning does not require gallons of solvent or thinner (even when working with oil-base paints).

First rub as much excess paint out of the bristles as possible by wiping the brush across the rim of the can, then by rubbing back and forth on a stack of old newspaper. Discard the top sheet as soon as it becomes loaded with paint. To clean the brush of water-thinned paint, simply wash it in running water, or in several changes of water, preferably with a little detergent added. Be particularly careful to wash up near the heel of the brush, and work the bristles between your fingers to make certain that you get all the paint out. Then smooth out the bristles and separate tan-gles with an old comb or a special metal brush comb that many stores sell. Lay the brush flat to dry, after which you should wrap the bristles as illustrated on page 164 top right.

Brushes used in solvent-thinned paints are most often washed in solvent or thinner—turpentine or mineral spirits for oil-base and alkyd-base paints, lacquer thinner for lacquer, and alcohol for shellac. First wipe out as much of the paint as you can, then pour about an inch of the thinner into a can wide enough to take the bristle easily. Press the bristles down and work them vigorously against the bottom of the container.

Pour the dirty liquid out into another container (don't throw it away yet), then pour another inch of solvent into the original container and repeat the process of working the bristles against the bottom until the solvent is saturated. Pour this dirty liquid into the second container, then rub the brush out hard on newspaper or scrap pieces of cardboard. Repeat this two or three more times, then finish by washing in a little warm water and detergent. Shake out the excess water, comb the bristles smooth, let them dry, then wrap as illustrated on page 164.

Most of the dirty solvent can be saved. Allow it to settle for a few hours, then pour off the top and discard the sediment-filled portion at the bottom—usually less than about one-fourth of the solvent used to clean the brush.

Brushes used in solvent-thinned finishes can also be cleaned effectively with a liquid brush

Rinse brush used in water-thinned paint (left), **then smooth and untangle bristles with comb** (right).

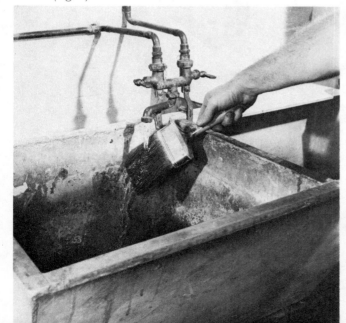
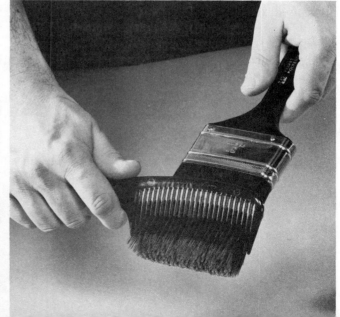

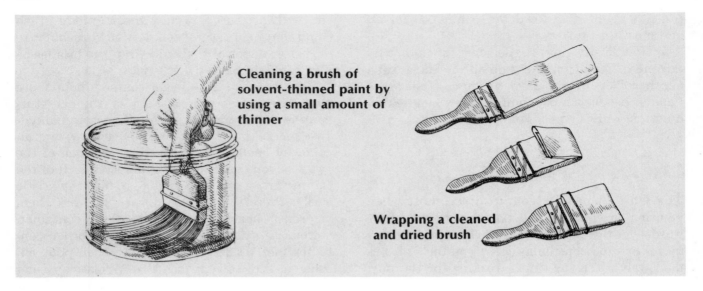

Cleaning a brush of solvent-thinned paint by using a small amount of thinner

Wrapping a cleaned and dried brush

cleaner. These liquids "emulsify" the paint so that you can then wash the brush out in a regular detergent solution. Directions for these products vary, so read the label.

CHOOSING AND USING PAINT ROLLERS

Paint rollers can apply almost any type of paint, and on many different surfaces. Most paint rollers are either 7 or 9 inches wide, but there are also special narrow models available for smaller surfaces—moldings and cabinets, for example—as well as models up to 18 inches wide for commercial and industrial work.

All paint rollers have removable covers or sleeves that are generally interchangeable with covers of the same width. These covers have fibers or naps of different length to suit the type of surface being painted and the type of finish you are applying. For flat wall paint, a cover with ⅜-inch or ½-inch nap is suitable for typical smooth-surfaced walls or ceilings. If the surface is heavily stippled or otherwise textured, then chances are a roller cover with a ¾-inch nap will do a better job of penetrating the crevices. And for painting really rough surfaces such as brick, stucco, or shingles, there are extra-long-nap covers with fibers up to 1½ inches long.

At the other end of the scale there are special mohair-type covers with very short fibers (more

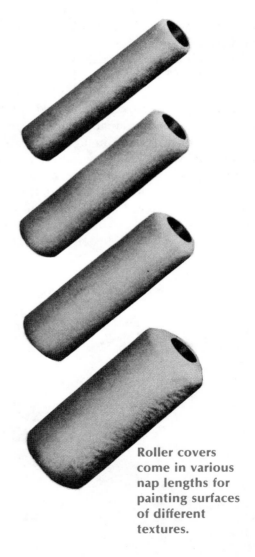

Roller covers come in various nap lengths for painting surfaces of different textures.

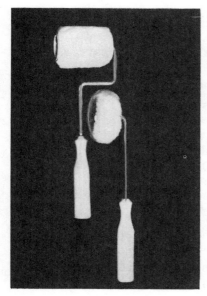

Narrow rollers are handy for corners and other small surfaces.

like a plush carpet) that are designed for glossy paints or varnishes when you want a really smooth job—though obviously these are practical only for very smooth, flat surfaces.

You can get special doughnut-shaped or V-shaped narrow rollers for inside corners, which an ordinary 7-inch or 9-inch roller cannot reach. These narrow rollers are also handy outside for the bottom edges of overlapping clapboard or shingles when painting with a roller or painting pad. And for furniture, cabinets, trim, and similar small surfaces for which a full-width roller would be impractical, narrow 3-inch rollers are also available.

Cleaning Paint Rollers

The most important thing to remember about cleaning a roller is that the job should be done immediately after you stop working. Start by rolling it back and forth on a stack of old newspapers to work out as much paint as possible. Discard the top sheet as soon as it is saturated.

Next, slide the cover off the roller handle for a thorough washing. Leaving it on when you clean it will cause paint to wash inside, where, after it dries, it will glue the cover on so that it will be impossible to get off later. Wash it in the appropriate solvent or thinner—water if the paint was a latex, and paint thinner if it was an oil paint. For washing in water you can use a bucket or container, but if you have a sink in the basement or can take the cover outside, rinsing under running water is probably the easiest.

Pointers on Using a Roller

To avoid spattering and spraying everything (and everyone) in the vicinity with a fine mist of paint, be careful not to spin the roller by working too fast. Roll with a slow, steady rhythm and with moderate pressure. When painting vertical surfaces always make the first stroke in an upward direction to minimize dripping or running.

For uniform coverage, get in the habit of picking up more paint as soon as you feel the roller running dry—don't just press harder to make the paint cover better. Even if the paint looks as if it is covering while it is wet, you'll find after it dries that the coating looks translucent and the color underneath shows through. As a result, another coat will be required. This is particularly true of latex paints, which have what is commonly called "false hiding" when they are wet.

For even coverage, pick up more paint as soon as roller feels dry.

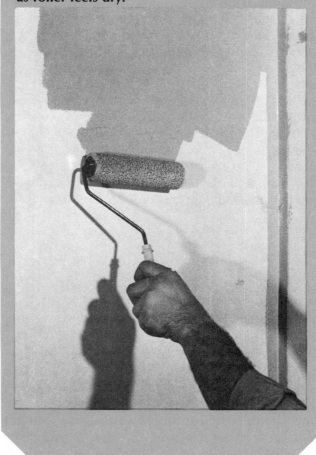

Cleaning roller of latex paint in a bucket of water and detergent

running or dripping, and may leave ridges of paint on the surface. Although pads are most appropriate for comparatively flat surfaces, special deep-pile or long-nap pads are available for rough or textured surfaces.

Painting pads can take most oil-base and alkyd paints, as well as all latex finishes, but they cannot take shellac, lacquer, and many other synthetics because the solvents in these finishes will attack the foam backing of the pad.

The most popular sizes of pads are about 9 or 10 inches in width, but smaller models are also available. There are even very small pads, only about 1 inch wide with wandlike handles. These are designed for painting moldings and for "cutting in" the narrow strips of wood that separate the panes of glass in windows.

Some painting pads are also designed to do a neat job of "cutting in" next to moldings or trim

To wash out oil paints, pour some thinner into the paint tray (after wiping most of the paint out), then roll the cover around and work the solvent into the fibers with your fingers. You will have to change thinner several times, but you don't need a lot each time—an inch or so in the bottom of the pan will do the job. Finish by washing in a warm detergent solution and rinsing with plain water. Squeeze out the excess by wringing the cover almost dry with your fingers. Stand the cover on end until it dries to avoid creating a flat spot in the nap. After the cover is clean, dip a cloth in thinner or solvent and wipe paint off the cage on the roller handle.

FLAT PAINTING PADS

Introduced primarily for painting striated shingles or "shakes" around the outside of the house, flat painting pads are now used on many other surfaces, both indoors and out.

These pads have a facing of plastic foam or nylon pile and are dipped into a tray much like a roller tray. Like rollers, painting pads are faster than a brush on large, comparatively flat and smooth surfaces, but unlike a roller, they do not spatter or spray if moved too fast. If you press too hard, however, you will have a problem with

Painting pad wipes paint on in wide strokes without spattering.

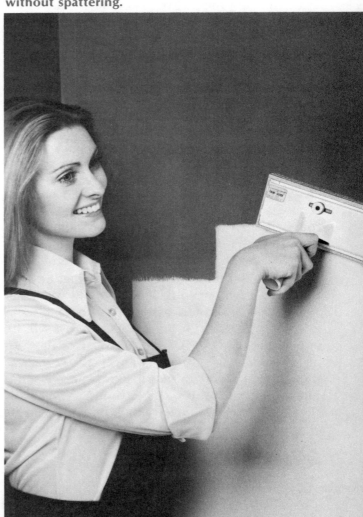

Painting masonry with a pad. Pads work best on flat surfaces.

with paint, dab off the excess by patting lightly on the upper part of the pan (above the paint).

Start painting with only the toe or forward part of the pad in contact with the wall, as illustrated in the drawing below. Then, as you move the pad along, gradually lower the rest of the face against the surface so that by the time you pass the middle of the stroke the pad is in full contact with the surface. As you near the end of the stroke, gradually lift the pad up and away—never lift it off suddenly, since this is likely to leave an uneven finish with small bubbles that will be difficult to smooth out. Bear down on the handle with only a moderate amount of pressure when applying the paint, and pick up more paint as soon as you feel the pad starting to run dry—resist the temptation to simply press harder.

Since replacement pads are quite inexpensive, most people do not bother cleaning them—they just throw the old one away at the end of the day and replace it with a new one. Actually, the pads

without getting any paint on the adjoining surface. There are two styles for this purpose. One has an overhanging lip or flange covering one edge of the pad. While the face pad is moved along the wall, the lip presses against the trim (or other surface you don't want to paint) to protect it. The second version has little wheels or rollers projecting out along one edge of the pad to keep the paint from spreading onto the trim or molding. Keep these pressed against the trim while you slide the pad along the surface and no paint will get on the trim. Needless to say, in both cases you must keep the flange or wheels clean when dipping the pad—otherwise paint will smear onto the surfaces you are trying to protect. Painting pads can be dipped into the same type of tray or pan used for a roller, but there are also deeper pans specifically designed to hold more paint for pad painters. Some also come with special wire handles for hanging the pan from the step of an extension ladder when working outdoors, and for carrying the trays from one place to another without spilling.

The best pad trays are those with a grooved or serrated roller that feeds paint as you roll the pad across it. This eliminates having to dip the pad directly into the paint, and avoids getting paint all over the edges and back (which causes dripping and running). After loading the pad

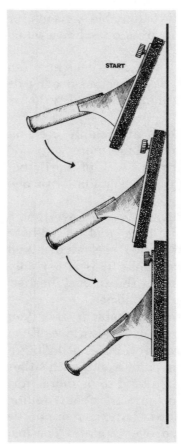

Applying pad to wall (top to bottom): **Start with pad "toe" against wall, then gradually lower pad to surface while continuing stroke.**

START

can be cleaned and reused without much difficulty, following the same techniques you would use for cleaning a roller cover (see page 165). Just be sure to clean all the paint off the back of the pad, as well as the face, and squeeze it thoroughly while washing to get all of the paint out of the foam.

INTERIOR PAINTS

Most interior paints fall into one of two broad categories: water-thinned latex paints, and solvent-thinned oil-base or alkyd-base paints. The latex finishes are by far the most popular, especially with do-it-yourself painters, because they offer a number of advantages:

They thin with water, so you can wash tools in water and clean up smears on hands or clothing with a damp cloth.

Latex paints do not have the solvent type of "painty" odor that many people find objectionable.

Because latex paints thin with water, there is no need to have highly flammable solvents, or rags soaked with solvent, around the house while you are working.

Since latex paints dry very fast, you can often put two coats on in one day, so rooms needn't be out of commission for more than a few hours after painting.

Latex flat paints, which are mainly used on walls and ceilings, tend to hide more with one coat than an alkyd flat paint will, primarily because they build up to a thicker film with one coat.

In spite of all these advantages, however, some painters still prefer oil-base and alkyd-base paints—mainly because they feel that alkyd paints are often more durable. This is partially true if you are talking about the enamel finishes, but questionable in the flat finishes.

Alkyd paints are less of a problem when you have to paint over an old glossy surface. Even though all manufacturers recommend dulling a glossy surface before you paint over it with either type of paint, alkyd paints tend to be more "forgiving" if you are a bit careless about dulling some parts of the old finish. Latex is more prone to peeling when applied over a glossy coating.

And as a rule, alkyd enamels are available in brighter, clearer colors than latex enamels, as well as in darker shades that are not as "muddy."

How Much Gloss?

The choice of either a flat, semigloss (also called satin-finish), or high-gloss enamel on a particular surface will depend on personal taste, as well as on the practical consideration of how much scrubbing and hard wear the surface is likely to undergo. Most people will prefer a flat paint for walls and ceilings, except in kitchens, bathrooms, and laundry rooms, where these surfaces are more exposed to dampness and are more likely to be washed at regular intervals. In these rooms a semigloss or high-gloss enamel will stand up better.

Likewise, for doors, windows, and other woodwork, most people will select an enamel paint because the finish will be easier to clean and less likely to absorb stains. If you object to a high gloss, a satin-finish or "eggshell-finish" enamel will not be nearly as shiny as a full-gloss enamel, yet will be almost as durable.

As a rule, when more than one coat will be required it is best to follow the manufacturer's directions as to applying the first coat. Latex paints usually do not require a separate primer—simply apply two coats of the same paint. However, alkyd paints usually need a separate primer or undercoat. Check the instructions on the label to make sure.

PAINTING WALLS AND CEILINGS

Before painting any room, always remove as many obstacles as possible—pictures, curtains or other hangings, area rugs, and furniture. Large pieces that cannot be easily removed should be pushed together in the center of the room, then covered with suitable drop cloths such as old bedsheets or inexpensive lightweight plastic covers. For covering floors you are better off with canvas or cloth covers, unless you can get heavier-weight plastic tarps; very lightweight plastic covers tend to lift and slide too easily.

If you do cover the floors with plastic—light or heavy—it is still a good idea to spread some old

Extension handle attached to roller enables you to reach high places without a stepladder in many places.

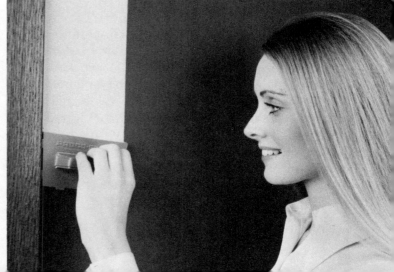

sanding. If you are using a latex paint, spot-prime any patched areas before you go ahead with the entire wall or ceiling. If you are using an alkyd paint, then a primer-sealer or an undercoat may be required for touching up.

Paint the ceiling first, then the walls. Woodwork and trim are normally done last. A roller is generally best on ceilings (painting pads are harder to control overhead). You can eliminate the need for a stepladder on most of the ceiling if you attach an extension handle to your roller—these handles simply screw into a threaded hole or socket in the base of most roller handles.

A standard roller will not reach all the way into the corner joints where the ceiling meets the wall, so you will need a brush to "cut in" this area. If the walls are the same color as the ceiling, then you don't have to cut in, but you will still need to reach into the corner. A brush, a narrow doughnut-shaped roller, or a small flat painting pad designed for cutting into corners will do the job.

As a rule, it is best to paint in the corners and around the edges first, with the brush or other applicator. Then go ahead on the main part of the ceiling with your roller. If you are fortunate enough to have a helper, then one person can paint around all the edges, while the other follows with the roller on the larger areas.

After the edges have been done, start with the roller in one corner and work across the shortest dimension of the ceiling in a wide band. When you reach the opposite wall, come back and start painting another wide band across the room. The

sheets, pieces of canvas, or even old newspapers on top; plastic doesn't absorb paint, so drips and spills will just get smeared around by your shoes if you happen to step on them. Papers or rags will help prevent this.

Use a vacuum to remove dust from walls and ceilings, and use detergent to wash sections that are really dirty or greasy. If you paint over dirt or grease, chances are that the paint will peel or wrinkle quite soon. So a thorough cleaning is especially important in kitchens and utility rooms.

In addition to cleaning the walls and ceilings, you should also patch all cracks and holes (see Chapter 6) and smooth over rough spots by

Narrow doughnut-shaped roller (left) and edger paint pad (right) are good for reaching into corners.

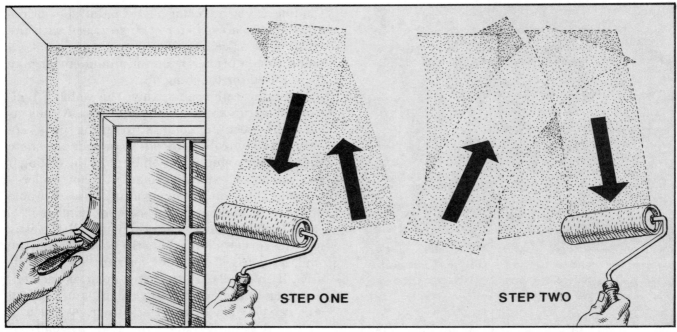

Paint corners and edges next to trim first.

When using a roller, stroke upward first to minimize drips, then downward at a slight angle (left). **Each stroke should overlap the last** (right).

idea is to always keep a wet edge for the next lap. That is why you should never stop in the middle of a ceiling or wall. Wait until the whole ceiling is done before you stop for a rest—or at least until you come to a break in the surface, such as where a room divider or other large built-in meets the ceiling.

Roll the paint on slowly in a series of diagonal back-and-forth strokes, applying only a moderate amount of pressure to the handle to avoid dripping or spattering. After you have covered several square feet, start smoothing the paint out by going back and forth over the same area with parallel strokes at approximately right angles to the direction in which the paint was originally applied.

When painting close to the wall with the roller, try to overlap as much of the brush-painted area as you can—the roller will cover any noticeable difference in texture between the brushed and the rolled areas. If the walls are to be painted the same color as the ceiling, there is no need for careful trimming or cutting in, so coat a band on the wall as well as on the ceiling with a brush or doughnut-shaped roller.

Painting walls is not much different from painting ceilings, except that you don't have to worry about reaching overhead or working in an awkward position. Also, on a wall there is much less dripping, running, and spattering than when painting overhead.

If you are applying paint with a roller, make your first stroke in an upward direction to minimize drips or runs, then come down at an angle to the first stroke before rolling upward again. Each stroke should overlap the previous one and go off at a slight angle so that you actually wind up painting a sort of inverted W on the wall.

As soon as you have completed these first three or four up-and-down strokes, cross-stroke lightly, alternating between strokes that are parallel to the floor and those that are more vertical. The idea is to smooth off the paint just applied and even up any noticeable irregularities. Pick up more paint as soon as you start to feel the roller running dry—don't just press harder to get more coverage out of the same amount of paint.

With a painting pad, the best way to coat each wall is in a series of vertical strips about 3 or 4 feet wide, starting each one at the top and working down to the baseboard. Start with only the toe (the leading edge) of the pad in contact with the wall, as described on page 167. Then continue with up-and-down strokes just as you would with a roller. Before starting on the wall, though, paint next to windows, doors, and other woodwork, with either a brush or a painting pad made for trimming. And be sure you remove switch plates and electrical outlet cover plates before you start, to avoid smearing them or painting them permanently in place.

PAINTING DOORS, WINDOWS, AND WOODWORK

A brush is the best tool for painting most woodwork and trim, but for flush doors and similar flat surfaces you can also use a roller or painting pad. Pads and small rollers are also good for cabinets, bookcases, and other built-ins, as well as wide baseboards or flat trim.

A brush about 1½ or 2 inches wide will be just about right for most trim, excluding doors. If you have wide baseboards or trim, then a 2½-inch brush is preferable. The idea is to use a brush that is not too narrow, since that would mean

Painting a flush door. Apply wide horizontal bands (left), smoothing each band with cross strokes (right).

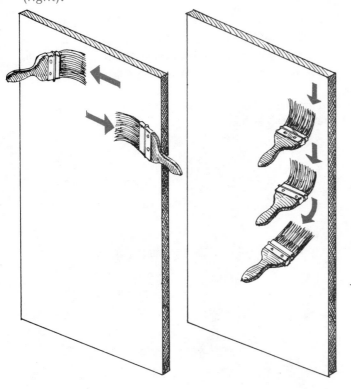

Sequence for painting paneled door. Paint sections labeled A first, B second, etc.

more brush strokes and a greater chance of leaving brush marks or lap marks.

Paint door edges first, then the two sides. On a flush door you just work from top to bottom in a series of wide horizontal bands, smoothing each one out by cross-stroking before moving down to the next band.

On paneled doors follow the sequence shown above. First paint the molded edge around each recessed panel, then the panel itself. Apply the paint to each panel with vertical strokes, and then, with an almost dry brush, cross-stroke lightly at right angles to the first strokes to smooth out the finish and eliminate any runs or sags.

After all the panels are done, paint the horizontal rails between them, starting at the top and working your way down to the bottom of the door. Paint the vertical rails (called stiles) last.

There is also a definite sequence to be followed when painting double-hung windows—that is, if

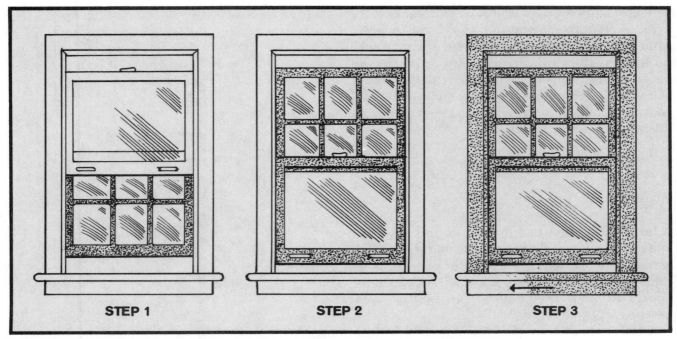

STEP 1   STEP 2   STEP 3

Sequence for painting double-hung windows (left to right): **Paint lower half of upper sash, upper and lower sashes, then frame and sill.**

you want to avoid skipping sections or having to handle sections you've just painted. Start by raising the lower (inner) sash as high as it will go, then lower the upper sash all the way down. Following the sequence shown, first paint the lower half of the upper sash, then slide each sash back into its normal position (the upper one at the top and the lower one at the bottom), leaving each one open an inch or two top and bottom.

Now paint the rest of the upper and lower sashes, first coating the narrow strips between the panes of glass, then the outer frame of each sash. Don't forget the top edge. The frame around the window is painted next, again from the top down. The windowsill is done last.

For many people, the hardest thing about painting windows is keeping the paint off the glass. Some use masking tape to avoid the need for careful "cutting in," but this is almost more trouble than it is worth—you have to be very careful when applying the tape, and you have to be sure to remove it promptly when the paint starts to get tacky. If you leave the tape in place for days you may find it difficult to remove, and it can pull some of the paint off with it.

A better way to keep paint off the glass is with a metal or plastic shield that you hold against the molding and move along with the brush as you paint. This works well if you remember to keep wiping the edge of the shield with a rag—otherwise it will start to smear as it becomes heavily coated with paint.

Cutting in freehand—that is, without any help from a shield or masking tape—is not as hard as it seems, but you need a good-quality sash brush that fans out to a nice sharp edge. Touch the

Cutting in window molding freehand with a good-quality sash brush

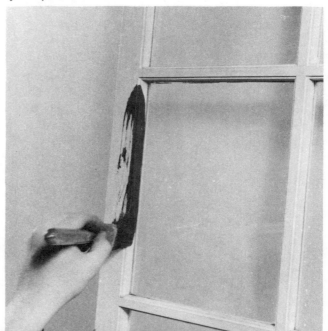

loaded bristles to the wood at a short distance from the glass, then move the brush along the length of the molding, pressing down enough so that the bristles fan out to a clean edge. Move the brush in a slight arc that will bring the bristle tips gradually in contact with the glass, then keep moving in a straight line along this joint. Remember: The paint should overlap onto the glass by a tiny fraction of an inch. This is essential for a truly tight seal.

CHOOSING AND APPLYING EXTERIOR PAINTS

While some exterior paints are good for many different surfaces, there is still no one paint for all surfaces, so make sure you check the specifications on the label before you buy. If you want a paint for both wood and masonry, read the label on the can—don't just take the word of a clerk.

Like interior paints, exterior finishes come with either a latex base or an oil or alkyd base. The latex types are far more popular with do-it-yourself painters, for in addition to their quick-drying and easy-cleanup advantages, you can start painting with them while surfaces are still damp after a rain, or in the early morning while surfaces are covered with dew.

All latex exterior paints have one other advantage over oil or alkyd paints—they are semipermeable. When wood or stucco gets saturated with moisture, either from condensation or from a structural defect that allows water to seep in behind the paint film, this moisture tries to push its way to the drier air outside, especially when the surface is warmed by the sun. Oil paints are not permeable, so the moisture literally pushes the paint off as it tries to escape. Latex paints let the moisture pass harmlessly through the film without blistering or peeling. Of course, this won't help much if you already have an oil paint on the surface and are merely applying a latex paint on top.

Exterior latex paints are semipermeable, thus less likely to peel on siding because of trapped moisture.

Choosing the Right Paint

Paint for the body of the house—siding, shingles, stucco, etc.—is usually referred to as house paint. For the windows, doors, and trim you will need a trim paint. Latex-base house paints are generally dull, while oil-base or alkyd house paints usually have some sheen. Trim paints dry to a high gloss and are very similar to an enamel in durability and gloss.

House paints are softer and more flexible so that they can "give" when large areas expand and contract, but the harder-drying trim paints are much more resistant to soiling and absorption of dirt. This makes them more durable for doors, windows, and other trim that gets lots of abuse; for large surfaces such as siding or exterior walls, however, they are too brittle.

Most latex house paints and some of the low-luster alkyd house paints (also called shake paints) are suitable for either wood or masonry,

For painting shingles, latex paints are better than oils—but ideally, shingles should be stained.

but as a rule, oil-base house paints that dry to a gloss are not for wood shingles or shakes because they are much more likely to crack and peel in a few years.

(Actually, shingles and shakes should not be painted at all—they should be stained. But if yours are already painted, then you have no choice, for you cannot use a stain over a paint. There are some "heavy-bodied" shingle stains that cover weathered paint, but these are more like paint than a true stain.)

If you have natural-finish redwood or cedar siding, then chances are you will want some kind of clear finish. Don't just apply an ordinary spar varnish. Varnishes are fine for boats, furniture, trim, doors, etc., but not for very large areas such as siding. Use instead a clear wood preservative, or a sealer made for exteriors, or one of the shingle stains with preservative added. If you want more of a gloss, there are slow-drying processed oil finishes specifically made for redwood and similar wood siding.

Applying clear finish to natural-finish wood siding

Surface Preparation Is All-Important

More outdoor paint jobs fail prematurely because of poor preparation than they do from any other cause, so make sure you don't scrimp on this part of the job. Applying paint over a dirty surface is probably one of the most common mistakes, though this doesn't mean that the whole house has to be washed down each time a new coat of paint is applied. It does mean that loose dirt, soil, and dust must be removed, and that greasy dirt and oily stains should be scrubbed off with a detergent solution. This is particularly true in areas that do not get much exposure to the natural cleansing effects of wind and rain—for example, under overhanging eaves or porch roofs, or inside a sheltered porch entrance.

When scrubbing off what appears to be dirt, be careful that you are not actually dealing with mildew—just scrubbing this off will not do much good, because it will probably come back worse than ever after a fresh coat of paint is applied. Instead, you have to kill the fungus that caused the mildew by scrubbing with a solution of 1 part fresh liquid laundry bleach and 3 parts water. Add some powdered detergent, then scrub the solution on and allow it to dry on the surface. Rinse off with plenty of fresh water.

If you are not sure whether a particular stain is

For a successful paint job, dirty surfaces must be scrubbed clean before being painted.

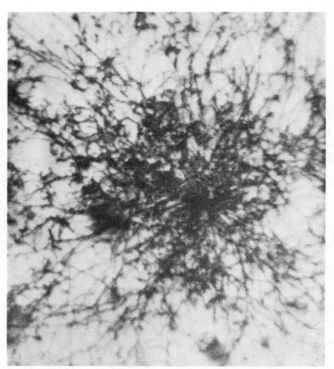

Mildew (here seen under a magnifying glass) can be scrubbed away with a bleach-water-detergent solution.

mildew or dirt (they do look alike in many cases), there is a simple test: Saturate a cloth with a little fresh laundry bleach and hold this against the stain for a minute or two. If the stain is mildew it will virtually disappear—or at least lighten dramatically. If it is dirt, it will hardly lighten at all. If you find yourself with a particularly bad mildew problem, ask your dealer about a paint that is truly mildew-resistant, or buy one of the additives sold for that purpose and add it to the new paint before you apply it.

Another common mistake when preparing the surface is not removing all paint that is cracked, peeling, or starting to blister and flake. If you just paint over such a surface, it will eventually fall off and take the new paint with it. The same precaution holds true for old paint that is powdering or chalking badly—unless you remove most of the powdery residue or use a special bonding primer recommended by the manufacturer, you'll be faced with early flaking and peeling of the new finish. A stiff wire brush, or even a scrub brush, will often remove enough to make a sound enough surface for repainting. If the condition is more severe, you may also need a surfacing primer or bonding sealer before the finish is applied.

Use a scrub brush, scraper, or sanding pad to remove flaking, peeling paint before applying new coat.

How do you remove all the old loose or flaking paint? With scrapers, wire brushes, sanding machines, and similar tools. If you really have a lot to remove, try a chemical paint remover, but this gets quite expensive if large areas are involved. Professional painters often prefer to burn the paint off with a torch. It's a faster way, but it is also much more dangerous because of the very real possibility of setting fire to the house (if you do use a torch, make sure you keep an extinguisher handy, and watch the area for at least an hour or two afterward). There are also electric heat guns and stove-type heating units that work like a torch to soften paint for easy removal. These are generally safer, but also quite a bit slower—and they can still scorch the wood if you are not careful.

One of the most important preparatory steps required before applying any exterior paint is replacing defective caulking compound and putty. These fillers seal out moisture that can work in behind the paint film and cause peeling, as well as rotting and cracking of wood and masonry. Caulk all open joints around window frames and doorframes, and also any place where two pieces of material meet to form a seam or joint that could possibly let water enter.

Use fresh glazing compound, rather than regular putty, to replace putty that is cracked or missing around windowpanes (see Chapter 5 for more information on using glazing compound).

SANDING PAD

Caulk all open joints around window frames and doorframes before painting.

In addition to replacing any missing or cracked caulking and putty, it is important to inspect the gutters to see if any repairs are needed before you start your paint job (see Chapter 14). Gutters that overflow or leak badly will not only leave ugly-looking streaks on your freshly painted siding or trim, they could also create moisture problems that would cause premature peeling.

If there are any rusted or exposed nails, countersink them with a nail set and fill the remaining hole with putty. If the nail heads cannot be countersunk (a limitation of large-headed nails) and if they are rusting and staining the paint, special steps are needed. Remove any rust with a piece of sandpaper or steel wool, then spot-prime the nail head, as well as any rust stain on the wood, with a shellac-base or latex-base stain killer and sealer. This will keep both nail and rust stain from "bleeding" through the top coats of paint, and the sealer dries so quickly it can be painted over within an hour.

Applying the Paint

Thoroughly mixing before you start is especially important with exterior paint, because of the amount of pigment in most brands. You cannot mix properly in a full can—you have to pour part of the contents into another container first, then stir up what remains in the original can until all the pigment is off the bottom, then pour all of it together into a larger bucket and stir again.

Since a complete exterior paint job will usually require several gallons of paint, you should buy enough right at the start to complete the whole job—especially if you are using a color. This is the only way to be certain all cans will be the same color. Check to see if the batch numbers on each can are the same—these numbers are usually stamped (embossed) on the top or bottom of the can. Different batch numbers could mean slight differences in shading.

You can apply most exterior paints with any of the common applicators—brushes, rollers, or painting pads. For stucco, smooth concrete, and similar large surfaces with moderate texture, a deep-nap roller with a long-fiber cover is the fastest and easiest tool. For surfaces with a really heavy texture, such as a brick wall, make sure you buy a roller cover with the longest fibers available (1-inch to 1½-inch pile).

On clapboard and siding a large brush is okay, but a roller or flat painting pad will make the work go much faster and will require less effort. You will need a narrow roller or brush for the edges on overlapping clapboard, and again a roller is faster. For painting wood shingles or shakes, a flat painting pad is the fastest tool.

A brush remains best for windows, doors, shutters, cornices, and other trim. Choose a reasonably wide brush that you can handle comfortably, yet not one that will be too wide for the surface. Spread the paint on liberally with moderate back-and-forth stroking. Never try to "scrub it on" by bearing down hard. If the paint does not flow easily, thin it a little, but don't add any more thinner than is necessary to make the paint spread easily. Too much thinning will not only weaken the film, it will also tend to make the paint run or drip and sag.

A rough surface such as brick needs the longest-fibered cover available (left). **For smoother surfaces, an ordinary roller can be used** (right).

Rollers are fast and easy on clapboard, but you'll need a narrow roller or brush for edges.

Work in Sequence

Although there is no set sequence for painting any house, as a general rule it is best to work from the top down, painting the body of the house first (siding, shingles, stucco, etc.), and the trim last. However, if you are working alone and doing the whole house, then your best bet is to complete one whole side or wall at a time before moving on to the next wall or section.

Following this type of routine will save a lot of unnecessary work in moving ladders and drop cloths. Another advantage is that if your job drags out over a period of months, or if you don't get it all finished in one season, at least the side or sides you have done will be complete. In fact, if tackling the whole house at one time is too much of a job, then it may be wise to plan on painting one or two sides each season.

PAINT FAILURES, AND WHAT YOU CAN DO ABOUT THEM

When a paint job starts to break down or show severe signs of cracking, peeling, or flaking, the first thing many people do is blame the paint. Yet in most cases paint is not the culprit—problems are most often due to one of the four following errors:

1. Poor preparation of the old surface before you applied the new paint.

2. Using the wrong kind of paint for the particular surfaces involved, or for the conditions to be encountered.

3. Not following the manufacturer's directions for mixing, thinning, or applying the paint.

4. Not first repairing structural defects—for example, not fixing a leak that then causes paint to peel.

Simply brushing a new coat of paint on right over the old one will seldom solve the problem. In fact, it may make things a lot worse. You have to determine what caused the problem, then take the necessary steps to prepare the surface so that the same thing won't happen again.

The most frequent type of breakdown is when paint blisters, then cracks and peels. There are many things that can cause paint to peel, and you can get a clue from whether or not the paint is peeling all the way down to original surface (wood, plaster, masonry, etc.) or if it is just the last coat that is lifting off. If the paint is peeling to the bare surface, then one of the first things you should suspect is that moisture is getting in behind the paint film and causing it to lift. Outside, look for cracks or open joints that may be allowing water to enter the wall, or look into the possibility of condensation problems inside the walls (see Chapter 15). Condensation is often a severe problem in older houses that have had insulation blown in without a vapor barrier, although it can also occur if there are gaps in an existing vapor barrier.

Installing small vents in the exterior siding is often the answer to condensation problems. You drill holes in the siding, then simply push the vents into the holes. They allow trapped moisture vapor to escape harmlessly without pushing the paint off in the process. For maximum effectiveness, you should have at least one of these vents between each pair of wall studs, though in some cases two will be needed—one near the top and one near the bottom.

If paint is peeling inside the house down to the bare plaster or wood, moisture is also likely to be the culprit. It can be coming in from an outside leak, or from a plumbing leak inside the walls or ceilings.

In many instances the leak will have caused rotting or deterioration of the plaster or wallboard, so that just eliminating the leak is not enough—you must also remove the rotten plaster or gypsum board and replace it with fresh

material if you want any new paint to stick to it for long.

Paint peeling all the way down to the original surface can also indicate that a poor primer was originally applied, or that the surface was covered with a film of dirt, grease, dust, or other foreign material when it was first painted. In any event, chances are that unless you remove most if not all of the old paint before you put any new paint on, you will continue to have problems.

What if only the top layers of paint are peeling, while the coats underneath remain sound? This is usually an indication of faulty preparation or improper priming; the particular sealer required was not used. Painting over a very glossy surface, or one that still has wax, dirt, grease, dust, or a chalky film on it, will cause the new paint to peel or crack. If you live near the seashore, the peeling can also be caused by a fine layer of salt that was deposited on the surface and did not wash off before the new coat of paint was applied.

To minimize the chance of peeling, you should always take time to knock off any gloss that remains on the old finish by sanding or wiping with

When condensation causes paint to peel, install two vents between each pair of wall studs (left); fit louver into predrilled hole (right) to let air in behind sheathing and moisture out.

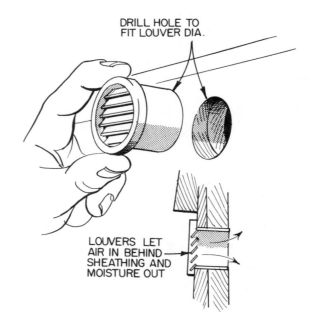

DRILL HOLE TO
FIT LOUVER DIA.

LOUVERS LET
AIR IN BEHIND
SHEATHING AND
MOISTURE OUT

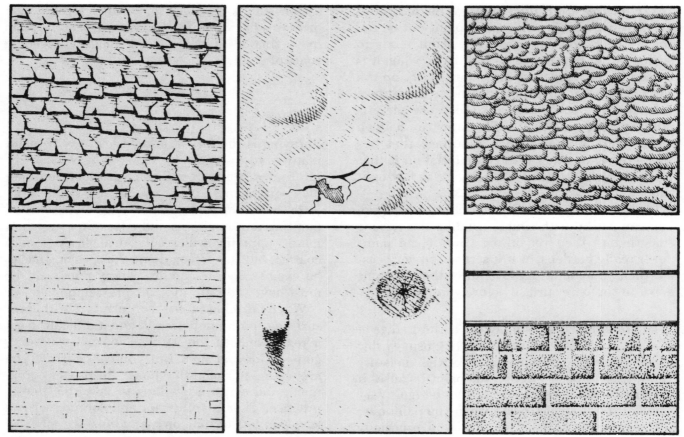

Common paint problems (clockwise from left): **alligatoring, blistering, wrinkling, checking, rust and sap stains, and chalking**

a deglossing liquid. Also, make sure that dirt, soot, and chalky residue or foreign material is cleaned off before you start, and follow the manufacturer's directions carefully as to what primer, if any, is required.

Of course, blistering and peeling are not the only types of paint failure. Here are some other common paint problems, along with suggestions for preventing or eliminating them:

Alligatoring. As its name implies, this occurs when paint develops a pattern of puckering and cracking that makes it look like an alligator's hide. It is caused by paint applied on top of a previous coat that was not completely dry and hard. Another cause is mixing the wrong kind of thinner or solvent in with the paint, or applying coats of incompatible paint.

To repair this condition, wait until the top coat dries hard and cures completely, then sand to create a smooth, sound surface. Apply a base coat of primer or undercoat before going ahead with the new finish coat. If the alligatored paint never does dry hard, your safest bet is to remove all of the old paint before applying a new coat on top.

Checking. Although this sometimes looks like alligatoring and is often confused with it, checking is more like a series of straight long lines, with short check marks crossing at right angles. It is usually caused by the wood underneath expanding and contracting over time. Most frequently encountered on painted plywood, the crisscross pattern of paint checking is smaller than that which occurs when paint alligators, and the cracks or check marks are usually thinner. Sanding and then applying a new coat of primer will usually solve the problem, but if the paint shows signs of letting go, complete removal of the old paint is advisable.

Wrinkling and puckering. The most frequent cause of this condition is paint put on too thickly or in too heavy a layer. Paint tends to shrink or tighten slightly as it dries, so when it is put on in thick layers it may start to dry on the surface before it does underneath. As the surface dries it may pucker or wrinkle because there is nothing solid underneath. The same can happen when paint is applied over a surface that has wax, grease, or other foreign material on it that prevents the new paint from drying as fast as it should.

If the wrinkled paint eventually dries hard, you can get by with simply sanding the surface smooth and then repainting. But if the paint never really hardens, or if it scrapes off very easily, then you should remove all of the old paint down to the bare surface before you repaint.

Blistering. This is simply the earliest stage of peeling—at least the kind of peeling usually due to moisture under the paint. As the moisture vapor tries to push through the paint it causes it to blister—then crack, peel, and let go. Very small blisters can also occur when you paint over surfaces heated in the glare of the sun, especially if you are applying an oil-base paint and are working with dark colors.

Chalking or powdering. Caused by qualities inherent in the paint itself, this is normally not a serious problem. In fact, most house paints are actually designed to chalk so that they will be "self-cleaning" as they weather. However, excessive chalking can interfere with proper bonding when a new coat of paint is applied, so scrub off as much as possible when it seems to be excessive. In severe cases you may have to apply a bonding primer or sealer as recommended by the manufacturer.

Stains that bleed through the paint. This is most often the result of knots or sappy streaks in the wood, but it can also be caused by rust from nails or other metal hardware. Sap will bleed through coat after coat of paint, as will rust, so repeated repainting is not the answer. Instead, sand with medium-grade paper to remove most of the surface discoloration, then apply a coat of stain killer such as a pigmented shellac-base sealer—the kind that thins with alcohol and dries to a flat white finish. This will seal the stain in so that it cannot bleed through succeeding coats of paint.

SPRAY PAINTING

Spraying is the fastest and easiest way to paint many hard-to-paint objects, such as wicker furniture, wrought-iron railings, yard tools, outdoor play equipment, fences, toys, and all kinds of objects that involve reaching into tight corners and painting multiple sides and edges. In competent hands, spraying will result in a glassy-smooth coating, but the person doing the spraying has to be experienced at handling spray guns, and he must have the right kind of spray equipment.

When finishing cabinets or furniture with large surfaces, most amateurs will find it difficult to get a really smooth job with an inexpensive spray gun—at least at first. But you can learn, if you are willing to spend the money for proper equipment, and if you are willing to take the time to practice. Then a spray gun and compressor can save you lots of time on many finishing jobs.

Spraying is quickest way to finish louvered removable shutters.

There are basically three types of spray equipment for jobs around the house: conventional spray guns that mix compressed air with the paint to atomize it and form a controlled mist; so-called "airless" spray guns that need no compressor because they have built-in high pressure pumps in the head which force the paint out through a tiny orifice in a mistlike spray; and aerosol-type spray cans that come packed with a small amount of paint and require no separate equipment at all—you just push the button on top of the can.

Spray guns also differ in the type of nozzle they have. In one type, known as an internal-mix nozzle, the paint and air are mixed together inside the nozzle and then come out through a single opening. In another type, known as external-mix, there are two separate holes, one for paint and one for air. The two streams intermix outside the nozzle before being carried onto the surface. Generally, external-mix guns are preferable for light-bodied, quick-drying finishes such as lacquer, while internal-mix guns are for heavier-bodied, slower-drying paints and finishes.

Conventional compressed-air spray guns are by far the most versatile. With the right type of nozzle and gun, almost any type of finish can be sprayed. However, when used with latex (water-thinned) paints, spray guns do tend to clog or cake up, especially the more moderately priced models. Yet they also give the smoothest and glossiest finish when used with enamels, lacquers, varnishes, and other fine finishes, and they do an excellent job of applying stains and most other paints and finishes.

These guns come in two basic types—pressure-feed and siphon-feed guns. In a pressure-feed gun the compressed air coming in through the hose (from the compressor) builds up pressure inside the cup to force the paint up and out through the nozzle. In a siphon-feed gun the air flows at high speed past the top of a small tube going down into the cup. This air "sucks" or siphons the paint up to mix in with it.

For the heavy-bodied finishes, such as outdoor paints, you will want a pressure-feed gun. But for finer atomization of light-bodied finishes a siphon-feed gun is better. Many of the quality spray guns have convertible heads that permit operation in either mode.

Airless paint sprayers are fastest—that is, they put out paint faster than a compressed-air gun

Two types of spray gun nozzles

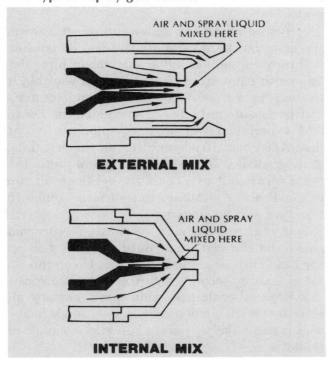

AIR AND SPRAY LIQUID MIXED HERE

EXTERNAL MIX

AIR AND SPRAY LIQUID MIXED HERE

INTERNAL MIX

Two types of compressed-air spray guns: pressure-feed (top) and siphon-feed

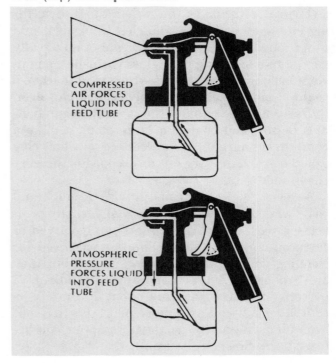

COMPRESSED AIR FORCES LIQUID INTO FEED TUBE

ATMOSPHERIC PRESSURE FORCES LIQUID INTO FEED TUBE

An airless paint sprayer makes fast work of painting shingles.

will, because the paint actually comes out in very tiny droplets, rather than as a mixture of air and paint. Most of the models for home use require no separate compressor because the tiny pump that atomizes and forces the paint out through the nozzle is built right into the head of the gun.

Their speed makes the airless units ideal for big jobs such as fences, shingles, brickwork, and other rough surfaces. But they cannot do a really good job of spraying high-gloss varnishes, enamels, and similar fine finishes—they tend to leave a slight "orange peel" or "pebbly" effect. However, there is one type of paint that an airless gun handles better, and that is a latex paint. Unlike a compressed-air gun, the airless model won't clog easily or cake up very often (except for the very cheap models).

Aerosol-type spray cans provide a quick and easy way to paint or finish many small projects—especially those with intricately carved or textured surfaces. They eliminate the need for cleaning and loading spray equipment, but they are expensive. A typical spray can is about 75 percent propellant, so only about 20 or 25 percent is actually paint. And some of this may not even be usable if the nozzle clogs up on you before you've finished the can.

Spraying Techniques

With any type of spray equipment there are certain rules to follow if you want to ensure the best possible results. There are also some working techniques that will make the job come out better.

1. Before filling any spray gun, make certain the paint has been carefully strained by pouring it through a piece of nylon stocking or a regular fine-mesh paint strainer, and be sure you thin it to the proper consistency. If the manufacturer's instructions do not tell you how much thinner to add, experiment with a small amount of paint first. Add about 10 percent thinner the first time, then gradually increase this amount until the paint sprays out in a fine mist, yet does not run or sag. Practice on some scrap surfaces similar to what you will be spraying.

2. If you are using an aerosol can, be sure you shake the can vigorously until the little ball on the inside rattles around loudly, and keep this up for at least 30 seconds before you start to spray.

3. Remember that two thin spray coats are always better than one heavy coat—a single heavy coat is more likely to sag or run after a couple of minutes.

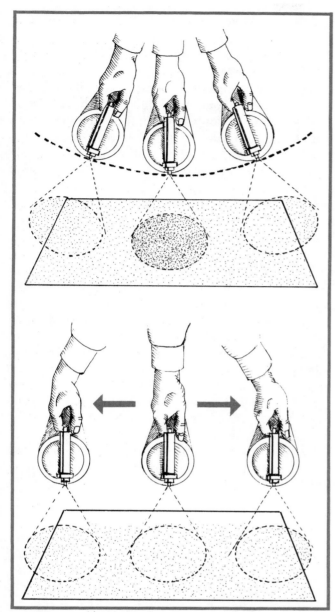

Starting and stopping a stroke with the trigger depressed will cause an uneven finish.

6. Do not arc your strokes by swinging your arm while holding your wrist straight. Instead, move the gun so that its stroke is parallel to the surface, with the nozzle always remaining at the same distance from the surface. This calls for arcing the wrist as you swing your arm from one side to the other.

7. When spraying a horizontal surface such as a tabletop, start spraying the part closest to you first, then work away from yourself till you get to the opposite side. This technique is less likely to result in some of the spray mist settling on parts that are already coated—a problem that often occurs when you start at the far side and work back toward yourself. (Since you are spraying

Right and wrong ways to spray paint. Spray past surface before releasing trigger, but move can in straight line, parallel to surface—not in an arc.

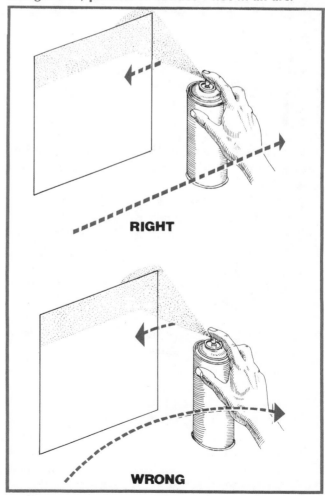

Right and wrong ways to move spray gun. Swinging your arm in arc will create an uneven finish (top); instead, swing arm while arcing your wrist to keep gun same distance from surface for even finish.

4. Hold the spray gun or can so that the nozzle is about 8 or 9 inches away from the surface, and if possible aim it so that the spray strikes at a right angle to the surface.

5. First press the trigger, *then* sweep across in a continuous stroke, releasing the trigger only after you are past the surface. The idea is always to have the gun in motion while paint is coming out.

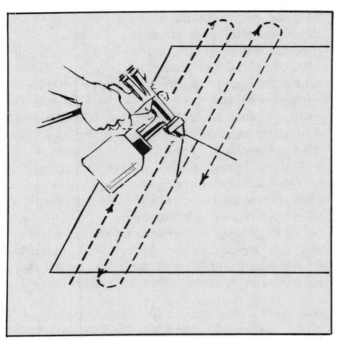

Work away from edge nearest you.

downward at an angle, the spray tends to spread away from you. If the farthest points are already coated, the spray will settle on top of those surfaces.) Also, paint the hard-to-reach areas first; leave the tops, fronts, and other prominent parts for last.

8. Avoid shooting straight into an inside corner; spray one side first, then the other. Spraying straight into the corner usually results in runs and drips.

9. When possible, take the work outside to spray it. If this is impractical, make sure everything nearby is covered to protect against overspray and drifting mist. If the object is small, you can set it up inside a large carton, or build a small "spray booth" out of large sheets of cardboard, or hang sheets of plastic around the spray area.

10. When working indoors, make sure there is plenty of ventilation, and no open flames or lit cigarettes, pipes, or cigars nearby.

HANGING WALLPAPER AND VINYL WALLCOVERINGS

Although we still call them wallpaper, many of the newer and more popular wallcovering materials are made of fabric, vinyl, canvas, and other materials. That's why the industry now refers to any material pasted up on walls or ceilings as a wallcovering rather than a wallpaper.

Wallcoverings are priced in units called a "roll" or a "single roll," but you will find that they all come packaged in multiple-roll bolts only—either in double-roll bolts that contain two single rolls, or in triple-roll bolts that contain three single rolls. A single roll contains about 36 square feet of material. But allowing for nominal waste, you can figure that you will get only between 30 and 32 square feet of usable material out of each single roll.

To figure the number of rolls you will need, measure the area to be covered, then divide by 30 to play safe. Measure the height of the walls, then the length of each wall. Add all the wall lengths together to get the perimeter of the room, then multiply this by the height of the wall (assuming all are the same height). At this point you do *not* subtract for openings such as windows, doors, fireplaces, etc.—measure as though all wall surfaces were solid. After dividing the total area by 30 to compute the number of single rolls required, you subtract one single roll for two average-size windows or doors.

There is also a much simpler method—just bring the room dimensions to your dealer and let him compute the number of rolls you need.

Preparing the Walls

Getting a wall ready for hanging wallcovering means first filling all cracks and holes, then smoothing over rough spots by sanding and spackling where necessary. A patterned wallcovering will hide or camouflage minor irregularities in a wall, but solid-color or mildly textured materials without a pattern will not. In fact, they may make rough spots even more noticeable.

If wallpaper is already up, you may be able to leave it on and put new paper up directly over it—but this only holds true if the old paper is adhering firmly, and if you are putting up a wall *paper*. Canvas or vinyl wallcoverings should never be hung over old wallpaper. In fact, most cannot be hung over any kind of old wallcovering. If in doubt, check the instructions that come with the material.

If the walls are covered with a vinyl or fabric

Use a wallpaper steamer to loosen old paper, then scrape paper off with putty knife.

easily (the machines are rented by many paint and wallpaper dealers, as well as by most tool rental agencies). The machine is a miniature kerosene-fired or electric boiler that makes steam and sends it through a hose to a flat metal pan with holes on one face. When you hold this side against the wall, steam comes out through the holes and saturates the paper. This softens the paper enough so that you can scrape it off the wall with a putty knife.

If you're removing wallpaper without a machine, you can make the job easier if you buy one of the special wallpaper-removing liquids that you mix with water. With a large sponge, brush, or garden-type sprayer, saturate the papered surface, then let it soak in for a few minutes. The liquid will soften and penetrate better than plain water will, making it easier to scrape off.

If you are ever faced with the job of trying to remove wallpaper that has been painted over or protected with a plastic coating, you will find that none of these techniques will work well because neither water nor steam will penetrate the paint or coating. The way to get around this is first to scratch the surface up thoroughly so that water or steam *can* penetrate. Buy some very coarse floor-sanding paper (open-coat) and rub it back and forth over the face of the paper to scratch through the paint or other coating. You will find that the water or steam can now soak through.

After the old wallcovering has been removed, scrub the wall thoroughly with hot water and detergent to remove any remnants of old paste or adhesive, then allow it to dry before hanging the new material.

wallcovering, removing this material is not much of a problem—all you have to do is work one corner loose, then start pulling or peeling it off. This technique will also work with wallpaper, if the paper was one of the strippable kind, or if a special strippable paste was used when it was put up.

With regular wallpapers the job will not be so easy—you will have to soak the paper and scrape it off by hand. The quickest way to get this job done is to rent a wallpaper steamer, made for steaming wallpaper loose so you can scrape it off

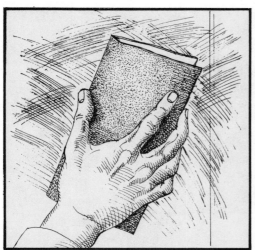

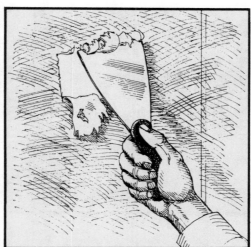

To remove paint- or plastic-covered wallpaper, scratch surface thoroughly with sandpaper so steam can soak through.

Cutting and Pasting

Measure the height of the wall, then unroll enough wallcovering to allow for a strip about 6 inches longer than the height of the wall. This allows a margin for trimming along the baseboard at the bottom, and along the ceiling-to-wall joint at the top after the wallcovering is in place. Before actually cutting the strip, however, look at the design to see how it looks along the top—you may want to cut at a point slightly farther along even if it means wasting a few more inches of material. For example, if the pattern has people in it, you might not want to cut strips in such a way that the top of the wall will have rows of headless people showing.

Now decide where to hang the first strip. The usual procedure is to work your way around the room in sequence after the first strip has been hung, so that the last strip will end up next to the first strip. Chances are the pattern on this last seam will not match; you will most likely have to cut one strip to less than its full width. So you want to select the starting point with care.

One of the best places to start is next to the doorframe through which the room is entered—a mismatch will be scarcely noticeable there, being visible only above the door. Another good starting point is in a corner behind an entrance arch or door, or next to a large window or built-in wall-to-ceiling bookcase.

Next, snap a vertical chalkline on the wall, using a chalked string with a plumb bob or weight of some kind on the end. This line should be at a distance from the starting corner equal to the width of the wallcovering, less about ½ inch. When you hang the first strip, line its edge up with this line and allow the extra ½ inch to fold around the corner onto the adjacent wall. If you are starting next to a door or window frame, this extra ½ inch will be trimmed off with a razor blade after the strip is up.

Don't make the common mistake of merely

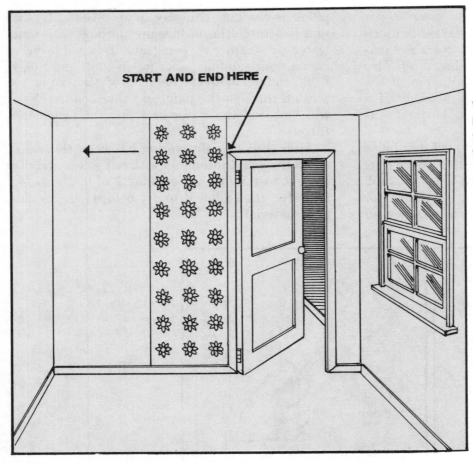

When hanging patterned paper, begin next to a doorframe so that the mismatched final strip will be inconspicuous.

lining up the edge of the strip with the wall corner, or with the edge of the door or window frame. These are seldom if ever really plumb (vertical), and if the first strip is not plumb all subsequent strips will not be plumb. The error will be magnified as you work your way along the wall.

After the first strip is hung plumb (along the line), subsequent strips on that wall will not have to be plumbed, because you will be butting adjacent strips together until you get to the next corner. Then the first strip on the next wall will have to be plumbed again before continuing on that wall.

Many of today's wallcoverings are prepasted—with these all you have to do is dip the rolled-up strip in water after cutting it to length. With those that are not prepasted, applying paste to the back of the material is the next step after cutting.

For this you will need a large flat surface. You can rent a special pasting table, or you can use a Ping-Pong table or a large kitchen or dinette table. Or place a large sheet of plywood across two sawhorses. The table or work surface should be about 6 feet long, and at least half again as wide as the wallcovering.

Lay the first strip face down on the table so that the top end is even with one end of the table as shown in the drawing. The edge closest to you should be lined up with the edge of the table, and the excess material left hanging over the other end of the table. To keep from smearing paste onto the table where it is exposed past the far edge, slide sheets of newspaper or other scrap material under the wallcovering to cover the exposed part of the table. After each strip is pasted, slide the paper out a little to expose a clean surface on which the next strip can rest.

The paste can be applied with a large brush or a roller. Make sure you use the adhesive recommended for that material by the manufacturer, and be sure there are no skips or misses. This is especially important along the edges, where even a small skip will leave a dry spot that can cause the seams to open or lift after the wall is finished. But don't apply the paste too liberally—just enough to cover the entire surface evenly.

As you finish coating the part on the table, lift up the pasted end and fold it over loosely, with the pasted sides on the inside, the pattern showing on the outside. The folded portion should now contain a little more than half the strip's length. Slide the strip along the table until all of the unpasted part (that was hanging over the end) is now up on the table. Paste this part, then fold it over in the same way so that the bottom end now meets the top in about the middle as shown. This makes it much easier to carry the strip over to the wall and simplifies handling when you start hanging it.

When you're ready to hang the wallcovering, unfold the top half and smooth it onto the wall with a couple of inches overlapping onto the ceil-

For applying paste to back of paper you'll need a long table and a roller or large brush.

Trimming Wallpaper Borders

Nowadays most wallcoverings are available pretrimmed—that is, with the selvages (unprinted borders) already trimmed off at the factory. However, many imported wallpapers and a few of the more specialized wallcoverings made in this country still come with a selvage or border that must be trimmed off before hanging. Trimming selvage is actually not that hard if you have a good straightedge at least 5 feet long (which can be rented along with a paper table from many dealers). After the strip has been pasted and folded as described above, place the straightedge on top of the folded strip so that its edge lines up exactly with the trim marks. Then hold the straightedge down firmly with one hand and with a razor blade in the other hand, trim off the border. Since the strip is folded, it is less than five feet long (the length of the straightedge), so you can trim the full length with a single cut. Just remember to bear down hard so you cut through with one clean stroke.

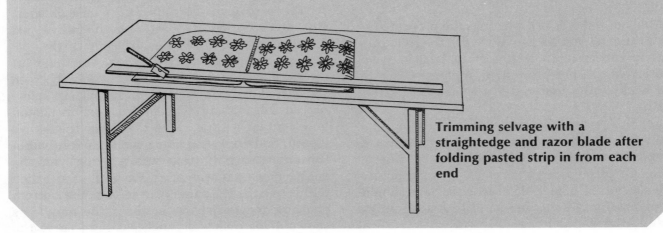

Trimming selvage with a straightedge and razor blade after folding pasted strip in from each end

ing and with the edge lined up with a plumb line tied to a nail driven into the wall up near the ceiling. For regular wallpaper and most lightweight vinyl or fabric wallcoverings, a paperhanger's smoothing brush is the best tool, but a large flat sponge can also smooth the paper onto the wall. For heavier-weight materials a wide metal trowel or a special type of roller may be required.

After the top half of the strip has been smoothed into place, the bottom half is unfolded and peeled down carefully. Smooth this part down in the same manner, then go over the entire strip with the smoothing brush once more to remove air bubbles and wrinkles. Work from the top down, and from the center out to each of the edges. If excess paste is squeezed out along the seams, immediately wipe it off with a cloth or clean wet sponge.

The next step is trimming off the excess material at the top and bottom. Crease the material

A plumb line helps you align first strip vertically. Hang strip close to line, then slide strip over.

into the corner joint with your smoothing tool, then trim along this crease with a single-edge razor blade. The razor blade will dull fast, so buy plenty of them and throw each blade away after you have used it on two or three strips (buy the commercial kind from a paint or hardware store—they are much cheaper than the ones in a drugstore). Wheeled cutters, called trimmers, are also sometimes used, but these require frequent sharpening and several passes—so razor blades are faster and cleaner. And the blades are cheap enough to throw away when dull.

After trimming the excess off along the ceiling and baseboard, go over the seams and top and bottom edges with a seam roller (made of plastic or wood) to smooth them down. Be careful to wipe off excess paste that gets squeezed out or else you'll smear it around.

Before you cut the second strip of paper, unroll it against the wall and hold it next to the first one to see how the pattern matches, as illustrated on page 192; in some cases the match is straight across, but in others there is a "drop match"— that is, to get a match at the top you will have to raise the material up by half a pattern.

Since this means wasting half a pattern length on each strip as you keep cutting from the same roll, cut the first strip off one roll and the second strip off another roll. Then back to the first roll to cut the third strip and back to the second roll for the fourth strip. By alternating rolls in this way you will only have waste on the second strip—after that you will be able to measure from the beginning of the roll each time without having to waste any at the top.

As each strip is pasted and hung, butt its edge against the edge of the previous strip by first applying it to the wall a fraction of an inch away, then sliding it over by pressing with your hands until it just meets the other edge. Then follow the same procedure of smoothing, trimming, and rolling the edges of that strip, before wiping excess paste off the face. Don't forget to keep rinsing the sponge frequently in clean water; otherwise you will just wind up smearing the paste over the covering.

When you get to an inside corner, do not simply fold the paper around the corner and continue on the adjoining wall with the same strip—this would almost certainly result in the material wrinkling and pulling out from the corner as it dries. Instead, stop and measure the

When hanging top half of strip, only uppermost section is unfolded. After smoothing, unfold bottom half.

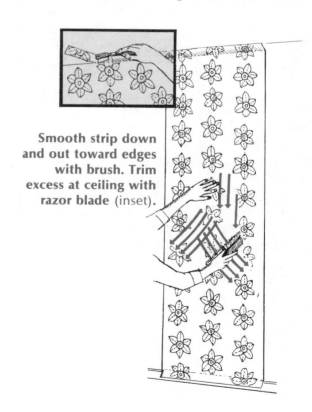

Smooth strip down and out toward edges with brush. Trim excess at ceiling with razor blade (inset).

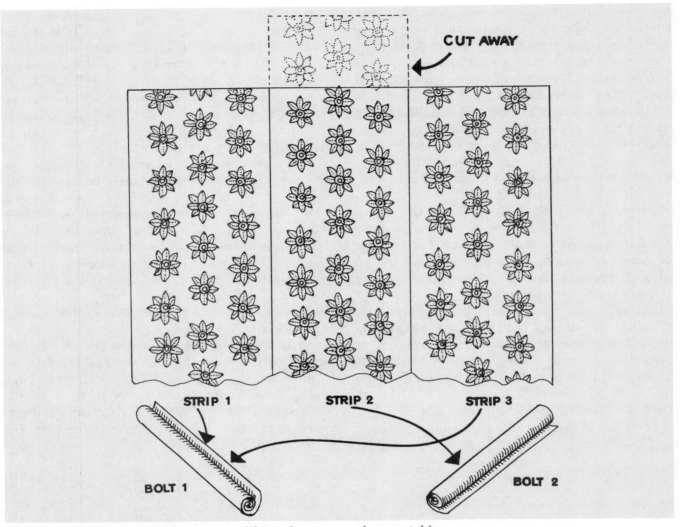

Cut strips from alternating bolts to avoid wasting paper when matching
a drop pattern.

space left between the edge of the last strip and the corner, then slice the next strip to the same length as the space left on the wall, plus about ½ inch. To ensure a straight cut, use a straightedge and a razor blade rather than the scissors you normally use to cut across a strip. Do this while the strip is still folded and on the table—that way you won't get paste on the straightedge.

When you hang this narrow strip, fold the extra ½ inch around the corner onto the next wall, then smooth it down and trim top and bottom in the usual manner. Be sure you press it tightly into the corner from top to bottom on both sides of the fold.

Take the rest of that same strip and hang it on the adjacent wall next to the folded edge. The match should be practically perfect, because both came from the same strip. If the corner is not straight, however, you may find it necessary to overlap the cut edge slightly here and there in order to avoid gaps between the two edges. On outside corners this is generally not necessary; you can safely fold a full-width strip around an outside corner if the corner is reasonably straight and plumb. If it isn't, then you should cut the strip as described above and apply it in two parts.

When trimming around windows, doors, and similar openings it is generally best to apply the full-width strip on the wall so that it overlaps the opening. Line up the one edge with the last strip hung, then carefully crease the wallcovering material into the joint formed between the wall and

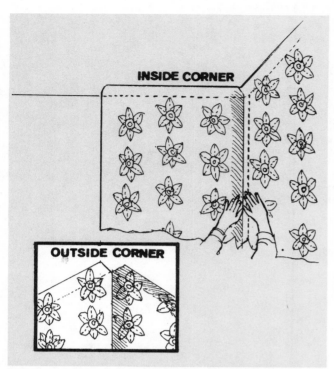

Paper can cover outside corner in one piece, but must be cut and slightly overlapped on inside corners.

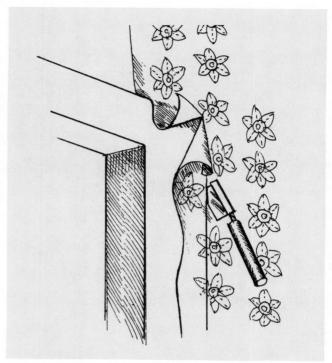

When trimming around frames, make a diagonal cut into the corner, then crease against molding and trim with razor.

the trim around the doorframe or window frame. To do this without tearing the paper, you will have to make several "relief" cuts so the material will lie flat against the wall.

Cut inward at a diagonal where the frame forms a corner joint as shown above right, then gradually trim away the largest areas of excess. Make enough cuts to permit the material to lie flat against the wall, then, with the single-edge razor blade, trim off the rest. On these strips it is generally better to trim around the window or

door before you go ahead with trimming along the ceiling and baseboard.

If the wall has light switches or electrical outlets, be sure you remove the cover plates first. Hang the wallcovering as though there were no opening. After trimming and smoothing, slit the wallcovering over the opening with your razor blade so that you can cut it out with scissors. Make sure you shut off power to that switch or outlet before doing this, and don't replace the cover plate until the paste has dried.

Chapter 9

Electrical Repairs

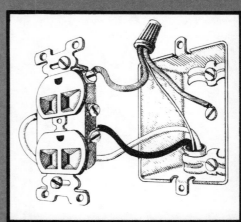

ALTHOUGH WORKING with 110-volt household wiring does call for observing some strict safety precautions, along with at least a basic knowledge of electricity and some idea of how electrical circuits are wired, doing your own simple electrical repairs need not be any more dangerous than most other home repair tasks.

Obviously, you don't want to start working with wires while current is still flowing through them—any more than you would cut a pipe or take apart plumbing connections when water is flowing through the system—so it is important that you always remember to shut off the power before you start. This means unplugging the appliance, if that is what you are working on, or taking out the fuse or turning off the circuit breaker that controls power to that particular circuit or fixture.

Fortunately, most of the electrical repair jobs commonly encountered around the home are comparatively simple and require only a minimum amount of knowledge and experience. Of course, rewiring entire circuits, or wiring a whole new addition to the house, is generally a job that only a qualified person can or should tackle—indeed, local building codes often forbid anyone but a licensed electrician from working on the house's wiring system—but there are still many repair jobs you can safely handle yourself.

SOME BASIC FACTS ABOUT ELECTRICITY

Electric wires are rated according to the maximum amount of current they can carry without overheating dangerously. If an appliance tries to draw more current than that wire can safely carry, or if a short circuit occurs, causing the flow of an excessively large current, the fuse will blow (or the circuit breaker will open) and thus shut off the flow of electricity.

If there were no fuse or circuit breaker in the line, its wires would try to carry the current and would overheat to the point where the insulation would scorch or melt, and eventually fire would break out. The same thing would happen if a fuse of oversize capacity were installed—which is why you should never replace a fuse with one that is "larger" than what is normal for that circuit. With circuit breakers, this cannot happen because you don't replace them; you just flip the switch to reset them.

Except for some large appliances that operate on their own circuits and draw 240 volts, most household circuits carry a current somewhere between 110 and 120 volts (it depends on your local utility company). The term "volt" is comparable to what we mean by the word "pressure" when we talk about water flowing through a pipe. The higher the voltage, the higher the "pressure" that is pushing that current through the wires.

The other measure of current is a term called amperes (usually abbreviated as amps). This refers to the "quantity" or actual amount of current flowing to, or actually consumed by, a particular appliance—similar to the way we talk about "gallons per minute" flowing through a faucet. In other words, the higher the amperage, the greater the quantity of current actually being consumed.

Since the total amount of electrical power consumed must take both voltage and amperage into consideration (you get more water through a pipe when it is being forced through at higher pressure), you measure total electrical comsumption in terms of watts. Wattage is computed by multiplying the volts in a circuit by the actual amperes consumed. Thus, an appliance that draws 10 amps at 110 volts is said to draw 1,100 watts (10×110).

How to Read Your Electric Meter

Knowing how to read your electric meter can be helpful in keeping track of power consumption, and in comparing energy usage at different times. Most electric meters have four or five dials similar to the ones illustrated here, with numbers running clockwise on alternate dials, and counterclockwise on the others.

Readings are cumulative—that is, they continue to increase from one reading to the next (they don't go back to zero). To determine how many kilowatt-hours you have consumed between readings you subtract the current reading from the last one (a kilowatt is 1,000 watts).

You read the dials from left to right, writing down the number of each in consecutive order to get the present reading. If a pointer is between numbers, always write down the smaller of the two. If the pointer seems to be right on the number, look on the dial immediately to the right of it. If that pointer is between 9 and 0, then read the dial in question as though the pointer had not yet reached the number it seems to be pointing at; if the pointer on the dial to the right has passed the 0, then read the number on the dial to the left as the one it is pointing at.

In the example pictured, the first dial is read as 3; the second as 5 (the dial to the right of it has not yet passed zero); the third as 9; and the fourth as 2. The final reading is thus 3592. To tell how much has been consumed since the last reading, subtract the previous reading from this number.

KILOWATT-HOURS

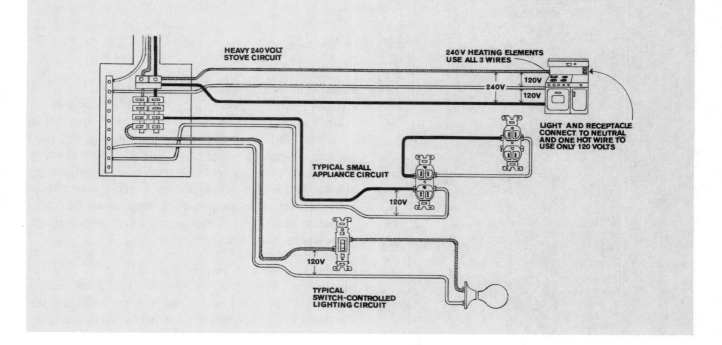

HEAVY 240 VOLT
STOVE CIRCUIT

240 V HEATING ELEMENTS
USE ALL 3 WIRES

120V

240V

120V

LIGHT AND RECEPTACLE
CONNECT TO NEUTRAL
AND ONE HOT WIRE TO
USE ONLY 120 VOLTS

TYPICAL SMALL
APPLIANCE CIRCUIT

120V

120V

TYPICAL
SWITCH-CONTROLLED
LIGHTING CIRCUIT

Some large appliances draw 220 (or 240) volts instead of 110 (or 120)—a stove or electric dryer, for example—so most modern houses have 240-volt wiring coming into the main service entrance. There it is broken up or divided—most circuits get the 120 volts they need, while the large appliances get the full 240 volts.

The way that this current is divided or broken up is fairly simple: The incoming 240 volts comes in on three wires—a common wire (which is colored white) and two "hot" wires that each carry 120 volts (one may be black and the other red, or both may be black). To get the full 240 volts, power is taken from the two "hot" wires, thus giving you 120 volts from each, or a total of 240 volts. For those circuits or appliances that need only 120 volts, power is drawn from only one side (called one phase) of the incoming circuits. In other words, the 120-volt circuit draws power from only one of the "hot" wires (red or black) and the common (white). You can consider the common as the "return," since all circuits must form a full unbroken loop if power is to flow. When this loop is broken—for example, when a fuse blows or a switch is opened (turned to the off position)—then no current flows. Switches and fuses are always located along the "hot" wire (the black or red wire), because breaking the common (white) wire only could still allow current to flow through a ground connection, inasmuch as the white wire is itself "grounded"—that is, connected at the fuse box to a common ground connection (see pages 201–202).

What You Should Know About Fuses and Circuit Breakers

Although fuses and circuit breakers often serve as safety switches that enable you to turn off power to a particular circuit when necessary, they are primarily designed to serve as "safety valves" that protect the wiring against dangerous overloads.

Electrical power enters the house through a large fuse box or circuit-breaker box that is normally referred to as the service entrance. The wires first go through a large set of main fuses or circuit breakers, then the current is broken up or divided into separate circuits—some for lighting, some for major appliances that are on their own circuits, and some for receptacles or outlets throughout the house. Each of these circuits has its own fuse or circuit breaker.

In older houses the main fuse or circuit breaker (called the main disconnect) controls the entire service entrance and may consist of two large cartridge fuses mounted in a removable block or panel that can be pulled out to shut off power. In others there may be a lever-action switch that you pull down to shut off power to the entire house.

In many circuit-breaker installations there will be one large circuit breaker, or a pair of breakers connected together, that controls power to the whole service entrance (and thus to the whole house).

Cartridge fuses that are rated at up to about 60

Typical circuit-breaker panel with main breakers clearly marked

amperes will have capped metal ends, while those larger than 60 amps will have flat-blade or knife-edge contacts as shown in the illustration on page 201. Cartridge fuses do not give any outward indication when they "blow." The only way you can tell is to test the fuse with a continuity tester or, better yet, replace it with a new one to see if this restores power. Needless to say, you should always have spares on hand, ready when an emergency does occur.

The fuses that are used in the lighting and small-appliance circuits throughout the house are normally of the screw-in type that has a transparent window on the top so you can see when they are blown (the window turns black or cloudy). The rating or capacity of the fuse (in amps) is marked on the top and is also stamped into the metal contact on the bottom of the fuse.

Lighting circuits normally have 15-amp fuses. Other circuits, such as those intended for appliances, may have 15- or 20-amp fuses, depending on the gauge of the wiring (the heavier the gauge, the more current the wire can carry). When any of these fuses has to be replaced, make sure you put in one that has the same rating. Putting in a fuse with a larger rating to keep it from blowing (because of an overload) can be downright dangerous, since it will allow wires to overheat and possibly start a fire.

When changing a fuse, make sure you are standing on a dry surface—put boards or a rub-

Main fuse box common in older houses: two cartridge fuses mounted in a removable block

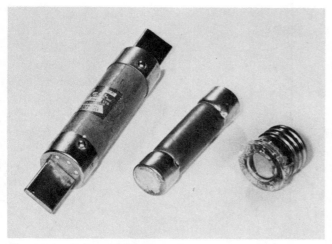

Common types of fuses

ber mat down if the floor is damp—and make sure your hands are dry. Plug fuses are easy to unscrew, but cartridge fuses have to be pulled out with a tug, so wear gloves and use a pair of pliers to grab the cartridge in the center. The large main fuses, mounted on a block as explained previously, can be removed by pulling on the handle of the block; the whole block, all the fuses mounted on the back, comes out to shut off all the power to that fuse box.

Circuit breakers perform the same function as fuses, but they do not have to be replaced when they "blow." They are like switches that flip to the off position when overloaded. They can be readily reset by simply pushing the toggle switch back to the on position after the overload is corrected (on some brands the toggle takes a middle position when the breaker opens; these have to be flicked to the off position before they can then be flipped back to the on position).

When a fuse or circuit breaker blows, simply replacing the fuse or flicking the circuit breaker back on is not the way to solve the problem. The overload that caused the fuse or breaker to blow must be corrected first; otherwise the same thing will immediately happen again.

How do you know what caused the problem? If the fuse blew just after you plugged in an appliance or power tool, chances are that the trouble is a short or other defect in that appliance. If it did not occur immediately, however, then the likelihood is that the circuit was overloaded by your plugging in that particular appliance in addition to all the other appliances or lights on that circuit.

If the fuse blows without any new load having

been added, then it could be an overload caused by something that kicked on automatically (a refrigerator, for example), or it could be a defect that has developed in the wiring, or in one of the appliances plugged into that circuit.

To try to locate the source of the trouble before turning the power back on, start by unplugging all of the lamps and other appliances on that circuit. Then turn the power back on. If the fuse or circuit breaker blows with nothing plugged in, then the trouble is in the wiring, or in one of the receptacles or permanently connected lighting fixtures. Unless you are pretty familiar with electrical wiring, you will probably have to call in an electrician at this point to track down the problem.

Assuming the fuse (or circuit breaker) does not blow with everything unplugged, you then start plugging lamps and appliances back in one at a time to see which one caused the problem. If there is a short or similar defect in one of the appliances, the fuse or breaker will pop immediately after the device is plugged in. If the fuse doesn't blow until a few seconds later, then the addition of that appliance has probably overloaded that circuit and you will have to move one or more appliances or lamps to a different circuit. You can, of course, check for this simply by plugging the suspect appliance into a different circuit (one that has very little or nothing else plugged in) to see if it works okay.

The Third Wire or "Ground"

All houses these days are supposed to be wired so that in addition to the black wire (the "hot" wire) and the white wire (the "common") in each circuit, there is a third wire called the ground. The purpose of this third wire is to do just what its name says: ground the metal housings of appliances, switch boxes, cover plates, and the like so that if a short develops along a current-carrying wire (the hot wire or the common) in contact with the housing, the current will be carried away by the ground wire (to the ground outside, by means of water pipes or a separate grounding connection that is part of the electrical supply system).

Without this ground wire the housing would be "hot" when an internal short developed and a

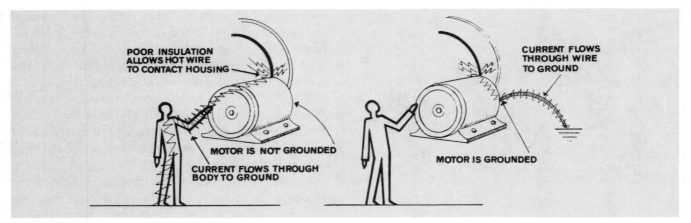

person touching it would get a dangerous shock—the current would, in effect, be grounding through his body. But the grounding system prevents this by causing the fuse to blow beforehand, thus protecting circuits and equipment against overheating, while also protecting users against shock.

In homes wired since 1962 this protection is accomplished by a separate ground wire (usually colored green) or a bare wire inside the cable that connects all switches, receptacles, and boxes in a continuous loop with the main ground in the fuse box. This is the same wire that is connected to the third hole in three-prong outlets, and to the third prong on three-prong plugs.

In houses that have BX cable, the metal housing of the cable may serve as the third or ground wire, while in older houses that have nonmetallic cable there should be a bare wire inside the cable that is connected to all metal outlet boxes and switch boxes.

If the house was wired in the days before three-prong receptacles were required, there will be a problem when you try to plug in motor-driven tools or appliances that come with three-prong plugs. This is usually solved by using an adapter between plug and receptacle; the adapter has a separate pigtail wire that you connect to the screw in the center of the receptacle plate to continue the ground connection. All too often people do not do this—or they don't first scrape paint off it to ensure a good connection. Even then, there is no guarantee that the screw holding the plate on is itself grounded properly—in a nonmetallic cable system a careless electrician may never have attached the separate ground wire to the metal box.

To make sure the screw in the center of the cover plate will work as a ground, use a small voltmeter or test light as shown in the drawing on page 203 top left. Push one prong of the test lamp into one of the slotted openings in the receptacle (if the test prod on the trouble light won't fit into the narrow slot, use heavy gloves to insert a paper clip or short piece of stiff wire into the outlet, then touch the test prod to this piece of metal; do not touch any of the bare metal with your bare fingers!). Hold the other prod of the test light against the screw as shown, pressing or rubbing slightly to ensure good contact. If the test light glows, the screw will make a good ground; if it doesn't, the screw is not properly grounded.

It is because of all these uncertainties that many communities now have codes that no longer allow the use of adapters. Old-style two-prong receptacles can be replaced by approved

Three-prong adapter with pigtail ground wire connected to screw

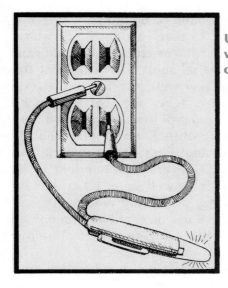

Using a test light to verify that ground is connected

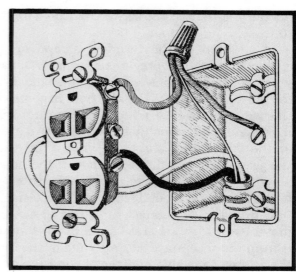

Proper wiring inside an outlet receptacle box

three-prong receptacles that have the third hole connected to a proper ground (the metal housing of the cable, or the third wire inside the box). It is a job best done by a licensed electrician or some-one who is qualified to do work of this kind, though you can do it yourself if you are reason-ably careful about following directions, and if there are no local regulations against doing your own wiring (check this with your local building department).

Start by first shutting off all power to that cir-cuit, then remove the cover plate and take out the two screws that hold the receptacle in place against the front of the box (see drawing above). Now pull the receptacle out of the box and dis-connect the two wires connected to it—one white and one black. If there is more than one white and one black connected to it, disconnect all of them, but make a note of where each wire was connected. If there are other wires inside the box, connected together, leave them alone.

Now connect the new three-prong receptacle to the same wires, making certain that all the same color wires go to the same connections on the receptacle. This means that all white wires go to the silver or lighter-colored screw on one side, and all the black (or red) wires go to the darker, brass-colored screws on the other side. It is essential not to mix this up. *Never* allow a white and a black (or red) wire to be connected together, or to be connected to the same terminal strip or screw.

When attaching the wires to the terminal

screws, always twist the strands tightly together, then wrap the wire around the screw in a clock-wise direction—in other words, in the same di-rection as the screw will be turned when you tighten it. As you tighten the screw head down on the wire, it will then tend to wrap the wire even more tightly around the terminal. If you wrap the wire in the opposite direction you will

Attaching wires. Twist strands, then wrap wire clockwise with no overlap.

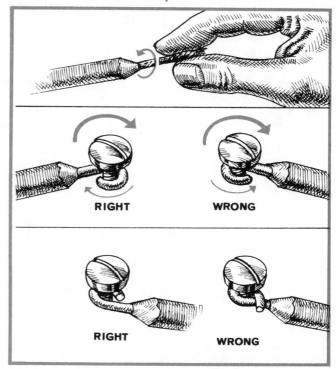

RIGHT   WRONG

RIGHT   WRONG

find as you tighten the screw that the wire tends to loosen, rather than tighten.

In addition to the terminal screws on each side, the new receptacle also has a separate green-colored terminal screw at one end. This is for the ground wire inside the box. In some cases this wire will itself be green, but in most it will be bare metal and probably be connected to a screw on the side of the metal box. Connect this wire to the green screw on the receptacle. If the house is wired with BX metal-sheathed cable, there may be no separate ground wire evident inside the box. In that case connect the green screw to the metal box with a separate piece of wire, running it from the receptacle screw to one of the screws that clamp the cable in place at the back or side of the box.

Once all wires have been connected, you push the receptacle back into the box and fold the wires neatly out of the way so none get crimped or pinched against the sides. Then tighten the screws that hold the receptacle against the front of the box and mount the cover plate on front to complete the job.

Ground Fault Circuit Interrupters

Even if all circuits and receptacles in your house are properly grounded, it is still possible for you to get a serious, even lethal, shock if you are standing on wet ground or holding a metal pipe while you happen to touch an appliance whose metal housing is "hot" or charged with current because of an internal short. It is true that the fuse or circuit breaker will blow, but in the fraction of a second it takes for this to happen enough current could flow through your body (on its way to the ground) to give you a fatal shock.

That is why ground fault circuit interrupters (usually called GFCIs) are now required in all outdoor receptacles, as well as for all outlets located in bathrooms, swimming pool areas, and other places where a person could be standing on a damp surface when using an electrical tool or appliance.

GFCIs are a special type of breaker that continuously monitor the amount of current flowing in each conducting wire (both black and white). Normally it should be exactly the same, and the GFCI does nothing. If, however, the slightest amount of current leaks out to ground—through the ground wire, or through contact with a person—there will be more current flowing in one wire than the other. When the GFCI senses this, even if the difference is only a few thousandths of an ampere, it immediately shuts off all current flow. It does this in a tiny fraction of a second—much faster than would a fuse or circuit breaker, and long before enough current can flow to ground to cause any bodily harm.

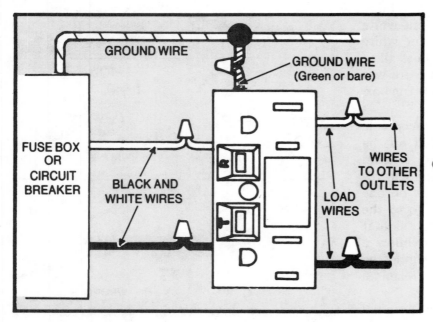

GROUND WIRE

GROUND WIRE
(Green or bare)

FUSE BOX
OR
CIRCUIT
BREAKER

BLACK AND
WHITE WIRES

LOAD
WIRES

WIRES
TO OTHER
OUTLETS

Circuit with ground fault interrupter

Problems with Aluminum Wiring

Many homes built during the late 1960s and early 1970s have wiring made of aluminum rather than copper, and in many of these houses problems have developed over the years because connections work loose on terminal screws of wall switches and receptacles. The condition is often first evidenced by such simple malfunctions as flickering lights or power interruptions to appliances, but it can result in overheating of wires, even the possibility of fire.

Aluminum wire is not in itself inherently dangerous, as long as the right size wire is used (it has to be one size larger than copper wire to carry the same load); its terminal connections are the problem. Aluminum expands and contracts more than copper; it also heats up more quickly when a heavy current is flowing through it. As a result, the wire that is wrapped around a terminal screw tends to work loose in time—especially if a careless workman crimped the wire severely or did not wrap the wire tight enough in the first place.

This problem can be prevented by using special switches and receptacles that are listed by Underwriters Laboratories as suitable for use with aluminum wire. They are marked with a stamp that says CO/ALR, indicating that they can be used with copper as well as aluminum wiring, and their terminal screws have oversize heads that will grip the wire more firmly when properly tightened.

If your house has aluminum wiring, but the switches and receptacles are still the original ones that do not bear this CO/ALR marking, it would be a good idea to have them replaced with the new ones as soon as practical. Another method that many experts favor for preventing trouble with aluminum wiring, and the one required by some codes that do not accept the use of CO/ALR fixtures, is to use special "pigtail" connectors. These are small solderless connectors or "wire nuts" that serve to connect a small length of copper wire to the end of each piece of aluminum wire with a special crimping tool. The piece of copper wire then makes the actual connection with the terminal screw on the switch or outlet.

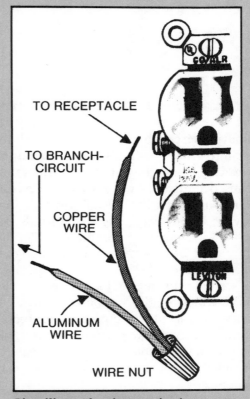

Pigtailing. Aluminum wire is connected to switches and receptacles through a short length of copper wire.

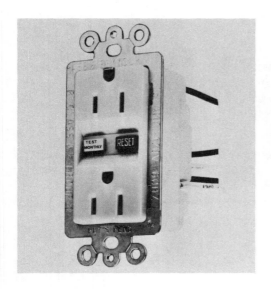

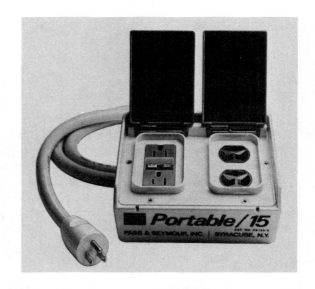

Left, a GFCI receptacle; right, a portable GFCI that plugs into a three-prong outlet

There are actually three different types of ground fault circuit interrupters. The first is a combination circuit breaker and GFCI that is installed in the fuse box in place of a regular circuit breaker. It protects the entire circuit, a safeguard that can be a nuisance when this type is installed in older houses. It will shut off power to that circuit even when very slight internal leakage occurs—as is "normal" for many older houses that have not been rewired—even though there is no real hazard.

The second type of GFCI is the receptacle type that is installed in the wall box in place of the conventional receptacle outlet. It protects anything plugged into that particular outlet, as well as all other outlets that are "downstream" from it, but not those outlets that are between it and the fuse box.

The third kind of GFCI is the portable type that merely plugs into an existing three-prong outlet and converts that receptacle to a ground-fault-protected outlet. Some models also come with extension cords for use around the outside, or in damp locations.

REPLACING A WALL SWITCH

Whether you have to replace an old switch because it is no longer working properly, or because you just want to update the system with an energy-saving dimmer switch that will permit you to lower the amount of wattage consumed when full brightness is not required, changing a wall switch is a fairly simple electrical repair that normally takes only a few minutes and requires no special tools or skills.

As with most jobs that involve the house wiring, the first step is to shut off the power by pulling the fuse or throwing the appropriate breaker. Next, remove the screw in the center of the cover plate and take the plate off. The switch has two screws to hold it in place against the front of the metal box, one at the top and one at the bottom, so loosen these screws until they come out of the threaded holes in the metal box. Now pull the whole switch straight out of its box so the terminal screws on each side are exposed.

Loosen these screws and disconnect the wires at each one. In many cases both wires will be black, because switches are always installed in the "hot" line, never in the white or "common" line. However, if the switch is at the end of the circuit and controls a light or outlet without

Wall switch has wire connected to each side.

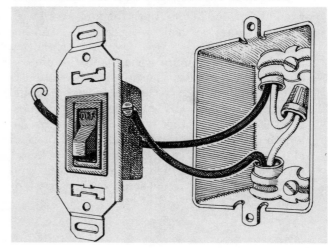

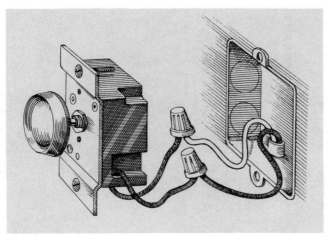

A dimmer switch installed at end of a circuit with only two wires coming into box

power going on from there to other parts of the circuit (as evidenced by the fact that only one two-wire conductor or cable will be coming into that box), there may be one white wire and one black wire connected to it. The reason for this exception is that electricians have no choice: There are no household two-conductor cables with both wires black. An electrician who installs a switch in this manner is supposed to paint the end of the white wire black, to show that it is actually serving as a black wire, but unfortunately this is not always done. So if you find both a black and a white wire going to the old switch, it probably makes no difference, though play it safe and hook them up on the new switch the same way they were on the old one.

If there are other wires inside the box joined together with solderless connectors or wire nuts, leave them alone. Push the switch back in place against the front of the box, then start tightening the screws at the top and bottom to hold it in place. Be careful to avoid crimping any of the wires as you fold them back out of the way, and do not allow any of them to become pinched or caught between the side of the switch body and the metal box.

If you are replacing a regular switch with one of the new dimmer types, a word of special caution. If the principal function of that switch is to control permanent overhead or wall-mounted lighting fixtures, fine, but if the switch you are replacing controls a number of wall outlets, you will have to be careful. For outlets that are also used for vacuum cleaners, fans, and other appliances, you will have to remember that the dimmer switch must be all the way on when these appliances are plugged in—otherwise you could damage them. Another thing to keep in mind when replacing a conventional switch with a dimmer type is to make sure the dimmer is rated to handle the total wattage that switch will have to control. Many have a maximum rating of only 300 watts.

If you are replacing a three-way switch—one that enables you to turn lights on and off from more than one location—make sure the new one is also three-way, and be very careful about tagging or labeling all the wires before you disconnect them from the old switch. You want to be certain that you are connecting them to the proper terminals on the new switch.

For some installations there is also another type of wall switch you might want to install—one that has a built-in timing device that turns the switch off automatically after a preset length of time (usually up to 60 minutes). This can be useful for controlling exhaust fans or built-in heat lamps in a bathroom, for controlling attic fans, or for similar uses where you want the power to go off automatically after a predetermined length of time. Like dimmer switches, timer switches are available to fit into standard wall outlet boxes, and they usually come with their own cover plates marked with numbers to indicate time spans. You turn a knob to set the length of "on" time, then a clock mechanism turns it slowly to off.

Solderless connector fits over and joins twisted wires.

REPLACING A RECEPTACLE

Although it doesn't happen often, there are times when a receptacle will go bad—either the fuse blows every time that receptacle is used, or the outlet remains dead even if the wiring to all other outlets on that circuit is okay. Another sign that you may need a new receptacle is finding that a light or appliance flickers or runs intermittently every time you plug something into its outlet (this could also be the fault of the plug or the cord on the appliance, so test with more than one plug and cord before deciding that the outlet is faulty).

Changing a receptacle or outlet is similar to changing a switch. You start by shutting off the power, then removing the cover plate and loosening the screws that hold the receptacle in place so you can pull it out to expose the terminal screws on each side (or on the back of some models). However, you have to be more careful about seeing how the old wires are connected before you disconnect them. With a receptacle it *does* make a big difference where the white and the black wires are connected.

To avoid mistakes, it can help to make a sketch to show where each white and black wire goes before you disconnect it, or to label each wire with a piece of marked masking tape before you disconnect it. You will notice that all the

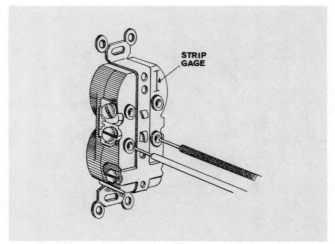

A back-wired receptacle with push-in connectors

white wires go to one side, and all black wires to the other side. Also, the screws to which the white wires connect will be lighter in color, while the black wire terminals will have darker-colored screws. Be sure you hook the new receptacle up in the same way. Some of the new receptacles are back-wired—that is, they do not have screw terminals; instead, they have holes in the back and you simply push the bared wire ends into these to make the connection without using the screw terminals.

All receptacles now have three-prong outlets with a green grounding screw on one side. If your old outlet does not have this there will be an extra wire that will have to be connected—a ground wire running to a screw inside the box (see page 209).

Adding an Extra Outlet

Adding an additional outlet to an existing circuit does not increase the total capacity of that circuit—it merely serves to locate outlets more conveniently, or it permits plugging in more lights or appliances at one time (so you won't, for example, have to pull the lamp plug every time the vacuum cleaner is to be used). Just remember that a typical lighting circuit fused at 15 amps can only carry a total load of 15 amps (about 1,650 to 1,750 watts), no matter how many outlets it has.

New outlets are added by tapping into, or connecting into, an existing outlet. In other words,

How black, white, and green wires are connected inside a receptacle

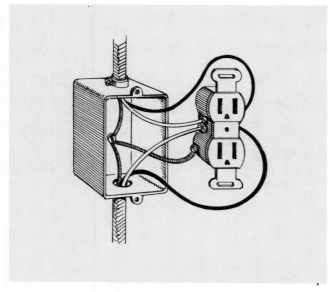

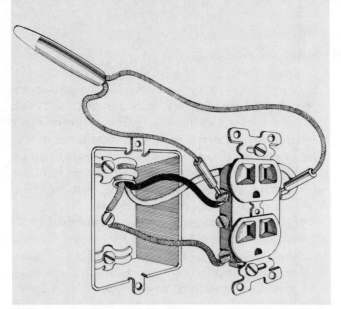

Using a test lamp to check for current in an outlet

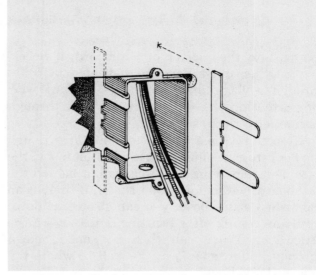

Metal "ears" for fastening a junction box to wall panels or plaster

you connect new wires to the switch box or lighting-fixture box. Of course, this means there must be current-carrying wires in the box you are tapping into ("hot" wires) that are not controlled by a switch (unless you don't mind the new outlet also being controlled by the same switch).

The easiest way to check the wires inside the existing box or receptacle (to see if they are "hot") is to use a small voltmeter, or a test lamp as shown in the illustration above. Touching the leads from the test lamp to the terminal screws on the existing outlet, or to the bared wires inside the box after you remove the wire nuts to expose them, will tell you whether they are "hot"—the lamp will glow if they are. Try this with the switch on and then with it off—if there is a switch in that circuit. The idea is to find a pair of wires—one white and one black—that remain "hot" even when the switch is off.

After you have located the wires or terminals (assuming you are attaching to the screws on an existing outlet or switch), hooking up the new outlet is simple: You connect the new length of

cable so that its white wire connects to the white wires in the old box, or to the same terminal screws as the existing white wire, then connect the black wires together in the same way. Remember the rule: *Always* connect white to white and black to black (or red). *Never* connect opposite colors.

Before cutting the hole in the wall for your new outlet, drill some small test holes to see where the studs are located. If possible you want to mount the outlet box next to a stud so that you will have something solid against which to fasten the box. Boxes also come with special "ears" for fastening to wall panels or plaster—electrical supply houses stock them in all types of configurations for every type of mounting situation, whether the box is to be secured at the side, back, top, or bottom.

The hardest part is often snaking the cables or wires from the source of power to the new location. Sometimes you can do this by ripping off a length of baseboard and running the cable in the space behind before you replace it (digging a

How extra outlet can be added by burying cable behind baseboard

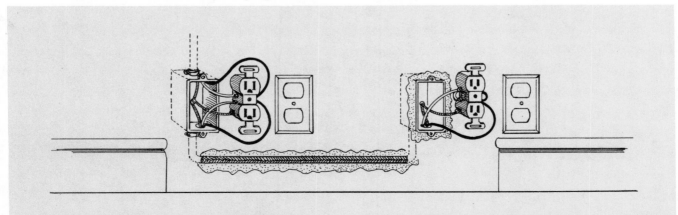

groove into the plaster or wallboard, if necessary). Other times you will have to cut holes through walls, ceilings, or floors, drilling with long extension bits and fishing the wires through with an electrician's "snake."

Often the easiest way is to come up through the floor from a ceiling fixture or outlet box in the basement (emerging next to a wall or behind the baseboard, so the hole won't show). If there is an unfinished attic above, you can also come down from the ceiling after bringing wires across the attic floor. Wires can then be snaked down through hollow spaces in the wall to where the new outlet will go.

Using Surface Wiring

To eliminate the need for all this drilling of holes and snaking of wires, there is another much easier method: You can add extra outlets by installing a system of surface wiring in which wires run inside metal or plastic raceways mounted on the surface of the wall or on top of the baseboard (some of these raceways serve to replace the baseboard entirely with a wide, hollow channel that carries the wires on the inside). These raceways or channels have recessed outlets mounted on their face and, being approved by most local electrical codes, can be used for permanent installations.

Some raceways are one-piece hollow channels (something like a flat conduit); you fasten them in place, then snake or pull the wires through.

The most popular types come in two parts—an open channel (back) that is fastened to the wall first, and a long, boxlike cover that snaps on after all wires have been run and connections made. The beauty of this setup is that the cover can be snapped off anytime to work on or add to the wiring, and there is no problem with snaking wires through a long enclosed space.

Most of these raceways come prefinished in an off-white or beige color, but they can be painted to match woodwork. They are ideal for kitchens, workshops, family rooms, and similar locations where surface conduits would not be objectionable, or where many outlets are desirable at different locations because of the many small appliances used in that room.

REPLACING A CEILING FIXTURE

Removing a ceiling fixture and replacing it with a new one is basically similar to changing a receptacle or light switch—you disconnect the wires from the old fixture, then reconnect them to the new fixture, with the wires going to the same corresponding terminal screws. Unlike the case with wall outlets and switches, however, the method used to mount ceiling fixtures can vary. All are hung from a recessed metal outlet box in the ceiling, which is nailed against the side of an overhead beam or bolted to a metal brace traversing two of the beams—but then the mounting methods differ. The drawings on page 211

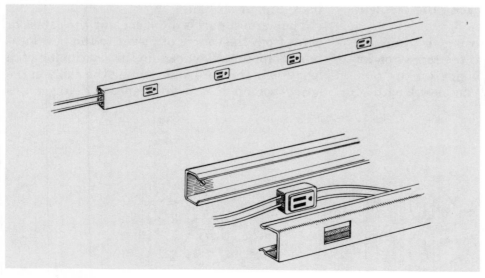

Hollow-channel raceways carry surface-mounted wiring.

the bottom of a threaded stud inside the box with the top of a threaded nipple that sticks up from the top of the fixture.

Chandeliers that hang from a chain are often suspended from a threaded stud at the top of the chain. This stud fits through a hole in the center of the fixture's ceiling canopy, then goes up through another hole in the center of the metal mounting strap, to be secured by a nut on top of the strap. In many cases there will be another nut under the canopy to hold it in place against the ceiling.

Most chandeliers and other ceiling fixtures are designed so that either the heads of the bolts that hold them in place are covered up by the canopy or globe that fits over the bulbs, or the canopy is held in place by a decorative escutcheon plate or collar that screws on over the bottom end of the threaded stud or pipe. When the fixture is the type that hangs from a chain, this decorative nut will often serve also as the securing point for the chain from which the fixture is suspended.

Whatever the type of fixture, the first step is to shut off the power, then remove the decorative globe or canopy. Glass globes are usually held in place by screws around the perimeter. After the globe is off, the canopy and the socket can be dropped by removing the two screws that go up into the metal supporting strap, or into the metal box itself. Taking these out will enable you to lower the canopy and expose the wiring. Remove the wire nuts or solderless connectors that join the incoming wires to the fixture, making sure you support its weight with one hand—or have a helper hold the fixture for you if it is an especially heavy one—then finish removing any bolts, nuts, or other hardware holding it in place.

During all this, note carefully how the parts go together so you will have no trouble mounting the new one. It's possible that the new one will mount differently, but if you note how the old one was hung you will know what adapters or other fittings will be needed for the new one. Hardware stores and electrical supply houses that sell fixtures have the metal straps, threaded studs, cap nuts, etc. used for hanging ceiling fixtures, so you should have no trouble getting any additional parts you may need if they were not included.

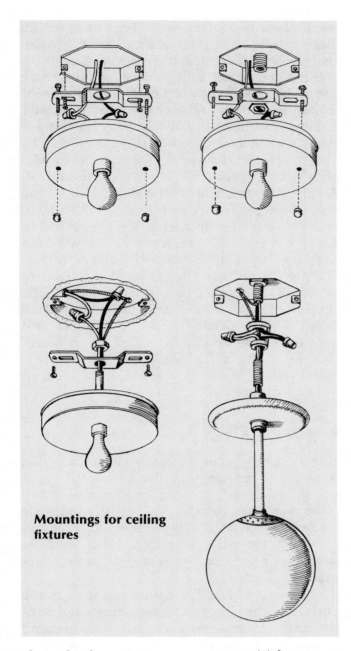

Mountings for ceiling fixtures

show the four most common ones: (1) by means of bolts that go through the canopy after passing through threaded holes at each end of the mounting strap; (2) by means of a large nut that holds the canopy and fixture onto the end of a threaded stud that sticks down from the outlet box and then fits through a hole in the center of the mounting strap; (3) by means of a threaded nipple at the top of the fixture that goes up through a hole in the center of the mounting strap and then is secured by a large nut; and (4) by means of a threaded coupling that connects

To mount the new fixture in place of the old one, simply reverse the steps. If the fixture is very heavy, have someone help you hold it while you insert the bolts through the canopy, or thread it onto the center stud through which the wires may also go—this all depends on the style and construction of the fixture.

Don't tighten anything yet; just secure the bolts or nuts sufficiently to support the weight of the fixture. Now connect the wires to the new fixture, using the old fixture's plastic twist-on, solderless connectors. If the old ones are cracked, or if you lost them, new ones can be purchased in any hardware store. Twist the bared wire ends together, then push them into the connector and twist firmly until the connector won't turn anymore. If any bare wire shows outside the connector, too much insulation has been stripped off. Take the connector off and cut a little of the bare wire off to shorten it.

After all connections have been made, with no bare wire showing, turn the power on and test. If all seems well, tighten all nuts and bolts, and finish mounting the fixture by installing the decorative globes or canopies that cover the bottom end.

REPAIRING LAMPS AND REPLACING PLUGS

When a lamp starts to flicker, or won't light at all, chances are that the trouble is caused by either a bad socket or a defective plug at the end of the cord—assuming you have checked the bulb by trying it in another lamp that you know works, and assuming there is power in the outlet into which the lamp is plugged (you test this by plugging something else in, something you know works).

Occasionally the problem is merely some dirt or corrosion on the metal at the bottom of the socket preventing good electrical contact with the base of the bulb. To eliminate this possibility, unplug the lamp and remove the bulb from its socket, then use a table knife or similar tool to scrape clean the metal strip at the bottom of the socket. If the strip is not bent upward enough to press against the base of the bulb, then pry it up a little, using the tip of the knife blade or a very small screwdriver. Wipe the base of the bulb clean with a small piece of fine abrasive paper, then replace the bulb and try the lamp again.

If it still does not light, you can be pretty sure the problem is either a bad plug, a bad socket, or a loose connection in one or the other. You can't tell which without actually checking the connections in or replacing each part, but you may be able to pinpoint the source of the trouble by wiggling the wires near the plug to see if this causes the light to flicker or produces sparking at the plug. If you see sparks, pull the plug out immediately. If you notice flickering, the plug is bad or one of the connections is loose, so you will have to take off the plug and possibly replace it.

When you still can't decide which is the source of trouble—the plug or the lamp socket—the simplest thing to do is change one and then the other. Since replacing a plug is cheaper and quicker, you're usually better off starting with this, especially if the plug is an old one that shows signs of cracking or whose prongs are bent or badly oxidized.

Replacing Plugs

Electric plugs come in many different styles, some made for use with flat lamp cords (also called "rip cords" because they consist of two conductors that you can "rip" apart), and some made for heavier-duty use with round cords and heavier-gauge wires (the type often used on power tools and appliances, as well as on many extension cords).

For lamps and similar light loads you can use one of the light-duty, flat plugs that do not have terminal screws—many do not even require stripping the insulation off the ends. As illustrated in the drawings, you simply cut the old plug off, then separate the two halves of the wire for a short distance and push the wire ends into the hole provided at the side of the plug. Pressing down a cam or lever forces metal prongs into each conductor and establishes electrical contact.

Another version of this type of plug that also eliminates the need for stripping allows you to slip the housing off the plug, then slide it back on over the wire. This causes pronged levers to close over the wires and pierce the insulation to make

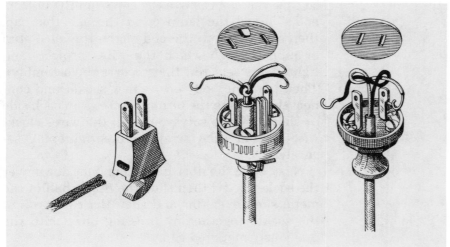

Electric plug on left pierces insulation to make connection. On right, an underwriter's knot is tied in wires before connecting to screw terminals of standard plug.

contact. Sliding the housing back on clamps the whole thing together.

Round plugs designed for use with heavier-duty wires, and flat plugs with terminal screws, do require that the ends of the wire be stripped bare of insulation. Use a knife or stripping tool to shave off about ½ inch of insulation at each end, taking care not to nick the wire.

The bared ends should be just long enough to permit wrapping around the terminal screws next to each prong. It is important that you wrap the wire *clockwise* around each screw so that the wire will tend to tighten as the screw is tightened. In this type of plug the wire comes in through the back, then the two conductors are separated and an underwriter's knot is tied to take strain off the cord before attaching it to the terminal screws. Make certain there are no loose strands protruding from under the screw head, which could cause a serious short.

Replacing the Lamp Socket

Most lamps have sockets with built-in switches, but some have separate switches on the base, so you should always make certain the switch is not the source of the trouble before you go ahead and change the socket. The easiest way to do this is to disconnect the wires leading to the switch, then simply join them together temporarily in order to "jump" or bypass the switch. If the wires happen to be soldered to the switch and you don't want to cut them, leave them connected and just run a short piece of wire from one side of the switch to the other for the test. If the lamp lights with the switch not in the circuit (when the wires are connected directly to each other), then you know the switch is defective and needs to be replaced. Replacement switches are widely available in most hardware and electrical supply stores.

If your lamp has no separate switch (other than the one in the socket), or if shorting out or "jumping" the switch does not solve your problem, replacing the lamp socket is your next step. Not only is this an easy job, it even offers you the chance to upgrade the lamp by replacing its conventional socket with a socket that takes three-way bulbs or, for maximum control of light, a socket with a built-in dimmer with which you can adjust the light from full brightness to all the way off by just turning a built-in rotary switch. These dimmer sockets fit all standard lamp bases and require no rewiring of any kind.

After taking the plug out of the wall, remove the lampshade and the harp that supports it, then take out the bulb. Pull the socket apart by pressing with your thumb just above the cap on the side where the word "Press" is embossed in the metal. Simultaneously, use your other hand to push the top half sideways and upward. The socket will snap apart, enabling you to lift off the top half of the metal shell as shown in the drawing on page 214 bottom left.

Inside the metal shell there is a fiber liner (resembling cardboard) that serves as an insulator. If this does not come off with the metal shell, slide it off separately to expose the terminal

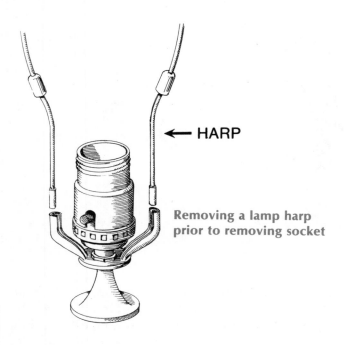

← HARP

Removing a lamp harp prior to removing socket

so that you can remove the cap from the bottom end. Thread the lamp wires through this cap, then screw it onto the end of the threaded stud or pipe through which the wires project (and tighten any setscrew that secures the assembly). Then take the body of the new socket and connect the wires to the terminal screws on each side as shown. Make sure you wrap the wires clockwise around each screw before tightening securely.

Next, slide the fiber insulating liner down over the socket body, then slide the upper half of the metal shell over this and snap the two parts of the socket together by pressing down into the previously mounted cap.

Rewiring the Lamp with New Cord

While replacing the lamp's socket, it is also a good idea to check the lamp cord itself to see if it is cracked or dried out, or if the insulation has been damaged or cut in any way. If any such conditions exist, this is a good time—while you have the lamp apart for replacing its socket—to replace the whole cord.

The lamp cord should run in one continuous length from socket to wall plug, so rather than trying to splice in a short section you should play it safe and replace the whole length of wire— even if only one section looks worn. You start by removing the lamp socket as just described. Then remove the felt or other material covering the base so that you can see up inside the lamp base. Very often there will be a knot tied in the

screws. Loosen each screw and pull the wires off, then remove the rest of the socket body.

The bottom half of the socket, called the cap, is threaded onto the top of the small metal pipe or hollow stud that comes up through the base of the lamp and contains the wires. To remove the cap, you simply unscrew it by turning counterclockwise while holding the lamp base firmly. (In most cases there will be a small setscrew that locks this cap onto the threaded stud to keep it from turning, so make sure you loosen this before you start unscrewing the cap.)

To install the new socket you first take it apart

Components of a typical lamp socket

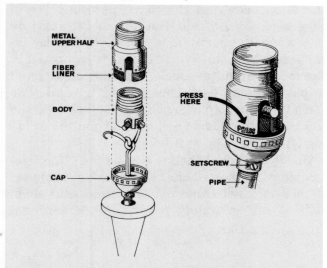

METAL UPPER HALF

FIBER LINER

BODY

PRESS HERE

PRESS

CAP

SETSCREW

PIPE

Knot in cord inside lamp base keeps it from being pulled out.

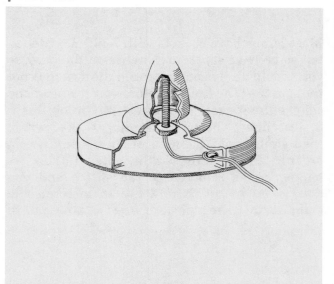

cord inside the base, and this will have to be untied before you can pull the cord out.

After disconnecting the wires from the lamp socket, tie a length of strong string to the upper end of the lamp cord, then pull the lamp cord out from the bottom (through the base). The string will be pulled along with it. As soon as the end of the wire emerges, untie it from the string, but leave the string in place inside the lamp. Now you can tie the new lamp cord to the bottom end of the string so that by pulling the string back up you will draw the new cord up through the lamp and socket cap. You finish the job by adding a new wall plug to the other end of the new wire.

TROUBLE-SHOOTING FLUORESCENT LIGHTS

Because most fluorescent lights give a "colder" or bluer light, they have never been very popular for home use except in kitchens, workshops, and similar utility areas. But they consume much less electricity than incandescent lamps of equivalent candlepower, and with the introduction of newer "warm" or "daylight" types, fluorescents have become increasingly popular for home use in recent years. The tubes or bulbs cost considerably

more than incandescent bulbs, but they last much longer, so that in the long run fluorescents tend to save money both ways—in the amount of power consumed, and in the cost of replacement bulbs.

There are two types of fluorescent lighting fixtures that are widely used in the home: those that have a separate starter, and those that don't but are known as rapid-start because they light almost instantly when the switch is turned on. Both types are relatively trouble-free, and when they do break down repairs are generally not difficult to make.

The drawings below and on page 216 show how fluorescents are wired, and how a typical fixture is assembled. Generally, the first thing you should suspect when trouble does develop is the tube. In home fixtures these are all of the two-pin type—that is, there are two pins at each end that go inside a socket at each end of the fixture. Fluorescent tubes use the greatest amount of current during the starting phase; once they are fully lit, current consumption drops off dramatically. That is why it is best to leave them on when vacating the room for only a short while (up to about an hour). Frequent turning on and off also shortens the life of the tube.

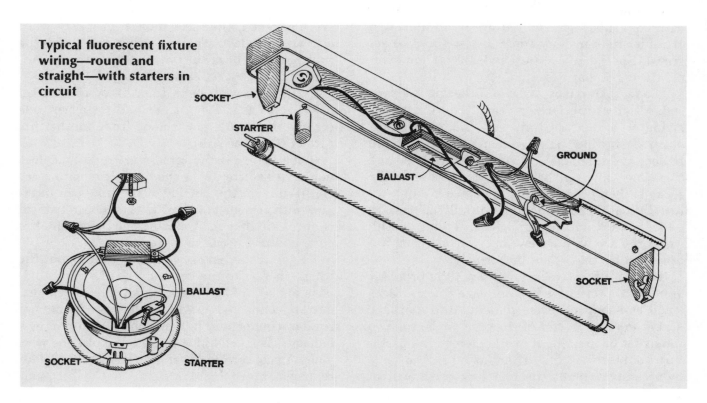

Typical fluorescent fixture wiring—round and straight—with starters in circuit

SOCKET STARTER BALLAST GROUND SOCKET

BALLAST SOCKET STARTER

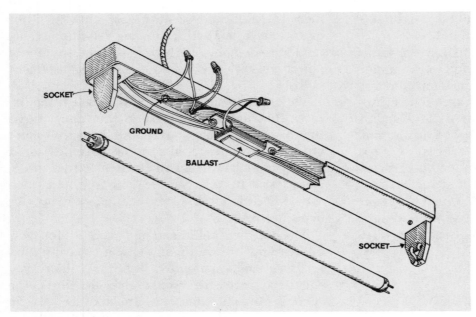

Wiring of typical "instant-start" fluorescent fixture

Here are the most common problems liable to crop up with fluorescent lighting fixtures in the home, along with the steps you can take to correct them:

Light flickers and blinks continuously. This is fairly common with brand-new tubes, but it should not occur after the tube has been on for an hour or two. It can also be a frequent problem with cold tubes—tubes that are in an unheated or colder-than-average room (below about 50 degrees). Special tubes are available for low-temperature installations.

The most frequent cause of flickering is a poor connection at the sockets. Take the tube out by giving it a quarter turn and pulling straight down, then wipe the pins clean at each end and replace the tube, making sure it is firmly seated this time—line up the pins with the slot in the sockets, then push in firmly and give it a quarter turn to seat it solidly. If the tube still flickers, try twisting back and forth slightly. If that doesn't work, replace with a new tube (or one from another fixture that is not flickering).

If none of these measures solves the problem, your next alternative is to replace the starter, a small can-shaped device that fits into a special socket under one end of the tube or lamp. You remove it by pressing it in and giving it a quarter turn counterclockwise. Then install the new one by pressing it in and turning clockwise a quarter turn. Starters come in sizes to match the tubes used, so make sure your replacement is of matching size (a 40-watt starter for a 40-watt tube, etc.).

Tube won't light at all. Check the obvious things that might affect power to the fixture— the fuse on that circuit and the switch that controls the fixture or circuit. If the ends of the tube are blackened, then the tube is probably worn out and needs replacing. Otherwise, take the tube out and check the pins to see if any are broken, or if the socket seems damaged.

If all seems well here, then likely the starter needs replacing. Take it out and try a new one (or one that you know is good from another fixture of the same size).

If the fixture is the rapid-start type that does not have a starter, wipe the tube clean with a dry cloth—dirt on the outside of the tube can interfere with proper starting. If that doesn't do it, chances are that the ballast inside the fixture has gone bad and needs to be replaced.

To get at the ballast you have to take out the tubes, then take the cover off the housing. Ballasts are secured with two small screws or bolts, and are connected up with solderless wire nuts or similar connectors. When shopping for a new ballast it is a good idea to take the old one with you to make certain of getting the right model for replacement.

Ends of tubes are discolored. A brown discoloration is fairly normal as the tube ages, but if it starts to turn very dark or black you will know that the tube is nearing the end of its life and is no longer working efficiently. If only one end of the tube turns black, take it out and turn it over (reverse its ends) before replacing it. If the darkening develops while the tube is still relatively new, then the starter is defective and should be replaced.

Fixture hums. This is almost always a problem with the ballast. Either it is the wrong type, or it is not properly secured and tends to vibrate slightly when current flows through it. In some cases the hum may be due to a defective ballast that is starting to go. First try tightening the mounting screws and checking all electrical connections to make sure they are tight, and if this doesn't help you will have to replace the ballast. Be sure to ask for one of the special low-noise types.

Tube glows at the ends only. First, try a new tube. If this doesn't work, the trouble is probably your starter. If the fixture is the rapid-start type, then it could be the ballast.

All of the above problems apply equally to circular fluorescents and those with straight tubes. Like the straight-line fixtures, circular fluorescents are available in both rapid-start (no separate starter) and regular types (with replaceable starter). Servicing them is exactly the same as servicing a straight fixture, the only difference being that circular fixtures have a single socket with a four-prong plug on the tube, instead of two sockets with two pins at each end.

FIXING DOORBELLS AND CHIMES

Because doorbells and chimes operate on low voltage—anywhere from 10 to 24 volts in most cases—this is one type of electrical repair that any do-it-yourselfer can safely tackle without fear of getting a shock.

The low voltage used to operate these signaling devices comes from a transformer connected to the house current, a device that reduces or "steps down" the voltage to the lower amounts required. This transformer is usually mounted on one of the electrical outlet boxes in the basement or utility room, or it may be on the outside of the fuse box in the basement. It has two wires that are connected to the 110-volt house current in-

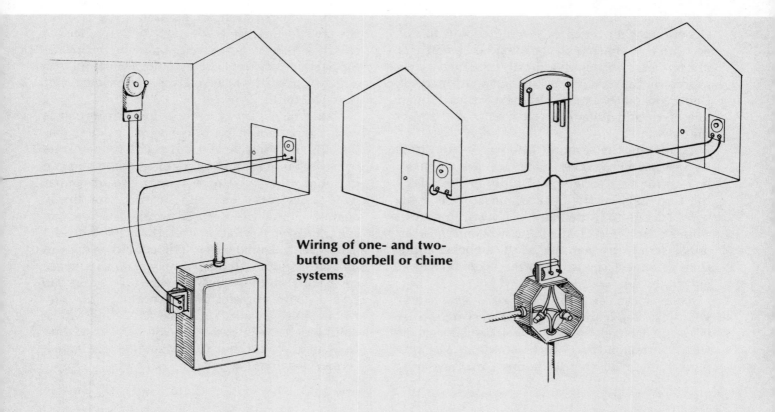

Wiring of one- and two-button doorbell or chime systems

side the metal junction box on which it is mounted, so you really can't get at them without opening that box.

The other exposed side of the transformer has two terminals that deliver the lower voltage needed to operate the bell or chime. You can easily connect wires to these more accessible terminals—the light-gauge wires that are normally used in circuits of this kind. Some transformers are made with multiple taps to take off different voltages—for example, 10 volts if that is all your bell requires, or 20 volts if you have a chime that needs greater power.

To intelligently troubleshoot a doorbell or chime that does not ring, it helps if you know something about how the system is wired. The drawings on page 217 show the most common installations, from a simple one-button system such as would be typical of an apartment, to the more common two-door installations with a second button at the back or side door. Two buttons usually means that the chime gives a different signal for the back door than for the front door, or indicates a bell-buzzer combination that sounds a bell for the front door and a buzzer for the back or side door.

Test the Button First

Generally, when a doorbell or chime fails to ring each time the button on the outside is pushed, or if it operates only spasmodically, the most likely source of the trouble is the pushbutton itself. Being constantly exposed to the weather, it tends to corrode and fail quicker than any other part of the system.

To test for this, unscrew the pushbutton from its position on the door frame or, if it is set into a hole in the frame, pry it out of its recess. Check the terminals on the back or side to see if the wires leading to it are loose or broken. If so, disconnect the wires, clean off the wire ends and terminal screws by scraping with a pocket knife, then reconnect the wires to the terminal screws and try again.

If this doesn't help, or if the wires seem sound, your next step is to "short out" the switch to see if the bell rings—in other words, connect the wires as though there were no switch. The simplest way to do this is to press a screwdriver

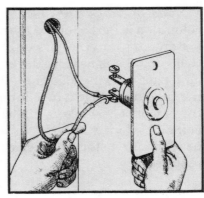

Disconnecting a bell pushbutton and shorting out wires in back will tell if a button is defective.

blade or similar metal object across the two terminals. If this is awkward to manage, just disconnect the two wires and rub them against each other for a moment. This should make the bell or chime ring. If it does, then you know that the pushbutton is defective. Buy a new button and install it in place of the old one.

Check the Power Supply Next

If shorting out the button or touching the wires together doesn't give you a ring (or a chime signal), you know that something else is wrong, most likely the power supply. First check the fuse or circuit breaker controlling the transformer's circuit to see if it has blown.

If it is okay, indicating that power is getting to the transformer, then the next thing to check is whether power is coming *out* of the transformer—in other words, that the transformer is still working (they normally last for years, but they can fail).

The simplest way to check the transformer is with a small voltmeter or continuity tester capable of reading low voltages. If you don't have one of these, there is another simple method you can use. Bare each end of a short piece of copper wire, then press one end of the wire firmly against one of the exposed terminal screws on the transformer while you rub the other bare end across the terminal screw. This should be done in dim light while watching closely. You should see some small sparks where the wire rubs across the screw—if the transformer is working. This may not be quite as sure a method as testing with a voltmeter, or with a small 12-volt test lamp wired to a small socket, but it does show if the transformer is delivering power.

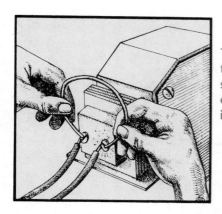

Testing a transformer with a short piece of copper wire to see if sparks are visible

If the transformer is not working, then it will have to be replaced with a new one. To do this, first shut off all power to that circuit, then open the junction box on which the transformer is mounted so that you can reach the wires on the inside. If it is mounted directly onto the fuse box, you will have to remove the front panel on the box—first making sure to shut off all power by pulling the main fuse.

The transformer is normally mounted with two bolts that can be reached from inside the box after the cover has been removed. The black and white wires coming from the transformer will be connected to matching black and white wires by means of solderless connectors or wire nuts. Untwist these and disconnect the transformer, then loosen the screws that hold it in place and remove the unit. Make sure the new one is the proper size for your particular system (some chimes require larger transformers than others, so if in doubt check the label on your unit), mount it in place, and connect up in the same way.

Sometimes It's the Bell or Chime

When the trouble is not the transformer or the pushbutton on the outside, the next thing to check is the actual doorbell or chime. Take off the cover to expose the terminal board or connecting screws and see if all connections are still tight. If so, inspect the exposed mechanism to see if the clapper or any other moving parts are clogged with dust or lint. Use a soft brush to clean them, or blow the dust out. Chimes have small plastic rods that slide up and down (or in and out) to strike the metal bars which make the sound, so check also to see whether these rods

are moving freely. Remove dust and lint with a small brush or by blowing it out, but do not use oil or other lubricant.

If you find nothing wrong here and can't decide whether the trouble is in the bell or chime itself or in part of the wiring that connects it to the transformer or pushbutton, you should test the bell or chime by running a pair of wires directly to it from the transformer terminals. Take the unit off, carry it down to the transformer, and run wires directly between the two, one from a transformer terminal screw to the bell terminal marked "TRANS" or "Transformer," and the other from the other transformer terminal directly to the terminal on the bell (or chime) where one of the pushbutton wires normally goes—marked "Front" or "Rear." This completes the circuit just as though one of the buttons were being pushed. If the bell or chime still fails to ring, and you have already tested the transformer, you know the unit is defective and has to be replaced.

If all these tests indicate that the bell or chime, the transformer, and the pushbutton are all okay, then the problem is obviously in the hidden wiring. Either there is break somewhere, or one of the connections where wires were spliced together has come loose.

Finding this spot may be tricky, even impossible if the wires are mostly buried in walls and floors. Usually it is simpler and quicker to just run all new wiring from the transformer to the chimes, and perhaps also to the pushbuttons. Use the type sold for low-voltage doorbell circuits.

Adding an Extra Bell or Chime

In homes that have a centrally located doorbell or chime it is sometimes difficult to hear this signal from more remote parts of the house such as a garage or basement—particularly if noise-making tools or appliances are in use. Adding an extra bell or chime to the circuit so that it will ring along with the central unit often solves this problem.

This is not an especially difficult wiring job, since you are working with low-voltage wires. Wires can be routed with safety anywhere that is convenient. In many cases you don't even have

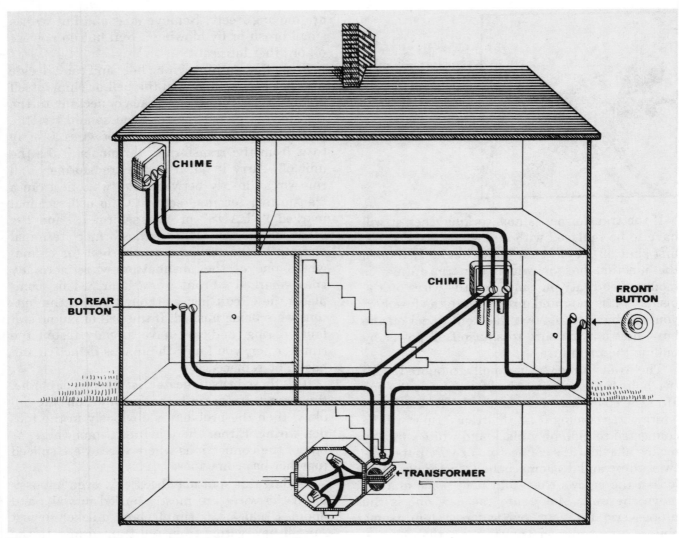

House system with extra chime added on top floor

to snake them through walls or floors—you may be able to go through closets, or even fasten them along the base of the wall.

There is one electrical problem you may encounter, though: The original transformer may not be large enough to carry the additional load of a second bell, buzzer, or chime. If in doubt about this, ask your dealer—tell him the size of the present transformer and the size of the unit it is now operating. He should be able to tell you if the same transformer can carry the additional load. If the transformer is too small, then you will have to change it for a larger one (see page 219 for more on this).

After deciding where the new bell or chime will go, you run wires from that point to the existing

bell or chime unit so that the two bells (or chime and bell) work in parallel. This means that when either of the door buttons is pressed, the new bell or chime will ring along with the old one.

In a typical installation that includes two door buttons (front and back, or front and side) there will be three wires going to your present chime— one from the front button, one from the back door button, and one from the transformer (see drawing above). In that case you will need three wires going from your new unit to the old one (or a single length of three-conductor wire) in order to connect each of the terminals on the old unit to the matching terminals on the new bell or chime. With three-conductor wire or cable, each wire is of a different color, so you cannot mix up the three. If you have to use separate lengths of single-conductor wire, try to get them of different colors.

When the job is done, both bells or chime units should ring at the same time. If they sound weak or barely hum, then the transformer is overloaded and a larger one is needed to supply the additional power for activating both units simultaneously.

OUTDOOR WIRING AND LIGHTING

It is usually best to have at least one separate circuit installed in your home to provide power for your outdoor lights and outdoor receptacles. But if only one or two outlets are needed for occasional operation of a small portable power tool, say a lawn trimmer or hedge clipper, it may be practical simply to wire an outdoor receptacle into an existing indoor circuit that does not have much of a load on it.

The easiest location for an outdoor outlet added in this way is on an outside wall opposite or close to one already fixed on an inside wall. As shown in the drawing below, this enables you to run a short piece of cable from the back of the existing box into the back of the new box after cutting the necessary opening in the exterior siding. The new box can then be installed on the outside—a weatherproof outdoor electrical box that comes equipped with a rubber-gasketed weatherproof hinged cover plate.

In the same way, outdoor lights are easiest to install if you mount them on the house wall—the cable can then be run from an inside power source or nearby junction box, or from a separate circuit set up for outside lighting only. That way none of the wiring will actually be exposed.

When an outdoor light or receptacle is needed at some distance from the house, the wires will probably have to be buried underground, as shown in the drawing. There is a special type of plastic-jacketed electric cable, designated as type UF, which can be buried directly underground. Other types of wire must be run through a metal or plastic conduit (pipe). Some local codes forbid plastic conduit, but where it is permitted plastic is a better choice, since it will never corrode (the same consideration also applies to the direct-burial UF-type cable mentioned above).

Using UF cable is the simplest and least ex-

How to wire an outdoor receptacle and connect it to existing indoor circuit

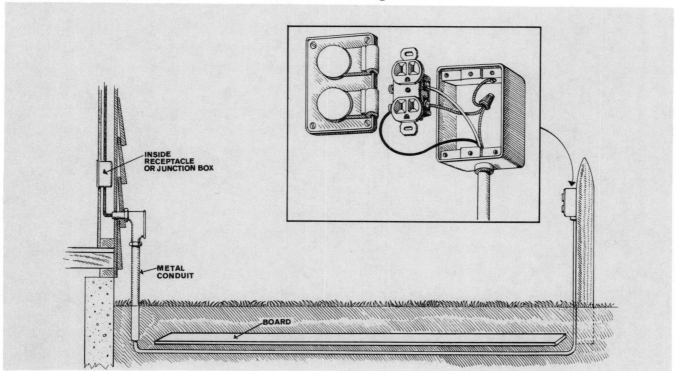

pensive alternative. It must be buried at least 12 inches deep, and should be covered by boards of rot-resistant lumber to protect it against physical damage if someone should start digging in the area. Or you can run the cable through conduit, in which case the conduit has to be buried only 6 inches deep.

Regardless of which material you use, wherever the cable comes up above ground it must be protected by a length of conduit as shown on page 221. Special waterproof connectors are used to connect the conduit to the openings in the outlet box, and plugs must close off any unused openings left in the box. If the outlet box is to be freestanding (not attached to a tree, fence post, or other structure), then the pipe or conduit that supports the box should be anchored solidly in concrete, or be secured by several concrete blocks buried around it. The same holds true for any outside freestanding electrical lamps or post lanterns—their bases should be firmly anchored in masonry.

Chapter **10**

Plumbing Repairs

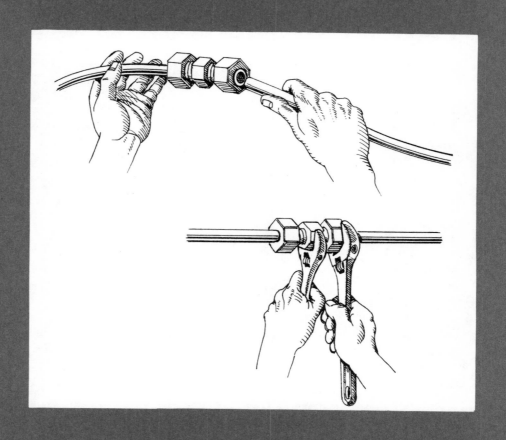

THE PLUMBING in your house (not including any pipes in the heating system) actually consists of two separate, unconnected systems: the *water supply* system, and the *drain-waste-vent* system.

The water supply system delivers cold and domestic hot water to the various sinks, toilets, and other water-using fixtures and appliances of the house. Part of the incoming cold water goes to the hot-water heater, which then supplies heated water to the various fixtures that need it; the rest goes directly to the cold-water faucets.

Because the water supply system is always under pressure (from the municipal supply system, or from your private well, from which water is pumped into a pressure tank), the pipes and fittings will have a much smaller diameter than those of the waste and drain system (which depends on gravity to keep waste water flowing). As a rule, each sink or fixture has its own set of shutoff valves (one for the hot water and one for the cold) located directly under or next to the fixture so that its supply can be shut off in an emergency without affecting the water supply in the rest of the house.

In some cases the shutoff valve will be located in the basement, or in an adjacent closet or utility room. Just make certain you know where all the valves are—including the main shutoff valve for the whole house. (Everyone in the house should know where that is—usually next to the water meter—and everyone should know that you shut it off by turning it clockwise all the way.)

The drain-waste-vent system (often referred to as the DWV system) is designed to carry waste and dirty water out of the house to be safely disposed of via the municipal sewer system or a private disposal system such as a septic tank.

This explains the first two words: "drain" and "waste." The last word, "vent," refers to the fact that the waste pipes also serve as vents that allow trapped sewer gases and noxious odors to escape through vertical pipes extending up through the roof of the house. The vents also prevent air blockages in the waste system that could interfere with rapid drainage.

The pipes in the DWV system are much larger in diameter than those in the water supply system, for two reasons: Some have to carry away solid waste as well as water, and the drainage system, unlike the water supply system, is not pressurized—these pipes only drain by gravity. So the diameter of the pipe must be larger, and these pipes must all slope downward or end in a vertical run that will carry the waste downward into the main waste line.

This type of drainage makes venting very important. If air could not escape easily from the pipes it would cause restriction and subsequent "glugging" sounds, and water might be siphoned out of the various traps located under or near each fixture. This would allow sewer gases to escape into the room through that drain opening.

Traps may be U-shaped or shaped like a P lying on its side—but regardless of shape, all traps work in the same way: The dip formed by the trap retains enough water to form a perpetual water seal which keeps noxious sewer gases from seeping back up through the drain. The water-filled trap also stops vermin and small rodents that might otherwise crawl up through the open drain in some installations. Without proper venting, however, there would be a constant danger that water would be siphoned out of the trap.

The largest waste pipes are the ones that the toilets empty into, normally referred to as soil pipes. The vent that serves these pipes is called a vent stack. Vents from the various sinks and other fixtures may connect to this same vent stack, but they will usually be made of smaller-diameter pipes. Throughout the entire system

A typical home plumbing installation showing the drain-waste-vent (DWV) system, as well as the water supply pipes

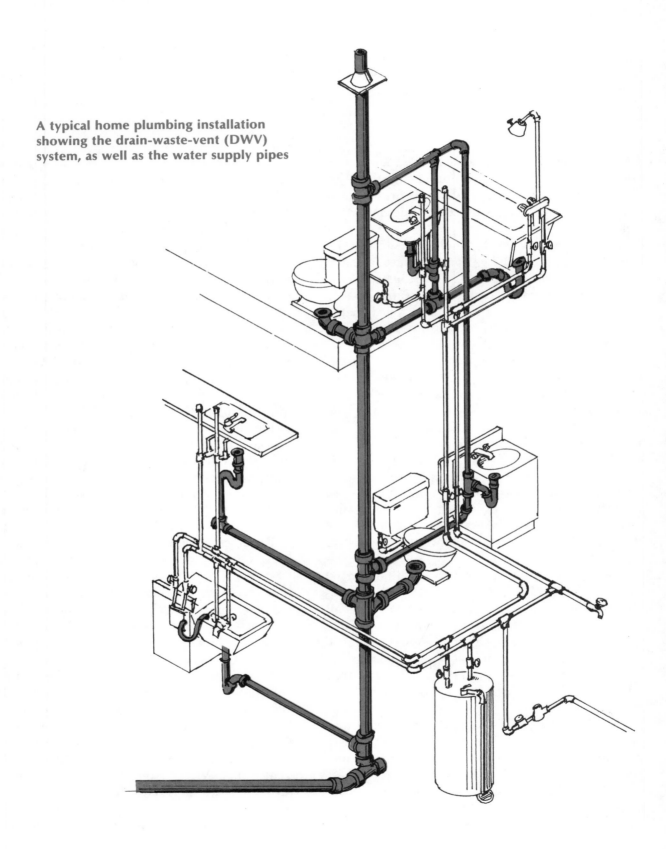

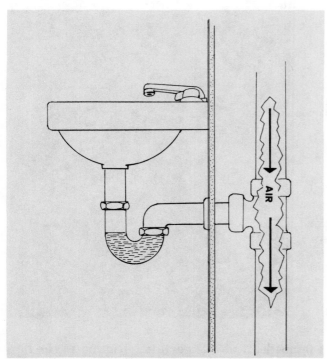

Trap holds water to seal out sewer gases.

there are numerous cleanout plugs that can be removed so that a large "snake" or power auger can be inserted to clean out obstructions in the line.

PIPES AND FITTINGS

Pipes in a home plumbing system are sized according to inside diameter—or at least nominal inside diameter. A 1-inch steel pipe, for example, is not necessarily 1 inch in inside diameter; it may be as much as ⅛ inch smaller or larger in inside diameter (depending on the thickness of the wall, and on different manufacturers), but you still call it 1-inch pipe and you buy 1-inch fittings for it. Copper and plastic pipe, which are more smooth-walled on the inside, generally are closer to their actual nominal inside diameters, probably because they are smoother and more uniform in wall thickness.

Depending on the age and location of your house, its water supply pipes may be steel, brass, copper, or plastic. In the DWV system, the pipes will be copper, steel, cast iron, or plastic. It's not unusual for one house to have pipes of several different materials in each system—it all de-

pends on local code restrictions and requirements, and on how many changes in or additions to the plumbing systems have been made since the house was first built.

Assuming that your local building codes are reasonably modern and permit a choice of pipe for additions or repairs, you should know something about the different types available. Here is a brief rundown describing the various types available, and their general purposes.

Threaded Pipe

This is usually galvanized steel or brass pipe that is joined with threaded fittings. Both were popular years ago for water supply systems, and steel pipe is also installed in many waste, drain, and vent lines. Threaded pipe comes in standard lengths of 21 feet, but some hardware stores and home centers stock shorter lengths of steel pipe—from 2 to 6 feet—that are already threaded on each end, as well as threaded pipe nipples in brass and steel. Some local plumbing supply shops and contractors will cut and thread to size for an extra fee, but you have to measure exactly, allowing for the extra length that projects into each fitting. There is no "give" with threaded pipe. As a rule, ½-inch and ¾-inch pipe will need an extra ½ inch at each end for the threads, while 1-inch pipe will need an extra ⁹⁄₁₆ inch at each end. For 1½-inch pipe you would add ⅝ inch at each end, and for 2-inch pipe, ¹¹⁄₁₆ inch.

Cutting threaded pipe to length so it will fit between fittings.

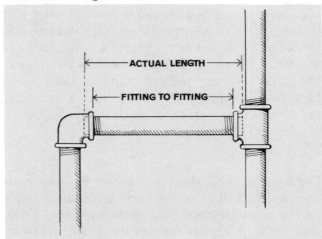

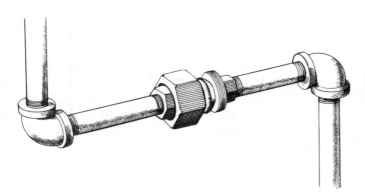

Left, threaded union allows installation of two new pieces of pipe in place of single length; right, Teflon tape is used on threaded joints instead of compound.

In each case, this extra length is added to the length of pipe measured from the face or edge of one fitting to the face of the fitting (valve, tee, elbow, etc.) at the other end. The drawing on page 227 shows how you measure length for threaded pipe.

One fitting that is especially important to know about when working with threaded pipe is the union. This serves as a coupling that enables you to take the joint apart without having to cut the pipe or unscrew fittings. Locating a union at critical points will greatly simplify servicing later. A coupling would be much cheaper, but you would have to unscrew the whole length of pipe on one side to take the connection apart.

Because it is bulky, cumbersome, subject to corrosion, and time-consuming to work with, and because of the expensive threading tools needed, threaded steel pipe is no longer as popular as it once was. Brass pipe will not corrode, but it is far too expensive for today's market. Both have been largely replaced by copper pipe and tubing or, where codes permit it, plastic pipe.

Copper Pipe

Copper is much lighter and easier to work with than steel. It does not corrode or build up scale on the inside as rapidly as galvanized steel does. And because copper pipe is much smoother on the inside, it offers much less friction to the flow of water. This means that smaller-size pipe can be used without cutting down on the quantity or pressure of water that will be flowing through the line.

Copper pipe comes in two basic types: rigid and flexible (the latter is also called tubing). Both are popular for modern water systems, and the most common nominal sizes are ⅜, ½, and ¾ inch. The choice of rigid or flexible generally depends on convenience and appearance. If the pipe will be visible, rigid pipe is neater-looking, and since it is somewhat stronger it does not require as many supports.

On the other hand, flexible tubing can be bent around obstructions and snaked through openings more easily, thus eliminating the need for many fittings. And it can be easily bent to form the curves often needed to correct for misalignment—hence measurements do not have to be as exact.

Working with Rigid Copper Pipe

Rigid copper pipe (also called hard copper) is usually joined to its various fittings by sweat soldering. Compression fittings are seldom used by professionals, because they cost much more and may be more prone to leaking over time. However, for small jobs, and for places where a torch

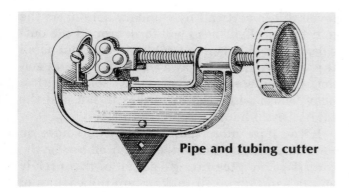

Pipe and tubing cutter

needed for soldering would be awkward or dangerous, compression fittings are sometimes simpler and quicker, especially for the amateur. Compression fittings are most often used with flexible copper pipe, so they will be discussed in more detail in the next section.

Sweat soldering is not at all difficult for the do-it-yourself plumber to master. All you need is an inexpensive portable propane torch (sold in all hardware and plumbing supply outlets) that takes disposable one-pound tanks of propane gas.

A pipe cutter, often called a tubing cutter, is the best tool for cutting pipe to length. As shown above, it clamps around the pipe or tubing, and has a sharp steel cutting wheel that digs into and cuts the pipe as you twist it around. After each full circle, tighten the handle about half a turn so that the cutting wheel digs in a little deeper, until

Soldering Pipe

In all soldering operations, it is important to take every precaution against fire. Use sheets of asbestos or similar fire-resistant material to shield wood or fabric next to the pipe, and play safe by always keeping a fire extinguisher or bucket of water handy—just in case.

When working on existing plumbing, make certain you shut off the water supply before you start, and make sure the pipes are drained before you try to heat them. If you are soldering a valve in place, take the valve apart and remove the stem, handle, and packing before you apply the torch to the body of the valve; otherwise the heat may damage the valve mechanism.

it cuts deep enough to finally snap the pipe in two. You can also cut pipe with a hacksaw, but this is time-consuming, and you're less likely to get the square cut necessary for a good fit when you are soldering.

After the pipe has been cut to length, remove any burrs left on the inside with a small file, a pocket knife, or a pipe reamer (attached to most tubing cutters). Then, with a piece of steel wool or fine emery cloth, clean and polish the outside of the pipe for the last inch or so where it will project into the fitting. This cleaning and polishing is not for looks—it is essential for a good soldered connection. So be careful, and don't touch the cleaned metal with your fingers, since the oil from your skin can contaminate the surface.

Now clean the inside of the fitting in the same way. Then apply a light coating of paste flux (rosin-core soldering flux) to the inside of the fitting and to the cleaned section of the pipe. Slide the fitting onto the end of the pipe and turn it back and forth once to distribute the flux uniformly, then line it up in its final position for soldering. As a rule, when there are a number of fittings and various lengths of pipe to be soldered, the surest procedure is to cut and fit all pieces first—without applying flux—to be certain everything fits, then take the whole thing apart and apply flux to each joint in preparation for the actual soldering.

Light the torch and direct its flame on the thickest part of the fitting, not on the pipe. In all sweat soldering you should direct the flame to the heaviest mass (the fitting), so that the other parts are heated by conduction. Have the solder ready in your other hand (see illustration on page 230) with a short bend in the end, but keep it out of the flame until the metal is hot enough to melt the solder instantly. Test for this after about 20 or 30 seconds by touching the end of the solder to the pipe just where it enters the fitting—but keep it out of the flame. The idea is to melt the solder by touching it to the heated metal, *not* holding it in the torch flame.

When the pipe is so hot that it melts the solder on contact, start feeding solder into the joint while moving it slowly and steadily around the perimeter of the pipe. Keep the flame aimed at the heavy part of the fitting, not at the pipe. The solder should melt and be sucked into the joint

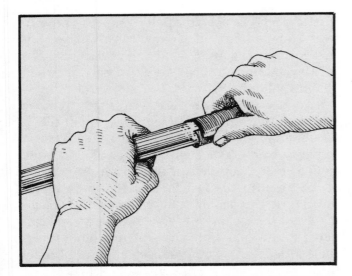

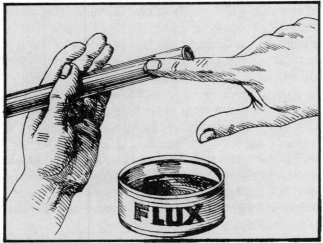

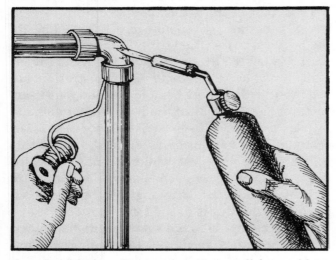

Sweat-soldering copper pipe. Top, polish outside of pipe and inside of union with steel wool or fine emery cloth; center, apply flux paste to end of pipe; bottom, solder union (see text).

(even if it is vertical) by capillary action. As the joint fills, a slight bead will form around the outside. When this bead of solder is continuous all the way around, take away both flame and solder. Immediately wipe off excess solder with a heavy cloth while the metal is still hot and the solder is still liquid.

If you have more than one joint to solder on the same fitting—both sides of an elbow, or the three legs on a tee fitting—get all of them ready at the same time. In making multiple joints of this kind it is even more important that you direct the flame at the fitting, not at any of the pipes that connect to it. Remember—the general rule in all sweat soldering is to direct the flame at the heaviest mass.

Sometimes in the course of making repairs or additions you will have to add to an existing fitting or valve that has a soldered joint on one side. To make sure the heat will not loosen up the old soldered joint, wrap the old joint with a thick layer of wet cloth and take extra pains to direct your flame away from this area. If the cloth starts to dry out or scorch, rewet it immediately. Use the highest flame so that the new joint is heated as quickly as possible.

For this kind of job one of the newer torches with "swirling flame" or "extra-hot" flame will work better, delivering more heat to the target area more quickly—before the heat is conducted away to the already-soldered joint at the other end.

Another way to make a new joint near a soldered one is with compression fittings, instead of "sweat" (solder) fittings (see page 231). These eliminate the need for a torch and for doing any soldering.

Working with Copper Tubing

As mentioned previously, the main difference between copper tubing and copper pipe is that the tubing is flexible and has a slightly thinner wall, though it is still strong enough to handle all normal household water pressures. It can be cut with a hacksaw, but a tubing cutter (see page 229) will do a much faster and neater job of cutting the end square.

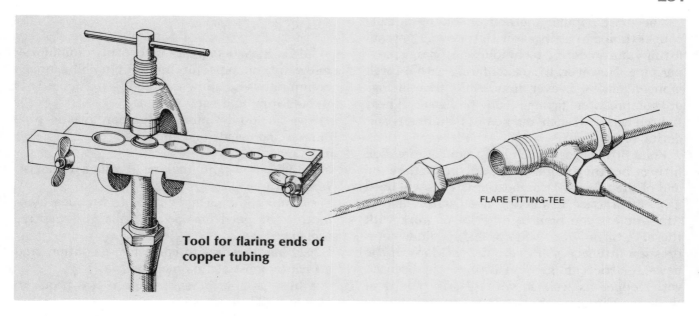

Tool for flaring ends of copper tubing

FLARE FITTING-TEE

Assembling Compression Fittings

As shown in the illustrations, each compression fitting has a tapered brass ring or ferrule that fits snugly around the pipe. A threaded collar or hollow nut is slipped on over it to join the two halves of the fitting and apply compression to the tapered ring, forming a watertight seal between the two halves.

To assemble one of these joints, first slip the nut or collar onto the pipe with its threads facing the end of the pipe. Then slide on the tapered brass ring over the end of the tubing. Push the end of the tube firmly into the compression fitting and then push the threaded collar forward and tighten it onto the fitting. This will squeeze the tapered ring tightly around the outside of the pipe and against the inner sides of the threaded collar to form a watertight seal.

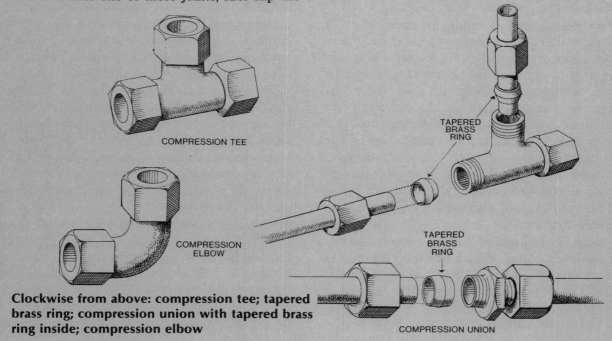

COMPRESSION TEE

COMPRESSION ELBOW

TAPERED BRASS RING

TAPERED BRASS RING

COMPRESSION UNION

Clockwise from above: compression tee; tapered brass ring; compression union with tapered brass ring inside; compression elbow

The most popular method of joining flexible copper tubing to fittings is with the same "sweat" fittings and soldering techniques as for rigid copper pipe. However, where soldering with a torch is inconvenient or even impossible, flare fittings or compression fittings can be used. These tighten with a wrench and do not require any soldering or heating.

Flare fittings cost much less than compression fittings, but they require a special tool to flare the end of the tubing. Also, most amateurs will need a bit of practice to make a good flare. That is why—unless you plan to do a lot of work with these fittings—you will probably find compression fittings easier and quicker. Many of the newer plastic compression fittings can be used with copper as well as with plastic pipe, and these too eliminate the need for flaring.

Compression fittings are more expensive than "sweat" fittings, but for small jobs only a few are required, and of course they eliminate any need for using a torch and solder. They are particularly helpful—with both rigid and flexible copper pipe—when there are already several nearby soldered fittings that might loosen up if heated by a torch. As a rule, though, compression fittings are best only in places where the pipe will be relatively exposed—not on sections of pipe that will be permanently closed up inside a wall or ceiling—because in time they may begin to leak.

Compression fittings come in many popular styles to fit all common copper pipe sizes. There are also reducers and adapters for attaching different sizes of pipe and for adapting soldered fittings to compression fittings (in those jobs that require tying in to lines that already have soldered connections). One big advantage to compression fittings is that any one can be opened or taken apart at any time after the joints have been assembled. In other words, the fittings function as threaded unions that you can break apart and reassemble without having to cut pipe or replace fittings.

In addition to regular brass compression fittings made for copper pipe and tubing, there are also a number of plastic fittings that are designed primarily for polybutylene plastic pipe and CPVC plastic pipe but can also be used with soft copper pipe and tubing.

WORKING WITH PLASTIC PIPE

While it may take years before all communities allow plastic pipe for indoor plumbing, many communities do allow it already—particularly in waste, drain and vent systems.

For the do-it-yourself plumber, plastic pipe offers some decided advantages:
• Lower cost
• Lighter weight, making it much easier to work with
• Simpler joining and cutting techniques, eliminating the need for special skills or expensive tools
• Imperviousness to corrosion, oxidation, and attack by most common chemicals
• Inside smoothness, making it less prone to clog or build up scale
• Better insulating quality than metal, helping to conserve energy in hot-water lines

There are presently two types of plastic pipe suitable for a home water supply system—flexible polybutylene (PB) and rigid chlorinated polyvinyl chloride (CPVC). Another flexible plastic pipe, polyethylene, is unsuitable for hot water, and some types of polyethylene pipe do not bear the National Sanitation Foundation (NSF) stamp indicating they are suitable for use with potable (drinking) water. Most localities forbid its use indoors, but allow it outdoors—for underground sprinkling systems, for swimming pools, and for bringing cold water in from a private well (provided it's a brand that is NSF-approved for use with potable water).

Where local codes allow, flexible PB pipe and rigid CPVC plastic pipe are suitable indoors for hot or cold water, and choosing between them is similar to choosing between the flexible or rigid copper pipe: The rigid material (CPVC) offers a neater appearance, while flexible tubing (PB) is easier to snake through walls and floors or around obstructions.

Flexible tubing is joined with special threaded plastic fittings similar to the brass compression fittings sold for copper tubing. In fact, some brands of PB fittings can join regular copper tubing as well as plastic. The fittings are screwed on and tightened by hand, then cinched up for an extra half turn with a wrench. You can take them

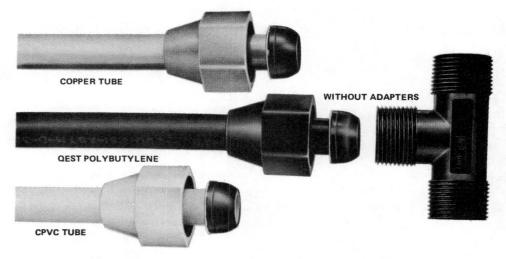

Plastic fitting accepts all three types of tubing

COPPER TUBE

QEST POLYBUTYLENE

CPVC TUBE

WITHOUT ADAPTERS

apart by simply unscrewing the compression collar, and they can be reassembled at any time like a threaded union.

Rigid CPVC pipe is usually joined with solvent-welded fittings, although some brands of screw-together (compression-type) plastic fittings, designed for use with PB tubing, are also effective. However, these fittings cost considerably more than the regular solvent-weld fittings.

When plastic pipe is to be connected to existing metal water lines, you will need special adapters. Most plumbing supply houses, as well as many hardware stores and home centers, carry a wide assortment of adapters for connecting to threaded or soldered fittings. They will have a "sweat" or threaded fitting on one end and a plastic coupling on the other. If you are not sure what you will need, bring your present fitting to the dealer and show him the transition

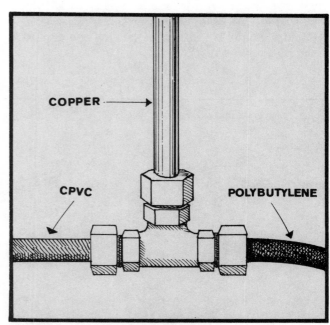

COPPER

CPVC

POLYBUTYLENE

A PB tee joining three types of tubing

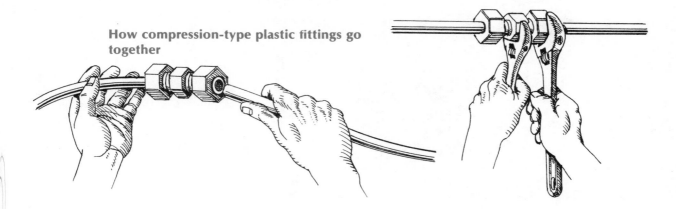

How compression-type plastic fittings go together

Joining Plastic Pipe with Solvent

Joining CPVC pipe with solvent-welded fittings is neat and quick, but requires some care to ensure leakproof joints. Use the solvent/cement recommended for CPVC pipe, and make certain the outside of the pipe and the inside of the fitting are perfectly clean and dry. You'll need a special cleaner that also serves as a primer to wipe on both surfaces with a clean cloth.

Apply the solvent/cement liberally to the outside of the pipe and the inside of the fitting, then push the pipe into the fitting's socket. Give it a slight twist to spread the cement around, then *immediately* line the fitting up in its final position before the cement gets a chance to set. Once the cement starts to set, the fitting cannot be shifted and the joint cannot be taken apart without destroying the fitting or cutting the end off the pipe, or both.

you have to make. Some of the newer plastic fittings eliminate the need for an adapter or transition fitting; they will accept copper pipe and tubing, as well as plastic.

Plastic Drain and Waste Pipe

In home plumbing, plastic pipe first became popular in the drain-waste-vent (DWV) system. Large-diameter pipes, essential for carrying away liquid and solid wastes, are extremely heavy when made of steel or cast iron, but plastic ones are quite light. They weigh less than copper and are considerably cheaper. Much smoother than cast iron or steel pipes, they are less prone to particle buildups, which can cause clogging.

There are currently two different types of rigid plastic pipe for home drain and waste systems: acrylonitrile butadiene styrene (ABS) and polyvinyl chloride (PVC). Both come in all standard sizes—from 1½ inches to 6 inches in diameter—and both are commonly joined with solvent-

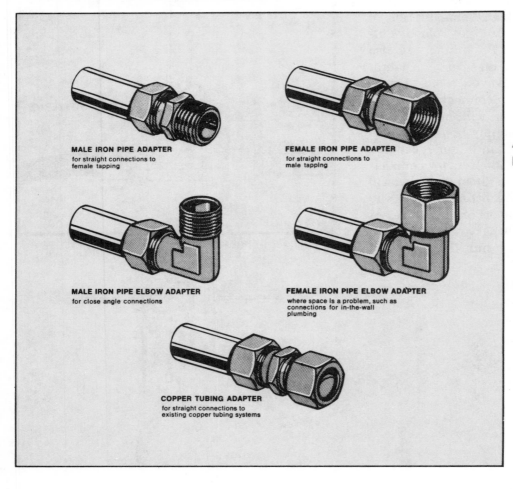

MALE IRON PIPE ADAPTER
for straight connections to
female tapping

FEMALE IRON PIPE ADAPTER
for straight connections to
male tapping

MALE IRON PIPE ELBOW ADAPTER
for close angle connections

FEMALE IRON PIPE ELBOW ADAPTER
where space is a problem, such as
connections for in-the-wall
plumbing

COPPER TUBING ADAPTER
for straight connections to
existing copper tubing systems

Adapters for joining plastic pipe to metal pipe

welded fittings, similar to those for CPVC pipe. The fittings, however, are designed with a more distinct shoulder inside that, when assembled, covers the edge of the pipe so that it does not project into the path of the flow. (Even a slight ridge will trap solid material that can eventually result in a partial blockage.)

There is a full range of elbows, offset connectors, tees, traps, and other fittings available for plastic drain pipes, and the techniques for joining them are much the same as those for joining CPVC pipe and fittings, described on previous pages. Special tees or Y-fittings are also available with removable cleanout plugs that you can twist off when major blockages or clogs must be removed. This type of pipe is also used for vents and for the stack pipes that go up through the roof.

SILENCING NOISY WATER LINES

If hammering or banging noises occur every time a faucet is turned on or off, or every time an automatic valve inside a washing machine or similar appliance snaps shut, it can be more than annoying. It may, indeed, signal the development of a condition that could eventually result in breaking open some soldered joints in copper plumbing, and in loosening the system's mounting straps. It could then further endanger the condition of the water lines and even result in the bursting of some pipes or fittings.

The banging noise is usually evidence of a condition known as water hammer. Water is not compressible, and when it is moving in a rapid stream and is suddenly brought to a halt by a swiftly closing valve, it tends to "bang" loudly against the walls of the pipes and fittings. If the pipe is also loose, it may actually move and bang against adjacent structural members or other pipes, making the noise louder.

To prevent such problems, plumbing systems often have "antihammer" devices (also called water-hammer arrestors) installed in various places—near washing machines and kitchen or bathroom sinks, for example. You can buy these devices ready-made, or you can assemble them yourself out of short lengths of pipe (see illustrations on page 236). All work on the same principle: A chamber with a cushion of air trapped

inside is spliced into the water line with a tee fitting as shown. When the water in that line comes to a sudden halt it forces itself partway up into the air chamber. Since air is easily compressed, this acts as a "cushion" that absorbs much of the water's kinetic energy and thus keeps it from banging around inside the pipe.

The illustrations show various types of anti-hammer devices: one that you can make yourself out of a straight length of pipe at least 18 inches high and at least as large in diameter as the water line, and others that you can buy in local plumbing supply outlets—some that look like dome-shaped metal cylinders, some that look like a coiled length of copper tubing.

Regardless of which type you use, the device should be installed next to or behind the fixture or faucet that causes the hammering noise when opened or closed. Cut into the supply line and install a tee fitting, then attach the antihammer device on top. If you assemble your own out of a length of brass or steel pipe, be sure you use compound on the threaded cap that closes off the top to ensure that it is airtight.

When the air chamber in an antihammer device becomes filled with water (even if it is absolutely airtight, some of the air in the chamber will be absorbed by the water over a period of time) it loses its effectiveness. To correct this condition, shut off the water supply to drain the pipes. Remove the air chamber and drain it, then replace it. Now turn the water back on. The air chamber will once again be filled with air and should work as it originally did (if it doesn't, it is leaking air and should be replaced). In many homes, these antihammer devices are required only near automatic washing machines; in other homes they may be required in several places—even near every faucet.

Another common reason for banging, hammering, and squeaking noises is loose mounts or not enough pipe straps to support the pipes. Where the pipes are exposed—in a basement or crawl space, for example—you can usually spot the loose straps easily and refasten them, or you can add more straps in places where the pipe seems to vibrate. Pay particular attention to places where the pipe bends at a right angle next to a beam it is almost touching—possibly the water, each time it slams to a halt at the elbow, is

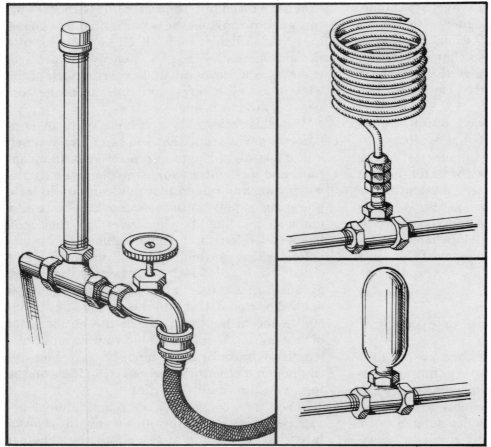

Three types of antihammer devices

Water hammer arrestor (shown being installed in washing machine hose) contains flexible membrane to absorb sudden pressure shocks.

causing the pipe to move just enough to bang against the beam. Inserting a pad of thick rubber or cork between the pipe fitting and the wood at this point will often solve the problem. Adding another strap on each side of the elbow is another solution.

Loose pipes inside the wall are a bit more difficult to repair, because you will have to rip a hole in the wall. If the situation is not too serious you can wait until that wall has to be torn open for other repairs or alterations, but if you can't wait, it may be worthwhile to cut the wall open, do the job, and then patch the drywall or plaster afterward.

When banging or clicking noises occur in a hot-water line, the problem may be due to ex-

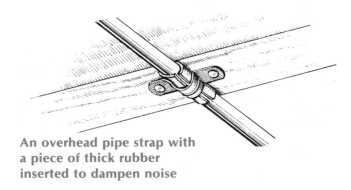

An overhead pipe strap with a piece of thick rubber inserted to dampen noise

pansion and contraction of the pipe as the water is run through it (heating it) and then shut off (allowing it to cool). This can cause pipes to rub up against beams or other structural members, even against loose-fitting metal hanger straps. You can solve this problem by inserting a pad of rubber or plastic foam between the pipe and its mounting strap, or between the pipe and the nearby wood against which it is rubbing.

A whistling or squealing that occurs while the water is running—particularly when one of the faucets is only partway open, or right after you open that faucet—is usually an indication of a loose washer, or one so badly worn that it no longer fits properly, or even one that is the wrong shape or size.

PROTECTING PIPES AGAINST FREEZING

Although water lines in a home plumbing system should be installed in such a way that they cannot freeze, all too often there is no insulation between pipes in outside walls and the exterior siding, or pipes are routed through unheated crawl spaces or attics. In both cases the pipes can then freeze up in very cold weather, particularly when the house is vacant for a while and the heat has been turned down. Or the freeze-up will occur at night when everyone is asleep and no one is using the water (moving water seldom freezes).

Unfortunately, water expands as it freezes, so a frozen pipe will usually split or burst if it is full of water. This makes quite a mess when the pipe finally thaws and the water starts running again.

To prevent this, pipes running through outside walls should have insulation installed between the pipe and the outer sheathing, not just between the pipe and the inside wall. And if pipes must run through an unheated crawl space, basement, or garage, they should themselves be insulated. You can use the self-adhesive foam type that comes in rolls with aluminum facing, or long foam sleeves that are slit down the middle so that you can slide them on over the pipe (the slit is then sealed with tape).

Bear in mind that insulation only conserves heat—if there is no heat inside the pipe it can still freeze. So if you leave the house unheated for days at a time while on vacation, or even if the heat is turned way down, even with insulation the pipes could freeze. The only sure way to prevent this from happening is to wrap the pipe with electrical heating cable (also called heating tape). It comes in various lengths, with automatic thermostat controls that will turn it on only when temperatures drop down close to freezing. You usually wrap the cable or tape around the pipes in a spiral, then wrap fiberglass insulation over it to keep the heat in and minimize energy consumption.

Obviously heating cables can be installed only on accessible pipes, and they help only as long as there is power—a power failure will render them

Electric heating cable keeps pipes from freezing.

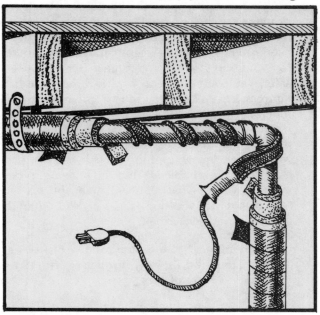

useless (though the insulation will help if the cold spell doesn't last too long).

Protecting pipes in enclosed outside walls is much more of a problem (even if you blow insulation into the wall later, you cannot be sure the insulation will get between the pipe and the outside sheathing). In extreme cases, where freezing is a frequent problem, your best bet is to cut an opening in the wall through which you can then cover the pipes with insulation.

Another trick that often works is to cut a small rectangular opening at the base of the wall and install a small louvered vent of the type used in hot-air systems. This will allow warm air from the room to get into the outer wall. The room will lose some heat, but you can keep the louver closed most of the time, opening it only in very cold weather when the water will not be running for many hours.

If the basement is heated, or is at least reasonably warm during cold weather, it may also be possible to cut openings from below that will allow some of the warm basement air to filter up into the hollow wall spaces where the pipes are located.

There are some occasions when none of these measures will help—when extra-cold weather will cause certain poorly located pipes to freeze every time: pipes in outside walls that have little or no insulation between the pipe and the outside, or pipes that come into a building from underground, but are not buried deeply enough

When Pipes Do Freeze

A frozen pipe must be carefully thawed or you can easily make matters worse. Heat must be slowly and gradually applied to keep the pipe from bursting, and you should always start at the faucet or valve end—making sure that this valve or faucet is all the way open. If the valve itself is frozen, thaw it first, then open it. Work your way along the length of frozen pipe so that the melting ice can run safely out through the valve or faucet. Otherwise trapped water might turn into steam—and this could literally explode the pipe open.

You can apply heat to the pipe with a small propane torch, but be careful about flammable materials near or behind the pipe, and be sure to use a small flame and keep it moving constantly to avoid applying too much heat in one place. A safer way to apply heat is with an electric heat lamp, but even here you must remember to keep moving.

An even safer way to do the job is to wrap the pipe with a thick layer of rags, then pour very hot water over the wrapping. Or you can wrap an electric heating cable around the pipe and plug it in for a while—the heat will melt the ice uniformly and safely (although more slowly than the other methods described).

Applying heat to a frozen pipe with (top) **a heat lamp and** (below) **hot water poured over a thick covering of rags**

When Pipes Crack

If a pipe does crack or split, there are emergency repairs that will keep the water running—sometimes you can even make permanent repairs yourself. For very tiny splits you may be able to get by temporarily by wrapping the leak with duct tape or plastic tape, but this will only slow the leak—it will seldom stop it completely. A better way to stop small leaks for a while, even completely, is with a couple of hose clamps and a piece of sheet cork or rubber (you can buy hose clamps at most hardware or auto supply stores, so it's easy to keep a few handy in sizes that will fit your household water lines). As shown in the drawing, you apply the clamps to secure the piece of rubber or cork around the pipe and hold it tightly against the crack. If the hole is really small, then a C-clamp and a block of wood, padded with cork or rubber, can also be used.

Leaks around fittings, or cracks and splits in fittings, can often be patched with a two-part epoxy putty or patching compound, but this is only effective if you can drain the pipe and dry the surfaces first. Clean the metal thoroughly to ensure a good bond, then butter the putty into and over the crack or split. A heat lamp or other mild source of heat can speed up the curing time.

To really do the job right you should cut out the damaged section of pipe and replace it entirely, along with any damaged fittings. Copper or plastic pipe and fittings are fine, as long as you buy the proper adapters (refer to the beginning of this chapter for information on how to work with different kinds of pipe).

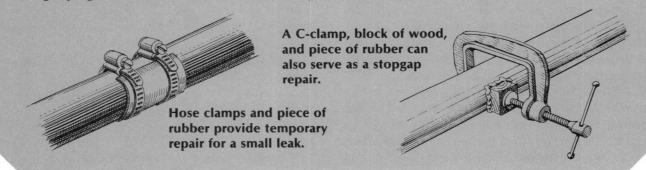

A C-clamp, block of wood, and piece of rubber can also serve as a stopgap repair.

Hose clamps and piece of rubber provide temporary repair for a small leak.

A small louvered vent allows warm air from the room into outer wall.

(they should be below the frost line for that area). In all of these situations, relocating or rerouting the pipes, or burying them deeper if they are outside, is the only sure cure. However, until you get around to doing this you can keep the pipes from freezing by allowing the water to run very slowly during very cold periods. A slow trickle or fast drip is all that is required in most cases, since moving water is much less likely to freeze.

Draining the Water System to Prevent Freezing

When a house is to be left vacant for a long period of time during the winter, especially if the heat will be turned off, it is necessary to drain the plumbing system in order to protect against freeze-ups. Even if the heat is left on, a danger still exists—there could be an extended power failure or some breakdown of the heating system. Pipes that freeze will often burst—and extensive flooding and other damage will result after the pipes thaw.

Some people feel safer if a plumber is called in to do this job, but if you are willing to take the time to do it carefully, there is no reason why you cannot do the job yourself. Here are the steps to follow:

1. On the day you are leaving, turn off the water at the main valve out in the street (you may have to call your local water company to have this done). Turning off the main valve at the meter inside the house is not enough—if the pipe bursts *before* the valve (inside the house), your basement will still be flooded.

2. Open all the faucets and spigots inside and outside the house, and leave them open.

3. Turn off the power or fuel supply to your hot-water heater, then drain the appliance by opening the valve or spigot at the bottom.

4. Check the plumbing lines to see if the water-heater drain in the basement is the lowest point in the entire system (no pipes or valves should be lower). If it isn't, then make sure there is some way to drain those lowest pipes in the system—either by opening a faucet or, if you must, by actually breaking open a connection. This is particularly important if you have a crawl space under the house with pipes running through it.

5. Disconnect and drain the hoses from your washing machine, then run the machine briefly in the drain cycle to remove the last of the water. Siphon out any remaining water. Do the same for your dishwasher.

6. Flush all the toilets, then sponge out any water that still remains in the tank (no more will come in because the water is off).

7. Pour about half a gallon of permanent-type auto antifreeze down each toilet bowl to fill the trap and to mix with any water left in the bowl, then pour at least a quart into each sink and fixture drain to protect the traps under each from freezing. Do the same in each shower drain, tub drain, laundry drain, and dishwasher and clothes washer drain, in addition to kitchen and bathroom sinks.

8. If your house has a central humidifier, it's best to drain it as well, rather than merely fill it with antifreeze.

9. If you have a hot-water or steam heating system, this too must be drained if you are planning to turn off the heat. There are many variations to these systems, however, and you should consult your local serviceman about the best way to close off your particular system. If you can get him to show you how to do your house once, then in subsequent years you can do it yourself.

FIXING LEAKY FAUCETS

A leaking or dripping faucet is more than a mere nuisance that causes unsightly stains in the bottom of a sink, tub, or shower; it can be a sizable energy waster—especially when the faucet supplies hot water. Yet in the vast majority of cases, fixing a leaky faucet is a fairly simple project that will normally take less than half an hour and will cost only a few cents for parts.

Faucets come in a variety of styles, but practically all of them fall into one of three broad categories:

Compression-type faucets have regular washers made of neoprene or rubber that are secured to the bottom end of the stem with a brass screw. The handle is attached to the top of the stem so that turning it causes the stem to move up or down on spiral threads inside the body of the faucet. Turning the handle one way raises the stem and its washer so that water can flow; turning the handle the other way lowers the stem and presses the washer against a seat to close off the opening.

Washerless faucets fall into two categories. One has a rubber diaphragm instead of a washer on the bottom end of the stem, and works similarly to the conventional washer-type faucet. The other is a noncompression type with metal or plastic disks to control the flow. The disk type usually has two disks—a movable one and a fixed one—with openings in both. Turning the movable disk in one direction will align the openings in both disks so water can flow through. Turning the disk in the opposite direction moves the openings out of alignment and thus cuts off the flow of water. Since this type of faucet has no washers to wear out and does not depend on a compression seal to shut off the water, it is generally much less prone to leaking than a regular compression faucet, and can often go for years without repairs.

Single-handle or single-control faucets are mixing faucets that have only one handle controlling the flow of both hot and cold water, as well as the volume of water that flows out through the mixing spout. They have no washers or diaphragms; instead they have a special ball or cartridge assembly that serves as a valve when turned or rotated (depending on the design) by the handle. On some models there is a round, knoblike handle that you turn to adjust for hot or cold, and that you pull out to adjust for volume. On others there is a lever-type handle that is moved from side to side to adjust for hot or cold, and pushed forward or back to adjust for volume.

Repairing Compression Faucets

When a compression faucet leaks or drips from the spout, it usually means that the washer has to be changed. If it leaks around the stem or under the handle, then the packing has to be replaced. And if the problem is a chattering or squealing noise when the faucet is turned on, it's likely that the washer needs tightening or replacing. In all of these situations you will have to take the faucet apart to get at the washer, so the first step is shutting off the water supply to that fixture. You can do this by closing the valve under the sink, or by closing the main valve that supplies water to the whole house.

Turn the faucet handle as far as it will go to the fully open position, then take the handle off the end of the stem by prying out the little decorative button or cap marked "Hot" or "Cold" in the center of the handle (it may just have an "H" or a "C") and taking out the screw underneath. With the screw out, you should be able to lift the handle straight off, though it may take a little coaxing or prying.

If your faucet has no removable decorative button or cap in the center, and if there is no screw visible on top, then look for a small threaded collar on the underside of the handle. Unscrewing this and letting it slide down will enable you to get the handle off.

The next step is removing the decorative bonnet or cap nut under the handle. This is a hollow metal housing that often is held down by a thin flat nut. Loosen this and you will be able to slide it and the bonnet straight up and off the stem. Under it you will find a large cap nut that holds the packing down. Loosen this with a wrench and the entire stem can be unscrewed by turning it counterclockwise until it can be lifted out of the faucet body.

On some faucets there will be no decorative bonnet or housing, just a chrome-plated threaded cap nut that can be unscrewed after the handle has been taken off, enabling you to then unscrew the entire stem and handle assembly by turning it counterclockwise until it comes all the way out. (When loosening this with your wrench—or when using a wrench or pliers on any chrome-

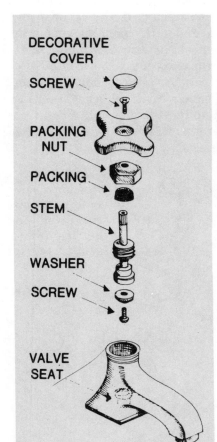

DECORATIVE COVER

SCREW

PACKING NUT

PACKING

STEM

WASHER

SCREW

VALVE SEAT

"Exploded" view of a typical bathroom faucet

plated fittings—protect the hardware with a few wraps of tape.)

With the stem out you can remove the small brass screw that holds the washer in place on the bottom, then replace the washer with a new one of the proper size and shape. The size (diameter) should be a neat fit inside the rim or hollow on the end of the stem, and the shape should match that of the original. Bear in mind that some washers are flat and some are beveled, so make sure you use the right kind.

If the old washer is so deformed that you cannot tell what it originally looked like, then your best bet is to take apart one of the other faucets—of the same type and brand—so you can see what the right washer looks like. If the brass screw that holds the washer in place is chewed up and corroded, replace it at the same time with a new one.

Screw the stem back into the body of the faucet, then slide the packing nut down on top and tighten it. Before you replace this packing nut, however, check the condition of the packing to see if it looks worn or stringy. If it does, or if the faucet was leaking under the packing nut, you should replace the packing with new material. It comes in string form that you wrap around the stem before you screw the packing nut down on top. Some faucets have a thick rubber washer instead of packing under the bonnet. If this is worn, it should be replaced with a new one of the same size and shape.

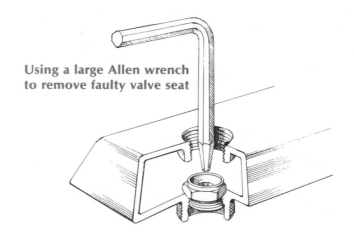

Using a large Allen wrench to remove faulty valve seat

One caution: When you screw the stem in, turn the handle (or rotate the stem) so that the faucet is left partly open and the new washer is not forced tight against its seat. This is important; forcing the washer down on top of its valve seat could crack the metal.

In general, don't tighten the cap nut more than is necessary to ensure a snug fit against the packing. Overtightening can cause the faucet to bind, or can even strip the threads on the nut. If it's too loose, at worst there will be a slight leak around the cap stem when the faucet is turned on; all you have to do is tighten the cap nut a bit more. If this still doesn't stop the leak around the stem, you will have to remove the cap nut and replace the packing under it.

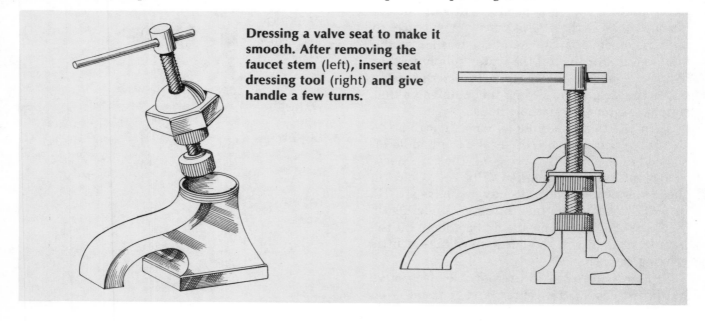

Dressing a valve seat to make it smooth. After removing the faucet stem (left), **insert seat dressing tool** (right) **and give handle a few turns.**

Sometimes you will find that even after the washer is replaced, the faucet continues to drip from the spout. This usually means that the valve seat—the metal seat against which the washer presses—has been damaged. In some faucets you can remove the valve seat by unscrewing it with either a large screwdriver or a special oversize Allen wrench (some dealers rent or lend these out), and then replacing the old seat with a new one. You can usually tell if your valve seat is replaceable by shining a bright light down the stem hole and using a small mirror to inspect the seat. If it has an octagonal-shaped opening in the center, there is a good chance that it is removable.

Instead of replacing the valve seat, you may be able to repair it with an inexpensive valve seat dressing tool. Sold in most hardware stores and plumbing supply outlets, these tools grind the valve seat down to remove burrs and scratches that may be preventing a proper seal. First remove the faucet stem as described previously, then screw the seat dressing tool down into the faucet body. A few turns on the handle while pushing down with moderate pressure will dress the seat to make it smooth.

Repairing Two-Handle Mixing Faucets

Most kitchen and bathroom faucets have two handles and a single mixing spout for hot and cold water to adjust the water temperature. In bathroom faucets this single spout is fixed, but in kitchen faucets the spout can usually swing from side to side.

When both handles are fully closed and the faucet drips, either the hot or cold side, or both, could be leaking. The easiest way to tell is to turn off one of the supply valves *under* the sink to see if this stops the drip. If turning off one eliminates the drip, then you know that is the one that is at fault. If that doesn't eliminate the drip, then turn the first valve on again and turn off the other. If the spout still drips water after a few minutes, then it could be that both faucets need new washers.

Either way, these faucets are repaired in ex-

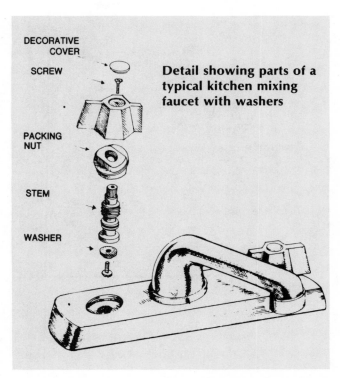

Detail showing parts of a typical kitchen mixing faucet with washers

DECORATIVE COVER

SCREW

PACKING NUT

STEM

WASHER

actly the same way as described above—depending on whether the faucet is a compression type or one of the washerless types.

If a kitchen faucet leaks around the neck of the spout when you turn it on, you can usually stop this by tightening the knurled collar around the base of the spout. If tightening doesn't do the trick, then unscrew the spout completely and pull it up and out of the faucet body. Under the collar you will see a rubber O-ring or washer. Remove this and replace it with a new one of the same size, then replace the collar on the spout and tighten it back down again.

Repairing Two-Handle Washerless Faucets

Faucets that have rubber diaphragms instead of washers are taken apart in almost the same manner as faucets with washers—and in many ways repair techniques are just about the same. The rubber diaphragm snaps on over the end of the stem (there is no screw to hold it in place). Like a washer, this diaphragm presses down against an internal seat when the faucet is closed, but it does not wear as fast as a regular washer

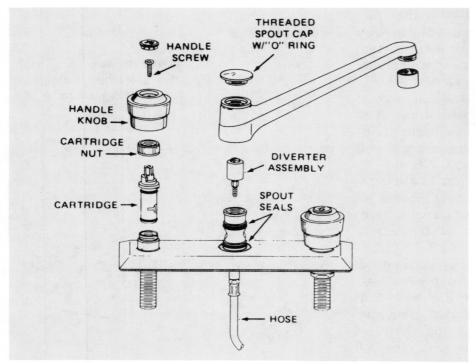

Parts of a cartridge-type kitchen faucet with spray attachment

because the diaphragm rotates when the handle is turned.

Many of these faucets do not have packing under the cap nut or bonnet to prevent leakage. Instead they have O-rings that fit into grooves around the shank of the stem, and these keep water from seeping up around the stem and then leaking out over the cap nut or bonnet.

To repair a diaphragm-type faucet that has no regular washers, follow the steps for repairing a conventional compression-type faucet with washers. After shutting off the water supply, take the faucet apart as described on page 241, then pry the old diaphragm off the end of the stem and replace with a new one of the same size and style (you simply press it on over the "button" or tip).

If the faucet is the disk or cartridge type, you

In a disk-type faucet, faucet is on and water flows freely when hole in cylinder valve is directly over inlet port (above); faucet is off when openings are out of alignment (below).

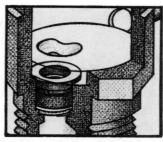

will probably have to replace the entire valve assembly when the disks are worn or damaged, although most disk models are designed so that only the rotating disks need be replaced (take the whole thing to your dealer if in doubt). If the O-ring around the stem looks damaged or worn, replace it with a new one at the same time.

When finished, reassemble the entire faucet by replacing the parts in reverse order, then turn the water back on.

One word of caution: Unlike washer-type faucets, which have parts that are more or less interchangeable brand to brand, washerless faucets usually do *not* have interchangeable parts, so check the brand before buying replacement parts. You won't run into this problem when you need only an O-ring, or possibly a diaphragm, but you might when you need replacement disks, stem assemblies, or other parts. So play safe and take the old parts with you when you go shopping for new parts—that way you will be sure of getting parts that fit.

Repairing Single-Handle Faucets

Often referred to as "one-arm" faucets, these are mixing faucets that have only a single handle to control both temperature and volume. The handle may move in and out to control volume, and from side to side to control temperature. These faucets do not have washers or diaphragms to wear out and will usually last for years without repairs.

Of course, like any faucet, single-handle faucets will eventually start to leak—especially if you live in a hard-water area where sediment tends to build up and clog the small orifices inside the faucet.

Although designs vary, most single-handle faucets are of the following three types: tipping-valve faucets, rotating-ball faucets, and cartridge-type faucets.

Tipping-valve faucets have a spring-loaded valve and a cam-shaped lever that is rocked or tipped when the handle is moved from side to side. The water enters from each side in proportion to how much this valve is tipped in either direction. The cam action also regulates the size of the openings to control the water volume.

Two problems are most likely to occur with this type of mechanism. The first is a partial clogging of the small internal screen that surrounds the tipping valve; the second is wearing of the small gasket that fits between the valve and its seat. Your best bet is to buy a repair kit that contains all of these replaceable parts, then follow the directions supplied with the kit. Most parts are not interchangeable between different brands, so when ordering be sure you specify the brand.

To take the faucet apart you first remove the spout (by unscrewing the threaded collar or by loosening the setscrew that holds it), then lift off the housing that covers the body of the faucet. You will see threaded plugs on each side, behind which the valves are located. Unscrew the plugs, then pull out the valves. Replace the damaged parts with the new pieces from your replacement kit, then reassemble in reverse order.

Rotating-ball faucets have compact ball-shaped valve mechanisms with holes or openings that allow hot and cold water to flow through.

Detailed view shows parts of a tipping-valve faucet.

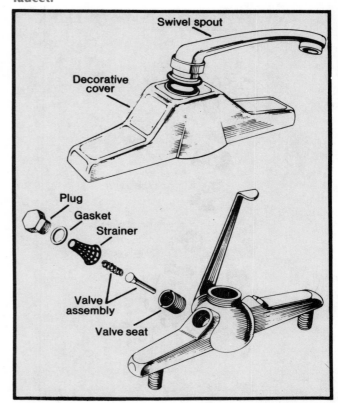

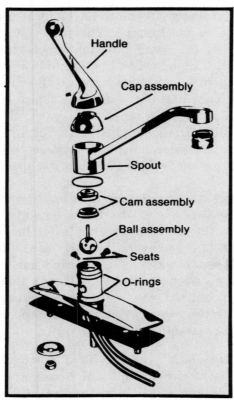

Kitchen (above) **and bathroom** (below) **single-handle rotating-ball faucets**

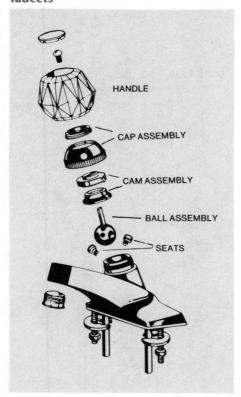

Moving the faucet's handle causes the ball to rotate so that its openings slide past openings in the seat in which the ball mechanism fits. When the openings are fully lined up, the maximum amount of water flows. When the handle is moved to bring the openings out of alignment, the flow of water (hot or cold) is diminished in proportion to the degree of the ball's rotation.

The most likely source of trouble with this mechanism is wear—either in one of the springs that maintain tension between the ball and the round housing inside which it fits, or on one of the gaskets or seals. The procedure for taking the faucet apart to replace the gaskets and springs will vary to some extent from one brand to another, but generally you first have to loosen a setscrew under the handle, then lift the handle off to expose the ball mechanism (in faucets with a swing spout the spout will come off with the handle).

Each manufacturer makes his own ball mechanism replacement kit, as well as a repair kit containing just the gaskets, springs, seats, and O-rings. Locate a plumbing dealer that carries your particular brand of faucet and get your parts from him. The instruction sheet that comes with the replacement unit or repair kit will tell you how to install the new parts.

Cartridge faucets, also called cartridge-sleeve faucets, have a rotating valve mechanism with several O-rings around the outside to act as seals. As the cartridge is rotated or moved in and out by the handle, openings in the cartridge line up with matching openings in the housing to control the flow of water from the hot or cold lines.

When this type of faucet starts to leak, the cure is simply to remove the entire cartridge and replace it with a new one. Replacement cartridges are generally available from plumbing supply houses, but again, brands are not standarized and not all are interchangeable, so make sure you buy one that will fit your particular model.

To take these faucets apart, first remove the handle, normally held on by a screw that goes through the top (it sits in a recess under the decorative button or cap on top of the handle). Pry the cap or button off, then remove the screw and

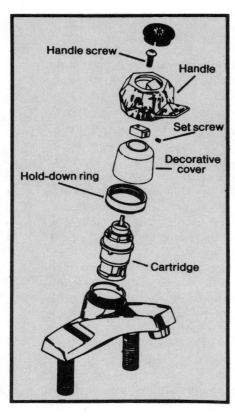

A single-handle cartridge-type bathroom faucet

stop tube that slides down over the entire assembly. You can slide this off after the handle has been removed. Then pull the retainer clip out by grabbing its edge with a pair of needle-nose pliers, or by prying it out gently with a small screwdriver blade. On some models the clip is under the handle; on others it fits in from the outside so you don't have to take the handle off first. Once the clip has been removed, the entire cartridge assembly can be slid out easily (the faucet stem is usually part of the cartridge).

Like the ball-type valve replacements, cartridges are not standardized. You have to buy the brand that matches your particular faucet. It will come with instructions for taking the old one out and putting the new one in. When installing the replacement cartridge, look for a flat spot or arrow on the stem; this will tell you which way to install it—usually with the arrow or flat spot pointing up.

Repairing Wall-Mounted Tub and Shower Faucets

Recessed faucets mounted in the wall above your tub or in the shower compartment are essentially no different from the faucets in your sinks. The only real difference is that they are horizontal instead of vertical. They also come in the same varieties, including compression faucets that have washers and single-handle or double-handle washerless types.

lift the handle off (in swivel-spout faucets, the spout will come off with the handle). With the handle removed you will have to take out a small clip or retainer, often called a keeper, that holds the cartridge in place in the faucet body.

In some faucets you won't be able to see this retainer clip or keeper until you remove a ring or

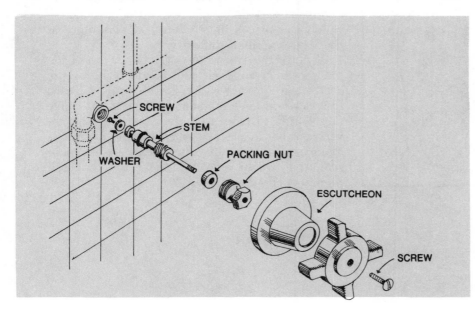

Detailed view of a wall-mounted tub and shower faucet

Repairing Sink Spray Attachments

Kitchen sink spray attachments divert water from the regular spout to the hose connecting the spray head with the faucet body—although in many cases there will still be a slight trickle from the spout even when the spray is working properly. The water is diverted automatically by a small valve assembly built into the body of the faucet and usually located under the base of the swing spout. Here's how it works:

While the water is running and before you press the lever on the spray head, the pressure on both sides of the diverter valve assembly is the same. But when you press the lever and allow water to escape, the pressure in the hose drops. This imbalance of pressure forces the valve to

Principal parts of a typical kitchen faucet with spray attachment

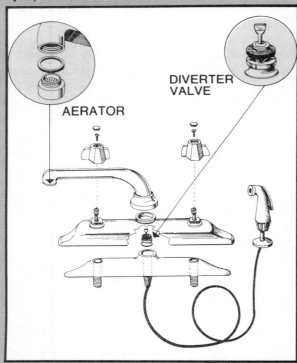

close, stopping the flow of water to the spout and diverting it to the hose that connects to the spray head.

When water somehow does not get diverted to the spray attachment, or when the spray is exceptionally weak, the first thing you should check is the hose. Look under the sink to see if it is kinked, cut, or damaged in any way. If so, remove it and replace it with a new one of the same length. The hose has a hex nut at either end so it can be easily unscrewed, and replacement units are available in all hardware and plumbing supply outlets.

If the hose is okay, check the condition of the spray head to see if its openings are partially clogged. Unscrew the head from the body of the unit and flush it out by running a strong stream of water through it from the back side, then clean out the little holes with a wooden toothpick.

If even this doesn't solve your problem, chances are that the diverter valve mechanism inside the body of the faucet has to be replaced. The first step is removing the spout by unscrewing the collar that holds it in place. You should then be able to reach down into the hole and lift the diverter valve out by pulling up on the little protruding stem.

In some models you will first have to take off the decorative housing that encloses the body of the faucet; then the diverter assembly will be accessible from the top, or through a hole in one side. As you remove the diverter valve, and any springs or gaskets, keep track of the sequence in which the pieces fit so that you can reinstall them later without difficulty.

With the diverter valve out, look for dirt inside the recess in which it fits, particularly on the seat. Clean this out with a cotton swab—or turn the water on for a moment to flush it out (have rags handy to mop up)—then install a new diverter valve in place of the old one, even if it looks okay to you (diverter valves are inexpensive and widely available in stores that sell plumbing supplies).

Single-handle washerless tub and shower faucets are taken apart in the same way as the sink-mounted faucets described on the previous pages. Buy a repair or replacement kit for that particular brand and install the necessary parts by simply following the directions supplied with the kit.

When a compression-type wall-mounted tub and shower faucet needs repair, however, there may be more of a problem, because the body of the faucet is recessed below the surface of the wall. In such cases the packing nut or bonnet may also be below the surface, so you cannot get at it with an ordinary wrench. Instead, you will have to use a deep-socket wrench—after you have removed the handle and the decorative bonnet or housing that fits over the stem and covers the opening in the wall. To remove this, take off the handle, then loosen the large, flat nut that goes around the stem and slide it off. The socket wrench is then slid on over the stem to remove the cap nut that holds the stem in place. Under this bonnet there may be a rubber seat washer below the packing, so slide this off carefully to avoid losing it. Now unscrew the stem and pull it out of the wall so that the washer can be removed and replaced with a new one. Before reassembling the faucet, replace the packing with new material (see page 242).

Replacing an Old Faucet

Although most deck-mounted faucets in bathroom and kitchen sinks are fairly standard in size, they do vary in the spacing required between the holes in the top of the sink or counter. So when shopping for a new faucet, buy one with the same spacing as your sink. Many of the newer units, including most single-handle faucets, come with decorative housings or escutcheon plates that will cover widely spaced holes, as well as an assortment of fittings that will enable you to hook up to most existing connections.

Every hardware store also carries a wide range of other adapters to simplify connecting up pipes of different diameters, or connecting one type of pipe to another, such as threaded pipes to copper. There are also flexible supply tubes (often furnished with the new faucet) that make it easy to achieve proper alignment between the old pipes and the new fittings.

The hardest part of the job will usually be getting the old faucet off—the new one is seldom a problem to install if its connections are properly spaced to match the openings in your sink. Specific instructions may vary to some extent, but in most cases here is the sequence to follow when replacing an old faucet:

1. Shut off the water supply to that fixture by closing the valves under the sink, then with a basin wrench (see illustration on page 250 top left) reach up under the sink and loosen the two supply pipes where they connect to the bottom of the faucet. There will usually be a threaded collar or nut that you loosen first, after which you can pull the supply tube down to disconnect it entirely.

2. Disconnect the supply tubes at the other end—where they go into the shutoff valve—to get them out of the way (sometimes you don't have to disconnect them entirely—you may be

Newer faucets come with flexible supply lines for easier installation.

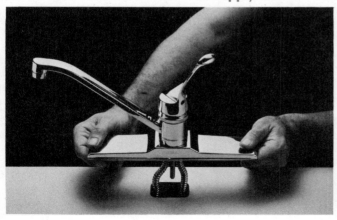
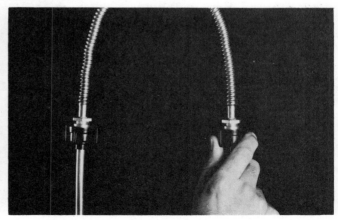

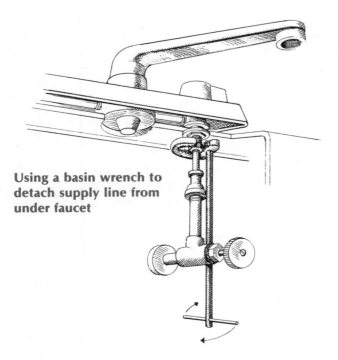

Using a basin wrench to detach supply line from under faucet

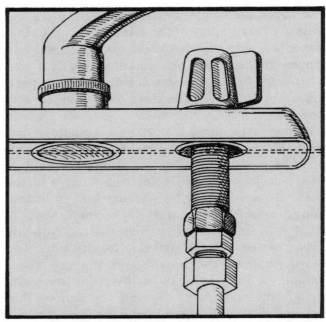

Nuts and collars to be disconnected in removing a kitchen faucet

able to just swing them out of the way temporarily). Next, with the basin wrench, remove the large locknuts holding the faucet in place from the underside. If these nuts are badly corroded and don't budge easily, squirt some penetrating oil on them and tap rapidly with a small hammer for a couple of minutes, then try again.

3. With the locknuts off (or dropped down along the supply pipe) you can lift the entire faucet off the sink top. Scrape off any old putty around the openings or the edge of the housing.

4. Take the locknuts and washers off your new faucet to ready it for insertion. Most new models come with plastic gaskets or bases that do not need sealing, but others will require bedding with plumber's putty before you set the faucet in place (the instructions should explain this). If you use putty, push down hard enough to bring the base of the faucet in contact with the surface so that none of the putty will show around the edges.

5. Reach up under the sink and screw on the locknuts and washers furnished with the new faucet. Tighten by hand, then finish tightening them with the basin wrench. You want these nuts snug, but be careful not to overtighten or you could crack the housing.

6. Connect the hot-water and cold-water supply tubes to the bottom of the new faucet with

the fittings supplied. If none of these fit, you'll have to buy new ones. To play safe, bring along what you have so the dealer will be able to determine what you need. If you have trouble lining up the old supply pipes, or if the fittings are corroded or deformed, replace them with new flexi-

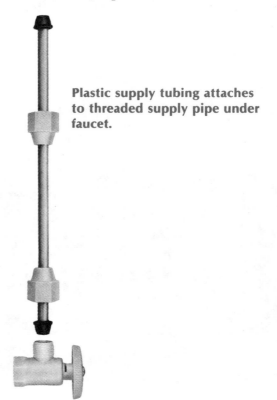

Plastic supply tubing attaches to threaded supply pipe under faucet.

ble supply tubes. You can buy chrome-plated supply tubes that bend to shape easily, or plastic ones with "universal" couplings for connecting up almost any kind of pipe or tubing.

7. Turn the water on and check all fittings for leaks. If you find one, tighten the fittings a little more—but go easy. Overtightening could strip the threads or crack the fitting.

FIXING CLOGGED DRAINS

Because the drain pipes in your house are not under pressure and depend entirely on gravity to carry away waste, it really doesn't take much to cause a blockage. Fortunately, in most cases, freeing up a blockage is usually not very difficult (though it may be a bit messy at times), unless the blockage occurs down in one of the larger main drains.

If drains are slow in more than one sink or fixture, the trouble is probably in one of the large drains or the main vent stack. If fixtures make glugging and bubbling noises as they drain and drain slowly, then there is a good chance that the vent pipe going up through the roof is clogged, or at least partially blocked. When air cannot escape freely up the vertical stack, drainage will be slow.

In many cases the simplest way to unclog a blocked stack is to go up on the roof and shove a hose down into the vent from above. Turn the water on full force for a while, with somebody inside watching some of the drains—just in case the water starts to back up. If this doesn't free up the blockage, try running a long plumber's snake down the pipe, or better yet a power auger (you can rent these from tool rental agencies in many communities).

If these measures fail, then you will have to remove a cleanout plug in the main drain line (usually in the basement) and run your drain auger in from there to the sewer to clean out the line. In most cases this cleanout plug will be at one end of a Y-fitting at the bottom end of the main stack where it connects with the large waste line leading out to the sewer or septic tank system.

To remove the cleanout plug you will need a large wrench and plenty of muscle. Be prepared for a small flood of dirty water when you do get this plug out—there may be a lot of water backed up in the vertical line behind it. When you find it necessary to remove this plug because of a problem in one of the main lines, very often your best bet is to call in a professional plumber, who has the equipment needed for this kind of job.

Cleaning Clogged Sink Drains

A clogged sink drain is usually not hard to fix, *if* you tackle it before things have gone too far. That's why it is best to take action as soon as you see a drain slowing up, rather than waiting until it is completely stopped.

In the case of a bathroom sink or tub, nine times out of ten the blockage is caused by an accumulation of soap and hair. If the trouble is in a kitchen or laundry sink, chances are that the blockage is caused by a mixture of soap, grease, and food particles congealed in the drain. In either case, the first thing you should do is check the drain opening inside the sink to see if it is clogged with hair or other solid material.

Kitchen sinks usually have a drain basket that you can remove and wash out. In bathroom sinks there is usually a pop-up metal stopper that closes the drain when a knob or handle behind the faucet is pushed down or pulled up. To clean out these drains properly this stopper will have to be removed first. Raise it as high as it will go, then turn it about half a revolution to disengage it from the linkage connecting it to the handle behind the faucet. Now lift straight up and remove it so you can clean off any accumulated hair or soap. If you can't lift the stopper out, take the linkage apart under the sink and pull the horizontal rod out of the drain pipe's tailpiece.

If the blockage is not in the drain opening, then the trouble is obviously under the sink in the trap or in one of the waste pipes leading from the sink or trap. In some cases—especially if the blockage is not yet complete—you may be able to clear it by just pouring a few potfuls of boiling water down the drain and then letting the hot water run for a few minutes before the drain can cool. The boiling water will soften up and liquefy the grease and soap, and the hot water will then flush it through.

When this doesn't solve the problem you have

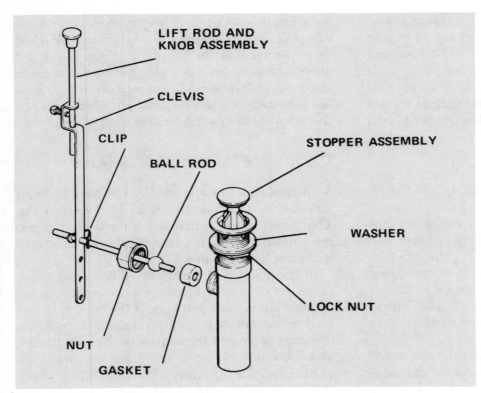

LIFT ROD AND KNOB ASSEMBLY

CLEVIS

CLIP

BALL ROD

STOPPER ASSEMBLY

WASHER

LOCK NUT

NUT

GASKET

Detailed view of typical bathroom sink drain assembly

two recourses that do not require any dismantling: a chemical drain cleaner, or a rubber force cup (also called a plunger or "plumber's friend"). Chemical drain cleaners are usually more effective on partial blockages, but if you are dealing with a completely stopped-up drain, then the positive action of a force cup will work better.

If you are in doubt, or if you think both will be needed, try the force cup first. If you use the chemical cleaner first, be careful. The caustic chemicals many of them contain will be mixed with the standing waste water, and you could be splashed when working with the force cup or when dipping out the waste water.

Although the rubber force cup is a simple tool, there are some "tricks of the trade" that will make it more effective. First, there should be enough water in the sink bottom to cover the rubber cup completely. Second, it's a good idea to smear a little petroleum jelly around the rim of the cup to ensure a tighter seal against the sink bottom. Third, make sure the overflow drain opening up near the rim of the sink is plugged (stuff a wet cloth into the opening). Fourth, if the sink is half of a double sink and shares a drain with the other half, make sure that that other

sink is plugged solidly—otherwise you will be merely forcing the water from one sink to the other.

After you press the rim of the force cup down over the drain opening, push up and down vigorously several times without lifting the cup off the bottom of the sink. The upward stroke creates a suction effect in the drain that is often even more effective than the downward compression stroke,

Using a plunger to unclog a sink

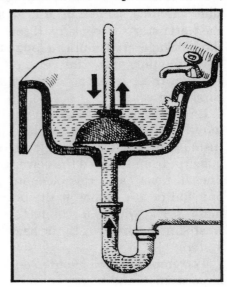

so put more effort into the lifting or yanking action. After four or five such up-and-down strokes, yank the suction cup off the bottom with a quick motion to create maximum suction. The alternate suction and compression action is what breaks up the clog so that it can be flushed away by the backed-up water. If it doesn't break up on the first attempt, don't get discouraged. Try again. It often takes four or five attempts to break through.

If you decide to go ahead with a chemical drain cleaner, then make sure you follow the manufacturer's directions exactly. Wear rubber gloves if the chemical is caustic (many are), and if the sink is full of water, dip most of it out before you start so that you can pour the chemical into the drain opening. Avoid contact with the porcelain if possible, and give the chemical plenty of time to work. The directions will specify how much time is needed; in some cases it may take several hours to really dissolve the blockage.

When you can't unclog the drain with a force cup or with a drain cleaner, then you will have to try cleaning out the trap under the drain. This is a U-shaped or J-shaped bend of pipe under the sink that always has some liquid in it, so more often than not debris that gets flushed down the drain will get caught in this section.

Some sink traps have a cleanout plug on the bottom so that you don't have to remove the whole trap to clean it out. Place a bucket under this plug, then carefully unscrew it; these plugs have fine threads, so go easy. As the plug comes off, the water inside the trap will run out. You then take a stiff piece of wire or a plumber's snake to probe the inside of the trap and dislodge or break up whatever is caught there (see drawing above right).

If the trap does not have a cleanout plug on the bottom, or if pushing the snake up through the plug opening does not remove the blockage, take the trap off completely by loosening the two slip nuts that hold it in place at each end. Slide these nuts up along the pipe, then pull the trap off—making sure you do not lose the rubber gaskets under each nut. Turn the trap upside down to clean it out thoroughly.

If you find nothing inside the trap, then the clog is in one of the drain pipes. First, look down the tailpipe (the short length of vertical pipe be-

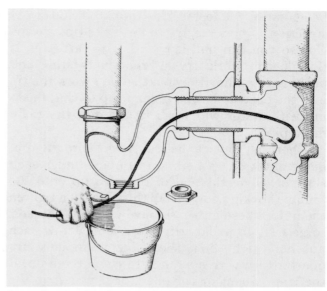

Inserting a plumber's snake through a drain trap

tween the bottom of the sink and the top of the trap) with a flashlight to see if anything's there. If not, use the plumber's snake to poke around inside the pipe beyond the trap, the one that runs into the wall or floor. Keep pushing and twisting with this flexible steel snake (it will go around

Using a plumber's snake beyond the drain trap (when trap has no cleanout plug or is not itself obstructed)

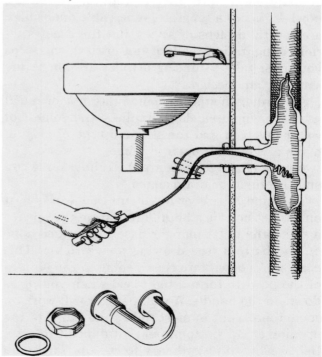

bends) until you feel it "bite into" the clog or obstruction. If possible, try to force the tip into the clog so you can pull it back out toward you. If this doesn't work, try alternately twisting and pushing or pulling the snake so you work the tip into the obstruction, to break it up so that flushing with water will wash it out into the main drain pipe.

When you replace the trap, make sure the rubber gaskets or washers are in place under each slip nut. Slide the end of the trap up onto the tailpipe sticking down from the sink, then tighten the nuts. These nuts also have very fine threads, so go easy to avoid stripping them. Screw each nut hand-tight first, then give them an extra quarter turn with a wrench to cinch them up. If the trap is bent or corroded, or if you strip the threads on the nuts, you'll have to replace the trap. Traps are not very expensive, and are widely available in local hardware stores.

Clearing Clogged Toilets

With toilets, even more than with sinks, it is much easier to free up a partial blockage than a complete stoppage, so take action as soon as you see the drain starting to act sluggish. Like a sink, a toilet has a trap, but unlike a sink the trap is actually built into the bottom of the toilet bowl—it is not a separate, removable one. There are several designs or styles, but the exact interior configuration really is not critical; the steps you must take to unclog a toilet are about the same for any design.

As a rule, chemical cleaners are not of much use in freeing up a clogged toilet—the volume of water involved and the size and type of clog all make a chemical much less likely to work. The two most effective tools are the rubber force cup and the auger or drain snake.

The kind of rubber force cup that works best on a toilet bowl is a bit different from the one for a sink—the toilet plunger has an extended cone on the bottom (see drawing above right). This cone sticks down into the opening in the bottom of the bowl to form a tight seal when you press down on the handle. A sink plunger will work on some toilets, but in most toilets the shape of the opening at the bottom makes it difficult to get a tight seal with an ordinary force cup. There are

some rubber force cups that have a folding cone designed for toilets, one that can then fold up inside the cup to leave a flat bottom that is just right for use on sink drains.

A rubber force cup is used on a toilet drain in the same way that it is used on a sink—you pump up and down vigorously and apply extra effort on the final upward yank.

If several tries with the force cup don't unclog

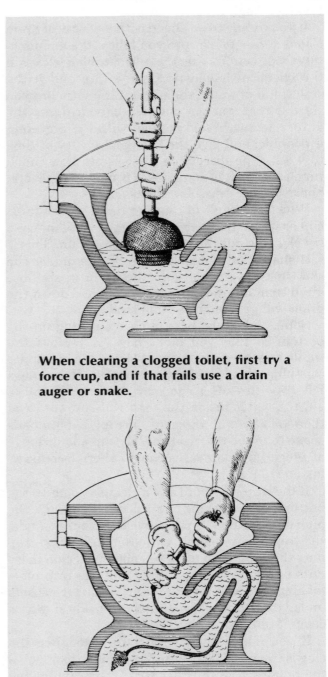

When clearing a clogged toilet, first try a force cup, and if that fails use a drain auger or snake.

the toilet bowl, you will need a drain auger or snake. An auger is more effective, especially if the clog is well inside the trap. You will have to do some pushing and twisting to force the tip of most snakes up and over the front rim of the trap. (It may help to slip a plastic bag over your arm, then reach down to the bottom of the toilet so you can guide the tip of the snake upward over the lip and into the trap.)

It's usually much easier to use one of the special augers designed specifically for toilets. Called a toilet auger or closet auger, this is a length of pipe with a sharp bend in the bottom end through which the first part of the spring-steel auger travels. This bent pipe serves to guide the tip of the auger up into the trap when you push it down into the opening at the bottom of the bowl. With the auger fully inserted, try to hook its tip into whatever is causing the blockage and then pull it back out. Augers come with a handle that enables you to twist the full length of the springy metal as you push into the drain, so keep turning and twisting on this handle as you feed the auger in. When you feel it dig into something, keep turning *in the same direction* while you slowly pull the snake back out, dragging the clog with it.

There are some rare cases when none of these measures will work—for example, when a solid object such as a hairbrush or plastic bottle, or something else that can't be hooked with the tip of the auger, has been accidentally dropped into the toilet and has worked it way up into the trap. The only solution is to take the entire toilet bowl off so you can turn it upside down and push the object out from below with a stiff piece of wire or a strong stream from a hose. Although some people may prefer to call in a plumber at this point, it is a job that can be handled by anyone willing to do a bit of heavy work. Here's how to go about it:

1. Shut off the supply of water to the flush tank, then empty it by dipping the water out.

2. Disconnect the toilet bowl from the tank behind it. If the bowl is connected to the tank by a large-diameter metal elbow, then the tank is hung on brackets which are fastened to the wall. Disconnect the elbow at both ends, then lift the tank off its brackets and set it aside. If the tank rests on the back of the bowl and is directly connected to it, there will be two bolts coming up

through the bottom that you'll have to remove. In some cases you can reach the exposed heads from underneath the flange of the bowl; in others you can get at the heads by reaching down into the bottom of the tank.

3. A toilet bowl is fastened to the floor with bolts around its rim, and in most cases the bolt heads are covered with decorative porcelain caps. These have to come off first, and usually you can simply pry them off, though sometimes they are threaded on and must be unscrewed to expose the nuts. Such decorative caps are also often filled with putty, which you'll have to scrape away to expose the metal nuts. If you find the nuts badly corroded and hard to loosen, soak them with penetrating oil and tap lightly with a small hammer for a few minutes, then try again. Be careful when using the hammer to hit only the metal, not the porcelain.

4. After the nuts are off, remove the bowl by lifting it straight up. The best way to do this is to straddle the bowl and grip the rim on opposite

In extreme cases it may be necessary to remove toilet bowl completely; if so, new wax ring may be needed to replace bowl.

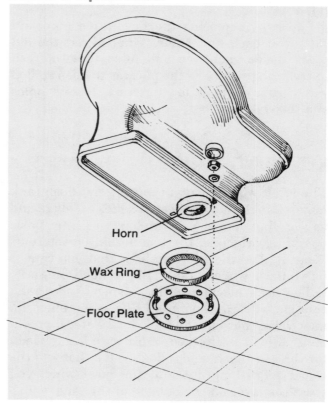

sides with both hands. Rock it gently from side to side till it breaks loose, then lift straight up.

5. Take the bowl outside and turn it upside down so you can probe the inside with a stiff piece of wire, or backflush with a strong stream from a hose.

Before replacing the bowl, you should buy a new wax ring or seal to replace the original one that fit under the bottom rim of the bowl (see drawing on page 255). Such rings are sold in all plumbing supply houses and fit over the horn that projects down from the bottom of the bowl. You will also need some fresh putty to put on the floor under the rim before replacing the bowl against the floor (having first scraped all the old putty off both floor and rim). Set the bowl into place by sliding it down over the original bolts that project up from the floor, then press down hard to compress the wax ring and the putty around the rim.

Replace the nuts and work your way around with a wrench, tightening each nut slightly before going on to the next one. Repeat this until all nuts have been snugged down firmly, being careful not to overtighten; you can crack the porcelain rim if you apply too much pressure on the nuts.

Finish by replacing the decorative porcelain caps over each nut, having scraped out the old putty inside each one and filled it with fresh putty. The purpose of the putty is to keep spilled water from washing down around the bolt holes and through the floor.

REPAIRING TOILET FLUSH TANKS

The inner workings of a typical toilet flush tank may seem like a complicated series of levers and valves, but once you understand the basic operating principle, there is nothing mysterious about it. And there is very little that you cannot fix yourself when a tank fails to flush properly.

The flush mechanism in a typical toilet tank consists of two separate valve assemblies: an inlet valve that fills the tank with water immediately after it is emptied in order to get it ready for the next flush, and a flush valve that lets the water go rushing out into the bowl when you press the lever on the outside of the tank.

The inlet valve mechanism is called the ballcock. It refills the tank and adds some extra water to the bowl itself, so there will always be some standing in the bottom. The ballcock is activated by the dropping water level as the tank empties, and it shuts itself off when the water level inside the tank rises up to a preset level. This level is determined by a float ball carried upward by the rising water, thus raising the float arm with it. The arm is attached to the inlet valve mechanism and serves to shut it off completely when the float ball reaches the proper level.

Some models do not have a float ball. Instead there may be a plastic float attached directly to the ballcock tube that rises with the water. In other models the float is replaced altogether by a pressure-sensitive valve at the bottom that senses the water level inside the tank and shuts off the inlet valve mechanism when the proper level is reached.

The flush valve is activated by the lever or handle on the outside of the tank. Pushing down on the lever raises the trip lever arm on the in-

Inside of a typical "old-fashioned" flush tank

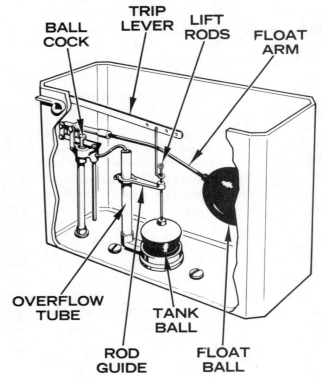

BALL COCK   TRIP LEVER   LIFT RODS   FLOAT ARM

OVERFLOW TUBE   ROD GUIDE   TANK BALL   FLOAT BALL

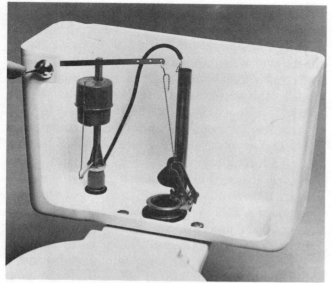

Newer tanks have plastic float instead of ballcock and flapper-type tank ball at bottom instead of old-style tank ball.

side (see drawing on page 256) and this in turn pulls up on the chain connected to the flapper-type tank ball on the bottom of the tank. As this tank ball comes up off its seat on the bottom of the tank, the water inside the tank rushes out through the opening at the bottom and into the toilet bowl. Simultaneously, the tank ball floats up to the surface, then drops with the water level until it finally falls back into its original position over the seat opening at the bottom of the tank. Incoming water then builds up pressure on the ball, serving to hold it down and keep the seat opening closed while the tank refills.

Instead of lift rods and a tank ball, most of the newer flush tanks have a chain connected to a flapper-type valve that fits over the seat instead of a tank ball and is hinged so that when the trip lever is raised, the chain lifts the flapper off its seat and allows the water to rush out and down into the bowl. The flapper valve stays in the up (open) position because it floats, but when the tank is almost empty the flapper automatically drops back down over its seat to close the opening again. The rising water holds the valve down and seals the opening at the bottom until the next time the toilet is flushed.

Now that you understand how a flush tank mechanism works, repairs should not be difficult to make when something goes wrong. You first determine the source of trouble, then make the needed adjustments, or replace any malfunction-ing parts with new ones (inexpensive repair parts are available in every hardware store and plumbing supply outlet). Here is a list of the most common toilet tank problems, and the steps that can be taken to repair each of them:

Water Keeps Running, Yet Tank Doesn't Fill Properly

This is often the case when you have to keep "jiggling" or flicking the handle up and down after each flush in order to stop the water from running out of the tank and into the bowl. It usually means that the tank ball (or the flapper valve) at the bottom is not seating properly, thus allowing water to continue running out through the bottom opening.

If the tank has a rubber ball that is pulled up by lift rods, the most likely cause of trouble is the lift-rod guide. The guide may have shifted slightly to one side or another, and as a result the ball does not fall squarely over the center of its seat. In other cases it may not fall at all and just get hung up over the seat until you jiggle the handle a few times. This problem can usually be corrected by realigning the guide slightly so the ball drops onto the center of the seat without binding. To move the guide, loosen the setscrew that locks it onto the overflow tube, adjust it, then retighten the setscrew.

Sometimes the problem is due to lift rods that are slightly bent and thus stick as they try to slide up and down through the guide. You can straighten the wire rods easily, either with your hands or with a pair of pliers. Binding or sticking can also be caused by an accumulation of slime or mineral deposits on the rods, so clean them off with fine steel wool while you are at it.

If the ball is falling onto the center of its seat and water still keeps running out of the bowl, check for any dirt, rust, or sediment on the seat that could be preventing a watertight seal. If the seat seems clean, then chances are that the rubber ball is dried out or cracked and has to be replaced with a new one. Just unscrew the old one from the bottom end of the lift rod, then screw the new one on.

A more permanent solution to this type of problem is to upgrade the entire mechanism by getting rid of the tank ball-and-lift-rod assembly

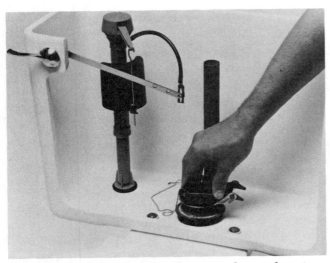

Cementing a combination flapper valve and seat on top of existing seat

(including the guide arm) and replacing it with a flapper-type tank ball similar to the one shown on page 257. Connected to the trip lever or handle with a simple length of chain, it will offer no chance of misalignment. And it can be installed in a matter of minutes to fit right over the existing opening in place of the old ball. For maximum efficiency you can buy a combination flapper valve that also comes with a new seat that you simply cement down on top of the existing one. You are thereby assured of a tight seal, and when these flapper-type valves do eventually wear out, replacement units are widely available in all hardware stores and can be quickly installed.

Tank Overfills and Water Keeps Running Out of Overflow

This happens when the inlet valve (the ballcock) does not shut off the incoming flow of water after the tank is full. As the water level rises above the top of the overflow tube, it runs through the tube and out into the bowl, making a hissing or running noise.

To check for this, take the tank cover off and look inside as it fills to see if the water level is reaching the top of the overflow tube and running over into it. If it is, lift up on the float arm to see if this stops the hissing sound and the incoming flow of water. If it does, then the problem can usually be corrected by bending the float arm

slightly *downward* so that it will reach its uppermost level when the water level is itself lower, and thus will close the ballcock that much sooner (before the water level rises as high as it does now).

In a few rare cases, bending the arm will not solve the problem because the float ball has developed a leak and is partially filled with water. As a result it will not float as high as it should—thus it never fully shuts off the flow of water. If you suspect this is the problem, and if manually lifting up the float arm shuts off the flow of water (so you know that the ballcock is working properly), then unscrew the float ball from the end of its arm and shake it while holding it next to your ear. If there is water inside you will hear it. Throw the ball away and replace it with a new one.

When you find that pulling the float arm up with your hand doesn't stop the incoming flow of water, you know that the ballcock valve is not working properly. Usually its washer or O-ring needs replacing, so you will have to take the ballcock apart. Shut off the water supply lines under the tank, then flush it once to empty it. Now disassemble the valve (at the top) of the ballcock so that you can replace the washer at the bottom of

Bending the float arm up raises the maximum level of water in the tank.

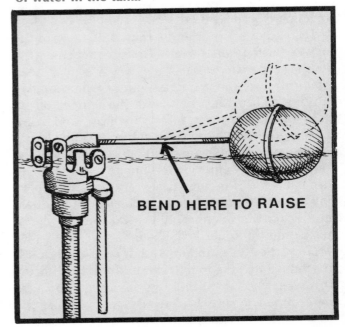

BEND HERE TO RAISE

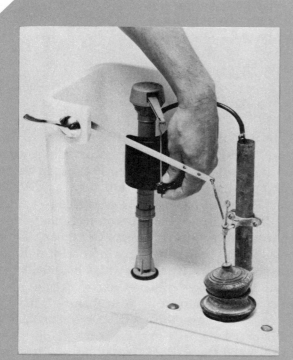

Adjusting the water level with one of the newer inlet valves

Some fill valves have no float ball, shaft-mounted float, or external levers. Instead, these compact units measure water level from *underwater* at the bottom of a toilet tank.

Adjusting the Newer Mechanisms

If your tank has one of the newer mechanisms that do not have a float ball and arm, then the inlet valve mechanism (the ballcock) will have an adjustment that controls the maximum height of the water level inside the tank. On most models there is a small adjusting screw on the top or side of the valve mechanism that enables you to adjust the water level to its proper height. (Most tanks have a line marked on the inside to indicate the correct water level when the tank is full.) If the valve mechanism cannot be adjusted to the proper height, then your best bet is to replace it with a new one.

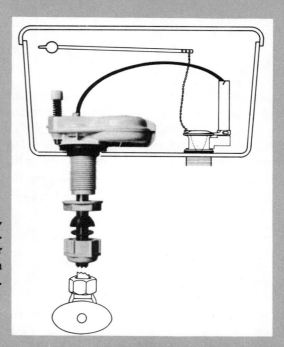

the stem along with the O-ring that fits into the groove around the body of the stem.

Simple as this repair sounds, taking an old ballcock apart is often a messy job because the screws are badly corroded and caked with sediment. In most cases when a ballcock needs repair your best bet is simply to replace the entire unit with a new one. All of the newer-model ballcocks are quieter and more efficient. They are widely available in hardware stores and home centers, and come complete with instructions for installa-

tion. Many of the newest models are made of plastic that cannot corrode, and since they eliminate the need for a float arm and float ball, they reduce the likelihood of future maintenance. (Some have an integral plastic float that rides up and down the length of the ballcock, while others have the pressure-sensitive valve described above that eliminates the need for a float of any kind. Either type can be easily installed in place of a conventional ballcock.)

After shutting off the water and draining the

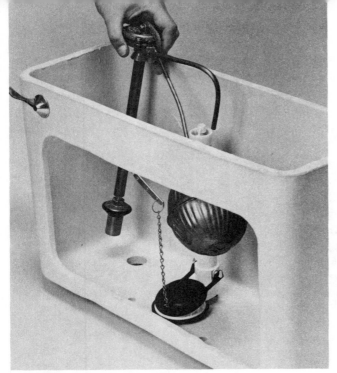

After emptying tank and sponging out water, disconnect water line, then remove all of ballcock assembly.

tank, disconnect the water supply line under the tank and loosen the large locknut that holds the ballcock in place. Lift out the old unit and install the new one in its place, then reconnect the water line. Adapters are usually supplied for fitting all types of pipe, but additional adapter fittings can be purchased if the new ones supplied don't fit.

Toilet Flushes Sluggishly or Bowl Doesn't Empty Completely

The most frequent cause of this malfunction is insufficient water pressure—that is, the water level inside the tank is not high enough to deliver the water at the pressure needed to properly flush out the bowl. If the water-level line on the back of the tank is not visible, then figure that the water should rise to about an inch below the top of the overflow tube. If the water level is lower than this, bend the float arm *up* slightly—or, in the case of one of the newer units without a float arm, turn the adjusting screw so the water will rise to a higher level before shutting off.

If raising the water level inside the tank doesn't correct a poor flushing problem, then the trouble lies in the drain and vent system, not in the flushing mechanism. Either the toilet or the

drain pipe is partially clogged, or the vent stack going up through the roof is partially obstructed (see page 226).

TAKING CARE OF SEPTIC TANKS AND CESSPOOLS

In rural and suburban communities where there are no municipal sewer lines, waste lines empty into either a cesspool or a septic tank. In a septic tank, natural bacterial action breaks the waste solids down into a sludge that settles to the bottom. The relatively clear liquid that floats to the top then flows out into a seepage or disposal field consisting of radiating lines of perforated pipe buried in the soil (there may also be one or more additional seepage pits at the end of the pipe in areas where drainage is a problem). This field serves to disperse the fluid harmlessly into the soil over a wide area so there is no chance any of it will reach the surface or pollute nearby water sources.

A cesspool, on the other hand, is nothing more than a large pit, usually lined with cement blocks or perforated concrete blocks. It receives and stores the sewage and then allows it—still relatively untreated—to seep into the ground through the bottom of the pit and through openings in the pool wall. In general, cesspools are not considered as safe as septic tanks—there is more danger of polluting nearby water sources—and many communities now forbid the building of new cesspools.

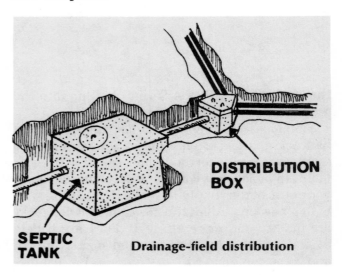

DISTRIBUTION BOX

SEPTIC TANK   Drainage-field distribution

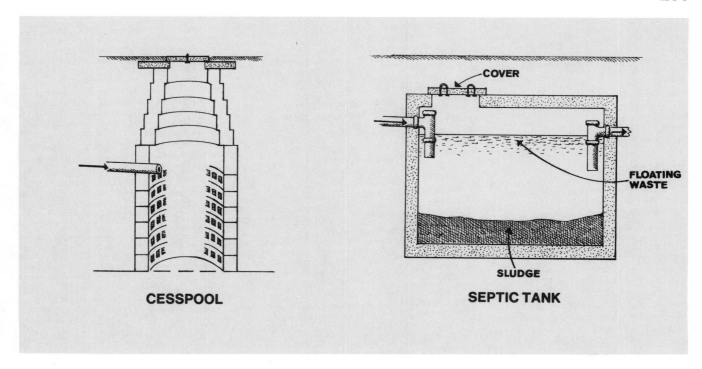

CESSPOOL   SEPTIC TANK

Regardless of the waste disposal system you have, avoid, if you can, letting solids in from the kitchen sink, and never send grease or oil down the drain. Some systems have a grease trap built in to collect waste before it reaches the septic tank; this should be checked at least once a year and emptied if it is more than half full.

Septic tanks do accumulate sludge at the bottom, and this has to be pumped out at regular intervals—usually when the sludge is more than 15 to 20 inches deep in a typical home-size tank. You can test the depth of the sludge by removing the access cover and pushing a long stick down. Wrap the end of the stick with an old piece of white toweling first, so when you push it down to the bottom you will be able to tell by the color on the toweling how deep the sludge is. Pumping this sludge out is a job for a professional. There are pumping services available in all communities that have septic tanks (you can find them in the local Yellow Pages).

Cesspools can also be pumped out when they start to fill up, but generally when this happens it is time to start thinking about replacing the cesspool, preferably with a septic tank. An accumulation of sludge often indicates that the walls of the pool are clogged with grease, and therefore drainage or seepage in the future will be very poor (it will fill up much quicker the next time). Some plumbers report mild success with using muriatic acid to "etch" or clean out the pores of the blocks that make up the walls of the cesspool, but the improvement is generally short-lived because the soil around and under the cesspool is already saturated with grease and waste and therefore seepage will continue to be poor.

Chapter 11

Heating and Cooling

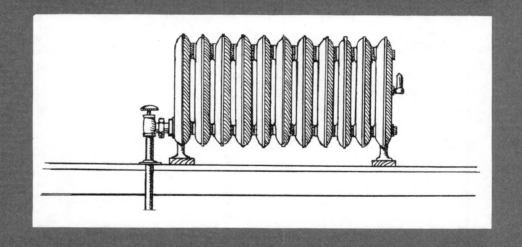

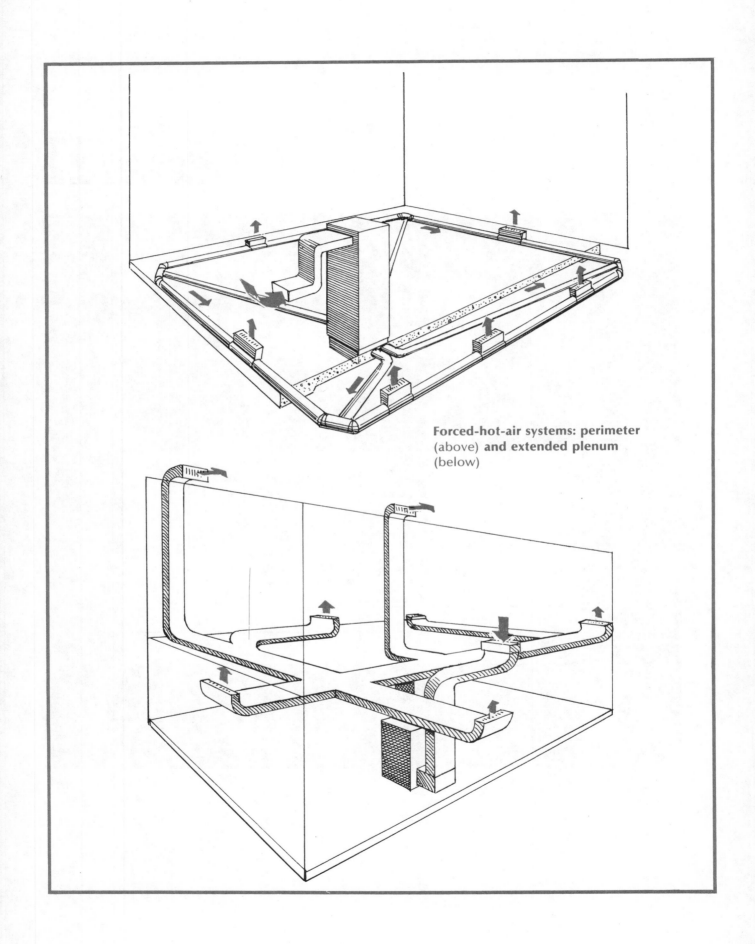

Forced-hot-air systems: perimeter (above) **and extended plenum** (below)

CENTRAL HEATING systems fall into three broad categories, depending on the medium used to deliver the heat from the furnace or boiler (a furnace heats air, a boiler heats water) to the various parts of the house: forced-air, circulating hot water, and steam. Heating systems also vary in the fuel they use—oil, natural gas, or electricity, with some home furnaces in rural areas using coal or wood. Some homes come with individual electric resistance heaters built into each room—usually with individual thermostats—but this is, strictly speaking, not a central heating system.

FORCED-AIR HEATING SYSTEMS

Years ago, hot-air systems depended on gravity to circulate the air. The furnace was centrally located, under the ground floor, and large-diameter ducts sloped upward to bring the heated air to registers in the floor of each room. The heated air rose by convection, and when it cooled it fell back down to the furnace to be reheated.

These systems have almost all been replaced with forced-air heating systems that eliminate the necessity for locating the furnace in the center of the house. The new systems also make it possible to use much smaller ducts that can be tucked up between the floor beams and inside the walls. A large squirrel-cage blower forces the heated air through these ducts to all parts of the house, and one or more return air ducts then serve to carry the air back to the furnace for reheating and recirculating (there will usually be at least one return duct for each floor of the house, though this varies with the design).

Forced-hot-air systems can be set up so that there are several heating zones in the house. For example, the upstairs bedrooms can be on one zone and the downstairs on another; or the bed-

rooms can be on one zone, the kitchen, dining room, and living room on another zone, and the family room on still another. With such a system you can adjust temperatures so that unused rooms are left much cooler without affecting comfort in the other rooms.

Zoning is accomplished by installing automatically controlled dampers inside the important ducts. The dampers open to let heated air from the furnace enter when heat is not needed in that part of the house. Although zoning is best built in when the system is installed, one-zone systems can be modified so there will be two or more heating zones inside the house, each with its own thermostat.

Most well-designed hot-air systems also have manually adjusted dampers in the ducts that run to separate rooms. You can regulate the amount of heated air each duct delivers, enabling you to "balance" the system when you find that some rooms are too hot while others are too cold. A

Adjustable dampers in hot-air ducts enable homeowner to balance system more effectively.

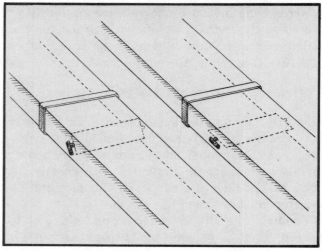

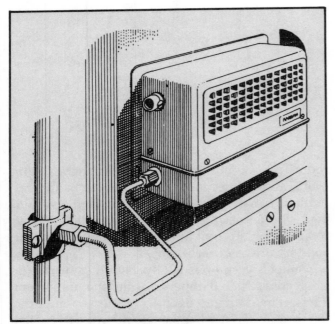

Humidifiers are connected to cold-water line and installed in plenum chamber or main duct.

further control is provided by the discharge registers, which have louvers that can be tilted open or closed—again to control the amount of heat actually delivered through each register.

Because hot air tends to dry out the atmosphere, many hot-air systems have a humidifier built in to add moisture to the heated air as it enters the plenum chamber after being heated by the furnace. The humidifier is connected to a cold-water line, through which water is drawn as needed, and vaporizes the water by adding it to the airstream.

For fully automatic control, there are some systems that measure the relative humidity of the air in the living quarters with an instrument called a humidistat, which then draws more moisture (water) as it is actually needed.

Maintenance of Hot-Air Systems

All forced-air heating systems have an air filter that screens out airborne dust and similar particles. This filter must be periodically cleaned or replaced when it gets dirty, or it will greatly cut down on the flow of air from the furnace and on the efficiency of the entire system.

To check the filter, remove it and hold it up to a strong light. If you can see the light through it easily, the filter is still okay. If the light is barely visible or hard to see, then the filter needs replacing (unless it is the kind that can be cleaned and reused).

Although not as important as the filter, the discharge registers in each room should also be checked regularly. Take them off and clean off the back side as well as the front to remove accumulated lint and dust.

The blower and motor on most hot-air furnaces will need oiling two or three times a year, although some of the newer machines have sealed bearings that never need lubrication. If in doubt, check the manufacturer's instructions for that unit, or ask your local heating serviceman about any lubrication that may be required. Use 20-weight motor oil to lubricate the motor and blower bearings; just two or three drops in each oil cup or oil hole. *Do not* use too much oil, as this can cause trouble eventually.

The belt that drives the blower should also be inspected at least twice a year—sooner if the furnace suddenly fails to deliver its usual amount of heated air, or if airflow from the upstairs registers becomes much weaker than normal. If the belt looks worn, or is starting to crack and split, you should replace it immediately; otherwise it

Many motors on hot-air furnaces and oil burners need regular oiling.

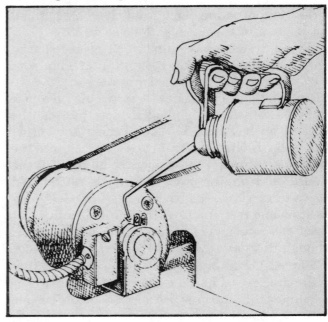

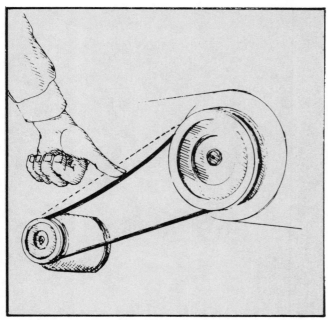

Pulley belt should depress no more than ¾ inch.

will surely go on a cold weekend night when you least expect it to.

While inspecting, make sure the pulleys on the blower shaft and motor shaft are accurately aligned so that the belt rides straight without chafing against the rim of either pulley. You can check this by placing a straightedge alongside the two. If necessary, a pulley can be realigned by shifting it slightly in or out: Loosen the setscrew that holds it in place on the shaft, then tap the pulley lightly sideways until it is exactly in line with the other pulley. Be sure you retighten the setscrew when done.

To check for proper belt tension, push the belt in toward the pulleys (while the motor is off!). It should depress no more than about ¾ inch from the straight line it normally assumes. If it does depress more, then the belt is too loose and is probably slipping when running—another reason for lowered efficiency and poor performance. Motor mounts usually have a bolt that can be loosened to permit swinging the motor in or out slightly, thus increasing or decreasing the tension on the belt.

If the system is equipped with a humidifier, it will usually need cleaning out at least once a year to avoid fungus buildup and accumulations of scale that could lower efficiency. Check the manufacturer's instructions to see what cleaning pro-

cedures are recommended and whether or not periodic replacement of elements is also required.

HOT-WATER HEATING SYSTEMS

Hot-water heating systems use a circulator pump to force heated water through pipes to radiators located throughout the house. The circulator starts when the thermostat calls for heat—but it won't come on unless the boiler water is hot enough to do the job. If the water is not hot enough, then the burner will come on first and there will be a short delay before the circulator motor actually starts sending hot water through the system.

All hot water systems form a continuous loop—that is, the water in the system goes through all the radiators, then comes back to the boiler to be reheated and recirculated. In the simplest and least expensive system, called a series loop, all radiators are hooked together as though they were attached end to end so that water flows through each one before proceeding on to the next one. Since water flows through all in series, none of the radiators can be turned off individually; all must be on or no water will flow through the system. This type of system is used only in smaller houses where cost is a primary consideration.

An improvement on the series-loop system is the one-pipe system. In this there is a continuous main pipe that circles the house and returns to the boiler. In other words, the water does not have to flow through each radiator before it can reach the next one. Each radiator is connected to the main pipe with a special type of tee (usually called a forced-flow tee) that shunts part of the water out of the main pipe and into the smaller-diameter line leading to the individual radiator. The rest of the water in the main pipe continues on to the other radiators.

The water that is diverted to each radiator goes through that radiator to release its heat, then continues out the other end and back into the same main pipe. With this system you can shut off individual radiators without affecting the others, so you have better control of the heat inside the house. However, as in the series-loop

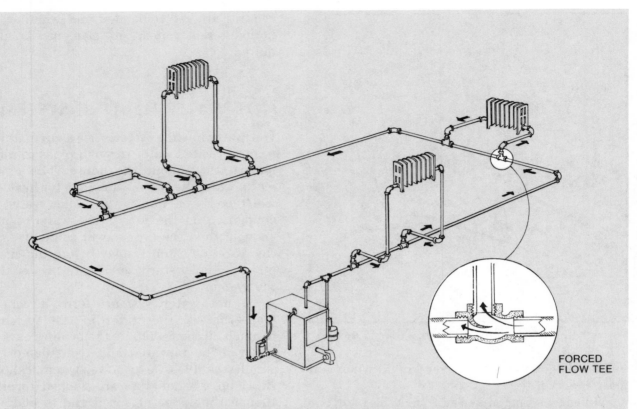

FORCED
FLOW TEE

One-pipe (inset shows forced-flow tee) and two-pipe (below) **hot-water heating systems**

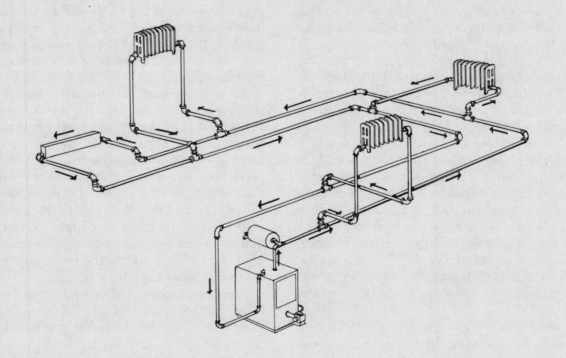

system, the water reaching the last radiator will be quite a bit cooler than it was at the start, so radiators must be balanced or arranged to have the larger ones at the end of the line.

The best type of hot-water system is the two-pipe system. It has two mains—a supply main and a return main—with each radiator drawing its hot water from the supply main and returning it to the return main. In this system the water getting to the last radiator is almost as hot as the water going to the first one (depending on the length of the pipe run, and whether or not it runs through an unheated area), so operation is more efficient.

One- and two-pipe systems can be set up so that there are two or more heating zones in the house, each controlled by its own thermostat. Solenoid valves control the water so that it flows to each zone only when the thermostat for that zone is calling for heat. The rest of the time the valve is closed and no water flows through its zone.

Radiators generally fall into two broad categories: cast-iron radiators, which are made of heavy castings, and convector-type radiators, which are actually lengths of copper pipe with metal fins around the outside to help them disperse the heat rapidly by convection. The convectors are usually recessed into the wall, although baseboard convectors are more often mounted flush against the face of the wall. The recessed models have a metal cover with louvers on the front so that air can flow freely into and out of the enclosure. Cast-iron radiators also come in baseboard models, as well as standard vertical units. They do not have fins like conventional radiators, just sections like freestanding radiators. Some are recessed into the wall, but most are freestanding.

Hot-water heating systems have an expansion tank—usually installed directly above or alongside the boiler—that contains a pocket of air, which serves as a compressible cushion to keep overheated water from turning to steam. As the water in the system is heated, it expands. This compresses the air inside the expansion tank and puts the water under pressure—preventing it from turning into steam while also helping to increase circulation throughout the system.

A gauge on the front of the boiler indicates the temperature of the water in the system, and the

An older-model aquastat

water pressure (there may be two dials on the same gauge, or two separate gauges to give these readings). The pressure gauge, which is often called an altitude gauge, usually has two pointers—one that moves to indicate the pressure in the system, and a fixed pointer that is set by the installer or serviceman to indicate the correct pressure.

The boiler will also have an aquastat, a device that controls the temperature of the water inside the boiler in the same way that a thermostat controls the air temperature. You set it to the desired water temperature and it automatically switches the burner on when the boiler water temperature drops below this setting. The aquastat has both a high-limit and a low-limit setting to determine when the burner comes on and when it switches off. On older models, the dials to set may be on top of or on the front of the unit, but on many newer models you will have to take the front cover off first—the dials are then easily accessible on the inside.

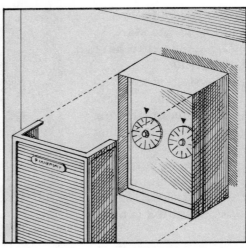

Aquastat dials may be on the inside or outside of control box.

The high-limit setting is essentially a safety device that will shut the burner off if the water gets too hot. Generally speaking, it is set between 180 and 200 degrees.

The low-limit setting actually controls the temperature of the water (within a variation of 15 to 20 degrees). A setting of 160 to 180 degrees is generally right for the winter, while a setting of 130 to 150 works well for the summer. If your boiler also makes your domestic hot water (for bathing, washing, etc.) and you have an electric dishwasher, you should keep your low-limit setting above 140 degrees, since that is the lowest temperature hot water can be if the dishwasher is to work properly.

Maintenance of Hot-Water Systems

The expansion tank in a hot-water system should be about half full of air, but periodically it will fill with water as the air in the tank becomes absorbed by the water over a period of time, or because of a leak in the tank. When this happens the tank must be drained. (Some of the newer sealed units are never drained, being equipped with a separate air bladder that keeps the air and water permanently separated; if these leak the whole tank must be replaced.)

The first indication you are likely to have that the expansion tank needs draining is when the pressure-relief valve above the boiler opens and

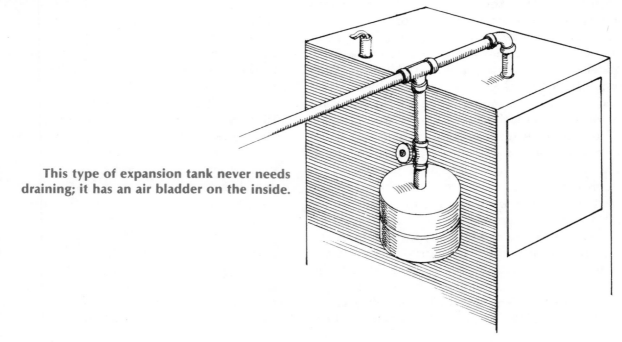

This type of expansion tank never needs draining; it has an air bladder on the inside.

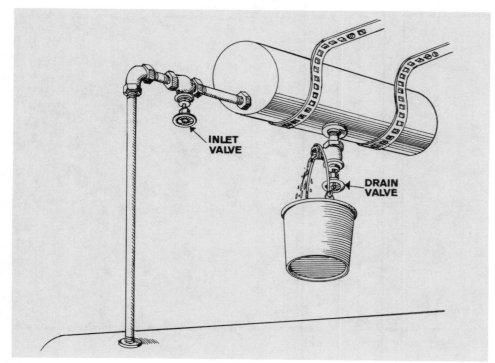

INLET
VALVE

DRAIN
VALVE

Draining a regular expansion
tank

water comes spurting out. When this happens, shut off the burner and allow the system to cool. The pressure-relief valve should close automatically as the water cools and the pressure drops (sometimes it helps to flick the lever on top up and down a couple of times).

Some expansion tanks have a purge valve that lets air in while you are draining off the excess water, but on most you first have to shut off the valve that lets water into the tank from the boiler. Open the drain valve at the bottom of the tank and drain all the water out; you can carry it off in buckets or attach a hose and let it run down a drain. Now close the drain valve or purge valve at the bottom of the tank and open the inlet valve from the boiler. Water will partially fill the tank and compress the air that is now trapped inside, once again restoring normal pressure to the system. Check the altitude gauge to make certain the pressure is normal again.

Although the boiler itself rarely needs flushing, it is a good idea to drain a little water out of the bottom about once a year so you can examine its condition. Pour the water into a clear glass container, then look for signs of rust. If a lot is showing, flushing out the boiler may be advisable.

Your first step in that case is to shut off the power to the system by throwing the main switch. Next, open the drain valve at the bottom of the boiler and let all the water run out. If the valve is so low you cannot get a bucket under it, connect a hose to the valve and run it to a drain. Now open the boiler's inlet valve and let the water run until it comes out of the drain clear. Close the drain valve and fill the boiler, then close the manual inlet valve and turn the power back on (if the boiler has an automatic inlet valve, it will refill automatically when the power is turned back on).

Very often when a boiler is refilled after draining, or when a system is first started up in the fall after having been off for months, the air inside the system collects near the top of one or more radiators. This keeps any such radiator from filling with hot water, so it either does not get hot all the way across, or does not get as hot as it should.

The cure for this is bleeding the radiator to let the trapped air escape. You open the small vent valve located at the top of each radiator, usually near the end opposite the water inlet valve. Some of these little vent valves can be opened and closed with a screwdriver; others need a special "key" with a rectangular socket or sleeve in the end (sold in plumbing supply outlets).

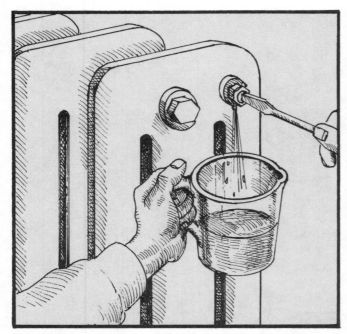
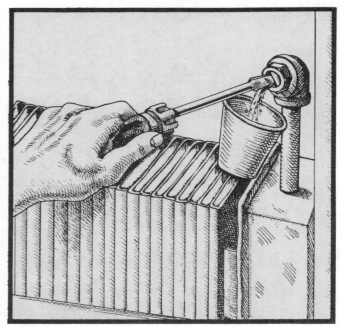

Bleeding a radiator, upright style, top, and baseboard, bottom

It's best to bleed the radiator when the circulator is running. Open the vent valve and leave it open until a solid stream of water is spurting out, then close it immediately. The trapped air will then have escaped and the radiator should be full of water again. After an entire system has been drained (when flushing the boiler, or after having made some major repairs or additions to the system), you may have to do this with each radiator—in fact, you may have to do some radiators more than once.

STEAM HEATING SYSTEMS

Although steam heat is seldom installed in new homes anymore—having been almost entirely replaced by less costly and more efficient hot-water heating systems—there are still many older houses that have steam heat.

A steam system is basically very similar to a one-pipe hot-water system: Heat is carried by means of pipes to radiators located throughout the house, and there is a boiler in which water is heated to generate the system's steam. Unlike a hot-water system, however, a steam system has no circulator motor; the heat and pressure cause the steam to rise naturally through the pipes. Also, there is most often only one pipe going to each radiator (a few two-pipe systems are still to be found in some areas).

After the steam comes into the radiator it gradually loses its heat to the radiator and condenses back into water. This water runs back down through the same pipe from which it entered (condensed water takes up much less volume than steam, so the water trickles out along the bottom of the pipe while the steam is rushing in along the top). The water runs back to the boiler by gravity and is reheated to create more steam. That is why in a steam system all pipes must slope downward from each radiator to the boiler. If there is a low spot or dip, water will be trapped inside the pipe at this point and the steam may not be able to get through.

Most steam boilers have glass gauges on the front to indicate the level of the water inside the boiler. There is also a pressure gauge with which you can compare actual pressure with correct pressure.

Maintenance of Steam Systems

When the pipes in a steam system start to bang and hammer every time the steam comes up, the first thing you should suspect is a low spot in one of the pipes—that is, a place where the pipe doesn't slope properly toward the boiler. As mentioned above, water becomes trapped there rather than flowing back to the boiler, and the steam cannot push its way through; what you hear is the water slamming against the walls of the pipe as the steam tries to force its way past. The only way to cure this condition is to correct the slope or pitch in that length of pipe, either by remounting it or by raising or lowering one end.

If the hammering and banging noises occur in a radiator, chances are that water is being trapped in that radiator. Place a spirit level on top of the radiator as shown to make certain the radiator slopes slightly *toward* the inlet valve through which the steam enters. The water should then flow out easily. If it doesn't, place a thin block of wood under the leg at the far end (the end away from the valve) to give the radiator a slight pitch toward the valve end. Make certain that the inlet valve is either fully opened or fully closed—partial opening is another common reason for knocking, banging, or failure of the radiator to heat up properly.

The cast-iron radiators that are used in steam systems (they may be the baseboard type or the freestanding type) have an automatic air vent built into one end (the end farther from the inlet valve). This vent allows air to bleed out automatically as steam enters, but does not allow the steam to escape. If it is not doing its job the incoming steam is blocked by the air that is al-

Placing a shim under the far end of a steam radiator to help trapped water escape

ready there and the radiator will not heat up properly.

If a steam radiator won't heat up when the steam comes up, even though the inlet valve is fully open, or if it only heats up part of the way across, then probably air has become trapped inside and is not getting out through the vent. To test for this, unscrew the vent and remove it while the steam is coming up. Air should come rushing out, then after a couple of seconds steam should be flowing out and the radiator should get hot all the way across. If this happens you know that the vent is at fault. Sometimes you can clean it by boiling it in vinegar, but in most cases your best bet is simply to replace it with a new one.

Steam boilers usually have a glass gauge on the front to indicate the water level, so check this regularly to see if more water is needed (in most older steam systems this must be done manually). If the water level is low, open the inlet valve and watch the gauge till the level rises to the desired height, then shut the valve off again.

This gauge can also show the condition of the water inside the boiler. If the water looks rusty, then draining and flushing the boiler is probably a good idea. To do this you shut off the power to the burner, then close the inlet valve and drain

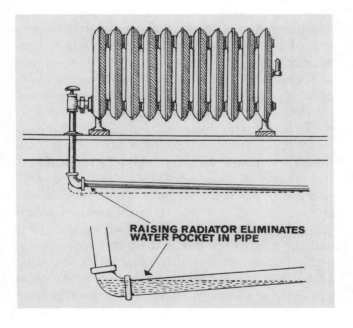

RAISING RADIATOR ELIMINATES WATER POCKET IN PIPE

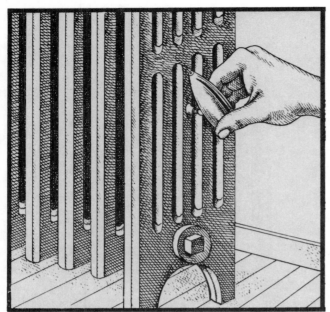

Unscrewing a steam radiator vent to see if air is trapped inside

as previously described for the boiler in a hot-water heating system (see page 271).

Sometimes the glass gauge will get so dirty that you cannot see the water inside at all. When this happens, take the glass tube out and clean it out by running a bottle brush through it—or replace it entirely with a new piece of glass tubing, available at plumbing supply outlets. To remove the glass tube, whether for cleaning or for replacement, shut off the valves at the top and the bottom of the tube, then loosen the compression nuts that hold the glass in place at top and bottom. You can then slide the glass up enough to permit lifting the bottom end out, after which you can tip it sideways slightly to slide the top end out.

WHAT YOU SHOULD KNOW ABOUT THERMOSTATS

Although a thermostat is the "brain" that starts and stops every central heating system, most homeowners pay little or no attention to this important little device until it actually fails to work. It's true that thermostats require very little, if any, maintenance, but it is still a good idea to remove the cover periodically and carefully vac-

uum out or blow out any dust or lint that has accumulated inside. Most thermostats have low-voltage wires coming to them, which pose no hazard, but there are some with a house-current line, so if you are not sure play safe and shut the circuit breaker off before opening the cover.

Other than this simple cleaning, a thermostat normally needs little or no maintenance on your part. It is a fairly delicate instrument that should not be fooled with by the average person, but there are some things you should know about it that can make a considerable difference in how your system operates—and, in fact, whether or not it operates at all.

First of all, if the unit is more than about fifteen years old it is probably a good idea to replace it entirely with a new one. New ones operate more efficiently with fewer spells of too much heat or too little heat, and they keep the temperature closer to the setting you desire. In addition, you can now buy models that have built-in timers or "computers" that can be programmed so that the heat will be turned down automatically each night, and up before you rise in the morning. These more sophisticated, computerized models allow for multiple setbacks each day—for example, they can also turn the setting down several times a day while everyone is out, yet raise it to the proper comfort level just before everyone comes home.

One thing that has an important effect on any thermostat is its location in the room. It can make a difference in the overall comfort level in the house (or at least in the zone that is controlled by the thermostat in those houses that are divided up into heating zones).

For example, a thermostat should never be located on an outside wall (where it will be affected by the colder surfaces in back of or inside that wall), and it should be at least 16 to 18 inches away from any corner where an outside wall meets the inside wall on which it is mounted. It should also be about 4 to 5 feet above floor level, and not where it can be subjected to cold drafts from an open window, intermittently opened door, or similar opening. Cold drafts will make it call for heat when the rest of the house is actually warm enough not to need it. By the same token, it is just as important that the thermostat not be located near a source of heat—a lamp, a

TV set, or a radio, for example. It also should not be in the same room with a fireplace that is used very often (or at least it should be as far away from the fireplace as practical). Generally speaking, it should be mounted where it will get a free and unobstructed flow of room air so that it will sense air temperatures fairly typical of the rooms (or the zone) it controls. Never block the thermostat by putting a large piece of furniture next to it, or by allowing heavy curtains or drapes to hang in front of it.

Most thermostats have a bimetallic coil or strip that senses small changes of temperature. This activates a set of contacts that close to call for heat when the temperature drops below the setting, then open to shut the heating system off when the temperature rises above that setting (there is actually a small "spread" of 1 or 2 degrees between the "on" limit and the "off" limit so that the unit won't be constantly turning itself on and off). In older models there are open contacts that come together when the circuit closes, and these can be affected by dust, lint, or even small amounts of corrosion. To clean them slide a sheet of ordinary writing paper or a new dollar bill between the contacts while gently rubbing back and forth. *Do not use sandpaper or other abrasives.*

The newer models use a sealed mercury switch, so there is no chance of dust or lint interfering with proper contact. However, dust and lint can accumulate on the bimetallic coil or strip that causes the mercury to tip (open and close), so cleaning the strip occasionally with a soft brush, or by blowing gently, is a good idea.

Replacing an old thermostat is not a particularly difficult job. After shutting off the power, you disconnect the wires from the old unit and unscrew it from the wall. You then pull the old wires through the opening in back of the new unit and remount it on the wall in place of the old one. Finally, reconnect the two wires to the two terminals on the new one.

Most thermostats operate on low voltages (15 to 30 volts) derived from a transformer that "steps down" the current, so they are safe for the do-it-yourselfer to change (even a 110-volt "line-voltage" model is not especially difficult to install if you make sure the power is off before you start). The voltage should be marked on the panel inside the thermostat (after you take the cover off), so check this before you go out and buy a new one. If you are not sure of the voltage needed, shut off the circuit breaker and remove the old unit from the wall, then take it with you so you can show it to the dealer to make certain you get one that operates on the same voltage.

When switching from an ordinary manually operated thermostat to one of the new clock-controlled models that give automatic setbacks, you may find that extra wires are required to run the clock mechanism, and this may mean fishing some extra wires up from the basement. There are other timed models, however, that draw their power from the same two wires, so that no extra wiring is required, and still others that have a built-in rechargeable battery to power the clock. (In these the battery is kept constantly charged by the low-voltage circuit.)

FIREPLACE PROBLEMS

Although the average wood-burning fireplace is not very efficient as a primary source of heat, it is still an extremely popular feature with homeowners for its aesthetic value—and for the warmth and pleasure that can be derived from watching a crackling fire on a winter night. But a fireplace that smokes incessantly and spews flying embers out into the room, or one that just won't keep a fire burning after it is lit, is hardly a pleasure—it is of little use to anyone, either for practical or aesthetic reasons. That is why it pays to learn how to use your fireplace properly and take steps to correct any defects that make it smoke or burn poorly.

The drawing on page 276 shows how a well-designed fireplace is constructed. Note that there is a smoke shelf directly behind or above the damper (at the base of the flue). This serves a very definite purpose—it deflects or turns back downdrafts so that they do not blow smoke out into the room; instead the smoke is sucked back into the upward draft and up the chimney.

There are fairly specific proportions that should be adhered to in the design of a masonry fireplace if it is to work properly. The total area of the opening in the front should be about 10 to 12 times that of the cross section of the flue

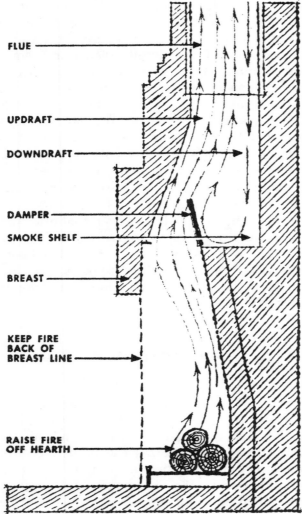

FLUE

UPDRAFT

DOWNDRAFT

DAMPER

SMOKE SHELF

BREAST

KEEP FIRE
BACK OF
BREAST LINE

RAISE FIRE
OFF HEARTH

Design and elements of a well-functioning fireplace

opening, assuming that the chimney is at least 15 feet in overall height. If the chimney is less than 15 feet in height, the fireplace opening should be proportionately smaller.

Even a well-designed fireplace will often smoke simply because the owner of the house doesn't know how to build a proper wood fire. Assuming that you start with seasoned wood (green wood will smoke a lot more easily and will make it much harder to keep the fire going), the first thing you should do is make sure the damper is wide open. Then spread a layer of crumpled newspaper over the floor of the fireplace, under the andirons (or inside the fire basket if you use one), and cover this with a layer of wood kindling, spreading the sticks or dried twigs so that

they crisscross each other on top of the paper.

On top of this kindling you build the actual fire, using three logs. Place the largest log at the back—that is, near the back wall but not quite touching it—and the second log about 2 to 3 inches in front of this one; then place another layer of kindling on top of these two logs so that it "bridges" the two logs. Put the third log on top between the other two so that the three logs form a sort of open pyramid.

Before starting the fire, light a large sheet of newspaper and hold it up near the throat of the fireplace, just under the damper. When it is almost burned up and flaming well, drop it on top of the logs and immediately light the layer of crumpled paper under the wood with another match. The reason for holding the flaming paper up in the throat of the fireplace is to warm the air in the chimney and start an upward draft that will help get the fire started and keep it from smoking before the chimney heats.

Probably the most frequent of all reasons that a fireplace smokes is that the fireplace opening is too large for the size of the flue, or the damper is too low (too close to the top of the opening). If the measurements of your fireplace opening do seem larger than they should be as described on page 275, or if you suspect that the damper is too low (not up inside the throat), then here is a simple test you can run to see if the problem can be easily corrected:

Insufficient Air Causes Smoking

One frequent cause of smoking in a home fireplace is a lack of sufficient combustion air—especially with a roaring fire going. Such a fire sends a large quantity of air up the chimney, air drawn out of the room in which the fireplace is located. This air must be replaced—either through an open door or window, or by means of natural infiltration from the outside (this is why the newest fireplace designs include ducts that go directly outside for intake of combustion air). If too little air gets into the room, the fire will not have sufficient draft, and smoke will back up into the room. If you suspect this problem, try opening a window in the room a few inches. The smoking may stop very quickly.

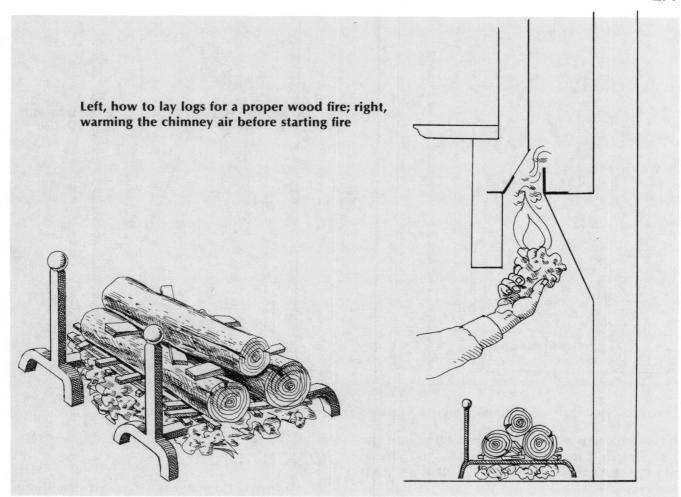

Left, how to lay logs for a proper wood fire; right, warming the chimney air before starting fire

Get a fire going in the fireplace, then hold a sheet of metal or a piece of water-soaked plywood across the top of the fireplace opening. It should be about 12 to 18 inches wide and at least 6 to 8 inches longer than the width of the fireplace opening. Starting at the very top, slide this piece slowly downward to give the effect of a decreased opening height for the fireplace. Keep moving it down till the smoking stops. This will indicate the correct size for the opening. You can then have a permanent metal hood or shield built across the top to close off the opening by this amount, or you can build the opening up from the bottom by placing extra rows of firebrick on the floor of the fireplace.

Another frequent cause of smoking is downdrafts—especially when a stiff wind is blowing. This condition can be due to the fact that the chimney is not high enough in relation to nearby dormers, peaks, or other structural parts of the

house, or it can be caused by an overhanging tree branch that may be interfering with a free flow of air past the top of the chimney. The chimney should project at least 3 feet above a flat roof, and at least 2 feet higher than the ridge of a sloping roof when that ridge—or any other part of the roof—is less than 10 feet from the chimney. Large trees or overhanging branches should also be at least 10 feet away if they are taller than the chimney.

Very often the simplest cure is just to extend the chimney higher, either by actually building the brickwork higher or by adding sections of metal chimney pipe to the top. The extension should have a flue that is at least as large as the original flue inside the chimney.

Sometimes it also helps to install a hood on top of the chimney, in the form either of a metal cap or a masonry slab supported by bricks set up on each corner of the chimney top. If the chimney

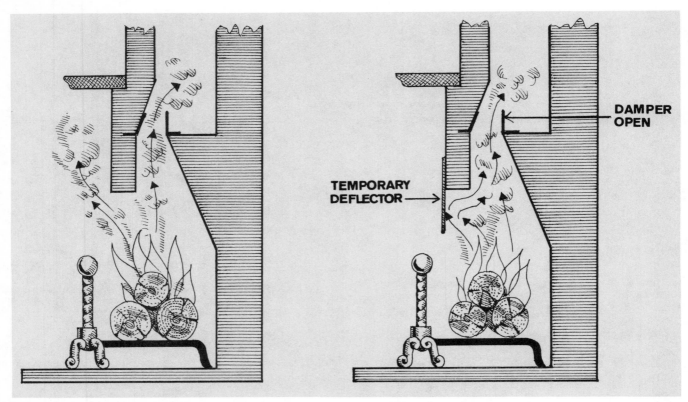

DAMPER OPEN

TEMPORARY DEFLECTOR

Temporary deflector will help determine if fireplace opening is too large.

has more than one flue (one for the fireplace and one for the furnace, for example), you should erect a vertical divider of brick (called a wythe) between the two.

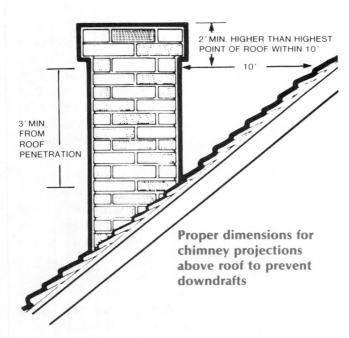

2′ MIN. HIGHER THAN HIGHEST POINT OF ROOF WITHIN 10′

10′

3′ MIN. FROM ROOF PENETRATION

Proper dimensions for chimney projections above roof to prevent downdrafts

MAINTAINING CENTRAL AIR-CONDITIONING SYSTEMS

The principal components of an air conditioner are usually factory-sealed (compressor and motor, for example), so there is actually very little maintenance required. This does not mean they should be ignored completely. There are some preventive maintenance measures that will help prolong the life of the equipment and that will often serve to prevent unexpected breakdowns.

Central systems that cool the whole house should have a "tuneup" in the late winter or early spring of each year by a competent professional. He will check for the possibility of leaking refrigerant, loose or worn drive belts, improper internal operating pressures in the system, and the need for internal cleaning of coils, fins, and other components. All central systems also have large filters through which the circulating air passes repeatedly, and these too will need inspecting, and replacing if they are dirty.

During the season a filter should be checked at least once a month to see if it needs cleaning or replacing (most are simply replaced when dirty, but some are washable and can be reused). The best way to check the condition of the air filter is to remove it and hold it up to a bright light, then try to look through it. If you can see the light easily, the filter is okay. But if it is hard to see through the filter or the light is very dim, the filter should be cleaned or replaced.

Although some air conditioners have permanently lubricated bearings that never need oiling, others may require periodic lubrication of motors, blowers, etc. If you are not sure about this, check your owner's manual, or ask your regular serviceman to tell you when and where lubrication is required.

If your air conditioner has an outside-mounted condensing unit, it should be cleaned of accumulated debris, especially near the inlet and outlet discharge grilles. Use a brush or hose to clean out leaves and windblown dirt or dust.

Make sure all indoor discharge grilles or louvers (in walls or ceilings) are kept free of dust and lint when the unit is in use, since this can cut down on airflow considerably. Use a vacuum cleaner once a month to clean off the louvers, and once a year remove them entirely so that you can clean off the back of the louver, as well as the inside of the ducts as far as you can reach easily.

MAINTAINING ROOM AIR CONDITIONERS

Room air conditioners also require comparatively little maintenance, since their important components are sealed units too. But since few people would think of calling a serviceman in for an annual checkup of a room unit, doing a little preventive maintenance yourself is a good habit if you want your machine to keep operating at maximum efficiency and to last a long time.

Regardless of whether the machine is mounted in a window or in a permanent opening in the outside wall, leakage of air around the case or housing will waste great amounts of energy and thus will sharply cut down on the effectiveness of the machine. If warm air seeps in from outside, it will add greatly to the load on that machine when it is running.

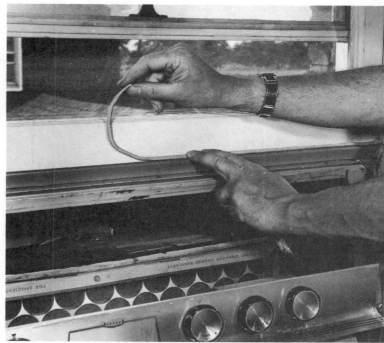

Foam stripping along top and sides of a room air conditioner helps prevent air leakage.

Window-mounted units usually have special panels at each side to close off the opening, and these should have foam stripping along the top and bottom to keep warm air from infiltrating around the outside of the cabinet. Units that go through the wall fit into a metal "sleeve" or shell that is permanently installed in the wall (the machine can be slid in and out much like a drawer when it needs servicing). This metal sleeve should be well caulked around the outside where it fits against the siding, and it should have some type of stripping on the inside to provide an airtight seal after the machine is slid into place. Both these seals—on the outside and the inside—should be checked at the beginning of each season to see if repair or replacement is needed.

It is also important that you clean the grille and the condenser coils in the outside part of the machine (these are behind the grille and can be cleaned after the grille has been removed). The condenser, in effect the outer half of the machine, consists of coils and fins that serve to disperse the heat removed from inside the room. Anything that interferes with a free flow of air to and from this mechanism will seriously hamper the efficiency of the unit and thus greatly add to operating costs.

Sometimes you can reach the condenser from the outside, but in other cases it is easier to work

Vacuum-cleaning an air-conditioner grille for improved efficiency

from inside, after sliding the unit inward to make it more accessible. With window units this may mean temporarily removing the unit from its place on the sill. With through-the-wall units the machine can be slid inward, out of its sleeve.

While cleaning the condenser and outside grilles, don't forget the coils and fins on the evaporator section (the inside part). Use a soft brush and a vacuum to remove dust and lint wherever you can reach, and wipe off the louvers or grilles on the inner half of the cabinet (the intake and exhaust grilles).

This is also the time to look for bent fins—which should be straightened very carefully—as well as for dust and lint on the fan blades—which should be wiped off with a soft cloth. Also, lubricate any motors or fans that need oiling by adding two or three drops of 20-weight oil to each oil hole or oil cup (most of the newer units do not need oiling; they are permanently lubricated at the factory).

Inspect the metal parts on the inside to look for signs of rusting, and scrape off any carefully with a little fine steel wool. Wipe off the dust,

then touch up the bare metal with a rust-resistant metal primer. Pay particular attention to the pan at the bottom that catches condensed water, to make sure the drain hole at the back of this pan is not clogged. Also, make sure that when the unit is in place the pan slopes slightly toward the back for proper drainage. (Some of the newer units no longer have condensate drains; instead, small heaters evaporate the water on the outside, so no drain is needed.)

After the unit has been cleaned, oiled, and replaced in its normal position, take the filter out and see if it needs cleaning or replacement (see page 281). If the unit is used daily, make sure you check this filter at least once every two to three weeks, and replace or clean it as soon as it shows signs of becoming partially clogged.

Whenever the machine is in use, make sure there are no curtains, shades, or large pieces of furniture positioned where they can block the flow of air to and from the front grilles. Also make certain the unit is plugged into a circuit of its own (a circuit that has no other appliance plugged into it—at least not one that is drawing current at the same time) and that it has the kind of heavy-duty cord required for a machine of that size.

Installing an Air Conditioner Through the Wall

Although a conventional room air conditioner designed for mounting in a window can be installed in an opening cut through the wall, it is

Lubricating oil holes of motors and fans may be necessary with some older models.

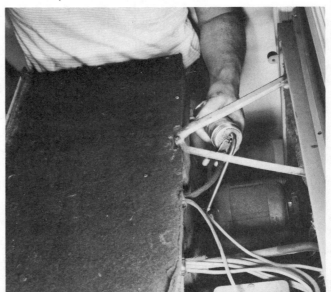

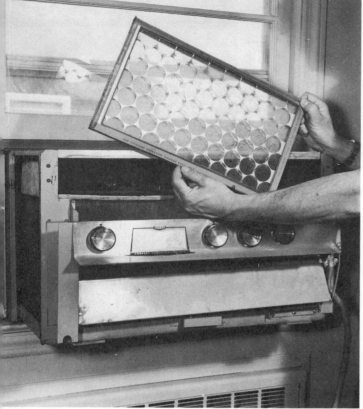

Air-conditioning filters should be checked after two or three weeks of continual operation.

far better to buy one that is specially designed for through-the-wall installation. Such a unit will have a metal "sleeve" or housing that is installed in the wall first to ensure the proper opening. The machine then slides into this housing from the inside. Also, through-the-wall units have their outside louvers or grilles (the ones used for cooling the condenser on the outside) positioned so as to project out past the wall and ensure a free flow of air on the outside. A window unit often has these openings on the sides, not far

enough back to clear the thickness of the house wall. In an ordinary frame house this will probably be no problem, but in houses with brick or block walls the cabinet may not project out far enough to provide clearance for the condenser openings near the back.

The illustrations below show the basic steps involved in installing an air conditioner through the wall. Mark the size of the opening needed for the cabinet on the inside wall first, if possible locating the opening so that only one wall stud will have to be cut. You can do this by placing one side of the opening alongside one stud and work over from there, or you can center the opening between three studs so that only the one in the center will have to be cut. Be sure the location you pick has no wires or pipes running through its part of the wall.

After marking out the opening, cut through the plaster or gypsum board on the inside to expose the studs, then cut off the stud that is in the way (the one that goes through the center in most cases). Use a drill with a long bit, or a hand brace and bit, to drill holes through to the outside at each corner of this cutout. These holes will mark the size and location of the opening on the outside, so that you can then go out and cut the same size opening in the exterior siding, using an electric saber saw or portable circular saw.

When this outside opening has been cut, you are ready to frame out the entire opening with pieces of 2×4, as shown. This can be done either from the inside or the outside, but it is generally more convenient to work from the inside. Nail one piece of 2×4 across the bottom of the open-

Installing an air conditioner through a wall: left, framing out studs from the inside; center, outside framing; right, air conditioner installed inside, with trim

ing and one across the top, then install the two short vertical pieces between them at each end of the opening.

To finish off the opening and create a casing against which molding or trim can be applied on both inside and outside, you install an inner framing of 1×6 lumber, as shown, nailing it flat against the 2×4s just installed along the top, bottom, and sides of the opening. This should create the exact size opening needed for the metal

sleeve, so you can then slide it in easily. When the sleeve or housing is in place, fasten it to the 1×6 framing with rustproof screws driven through the sides. Make certain it slopes slightly toward the outside to ensure proper drainage of condensation and rainwater.

Finally, finish the job off by nailing the desired trim around both the inside and outside of the new opening, and then applying caulking around the outside edges.

Chapter 12

Working with Concrete and Masonry

ALTHOUGH MOST people use the words "cement" and "concrete" interchangeably, there is a big difference between the two. Cement—more accurately referred to as portland cement—is one ingredient in concrete (as well as in mortar and stucco). It is made by firing a special type of crushed rock, then grinding it to a fine gray powder. Mixed with sand, water, and lime, cement forms mortar; mixed with sand, water, and gravel, it forms concrete.

Portland cement is normally sold in 94-pound bags, which contain 1 cubic foot by volume. When making concrete, professional engineers vary the proportions of aggregate (sand and gravel) used per bag of cement, depending on the need for extra strength or extra resistance to water penetration, but for most jobs around the house a good all-purpose formula is 1 part cement, 2½ parts sand, and 3 to 3½ parts gravel. All parts refer to volume (1 shovelful or 1 bucketful of each ingredient being 1 part). A full bag of cement, mixed with the sand and gravel, will make about 4½ cubic feet of mixed concrete when the right amount of water is added.

For patching stucco and concrete (more about this in the pages that follow), cement is mixed only with sand and water. While proportions may vary for specific purposes, as a rule a good all-purpose mix is 1 part cement and 3 parts fine sand (a special mortar cement is generally used for making mortar, rather than regular portland cement).

Although mixing your own from scratch is cheapest for sizable amounts of concrete or mortar, for small jobs you will probably find it quicker and easier to buy the dry ready-mixed material that comes in bags and requires only water. Three basic types are sold in hardware stores and home centers:

Sand mix contains only cement and sand and is good for small patching jobs in all types of masonry.

Concrete mix contains gravel or coarse aggregate in addition to cement and sand. It is the right mix for making sizable patches in concrete, for building up broken or missing sections of walks and driveways, and for most general concrete work around the house.

Mortar mix is, as the name implies, mainly for laying brick and block, but you will also need it for tuck-pointing existing mortar joints (replacing old mortar that is cracking or crumbling—described later in this chapter).

All of these ready-mixed products come in bags of various sizes. They are not only more convenient than buying separate ingredients and mixing your own, they may also be the only practical solution, because in some communities it is often difficult to buy small quantities of sand and gravel. If you don't intend to use the whole bag, pour all of the contents out and mix the dry

Small amounts of concrete or mortar can be mixed in a wheelbarrow.

ingredients thoroughly. Then, before adding water, put back in the bag what you don't think you'll need. Follow the recommendations on the package as to how much water to add.

Mixing Your Own Concrete

Adding the right amount of water to the mix is just as important as having the right proportions of cement, sand, and gravel, because this can greatly affect the strength of the cured concrete. The exact amount of water will usually depend greatly on the wetness or dryness of the sand.

If the sand is of average dampness (when you squeeze it into a ball it retains its rough shape, but leaves no moisture on your fingers), you can generally figure on adding about 5 gallons of water to each batch that uses a full bag of cement. If the sand is wet enough so that water runs out when you squeeze it, cut the amount of water down to a little over 4 gallons. And if the sand is fairly dry and doesn't hold its shape when squeezed, add from 5½ to 6 gallons of water to each batch.

Another way to test for the right consistency of a mix is to jab the back of the shovel into the surface of the mix while dragging it backward over the heaped-up material. The dragging motion will tend to smooth the top over, while jabbing the shovel in will cut or groove the surface to form a series of ridges.

Concrete can be mixed on a plywood sheet, using a hoe or shovel.

If each groove or ridge remains distinct, the mixture is just about right. If the grooves crumble or are not distinct, then more water is needed; if they tend to fill in or level out, then too much water has been added and you will have to add more cement, sand, and gravel to absorb it.

The actual mixing of ingredients can be done by hand with a shovel or hoe, or with a power mixer, which you can rent from local tool rental

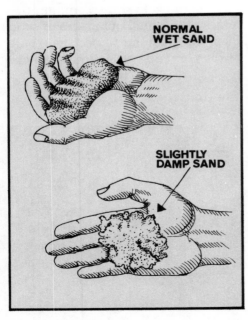

NORMAL WET SAND

SLIGHTLY DAMP SAND

When mixing concrete, squeeze sand to determine how damp it is, thus how much water to add.

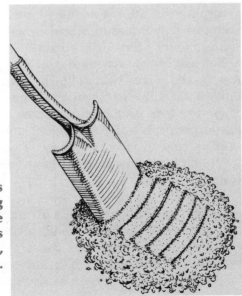

Check concrete's consistency by making ridges in mix with the back of a shovel. If ridges stay the same, consistency is correct.

Working with Ready-Mix or Transit-Mix

If you really have a lot of concrete to mix, then you may want to buy ready-mix or transit-mix, which is delivered in large trucks that do the mixing en route. Concrete companies usually have a minimum delivery requirement, so check with local suppliers to see if you need enough to meet this minimum. If you tell the dealer the size of the project he will be able to tell you how many cubic yards of concrete you need.

Before the delivery is made, try to arrange for the truck to back up to where the concrete can be poured directly into the forms. If this is not possible, you will have to arrange for wheelbarrows to carry the mix from the truck to the forms. Lay planks for the wheelbarrows if the ground is soft, and remember that most companies allow only a short time for unloading (30 minutes is typical).

Often this means you will need some helpers to get the truck unloaded (if you have to use wheelbarrows), and you may also have to rent one or two extra wheelbarrows for the time it takes to unload. Also, make sure your forms are all ready for pouring before the truck arrives, and that you have all necessary tools and equipment on hand for filling the forms and smoothing the concrete after it is poured.

If possible, arrange for transit-mix to be poured from truck directly into forms (left). **Otherwise, a wheelbarrow can transfer concrete from the truck to the forms** (right).

Renting a power mixer is best when large quantities of concrete are needed.

agencies. When mixing by hand, measure out the sand and gravel first, then add the cement on top. Work on a sheet of plywood or a clean paved area, and turn and mix the pile with the shovel until it is uniform in color and texture. Then spread the material around in a "ring" with a deep depression in the center as shown on page 286, and start adding water to the center.

Add the water in small amounts, and mix the dry ingredients thoroughly into the center until the water is absorbed and the mixture starts to get crumbly. Then add a little more water. Remember—it is much easier to add more water if the mixture is too dry than it is to add more cement, sand, and gravel if the mixture is too wet. So add water slowly and mix it in well as you go.

If you have more than one or two bags to mix, you will find it worthwhile to rent a power-driven mixer. When using one, you start the drum while it is still empty, then begin shoveling in the gravel. Add some of the water, then add the required amount of sand and more water, then the cement. Finally, add the rest of the water. Again, don't forget to add water slowly, stopping when the mix is a uniform gray color and looks reasonably damp, not yet soupy.

Pouring a Walk or Patio

Regardless of whether you mix your own or buy transit-mix, forms must be set up before you start to pour. The forms are most often made of 2×4s set on edge, but they can also be made of thinner material (1-inch boards) if the lengths are not too great and if you have enough stakes to keep the form boards from curving or bulging. Of course, if you want a curved form, then you will need thinner boards—in fact, for real free-form outlines, strips of ¼-inch plywood supported by stakes spaced close enough together will maintain the overall shape.

A walk or patio should be at least 3½ inches thick, so you will have to excavate the soil at least this deep if you want the surface of the walk to be flush with the ground next to it. Set the 2×4 form boards in place around the perimeter of the excavation, and space supporting stakes no more than about 3 feet apart along the outside. Nail the form boards to the stakes to secure them.

If the soil has a high clay content it will drain poorly, so dig down an extra 3 inches and spread a 3-inch layer of coarse sand or fine gravel over the bottom before pouring the concrete on top.

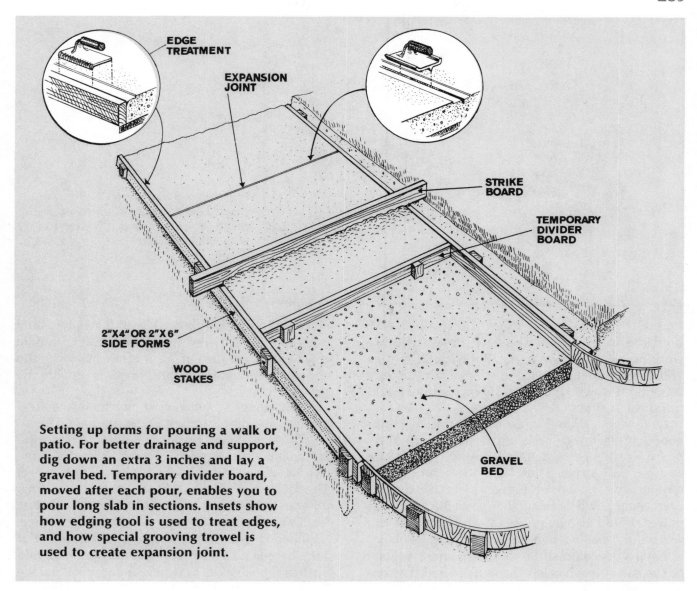

EDGE TREATMENT

EXPANSION JOINT

STRIKE BOARD

TEMPORARY DIVIDER BOARD

2"X4" OR 2"X 6" SIDE FORMS

WOOD STAKES

GRAVEL BED

Setting up forms for pouring a walk or patio. For better drainage and support, dig down an extra 3 inches and lay a gravel bed. Temporary divider board, moved after each pour, enables you to pour long slab in sections. Insets show how edging tool is used to treat edges, and how special grooving trowel is used to create expansion joint.

This sub-base will help ensure good drainage and minimize the likelihood of future heaving and cracking—especially in areas where the ground freezes during the winter.

Driveways have to carry heavier loads—the family cars plus an occasional large delivery truck—so they should be approximately 6 inches thick. This means using 2×6s for the form boards, instead of 2×4s, and it means digging down a couple of inches farther to provide the extra depth for the concrete. Here again, if the soil does not drain well, it's a good idea to dig down an extra 2 or 3 inches and put down a sub-base of coarse sand or fine gravel.

As the concrete is poured into the forms, use your shovel to spread it around and poke it into all corners. Make sure you eliminate all air bubbles and hollow pockets, and continue pouring until the forms are filled to about ½ inch higher than the form boards to allow for settling and compacting. Avoid handling or moving the mix around any more than necessary. Too much working and turning causes the concrete to separate or settle, and may result in a surface that will powder excessively later on.

When the form has been filled, hold a long 2×4 on edge as shown on page 290 top and "strike off" or screed the surface so it is level with the

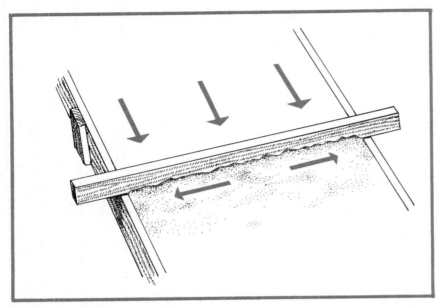

After concrete has been poured, hold a long 2×4 on edge and move it back and forth while pushing forward to strike off the surface and level it with the tops of form boards.

tops of the form boards. You will need a helper to hold the other end of the 2×4, unless you are working on a narrow walk. Work the 2×4 back and forth with a seesaw motion, lifting it and bringing it down sharply at intervals in order to tamp the concrete down.

Long walks should be broken up into sections about 10 feet long. Set up a temporary form board at the end of a 10-foot section, fill up the section, and strike it off. You then remove the temporary form board and set it up 10 feet farther along, and repeat the procedure. (Large patios should also be poured in sections that you can handle easily when striking off and leveling.)

Final surface finishing should be done as soon as the wet sheen has left the surface and the concrete has started to stiffen slightly. Don't do your final troweling or floating (with a wood float) before this, or the surface will be weakened considerably and will be much more likely to flake and powder later on.

For a textured, nonskid surface, use a wood float (also called a darby) for the final troweling, rubbing it over the surface in a series of circular motions and making no more than one or two circles over each spot. A wood float is something like a regular trowel, only its blade is wood instead of metal. A wood float the size of a conventional steel trowel is fine for most jobs small enough so that you can reach across from one side to the other, but for wider areas you can make a larger version known as a bull float. This

consists of a straight board about 3 to 4 feet long and 7 to 8 inches in width. Attach a long handle so that you can drag it back and forth over the surface of the concrete while kneeling outside the forms.

For a smoother or slicker finish, use a steel trowel immediately after using the wood float. Go over the concrete once, holding the trowel flat against the surface, then trowel the same area again with the leading edge of the trowel slightly raised. Finish with a third troweling, holding the leading edge still higher, pressing down harder and moving your arm in wide arcs.

Finishing off the edges is the final step. For this, there is a special trowel that rounds off and finishes the edges as you slide it along just inside the form boards, as shown in the illustration on

For a textured nonskid surface, rub in an oval pattern with a wood float.

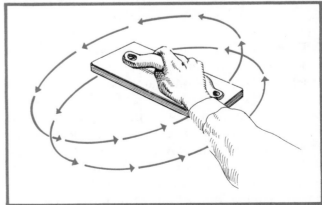

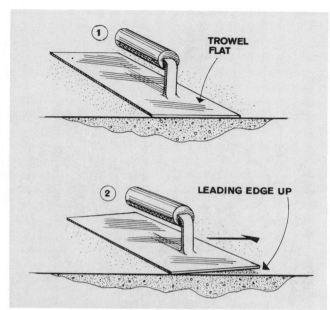

For a smoother finish, apply a steel trowel to surface after using wood float. Trowel three times: once while holding trowel flat, then with its leading edge up, and again with the leading edge still higher, but pressing harder.

page 289. This should not be done until after the concrete has begun to stiffen and there are no signs of wetness still evident.

For concrete to achieve full strength it must cure properly—and this means it must dry slowly. This is especially important in hot weather when the sun is shining on the surface. To keep the concrete from drying too fast, keep the surface covered with a layer of burlap, straw, or similar lightweight, porous material. Wet this

covering down with a fine spray right after you put it on, then keep it damp continuously for at least 72 hours.

Another method is to cover the damp concrete slab with a layer of lightweight plastic—this will slow up drying for quite a while without need for continuous spraying during the curing period.

PATCHING CONCRETE AND MASONRY

Although concrete and masonry structures are supposedly maintenance-free, repairs are often necessary because of cracking, settling, and heaving of the soil on which the paved area lies. If cracks are not filled promptly, water will enter and cause further deterioration, especially in the winter when freezing causes the water inside to expand.

Very small cracks in stucco or concrete can be filled easily with a caulking compound containing butyl or silicone rubber. Just dust the crack out thoroughly and make sure it is dry, then force the caulking compound in and smooth off the excess with a putty knife.

For a more permanent repair, and for filling cracks larger than about 1/16 inch wide, you'll need patching cement—either one of the cement-and-sand mixes that come in bags, or one of the vinyl-concrete patching cements. If you use a sand-mix patching cement, then you will have to "undercut" the edges of the crack first. With the corner of a cold chisel, cut out the crack so that it

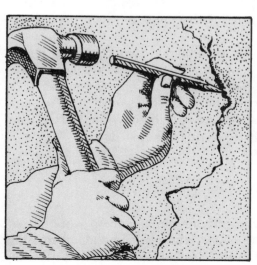

For patching a large crack in masonry, undercut the crack with a hammer and chisel (left), wet crack thoroughly, then trowel in fresh patching compound (right).

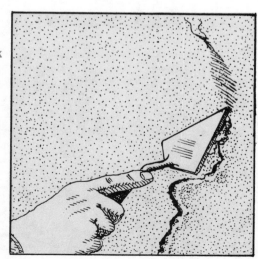

is wider on the inside than it is at the surface. Brush out all dust and chips, then wet the crack thoroughly before troweling in the freshly mixed patching cement.

For many small repairs, vinyl-concrete patching cement is easier and stronger than a conventional sand-mix cement. It costs more, but it has a much finer consistency, and its vinyl or acrylic binders greatly increase bonding strength. It bonds best when applied in small sections, and it can be "feathered out" in thin layers without flaking off later on (sand-mix patching cement must be applied at least ½ inch thick or it will flake off). These vinyl-concrete patching cements also eliminate the need for prewetting the surfaces, and for undercutting the cracks ahead of time (because their bond is much stronger). They come in the form of a dry powder that must be mixed with water.

When a larger patch is required—say to build up the broken corner of a stoop—then a cement-and-sand mix will generally hold its shape better and be easier to work with. Brush away loose dust and dirt, and wet the area thoroughly with water. Mix the dry ingredients with water according to the directions on the package, and trowel the patching cement on, packing it into

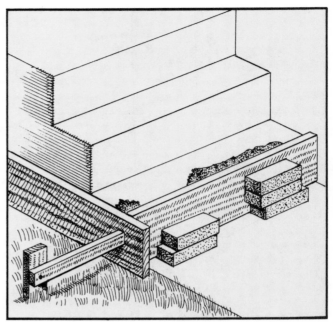

To hold corner patch in place while it hardens, erect temporary form boards, propping them in place with stakes.

When patching broken corners, add latex masonry adhesive to cement patching mix to strengthen the bond.

the crevices firmly, then smooth it off neatly around the outside.

To increase the strength of this kind of patch, and to make it bond better, it is a good idea to add some latex masonry adhesive to the mix. Also, brush some of the adhesive over the surface of the old masonry before you apply the new cement. This will help increase the strength of the bond between old and new concrete.

Where necessary, temporary form boards of plywood or lumber can be erected to keep the patch in place and prevent sagging. Prop these boards in place with stakes or with any convenient prop.

Try to avoid working in the hot sun, but if you must, make sure the surfaces are wet before you start and keep the patch damp for at least 24 hours after you have finished—either by using a fine spray at intervals, or by covering with a thin sheet of plastic during the first day.

PATCHING STUCCO

Ordinary sand-mix patching cement can be used for patching cracks and replacing small missing sections of stucco, following the techniques de-

Patching a Sidewalk or Driveway

When repairing a broken section on a concrete sidewalk, patio, or driveway, the best procedure is to break out and remove the badly cracked or settled section first. You then compact the exposed earth by tamping firmly with the end of a piece of 4×4, and set up a temporary form board of 2×4 or 1×4 as shown here. The upper edge of this form board should be exactly level with the surface of the existing pavement. The board is held in position with a couple of wood stakes driven in along the outside.

Clean off the exposed, broken edges of the old concrete, then apply a liberal coat of latex ma- sonry adhesive as described on page 292. Now mix up a batch of fresh concrete, either with a bag of dry ready-mix concrete (sold in hardware stores and home centers), or by mixing your own from sand, gravel, and cement (see page 286). Then shovel this into the cavity enclosed by the form boards.

Poke it firmly into all corners to eliminate air pockets, then "strike off" the surface with a length of 2×4 held edgewise as shown. Move this back and forth with a zigzag motion, compact the surface, and scrape off all excess so the surface is level with the old concrete. Wait until it starts to stiffen slightly, then smooth off with a wood float and trowel as described on page 290.

When patching a sidewalk, erect a temporary form board level with the surface of the existing pavement (left). **After applying patching mix, strike off the surface with a 2×4 held on edge** (right).

scribed in the previous pages for concrete and masonry. Make sure you undercut the patch or edge of the broken stucco to help "lock in" the patch firmly, so it will be less likely to crack out or break loose later on. Use a cold chisel or stiff putty knife to chip away all the loose or crumbling material, and don't start patching until only sound, firmly bonded material remains.

If the stucco has come off down to the wire lath, or down to the masonry backing (if there is no wire lath), then apply the new material in two or three coats, rather than in one thick layer. Wet the surface thoroughly, then apply the first coat in a ⅜-inch-thick layer, pressing it firmly into the wire mesh so that you completely cover it. Wait until this first coat, called the "scratch" coat, starts to stiffen, then use a scrap piece of wire mesh or board with a row of nails driven through it to scratch multiple lines in the surface of this first coat. This helps to ensure a better bond when the second coat is applied.

Allow the scratch coat to harden for at least 5

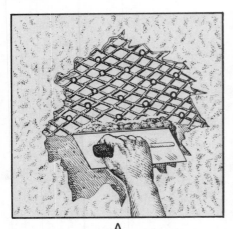
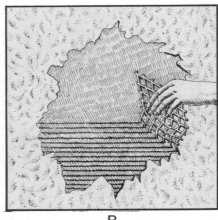
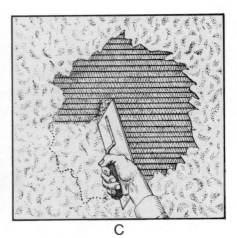

A B C

A. Coat of cement is troweled on over lath after nailing wire lath over area where material has been removed. B. First coat is scratched with scrap of lath while material is still soft. C. Final coat is troweled on over scratch coat, and textured to match original surface.

to 6 hours, then apply the second coat, called the brown coat. This is troweled on to bring the mass up to within about ⅛ inch of the surface, and when finished it is rubbed with a wood float to give it a slight texture. The brown coat should cure for at least 24 to 36 hours before the finish coat is applied, and it should be kept damp the

To achieve one popular type of stucco texturing, dip a large brush into the stucco mix, then spatter it onto the surface.

whole time. Then, the finish coat is troweled on and textured to match the surface of the existing stucco. It too should be kept damp for about 24 hours after you are done.

Matching the texture of the patch to the old surface may take some experimentation for a reasonably close result. In some cases you can use a stiff brush (like a small whisk broom), swirling it back and forth as you drag it over the surface. In other cases, the texture is created by working the wet finish coat with a trowel; you make a series of swirl marks by twisting the handle as you swing your arm back and forth in an arc. Another popular type of texturing calls for dipping a large brush into the stucco, then using it to spatter the material onto the surface.

In each case, if color must be added it is mixed in with the wet finish coat before you trowel it on. Just remember that the dry color will be much lighter than the wet color, so experiment with small batches applied to a scrap surface, letting these dry so you can check the color before going ahead with the actual job.

MORTAR JOINTS AND LOOSE BRICKS

A problem in a brick wall or chimney is almost always due to a failure of one or more mortar joints. Either the mortar has cracked and crumbled, or it is no longer bonding properly. Sometimes this is simply the result of aging, but more often it is due to the improper mixing or application of the mortar in the first place. Either way, defective mortar joints should be repaired as soon as possible in order to prevent excessive penetration of moisture, which can hasten deterioration of the entire structure.

The process of repairing mortar joints is normally referred to as tuck pointing. It involves scraping or chipping out the old mortar to a depth of at least ½ inch, then filling in with new mortar. To scrape out the old mortar you can use the corner of an old cold chisel, or a special type of masonry chisel called a cape chisel. Sometimes scraping is enough, but often you will have to tap lightly on the handle of the chisel with a hammer in order to remove stubborn sections. Work carefully to avoid chipping the brick or loosening adjoining ones, and use a wire brush to clean out chips. Finish with a stiff brush to remove loose dust and particles.

For mortar you can buy dry ready-mixed mortar cement, or you can mix your own out of cement and sand. If you do decide to mix your own, buy mortar cement rather than portland cement—it makes a more plastic and better-bonding mortar. Mix 1 part of this cement with 3 parts fine sand. If you use portland cement, mix 1 part cement with 1 part hydrated lime and to this add 6 parts fine sand (all measurements are by volume).

Mix the dry ingredients thoroughly, then add water slowly until you create a buttery mix that will hold its shape without sagging when heaped up on a trowel, yet will not crumble when worked with the trowel. Spray the bricks with a hose, then pack the mortar in firmly with a triangular-shaped bricklayer's trowel similar to the one illustrated below center.

The mortar is carried to the wall on a tool called a hawk. You can buy a metal one, or you can make your own by nailing a 12-inch-square piece of plywood to the end of a short piece of broomstick for the handle (see drawing on page 296 top). Scrape the mortar off the hawk with your trowel, then pack it into the joint while holding the hawk underneath. Excess mortar will be caught by the hawk and easily reused.

After each joint is filled, allow the mortar to set for about 5 minutes, or until it just starts to stiffen. Then finish off the surface of the joint by tooling it so that it matches the appearance of the surrounding joints. This finishing off is not merely for aesthetic reasons—tooling compresses the surface of the mortar and makes it much more resistant to moisture penetration.

The drawing on page 296 bottom shows some of the most common styles for finishing off mortar joints. Many patterns can be achieved with the point of a trowel—such as the vee, struck, weathered, and flush designs. The concave finish can be achieved by dragging a round piece of wood or metal rod along the joint, while the

Tuck-pointing mortar joints (left to right): Scrape out old mortar with chisel; apply mortar mix from a hawk with a bricklayer's trowel, holding hawk underneath to catch excess mortar; then tool surface to match finish and to compress the mortar.

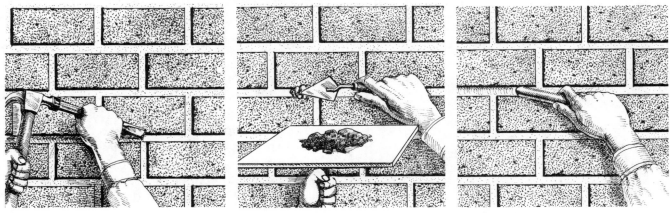

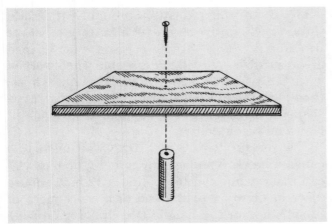

Constructing a hawk out of a 12-inch-square piece of plywood and a short piece of broomstick

raked joint can be finished by using the edge of a piece of wood whose thickness is just slightly less than the width of the joint.

While finishing off the joints, scrape off any excess mortar on the face of the brick with the edge of the trowel, or scrub it off with a stiff brush. Try to keep the newly pointed mortar joints damp for at least 12 hours by spraying with a fine mist as needed, especially in hot weather.

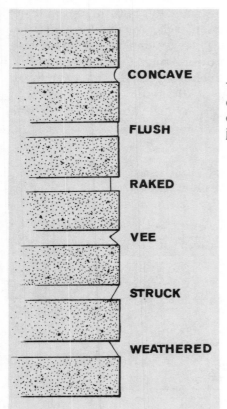

CONCAVE

FLUSH

RAKED

VEE

STRUCK

WEATHERED

The most common styles of brick mortar joint finishes

When a brick works loose on an old wall, it may not be possible to use mortar to cement the brick back into place unless you first remove most of the old mortar to make room for the new material (mortar must be applied at least ½ inch thick to bond properly). In some cases you will have no difficulty in chipping out the old remaining mortar, especially if you are careful to tap the corner of the chisel under the mortar so you work the tip between it and the brick. But in other cases the mortar may be so tightly stuck that chipping it off means damaging the brick or loosening additional ones.

If you do find that the old mortar is still sticking tightly, the simplest solution may be to leave it in place, and cement the loose bricks back with an epoxy adhesive. A two-part epoxy adhesive will bond to any clean, dry masonry surface and is particularly useful for corner bricks, which always seem to be getting knocked loose on stoops or walls.

An epoxy can also be used to permanently repair cracked or split bricks when the crack is too fine for patching with cement. The epoxy will penetrate and bond the pieces together as it cures.

PATCHING AND SEALING BLACKTOP

Asphalt walks and driveways, more commonly referred to as blacktop, are comparatively easy to repair when holes or cracks develop—but since blacktop is softer than concrete and not as tough, repairs will be required more frequently. It is best to do this kind of work when temperatures are above 60 degrees, because the material will be easier to work and patches will bond better.

For most patching jobs you can use one of the ready-made cold-mix asphalt patching materials that are sold in most lumberyards and hardware stores. The material should not be lumpy in the bag; if it is, bring the bag indoors and store it in a warm location overnight (be careful where you place the bag—most leak a little and will stain a floor—or put a sheet of plastic under it).

Clean out the hole or crack to remove dirt, leaves, and other debris. If the hole is more than

Patching asphalt. Apply ready-mixed patching compound with a shovel, packing it hard into corners to eliminate air pockets.

Next, shovel enough additional material into the hole to make it slightly higher than the surrounding surface, then tamp again to bring it down. If necessary, add more material to once again bring the surface up higher than the surrounding area. Finally, drive one wheel of your car back and forth over the patch to pack it down completely. To keep the fresh asphalt from sticking to the tire, sprinkle a layer of fine sand over the surface of the patch before rolling the car over it.

Small cracks that are too fine for patching in this manner are best filled by making your own "putty" out of fine sand mixed with some liquid driveway sealer (also called blacktop sealer). Mix to a stiff consistency, then trowel it into the crack and pack it down as much as you can. Allow it to stick slightly higher than the surface when finished, then tamp firmly to bring it down flush.

Most experts recommend that blacktop driveways be given a coat of sealer at least once every two or three years. This not only fills in hairline cracks that would otherwise allow moisture to enter and freeze (thus causing faster deterioration of the entire driveway), it also helps protect the surface against stains caused by penetration of oil or grease. Blacktop sealers come in 5-gallon cans and are poured onto the surface, then spread around with a long-handled brush, roller, or squeegee. Two coats are generally recom-

about 4 inches deep, shovel in some gravel or coarse sand to fill it up to within 3 inches of the top, then tamp this down firmly with the end of a piece of 4×4. Now shovel the cold-mix patching material in, packing it hard into all corners to compact it and eliminate air pockets. Fill the hole about halfway up, then tamp this layer down.

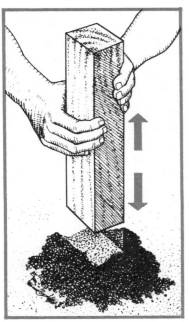

Fill the hole slightly higher than the surrounding surface and tamp it down with a 4×4 (left), then with the wheel of a car.

Blacktop sealer protects driveways from cracking as well as staining. Pour sealer onto the surface and spread it around with a squeegee.

mended, but check the manufacturer's instructions on this, and on how long you should wait between coats.

DAMP BASEMENTS

The first step in drying out a damp basement is to make certain that the dampness is coming from outside—that is, that moisture is really coming through the walls or floor. In many cases dampness is due to condensation, rather than to seepage or leakage from outside. Warm, moist air from inside the house finds its way down to the basement and comes in contact with the cold masonry walls or floor. The moisture in the air then condenses to form wet spots on the surface resembling a leak.

To see if this is your problem, here is an easy test: With strips of tape or some type of mastic, fasten a shiny piece of metal or small mirror against the wall where a damp spot usually appears. Keep it there for at least 24 hours, then look at the surface of this metal. If drops of moisture are noticeable, condensation is the problem. If the surface is dry, but moisture is evident in the masonry behind it after you pull the mirror off, then chances are the moisture is coming through the masonry from outside.

If condensation is the problem, you need more ventilation and may want to install a dehumidifier (the windows must be kept closed for this to work). If you have a clothes dryer in the basement, make sure it is vented directly to the outside. And if there are "sweating" pipes to add to the indoor humidity, cover them with pipe insulation.

If, on the other hand, water is actually coming through the walls from the outside, you should see what steps can be taken to minimize the amount of water accumulating in the ground around the foundation. This water builds up a hydrostatic pressure that literally forces it in through tiny cracks, holes, and porous sections in the basement walls, so minimizing the amount of water will minimize the pressure that builds up outside during rainy weather.

Check first on whether roof drainage is being carried away from the house foundation by gutters and downspouts—before it soaks into and saturates the soil next to the basement walls. Ideally, the water coming out of each downspout should be carried out to a storm sewer (where local codes permit) or a large dry well (a seepage pit) that is at least 15 to 20 feet away from the foundation and lower than the footings. The drawing on page 299 shows how such a dry well can be built with an old 50-gallon drum that has both ends cut out. A number of holes are punched at random through the drum, which is then filled with large rocks or broken cement blocks. A heavy slab of wood or concrete is placed over the top, then the drum is covered with earth.

If this is impractical, you should at least install a sizable splash pan on the bottom of each downspout opening so that water will be carried a minimum of several feet away before it is allowed to spread out over the ground and soak in gradually. In addition to all this, it helps if the ground slopes away from the foundation in all directions around the house, so that water will tend to run off rather than soaking down next to the basement walls.

Gutters and downspouts can be connected to perforated pipe to carry roof drainage away from the foundation and disperse it gradually into the soil.

A splash pan placed at the bottom of each downspout will carry drainage several feet from the foundation.

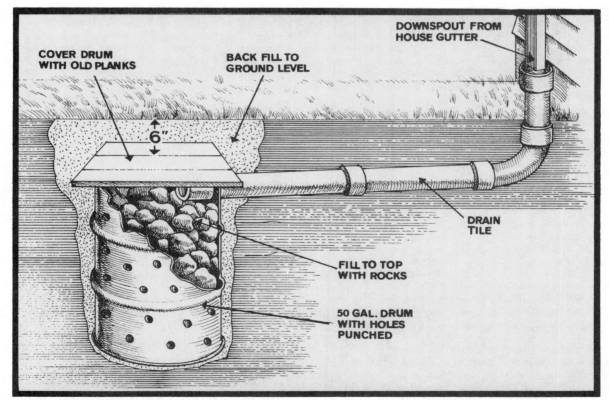

Constructing an underground dry well with a 50-gallon drum. Cut out both ends of drum, punch holes in drum, and bury it. Then fill with rocks and place concrete or wood blocks on top.

Dealing with Water Runoff

If your house is built on a sloping site, water running down from higher ground may be the culprit. To cure this, dig a 12-to-15-inch-deep trench on the high ground above the house. The trench should be approximately parallel to the house, but should pitch slightly off to each side, as shown in the drawing below. As water comes flowing down off the hill the trench will catch it and deflect it off to either side of the house, where it will flow harmlessly on its way to lower ground. In some cases it may be practical to run it, by means of underground plastic pipe, to a dry well or storm sewer, filling the trench with gravel so no one will trip over it.

A trench dug on the high ground above the house will catch water running downhill and deflect it away from the house.

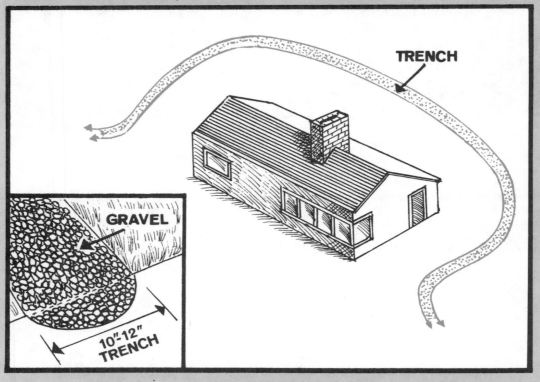

Working from Inside

In a properly built house, the basement walls should originally have been waterproofed with alternating layers of heavy roofing felt (or plastic) and asphalt applied to the concrete—before the soil was replaced around the outside of the foundation. All too often, however, builders skimp on the number of layers applied, or even apply none at all, and leaks will occur through seams, cracks, or porous sections.

If the condition is not severe, you may be able to fix it from the inside by first filling the cracks with a waterproof hydraulic cement, then applying a damp-proofing coating to the entire wall. For fine cracks you can simply brush on one of the epoxy sealers sold for basement walls, working it into and over the crack with a paintbrush when the surface is perfectly dry.

Larger cracks, such as open seams along the floor-to-wall joints, can also be filled with epoxy, but sometimes the material will be too thin to bridge the opening completely. In those cases you can use one of the two-part epoxy putties,

Applying waterproof hydraulic cement to fill crack in a basement wall

while water is still flowing through the opening. To do this, mix up a small batch and hold it in your hand for about a minute or two—or until it just starts to feel warm. Then jam it into the hole or crack and hold it in place with your hand, or with a trowel pressed against it, for a couple of minutes. It will set up and hold back the water in a short while.

When filling any crack or open joint, especially along the seam where the wall meets the floor (a common source of leakage), use a chisel and hammer to undercut the edges of the crack and ensure a better grip for the patching compound. Brush out all loose dust and chips before applying the patching compound.

Minor seepage and small leaks can often be cured by sealing the walls on the inside with one of the various coatings sold for this purpose in paint stores and lumberyards. Some are powders that must be mixed with water and some are ready-mixed coatings to be used as is, or thinned slightly with water. In addition, there are the two-part epoxy sealers mentioned previously— these are probably the strongest and most effective of all when used according to directions. They are also much more expensive than any of the others, so the cost may be impractical for an entire wall. However, you may want to apply them on cracks and porous areas, then switch to one of the other heavy-duty coatings for the entire wall.

Most of these coatings work best when there is no paint on the wall, or when most of the old

which are thicker (sold for use on boats), or you can use a quick-setting hydraulic cement. These cements look like regular cement, but they have special binders added and are designed to expand as they cure. Thus they will lock firmly into the crack to form a waterproof joint that will withstand most normally encountered hydraulic pressures.

This characteristic of hydraulic cement, combined with the fact that it sets up in minutes, makes it possible to use it for plugging leaks even

An epoxy sealer can be brushed on to fill fine cracks.

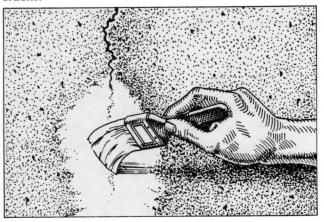

Quick-setting hydraulic cement expands as it cures to provide a firmer, more waterproof joint for larger cracks.

Apply hydraulic cement to an actively leaking crack by hand, and hold it there until it cures—in a matter of minutes.

Sealing basement walls by applying coating to the inside is one way to repair small leaks and seepage.

paint has been removed, but some can be applied over old cement-base paints—as long as the paint is still adhering solidly and not flaking or peeling. Regular oil-base or latex-base paints will generally have to be removed. You can do this yourself with a wire brush and a paint remover, or you can have a contractor come in to sandblast the old paint off. None of these coatings can be applied on a floor, since they cannot take the kind of wear that would result from people walking on them.

When Painting the Inside Is Not Enough

When water comes up through the floor of a basement it is usually due to a fairly high level of groundwater and considerable underground pressure from the outside. There are two ways to solve this problem.

Install a sump pump in the lowest part of the basement, then dig shallow trenches in the floor (usually next to the walls) to carry accumulated water to the sump where the pump is located. The pump, activated automatically when water accumulates, then pumps this water through a hose or pipe to a safe disposal point outside the house.

A much better way to eliminate dampness is to install drain tile under the floor, below the level of the footings. Drain tile is a type of perforated ceramic or plastic pipe that allows water to enter

through openings at the top, then carries the water away to a storm sewer, dry well, or other safe drainage area. Installing this pipe requires chopping through the basement floor next to the walls. You then shovel in a bed of gravel to facilitate drainage, and lay the drain tile in the trench, on top of or next to the footings. Cover the drain tile's joints with wide strips of roofing felt, then add about 6 to 12 inches of gravel on top (depending on how much room you have). When finished, cover the whole thing with a layer of fresh concrete.

Working from the Outside

Generally speaking, serious dampness problems in a basement can be corrected only by working from the outside—that is, by digging down to expose the outer foundation walls so that a waterproof membrane can be applied directly to the masonry. This is much more effective than any interior coating. At the same time, drain tile should be laid along the outside of the footing so that water accumulating in the soil will be safely carried away before pressures build up to force water up through the floor, or through the floor-to-wall joints around the footings.

As shown in the drawing on page 303 bottom, the drain tile is laid along the bottom of the excavation to slope or pitch downward about ¼ inch every 6 feet. The pipe is then connected at its lowest point to another underground pipe that will carry the water away to a dry well or

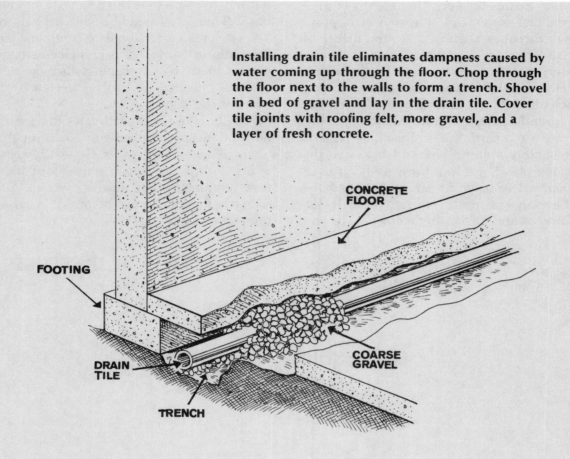

Installing drain tile eliminates dampness caused by water coming up through the floor. Chop through the floor next to the walls to form a trench. Shovel in a bed of gravel and lay in the drain tile. Cover tile joints with roofing felt, more gravel, and a layer of fresh concrete.

CONCRETE FLOOR

FOOTING

DRAIN TILE

TRENCH

COARSE GRAVEL

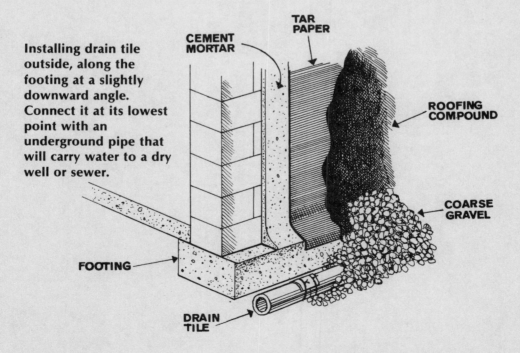

Installing drain tile outside, along the footing at a slightly downward angle. Connect it at its lowest point with an underground pipe that will carry water to a dry well or sewer.

CEMENT MORTAR

TAR PAPER

ROOFING COMPOUND

COARSE GRAVEL

FOOTING

DRAIN TILE

storm sewer. Seams between the lengths of pipe are covered first with strips of heavyweight polyethylene or tarpaper, then with several inches of gravel.

To waterproof the foundation walls, first scrub off all dirt and soil to expose the clean concrete, then patch all visible holes and cracks by troweling on hydraulic cement. Allow this to dry hard. Next, trowel on a thick layer of asphalt cement and immediately apply a sheet of heavyweight polyethylene plastic on top, pressing it on over the wet cement to leave no air pockets or bubbles. Where sheets meet, overlap them by at least 8 inches, and carry them down over the footing, to just above the drain tile laid along the base. Then trowel additional asphalt over all seams. Some professionals recommend troweling an additional layer of asphalt cement over the plastic to protect it against damage when the earth is replaced, and to further ensure against leaks at the seams.

Finally, shovel the earth back in carefully so as not to damage the plastic or cut through the asphalt cement on the walls. Generally speaking, it is best to fill the trench only about halfway at first, tamping the soil down as you go. Allow this to settle for a few days before filling the trench the rest of the way.

Chapter 13

Roof Repairs

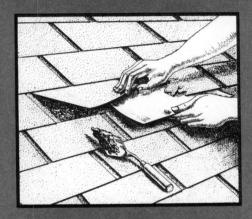

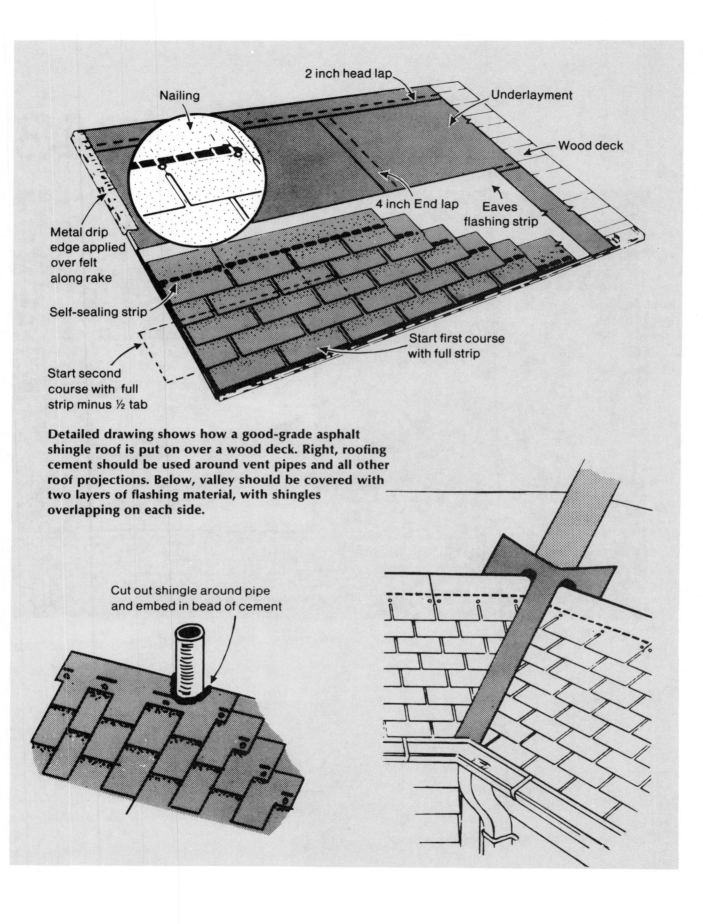

Nailing

2 inch head lap

Underlayment

Wood deck

Metal drip edge applied over felt along rake

4 inch End lap

Eaves flashing strip

Self-sealing strip

Start second course with full strip minus ½ tab

Start first course with full strip

Detailed drawing shows how a good-grade asphalt shingle roof is put on over a wood deck. Right, roofing cement should be used around vent pipes and all other roof projections. Below, valley should be covered with two layers of flashing material, with shingles overlapping on each side.

Cut out shingle around pipe and embed in bead of cement

BECAUSE MOST roofs will last for a great many years and are not really very visible most of the time, homeowners generally pay little or no attention to them until a leak develops—or until a storm rips off some of the shingles. By making an annual inspection that takes only an hour or so, potential trouble spots can be located early enough to be easily repaired or patched with a minimum of expense—thus prolonging the life of the roof considerably and sometimes preventing leaks before they actually occur.

If the roof slopes or is pitched, it is probably covered with shingles—such as those made of asphalt, slate, wood, or fiberglass mixed with asphalt. If the roof is flat, or if it has only a very slight pitch that is not steep enough to permit the use of overlapping shingles, then it is probably covered with roll roofing—that is, with layers of heavyweight roofing material laminated with alternate layers of hot tar or asphalt roofing cement. In most cases either the top layer consists of gravel-coated roofing, or the roof was covered with a layer of gravel after the last layer of roofing was put on (the gravel serves to protect the roofing from the drying effects of the hot sun and to reflect away some of the sun's heat in the summer).

FINDING LEAKS

Even when signs of a leak are evident from the inside, it's not always easy to pinpoint the source of the problem on the roof. If the roof is not finished on the inside and there is no insulation between the rafters (so that the sheathing or roof boards are visible from below) you may be able to spot the source of the actual leak—that is, the actual point of entry from the roof. You can't be sure, however, because water can seep in at one point, then travel for many feet along a beam or rafter before finally dripping down onto the attic floor.

That is why water stains on a top-floor ceiling (just under the attic) do not necessarily mean that the roof leak is directly above that spot. In addition to traveling downward along pitched roof rafters, water can also run horizontally, along ceiling beams on the attic floor, or along the top of the ceiling; it can even travel down along some of the wall studs.

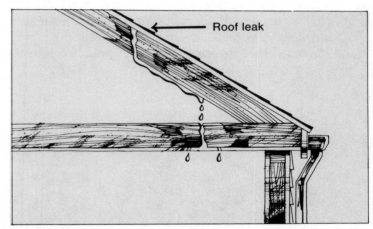

A leak can run down the inside of the roof (above) **or even across for some distance before dripping down** (below).

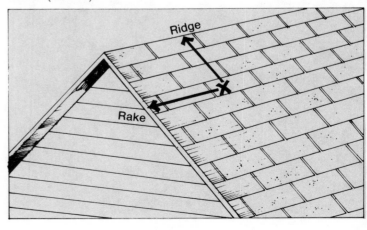

Given all these possibilities, if the attic is unfinished it pays to try to locate the leak from underneath by shining a bright light up at the underside of the roof while it is raining heavily (sometimes a leak will become evident only after it has been raining for an hour or two). Look for signs of dampness on the roof sheathing or rafters, then try to follow this trail back to its source—even if this means pulling down some of the insulation. When you do locate the spot where water is entering, try to poke a stiff wire up through the opening so you will be able to spot it from above after the rain stops. It may even pay to drive a nail up through the roof so you will be able to see it sticking out on top later.

If you still aren't able to locate the source of the leak, or if the ceiling below the roof is finished so that you cannot see the underside of the roof, then you will have to do your searching from above.

Start by measuring from some fixed object that is present both inside and outside—for example, a chimney, a dormer wall, a vent pipe, etc. Measure the distance from this point to where the water is first seen on the inside, then measure the same distance along the roof on the outside. Start looking around this area first, keeping in mind that water can travel quite a way on the inside or under the shingles and along the sheathing before it ever shows up on the inside. Also remember that while it can travel horizontally in some cases, it never travels uphill—so you can limit your search to the areas that are level with or higher than the measured point only; no sense in looking at points that are lower.

What do you look for? Cracks or splits in the shingles or roofing; rusted, cracked, or rotted flashing materials; open seams, particularly where parts of the roof meet a brick chimney or house wall; shingles that are missing or curled upward, or have pieces missing; blisters in roll roofing that also has cracks or check marks in the blistered area (blisters alone do not necessarily mean that the roof is not watertight at that point); and anything else that looks like a possible point of water entry, especially when the wind is blowing.

Dark blotches on roof show where granules have worn off and shingles may soon need replacing.

REPAIRING ASPHALT SHINGLE ROOFS

A shingle that is curled or raised up by the wind can almost always be cemented back down by smearing a thick dab of asphalt roofing cement under it, then pressing the raised shingle down on top of this. Hold it down for a couple of minutes (or place a brick on it for an hour or so) if it won't lie flat by itself. If the shingle is so stiff that it won't stay down, you may have to nail it down with a large-head galvanized roofing nail, but be sure you smear another layer of cement over the nail head to protect against water seeping down through the nail hole.

If no more than one or two shingles are torn, roofing cement will probably be adequate for the necessary repairs—just be sure you smear it both under and over the damaged area, then press down (or nail down) as described above. However, if pieces of some shingles are actually missing, or if a shingle is so dried out and split that this type of simple repair will not do the trick, some kind of patch will be required. In most

Safety Precautions When Working on Roofs

When you have to climb up onto the roof for any inspection or roof repairs, make sure you pick a dry day when there is little or no wind and wear sneakers or rubber-soled soft shoes to ensure safe footing and minimize damage to the roofing material. Avoid walking around on the roof any more than you have to, and don't go up on the roof on very hot, sunny days when the shingles or roofing material is very soft.

You will need an extension ladder tall enough to reach up above the eaves by at least 2 to 3 feet to give you something to hold on to as you climb onto and off the roof. Arrange to have someone hold the bottom end of the ladder while you are climbing on and off, and if possible tie the top end of the ladder to something solid in order to keep it from slipping sideways (see page 38 for more information on how to work with extension ladders).

On pitched roofs with a fairly steep slope, always clamber up or down the slope on all fours, rather than walking straight up. Haul tools or equipment up after you, once you are in place, with a long rope—unless you can fit everything into your pockets or into some kind of tool pouch that can be tied around your waist.

One trick often used by the pros to provide a safe footing while working on a sloping roof is to use half of an extra extension ladder, or a suitable length of any straight ladder, as a temporary "catwalk" as shown in the illustration below. Lay it flat on the surface of the roof so that one end sticks up past the peak of the roof, or as close to it as you can safely reach; you can then sometimes hook the ladder brackets over the peak to keep the ladder from sliding down, though it is better to tie a long rope to the top of the ladder beforehand, then throw the other end over the ridge so that it hangs down on the other side. The free end is then tied to a tree or to some solid object on the house.

Although placing half of a regular ladder flat on the roof will provide a reasonable foothold for most small repair jobs, when there is much work to do, or when the slope is particularly steep, the safest procedure is to build yourself a simple gangplank (often called a "chicken ladder") similar to the one shown here.

Made of ordinary lumber, the plank consists of two 8-inch or 10-inch boards held together with 2×2-inch cleats nailed across the top as illustrated. Space these cleats about 12 to 14 inches apart for a properly spaced series of footholds or "steps," then nail on the strips of wood to form a right-angle brace that will fit over the peak of the roof to hold it firmly in place. The overall length of this gangplank should be such that it reaches from the peak of the roof down to within about 2 or 3 feet above the gutters or edge of the eave.

Left, ladder positioned on a pitched roof, with secured rope running down other side. Right, a gangplank or "chicken ladder" can be constructed for steep roof instead of using ladder.

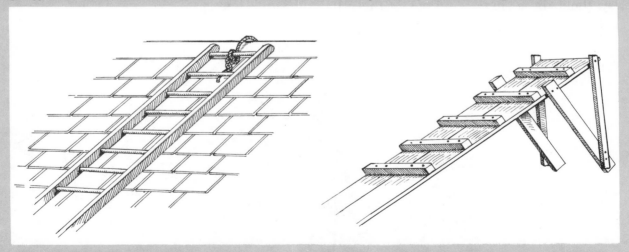

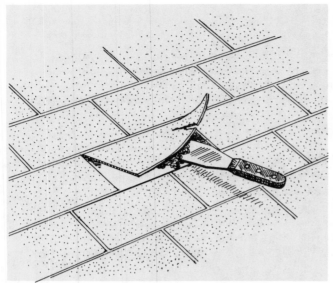

Asphalt roofing cement can be worked under a split shingle.

Inserting a metal patch to replace a badly damaged or missing shingle.

cases the simplest alternative is a sheet of copper or aluminum flashing material (sold in lumberyards and hardware stores).

Cut a piece of the metal large enough to completely cover the area of the original shingle or shingles, plus about 3 inches extra on all sides so the piece will reach under the shingles next to it. Next spread a layer of roof cement over the bottom side of the metal patch and slide it up into place so that its edge goes up under the shingle above, as shown in the illustration above right. Now spread more cement on top of the metal along the sides where the adjoining shingles overlap (hold those shingles up out of the way while spreading the cement onto the metal), then press the shingles back down onto the cement to hold everything in place. Nailing will not be required in most cases, but if the metal won't stay put, then a couple of nails may be advisable to keep it in place. Use rustproof nails with a large head, then cover the heads with a liberal dab of the cement.

If one of the shingles along the hip or ridge of the roof is missing or damaged, then the same patching techniques can be used—roof cement alone if the crack or tear is very small, plus a piece of metal flashing or an extra shingle if a piece is missing.

Shingles along the ridge of a roof are patched or replaced in the same way as row shingles.

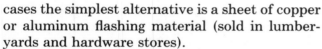

PATCHING FLASHING

Hard-to-find leaks are in many cases due not to a defect in the roofing material but to cracks or rusted-out sections in some of the flashing, especially where it comes up against the house walls (next to a dormer, for example), or where a vent stack or chimney protrudes through the roof. Flashing is usually made of metal—copper or aluminum—but in some instances it may be a heavy type of roofing felt or even several layers of tar paper.

The smallest split or crack in this material will allow water to seep in underneath, so examine all the flashing carefully to look for breaks in the surface, or for places where it seems to be pulling away from the brick or other material adjoining the roof.

When you find a place that needs patching, brush away the dust and dirt, then spread a liberal layer of asphalt roof cement on with a small trowel, or use sealant out of a caulking cartridge, forcing it into all the cracks and crevices. Feather the compound out to cover the edges of the flashing material. If brickwork is involved (a chimney or wall, for example), make sure while you're at it that the mortar joints immediately above the flashing are sound. If in doubt, repoint

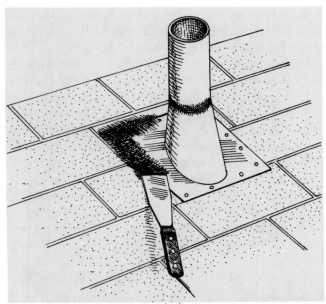

Spread roofing compound liberally over the edges of flashing material and nail heads.

the joints by scraping out and replacing the mortar (see pages 294–95), or caulk them with a silicone rubber sealant.

REPAIRING SLATE ROOFS

Properly installed slate shingles will normally last as long as the house they cover, but sometimes a piece will get damaged or need replacing because of an accident—a tree branch falling on the roof, for instance.

If a slate shingle is cracked, and if the crack is not too big (or if only a small piece is missing), you can probably get by with smearing on a liberal coat of roofing cement, then sliding a sheet of aluminum or copper under the cracked or missing section. Coat the underside of the metal with cement first, then smear more cement on over the metal after you have it in place. Nailing should not be necessary.

When an entire shingle is missing, you will have to buy a new piece of slate and install it in place of the missing one. To cut slate to the size needed you can use a masonry cutoff wheel in a portable circular saw. You can also cut it by hand: Score it deeply on each side with repeated strokes from the corner of a cold chisel, making certain the score marks on each side are exactly in line with each other; then lay the slate over a

Flashing around the base of a chimney is a common site of roof leaks.

piece of dowel, directly on the scored line, and smack down hard on both sides. This should snap the piece neatly in two.

Before you can slide the new slate shingle in place you first have to remove any pieces of the old shingle, as well as the nails that originally held it. For this there is a special nail-pulling tool that can be used to reach up under the shingles from below. Usually homemade, it is nothing more than a piece of strap iron with a notch filed or ground in one end, as shown. The other end is bent over so that you can drive it downward with a hammer. You slide it up under the shingle, hook the notch over the nail, then hammer down on the other end to pull the nail out, or simply cut it in two.

You can also use an ordinary hacksaw blade. Wrap one end of the blade with tape to provide a grip, then reach up under the shingle and saw the nails off.

After the nails are cut or pulled out, you can slide the old slate out, then slide the new piece up and nail it into place. To avoid splitting the slate, drill holes for the nails first, using a carbide-tipped masonry bit in your electric drill. The holes should be about an inch below the bottom edge of the shingle above. Spread roof cement under the new shingle before you slide it into place, then apply more cement over the nail heads after the job is finished.

PATCHING FLAT ROOFS

Repairing leaks and damaged areas on a flat roof that is covered with roll roofing is relatively simple in most cases because you don't have to

You can make or purchase this special nail-pulling tool for reaching under shingles.

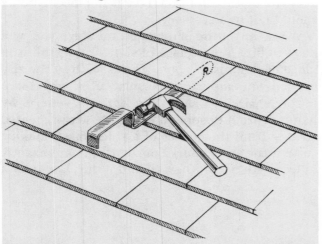

worry about climbing slopes or working at a steep angle, and you don't have to be concerned about reaching up under overlapping shingles. Also, leaks are often easier to spot—at least the defective area is usually more noticeable from on top. But there is also a much greater chance that the actual leak is due to a defect not in the roofing material itself but in the flashing around vent stacks or chimneys where they come up through the roof.

Although blisters are not always a sign of water entry, water can seep in and work its way under roll roofing to cause bubbles or raised pockets where the water accumulates. Check these areas carefully and look for signs of cracking or checking, as well as for loose nails or open seams. A blister that looks sound and is not anywhere near a suspected leak can often be left alone. The mere fact that the spot is blistered does not mean that water is entering there.

If, however, the blister is directly above (or not far from) the place where water is entering, then it should be cut open. Also, if you can't find any other signs of a leak, or any other place where the roof looks suspicious, you should suspect any blisters that you see.

Start your repair by slitting the raised section open with a straight cut down the middle, using a sharp knife and pressing no harder than necessary to cut through the top layer of roofing material (you want to avoid cutting through the layers below, if possible). If there is gravel on the surface, this should be swept or brushed away first. Next, use a putty knife or small trowel to force roofing cement under each half of the blister by working first under one side, then under the other.

Press the two sides down, then drive large-headed rustproof roofing nails in along each side of the cut, spacing them no more than 3 to 4 inches apart. Cover the entire area with a layer of roofing cement, then cut a piece of heavyweight roofing felt large enough to make a patch that will cover the whole blister.

In place of regular roofing felt you can use some of the heavy asphalt-impregnated flashing material that most lumberyards and building materials dealers sell as a replacement for metal flashing. Nail this patch down on top of the fresh cement by using roofing nails spaced every few

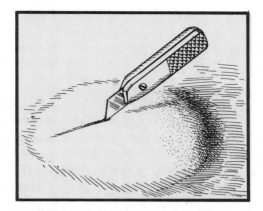

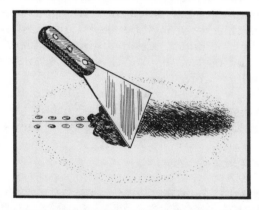

Repairing a flat-roof blister. Cut through the middle of the blister, force roofing cement underneath, nail along each side of cut, and cover seam with more roofing cement; then apply a patch of roofing felt or flashing on top, nailed around the edges and covered by still more cement.

inches around the perimeter, then spread a heavy layer of roofing cement over the edges of the patch and over all the nail heads.

When the old roofing is so badly cracked and dried out that you have to replace a whole section, the technique is a bit different. As shown in the drawing below, you start by cutting out the damaged section entirely, using a sharp utility knife and a metal straightedge (straight cuts will make it easier to cut a patch to fit). The cutout should be square or rectangular in shape, and

Repairing a large hole in a flat roof. Cut out a square piece around the hole; replace it with a patch of exact same size, nailed all around and with cement underneath; then cover with another, larger patch, again nailed down and with cement underneath. Then cement all edges.

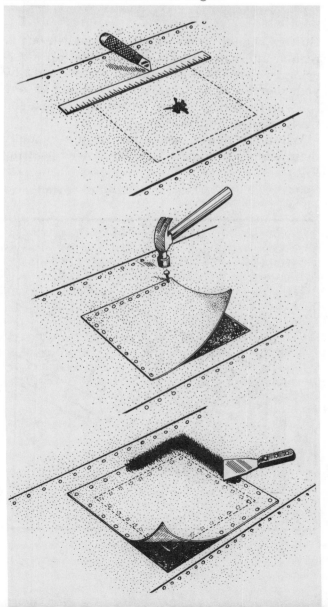

large enough so all the damaged material will be removed when you lift the piece out.

Sweep away all dirt or debris and dry off any noticeable moisture, then cut a new piece of roll roofing to form a patch that will fit neatly into the recess just created. Coat the inside with roofing cement and press the patch down on top. Drive nails in around the edges at 3-inch or 4-inch intervals, then cut a second patch at least 3 inches larger than the first one on all sides. Coat the top of the first patch with roofing cement, spreading the cement about 3 inches past it on all sides, then press down the new patch and drive nails around the edges. Cover the nail heads, and the edges of the last patch, with a final layer of roofing cement.

REPAIRING GUTTERS

Gutters should be inspected and cleaned out at regular intervals if they are to do their job of carrying away the vast amounts of water caught by your roof during each rainstorm. Without gutters the water could flood your basement or cause soil washouts around the foundation.

While the newer plastic gutters are virtually maintenance-free, since they don't need painting or other protection against the elements, even they can and do get clogged if they are not periodically cleaned out . . . unless they are protected with mesh-type covers or guards. These "gutter guards" consist of long strips of plastic or metal mesh that fit over the gutters to keep out leaves and other debris. The outer edge of the mesh snaps on over the rim of the gutter; along the other edge it either attaches to the bottom row of roof shingles with metal clips, or its edge slips up under the shingles. Leaves may accumulate on top at times, but they soon get washed off or blown off by the wind.

In lieu of full-length gutter covers, many homeowners find that simple wire "cages" that protect the downspout opening are enough— especially if there are not many tall trees nearby. Such cages are merely pushed into the downspout opening from above. They don't keep leaves out of the gutter, but they do keep them from being washed down the downspout opening and getting stuck in the vertical pipe or—worse yet—in the underground drain pipe that connects the bottom end of the downspout with a dry well or storm sewer.

At least once or twice a year, clean out leaves and other debris and check the gutters to make certain they are draining properly. If they over-

Plastic or metal screen can be used to cover gutter and keep out leaves and debris.

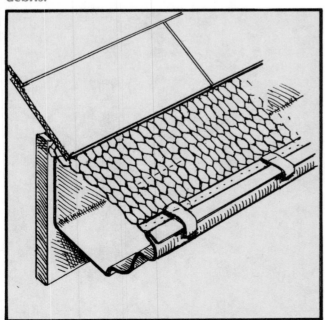

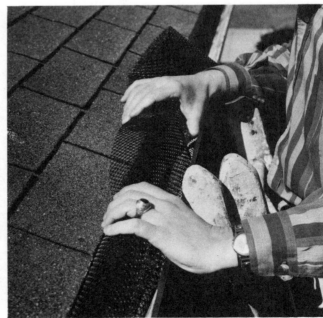

A wire "cage" will protect most downspouts from debris.

necessary to replace some brackets or hangers entirely, while in other cases it may be advisable just to add extra supports where the gutter tends to dip or sag. Use the same type of hanger or bracket, and position it where it will maintain an even slope (about a 1-inch drop for every 10 feet of gutter length).

If there is leaking in the seams between lengths, or where the gutters are joined to corner fittings or downspouts, apply a silicone rubber or butyl rubber caulking compound on the inside of the joint (don't try to seal it from the outside—it won't hold). You can also use a thick layer of asphalt roof cement on the inside, though silicone rubber will last longer. Just make sure the surfaces are clean and dry before you apply any of

Three types of gutter supports (from top to bottom): **spike and ferrule, hanger bracket, and hanger strap**

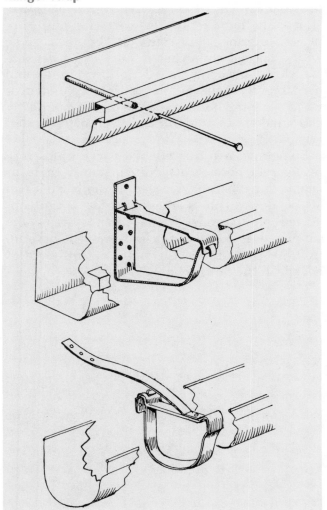

flow periodically during heavy rains, or if running water into the gutters from a hose shows the water pooling or overflowing in some places, chances are that the gutter has sagged in those places because of some bent or broken hangers or supporting brackets. Hangers and brackets can be damaged by heavy snow loads, by someone carelessly stepping on a gutter when climbing onto the roof, or from leaning a heavy ladder against the gutter where it is not adequately supported.

Gutters are supported by three common methods: (1) by use of hanger brackets that are nailed to the fascia board, the gutters then being snapped into them (this system is used most often with plastic gutters); (2) by using hanger straps that hook into or over the outer edge of the gutter, while the other end is nailed to the roof up under the first row of shingles; and (3) by using a ferrule-and-spike support. The last consists of a long spike which goes through the upper edge of the gutter and into the fascia board behind it; the metal ferrule fits inside the gutter, and the spike goes through it before going into the fascia board.

If sagging is evident, check the mounting brackets or hangers to see if any are badly bent, or if some of the nails that hold them in place have been pulled out. Sometimes you may find it

these sealants. Use a wire brush to clean off rust and accumulated dirt, and steel wool to remove corrosion or rust. Spread the caulking on liberally, forcing it well into the joint or seam to ensure a watertight seal.

If a small section is rusted out or badly rotted, you can repair it effectively with a patch on the inside, using layers of roofing cement and heavyweight aluminum foil. Clean the surface on the inside as described above, then spread a thick coat of cement over the damaged area, feathering it out around the edges so no ridge is left. Press the sheet of aluminum foil down on top of the wet cement, then trowel a second layer of cement on over this, carrying it well out past the edges of the foil. Again feather it out to a smooth edge that blends in to leave no ridges that could interfere with rapid drainage.

For a more permanent patch you can use one of the fiberglass patching kits sold in hardware stores and home centers, as well as in auto supply and marine supply outlets. These kits come with a special resin that is used to impregnate the cloth and bond the whole thing firmly and permanently in place. The resin can be used over wood or metal, but the surface must be perfectly clean and dry in order for the resin to bond properly.

Sometimes a gutter will overflow during every heavy rain because its vertical downspouts or leaders have become clogged. If the bottom end of this downspout is accessible—i.e., is not connected to an underground drain system—the simplest way to unclog it is to shove a hose up from below and turn the water on full force to backflush the downspout.

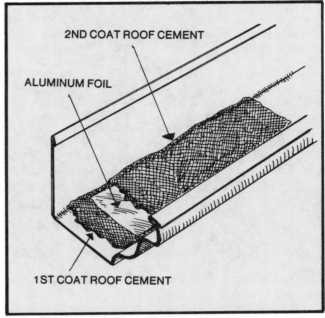

Repairing rusted or rotted sections inside a gutter

If this fails, or if the bottom end of the downspout is not easily accessible, you may have to use a long plumber's snake or drain auger from the top. Should the bottom end of the downspout be connected to an underground drain pipe that carries the water away to a dry well, or to a storm sewer or sump, you should avoid pushing the obstruction down into this pipe. You can make sure by disconnecting the bottom end of the vertical pipe before you push the snake or auger down from the top. In fact, your best bet is to start by pushing the snake up from the bottom end of the pipe; then push it down from the top through the opening in the bottom of the gutter.

Chapter **14**

Exterior Repairs and Maintenance

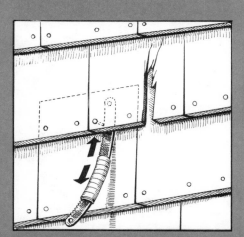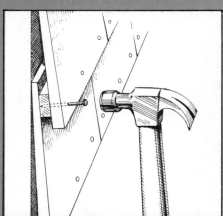

IF YOU'RE like most homeowners you do not pay much attention to the need for preventive maintenance around the outside of your house—other than to note when it is time for a new paint job. Yet if you get in the habit of making regular inspections—and then making small repairs as soon as minor problems are noticeable—you will help prevent further damage and can often ward off the need for larger and more extensive repairs later.

For example, if you spot a place where the paint has chipped off and left the bare wood exposed, touching it up even though the rest of the house doesn't need painting will help prevent the entry of moisture that can cause extensive blistering and peeling, necessitating an entire paint job much sooner than would otherwise be required.

By the same token, renailing a loose piece of trim or siding will help keep adjoining nails from working loose—a condition that can sometimes lead to splitting and eventual rotting of the wood so that you finally wind up having to replace whole sections of siding or trim.

REPAIRING SIDING AND SHINGLES

Cracks or splits in clapboard siding should be repaired as soon as they are noticed in order to keep water from penetrating and causing further damage. If the crack is narrow and not too long, you can usually get by merely with filling the crack with a good grade of caulking compound. Brush out loose dirt and make sure the wood is dry, then use a flexible putty knife to press the compound firmly into the crack. Smooth off the excess, then apply a coat of paint as soon as the filler has cured.

For a more permanent repair you can use exterior wood glue to fix the split. This method works best on long or wide cracks when the rest of the wood is still solid. You start by using a few screwdrivers and chisels to wedge the split open a little more, forcing them in at intervals and keeping them in place to hold the crack open. You don't want to make the crack a lot worse, you just want to wedge it open enough to permit forcing some waterproof glue into the crack. Use a plastic squeeze bottle with a narrow spout to force the glue in, and spread it around on the inside with a thin spatula of some kind. Now remove the screwdrivers and/or chisels that were holding the crack open and force the crack closed by hammering up against the bottom edge of the board with a block of wood as shown on page 320. While you have a helper hold the split closed, drive a few rustproof nails (aluminum or bronze)

Using screwdrivers or chisels to wedge open a split board for gluing

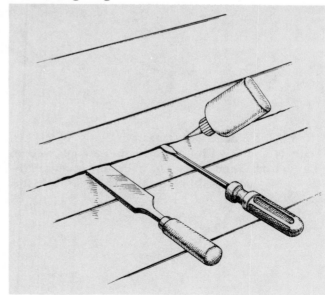

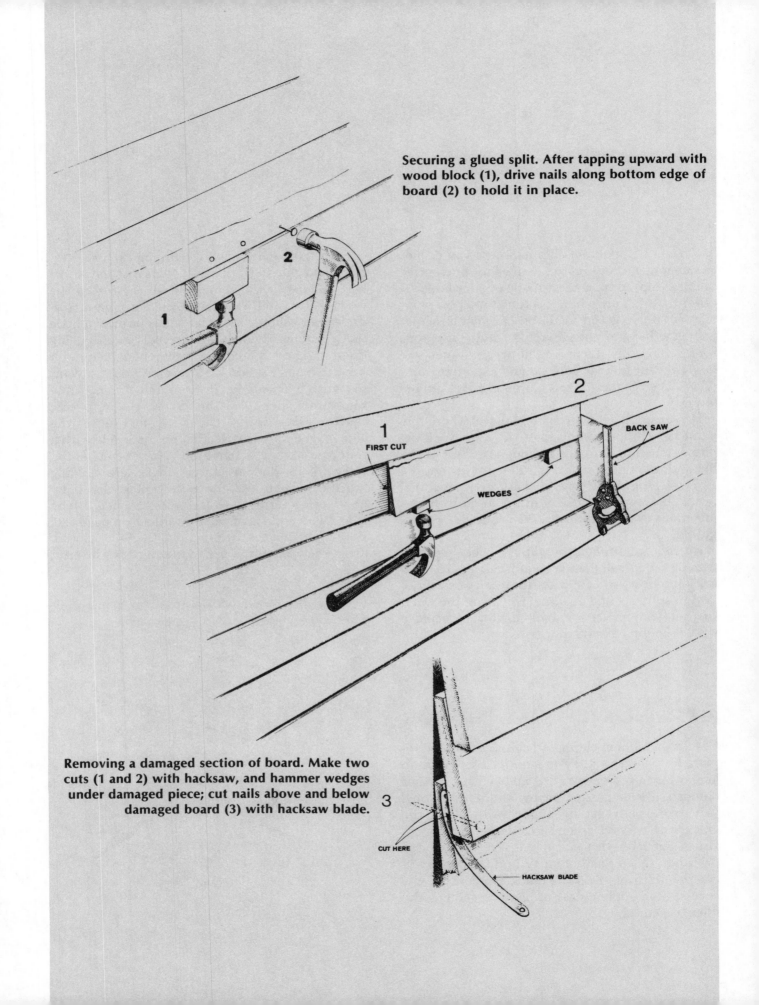

Securing a glued split. After tapping upward with wood block (1), drive nails along bottom edge of board (2) to hold it in place.

1

2

1
FIRST CUT

2
BACK SAW

WEDGES

Removing a damaged section of board. Make two cuts (1 and 2) with hacksaw, and hammer wedges under damaged piece; cut nails above and below damaged board (3) with hacksaw blade.

3

CUT HERE

HACKSAW BLADE

into or under the lower edge of this board to keep the crack closed. Allow the glue to dry hard before painting.

When a piece of siding is too badly split for this kind of repair, or when there are rotted or missing pieces, the only way to do the job properly is to cut out the damaged section and replace it completely with a new piece of matching siding. However, since the boards usually overlap from the top down, cutting out the damaged section can be a bit tricky without also ripping out the boards above. Here's how to do it:

1. Draw a vertical line on each side of the damaged area to mark off the section you want to cut out, then saw the board vertically along each of these lines. Any sharp woodworking saw can be used, but a backsaw similar to the one illustrated on page 320 is easiest for this job. Don't cut any deeper than necessary; you don't want to damage the board underneath. Near the top where the board above overlaps, you may have to use a sharp chisel and hammer to complete the cut.

2. Next, use the chisel and hammer to split the damaged section of board so you can pull the pieces out, working carefully to avoid damaging the board underneath. Pry out the pieces under the overlapping board above if you can (usually these are held by the nails that go through both boards).

3. Remove the nails that originally went through the top of this board and the bottom part of the overlapping board above. Sometimes these nails can be pulled out with a claw hammer after whacking the surface of the board a few times to make the heads stick up slightly. If this doesn't work, your best bet is to reach up from underneath with a hacksaw blade and cut the nails off from below (see drawing). To provide a grip for the hacksaw blade, wrap one end with several thicknesses of tape, and to make it easier to slide the blade up under the board, wedge the board's bottom edge out slightly by forcing a couple of small tapered pieces of wood in from below.

4. After the nails have been cut off or pulled out and the old wood has all been removed, cut a new piece of clapboard to length for a snug fit between the cut-off edges of the old board. If the building paper under the siding is torn, cover the torn areas with a layer of asphalt roofing cement,

or nail on a whole new piece of tarpaper or weather-resistant building paper.

5. Spread caulking compound over the cut ends of the old board and the ends of the new piece of siding, then push this piece into place so it fits up under the overlapping board on top. Use a block of wood and hammer to tap it into proper alignment with the edges of the old board on each side, then fasten it in place with rustproof nails along the bottom edge. Drive extra nails into the top edge through the bottom half of the board above where it overlaps the new piece, then countersink the nail heads and fill the resulting holes with putty before painting.

Replacing a Damaged Wood Shingle

A badly split or missing wood shingle is a lot easier to replace than a damaged section of clapboard. The shingles do not have to be cut apart the way long pieces of clapboard do—you can remove one shingle and replace it with another one by using the technique previously described: cutting the nails off by using a hacksaw blade, removing the pieces of old shingle, then inserting and nailing the new shingle in place.

As a matter of fact, most split or cracked shingles do not have to be replaced at all—you can merely nail down the pieces on each side of the split, using rustproof aluminum or galvanized nails. If the split looks as if it will leave a sizable gap, then it may be a good idea to also slide a sheet of heavyweight paper or tarpaper up under the shingle before driving the new nails in.

When a shingle does need replacing, however (usually because it has pieces actually missing), then the simplest method is to split the pieces away with a hammer and chisel so you can pull them out from under the shingle above. Work carefully to avoid damaging the shingle underneath, then cut off the nails that go through the bottom edge of the overlapping shingle above. Use a hacksaw blade to cut the nails, as illustrated in the previous section.

After the nails have been removed, slide the new shingle up in place of the old one, then drive rustproof nails in along the top and bottom edges (the nails that go through the top edge of the shingle will go through the bottom edge of the one above it first).

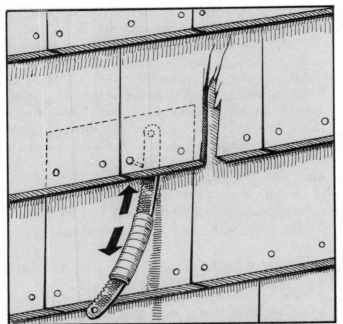
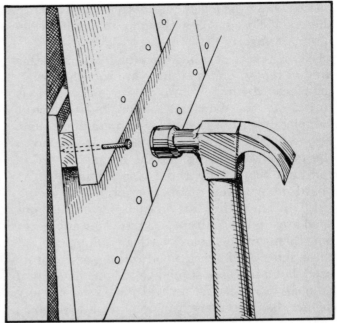

Replacing a damaged shingle. Left, cutting the old nails; right, driving new ones in through shingle and "shadow" strip that some installations have.

Replacing a Damaged Asbestos Shingle

You replace a damaged asbestos shingle using basically the same method as to replace a damaged wood shingle, but since asbestos shingles are very brittle, and since nails are only driven through the bottom edge of each shingle (seldom through the top edge), there are a few differences in technique. The top edge still fits up under the overhanging edge of the shingle above, but the nails that go through the bottom of the overhanging shingle are high enough up from its bottom edge so that they do not go through the top of the shingle below (see drawing above).

Start by splitting out the damaged shingle with a few blows from a hammer, being careful to avoid damaging the adjoining shingles, which are very brittle. The nails can then be pulled out with a claw hammer, and you won't have to use a hacksaw as with wood shingles because there are no nails under the overhanging shingle above to get in the way.

Slide the new shingle up in place of the old one, shoving it well up under the shingle above so that its bottom edge lines up with the shingles on

each side, then drive rustproof aluminum nails through the predrilled holes along the bottom edge of the shingle. If your new shingle doesn't have predrilled nail holes, you'll have to drill your own. Never try to drive nails through an asbestos shingle unless you drill pilot holes first—you will probably split or shatter the shingle if you do.

CHOOSING AND USING CAULKING COMPOUND

A caulking gun loaded with a good grade of caulking compound and used regularly around the outside of your house to seal up cracks, seams, open joints, and small holes is one of your best weapons in the continual battle of protecting your house against the ravages of the weather.

Caulking is most often used around window frames and doorframes to ensure a watertight seam that will also seal out cold drafts and thus conserve fuel during the heating season and electricity during the summer when air conditioners are in use. But this is by no means the only place

Caulking around a window frame (left), **and where different surface materials meet** (right)

where caulking compound is important around the inside of the house.

It should also be used to seal joints wherever two different materials meet to form a seam that must be watertight or airtight, or both. This includes such places as where wood trim meets siding, where wood siding meets brick or masonry, where siding or trim has open joints or seams that do not fit properly, and along all inside and outside corner joints where pieces of siding or trim fit against each other.

Other places where caulking compound is

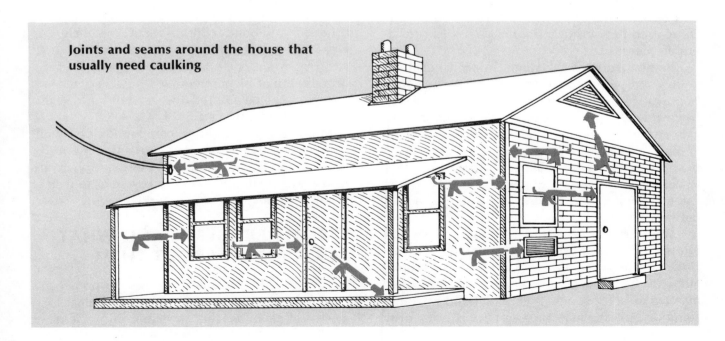

Joints and seams around the house that usually need caulking

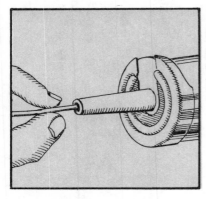

Puncturing the plastic seal of a new cartridge with a stiff wire

needed include wherever posts or columns rest on top of stoops, porch floors, or concrete slabs; any openings where pipes, conduits, or wires pass through the house walls from outside; around air conditioners and exhaust fans or dryer ducts that go through the house wall; and around attic vents, ventilating louvers, and similar framed openings in the walls or foundation.

Caulking compound is generally sold in disposable cartridges that fit into standard "half-barrel" or "drop-in" caulking guns. The cartridges all fit the same size gun and come with a tapered plastic nozzle that can be clipped off to give the size opening desired (the larger the opening, the larger the diameter of the "bead" of caulking the cartridge will dispense). A piston-like plunger in the caulking gun is pushed forward by a ratchet mechanism whenever you pull on the trigger of the gun, thus forcing the compound out through the nozzle under considerable pressure.

The first time the cartridge is used you should poke a stiff piece of wire down through the nozzle to puncture a plastic seal on the inside. If you fail to do this, the pressure that builds up on the inside can burst the cartridge and create a mess. (Before putting a half-empty cartridge away, push a screw or large nail into the nozzle opening to act as a temporary stopper; this will also keep the compound from hardening inside the nozzle between jobs.)

For exterior use around the house there are four basic kinds of caulking compound to choose from: oil-base caulking, latex-base caulking, butyl rubber, and silicone rubber. All are thick, masticlike compounds that will bond to most common building materials without turning brit-

tle and that can flex or "give" with the expansion and contraction of these materials.

Oil-base caulking is the oldest type, and it is the least expensive of the four. But it is also the least durable, being likely to dry out and crack or peel away sooner than most of the others. Accordingly, and because an oil-base caulking will "burn through" latex paint, most homeowners (and contractors) have switched to one of the latex-base caulking compounds.

Latex compounds have either an acrylic or a vinyl base and dry much faster than oil-base caulking. They also tend to bond better on most surfaces and will stay flexible longer without drying out or cracking as easily as an oil-base compound. Also, they are compatible with latex paints—they will not "burn through"—and can be painted over almost immediately.

Butyl rubber caulking tends to form a stronger bond than either the latex or the oil-base caulks, especially on masonry and metal. It also stays flexible and resilient for years longer. However, butyl caulking usually costs considerably more than latex compounds, and most butyl caulkings cannot be painted over for at least 10 to 15 days after they have been applied (a few cannot be painted over at all).

Silicone rubber caulking is the most expensive of all, and also probably the longest-lasting under normal circumstances. It forms a stronger bond than most of the other caulking compounds, and will stay flexible and "rubbery" longer than the others. It will bond to almost anything, including glass and plastic, as long as the surface is clean and dry when the compound is applied. Many brands cannot be painted over, however, and the ones that can be painted over are not quite as durable as those that can.

Most of these caulking compounds are available in white, black, or gray, but some brands of latex caulking, and some of silicone rubber, are also available in other colors, as well as in a clear or colorless shade.

TERMITE PROBLEMS AND WHAT YOU CAN DO ABOUT THEM

Termites really have nothing against homeowners—it's just that their only food is cellulose, and since cellulose is the principal ingredient of

Applying the Caulking

It may take a little practice to learn how to do a neat job of caulking, but it's not really difficult.

What you must do is make sure the surfaces to be caulked are clean and dry, and you must also scrape out all of the old caulking so the new material can bond directly to the surface. Hold the gun so that its tip is pointing into the joint at about a 45-degree angle, then squeeze the trigger slowly with a steady pressure to force the compound out in a steady stream, not in sudden squirts.

As soon as the compound starts flowing out of the nozzle, start moving the tip toward you along the seam. Keep going at a steady pace while maintaining constant pressure on the trigger, and try to coordinate the rate of movement with the amount of pressure you apply on the trigger so that a "bead" of uniform width and thickness comes oozing out. With practice you will learn how slow you have to go to dispense a bead of uniform size. When you reach the end of the trigger stroke, release pressure on the trigger to let its spring action return it to its starting position, so that you can then begin pressing again at the same rate.

An important point to remember: Contrary to popular opinion, the bead of caulking should be slightly convex at the surface, not concave. This means that you should not smooth it down with your finger, trying to leave a neat-looking curve on the surface. Caulking shrinks slightly as it dries, and it tends to dry first on the surface, so smoothing it down with your finger creates a concave surface that is more likely to crack or split as it shrinks. Leaving the surface raised or with a convex bulge down the center gives the bead plenty of allowance for shrinkage.

One nuisance that often plagues users of caulking is that the compound continues to ooze out of the nozzle after one gets to the end of the joint and stops pressing on the trigger. You can prevent this by turning the handle over to release the ratchet mechanism and pulling the handle back slightly to relieve pressure that has built up on the inside.

Correct caulking angle. Beads should be convex rather than concave at the surface.

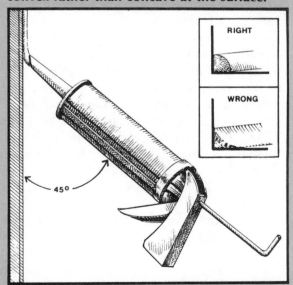

RIGHT

WRONG

45°

To stop oozing action, turn handle to disengage ratchet mechanism and pull back to release pressure.

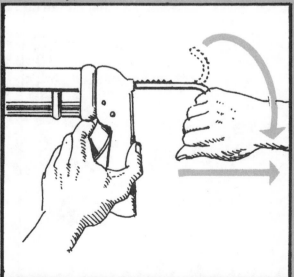

wood, they see the wood structure of a house as an ideal source of food for their colony.

There are many different species of termites, but the ones that do the kind of structural damage that most homeowners are afraid of are the subterranean termites. They are called subterranean because that is exactly where they live—underground. They establish colonies in the ground near the house and forage out daily through tunnels dug in the soil, and in any wood through which they travel, to bring the cellulose back to the nest. When the colony cannot find enough wood (cellulose) in the soil near the nest, they extend their tunnels farther and farther until they find another source—even if it happens to be the house in which you live.

Termites have an uncanny ability to know when wood is not far off, even when it is overhead and well beyond any soil. That is why they will sometimes travel straight up through mud tunnels built along the vertical surface of a concrete foundation—or in some cases straight up in the air through unsupported vertical dirt tunnels they have erected themselves. In the same way, they will also build tunnels along outside pipes and conduits, should these lead to a source of wood above the soil.

Termites dig through soft grain, but never break through the surface.

Photograph shows actual tunnels along inside of foundation wall.

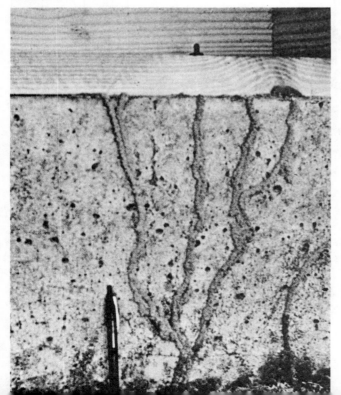

Why do they build tunnels instead of merely crawling over the surface? Because termites never want to expose themselves to daylight or to the drying effects of fresh air (except when they sprout wings and swarm once in their lives—but more on that shortly). They need a dark, continuously damp environment in order to survive, and they must return to the soil each day (usually once in 24 hours) to replenish their source of moisture.

That is why you never see them actually at work. They dig their way through the soft grain of the wood, somehow sensing when they have weakened that member enough to cause it to collapse and stopping just before this happens. Then they move on to the next section. If they accidentally break through the surface of the wood, they will pull back and plug the hole to protect themselves, then continue on to the next section.

Given these ways of termites, a properly built house should have metal termite shields installed along the top of the foundation to keep them from climbing up the masonry and entering the wood, and it should be built so that none of its wood comes close to or in contact with the soil. Termites can still enter through minute cracks that develop in masonry foundations or concrete slabs that adjoin the house, however, as well as by building tunnels along the surface of pipes, concrete foundations, etc.

The one most effective means of preventing termite entry, and getting rid of them once they do enter, is poisoning the soil around and under the house. This creates a barrier through which they must pass on their daily trips to and from their underground nest, causing them to carry the poison with them and thus to kill off the colony. Any termites that remain inside the house will die off by themselves in a few days, for they will not live long if they cannot get back to the damp soil.

The only time a termite actually leaves its underground colony and the safety of its tunnels is in the early spring when a colony is big enough for the reproductive members to go out and start a colony of their own. That is when termites sprout wings, for these members of the colony fly out in search of a new location nearby. Once that location has been found, they shed their wings and crawl back underground to start the new colony, and to remain there for the rest of their lives.

Since termites shed their wings right near where they have reentered the soil or the wood structure of the house, this is often the only sign of termites the homeowner sees—the swarming period itself is relatively short and is seldom seen by the occupants of the house; but the discarded wings are a certain indication that you have a well-established colony of termites nearby.

Sometimes a homeowner will see a swarm of flying ants—or crawling small ants—and mistake them for termites. Though ants do look something like termites, they are actually quite different. As the drawings above here show, an ant will have wings that are of different lengths, with the two forward wings longer than the two back ones; a termite's wings are all the same length. An even more distinctive difference is in their body shapes. Ants have a two-part body with a thin waist joining the two sections. Termites have a relatively straight body without a narrow waist. Also, they are usually black in color (ants can be many different colors, depending on the species).

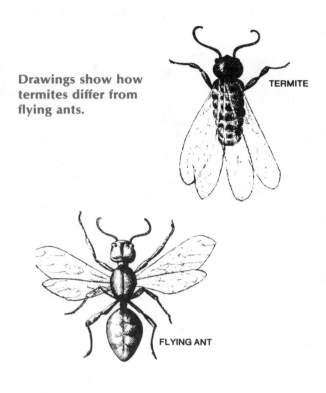

Drawings show how termites differ from flying ants.

TERMITE

FLYING ANT

Dealing with Termite Infestation

Although it is best, when you suspect the presence of termites in your house, to call in a professional exterminator who specializes in termite detection and prevention, there are some things you can do to help eliminate possible points of entry—steps that are worth taking even if you do not yet have a termite infestation.

Make sure that the soil around the outside of your house is never banked up so high that any wood comes in direct contact with the ground, and never pile firewood or lumber directly on the ground for any length of time. It should instead be stacked on cement blocks or bricks that will keep it raised off the ground, with the stacks not next to the house or other structures. Fence posts, columns, and other wood members that do come in contact with the ground, or that rest on concrete slabs that are directly on top of the ground, should be made of pressure-treated lumber that will resist rot and attack by insects. If they are not, they should be soaked in a wood

Termites enter house in various ways (left to right): **over foundation, through cracks in concrete slabs, across porches, behind brick veneer.**

preservative containing pentachlorophenol or zinc naphthenate, which will help protect against rot and termite attack (while these wood preservatives definitely help, wood treated at home is not as long-lasting as commercially treated lumber).

At least once a year, look around the outside of the house and inside the crawl spaces for possible signs of termites. Remember that termites will never bore completely through the surface of the wood, so beams, sills, posts, and other members susceptible to attack may look perfectly sound on the outside. But there is a simple way to test for damage if you suspect termite activity—poke the wood in suspected places with a sharp knife or icepick. If the point goes in easily to a depth of more than about ½ inch, then you may have a problem, though not necessarily termites. It could also be rot (sometimes called dry rot). To check for the difference, chisel out a small section and see if the wood is hollowed out in galleries or tunnels that parallel the grain while the wood on the surface looks fine. If it is, you can be sure the damage was done by termites. If, on the other hand, the wood is just spongy, or if it crumbles easily and is just as soft on the surface as it is underneath, then chances are it is simply rot.

While you are looking for signs of termite activity, don't forget to look for tunnels along the face of masonry walls and along pipes that enter the house. And don't overlook cracks that may have narrow mud tunnels built on the inside—another favorite means of termite entry. Small cracks in a concrete slab next to the house, or in

a concrete stoop that adjoins the house, should be patched promptly.

If you find evidence of termite infestation, don't panic. Termites can do a lot of damage in time, but it takes years for them to have any serious effect on a building.

The method of treatment to get rid of termites involves poisoning the soil under and around the house with a powerful insecticide such as chlordane, but this is a job for a professional who knows how to handle this strong and potentially hazardous chemical (only a licensed professional can buy such chemicals anyway). An exterminator will also have the equipment to drill the holes needed to pump the chemicals into the soil under the basement floors and under all concrete slabs

Termite exterminator pumps chemicals through hole drilled in basement floor.

and stoops next to the house. It is possible to do this part of the job yourself by digging a trench around the entire house and renting the equipment for boring holes through the concrete basement floor, and through the floor of the attached garage and patio (if you can buy the necessary chemicals), but this can be quite a project, and you still won't have the pumping equipment needed to saturate the soil properly.

REPAIRING OVERHEAD GARAGE DOORS

There are two basic types of overhead garage doors used on home garages: the one-piece swing-up type that consists of a single panel that swings up to open, and the sectional or roll-up type that consists of several narrow panels joined together by hinges so that the whole thing can roll up on tracks—much in the way that the cover on an old-fashioned rolltop desk rolls up and out of the way.

One-piece, swing-up doors are generally cheaper than sectional doors, but they do not work as smoothly or open as easily. Also, many people feel that they are less attractive than the sectional roll-up models.

Both door types depend on heavy coiled metal springs to counterbalance the weight of the door so it will be easy to open without having to actually lift the entire weight of the door. These springs also serve to "hold back" or help support the weight of the door when closing, so that it doesn't come crashing down.

Some models have coil springs that are wound up as the door is lowered in order to build up the tension needed to raise it when you are ready to do so; in others the springs are stretched as the door is lowered, thus also serving to build up tension to help lift the door the next time you want to raise it. Almost all of these doors have overhead tracks on each side in which rollers, attached to the edges of the door, guide the door as it moves up and down in the process of opening or closing.

When the door's springs are properly adjusted and all moving parts are working smoothly, the tension in the springs should be such that the door will stay in place, not sinking or rising by it-self, when you let go of it with the bottom edge of the door about 3 feet off the ground. If you let go of it when it is higher than this, it should tend to rise slowly; if you let go when it is much lower than 3 feet, it should tend to drop the rest of the way by itself.

The drawings on page 330 show how a typical sectional roll-up door and a typical one-piece swing-up door are assembled. In the swing-up model the springs are always the type that gets stretched as the door rises; one end is attached to the door and the other end to the garage wall or ceiling. The roll-up models may have either a torsion spring (the kind that gets wound up) or a tension spring (the kind that gets stretched), depending on design. In both cases the spring is not attached directly to the door; it transfers its energy to the door by means of an arrangement of pulleys and cables so that the spring is tensioned as the door comes down, then releases as the door goes up.

When an overhead door fails to work smoothly, chances are that the trouble is due to one of the following:

• The mounting screws or bolts that hold the rollers in place have started to work loose, so that the door tends to wobble or bind as it goes up and down.

• The rollers have jumped out of the overhead track, usually because the track is bent, or because the bolts holding the rollers to the door have worked loose.

• The hinges, rollers, or other moving parts have become bent or corroded, or they need lubrication.

• The springs have lost some of their tension, or the weight of the door has increased (because of many coats of paint), making it necessary to shorten the cables that connect to the springs (and thus increase tension on the springs).

If the problem is one of sticking or binding in certain places as the door goes up or down, start by checking the bolts or screws used to fasten the roller brackets to the door. If any of these have started to work loose, the door may have sagged out of alignment, causing binding in the tracks at some places. Binding can also be caused by brackets that are bent, or by sections of track that have been bent out of alignment—as from an accident of some kind, or because the brackets

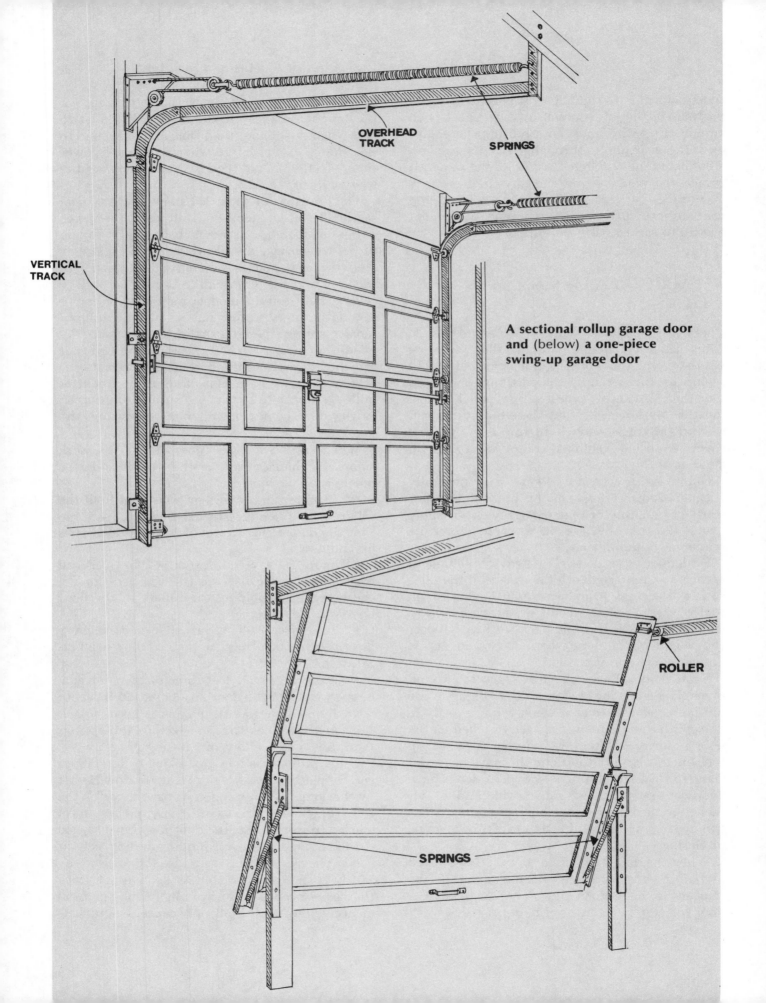

OVERHEAD TRACK

SPRINGS

VERTICAL TRACK

A sectional rollup garage door and (below) a one-piece swing-up garage door

ROLLER

SPRINGS

that hold the track in place on each side of the garage door have been bent or worked loose. Also, check all the screws or bolts that hold the hinges in place between sections (on roll-up doors); should any have come loose, the result could be sagging or binding when the door moves up or down.

If all the hardware seems tight and in proper alignment, it could be that lubrication is needed in some of the moving parts. Squirt a few drops of lightweight oil on each hinge pin and into the oil holes on each roller bearing. Also oil the pulleys over which the cables ride, and while you're at it, wipe the cable itself down with an oil-soaked rag to help protect against rusting.

If the door still tends to stick or bind after all this, the next thing you should check is the stop molding or trim on each side, to see if the door is rubbing against it as it moves up or down. If you find places where this kind of rubbing occurs, the simplest cure is to pry the molding off, then re-nail it slightly farther away from the face of the door, using new nails driven in an inch or two away from the old nail holes.

If you suspect that the tracks are out of alignment—either because they have been bent or because the mounting bolts have loosened—use a level to check that the vertical sections are

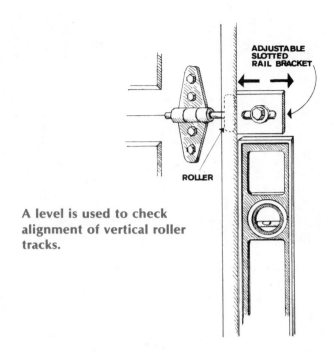

A level is used to check alignment of vertical roller tracks.

plumb (vertical) in both directions (from side to side, as well as from front to back); then use the level to make certain the horizontal sections along the top are level or, better still, are pitched very slightly toward the back of the garage (this helps ensure that the door will stay open when fully raised).

For a door to operate smoothly, the tracks on each side must be parallel to and equidistant from each other at all points along their length. Use a rigid ruler or straight length of wood to check this, measuring the distance apart at several different places along both the horizontal and vertical sections. The mounting brackets for these tracks usually have slotted mounting holes so that you can make minor adjustments without having to completely remove and reinstall them.

When Springs Need Adjusting

If an overhead garage door tends to come crashing down when you close it, or if it becomes very hard to lift, chances are that the tension in the springs needs to be increased (unless the spring is broken—in which case it must be replaced). The first thing you should do is check to see if the hooked end has come off where it is fastened to the bracket against the overhead on each side of

Lubricating hinge pins can help free a balky garage door.

Lift cable can be tightened on some models by moving the S-hook into another hole. A torsion-type spring provides tension on other models.

the door. If it is still secured, see if the cable has jumped out of the groove in one of the pulleys over which it runs. If it has, open the door as high as it will go to release the tension, then use a stick to pry the cable back into its proper path.

Sectional roll-up doors have two springs mounted horizontally next to or above the overhead sections of track on each side. Each spring is connected by cable to the door (usually to the bottom corner on each side), so the easiest way to increase tension is to shorten the cable. First raise the door all the way up, then use blocks or clamps to hold it in this position. There should now be no slack in the cable, and the spring should be under little, if any, tension. Disconnect the cable where it is connected to the door, then pull it tight enough to stretch the spring a little before you connect it back up again.

On some doors the cable is attached to an S-hook that then fits into one of a series of holes, so shortening the cable to add more tension is accomplished simply by pulling hard enough to permit moving the hook to the next hole. Make sure you take up by the same amount on each side to keep tension on both springs the same. Repeat the process if you find that increasing tension makes it work a little better, but that it still needs a bit more to counterbalance the door properly.

Some overhead doors have a single torsion-type spring that goes across the top of the doorframe. To increase tension on this type of spring you have to use a strong metal bar that fits into a hole provided for it. The metal bar serves as a handle for a ratchetlike winding mechanism de-

signed to wind the spring a bit tighter. This requires care—and lots of muscle!—and frankly it can be dangerous if the "handle" gets away from you. That's why this job is best left to a professional. A tremendous amount of tension is involved in winding these springs tighter, posing a real chance of serious injury when the job is tackled by those unfamiliar with the techniques involved.

In swing-up-type one-piece doors, the springs are generally mounted vertically on each side of the door, and there is usually no cable. Instead, the end of the spring is attached to an S-hook that can fit into any one of several holes, so to increase tension you simply move the hook to the next hole—though this in itself may take some heavy muscle power.

There is one other problem that can interfere with proper operation of an overhead garage

Alignment of locking bar can be adjusted by moving bracket up or down.

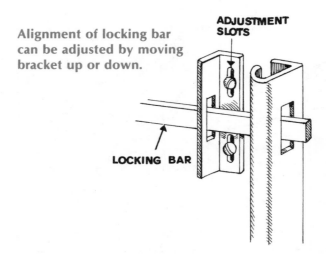

door: The door may close and open easily, but it doesn't lock or latch properly because the locking bar does not line up with the hole in the rail or track on each side. Sometimes this is simply because the bar has been bent, so taking it off and straightening the bar will solve the problem. Otherwise, the most likely solution is to loosen the screws that hold the bracket through which the end of the locking bar slides, then move this up or down as necessary to align the bar with its opening.

REPAIRING FENCES AND POSTS

For maximum durability and longest protection against rotting or attack by insects, fence posts should always be made of pressure-treated lumber. If this lumber is not available, then the bottom end of each post should be soaked overnight in a pail of wood preservative such as one containing zinc naphthenate or pentachlorophenol. Just painting this preservative on is not enough—the wood must be soaked in it, preferably after pieces have been cut to size so the end grain can absorb the liquid completely.

The preferred method for setting a wood fence

Secure anchoring of a fence post, using temporary braces to hold post in place while concrete hardens

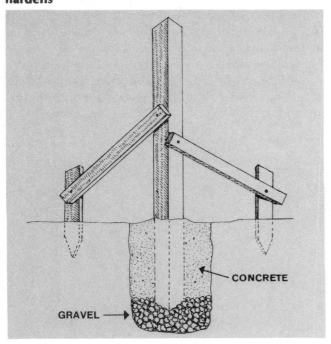

post into the ground is illustrated in the drawing below. The hole must be deep enough so that you can first put in a base of gravel several inches deep, then rest the post on top of it. The gravel ensures good drainage at the bottom of the hole so that the post is not sitting in water after every rain. The rest of the hole, around the post and up to about an inch above ground level, is then filled with freshly poured concrete; tamp it down repeatedly as you pour so as not to leave any air pockets. The top of the concrete is troweled off so that it slopes away from the post in all directions to help shed water.

To hold the post vertical while pouring the concrete, nail two temporary braces to the sides of the post at right angles to each other. Use only one nail so that the brace can swivel up or down while you are aligning the post vertically. Use a spirit level to check if it is plumb (be sure you use the level on two sides to make certain it is plumb from side to side, as well as from front to back). The bottom end of each brace is then nailed to a sturdy stake driven into the ground, as shown. Leave the braces in place for several hours after the concrete is poured, then remove them.

Bracing Wobbly Posts

When an existing fence post starts to wobble, steps should be taken to repair it as soon as possible—otherwise adjoining posts and other sections of the fence will also start to work loose. If the loose post is still solid—that is, not rotted or cracked—you can probably reinforce it without taking a section of the fence apart. Use a narrow post-hole shovel, or a post-hole digger, to dig down around the post, then pour concrete around it as just described.

More often than not, a wobbly fence post will also be cracked or partially rotted, at least in that part close to or below ground level. One quick way to repair a post of this kind is to add 2×4 braces as illustrated on page 334 top left. Taper the end of each piece so it comes to a partial point, then drive them down alongside the post—one on each side. The 2×4s should be long enough to extend lower than the bottom of the existing post, yet project up at least 18 to 24 inches above the ground. And they should be

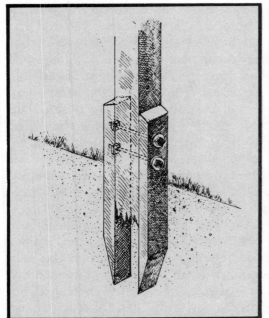

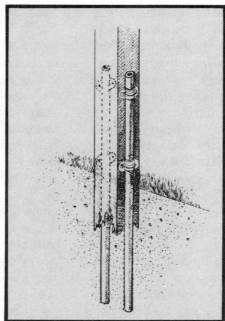

Two expedient methods of bracing a rotted fence post

made of rot-resistant lumber, or treated to resist rot as previously described.

After the braces are in place next to the damaged post, use a long drill bit or brace and bit to bore holes through the two pieces of 2×4 and the post. Then insert long galvanized bolts as shown to join the three pieces firmly together, using large washers under the heads and nuts so you won't crush the wood when you tighten them up all the way.

Another way to accomplish the same thing is to use two lengths of 1-inch galvanized pipe instead of pieces of 2×4. Such pipes should have holes for bolts or lag screws bored through them ahead of time. They are hammered into place on each side of the post, then fastened to the post with long screws or lag bolts, rather than with regular bolts (it would be very difficult to line up all the holes if you tried to insert long bolts through both pieces of pipe and the post).

Posts that support gates are particularly susceptible to loosening and becoming wobbly because of the extra stress placed on them. They can be stiffened or braced by installing angular braces, though you should make sure to install these braces where no one will trip over them (especially in the dark). If there is no safe spot to install a brace of this kind, then use the techniques described for a conventional post—or give some thought to replacing the gate post with one of a larger size that also goes deeper into the ground.

Chapter 15

Energy-Saving Techniques

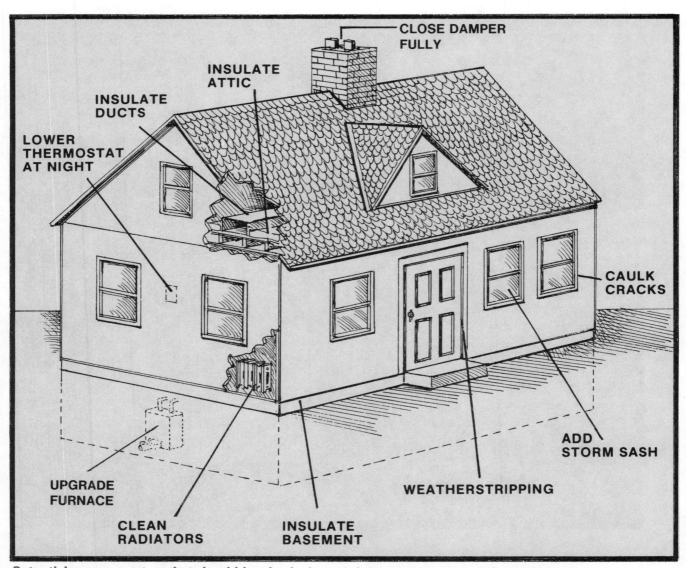

Potential energy-wasters that should be checked around the inside and outside of the house

ANYTHING THAT can be done to reduce fuel costs for heating, or energy costs for air conditioning and similar equipment that consumes electricity, gets high priority from most homeowners these days—and rightly so. Energy conservation is essential for our long-term survival, as well as for our economic well-being.

The biggest single consumer of energy in the average house is the central heating system, so it makes sense to give this top priority when trying to lower energy costs. There are actually three ways to approach the problem: (1) Do everything possible to keep heat indoors during cold weather. (2) Seal off openings through which cold air can enter, especially on windy days. (3) Try to improve the efficiency of your heating system so that you get the maximum amount of heat out of every dollar spent on fuel and/or electricity.

Most houses—especially older houses that were built in the days before we all became so energy-conscious—are not adequately insulated by today's standards. They also are apt to have many gaps or openings through which cold air can enter. So it makes sense to start your battle against higher heating costs by first doing everything possible to contain the heat that is generated on the inside. You do this by adding insulation to outside walls, windows, and attics, and by using weatherstripping and caulking compound to plug as many potential "leaks" as possible. (During the air-conditioning season, the same measures will keep the summer heat out, and thus will help to lower air conditioner operating costs.)

ADDING INSULATION

Most conventional building materials—wood, brick, concrete, and all of the other materials commonly used in building houses—offer comparatively little resistance to the passage of heat, so additional insulation should be added to any wall, ceiling, or floor that separates a cold, unheated area from a heated space.

There are many different types of insulating material available, but the ones most often used in the home generally fall into three broad categories: (1) batts and blankets made of fiberglass or mineral wool; (2) loose fill, which is blown into cavities in existing walls or spread over unfinished attic floors, and which usually consists of fiberglass or cellulose (specially treated shredded paper); and (3) rigid boards or panels of plastic foam, which are more often used as exterior sheathing (under shingles and siding), but which can also be used inside when covered with a fire-resistant panel such as gypsum board.

All insulation is rated according to its R-value, a number that indicates how much resistance it offers to the transmission of heat. The larger a material's R-value, the better it is as an insulator. R-values are cumulative, increasing in direct proportion to that material's thickness. However, not all insulations have the same R-rating for a given thickness; 4 inches of one insulation may have just as high an R-rating as 5 inches of another. So when shopping for insulation, use the R-ratings to compare values, not just the thickness of the material. And remember that these add up; if you add an R-11 insulation to an existing R-9, for example, you will wind up with a layer that has a rating of R-20.

How much insulation do you really need in the walls and ceilings? This depends on where you live, on whether or not you regularly use air conditioning in the summer, and to some extent on the type of heat you have. A house that is heated by electricity should have more insulation than one that is heated by oil or gas, because electric heat is much more expensive than the other types in most parts of the country. The map and the charts on page 338 show the recommended

Climate Zones of the U.S.

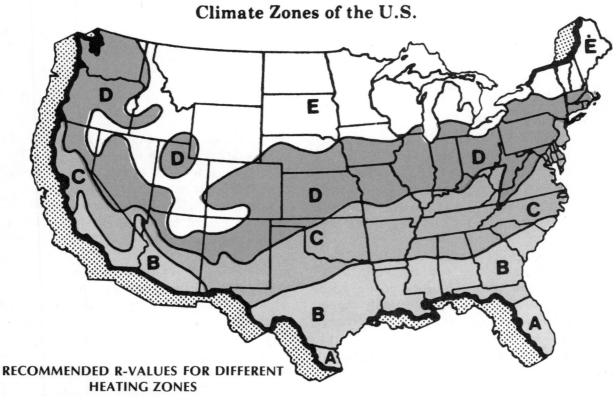

RECOMMENDED R-VALUES FOR DIFFERENT HEATING ZONES

	A	B	C	D	E
CEILINGS (Attic Floors)	R-19*	R-19*	R-30	R-38	R-44
FRAME SIDEWALLS	R-11*	R-11*	R-13	R-13	R-19**
FLOORS OVER UNHEATED SPACES	R-9*	R-9-11*	R-13	R-13	R-19

Recommended R-values for different geographical heating zones in the United States

*Since these are not in zones that normally require heating, insulation can be reduced or eliminated if house is not air conditioned.

**Ordinary frame walls can only take insulation about 3½" thick (equal to R-11 or R-13) so this much insulation will only fit if walls are framed out with 2×6's.

amounts of insulation required for walls and ceilings of a typical house located in various parts of the United States. Use it to figure out how much more you would have to add if you wanted to bring your house up to today's standards for your climate area.

Of course, adding insulation does cost money, so there comes a point when it may not be cost-effective to keep on adding more. A lot depends on whether you can do the work yourself and thus save on the cost of professional labor, which can run so high that it may take you many years to recoup the amount you spent on having the extra insulation added.

Adding more insulation to the floor of an unfinished attic (the ceiling of the room below) is a fairly simple job that you can do yourself, and it will usually pay for itself in fuel savings in a few years. To check the R-rating of any fiberglass insulation that is already down, measure its thickness and assume an R-rating of a little over 3 for each inch of thickness (R-9 for a 3-inch layer of fiberglass, for example). If the insulation in your attic is less than 4 inches thick, adding more is definitely worthwhile. But if there is already more than 4 inches in place, adding more insulation may be only of slight benefit—in some cases saving as little as $20 to $40 for the entire year. At that rate it would probably take many years to save enough to pay back the cost.

If the insulation in the attic is up between the roof rafters, then the amount you can install is limited by the size or width of the rafters—it should not be quite as thick as the full depth of the rafters, for you want to make certain there is room for air to circulate between the top of the insulation and the underside of the roof sheathing (more about this later when we talk about the need for ventilation and vapor barriers).

Adding insulation to the walls in an older house that has none is generally a job for a professional, who will either blow in loose fill or pump in a foam that expands to fill in the hollow spaces. Loose fill may be either cellulose, fiberglass, or mineral wool. This is a fairly expensive project that calls for drilling holes in the exterior walls at regular intervals, then neatly covering or plugging these holes at the end of the job. The holes must be carefully spaced so all cavities are filled, with no large air pockets remaining.

In a fairly cold climate, or in a house that is centrally air-conditioned, wall insulating is economically worthwhile, although the payback period will vary considerably—from as little as five years in really cold climates where indoor temperatures are normally maintained at close to 70 degrees during the winter to as much as ten to fifteen years in milder climates where people may be content with 68 degrees on the inside (the greater the difference between indoor and outdoor temperatures, the faster the heat loss and the greater the number of BTUs lost during a given length of time).

If the walls already have some insulation in them, chances are that it would not pay to add more, even if there is space available inside the walls. The cost would be too high for the amount of additional savings you could expect to achieve. If you are planning major alterations, however, it may be practical to add more insulation at that time without adding greatly to the cost. For example, if you're putting up new siding, it may be practical to install board-type insulation underneath—adding to the R-rating of that wall while

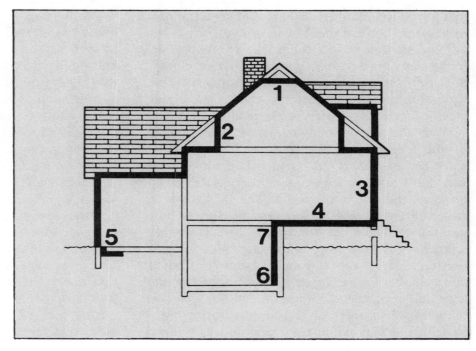

Where to insulate a home: (1) ceilings with cold spaces above; (2) rafters and "knee" walls of finished attic; (3) exterior walls or walls between heated and unheated spaces; (4) floors over unheated or outside spaces; (5) perimeter of a concrete floor slab on grade level; (6) walls of finished or heated basement; (7) top of foundation or basement wall

also sealing any open cracks or seams through which cold air may have been entering.

Besides the attic or roof, and the regular outside walls, there are several places in the average house where adding insulation is economically worthwhile. These would include the following:

• Any wall that separates the living quarters of the house from an unheated area—such as an attached garage or an unused part of the attic adjoining one of the upstairs bedrooms

• Floors that are over an unfinished, unheated basement

• Floors that are over an unheated garage, or over an unheated crawl space or open porch

• Exterior walls of a heated basement where these walls project above ground level

In many of these locations, insulation may be missing entirely, because years ago builders didn't think it necessary to insulate such places. Adding insulation now where possible will be worthwhile, in terms both of comfort to occupants during cold weather, and of fuel savings likely to accrue over the years you expect to live in that house.

Insulating the Attic

Laying insulation over an unfinished attic floor is probably the easiest type of installation—you just unroll the blankets or batts between the rafters and the job is done. Make sure you buy batts or blankets that have a vapor barrier on one side (a specially treated heavy kraft paper or aluminum foil) and put the insulation down with the vapor barrier on the bottom—that is, with the barrier facing the heated or warm side.

If the attic floor already has some insulation on it and you want to add more, you can simply place the new material on top. Just make sure you don't add a second vapor barrier: Pull up some of the old insulation to see if there is a vapor barrier on the bottom, and if there is, buy new material that has no vapor barrier. If you already have or can only buy material with a vapor barrier, slash it every few inches before putting it down. If there is no vapor barrier under the old material, pick the old material up (or push it temporarily to one side if you are dealing with loose fill) so you can put the new material down

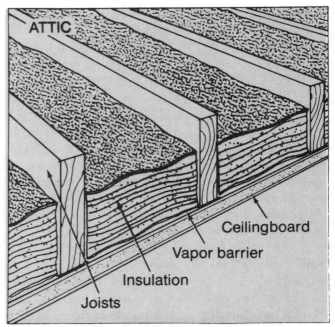

How insulation is installed on attic floor

first with its vapor barrier on the underside; then put the old material back on top.

You can install insulation that is thicker than the height of the floor joists by putting it right on top of the old material, but for best results, run it *across* the joists as illustrated. In other words, put it down at right angles to the original layer of insulation (making sure you don't add a second vapor barrier, unless you slash it as described above) so that it actually covers the wood joists, as well as the spaces between the joists. This helps cut down on heat losses through the wood itself (solid wood is a poor insulator).

Never compress batts or blankets of insulation in an effort to squeeze extra material between floor joists (or between wall studs). Compressing the fiberglass actually reduces its overall efficiency, squeezing out the millions of tiny trapped air pockets on the inside that are essential for the insulating effectiveness of the material.

When applying insulation to an attic floor on the part that extends out over the eaves, make sure you do not cover up any vents or openings. These openings are necessary for proper ventilation *above* the insulation (to prevent condensation during cold weather, and to help heated air escape during hot weather). Also, keep the insulation away from any recessed lighting fixtures or

Laying second layer of insulation across unfinished attic floor, on top of joists

Insulation should be cut out around recessed ceiling lights that generate heat.

vent fans that stick up through the ceiling from the rooms below. These fixtures generate heat that must be allowed to escape freely to avoid a fire hazard, so keep insulation off them (if you are spreading cellulose insulation, keep it at least 3 inches away on all sides).

The same holds true if you are putting down loose fill insulation (fiberglass or cellulose) on the attic floor—keep it away from lighting fixtures, fans, etc. Plywood or sheet-metal barriers will keep the material from moving or drifting later

on, and you can put cardboard or hardboard barriers around vent openings (over the eaves) to keep loose insulation from blowing into or over these openings. To spread the material, use a rake or a piece of wood the width of the space between the joists. Remember that the R-rating will depend on the depth of the material, so keep this constant to provide the rating you want.

If your plans call for finishing and heating the attic at some future date, the insulation should be installed up between the roof rafters instead

Pouring loose-fill insulation between attic joists

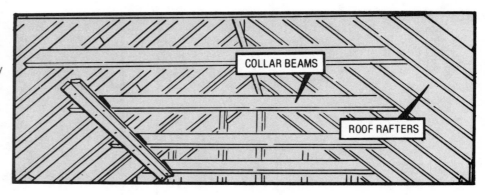

Insulation under a pitched roof in an attic still to be finished should extend only up to (and across) collar beams.

of on the floor. Fiberglass batts or blankets are stapled up so they fit between the overhead rafters, with flanges overlapping on the face of each rafter. The insulation should *not* go all the way up to the peak, just across the horizontal collar beams that span the rafters near the top (beams that will form the ceiling of the finished room when you are done). If your attic does not now have such collar beams, even though it has a sloping roof, you will have to nail up your own alongside each pair of rafters, as shown.

This is also a good time to put up the short studs that will frame out the "knee walls" (the short walls that separate the finished from the unfinished parts of the attic over the eaves). That way you will be able to carry the insulation down behind these knee walls and then out along the rest of the floor joists to the eaves. This is more efficient than carrying the insulation all the way down the roof rafters to the eaves only to have to put more insulation up behind the knee walls at some later date.

Attics that are already finished are, of course, much more difficult to insulate: You have to get behind the existing knee walls and above the finished ceiling in the attic (assuming there is no insulation up between the rafters). But it can be done. To get behind the walls that separate the heated rooms from the unfinished areas you have to cut an opening in the panel or wallboard so you can crawl out between the studs to apply insulation behind them. When finished you can

Insulating Existing Walls

To insulate finished walls there are really only two things you can do—rip the wall open from inside by removing all plaster or paneling so that you can install insulation between the studs from within, or have a professional contractor come in to pump in loose fill or cellulose insulation. Either way, there is considerable cost involved, but in a cold climate it can still pay off—in many cases you can save enough fuel to pay for the cost of the job over a period of about six to eight years.

Of course, installing insulation is simple if the walls are unfinished and the studs are still exposed—as when new additions are being made to an existing home, or when an interior remodeling job calls for ripping walls open to expose studs on the inside. The insulation is installed between the studs, with the thickness you can use being limited to the width of the studs. Remember that the 2×4 studs in an ordinary wall are actually only 3½ inches wide, so this is the thickest insulation you can install in normal circumstances. (That's why many of the newer, energy-efficient houses are being built with walls made of 2×6 studs—these are spaced 24 inches apart, center to center, instead of the usual 16 inches apart.)

When you put up the insulation make certain the vapor barrier is facing inward, and staple the flanges to the inner face of the studs so that the flanges overlap. If you are putting up insulation that does not have a barrier and are planning to install a separate vapor barrier by stapling up sheets of polyethylene plastic, make sure the sheets overlap where they meet on the edge of a stud (never between studs) and avoid cuts or tears that will break the continuity of the film. Do a neat job of cutting around electrical outlets, switches, and other openings in the wall so as not to leave gaps in the film.

patch the opening by following the techniques described in Chapter 6.

To get insulation up above the attic ceiling (between the roof rafters) in a finished attic room, you have two choices: You can call in a professional contractor to blow in loose fill, or you can cut a sizable opening in the ceiling so that you can crawl up above the collar beams, then slide insulation in from above, allowing it also to slide down the sloping part of the ceiling. You can then patch the ceiling just as you would a wall.

Installing Insulation Under Floors

Floors over an unheated area are most often insulated by pushing fiberglass batts or blankets up between the floor joists from beneath. The rule about vapor barriers still applies: They should face the warm (heated) side of the floor.

Most insulation has the vapor barrier and the flanges used for stapling on the same side, and this can pose a problem when putting the insulation under a floor—the flanges (and the barrier) will be on top, so you'll have difficulty stapling the batts or blankets to the underside of the floor joists. The easiest way to solve this problem is to buy batts that have "reverse flanges," which are on the side *opposite* the vapor barrier. These are not widely available, so the more usual procedure is to push the batts up between the joists, then hold them in place either by stapling some wire mesh underneath or by using wires woven back and forth between nails driven into the bot-

tom edge of each joist, as shown. (Even with reverse-flange insulation, you still need this wire to keep the insulation from sagging later on.)

An even simpler method to support insulation under a floor is to use short pieces of stiff wire that you simply jam up between the joists at intervals of 18 to 20 inches, as shown below. These have pointed ends that stick into the wood and keep them from slipping out while they support the insulation and keep it from sagging. This method eliminates the need for driving in nails or stapling up wire mesh.

Insulating Basements and Crawl Spaces

Adding insulation to basement walls pays if you live in a fairly cold climate, and if you plan to finish and/or heat the basement in the future. But if you live in one of the northern states (like Maine or Minnesota) where winters are really severe and where the frost line goes down below the level of your basement, then insulating the basement could cause structural problems (heaving of the foundation, etc.). Should you wonder about your own location, contact your local HUD/FHA field office for recommendations before you insulate your basement.

An ordinary basement with masonry walls of poured concrete or cement block is best insulated by putting up studs to frame out a partition wall in front of the existing masonry wall, as shown in the drawing on page 344. Fiberglass batts or blankets can then be put up between the studs

Holding insulation in place under a floor with (left) woven wires and (right) stiff pointed wires jammed between joists

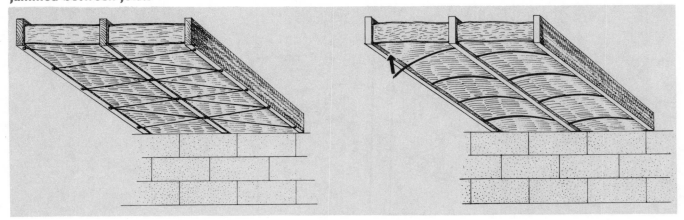

by stapling the flanges to the inner faces of the studs and putting them up so the vapor barrier is on the inside. If there is a possibility of water seeping through the masonry at times, then don't do a job of this kind until the moisture problem has been cured.

Generally speaking, it is not necessary to carry the insulation all the way down to the floor; usually it is sufficient to carry it to about 18 inches below the outside ground level. (Carrying it all the way down will do no harm, of course, and will save a little more heat.) With the insulation installed between the studs, the inside of the framed-out partition wall is covered with gypsum board or some other type of paneling to finish it off.

Another method sometimes used to insulate basement walls is to cement up rigid panels of insulating foam board, using a mastic cement sold for this purpose. Foam panels have a higher R-rating per inch of thickness than most other insulating materials, but they are highly flammable, so all building codes require that they be covered with ½-inch-thick gypsum wallboard on the inside after they are installed.

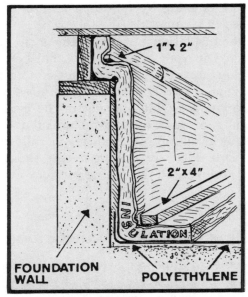

Proper way to insulate a crawl space

A crawl space can be insulated along its walls and the inside of the rim joists around the top of the foundation walls. The most effective way is usually to run insulation from the rim joists down the walls and out onto the floors for a few inches, as shown in the drawing above.

Basement wall insulation should extend at least 2 feet below ground level.

WHY VENTILATION AND VAPOR BARRIERS ARE NEEDED

Years ago when houses were loosely built with lots of "natural ventilation" from loosely fitting windows and doors and many open joints along foundation walls and attic eaves, and when most had little, if any, insulation in the walls, there was never a problem with condensation developing in walls, crawl spaces, or attics. But as insulation, weatherstripping, and storm windows were added to seal the house more tightly, the need for vapor barriers and venting of attics and crawl spaces became apparent.

During cold weather the air inside the house is not only much warmer, it also has much more moisture in it—moisture that is added by normal day-to-day cooking, bathing, washing, even the breathing of the occupants. Air that is warmer and has more moisture always tries to find its way to cooler and drier air, so the inside air tends to work its way out into the colder hollow wall spaces, as well as up into the attic, carrying its extra moisture with it. There the moisture vapor comes in contact with the colder surfaces of the wall sheathing (or the roof sheathing in the case of an attic), causing the moisture to condense and form droplets of water—much in the way that a pitcher of icewater "sweats" on a summer day. This water soaks into the insulation, causing it to lose much of its effectiveness, and can cause

rotting of wood structural members and rusting of nails or other fasteners.

To prevent this, a vapor barrier is installed—a nonpermeable film of foil or specially treated kraft paper that will not allow moisture vapor to pass through (ordinary walls of wood, concrete, plaster, gypsum board, or similar materials offer little or no resistance to the passage of moisture vapor). If it is properly installed and unbroken, this barrier prevents the moisture vapor from passing through to reach the cold surfaces, and no condensation takes place.

So why is there still a need for ventilation in attics and crawl spaces? Because no vapor barrier is ever really perfect—there are always places where the barrier is torn or where pieces are missing so that moisture vapor can get through. There are also openings in the barrier that can never be sealed off completely (around outlets, built-in cabinets, recessed radiators, etc.). All this means that some moisture vapor will still work its way up to the attic (including through the hollow spaces inside the walls).

That is why vents are needed—to provide openings that will allow fresh air from outside to flow freely above the insulation and thus permit the moisture-laden air to escape harmlessly to the outside before condensation can form. In other words, they serve to "dry out" the air above the insulation so that it cannot form drops of water on the underside of the roof beams or sheathing.

How a vapor barrier keeps moisture from coming in contact with cold outer surfaces to condense inside hollow wall spaces

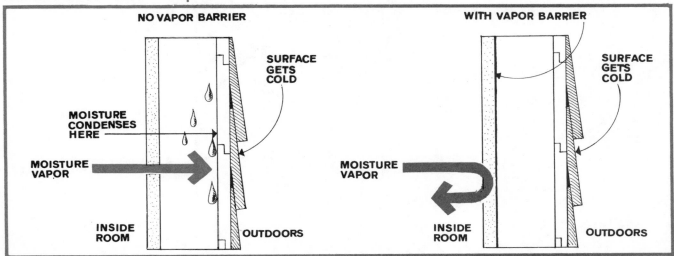

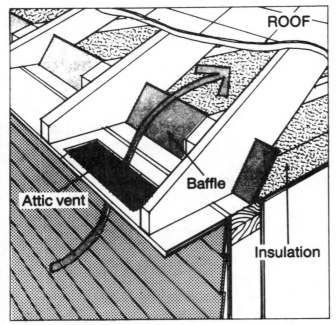

Properly installed attic insulation allows for free flow of air above the insulation.

The vents can be located in various places, but the most common type of attic venting is provided by louvered and screened openings that are cut into the top of each of the end walls. For best results this method of installation should be combined with additional screened openings in the overhanging eaves. The idea is to permit air to flow in at the bottom of the attic (through the vents in the overhanging eaves), then up over the insulation and out through the openings near the peaks.

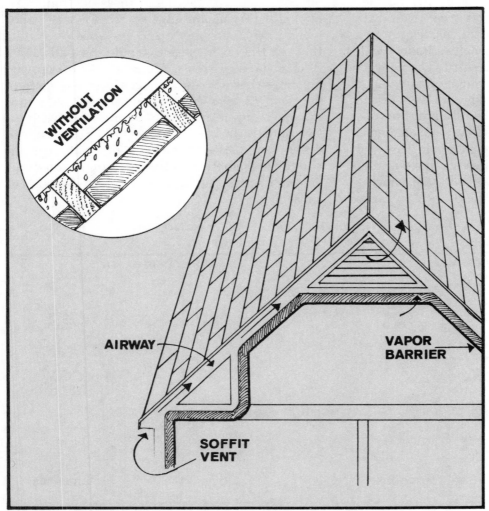

Insulation lets air flow under roof and through vents; detail shows how condensation forms without such ventilation.

All vents should be located where they will provide efficient cross-ventilation—you don't want one large vent at one end of the attic without any vents at the other. They should be large enough to provide a total of at least 1 square foot of unobstructed opening for each 300 square feet of attic floor space (make it 2 square feet if the attic insulation does not have a vapor barrier under it). Bear in mind that this figure refers to "unobstructed" openings. A vent that has louvers and mesh screening over it is not an unobstructed opening—the louvers and mesh cut down on the actual size of the opening by about half, so the overall size of the vent must be doubled to provide an equivalent amount of ventilation.

Ventilation is equally important in a closed-off crawl space—especially if it has an unfinished dirt floor. Large amounts of moisture vapor are given off by the uncovered soil, and this moisture can find its way up into the house walls and other parts of the structure.

To prevent this spread of moisture, cover the soil with a layer of heavy roofing felt, or with sheets of heavyweight polyethylene. Overlap sheets at least 12 inches where they meet and weight the material down with bricks or stones along the seams, as well as around the edges. The walls of the crawl space should have vents located on opposite sides of the area to ensure through-ventilation for moist air to escape easily.

These vents should be large enough to provide at least 1 square foot of unobstructed opening for every 300 square feet of crawl-space area, assuming the floor of the crawl space is paved or covered with a vapor barrier as described above.

If the floor above the crawl space is insulated, and if the floor of the crawl space is either paved or protected with a layer of plastic or roofing felt, then the vents can be covered up during the heating season to conserve fuel. However, in many cases this may lead to condensation forming in the crawl space, so it may still be necessary to leave the vents open in the winter. If in doubt on your own situation, close the vents and check periodically during the winter to see if condensation is forming under the floor or under the insulation; if it is, leave the vents open.

INSULATING PIPES, AIR DUCTS, AND WATER HEATERS

In a forced-air heating system, the ducts that carry heated air through the house often have to run through basements, attics, crawl spaces, and other unheated areas. If these ducts are not insulated there can be sizable losses of heat through the walls of the duct (this also holds true if the house is centrally air-conditioned—ducts that pass through spaces that are not air-conditioned

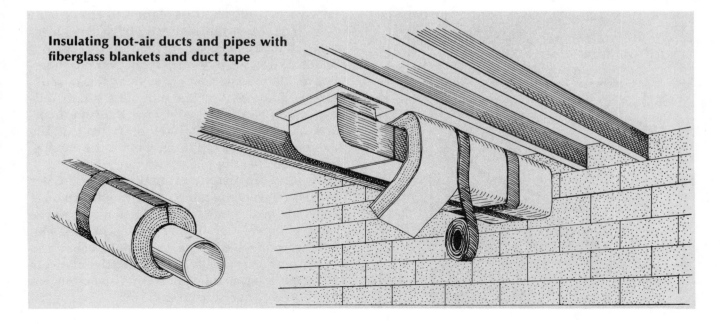

Insulating hot-air ducts and pipes with fiberglass blankets and duct tape

should be insulated to retain the system's cooling capacity). Of course, in the case of heating ducts, you may *want* this heat to be dispersed along the length of the duct—for example, in an otherwise unheated basement, "waste" heat from these ducts may be desirable to keep the basement more comfortable and to cut down on condensation problems. Just remember that the more heat the duct loses as it passes through these areas, the less heat there will be left for the rooms upstairs, and the more the furnace will have to work to keep temperatures at a comfortable level over the rest of the house.

Ducts can be insulated where accessible by wrapping with fiberglass blankets sold for this purpose. Usually 1 or 2 inches in thickness, they come with or without an aluminum-foil vapor barrier on one side (the vapor barrier is needed for air-conditioning ducts, but seldom for heating ducts). After the duct has been wrapped, the insulation is secured with duct tape or with plastic or wire ties.

Steam pipes and hot-water lines should also be insulated—at least wherever these pipes pass through unheated basements, crawl spaces, or attics. The insulation will keep the water or steam inside that much hotter, so more heat will be delivered to each of the radiators. Of course, you can't do much about insulating pipes that run inside the walls, though in most cases this heat is not completely lost anyway; any heat that is given off inside a wall tends to help keep its room warmer, especially in the case of an outside

Hot-water pipes can be insulated with foam "sleeves" that are slit open along one side.

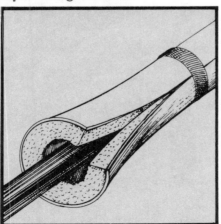

wall that has insulation between the outer side and the pipe.

Everything said thus far about insulating the pipes in a hydronic (steam or hot-water) heating system also applies to insulating pipes that carry your domestic hot water (the water used for bathing, washing, etc.). Losses that occur as the heated water travels through many feet of metal pipe on its way to the various sinks, tubs, and other water-using fixtures in the house can be considerably reduced in most cases by covering the pipes with insulation, where the pipes are accessible.

The quickest pipe insulation to install is the kind that comes in "sleeves" or tubes and is made of flexible plastic foam. Sold in sizes to fit all common pipe diameters, these insulating sleeves come slit open along one side so that you can readily slide them over the pipe. The slit is then sealed with duct tape, although some brands have self-sealing, zipperlike closures. Pipes can also be insulated with wraparound insulation that comes in the form of an adhesive-backed foam tape with a foil facing on the outside. This insulation is wrapped spirally around the pipe with a slight overlap as shown on page 349.

The hot-water heater is the second-greatest consumer of energy in the average American home (heating is the first), so anything you can do to cut down on waste from this appliance is a big help in reducing energy costs. One simple but effective step is to add insulation to the outside of the tank. Most tanks already have some insulation, but by today's standards this is not enough. You can buy one of the various fiberglass insulation kits that are sold for this purpose in many home centers and plumbing supply outlets, or you can make your own by using fiberglass blankets rated at R-11 or R-14. Cut the pieces to size and wrap them around the outside, then fasten them in place with duct tape.

If you have a gas heater, make sure you don't obstruct the vent openings at the top. If you have an electric heater, make sure you don't cover the electrical connection box where the heating element is connected, since this could cause the wiring to overheat (if you buy a kit, the blankets will be cut to size and come with instructions on how to avoid these mistakes).

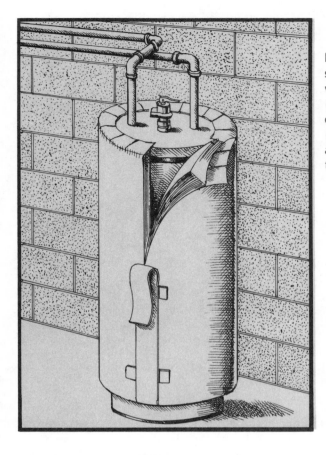

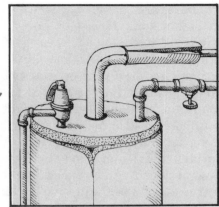

Hot-water heaters should be insulated with fiberglass blankets (left) **and, for the pipes, either special sleeves** (right) **or adhesive-backed foam tape** (below right).

WEATHERSTRIPPING WINDOWS AND DOORS

Adding weatherstripping to doors and windows is one of the least expensive and most effective ways to conserve energy in any house that is heated in the winter or air-conditioned in the summer. It is also one job that can be easily done by a homeowner without need for calling in a professional.

Because doors and windows have to be opened and closed regularly, there is a limit to how tight they can fit—if they fit tight enough to seal out all air leaks, they can be difficult to open or close; yet if they fit loose enough to work easily, they can allow a good deal of cold air to enter from outside (in addition to rattling noisily and allowing windblown dirt and moisture to enter). Good weatherstripping can prevent this by providing a happy compromise: It seals the window or door without seriously hampering easy opening and closing.

Some of the most popular types of weatherstripping: (A) spring-bronze weatherstrip; (B) tubular vinyl, with adhesive backing; (C) foam weatherstripping, with adhesive backing; (D) foam-filled vinyl (tubular), with flange for nailing; (E) V-shaped plastic; (F) metal-and-vinyl rigid strip; (G) foam-edge and vinyl-edge wood strips

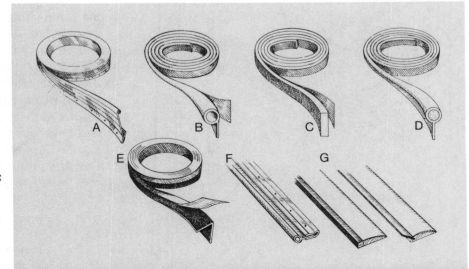

There are many types of weatherstripping available, some for use on doors, some for use on windows, and some that are suitable for both purposes. All have some kind of resilient or springy material that presses against the face or edge of the sliding or hinged frame in order to maintain a continuous airtight seal without seriously restricting movement. The resilient material may be felt, plastic, rubber foam, or springy metal, and it may be fastened to the window or doorframe by tacks, staples, or screws, or by means of a self-adhesive backing on the stripping.

As a rule, felt and foam materials are the lowest in cost, though they are not as permanent as those made of springy metal or heavy vinyl. The illustrations on page 349 show the most popular, and most useful, types available.

Weatherstripping Windows

Weatherstripping materials designed for use around windows generally fall into two classifications: (1) flexible materials that come in rolls and are fastened to the stop moldings so that the

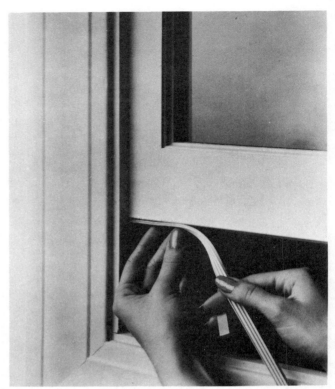

Weatherstripping is also advisable along bottom rail of lower sash.

Stop molding around window jambs should be insulated, with flexible face of weatherstripping in light contact with closed sash.

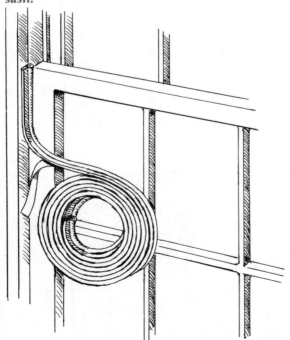

resilient facing of felt, plastic foam, or hollow vinyl presses lightly against the moving surface of the sash; and (2) spring-metal and V-shaped plastic strips that fit *inside* the window channel to press against the edges of the moving sash frame, instead of against the face of the sash frame the way the first type does (these springy metal and plastic types are completely invisible when the window is closed).

All those in the first group are installed by fastening the strip to the stop moldings on each side of the window jamb. Mount the strip so that its flexible or resilient face just comes in contact with the sash frame when closed, but not so tight against it that it will interfere with easy movement when the sash is raised or lowered.

For the upper sash, the weatherstripping is nailed to the parting strip—the narrow molding that separates the two window channels. An extra length of weatherstripping is then fastened to the bottom rail of the lower sash so that it presses against the sill when the window is closed, and another strip is nailed across the top of the lower sash where it overlaps the bottom rail of the upper sash in order to seal off the space between the two when the window is closed. Sometimes adhesive-backed strips of foam are used along the bottom edge of the lower sash and the bottom inside face of the upper sash to seal these joints in windows that are not opened during the winter.

Spring-bronze metal and V-shaped plastic weatherstripping provide a much neater installation that lasts almost indefinitely. Neither is visible from inside when windows are closed. As the drawings show, the metal strip is nailed along one edge only—the other edge springs away from the surface and presses against the edge of the sash to form a relatively airtight seal. Both types are installed so that the free edge faces toward the outside. With the metal type the nailed edge is against the inside stop molding or parting strip. With the plastic type the pressure-sensitive adhesive is only on one half of the V. When this is in place against the channel, the other half of the V springs free to press against the edge of the sash. Additional strips are then fastened under the bottom rail of the lower sash, and to the inside face of the bottom rail on the upper sash (to seal off the joint where the lower sash overlaps the bottom of the upper sash after the window is closed).

Separate weatherstripping is fastened on the inside of both upper and lower sashes, as well as along the bottom of each.

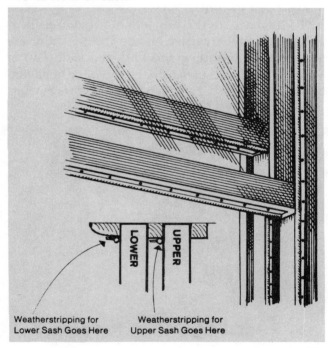

Weatherstripping for Lower Sash Goes Here   Weatherstripping for Upper Sash Goes Here

LOWER   UPPER

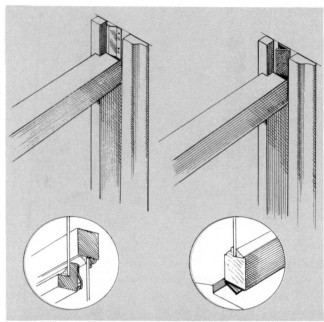

The neatest and longest-lasting installation is provided by spring-bronze metal (left) **or V-shaped plastic** (right) **weatherstripping that fits between sash and jamb.**

Weatherstripping Doors

Most of the weatherstripping materials described above for use on windows can also be used on doors, but a neater job will result if you use a rigid weatherstripping material. Rigid strips are made of wood or aluminum and may have either rubber or plastic foam along one edge, or a flexible vinyl tube or strip fastened along one side. The strips are nailed or screwed to the stop moldings on the inside of the jamb—on each side, as well as along the top—so that the door closes against the resilient or flexible edge. In some installations the wood or metal strip actually serves as, or replaces, the regular stop moldings.

The simplest way to weatherstrip a door is to use self-adhesive plastic foam or sponge-rubber strips. These can be applied to the inside face of the stop molding so that the door closes against them to form a tight seal when closed, or they can be fastened to the edge of the door so as to press against the stop molding as the door closes. Extra strips can be applied along the hinge side to seal that edge when the door is closed.

The most permanent weatherstripping you

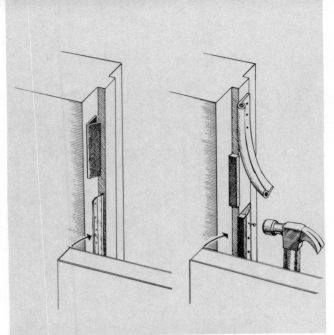

Insulating a door with various types of weatherstripping: along inside face of door jamb with V-shaped plastic or spring bronze (left), or against stop molding on its inside edge or face (right)

When nailing weatherstripping to stop molding, make sure free edge faces stop molding.

can install around a door is the spring-bronze metal or the plastic V-type shown on page 349 and above. Either is fastened to the inside of the jamb as shown, so that the free (unnailed) edge faces toward the stop molding. This edge will spring up to press against the edge of the door as it closes. Make sure this free edge is not too close to the stop molding when the door closes over it—you have to allow for clearance so that when the free edge is compressed (flattened) by the closing door it will not bind against the molding.

To keep drafts from coming in *under* an entrance door, there are a variety of special "door bottoms" and weatherstripped thresholds you can install. A door bottom is a metal, wood, or

plastic molding that has a vinyl, felt, or rubber strip along one side. This acts as a "wiper" or sweep which presses against the top of the threshold to seal out drafts when the door is closed. All of these door bottoms are fastened along the inside bottom edge of the door with screws or nails so that the flexible or resilient material comes in contact with the top of the threshold as the door closes (most entrance doors open inward).

To take care of the problem of providing clearance for a thick carpet on the inside, there are special door-bottom strips designed to flip up or slide upward automatically as the door opens inward (over the carpet). When the door is closing,

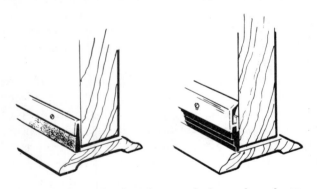

Weatherstripping fastened along door bottom acts as a "wiper" or sweep to keep out cold drafts.

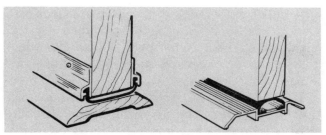

A standard door-bottom shoe (left) and a special aluminum threshold with recessed gasket running down the center of the metal (right)

the edge of the strip folds (or slides) down again to make firm contact with the threshold or floor by the time the door is fully closed.

In place of a regular door-bottom strip that fastens to the inside of the door and thus is always visible, you can also install a special type of door-bottom weatherstripping that fastens to the bottom edge of the door where it is almost completely invisible from either side. Sometimes called a door shoe, it consists of a metal retainer strip that fastens to the bottom of the door, as illustrated above left. A vinyl "bulb" or hollow tube of ridged vinyl runs down the center (under the door) so that it rubs against the top of the threshold as the door closes. Door shoes work fine with conventional wood thresholds that are in reasonably good condition, but probably you will still have to trim a little off the bottom of the door in order to provide the additional clearance needed.

Instead of fastening the vinyl "bulb" to the bottom of the door, many people find it preferable to install a special aluminum threshold that has this same type of flexible vinyl gasket or bulb inserted into a recess which runs down the center of the metal, as illustrated above right. These metal-and-vinyl thresholds can be installed in place of the existing wood or metal threshold, or they can be fastened down on top of it—though in the latter case you have to trim off the bottom of the door to provide the needed additional clearance.

STORM WINDOWS—INSIDE OR OUTSIDE

Windows are one of the greatest energy wasters in a heated house, especially if the windows have only single panes of glass. Heat escapes through the windows in two ways: by seepage of air around loose-fitting sashes or poorly fitted window frames, and by conduction of heat directly through the glass itself (a single pane of glass is a very poor insulator).

Seepage can be greatly reduced by making sure the outside of the window is properly caulked so there are no air gaps around the window frame, and by making sure that all windows have good weatherstripping installed. Cutting down on the amount of heat that is lost through the glass itself is best accomplished by double-glazing—adding another layer of glass—either by adding storm windows or by replacing the sash with double-pane insulating glass. This serves to trap a layer of dead air, which adds greatly to the insulating qualities of the window.

If storm windows are installed they can be either the permanent metal or wood type that are installed on the outside, or they can be plastic units that are easily installed on the inside. In both cases the result is a sizable increase in the window's insulating qualities, with a corresponding reduction in the amount of heating energy wasted. In houses in very cold climates where there are already storm windows on the outside, adding a third layer of glazing material by installing another storm window on the inside may be advisable—to eliminate condensation problems on the windows, as well as to save on fuel.

Windows that have double-pane insulating glass (commonly called Thermopane, which is actually a specific brand) supposedly eliminate the need for storm sashes—as is basically true in moderate to average cold climates—but studies have shown that in a really cold climate adding a third layer of glazing material (a storm window) is usually a worthwhile investment that saves enough fuel to pay for itself within a few years.

Permanent exterior storm windows are usually made of aluminum and have movable panels that permit replacing one section with a screen during the summer. Most of these have to be custom-made and installed by the dealer. Some older houses still have one-piece wooden storm sashes that are put up each winter and taken down each summer, but these are a maintenance headache, and more and more homeowners are replacing them with the combination aluminum units permanently installed on the outside.

Inside Plastic Storm Windows

The cheapest and easiest way to add your own storm windows is to install plastic windows on the inside, using one of the many kits sold for this purpose in hardware stores and home centers. These range from simple sheets of thin plastic that you put up with staples, tacks, or tape to more substantial semipermanent variations that can be taken down and reused in following years.

These semipermanent types generally fall into two broad categories:

1. Some are made of a clear flexible vinyl material that is held in place with a plastic molding premounted on the window frame, often by means of a self-adhesive backing. The clear vinyl film is then positioned over this and secured around the edges by pressing a special plastic spline or strip into the groove provided for it in the plastic molding. There are also several brands available that hold the thin plastic in place with adhesive, then permit you to "shrink" it tight by heating with a hair dryer—thus eliminating wrinkles.

2. Others are a rigid sheet of clear plastic that fits into a frame so that the entire unit can be removed in one piece when the season is over (or when you want to clean or open the window). Some of these have a plastic molding (with a self-adhesive backing) that remains in place on the window frame; in others the framed sheet of plastic is held in place by small clips so that when the clips are swung out of the way the entire unit comes off for storage.

All of these indoor storm sashes have one disadvantage over the conventional outdoor-mounted types—they must be removed every time you want to open a window or clean it. But this is seldom a real problem, since most windows are rarely opened in the winter anyway.

CUTTING THE COST OF KEEPING COOL

Although much has been written about the need for saving energy by doing everything possible to cut down on fuel consumption during the winter, many people do not realize that all of these same measures—adding insulation and weatherstripping, putting up storm windows, etc.—also serve to conserve energy during the summer when air conditioners are running. In other words, the same things that help to keep heat *inside* during the winter also serve to help keep heat *out* during the summer.

That is why it is wise to leave storm sashes up

Inexpensive semipermanent storm windows: left, clear vinyl sheet held in place with adhesive strip around window frame; right, rigid sheet of clear plastic that fits inside frame

in rooms that will be air-conditioned, or to leave the two panes of glass in place if you have combination storm-and-screen units (you can still remove or open them when the air conditioner is off and fresh air is desired). The extra layer of glass, coupled with the dead-air space that is trapped between the two panes, will help insulate the windows against the outside heat, and thus will help to lower the load on the air conditioner while it is running.

Another way to cut down on the amount of the sun's heat absorbed through the window glass is to apply one of the various heat-reflecting "solar" films to the glass. Sold in home centers, these tinted transparent films have a clear adhesive backing that enables you to stick them on over the existing window glass. They will reflect away as much as 70 percent of the sun's heat, yet will cut down on interior brightness by a much smaller amount. During the day they add privacy, because from the outside the window tends to look like a mirror and people cannot see in. At night, however, when it is dark outside and light inside, the reverse holds true—you won't be able to see out easily, but if your blinds are open people will be able to see in.

Ordinary window shades and blinds will also help to keep out the sun's heat during the day, and thus will help lower the load on the air conditioner. The same holds true for awnings or anything else on the outside that shades the windows against the direct rays of the sun.

If you have a window air conditioner located in direct exposure to the hot afternoon sun, it's a good idea to erect some type of shade for that machine. Allowing the sun to beat down on the condenser (the part that sticks outside and gets rid of the heat) only adds to the amount of heat the machine must disperse, and this means it will have to work that much harder and longer. If your house is centrally air-conditioned and has a separate condenser that is located on the outside, by the same token make sure this part of the unit is shaded from the sun in hot weather.

Applying "solar" film to window glass. Left, press top, adhesive side down, to glass; right, press entire film smooth with squeegee.

Two ways to cut down the effects of solar heat during the day: drawing window blinds down, and shading the condenser on window air conditioners to lower running costs of unit

Another energy-saving idea worth considering if you are planning to make new screens for your windows, or if you need screens for a newly built room, is to use one of the special "solar screening" materials that also serve as regular screen mesh. In addition to keeping out insects, these block some of the sun's rays and cut down on the amount of heat absorbed by the windows, thus further easing the load on the air conditioner. Usually made of fiberglass, the mesh of this screening consists of tiny louvers that shade the window glass while not obstructing vision—although there is some reduction in the amount of light admitted.

One of the most frequent causes of wasted energy when a room air conditioner is in use is cold-air seepage around the unit itself, where the air conditioner fits through the wall or into the window. Gaps or open seams that allow hot air to enter add to the number of BTUs the air conditioner must get rid of—and to the amount of energy the machine consumes. To seal such openings, use thick strips of foam-type insulation or weatherstripping pushed into the crevices around the perimeter of the cabinet, and apply caulking around the outside where the cabinet comes through the wall. Window units have filler panels on the sides that should fit snugly—but if they don't, use weatherstripping to close the gaps. You can also use foam strips to seal the joint where the bottom of the window sash frame comes down on top of the air-conditioner cabinet.

"Solar screening" blocks out some of the sun's rays and reduces the amount of heat windows absorb.

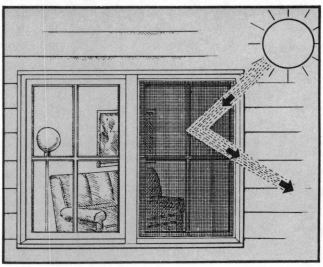

Using Fans to Get Rid of the Heat

Cooling with a fan—or even several fans—is a lot cheaper than using an air conditioner, and in many cases it can actually eliminate the need for air conditioning. This is especially true of large, whole-house exhaust fans, usually installed in the attic. When one of these is turned on after the sun sets and outside temperatures have dropped lower than the indoor temperature, an exhaust fan draws cooling breezes in through several open windows, while at the same time exhausting hot air through louvered vents in the roof or attic.

When we speak of an attic fan, we must consider that there are actually two different classes

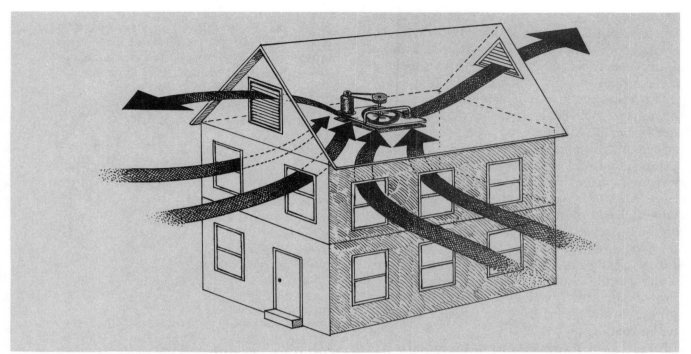

Ventilating and cooling action of an attic exhaust fan when upstairs windows are open and downstairs windows are closed

or types in use: the large ones that are capable of cooling an entire house by drawing hot air up from the rooms below and then exhausting it through a large opening in the wall of the attic; and the smaller fans that are usually mounted on the roof and serve only to draw trapped air out of the attic.

These smaller fans do not directly cool the living quarters of the house in the way that a whole-house fan will, but by drawing trapped hot air out of the attic they do help keep attic heat from being radiated downward (through the ceiling) to the upstairs rooms in the house. For the fan to do its job properly, however, there must be other vents or openings in the attic through which air can enter to replace the air that is expelled.

In order for a large attic fan to be capable of cooling an entire house, it should have a cubic-feet-per-minute rating (CFM) approximately equal to the cubic content of the living quarters inside the house (not counting closets, basements, utility rooms, etc.). The fan itself is usually mounted in the attic in one of three ways: (1) by laying it flat on the floor over an opening cut in the ceiling; (2) by installing it vertically in

one of the end walls of the attic; or (3) by installing it vertically in a suction box built on the inside, directly over an opening cut in the ceiling.

The simplest method is the first one—installing it horizontally on the attic floor over an opening cut in the ceiling. A set of spring-activated louvers is located directly under the fan. The springs keep the louvers closed when the fan is not running, but allow them to open automatically when the fan starts up. A second set of louvers (at least as large as the one under the fan) is then installed in an opening cut in an outside wall to provide a means for the hot air to escape to the outside as it is drawn up from below by the fan. These louvers may either be open all the time or designed to open only when the fan is on.

One drawback of this setup is that the noise of the fan is sometimes quite noticeable in the rooms directly below. To get around this, some people prefer the second setup—with the fan mounted vertically on one of the end walls of the attic. This still provides a louvered opening in the attic floor through which air is drawn up from below when the fan is on, but that way you can hardly hear the fan operating. This method will work effectively, however, only if the attic is reasonably airtight, so that air that is being exhausted from the attic is replaced only with hot air drawn up from the rooms below, not with hot air drawn in from outside through other openings in the attic.

The third method is a compromise between the first two. The fan is vertically mounted over a suction box built directly over an opening in the attic floor. This opening is covered with the same spring-activated louvers described above. Air is drawn up through the ceiling from the rooms below when the fan is running, but the louvers remain closed to seal off the opening when the fan is not in use. Since the fan is not resting on the floor directly over the opening, its sound is scarcely noticeable, and since the fan is enclosed in an airtight box, the problem of drawing air in through the attic openings is also eliminated (it can only draw air up from the louvered vent at the bottom of the box).

An attic-mounted whole-house exhaust fan will help only if used after the air outside cools off (usually after the sun sets) and while the air inside the house is still hot. Turning the fan on then, after opening several windows in the living quarters of the house, will expel large quantities of hot air through the top of the house and draw an equal amount of cooler air in through the open windows. This creates the effect of a continuous breeze coming in through each of the open windows. This is not to say that you can open every window in the house and expect a "cool breeze" through all of them. No fan will be large enough to handle this much movement of air. The idea is to open windows only in those rooms where people are present—for example, at night, open one window in each bedroom; or during the early evening, open one or two windows in the family room or living room where people are reading or watching TV.

Powered attic ventilator draws hot air out of the attic to cool it.

Three ways of mounting a whole-house attic fan (top to bottom): flat on the floor over an opening in the ceiling; vertically in one end wall; and vertically in a suction box over the ceiling

Chapter 16

Home Security

YOUR HOME is proverbially supposed to be your castle—a place where your whole family can feel safe and free from danger. Unfortunately this is not always true. Aside from accidents, which can occur inside the house even more readily than outside, there are two dangers we all must live with continuously—fire and theft.

Statistics show a steady increase in the number of burglaries that take place each year in the United States (one of the highest rates of any country in the world), and in the amount of property damage lost by fire (there are close to a million residential fires each year). All of this results in many thousands of fatalities, hundreds of thousands of injuries, and many millions of dollars in property damage and loss each year.

While we can hardly prevent all of these tragedies and losses, modern technology has provided the homeowner with many devices that help protect life and property by at least minimizing the likelihood of serious injury or death when an intruder tries to break in, or by giving us adequate warning so occupants can escape safely when fire does break out in the middle of the night (most deaths from fire occur while people are sleeping). These include a variety of different types of burglar-alarm systems that can be easily installed to warn of intruders by sounding an alarm, as well as smoke detectors and heat sensors that will sound an immediate alarm if a fire breaks out in any part of the house.

This chapter describes these devices and systems, and outlines the steps everyone can take to combat the growing threat of damage to property—and to life and limb—from the twin dangers of fire and theft.

PROTECTING AGAINST BURGLARY AND BREAK-INS

A few decades ago it was perfectly common in many communities for residents never to worry about burglars or crime—they would often go out and leave their windows open and doors unlocked. It was not uncommon to have back and side doors protected by nothing more than an old-fashioned warded lock—the kind that can be opened with a simple "skeleton key," or even with a bent piece of stiff wire.

But the realities of home security have changed dramatically. In many communities today the police seem almost helpless to do anything about the rising crime rates, and as a result thieves have become bolder than ever, striking modest homes almost as often as they do the palatial homes of the well-to-do.

That explains why so many new types of burglar alarms have been introduced in recent years—and why almost every home or apartment now has extra locks, intruder alarms, and other security devices. Yet for all these new measures, it must be remembered that, regardless of how sophisticated an alarm system you install, and regardless of how many "burglar-proof" locks you add to your front door, none can completely prevent or stop a determined professional burglar who knows there are valuables in the house.

The professional thief also may not consider an ordinary alarm system much of a deterrent—he probably will know how to deactivate it—and he may be perfectly capable of picking any lock that you install. Still, these devices do add to the time it takes to break in, and thus to the risk involved. So unless a burglar is really intent on *your* particular home, these safeguards may be enough to make him think about moving on to a "job" where he is less likely to be detected or interrupted.

A good alarm system and good locks *will* help to deter, and often completely discourage, the thief who is casually traveling through a neighborhood and looking for an "easy mark." He prefers a house that will not give him much trouble. Alarms and locks will also help to discourage and/or scare off drug addicts, young hoodlums, and similar housebreakers who often decide to burglarize or break into a house on sudden impulse.

Door Locks

The locks on your entrance doors are your first line of defense against unwanted intrusion. Today most locks are of the pin-tumbler variety that are opened with a matching key that has the right number of accurately spaced notches, each cut to a precise depth so that a number of individual tumblers inside the lock cylinder will be raised by the correct amount when the key is inserted and turned. These tumblers must all be lined up by the key before the cylinder can be turned, and the more pins a lock has, the harder it is to pick. But even the best-quality pin-tumbler lock can be picked by a skilled burglar equipped with the right tools (though it will take him much longer to pick a good-quality five-tumbler lock than an inexpensive three-tumbler lock).

There are also a number of more specialized types that are even harder to pick—some with multiple rows of pins instead of a single pin. Very often these more exotic mechanisms involve the use of special keys that cannot be duplicated locally, but only by the manufacturer of that lock (which can pose a problem if you ever lose your key).

On many homes, the lock originally put on by the builder is an inexpensive model that has an easy-to-pick mechanism. Rather than changing the whole lock one can often upgrade it simply by changing the cylinder—the part that the key activates. However, this only makes sense if the lock itself is a good-quality unit with deadlocking

capabilities (described on the pages that follow) and the strength to withstand easy forcing.

The type of lock that offers the least amount of security—and should never be used on an entrance door—is the spring-latch type. In this door lock the key fits into a keyhole in the knob (hence they are often called key-in-the-knob locks) and the spring-driven latch bolt (the piece that slides into the strike-plate opening in the door jamb) has a beveled face so that it can snap into place when the door is slammed shut. This type of lock is one of the easiest to force open—all you need is a stiff piece of plastic (such as a credit card), or a thin strip of flexible metal. If this is forced between the door and the jamb until it comes up against the sloping face of the latch bolt, the plastic or metal strip will push the bolt back into its recess in the edge of the door, releasing the lock and permitting the door to be opened.

Some additional protection is provided by those spring-latch locks that have a separate guardbolt or deadbolt located directly behind the main latch bolt. This extra bolt is also spring-driven—that is, a spring pushes it out—and it moves separately from the main latch bolt, so that even if the sloping latch bolt is forced back, the plastic or metal strip will encounter

A tubular spring-latch lock is the easiest type to force open; it is not recommended for entrance doors.

SPRING BOLT DOOR LOCK

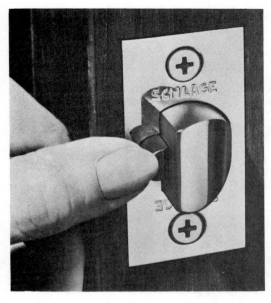

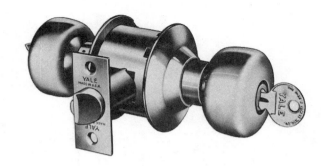

Lock with separate deadbolt, located behind the main latch bolt of a spring-latch lock, offers some additional protection.

this second bolt, which cannot then be released by pushing past it. Thus it is almost impossible to force the bolt open with a credit card or similar tool.

These secondary bolts are not very strong, however, and are easily bent out of the way or even sawed through with a hacksaw blade. In addition, they don't project very far into the strike-plate opening, so if the door fits loosely inside its frame the burglar can use a pry bar to force the frame open enough so that the latch bolt slides out of its opening in the strike plate, thus permitting the door to swing open.

The best type of lock to offer full resistance to forcing or prying is the deadbolt or deadlatch. This has a steel latch bolt that projects far enough into the doorjamb to make prying difficult—a ½-inch projection is considered minimum, but 1 inch is even better. The bolt has a blunt end, not a sloping one like a spring latch, with a square or rectangular cross section. It should be at least ½ inch thick, and the best ones will have a round steel roller on the inside so that cutting through with a hacksaw blade becomes almost impossible.

A deadbolt may be incorporated as part of the basic door lock, or it may be installed as a separate auxiliary lock activated by a separate key. One of the best is the heavy-duty mortise-type lock that is recessed into the edge of the door and has both a deadbolt and a spring latch with an extra guardbolt behind it. With this type of lock the door latches and locks automatically when the door is slammed shut, but then an extra turn

of the key throws the deadbolt for extra "double-locking" security. This may not be practical unless you are installing a new door, since it can require a lot of patching and redrilling on an old door. So for those who have older houses with a lock already installed, it is often easier to add a separate auxiliary deadbolt.

Auxiliary deadbolts are installed in one of two ways: by mounting on the inside face of the door, or by recessing (mortising) into the edge of the door. Surface-mounted auxiliary locks are easier to install, but many people object to their appearance on the inside. Most auxiliary deadbolt locks have a knob on the inside for opening and closing, with a key tumbler on the outside. The better-quality ones will also have a special ta-

A deadbolt lock with spring latch and extra guardbolt offers double-locking security.

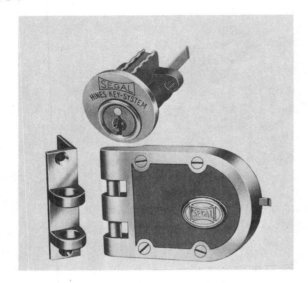

Some surface-mounted auxiliary deadbolts or locks have a key tumbler for opening and closing from inside, but most have a knob inside and a key tumbler outside.

pered ring around the cylinder on the outside so that a burglar cannot use a wrench to unscrew the cylinder.

Deadbolts that are recessed into the edge of the door are a feature of single-cylinder locks that use a key on the outside and a knob on the inside; or they come in double-cylinder locks that require a key on both sides for opening and locking. The latter type is recommended for doors that have glass panes in them or next to them, so that if the burglar breaks the glass he still can't unlock the door. With this type of twin-cylinder deadbolt, however, a key should be left in the lock or hung close by when you are at home, so that in the event of a fire or other emergency no time will be lost in getting the door unlocked.

Since every door lock can only be as secure as the door itself, and the frame in which the door fits, attention should be paid to making certain that all entrance doors (back, side, and front) are secure and solid (hollow-core doors offer poor protection against break-ins). They should fit snugly in their frames with no large gaps between the jamb and the door, and they should be mounted so that the hinge pins are on the inside, not the outside.

An entrance door's frame should be solidly mounted against the studs. When installing doorjambs builders often leave a hollow space between the jamb and the 2×4 studs against which it is nailed, then fill this hollow space with shims in order to plumb up the jamb more easily. You can check for this by pushing hard against the doorjamb—away from the opening—while

the door is opening. If the jamb seems to "give" or acts springy (as though it has no solid backing behind it), it would be worth the trouble to remove the jamb and fill in the spaces behind it with full-length strips of solid wood. This will make it much harder for a burglar to pry the

Two types of recessed separate deadbolt locks. Right, the single-cylinder lock uses a key outside and a knob inside; below, a double-cylinder lock uses a key both inside and out.

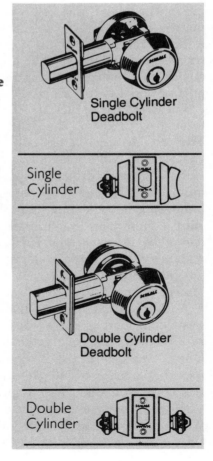

Single Cylinder Deadbolt

Single Cylinder

Double Cylinder Deadbolt

Double Cylinder

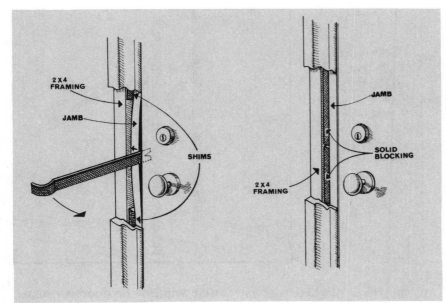

A doorjamb, easily bent with a pry bar (left), can be reinforced with full-length solid wood strips so that the door can't be pried open as easily (right).

doorframe apart so that he can unlatch the lock without ever actually unlocking it, a common technique.

Equally important is making certain that the strike plate into which the latch bolt slides is solidly mounted with long screws that go into the studs behind the jamb or frame; short screws can be easily pried out when the door is given a hard kick. Hinges should also be mounted good and tight with long screws that go into the 2×4 studs behind the jamb, not just into the jamb frame. Loosely mounted hinge screws can make it easy to pry the whole door out without ever having to unlock it.

Window Locks

The conventional latch used on most double-hung windows—a rotating catch that merely secures the two sash frames together—is of very little value in keeping intruders out. Such catches can be easily opened from the outside by sliding a thin metal blade up between the two sash frames from outside. Pushing sideways will then release the catch in most cases.

Windows located on the first-floor or ground-floor levels should be secured with either a key lock that is made for use on windows, or with a simple pin (heavy nail) inserted from the inside. The pin goes through the upper rail of the lower sash and the bottom rail of the upper sash (see drawing below) so that both are secured. To install one of these pins, close the window all the way, then bore a hole through the top rail of the inside sash and partially (not all the way) through the bottom rail of the upper sash. The hole should be just big enough to accept a heavy nail easily, and should be bored at a slight downward angle to keep the nail from falling out. Cut off the pointed end of the nail so it is just long enough not to protrude, and paint the head of the nail the same color as the window to make it less noticeable.

Secure a window sash with a pin (heavy nail) inserted at an angle through the lower, inside sash and partially through the upper, outside sash.

Window key locks are available for double-hung windows (left), and for hinged casement windows (right).

You can also buy keyed locks that are specifically made for use on windows. Some have barrel bolts that go into holes bored in the window channel while the lock is fastened to the movable sash frame; others are wedge-type locks fastened to the upper sash and designed to jam down hard against the top of the lower sash and thus keep either one from being moved. Since these locks can only be opened with a key, even breaking the glass will not permit the burglar easy entry.

Special locks are also available for use on casement windows and sliding windows (as shown in the drawings above)—although on the latter a simple wood or metal bar dropped into the track will often do the trick.

BURGLAR ALARMS

The least expensive alarm units are one-piece "spot" alarms that protect a single window or door by sounding a horn, bell, or loud buzzer

Special locks are also available for sliding windows and doors.

when that particular window or door is opened by an intruder. These are self-contained, and usually battery-operated, but they are easily disarmed simply by closing the window or door—or by ripping them open and disconnecting the battery. Most experts feel that spot alarms are hardly worth the money.

More dependable home burglar-alarm systems generally fall into two categories: perimeter-type alarms that go off as soon as someone tries to force his way in through a window or door that is protected with one of the system's various sensing devices; and space alarms that sound off when someone is detected inside the room or area that is being protected.

Perimeter Alarms

These systems usually make use of two-part magnetic switches as sensors, installed on each window and door to be protected so that one half is mounted on the frame and the other half on the movable part of the door or window. When the door or window is closed, the two halves of the switch are next to each other and the circuit is unbroken—that is, it is joined in a continuous loop of low-voltage wires to the central control box and alarm unit. Once the system is "armed" (switched on), breaking this loop in any way—by cutting the wires, or by separating the two halves of one of the magnetic switches (when the window or door is opened)—will cause the alarm to be activated.

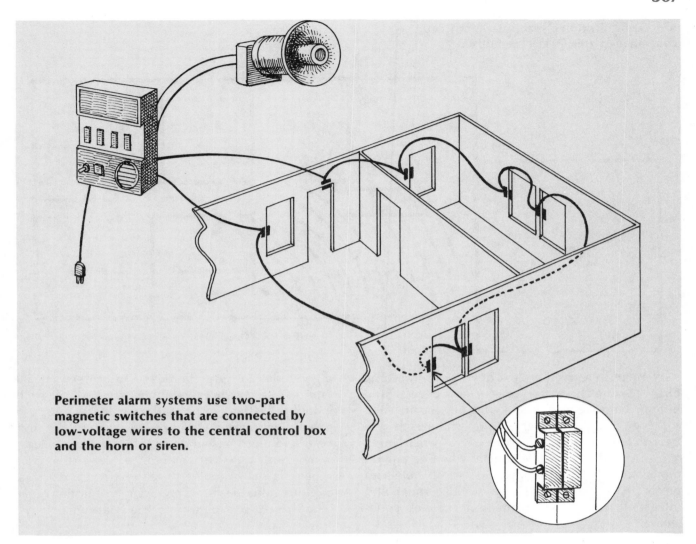

Perimeter alarm systems use two-part magnetic switches that are connected by low-voltage wires to the central control box and the horn or siren.

In addition to these switches, the continuous wire loop can also include magnetic tape applied to the glass on windows and doors so that breaking the glass will also set off the alarm. There are even pressure-sensitive mats that can be placed in front of doors or hallways to sound the alarm when anyone steps on them.

The actual alarm can be a loud horn or siren mounted inside or outside the house, or both. Or it can be a relay that also turns on lights and even dials a preset number on your home telephone to alert a friend or neighbor (who can then call the police). The hope is that the loud noise and the lights will scare the burglar off, but even if they don't, at least anyone at home (and nearby neighbors) will be notified of the intruder's presence.

Most systems have a time delay built in so that when you return home and open the door with your key, you have a short period of time (usually from 15 to 60 seconds) to deactivate or disarm the system by turning the controller off with another special key. This control box should be located close enough to the entrance door so you can get to it quickly, but not out in the open where a burglar could spot it upon entrance.

Space Alarms

These alarm units have special sensors that detect the presence of an intruder inside the room or part of the house where the alarm unit is located. Some use ultrasonic sound waves to detect

A radar or ultrasonic space alarm protects a cone-shaped area inside the house.

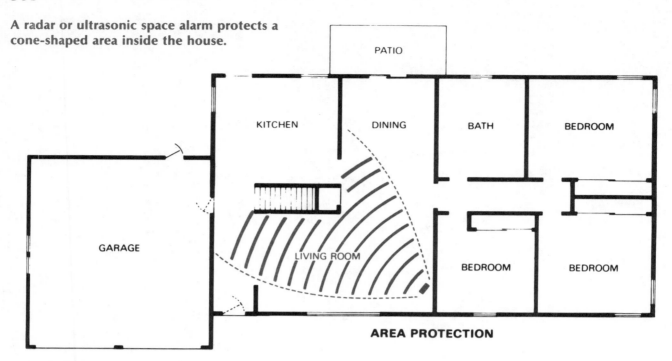

AREA PROTECTION

movement in a given area—they work something like radar. Others use photoelectric cells and hidden light beams that sound an alarm when someone breaks a beam. And still others use heat-detecting infrared rays that sense body warmth and sound the alarm when a person moves into the cone-shaped pattern of the alarm unit's protective area. There are also radar and ultrasonic units that protect a sort of cone-shaped area.

The appeal offered by most of these alarms is that they require little or no wiring, other than perhaps plugging in the power cord, and that they come in compact, portable, self-contained units. The disadvantages are that they don't sound the alarm until *after* the burglar is already inside. Also, they are prone to false alarms, especially during the night, since they can be set off by roaming pets or even, in some cases, by swaying curtains. And since they are one-piece boxes that have to be out in the open so you can aim the beam properly, it isn't too hard for a burglar to spot the box and shut the alarm off when it sounds (most are powered by house current, although a few have a battery-powered backup to keep them going even if the plug is pulled).

Because of these drawbacks, most security experts recommend perimeter-type alarms instead—unless both types are used together, often

a good idea for large homes or to protect special "target" areas where valuables are kept. In such a double system, you install a perimeter alarm to protect windows and doors—at least on the first floor and on those windows that are easily accessible from a nearby roof or a tree—then add space alarms in hallways leading to rooms that contain valuables or in areas that a burglar must pass through on his way to the bedrooms.

Portable, self-contained space alarms can be set up almost anywhere.

Wireless Perimeter Alarm Systems

One drawback that often keeps homeowners from installing a perimeter alarm system is the need for running wires from each window and door to the central control unit, and then from the control unit to the alarm devices (horn, siren, etc.) that are activated when one of the sensors detects an unauthorized entry. Having this job done professionally gets quite expensive—the labor can cost more than the actual equipment—and doing it yourself is time-consuming and tedious.

To eliminate the need for such wiring, there are wireless perimeter alarm systems that require no running of wires to a central control unit or panel. Each magnetic switch has its own tiny transmitter that sends a radio signal to the console when the door or window is opened. In some, half of the switch is inside a small case with the transmitter (a small 9-volt battery fits inside the housing); in others, the switch is wired to a separate little transmitter mounted next to it on the window frame or doorframe. Otherwise the switch is basically the same type as is used in the wired systems (the wires go to the little transmitter, instead of all the way back to the console).

As long as the two halves of the switch are not separated (while the window or door is closed) the alarm won't sound. But once the central unit is armed (turned on), separating the two halves of the magnetic switch (by opening the window or door) will cause the transmitter to send a signal to the central unit. This central unit can be located anywhere in the house, but it should be out of sight so a burglar cannot find it easily. As soon as it gets the signal it sounds a loud built-in horn. Most models can also serve to activate a remotely located second horn, bell, or siren, and many have receptacles that enable them also to turn on lights and other devices inside or outside the house.

Wireless perimeter systems are often sold in kits that include a central control unit and one or more sensor/transmitters for windows and doors, but you can also buy the various units separately—one transmitter for each window or door you want protected, plus the central alarm console and any remote horns or sirens you desire. In most cases the control console is powered by regular 110-volt house current, while in others there is a standby battery pack that will take over in the event of a power failure, or if the power line is cut off by the burglar.

Another feature offered by many of these wireless systems is a remote personal-emergency or "panic" transmitter. This is a small compact transmitter (about the size of a pack of cigarettes) that can be kept at bedside or carried in a

Two kinds of wireless perimeter door alarms. Left, half of the magnet switch is inside a case with the transmitter; right, the switch is wired to a separate transmitter mounted next to the door.

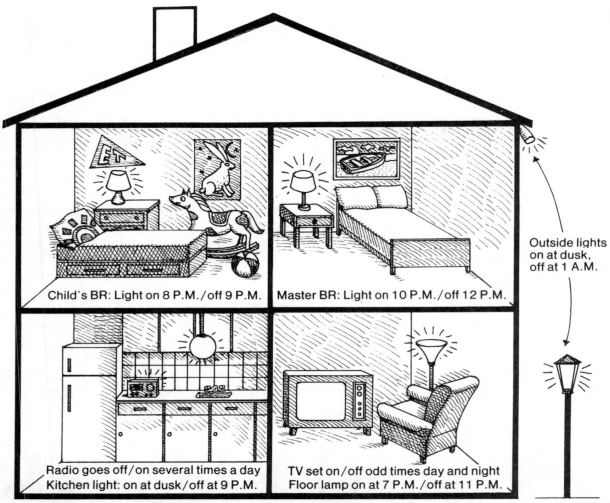

Child's BR: Light on 8 P.M./off 9 P.M.

Master BR: Light on 10 P.M./off 12 P.M.

Outside lights on at dusk, off at 1 A.M.

Radio goes off/on several times a day
Kitchen light: on at dusk/off at 9 P.M.

TV set on/off odd times day and night
Floor lamp on at 7 P.M./off at 11 P.M.

Setting timers to turn lights and other household appliances on and off gives the appearance of an occupied house.

Timing Devices to Discourage Burglars

Since burglars always prefer an empty house to an occupied one, it is a good idea to do everything possible to make the house look occupied even when no one is at home. Using timers to turn on lights in various rooms that would be normally occupied at night is one of the best ways to do this (leaving lights on continuously is *not* a good idea). The timer effect will look "natural" since it can be set to turn the lights off at approximately the hour when the family normally would turn them off if they were at home.

Some timers are simple plug-in models—you plug them into the wall, then plug your lamps or other appliances into an outlet on the timer. Other timers are permanently installed devices that fit into a standard wall outlet box. Generally, the plug-in types are simpler to deal with since you can use them only when needed.

The best kind of timer is one that allows for several settings each day (or night) rather than for just one on and one off setting for each 24 hours. That way you can have lights go on and off several times during a night in different rooms—to simulate people moving about in a normal routine. It is also a good idea to use one timer to turn a radio or TV set on for several hours, and tuned to a talk station so that the impression of people talking will be added to what the potential burglar hears.

Finally, remember that lighting up the outside is just as important as having lights on the inside—especially around all entrance doors and windows (and don't forget the side and back doors). Burglars prefer to pick locks or force doors where they can work in the dark.

Attaching a lamp (left) **or TV set** (below) **to an outlet on a plug-in timer**

pocket. Anybody near one or carrying one in the house can use it to sound the alarm (and turn on the lights) simply by pushing a button on the transmitting unit.

Some brands of wireless alarms can also be integrated with smoke alarms to warn of fire. Such smoke-alarm units not only have their own built-in horn or buzzer to warn of smoke or fire in any part of the house, they also have a tiny transmitter that sends a signal to the central control unit so that its horn or siren, as well as any remote wired alarms, will sound the alarm when smoke or fire is detected in any part of the house.

SMOKE AND FIRE ALARMS

Until a few years ago, the only type of fire detector that a homeowner could install was a heat sensor, a device containing a heat-sensitive strip of metal that melts when subjected to temperatures in excess of about 130 degrees (the actual melting point varies with the type of heat detector). The trouble with this type of fire detector is that by the time enough heat builds up to set it off, it can be too late for those in the house to escape—especially if occupants are asleep when the fire breaks out.

The development of early-warning smoke detectors some years ago resulted in a vastly improved margin of safety for homeowners and apartment dwellers, and these warning devices have now almost completely replaced heat detectors in most homes. They give warning of a fire by sounding an alarm before flames are even visible in most cases.

Heat detectors still have some practical value in areas where it is possible for a fire to flare up quickly and produce high heat with very little smoke at first—such as furnace rooms or kitchens, for example. But for whole-house protection of occupants at night, experts agree that smoke detectors are far better. In fact, many communities now require their installation in all apartment houses, as well as in all newly built houses. The Federal Housing Administration has long required the installation of smoke detectors in all homes that it finances.

When fire breaks out while people are asleep, it is usually not the flames that cause injury or

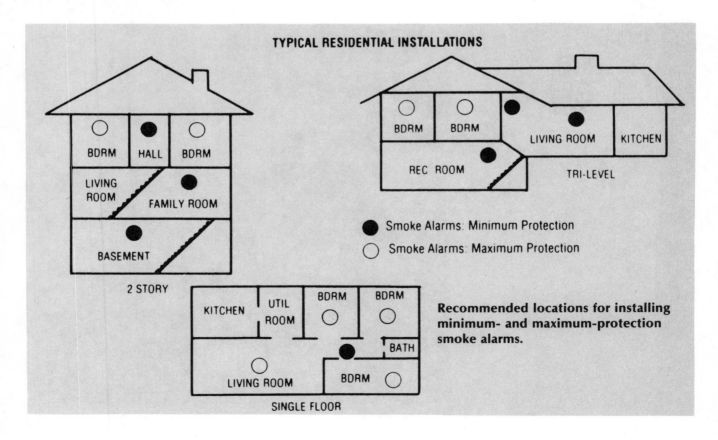

TYPICAL RESIDENTIAL INSTALLATIONS

● Smoke Alarms: Minimum Protection
○ Smoke Alarms: Maximum Protection

Recommended locations for installing minimum- and maximum-protection smoke alarms.

death, it is the asphyxiating smoke and heat from the fire. That is why most fatalities occur at night. Occupants inhale smoke and fumes while still asleep—before the flames ever reach them—so they never really wake up in time to escape.

A good smoke detector will sound the alarm long before this happens. Located outside the bedroom door, or in the hallway that leads to the bedrooms, it detects the smoke or fumes while the fire is still in its earliest or incipient stage. It then sounds the alarm to waken occupants before the actual fire gets close enough to create a dangerous amount of smoke or heat.

Most models have a loud horn built in so that the detector is a self-contained, one-piece unit. Some are designed so that they also transmit a signal to a central alarm console or control panel (usually part of a fire-and-burglar-alarm system). This causes the detector to also sound a louder central alarm that will be more easily heard throughout the house. (See also previous section on wireless units.)

Smoke detectors come in two basic types: ionization and photoelectric. In the ionization type there is a chamber containing an infinitesimal particle of radioactive material that electrically charges the air inside that chamber. When the airborne fumes or tiny particles that are the by-product of all combustion (and are too small to be seen by the eye) enter this chamber, they affect the flow of electrical current. The detector

Smoke alarms have battery on inside and test switch or button on outside.

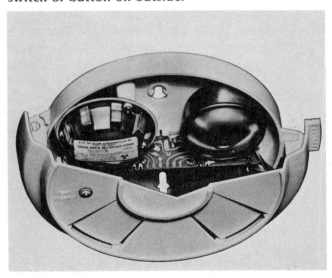

senses this change in current and sets off the alarm.

In a photoelectric-type smoke detector, the sensing chamber has a tiny light beam that shines across it and strikes a photosensitive cell on the other side. Smoke entering this chamber cuts down on the amount of light that reaches the cell—and again the effect is to sound the alarm.

Each type has advantages and disadvantages in responding to different types of fires, so most experts now agree that for maximum protection the homeowner should install both types in strategic locations. The ionization detector is quicker to sense a quick-spreading "clean" fire that gives off little or no smoke at first—for example, the kind of fire that is caused by burning paper, a blazing Christmas tree, or flaming drapes. A photoelectric detector, on the other hand, will give quicker warning of a slow-burning, smoldering fire that gives off lots of smoke even though there is very little flame or even heat at the beginning—for example, the kind of fire that results from a cigarette smoldering in upholstered furniture or in a carpet.

It is a good idea to have one of each type outside the bedrooms or sleeping areas—you can never tell which type of fire will break out first. Adding a second detector is inexpensive insurance, because even a few seconds' delay can make the difference between getting away safely and becoming trapped behind a flaming barricade.

Another important factor to consider when selecting a smoke alarm for your home is the power source it will use. You can choose either a battery-powered model or one that is powered by plugging into a 110-volt household outlet—as well as a few that can be powered by both. The latter, while normally powered by house current, also contain a standby backup battery that takes over automatically in case of a power failure (the battery is usually the rechargeable type that, as long as it is plugged in, is kept continuously charged).

Battery-powered models are the simplest to install—you just screw them to the ceiling. Those powered by household current have a cord that must be plugged into a wall outlet, which means running wires down the wall to the

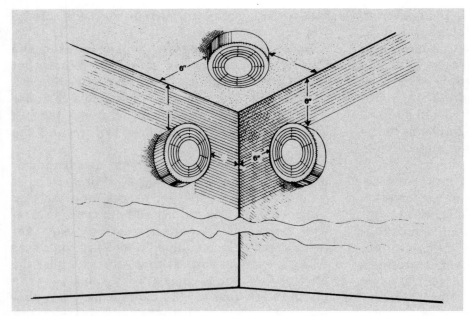

Smoke detectors should be mounted on an upper wall or ceiling, at least 6–8 inches away from the nearest wall, and away from drafts from windows or doors.

nearest receptacle—unless a wall outlet is provided up near the ceiling, or unless the unit is permanently wired into a junction box near the ceiling.

The advantage of battery power is that the alarm will still work even if there is a power failure. Approved models have a built-in warning beeper that sounds automatically at regular intervals when the battery voltage is dropping below a safe operating capacity (the beep will continue at steadily increasing intervals for several days). You therefore know when it's time to put in a new battery. A word of caution: *Don't* take the battery out to stop the beeping until you actually have a new battery to put in.

Make sure you locate the detector close enough to the bedroom door to hear it even if you are sound asleep. All smoke detectors should be mounted on the ceiling—at least 6 to 8 inches away from the nearest wall, and out of natural drafts from open windows or doors. Use the test button to check the detector's operation at least once a week, and always test it immediately after returning home from a vacation or a long trip when the house has been left vacant for more than a few days.

Chapter 17

Dealing with Contractors- for Large Jobs and Major Remodeling

ALTHOUGH THE primary aim of this book is to help free you of the need for hiring home repair professionals for most routine remodeling and repair projects, there does come a time when a project is too large, too complex, or possibly too dangerous to tackle yourself. There are also some jobs that require specialized or expensive tools and equipment that you do not own (and can't even rent), so that you do have to hire a contractor to get the work done. In addition, there are occasions when you just don't have the time to do the work yourself—although you will still want to know what's involved so that you can deal intelligently with the people you hire.

In all of these situations, as well as when a project may be physically beyond your capabilities, your obvious recourse is to hire a professional contractor. Unfortunately, this all too often leads to frustration because of misunderstandings and a lack of knowledge on the homeowner's part. In some cases it ends up as an expensive disaster, with costs climbing much higher than anticipated, and delays and misunderstandings often wind up with the homeowner and the contractor fighting it out in court.

Contrary to what many homeowners think, however, problems of this kind do not necessarily mean that all servicemen and remodeling contractors are thieves, or that everyone in the home remodeling business is out to "get" the homeowners on whom they depend for a living. As in any business, there are some unscrupulous practitioners whose specialty is preying on the unwary and getting away with as much as they can. Be wary, for example, of those who come knocking on your door without invitation saying they are working in the neighborhood and therefore can give you a special price. Also, avoid anyone who uses high-pressure tactics and wants you to sign immediately without giving you a chance to study the contract or think over the whole proposition. Be doubly wary if he says that prices will be higher when he comes back.

On the other hand, there are still many reliable and honest contractors who will conscientiously try to fulfill their part of the contract, or at least what they honestly believe is their part of the bargain. And that is exactly where most disagreements occur.

All too often arguments—even lawsuits—develop simply because of a lack of proper communication, and because the homeowner has not clearly spelled out *in writing* exactly what he or she expects from the contractor, as well as exactly what the contractor expects from the homeowner.

No matter how well-established and honorable the contractor is, and no matter how well-intentioned the homeowner is about not trying to "get something for nothing," unless both parties write everything down by spelling out the terms, conditions, and specifications that both have agreed to, there are bound to be differences of opinion later on. When these differences do arise, each party will think that he or she is right.

To avoid such unnecessary grief, there are two important steps the homeowner must take: (1) Make every effort to hire a well-established, reliable contractor or service company with a good reputation in the community; and (2) make sure the contractor submits a clearly written detailed estimate, and then have an equally clear contract drawn up that spells out every detail of the work to be done, the materials to be used, the amount of money that the contractor will be paid, how and when he will be paid, etc. (more about all this later on). *Never* depend on oral or "handshake" agreements, no matter how friendly you are with the contractor, how much of a gentleman you feel he is, or how well recommended he comes.

Should You Hire an Architect?

This depends to a great extent on the size and complexity of the project. You should hire an architect if your project involves a major addition to the house or extensive alteration of the inside, particularly if it calls for the moving of load-bearing walls, staircases, etc. This is because accurate plans must be drawn in order to get the necessary building permits and to make certain that the structure will be sound when finished. An architect will consider aesthetic factors, in addition to structural integrity, so that you don't wind up with an eyesore you will long regret.

The architect can serve you in one of two ways: He can merely draw up the necessary plans and then give these to you so that you can make all the necessary arrangements for hiring a contractor and getting the work done; or he can draw up the plans and then supervise the entire project for a fee (usually a percentage of the total cost of the job). Either way, his plans will enable you to get accurate estimates from local contractors or builders, because the plans and specifications provided will ensure that all are bidding on the same amount of work and the same type of materials. (He should furnish you with enough copies of the plans so that you can give one to each of the contractors who will bid on the job.)

Generally speaking, if the job is large enough to warrant hiring an architect for drawing up the plans and designing the project, then it is usually worth also hiring the architect to supervise the job. He can often save you more than his fee because he knows how to deal with contractors and how and where to purchase supplies. An experienced architect can also help avoid needless delays and unpleasant disagreements by attending to all the details involved in getting the necessary permits and making certain that all work conforms to local code requirements.

Finding a Contractor

The best way to find a contractor is through personal recommendation—from friends, neighbors, relatives, or other people whose opinion you trust. Unfortunately, this is not always easy, because most homeowners do not hire contractors that often, so many will have had limited experience of their own, if any. Then too, perhaps you are new to the area and have not built up a set of reliable acquaintances.

Your next best source of recommendation is the branch office of one of the local trade associations such as the National Association of Home Builders, or the Home Remodelers Association. Membership in these organizations, or in the local Chamber of Commerce or similar community organization, is not necessarily a guarantee of reliability or honesty, but it does indicate that the contractor at least has roots in the community, so it is more likely that he will be interested in maintaining a solid reputation. He will also be more familiar with local building codes or restrictions, and with local problems of drainage, soil conditions, etc.

Another way to get recommendations is to check the local dealers and supply houses in your area—paint stores, lumberyards, building supply outlets, electrical wholesalers, plumbing supply houses, etc. They know all the local contractors and will sometimes be willing to make recommendations. Still, don't follow these recommendations blindly. Each dealer will naturally favor his own customers, and may even recommend an otherwise undependable firm just to get a customer some work. If, however, you compare recommendations from several different dealers and find that the same name turns up several times, you can be pretty sure that the firm mentioned is a good one to deal with—the man obviously has a good reputation.

Very important sometimes is the credit standing of the contractor. You can ask dealers or supply houses about this, although they may not be willing to give you the information you want. But if you are tactful you may get comments that indicate that the contractor buys only for cash, or that his credit is shaky. If so, it is best to stay away from that one. While you're at it, also check with the local office of your Better Business Bureau. That organization usually won't recommend anyone, but it can tell you whether or not the names you are considering have many complaints listed against them.

Also, try to get some idea of how long a contractor has been in business in the area. "Fly-by-night" contractors who set up shop and then disappear after doing a few jobs are a frequent source of trouble for unwary homeowners. Not only are they likely to leave you with an unfinished or unsatisfactory job; there is also the chance that you will no longer be able to find them if something goes wrong after the job is finished.

From all of these sources try to compile a list of at least three contractors from whom you can solicit bids.

Soliciting Bids

When you ask for estimates or bids, make sure each contractor is bidding on the same set of plans, on the same amount of work, and on the same brands or quality of materials that will be used. If you have a *particular* brand of paint, bathroom fixture, or roof shingle in mind, make sure that this is indicated in the specifications you send out with your plans. If colors are involved, this too should be spelled out, because in some cases it can affect the price of the materials.

Always make sure you get a written estimate from each contractor, and only consider those that spell everything out clearly. The estimate should be, basically, the same document you will eventually use as the contract between you and the contractor—though you will want to add such details as the schedule to be followed for making payments as work progresses, the starting and finishing dates, etc.

As an example, if painting is involved, the estimate and the resulting contract should both spell out how many coats will be applied over each surface, what kind of preparation will be done to get those surfaces ready, the brands of paint that will be applied, and who will supply (pay for) the paints, wallcoverings, and other materials to be used.

Or, if you are contracting for a new kitchen, the contract should include such details as: Who will buy the appliances? What brands (including model numbers) will be installed? Will cabinets be replaced or merely refinished? Who will pay for any wiring or plumbing that is required? Who will get the permits needed, if any? Who will re-

move and dispose of the old fixtures and appliances?

If you are hiring an insulation contractor, make sure the R-rating of the insulation is specified, along with the type that will be used in each location. And if the insulation is to be blown in through holes drilled in the outside, determine who patches the holes and if it is the contractor who decides if the patch is "acceptable," both in appearance and in durability.

Here are some other considerations that should be clearly spelled out in the final contract before it is signed by both parties:

• Make sure a set of plans and specifications is attached to and becomes part of the contract so that both parties understand the precise details of the work to be done.

• In addition to predetermining brands and model numbers, where applicable, make sure, where the type or species of wood is important, that this too is specified (for example, if you want redwood for an outside deck, the contract should say so).

• Be very careful about accepting the common phrase "or equal" when specifications include brand names or quality grades. It is a perfectly acceptable clause that typically appears in every building and remodeling contract, but it should be considered with caution. What it means is that if you specify a certain brand of window, for example, and that brand is not available in the size you want, or at the time that you need it, then the contractor can substitute another brand of equal quality. There is nothing wrong with this, but be sure a proviso is included stating that you (or your architect) must give approval for the "equal" brand selected.

• If an architect is involved, he should be mentioned in the contract and his role (if any) clearly spelled out—especially if he will be supervising the project.

• If there are subcontractors to be hired, make the general contractor responsible for hiring them, for paying them, and for coordinating their work so that no unusual delays are encountered.

• When time is important, starting and completion dates should be included. Just remember that these are not really very binding when it actually comes down to a court fight (if it ever does). The clause will be much stronger—and more enforceable—if the wording says something like "Time is of the essence," or "Dates are of the essence of this contract." You will still have to allow for unavoidable delays because of weather, strikes, etc., but a completion date gives you something to fall back on if you feel the contractor is deliberately stalling or leaving for another job before yours is finished.

• Insist on seeing proof of adequate insurance coverage on the part of the contractor before he starts, including proof of such an agreement with his subcontractors. There should be a compensation policy covering any workers he brings to the premises; otherwise you could be liable if a worker injures himself while working on your property.

• The contractor should also have liability insurance to cover any property damage that may occur, so if possible ask for a written release that relieves you of any financial responsibility for unpaid bills incurred by the contractor (for labor and materials) in the event he goes bankrupt, or even should he suddenly die while the job is in progress. This may be a separate agreement which your lawyer can draw up, or it can be included as part of the basic contract.

• The contract should spell out who will clean up the premises and remove any debris. It should also clarify just what is meant by "cleaning up." One commonly used expression is leaving the premises "broom clean"—which means the contractor will sweep up after taking away all the debris, not just pick up the large pieces. This still doesn't detail who will be responsible for actually carting the refuse away and for paying any of the costs involved.

• If lawns, plants, trees, or other shrubbery are damaged, it should be clear who will pay for making the needed restorations or replacing the damaged shrubbery.

• If approvals are required from the local building department as work progresses—for example, they may want to see foundation footings before the soil is replaced, or they may want to inspect plumbing and wiring before the walls are enclosed—the contract should spell out the contractor's responsibility for getting these inspections made, and for getting the necessary approvals by making certain his work conforms to all local codes.

• Any changes requested by the homeowner, or suggested by the contractor, or any additions to the original contract, should be written down and signed by both parties—including an agreed-on price for these changes. This is probably the most frequent cause of disagreement between otherwise reputable contractors and trustingly honest homeowners: Changes are made (at the customer's request) but without a clear understanding beforehand as to how much extra they will cost.

• The contract should spell out the terms of payment—specifically how much money is to be paid to the contractor at different stages, and what percentage of the total he is to get in each case. For self-protection, you should always be ahead of the contractor—that is, at any time during the job you should have paid the contractor for less than the total amount of work actually completed. That way, if he fails to finish for any reason, you will have a balance in your favor.

• The payment schedule should be such that at the end there is a balance of at least 10 to 15 percent of the total still due when the job is finished. The idea is to give yourself a reasonable length of time (from 10 to 30 days, depending on the size and complexity of the job) to check out that all work has been done satisfactorily.

• When making the final payment, insist on an affidavit certifying that all subcontractors who worked on your house have been paid, and all materials used in the job have been paid for (without this document, unpaid suppliers or unpaid subcontractors could eventually file a lien against your house—even though you would have paid the general contractor for everything).

• Never sign any letter or form that says the job is finished when it really isn't—no matter what kind of story you are told. Wait till the job is actually finished, and everything is inspected, before you sign any such document.

• For building on new additions, a certificate of occupancy will be required by most local building departments. The contractor should be responsible for getting this certificate, and for meeting all the local requirements necessary to receive it. He should not get his final payment until this is taken care of.

Appendix

Furniture Finishing and Refinishing

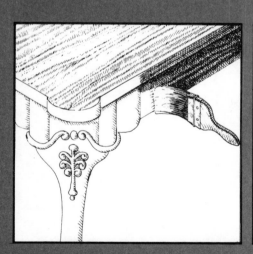
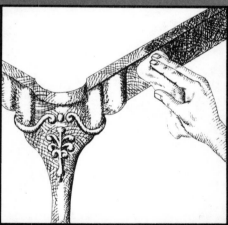

WHEN TACKLING a job of finishing or refinishing a piece of furniture, the first thing you have to decide is the type of finish you want. This will depend to a great extent on the style of that particular piece, on the kind of wood it is made of, on the condition and color of that wood (clean or dirty, previously stained or unstained, etc.), and on how much preparatory work you are willing to do.

CHOOSING YOUR FINISH

All of the commonly used furniture finishes can be classified in three broad categories: transparent or clear natural finishes that allow all of the wood's existing grain and color to show through; translucent finishes that allow most of the grain and at least some of the existing color to show through; and opaque finishes, such as paint, that completely hide the color and grain of the wood.

Generally, the more formal and more traditional a piece is, and the better the quality of the wood used in its manufacture, the more likely you are to want a transparent finish with no stain or other coloring to change the tone of the wood.

On the other hand, if the piece is made of inexpensive woods, or if there are several different shades of wood involved, then chances are you will be better off with a translucent finish that calls for the use of a wood stain before the final clear finish is applied. The same holds true if the original wood is an uninteresting color—a stain may be advisable in that case to partially hide the existing color and give it a more interesting tone.

Opaque finishes, such as enamels and "antique" finishes that use paint as a background or base coat, are best used over really battered pieces or those needing many repairs. They may also be advisable over pieces that are so hopelessly stained or poorly finished that you can never get the natural wood to look right again.

An opaque finish may also be the answer for a piece you don't want to bother stripping completely, or one that would require so many patches that a "natural" finish is not really practical. It is also the quickest way to rejuvenate an old piece that is still serviceable, but not worth all the extra work involved in applying a transparent or translucent finish.

STRIPPING OFF THE OLD FINISH

There are basically two methods for stripping off an old finish—mechanically with sandpaper and scrapers, or chemically with a paint and varnish remover. Sanding is cheaper and makes less of a mess, but it requires a lot more time and effort. Also, many experts frown on this method of stripping—especially for older pieces that have delicate carvings or turnings.

The wood on old furniture darkens a certain way with age, and acquires a special appearance or "feel" that is the result of years of being touched, polished, etc. It's what is known as the "patina," and it's almost impossible to duplicate. With the kind of sanding required to strip a piece, a thin layer of wood usually disappears with the finish, and this kills the patina.

It's possible, of course, to sand with a very fine abrasive and a gentle hand—it's done all the time between coats of finish. But removing a finish calls for a heavier paper and a heavier hand—heavy enough, say experts, to mar carving or even change the shape of a curved leg. Even on plain pieces, you have to be careful not to round corners.

Sanding is most effective on flat surfaces, so if you've got a relatively uninteresting chest, say, that's not old enough to have a patina, and it's covered by some tough old paint, sanding may be the fastest and easiest way to get it off. The same goes for a table with plain legs, one that only your refinishing will make beautiful.

It is possible to give wood a more aged look by staining and refinishing, so don't be afraid to get down to the bare wood—*if you have to.* Most times you will have to sand even after the finish has been removed chemically.

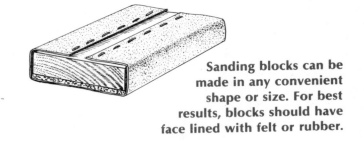

Sanding blocks can be made in any convenient shape or size. For best results, blocks should have face lined with felt or rubber.

Stripping by Sanding and Scraping

Although we tend to refer to all abrasive papers as "sandpaper," they don't actually have any sand in them. The oldest type is flint paper, which is coated with grains of quartz, a natural mineral that looks very much like sand. It's the cheapest of all abrasive papers, but it dulls quickly, clogs easily, and wears out much more rapidly than other types. Ultimately it costs no less than the newer and better types, which are coated with synthetic minerals.

The most versatile and most widely available type of flexible abrasive is aluminum oxide paper (also called production paper). Aluminum oxide is a synthetic mineral that is much harder, sharper, and longer-lasting than flint or quartz in normal use. In addition, aluminum oxide papers have a stronger, more tear-resistant backing than flint papers. Garnet paper is not quite so hard or long-wearing as aluminum oxide, but many finishers prefer it because it works particularly well on raw wood.

Sandpapers are also graded according to the size of the abrasive particles coating them. The lower the number, the coarser the grade—30 is very coarse and will leave deep scratches, while 600 is very fine, and is mainly used for polishing. Sometimes papers are simply marked Very Coarse, Coarse, Medium, Fine, etc., or simply M for medium, F for fine, and so on.

For stripping purposes, 80 is best. It's somewhere between coarse and medium, and is rough enough to take off the finish without taking a lot of wood with it. On flat surfaces, it's best to use a sanding block. You can apply more pressure without tearing the paper or having it clog, and it helps you to apply pressure more evenly so you're not sanding down one part more than another.

You can buy commercially made sanding blocks padded with foam rubber or felt in different sizes and shapes in most paint and hardware stores. Most experienced finishers, however, prefer to make their own. They simply cut blocks of wood to the desired size and shape, then cover the working face with thick felt, foam, or sponge rubber.

Don't leave off the padding. A block without any resilient material between it and the paper can cause deep scratches—especially if the paper tears or if a large particle of abrasive grit gets caught between the block and the surface being sanded.

For sanding areas where a block is not convenient, tear a standard sheet of sandpaper in half, then fold each piece in half with the abrasive sides facing out. You can now hold each of these folded sheets comfortably in the palm of your hand and work with the double thickness. When one side becomes dull or clogged, simply flip the folded sheet over to expose the other side. The

For convenient hand sanding, tear a sheet of sandpaper in half and fold each piece in half, with abrasive sides facing out.

reason you tear the sheet in half before you fold it—instead of folding the large sheet four ways—is to keep the abrasive faces from rubbing against each other. That would only shorten their life by causing them to dull prematurely. Sand with the grain, where possible, and after sanding make sure you remove all dust by wiping with a tack cloth (see page 399).

Sanding machines. Some purists still feel that the only way to do a proper job of smoothing fine wood is to do your sanding by hand. On some valuable antiques and heirlooms, this is probably the best way. However, for many projects with flat surfaces, sanding by machine is much faster and easier, but you must be careful to avoid cutting too deeply or accidentally scratching the surface.

Electric sanding machines fall into three broad categories: disk sanders, belt sanders, and orbital sanders. Descriptions of these machines and of their general methods of usage can be found in Chapter 1, pp. 36–37.

When using any power-driven sanding machine, never make the common mistake of bearing down hard while the machine is working in an effort to make it cut faster. Pressing hard does just the opposite. It tends to overload the motor and actually makes the machine cut slower. It can also result in scorching the sandpaper and overheating the motor.

You can press down lightly to ensure firm contact with the work, but never so hard that you slow the machine down. On horizontal surfaces the weight of the machine is almost enough—just press lightly. On vertical surfaces you'll have to compensate for the weight of the machine and thus will have to apply a little more pressure.

For safety's sake it is a good idea to wear goggles with any electric sander—especially when working overhead. If the dust bothers you, wear a spray mask similar to the kind sold for use with paint sprayers. (Inexpensive, disposable models are sold in almost all paint and hardware stores.)

Scrapers. Hook-type scrapers, of the kind illustrated on page 386, are useful for what finishers call rough work—taking off finishes. To use, hold the handle almost parallel to the surface with one hand, while you bear down on the blade end with the other hand. Then drag the tool toward you. Use this tool cautiously until you get the feel of it, and don't try it with fine pieces. It's too easy to gouge the wood. Cabinetmaker's

Belt sanders do a fast job of removing finishes and smoothing rough surfaces, but they can only be used on flat surfaces.

Orbital sanders, also known as finishing sanders, are generally easier to control than other power sanders, and are more useful in fine finishing.

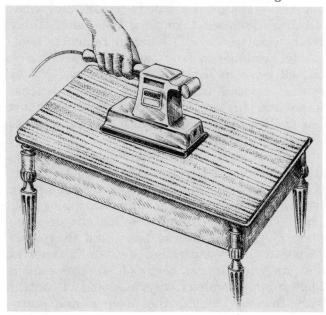

A hook scraper is often the only way to get into corners and up against dividers where you cannot reach with sandpaper.

wood scrapers, available from mail-order houses, can also be useful, but some practice will be required before you learn how to use them.

Steel wool. This is a much finer abrasive than sandpaper, and you'll use a lot more elbow grease taking off a finish with it. It's likely to be more useful in the final smoothing operations, and for getting into curves, carvings, and turnings you can't work with sandpaper. Like sandpaper, it's graded according to coarseness—3 is the coarsest, 1 is fine, and very fine grades go from 0 to 0000.

Stripping with Chemical Removers

When we talk about a "finish," what we're really referring to is the product that seals the wood—not the stain or the wood's color—and what chemical removers take off is this finish. There are a wide variety of chemical removers commonly available in paint and hardware stores, but all work in basically the same way. They contain special solvents and chemicals that soften and "lift" or blister up old finish so that it can easily be wiped, scraped, or washed away to expose bare wood.

Some removers are liquid and some are creamy or semi-paste in consistency. As a rule, the liquids cost less, but the thicker semi-paste types are better for most furniture-stripping jobs. They "stay put," without running and dripping when used on vertical surfaces, and they don't evaporate or dry out as quickly. And a remover that stays wet longer keeps on working longer. The longer a remover stays wet and in contact with the old finish, the deeper and more

thoroughly it will penetrate in a single application.

Another important difference between removers is their flammability. Many are highly inflammable and must be used with extreme caution when working indoors. Weather permitting, you should work outside or in the garage (with the door open). Others are nonflammable and cost only slightly more, so choose one of these when you must work indoors.

To keep paint removers from drying out or evaporating before they can completely penetrate and soften the old finish, manufacturers usually add special ingredients that retard evaporation by keeping air out. In many removers, this is a waxlike compound, which leaves a residue that must be neutralized or washed away when the job is done. Otherwise a new finish will not adhere properly. However, many removers use a retardant that contains no wax, and these supposedly need no washing with solvent. Usually labeled as "no-wash" or "self-neutralizing," these removers come in both liquid and semi-paste forms, and they create fewer problems than those that contain wax. Nevertheless, it is best with either type to play safe and wipe the surface down with paint thinner or denatured alcohol after using the remover.

One of the easiest types of varnish remover you can use is a water-wash type. Most widely available in semi-paste form, it is also usually nonflammable. The advantage of using this remover is that after the old finish has been thoroughly softened with a heavy application, you can wash everything off by simply scrubbing with a brush or a piece of steel wool dipped in water. You can even take the piece outside and hose it down with water, while you scrub the finish off with a stiff brush. But you do have to be careful about using water on old pieces of furniture. Many of them are assembled with glue that is not water-resistant. And *never* use water on a piece of furniture that is covered with veneer. The surface will almost always wrinkle or loosen, destroying the veneer.

When using remover, cover the floor and nearby areas to protect them. But don't depend on plastic drop cloths. Many chemical removers dissolve plastic. Put a few layers of old newspaper down, or use an old bedsheet or blanket cov-

To prepare for chemical stripping, remove hardware and position the parts of the piece, such as bureau drawers, so that the surfaces to be stripped are horizontal. The bureau case can, of course, be tipped on its side or back when stripping sides and front.

ered with several layers of newspaper. Wear rubber gloves to protect your hands, and if you will be working on surfaces above eye level, wear goggles to protect your eyes.

Before starting to apply the remover, take off knobs, hinges, handles, and all other hardware. Stand the drawers up so the fronts are horizontal, and lay doors flat after the hinges have been removed.

Some repairs are done after stripping, and some before (see page 419), but now is the time to look for loose joints. If there are many that need repair, take them apart before stripping.

The easiest way to apply the remover is with an old paintbrush, or with an inexpensive brush that you can throw away afterward. Lay the remover on in thick layers with a minimum of back-and-forth brushing so that you don't disturb the film any more than necessary as you apply it.

Too much brushing only slows up the chemical action, because it allows air to enter the solution and speeds evaporation of the solvent. If you are working outdoors, avoid working in direct sunlight, since this too hastens evaporation and shortens the working time.

As a rule, it is best to concentrate on one side or section at a time. Apply the remover to the area in a heavy layer, then wait about 15 to 20 minutes and test one corner with a putty knife to see if the old finish is softened all the way down to the bare wood. Ideally, all layers of finish should come off down to the bare wood with a single scraping. If your test indicates that the finish is not soft all the way down, and if the remover is still wet (and therefore not working), wait another 5 or 10 minutes and try again. If the remover has still not softened the finish all the way down to the raw wood, stop scraping and apply a second coat of the remover right on top

Lay remover on in thick layers, using the flat side of the brush more than its tip.

Softened finish should come off down to the raw wood with one scraping. If not, put more remover on and allow a longer working time.

of the original one. Allow this to work for another 10 or 15 minutes and then try again. Whatever you do, don't skimp on remover, and don't wait longer than about 20 minutes before scraping off everything that you've put on thus far. It's too hard to scrape off otherwise.

On flat surfaces a putty knife is probably the quickest and easiest way to scrape most of the softened material off. In grooves or crevices, or where there are many carvings, you'll really appreciate the advantages of using a water-wash remover. All you do is dip a stiff-bristled brush into water or a detergent solution, and then simply scrub the softened residue out.

If you're not using a water-wash remover, you can accomplish the same thing with coarse steel wool and a wire brush. Read the label on your product carefully, and know what you're buying. Then you'll best know the most effective way to scrub up.

After the entire surface has been scraped clean, look over the piece carefully to make sure there are no spots where small patches of the old finish are still visible. Often these will show up as dark spots, or as "glazed" spots that are still slightly glossy. Although barely noticeable on the raw wood, these will really stand out after the new finish is applied, especially if the refinishing process requires a penetrating type of wood stain. In those spots, the stain will not soak in as much as it does on the rest of the wood—if at all. To prevent this, recoat the missed spots with remover and then scrub with steel wool or a wire brush.

When the wood has been stripped clean, allow it to dry thoroughly, then sand lightly with 220 sandpaper. This not only gives the wood a final smoothing, it also removes any film or chemicals that may still be left on the surface, and helps to open the pores of the wood so that the new finish will penetrate properly.

Wire brushes. Invaluable for degunking after using paint removers, especially carved and

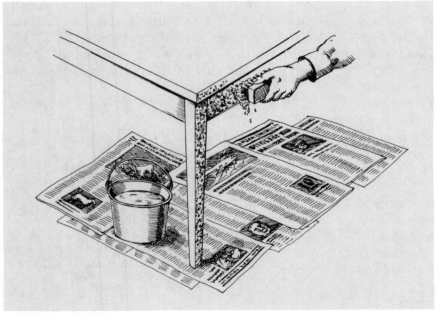

When using a water-wash remover, softened paint or varnish can be scrubbed off with a stiff brush dipped into water, without need for scraping.

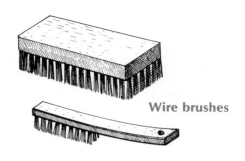

Wire brushes

turned areas. Nothing scrubs up like these, and you'll want several in different sizes.

USING BLEACHES TO LIGHTEN WOOD

As mentioned earlier, paint and varnish removers take off only the finish—not the stain, or at least not very much of it. So if you are working on a pine or maple piece that has been stained to look like walnut or mahogany, and you want to lighten it to look more like oak, you may be able to do it with bleach. Or maybe you are hoping to get down to light wood so you can restain it to match the rest of the furniture in the living room.

Bleach is not only capable of lightening wood all over, it can be very effective in removing blemishes and discolored areas that have penetrated too deeply into the wood to be removed by sanding.

There are three types of bleach you can use on furniture: liquid laundry bleach; oxalic acid; or one of the two-solution wood bleaches that are specifically sold for this purpose. All are effective only on bare wood, so all the old finish must be taken off before bleaching—and there must be no skips or missed spots or the bleach will not soak in and you will wind up with a blotchy, uneven job.

For the same reason, it's important that close-grained woods, such as maple, be thoroughly sanded to open the wood's pores before bleaching. Otherwise, you get an uneven job.

Of the three bleaches mentioned, laundry bleach is the weakest and the hardest to control. However, applying it several times is often convenient when you don't want to bleach an entire piece but just lighten some discolored areas. It's also good for taking out ink spots or watermarks that have darkened the wood in places.

Oxalic acid is stronger and easier to control than laundry bleach, and comes in nonspillable crystal form. To use, dissolve as many crystals as you can in a container of hot (hot is important) water. Mop this solution over the piece while it's still hot, then allow the bleach to dry. Rinse off with plenty of clear water. Repeat the treatment if you want the wood even lighter.

If you're still not satisfied, try strengthening the action by combining oxalic acid with hypo-sulfite—ordinary photographer's hypo, available in any camera store. Apply the oxalic acid first. As it begins to dry, mop on the hypo solution (3 ounces of hypo in 1 quart of warm water). Let sit for about 15 to 20 minutes, then rinse off with plenty of clean water.

If even this is not light enough, you can try the two-solution chemical wood bleaches.

These are the most expensive of the bleaches, but they're also the strongest, the most effective, and probably the fastest-acting. You spread one solution on the piece first, then follow up with the second.

Pour the first solution into a plastic or glass bowl (not metal). Then take a synthetic nylon brush or rubber sponge, dip it into the solution, and spread the solution on the surface of your piece.

Allow the first solution to remain on the piece for the length of time recommended on the label or in the directions, usually 10 to 20 minutes. Then apply the second solution in much the same way. Again, let stand for the recommended

Two-solution chemical wood bleach is the most effective type for lightening dark woods. Wear rubber gloves to protect hands.

amount of time, but this time, keep your eye on the wood. If it looks as if it is getting lighter than you want it to, you can stop the action at any time by flooding the surface with ordinary household vinegar.

When working with any bleach, wear rubber gloves and old clothes with long sleeves to protect hands and arms. If bleach spills on exposed skin, wash immediately with lots of water. After you've finished, throw out any bleach that remains in the bowl. Don't pour it back into the original bottle because it will ruin whatever's left for further use.

No matter what brand of bleach you use, or what it says on the label, it's always best to use a neutralizing rinse afterward. The simplest is ordinary white vinegar, and it works as well on two-solution bleaches as on laundry bleach.

First rinse the bleached piece with plain water. Then pour on vinegar, full strength, and let stand for a few minutes. Wipe off with clean rags and rinse with more water.

Instead of vinegar, you can use a borax solution as a neutralizer. (This works as well on oxalic acid as on any of the others.) Dissolve 1 cup borax in 1 quart of hot water, and apply to wood while still warm. Rinse off with clean water and allow wood to dry thoroughly before going ahead with any finish.

Since all bleaches have a water base, and since they have to be followed with a water rinse afterward, bleaching will almost always tend to raise the grain of the wood to some extent. This creates a slight fuzziness, which can be removed after the wood is dry by rubbing lightly with fine sandpaper. If several bleaching applications will be required, don't do any sanding until after the final rinse.

MAKING NEEDED REPAIRS

Although surface repairs—the filling and patching of dents and gouges, smoothing of uneven areas, etc.—should be done after the finish is off, loose joints—wobbly legs or spindles—should be repaired *before* stripping if you're going to use a chemical remover. Because removers are liquid, they inevitably seep into the open cracks of loose joints, and not even a strong flushing with water

or solvent will get all of the stuff out. The slightest residue will keep the wood from drying or bonding properly.

You could take the joint completely apart, without regluing, during the stripping process, and have greater success flushing out residue. Sometimes the joint doesn't come apart until the stripping process, and that's what you have to do. But it's best and safest to do it all first.

If you're stripping mechanically by sanding and scraping, then it makes no difference when you glue.

Of course, if you're not going to strip at all—if you're going to paint or antique—your repair problems are just a little different. Wood with a transparent or translucent finish shows blemishes, so you've got to be very careful about filling and patching in terms of color and how fillers match the wood. But with an opaque finish, only smoothness counts, since nothing else shows.

Using Glue and Dowels

When chair or table legs or rungs work loose from the holes in which they were fitted, the only way to do a thorough, permanent repair job on these joints is to take them apart completely so that they can be properly reglued. This means all the joints, not just the loose ones, because it's just too hard to take one joint apart without cracking or splitting the others.

When taking joints apart, watch for concealed screws, nails, and other fasteners. They're sometimes driven in from the side or back or at such an angle that they're almost impossible to detect if you don't look carefully, and they can really damage a good piece of wood if you don't find and remove them first.

Pry the joints apart by hand if you can, but you may use a rubber or plastic mallet, which won't mar the wood, to tap the pieces apart if necessary.

Most of the glues that were used years ago were not water-resistant and had an organic base, so if you find the joint difficult to take apart, you may be able to soften the old glue by wetting it with vinegar.

An even stronger solvent can be made by using glacial acetic acid (sold in photo supply stores), diluted with 3 or 4 parts of water. (When mixing acid with water, always pour the acid into the water rather than the water into the acid, and mix in a glass or plastic bowl. Concentrated acetic acid is very strong, so handle it with extreme care.)

After you have taken the joints completely apart, use a fine wood rasp or medium-grade sandpaper to clean the old glue off the ends of the rungs or legs, and use a pocketknife or similar tool to scrape all of the old glue out of the holes into which they fit. Sometimes hot water or vinegar will help clean out these recessed areas completely.

To reglue the joints you can use ordinary white glue that dries clear, but for a stronger bond and a "stickier" grip that will hold pieces in alignment more easily while you're setting them into position, use one of the pale-yellow or beige-colored aliphatic resin glues, which also come in plastic squeeze bottles and dry almost clear.

For some jobs, two-part epoxy glues are useful. They are exceptionally strong and completely waterproof, and they do not require clamping. All you have to do is keep the pieces in firm contact with each other while the adhesive sets. What's more, they have the ability to fill in voids when pieces fit loosely or when joints have decided gaps in them. However, they cost considerably more than other glues, and, worse, they form a dark-colored joint that is more noticeable when dry, so while they are okay for opaque finishes, they may not be suitable for transparent ones, on light woods.

When the end of a rung or leg has shrunk so much that it no longer fits snugly in its hole, there's no sense in merely pouring more wood glue into the joint. You have to take steps to make a snug fit first if you want to be sure the repair will be permanent and invisible. One easy method is to wrap the end of the loose-fitting member with fine cotton or linen thread to enlarge its diameter slightly. Then coat with glue and assemble in the usual manner.

Another way to do the job is to saw a slot in the end of the loose-fitting piece, then force a thin, wedge-shaped piece of wood into the slot as illustrated. When the piece is hammered into place, the wedge will be forced in and will spread the end of the loose-fitting rung slightly, expanding it enough to ensure a tight fit.

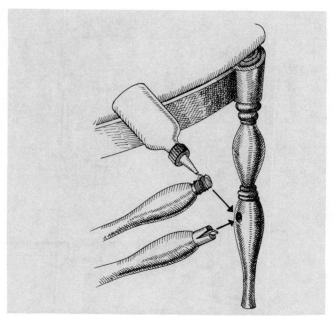

Two ways to ensure a snug fit when rung fits loosely. Wrap end with thread until it's the right thickness (above), or fit wedge into slot cut in end of rung beforehand (below). In both cases, coat with glue and then force into place.

When reassembling pieces, coat each surface with glue and then clamp or tie the parts together to apply the pressure required to achieve a permanent bond.

Bar clamps or pipe clamps are useful for this kind of project. So are C-clamps and other woodworking clamps. If you don't have any of these handy, there are several other ways you can apply the needed pressure.

Where practical, simple weights (books, buckets of sand or water, bricks) set on top of a piece will do the trick.

In other cases, a rope tourniquet will serve almost as well as a professional web clamp. To make a rope tourniquet, wrap a piece of stout clothesline twice around the chair, drawer, or other piece being assembled. Then tie a knot to hold it in place. Pressure is applied by using a stick between the two turns of rope and then twisting, as pictured on page 392 bottom. Before doing this, insert pieces of heavy cardboard or similar padding over each corner to protect against damaging the wood as the rope tightens. Scrap pieces of cardboard or plywood should also be used under the jaws of all clamps to keep the metal from marring the wood.

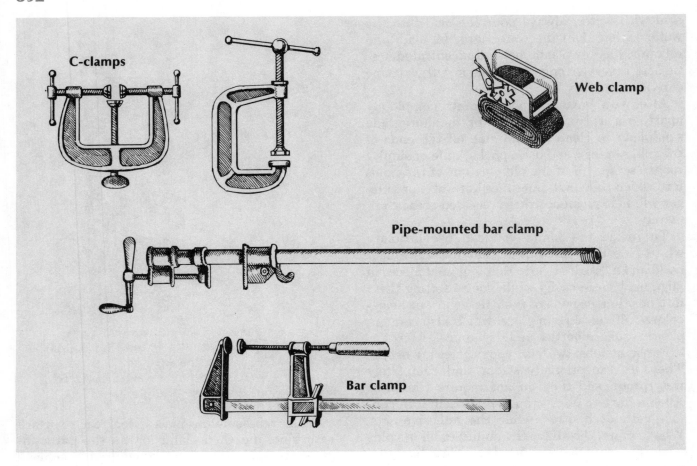

C-clamps

Web clamp

Pipe-mounted bar clamp

Bar clamp

A rope tourniquet can be used instead of a web clamp to hold parts of a chair (or other piece of furniture) together while glue is setting.

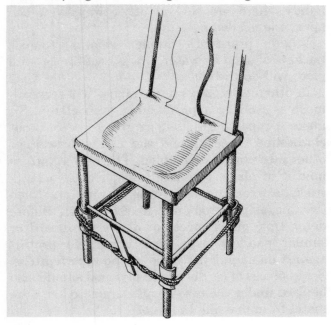

There are many times when it is impractical to take loose joints apart in order to do a proper job of regluing. Sometimes taking them apart will cause too much damage. Or perhaps only one or two joints are loose and it is not worth taking all the other joints apart.

In these cases, first force the pieces apart as much as you can without actually disjointing them. Then use a thin blade to scrape out as much of the old glue as possible. One tool that is handy for this job is a small fingernail file; another is a stiff piece of wire with a very small hook bent at the end.

Blow out as much of the dust and scrapings as possible. Then work glue into the joint with a piece of wire or a flexible artist's palette knife.

It helps if you can turn the piece so that the joint is vertical, with the open end up, so that gravity will make the glue flow down into it.

After you have worked in as much glue as possible, open and close the joint a few times by pushing the loose pieces back and forth to spread the adhesive around on the inside. Then press the pieces together, and clamp them to apply the needed pressure while the glue sets.

A very handy gadget for working glue into a loose joint is a syringe type of glue injector—a larger version of the syringe doctors use for hypodermic injections. Made of metal or plastic, and sold in many hardware stores as well as through mail-order houses that specialize in craftsmen's supplies, these tools have a narrow nozzle with a hole in the center. A plunger fits snugly inside the hollow barrel, which you fill with glue. Pushing on the plunger then forces the glue out through the nozzle.

To get the glue into the joint, drill a small hole where it will be least noticeable—the back of a leg on a chair, under the seat for bench slats. Inject the glue through the hole so that it penetrates the joint. Keep pumping glue in until it oozes out around the assembled pieces. Apply clamping pressure and wipe off excess glue afterward. The little hole that remains will be filled with a wood or plastic compound later on.

There is one other method you can use to tighten a loose rung or similar joint when simple regluing doesn't seem to work. Drill a small hole completely through the joint, again in a not-too-visible place, and just big enough to drive a small dowel through it. It's easiest to match the hole to the dowel—if you have a ¼-inch dowel, use a

A syringe-type glue injector is used to force glue into a joint through a small hole drilled in an inconspicuous spot on part being repaired.

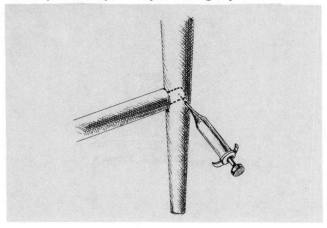

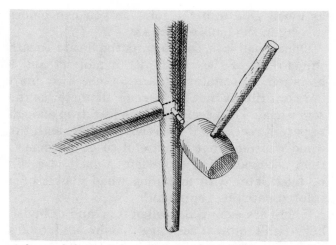

A loose joint can be reinforced by drilling a small hole through it, then inserting a short length of small-diameter dowel.

¼-inch drill. Next, work glue into the loosened joint by one of the techniques just described. Then dip the dowel into more glue, and drive it home with a wooden mallet.

The hole you drill for the dowel should be snug enough to ensure a tight fit, but not so tight that the dowel will be smashed when you try to drive it home. Your best bet is to drill trial holes in scrap material first to make sure you are using the right size bit for your particular dowel. To provide room for the glue, it helps to file a small flat area along the length of the dowel, using a rasp or piece of sandpaper. Cutting grooves lengthwise with a knife or fine saw is another method. Make the dowel longer than necessary and leave the excess sticking out until after the glue dries, then trim it off neatly with a hacksaw blade or coping saw and use sandpaper to contour the exposed part for a flush fit.

Using Nails and Screws When Necessary

On some pieces where you can't use dowels and glue you may have to use small nails or screws. Drill small pilot holes before driving the nails or screws in, so that you don't split the wood. The nails or screws will be driven in through the side of a joint, where they are least visible, so that's where you can drill your holes. Again, try to work as much glue into the joint as you can before driving in the nails or screws.

Once a nail is in, countersink the head beneath the surface of the wood with a nail set and a hammer. To countersink screws, use a counter-bore or drill bit that is the same diameter as the screw head. Drill a shallow hole just deep enough to permit recessing the screw's head beneath the wood's surface, but be careful to go no deeper than necessary. The holes left in each case will be filled later with matching wood plastic or a colored patching compound.

There are even times when this kind of invisibility isn't quite necessary. Chairs and tables that have aprons or skirts beneath the seat or top, for example, with legs that butt up against the underside, will often get wobbly because the brace that goes across the corner joint has worked loose. The brace may be a piece of wood secured by screws driven into the frame on each side, or it may be a steel brace, with a threaded lag bolt going through the center to the inside corner of the leg.

In the latter case, tightening the wing nut will draw the assembly together more firmly. In the case of a wood brace, the screws may have worked loose and merely need tightening. If tightening the screws doesn't do the trick, or if the screws have gouged out oversized holes in the wood, then you may be better off installing a new wood block, slightly oversize, and securing this with both glue and screws.

Repairing Damaged Veneer

Veneer is a thin layer of beautiful wood that is bonded to a lesser wood to make it richer-looking. In time, the glue may come loose and the veneer may loosen and lift in spots. Blistering and lifting repairs are not very difficult, but replacing a missing piece of veneer can be tricky.

If the veneer is loose along one edge, pry it up carefully and slide a knifeblade or fingernail file under it to scrape out as much of the old glue as you can. An emery board, the kind used on fingernails, is especially handy for jobs of this kind. Just be very careful not to lift the veneer any more than necessary to avoid splitting or cracking it.

Use a soda straw to blow all dust and dried glue flakes out from under the veneer, then work fresh glue underneath by poking it in with a piece of wire or a knifeblade. Ordinary white glue is probably the easiest material to use, since it dries clear and is virtually nonstaining.

After the glue has been spread around as much as possible, move the loose veneer up and down a few times to make certain both surfaces are coated. Now press down hard and use clamps or weights to keep the two surfaces in contact until the glue dries. Be sure you wipe off excess glue that oozes out before it dries.

If the veneer is loose in the center of a panel, creating a noticeable blister, use a *very sharp*

Chair or table leg may be loose because wood brace (left) has worked loose and needs retightening—or because metal brace (right) needs to be tightened by taking up on wing nut in center.

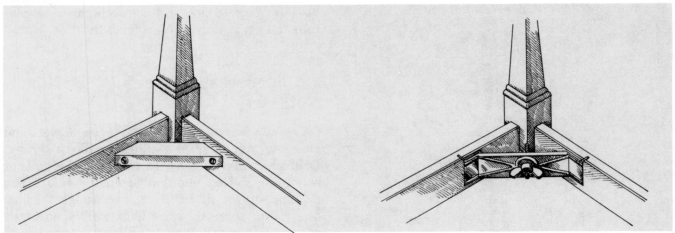

knife or razor blade to slit through the middle of the blister. Then press one half down while you work glue under the other half with a thin spatula or piece of wire. (An artist's palette knife, with a thin, long, flexible blade, is ideal for this job.)

After you have spread glue under one half of the blister, press that half down and then work glue in under the other side.

Now press the entire blister up and down several times to spread the glue around and apply weights or clamps to hold both sides of the veneer in place while the glue hardens. To keep the weights or clamps from sticking to the surface (some glue will ooze up through the slit you made in the middle of the blister), cover the veneer with a piece of waxed paper, after wiping off as much as possible of the oozed-up glue with a damp cloth. There will be a barely visible slit, but on old pieces it sort of adds to the antique look.

When a piece of veneer is missing entirely, the only way to make a repair that won't be noticeable is to insert a patch of the same veneer. There are very few lumberyards that stock wood veneer these days, but it can be ordered from some mail-order houses that cater to home craftsmen, as well as from some dealers that specialize in cabinetmaker's supplies.

However, since wood is a natural product, even if you can find the veneer, chances are it won't match the tone and grain of your surface exactly, so in many cases you are better off trying to remove a small piece of veneer—enough to make the patch you need—from the same piece of furniture. You do this by cutting out a piece in a place where it is not easily visible. For example, the back of a piece may be covered with the same veneer, or there may be veneer on the inside of a

When a piece of matching veneer cannot be found, it may pay to cut out a piece where it will not show, and use it for making a repair in a prominent area.

door or drawer front. Sometimes you can even get away with cutting a piece out of one side of a large unit that stands in a corner or against another large piece. A small patch of veneer removed from the hidden side, near the back or near the floor, won't be noticeable.

The easiest way to "steal" such a piece is to cut it out near an edge. This will enable you to slide a knife or sharp chisel in from that edge in order to lift off a small piece of the veneer.

If this is not practical, then you can use a sharp knife to cut out a rectangular or oblong piece that will be large enough to make the size patch needed. Use a metal straightedge to guide your knife and cut along each side three or four times to make certain the piece will lift out cleanly. Then carefully slide chisel or knife blade under this cut-out section to slice the glue away until you can lift it out neatly.

The next step is to trim this piece to a neat rectangle, square, or diamond shape, so that when laid over the area where the veneer is missing, the new piece will fully cover it.

If you have a choice, try for a diamond-shaped patch with the grain running in the long direction of the diamond. This shape tends to blend in more easily than a rectangle or square that has two edges running straight across the direction of the grain.

A blister in veneer can often be cured by cutting a slit across the middle, then working glue under each half with an artist's palette knife and pressing flat with weights or clamps.

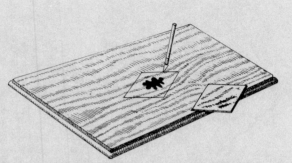

Trace outline of patch over damaged area. Then cut out piece to be replaced with a sharp knife.

Use hammer with knife or very sharp chisel to gently pry off piece that is damaged in the center.

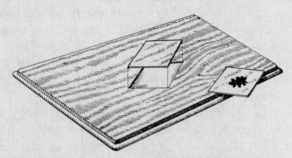

Scrape out all old glue, apply fresh glue, and fit new patch in place. Old piece can be reinserted in place where new patch was cut out (side or back), and damage may be scarcely noticeable there.

After the patch has been trimmed to a size slightly larger than the damaged area, lay it directly over the damage and trace its outline onto the existing veneer with the point of an awl or icepick. Now lay the patch aside and carefully cut out the old veneer to match the pattern just outlined.

Don't cut on the outside of the line. If anything, cut slightly inside the line. You can always trim the patch slightly if needed to make a snug fit. Be particularly careful about matching the direction of the general grain pattern. If trimming is needed, use a single-edge razor blade until the patch drops neatly into the area where the damaged veneer has been cut out.

After the old veneer has been removed, scrape the dried glue out from underneath, blow all dust away, and glue the new patch in its place. Use weights or clamps to apply pressure until the glue sets, and wipe away any glue that may have oozed out. The hairline seam or joint will fill in when the new finish is applied and—if you have worked carefully—should be scarcely noticeable when the job is done.

Patching Cracks, Holes, Dents, and Gouges

Some old pieces of furniture have "distress" marks that add to the character and appearance of the piece and should be left as is when refinishing. However, there are times when scratches, dents, gouges, and other defects are just plain unsightly and should be patched or smoothed over if you want the final finish to have a smooth, professional look.

Patching compounds for filling cracks, holes, and gouges in wood generally fall into two categories: ready-mixed plastic compounds that dry quickly, and powdered compounds that you mix with water to form a puttylike material for use on wood.

Generally, the powdered wood-putty compounds are available only in a kind of light tan or buff color that is fine for opaque finishes, while ready-mixed wood plastics come in a variety of wood-tone shades so you can blend them in better with different-colored woods and finishes.

These wood patching compounds differ in porosity when hard—that is, in their ability to absorb stain. Some are fairly porous and will "take" stains to some degree, while others are extremely hard and dense and will not absorb any stain at all. This means you have to be very careful about using them on a piece that you plan to eventually treat with stain. The stain will not be absorbed uniformly, so that all the patch marks will stand out when the job is done, or the stain may not "take" on any of the patched areas.

For best results, it's smart to experiment beforehand with various brands and types. Make some gouges on a few pieces of scrap wood, then apply the patching material and let it dry hard. Sand smooth and apply stain over this to see how the patch absorbs the stain. Don't rely on a manufacturer's claims that its filler absorbs stain. Even it it does, it won't absorb it in exactly the same way as the wood around it.

The usual way to avoid this headache is to apply the stain to the wood first, then use a colored filler or patching compound that matches the stained wood when dry. If you can't find a patching compound to match the color of your stained wood, remember that colors can be intermixed or "doctored" by adding tinting colors, which you can buy in most paint stores. This will take some experimenting, especially since patching compounds dry to a different shade than they appear in the can. But this is really the only way you can be sure what the final results will look like, and you'll learn a lot in the process.

Never try to fill a deep crack or gouge with a single application of patching compound. Although some of these materials are labeled "nonshrinking," most will contract to some degree when applied in heavy layers. Also, they may not dry properly if you put them on in thick layers. The compound dries at the surface first and remains soft underneath for quite a while. To prevent this, apply the material in layers, allowing each one to harden before applying the next one. The last layer should be slightly higher than the surrounding surface so that you can trim it flush by sanding or shaving carefully with a very sharp chisel or scraper.

When using any of these compounds to build up a chipped edge or corner, you can increase the strength of the patch by drilling a few small holes in the bottom of the recess or cavity before ap-

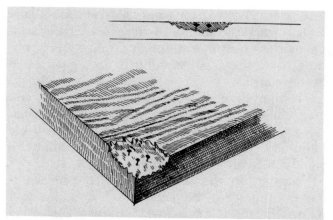

To increase strength of bond when patching broken corners or edges, drive very small staples or brads partway into the wood first, making sure heads won't stick up above the surface. These will help ensure a firm grip on the compound when it hardens.

plying the first layer of patching material. As you press the compound into position, with a little extra pressure you'll force some of it into the holes, increasing the strength of the bond.

Another method is to drive a few small staples or brads into the cavity, allowing the heads to protrude slightly—but not high enough to interfere with the smoothing over of the final patch. When the wood plastic is packed around the staples or brads, the heads will firmly lock the patch into place and greatly reduce the chances of its being knocked or chipped away later on.

Sanding and Smoothing

The last step before applying any finish is the final sanding and smoothing. This requires more care when refinishing an old piece than it does when applying any finish to a new piece. On new wood your only concern is to get the wood as smooth as possible—no matter how much sanding is required. On old pieces, you want to retain that aged patina we've talked so much about.

On most small surfaces, and on older pieces that require special care, hand sanding is probably the safest and simplest procedure. Even if you use a finishing sander for preliminary smoothing, it's still advisable to switch to hand sanding for the final smoothing.

On curved, carved, or contoured surfaces, steel

wool works better than sandpaper. It's less likely to leave scratch marks in the wood than sandpaper. It is slower-working and takes more rubbing to do the same job, but it does give much better control.

For round pieces, such as legs or spindles, you can tear the steel wool in long strips, and then use it shoeshine-style. Grab each end with one hand and pull back and forth, maintaining a steady pressure on each end.

You can do the same with fairly fine sandpaper. Simply cut the paper into long strips, and follow the directions above. To keep the strips from tearing, reinforce the backs with strips of cellophane tape.

Start on the raw wood with 100 or 120 paper. Sand at a slight angle to the direction of the grain, but no more than necessary to level off any ridges or scratches left after stripping. Then switch to 200, this time working parallel to the grain wherever possible so no visible scratches remain.

The 220 paper will give you a satin-smooth finish, but you can go on to an even silkier surface with 280 or 320 paper. Before switching to this fine grade, wipe the surface clean with a rag lightly moistened with paint thinner to get rid of any grit left by the coarser papers, and once again go with the grain.

Check the surface frequently with your fingertips; you can feel rough spots more easily than you can see them. You can also hold a bright light behind the surface, and almost parallel to it. This angular light will show up the slightest irregularities.

And remember, when hand sanding on a flat surface, it's best to use a sanding block.

On some types of wood, especially in the softer varieties, sanding with even the finest grit does not always leave the surface perfectly smooth, because the wood fibers tend to stand up along the grain. This creates a fuzzy surface that never really looks or feels smooth. Sometimes this isn't noticeable until the first coat of stain has been applied, while in other cases it can be clearly seen even on the raw wood. Here's an old preventive trick that many professional finishers use. Just before the final sanding, dampen the wood slightly by wiping with a sponge that has been moistened in water. The water will cause

the wood fibers on the surface to swell slightly so that when they dry, these fibers will remain erect. The final sanding will remove this fuzz and leave the surface very smooth. It also minimizes the likelihood of more grain-raising when the stain is applied.

If the wood is very soft and fuzzy, here's another method that works even better. Dilute some 4-pound-cut shellac with 2 parts of denatured alcohol. (The "pound-cut" of shellac is explained on page 408.) Apply a very thin "wash" coat to the surface. Avoid overlapping strokes with a brush. You want to make sure the wood gets only one coat over its entire surface.

The shellac will not only raise fibers, which can be sanded down, it will also partially seal the surface and tend to stabilize the grain and make it uniform in porosity. Partially sealing the grain also helps ensure that a wood stain applied over it will "take" uniformly without blotchy spots where the stain soaks in more rapidly in some places than it does in others, a common problem with very soft wood.

After sanding, it is important that you remove every bit of dust and grit before you apply the first coat of stain, sealer, or other finishing material. Slight specks and fine dust particles, which may be practically invisible on the raw wood, will stand out conspicuously after a finish has been applied.

Wiping the surface down with a dry cloth or brushing the dust off is not enough. Using a vacuum cleaner is better, but even this will not remove all of the dust.

The best thing to do is vacuum to remove the heaviest accumulations. Then wipe the entire surface down carefully with a "tack rag."

Sold in most paint stores as well as in many hardware stores, and often referred to as a "tacky cloth," a tack rag is nothing more than a piece of coarse-mesh cotton or cheesecloth that has been impregnated with a varnish-and-oil mixture to make it sticky. It picks up dust without leaving any residue on the surface of the wood.

To use the tack rag, fold it to a convenient size and wipe it over the surface of the wood carefully. Don't skip any spots. As the exposed side of the cloth gets loaded with dust, keep folding it to expose a fresh surface.

Making a Tack Rag

If you cannot find tack rags in your local paint or hardware store, make your own out of a piece of cheesecloth. Start by folding the fabric into a pad and wetting it with water. Then squeeze almost dry.

Next, with the damp cloth still folded, pour a little turpentine over the fabric and work this into the cloth by squeezing or kneading it with your hands.

Now with the cloth still folded flat, pour a small amount of varnish over the fabric, or sprinkle it through the folds. (Use about 1 ounce of varnish for a piece of fabric that's about a yard square when completely unfolded.)

Work this varnish through the pad, again by kneading the cloth with your hands, until the varnish has spread uniformly through the entire piece of cloth.

Unfold it to see if there are any dry spots remaining, and if so, sprinkle on a little more varnish and knead again. The cloth should be uniformly amber or light yellow in color and damp enough to feel kind of sticky. But it should not be so damp that it drips liquid when squeezed hard.

The tack rag is now ready for use. Store the rag in a tightly closed screw-top jar or airtight plastic bag to keep it from drying out.

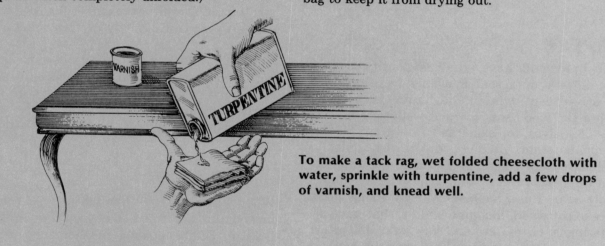

To make a tack rag, wet folded cheesecloth with water, sprinkle with turpentine, add a few drops of varnish, and knead well.

WHEN AND WHY TO USE STAIN

Most home finishers use stain for one of two major reasons—to make the wood look the way it's "supposed" to, or to change it considerably to suit either one's taste or some specific purpose.

It's amazing how few people associate raw wood from the lumberyard with the same wood used in making furniture.

Even if new wood is your idea of beauty—as natural as you can get it—a light stain, just enough to strengthen color and highlight grain, can give a less-than-prime piece of lumber a lot of character.

Wood stains have also been used for years to "upgrade" wood—to make a relatively inexpensive or unfashionable species look like something "better." It was back in colonial America that pine began masquerading as mahogany, so beloved back in Europe, or walnut, which ran a close second. But remember, stain changes only the *color* of the wood, not its grain pattern. True, color may be the first thing most people will notice, but some species have such a distinctive grain pattern that any attempt to duplicate their appearance by mere stain is almost certain to result in disappointment.

That doesn't necessarily mean a camouflaged piece will always look bad. But if you try to use a walnut or mahogany stain to make an inexpensive pine piece look as if it actually were made of walnut or mahogany, don't expect to fool anyone who knows much about wood.

There's another good reason why stain is sometimes used on furniture made of several different types of wood, or pieces that are not uniform in tone or color. A dark stain will often help blend these lighter and darker parts together for a more consistent overall tone before finishing.

In all "matching-type" problems, of course, you must remember that a stain will look different on different types of wood. Walnut on pine, for example, does not always look the same as walnut on walnut—or even the same from one piece of pine to the next.

Presealing Soft Woods and Edges

Many hardwoods have a uniform density of grain that allows stain to soak in evenly over the entire surface—except where end grain is exposed (where the wood was cut across the grain—the ends of shelves, for example). End grain is very porous, so stain will soak into it very quickly, penetrate deeply, and make it look much darker than the rest of the wood.

The same thing happens when staining some types of softwood, like pine and fir, that have alternating layers of hard and soft grain, and alternating areas of porosity. You wind up with a streaky, blotchy, "wild" grain effect, which is a lot less interesting than it sounds, and definitely unattractive.

There is a cure. A thin coat of sealer is applied first—thin enough to seal the surface partially so that the stain doesn't soak in too deeply in porous areas. It's important *not* to seal the wood completely. You want to limit the stain's penetration, not prevent it entirely. If you're not sure whether a sealer is needed, test the stain first on a scrap piece of the same kind of wood, or on the back or bottom of the piece.

The two products most often used to seal porous wood are thinned shellac and penetrating wood sealer.

Professionals generally prefer a "wash" coat of shellac. It dries very quickly, for one thing, and you can stain over it in about an hour. It's made by mixing 4 parts denatured alcohol with 1 part 4-pound-cut shellac. (See page 408 for more about various "pound-cuts" of shellac.)

Brush the shellac wash on rapidly with a wide brush, making every effort not to overlap or cover any area more than once. Because shellac dries so quickly, overlapping, or even too much brushing back and forth, can result in some spots getting two coats of shellac instead of one, which means some spots are sealed more than others, and gone is that uniform staining job you've just taken this extra step to ensure. As a rule, a light rubdown with very fine steel wool, before the first coat of stain is applied, will help.

If all those precautions about overlapping have you feeling a bit nervous, here's another method that's much safer for the amateur, although you'll have to wait a bit longer for it to dry. It's easier to control, and there's less likelihood of buildup.

Mix 1 part clear penetrating wood sealer with 2 parts thinner, and brush on over the surface. Wait a minute or so, and wipe down with a clean cloth to remove any excess still on the surface. Allow it to dry overnight before applying wood stain.

Types of Stains

Wood stains are a lot like fabric dyes; they soak in and tint the wood fibers without hiding the texture. Unlike opaque finishes such as paint, they allow natural grain and some of the color to show through—the exact degree varying with the type of stain used. Stains run the gamut from translucent to totally transparent and from easy to use to tricky.

The stains you're most likely to use fall into three broad categories: pigmented stains, sometimes called pigmented wiping stains; penetrating or dye-type stains; and powdered aniline stains designed to be mixed with water or alcohol.

Pigmented stains are made up of tiny particles of pigment suspended in either an oil or an emulsion-type latex base. The pigments never really dissolve, which means the stain has to be stirred frequently when you're using it, or the particles will settle to the bottom of the container, and your stain will vary in both consistency and color. It's the easiest to use and the most forgiving of errors. If you think you've put too much on, you can usually wipe off as much as you want by rubbing promptly with a dry cloth or a rag saturated with paint thinner. Since pigmented stains don't penetrate as quickly as the dye types, there's very little likelihood of streaking or lap marks, and if necessary, you can sand to take some of the color off even after the piece has dried.

There are drawbacks to stains that don't penetrate very deeply. They will fade more quickly if exposed to sunlight, for example, and they're not as transparent or clear as the penetrating dye-type stains. Therefore, color tends to be a bit "cloudier" when dry. The tiny particles of solid pigment will also partially conceal or "cloud" some of the grain, but this can be an advantage on poor-quality woods.

There's very little difference between oil-base pigmented stain (loosely referred to as an oil stain) and latex-base pigmented stain, except that the latter can be thinned with water (that means you can also clean your tools and hands with water).

Penetrating oil stains are more like true wood dyes. No pigments or other solid particles in suspension here. Colors are completely dissolved, which makes this type of stain much more transparent and brilliant in color than pigmented stains. No grain is hidden, and the dye penetrates deep into the wood, making it far more resistant to fading.

Most of the ready-mixed penetrating stains available from the local paint store have an oil base, and are marked with the words "penetrating" or "dye-type" on the label so you can't mistake them for pigmented stains.

On really fine furniture made of good-quality wood, penetrating-type stains are always preferable to pigmented stains. They not only allow everything to show through, they're not as likely to mask a patina if used judiciously. However, they're not quite as foolproof as the pigmented stains. On the less expensive or softer woods, or pieces that have an uneven porosity because of surface damage of some sort, a preliminary sealer may be needed to avoid blotchiness. This type of stain will penetrate far more deeply in the softer parts of the grain than it will in the denser parts.

Powdered water stains are aniline-type wood dyes. You buy them in powder form, and dissolve them in water or alcohol. Widely preferred by professionals because they dry very quickly and provide the clearest, purest color and deepest fiber penetration, they can be very tricky for the amateur. They're not widely available except from mail-order houses, and you have to do a lot of experimenting when you mix anything yourself. But there are more important objections:

1. They raise the grain of the wood, so you not only have to sponge with water and sand the wood before applying the stain, you also have to rub down with fine sandpaper after the stain has been applied.

2. They dry very quickly, so you have to be careful about lapping and streaking when putting them on with a brush (professionals prefer to spray them on); amateurs find it difficult to achieve uniform results.

3. Most important, perhaps, water stains are not suitable for use on old wood that has been previously finished. Even if all the old finish has been carefully stripped off, water stains often will not penetrate properly and you'll wind up with a blotchy, uneven effect that's difficult to correct.

Powdered aniline-type stains that are designed for mixing with alcohol rather than water dry even faster. They have the advantage of not raising the grain the way a water stain will, but they are even harder to apply evenly, because they dry so quickly that it is almost impossible to brush them out smoothly—even on moderate-size surfaces. As a rule, amateur refinishers are better off staying away from them.

All the same, they can be important and are beautiful, so you may want to experiment. And there are certain finishes you may want to use that just won't work with any other stain—a French polish, for example (see page 409).

Choosing a Color

You can't simply wipe a stain entirely off the surface of wood and start from scratch if you don't like the color. You can come pretty close with pigmented stains, but some stain always soaks into the fibers, so it may take some sanding to get it all out. That's why it's important to go to the trouble of picking the right color to start with.

Manufacturers supply color cards and stores display samples, but you can't let them be your only guide. Unlike paint, which is opaque and looks the same on all surfaces, stain is very much affected by the color of the wood that shows through. Stains also "take" differently on different pieces of wood—sometimes of the same kind.

Some manufacturers try to show you what several different stains look like on a variety of woods, but the variety is rarely broad enough, and the samples often don't look like real wood. The best way to be sure is to actually try the stain on the same type of wood as your piece, or a very similar one. If you can't find any scrap pieces, try your stain on an inconspicuous part— back, bottom, or corner—where discoloration left over by the wrong stain won't be noticed.

Unfortunately, there is no standardization of names to describe colors between different companies. One brand's black walnut may be very different from another's. In fact, the same colors by one manufacturer may vary from batch to batch.

The lesson to be learned here is that if you find a color you like, and you're planning to use it on a big piece or a whole suite of furniture, buy enough for the whole job. Then, before you begin, mix all the cans together. It's your only way to ensure a uniform color.

If you don't find a ready-mixed shade you like, don't be afraid to mix two or three colors together. In many cases, it's the only way to get a shade you want. Once you find it, don't forget to mix up a batch of it big enough to finish your project.

Don't forget, no wood, not even a freshly stained piece, looks the way it will with a clear finish on it, so if you've got scraps with stain tests on them, try the actual finishes over them. You'd be surprised what a finish with an amber or orange cast can do to a stain color. Even a supposedly perfectly clear finish makes a big difference.

Staining Techniques

Except for some special preparation for water stains, methods of applying most stains are pretty much the same. They can be put on with a brush, rag, sponge, or one of the flat painting pads that are so popular today.

Generally, after a few minutes excess stain is wiped off with a rag. Most stains should be wiped for uniformity of color, but exactly how long you wait before wiping it off depends on the type of stain you're using, the porosity of the wood, and the depth of color you're after. A penetrating stain, for example, soaks into wood more rapidly than a pigmented product, and should generally be wiped sooner.

There is no set rule that governs how long you should wait before wiping. Only experimentation and experience with similar stains and woods will tell you how long to wait. Just remember that it's easier to correct the effects of wiping off too soon—with another coat or a darker stain—than it is to sand, bleach, and otherwise strenuously lighten a piece on which the stain's been left too long.

Start by applying the stain to a small section of wood at a time, and begin wiping with a dry rag as soon as the wood looks dark enough. If you find yourself removing too much of the stain, try waiting a little longer. If this doesn't help, you may have to switch to a darker stain. Or you can darken your original stain by adding tinted pigments available in most paint stores.

When you're dealing with matching problems, like lighter and darker woods next to each other on the same piece, you can control the final effect to some extent by wiping the dark piece sooner or more vigorously than the other. Or you can first stain the lighter piece with a stain that will bring it closer to the darker wood in tone. After the stain dries, apply another coat over both pieces. This minimizes any differences in color that remain.

To prepare wood for aniline or water-stain dyes, follow the suggestions on page 400 for getting a soft wood smooth, with no fuzzy wood fibers sticking up. Only this time, dampen the wood—all of it—with a sponge moistened in warm water. After the piece has dried, sand as you would for a final sanding. This will probably eliminate any grain-raising after staining. If not, sand again. Since staining does not tend to be uniform with this type of dye, sanding may help you control color. You can always stain again for a darker color, but keeping an entirely even tone won't be easy.

Aniline stains can be dissolved in alcohol, too, as mentioned, and they don't raise the grain. But they dry so quickly that splotching becomes an even greater hazard. Investigate these only if you intend to spray.

Using a Pigmented Penetrating Sealer as a Wood Stain

Penetrating wood sealers come in clear as well as in wood tones, so it's possible to use them as stains as well as finishes. In fact, if you're going to use this kind of finish, and your piece needs added color, this is the best way to stain it.

A penetrating sealer is not a surface finish; it is rubbed *into* the wood to penetrate its fibers and has little or no shine. The effect is more of an "oiled" look, and bears a resemblance to the old beloved "rubbed" linseed-oil finish, which generally takes half a year to build up, and an eternity to maintain.

The important thing here is that you can use this staining and finishing technique to take advantage of open-grained, beautifully textured wood, yet these penetrating sealers can look lovely on close-grained woods, too.

Clear sealers can also be used as a medium if you want to mix your own stain. Thin the sealer with about 25 percent paint thinner, then add tinting colors to get what you want.

Tinting colors are available at most paint stores, and are called by such names as raw umber, burnt umber, sienna (also raw and burnt), Venetian red, ocher, black—in short, the basic colors that can be mixed to get a wood tone. You have to experiment a bit to get what you think is a rich oak or walnut or teak, but here are a few general rule-of-thumb suggestions to get you going. Burnt umber and a touch of Venetian red are mixed to get a mahogany tone. (Caution: A little red goes a long way.) You can use burnt umber with a little raw umber for walnut. Raw umber with a small amount of burnt sienna will give you oak. Here, testing on scrap wood is really a must, and bear in mind that your colors will often look considerably different dry than wet.

Whether you buy them ready-made or mix your own, the agents used to color the sealer are pigments, not dyes, and in most cases, results will be very similar to what you get with pigmented oil- or latex-base wiping stains. Colors are not quite so clear or rich as they are with a true penetrating-type dye. However, grain shows through very well, and texture is marvelously emphasized; sealer finishes compare well in beauty to most other stains and finishes.

When and How to Use Paste Wood Filler

Although open-grained woods such as oak, teak, walnut, and mahogany are often finished with a penetrating sealer that does not fill in the pores of the wood, there are times when you will want to give wood pieces of this kind a smooth, built-up "piano-type" glossy finish. But to do this you will have to fill in the open pores first by using a paste wood filler. Otherwise it makes no difference how much sanding you do—you will never get a really smooth finish on the open-grained wood. This also holds true when you are refinishing older pieces that were originally treated with wood filler—if you used a chemical remover to strip off all of the old finish, then you probably took a good deal of the filler off at the same time. So plan on reapplying filler when you start refinishing.

If your piece is to be stained, do it *before* applying the wood filler. Then the wood filler must be tinted to a tone slightly darker than your piece before you start working with it. The reason for this is that paste wood fillers come in a "natural" or "neutral" shade about the color of cashew butter—a bit lighter than peanut butter. If applied as is to raw wood, any subsequent stain will soak much more into the wood than it will into the filler, leaving lots of light spots and streaks just where you might want them a little bit darker.

One of the advantages of wood filler, aside from its smoothing qualities, is that, if colored, it allows you to darken the pores, giving the wood a much grainier look.

Several manufacturers make paste fillers in wood tones, but most stores stock them only in "neutral," so to get what you want, you'll have to add tinting colors. Again, you'll have to experiment a bit, to get the shade or color you want.

To simplify mixing, dilute the tinting color with a little solvent first, then mix this in with the paste wood filler. This will, of course, thin the filler a little, but since you have to thin it anyway, no harm is done.

Another way to tint filler to the shade you want is to mix it with some of the actual stain you'll be using—but only if you're using an oil-base stain. Use the thickened sediment that settles to the bottom of the stain can after you've poured off some of the liquid on top.

When applying a tinted wood filler, you'll actually be staining the wood as well as filling the pores, since the wood will absorb the color contained in the solvent. It won't make much noticeable difference on an already-stained piece, but it offers you another staining alternative for open-grained woods—you can tint your wood and fill its pores in one step.

Whether you're filling pores, staining, or both, before using any paste wood filler you have to thin it with turpentine or a similar solvent in order to reduce it to brushing consistency. The manufacturer's directions will usually suggest the amount of thinning required, but as a rule the filler should be about the consistency of a heavy-bodied interior flat wall paint.

Spread the filler on liberally with a brush, covering only a few square feet at a time. Brush across the grain to work it into the pores. Allow it to set for a few minutes until the filler starts to lose its wet look and begins to get slightly dull-looking, then take a folded pad of coarse cloth (burlap is excellent) to wipe off the excess. Rub vigorously with a circular motion and turn the cloth frequently as it becomes saturated.

For best results, switch to a second piece of clean cloth and rub hard *across* the grain to remove all excess from the surface before it dries. Finally, finish by wiping almost parallel to the grain, but this time don't rub hard. You don't want to wipe the filler out of the pores of the wood, just smooth it all down.

Actually, the wiping-off process is the most critical part of the whole operation, and it may take some experimenting before you learn how to do it correctly. If you start wiping too soon, you will rub most of the filler out of the pores, but if you wait too long, the filler will start to harden

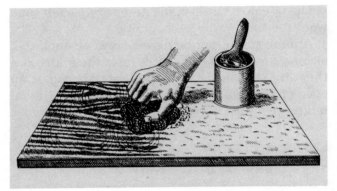

Paste wood filler must be rubbed off before it gets completely dry. Use circular motion for the first wipe.

and become sticky and will be extremely difficult to remove. You may even have to sand it off.

After the entire surface has been filled and wiped, let it dry for at least 24 hours. Then sand lightly with very fine-grit paper. On flat surfaces, use a sanding block that has been faced with felt or sponge rubber.

On curved surfaces, use fine steel wool instead of sandpaper. Dust thoroughly with a tack rag before going any further.

A Shortcut: Finishing with Varnish Stain

Since varnish stains apply color and finish in one application, they are not something you'd use on your finest pieces, or where you want a good wood to show through, or on a piece that's going to take a lot of scrutiny. However, if you feel it isn't worth stripping and refinishing the inside of an old cabinet or the inside of a drawer or the bottoms of shelves that are not normally seen, but you want a decent, durable, cleanable surface there all the same, varnish stain may be the answer.

The very name, varnish stain, suggests that it allows you to stain the wood as you varnish. However, you're dealing with pigments, not wood dyes, and the effect is more like a thinned-down paint or translucent color wash.

Since varnish stain colors and finishes in one step, and can be applied over an old coat of shellac, varnish, or similar finish without stripping, it can be a time and work saver on some jobs. And you can save your time and energy for the finer stuff.

CHOOSING AND USING CLEAR FINISHES

All furniture falls into two broad categories—surface coatings and penetrating types. Penetrating finishes are used mostly on modern and country pieces, where a casual look is wanted, although there are other imaginative ways to use it. Surface finishes, as the name suggests, build up a protective film that can be either glossy or dull, and are used on many traditional pieces—what have often been called the pride of the household.

Varnishes

Originally made of natural oils and resins, most varnishes today are based on man-made or synthetic resins and have either an alkyd, a phenolic, a vinyl, or a polyurethane base.

Alkyd-based varnish is the least expensive, but not the toughest. Varnishes with a phenolic base work better outdoors than indoors. In most cases, they don't really dry hard enough for indoor use. (Most spar varnishes belong to this category of finish.)

Vinyl-based varnishes are the clearest in color. They dry more quickly and darken the wood less than any other varnish. They aren't as tough as most of the other types, but if clarity, trueness of color, and quick-drying capability are top priority, this is a good choice.

Polyurethane, the newest type of varnish, is the most durable and expensive of all ready-mixed varnishes. It offers maximum protection on surfaces that take a lot of punishment, such as tabletops, serving bars, and other places where food and liquid spills are common, and can be very useful on floors and other surfaces.

The thing to remember about polyurethane is that it dries to an exceptionally hard finish. That means if you are varnishing over an old piece that already has a polyurethane finish, a thorough sanding is required between coats to ensure

proper adhesion. If you miss any spots with this sanding, chances are in those areas the bond will be poor and peeling or cracking is likely. If you're varnishing on raw or stained wood—with no finish—the rules are different. With some polyurethane and vinyl formulations, you will note that a second coat must be applied *within* a certain number of hours—usually a lot less time than other varnishes. If you follow those directions, you will eliminate the need for any sanding between coats. But if you wait too long, you will have to sand thoroughly, as above.

Other factors to consider when choosing a varnish are color—actually, lack of color, or clarity—and the amount of gloss.

As mentioned earlier, vinyls are the "clearest," and although all varnishes are labeled "clear," most of them do have a slight amber tone. On a dark wood, it's not likely to make much of a difference, and may even enhance some woods by "aging" and enriching them just a bit. But if it's a light finish you want, or if you're trying to retain the original color of the wood, then the degree of amber may become important. Then it's best to test on scraps of the wood you'll be using.

Many varnishes come in either a high-gloss, a semigloss, or a completely flat finish. Not every finish is available in all three choices, but you can probably find what you want among the various types available.

If you want a piece to have a built-up, highly polished, piano-type finish, then you'll use a high-gloss finish. But if you want the duller "rubbed" finish, you can choose the rich luster of one of the various semigloss or satin-finish varnishes.

Years ago, when all varnishes were glossy, the only way to achieve a low-luster finish was to apply many coats of varnish, then rub the glossy finish down with powdered pumice and rottenstone. Nowadays, you can get much the same effect—with little or no rubbing—by using one of the low-luster varnishes. Most manufacturers differ in describing the amount of gloss their varnish provides; one company's semigloss may be duller or shinier than another company's satin gloss. Ask to see samples and experiment on scraps.

Regardless of the type of varnish you select, or whether you're going shiny or dull, if you want to achieve professional-looking results you must make sure the surface of your piece is dust-free. In addition to wiping the wood down carefully with a tack rag (see pages 398–99), try to work in a room that is as free of dust as possible. If you use a vacuum cleaner in that room, wait at least a few hours before varnishing in order to allow the airborne dust (blown around by the vacuum's exhaust) to settle.

As a rule, varnishes are ready for use in the can without need for additional thinning. However, for the first coat on raw wood, you'll generally find it advisable to thin slightly so that it soaks in more and does a better job of sealing the surface. Consult the instructions on the label for the amount of thinning recommended, or experiment with a small amount of the varnish beforehand. Periodic thinning as you work may be required to maintain a consistency that works easily and flows out smoothly.

Never shake a can of varnish before opening it. It may cause air bubbles in the liquid, which will be difficult to brush out later on. For the same reason, stir gently when adding thinner to varnish.

It's best not to work out of the full can. Pour off what you expect to use in a single session into a separate container and work from this.

Dip the brush into the varnish by no more than one-third its bristle length, and remove ex-

When varnishing, never dip brush bristles in by more than about a third of their length, and remove excess varnish by tapping the tips against the rim of the can—never by wiping across the rim. This holds true for enameling as well.

cess by tapping the bristle tips lightly against the inside rim of the can above the level of the liquid. *Never* wipe the brush across the rim. That kind of action is another cause of tiny air bubbles that run back into the can.

Whenever possible, try to work on surfaces that are horizontal. If the piece is small enough, turn it on its side or back, and remove as much hardware as you can.

On most pieces, it's best to coat all hard-to-reach places and the least conspicuous areas first. For example, do the backs and legs of a chair, as well as the rungs, before you do the seat and arms. In the case of a cabinet or chest, do the insides of doors before you do the outsides. The idea is to try to work toward yourself so that you are not reaching over or dripping on previously coated areas in order to varnish an unfinished area.

Varnish is applied by "flowing" it on, rather than by "scrubbing" it on. Brush with light, rapid strokes *parallel* to the grain. Then immediately cross-stroke lightly, with just the bristle tips, using long strokes *across* the grain. Follow this by cross-stroking again, *parallel* to the grain. (Cross-stroking simply means brushing at right angles to the direction from which you just stroked.) For this the bristles should be almost dry, and the tips should be dragged along the entire length of the panel in one single stroke.

If it is impossible to go from one end of a panel to the other with a single stroke, touch the tips of the bristles to the surface at one end and then drag them about halfway across before curving gently up and away from the surface in an arc. The next stroke is then started at the opposite end of the panel and brought forward until it overlaps the end of the stroke just completed—again in an arc up and away from the surface with a gradual motion. The idea is never to touch the bristles to the surface in the middle of a panel when you're smoothing off, since this will always leave a mark or blemish that will be clearly noticeable.

When varnishing recessed panels or doors that have carvings or moldings around the edges, always coat the molded or carved edges first, then complete the flat area in the center. Avoid dragging the brush across the edges of a piece or a door, as this will cause runs and dripping.

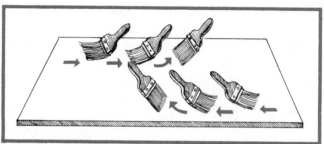

When you can't coat a full length of panel in one stroke, start at one end and go more than halfway, curving up and away from the surface at the halfway point. Then work from the other end and repeat, making sure that the second stroke overlaps the first before the brush again curves up and away.

Although most varnishes specify the minimum drying time required between coats, it's usually best to play it safe and wait a little longer. The only exceptions are some polyurethane and vinyl formulations. On some of these the manufacturer specifies that the second coat go on within a pre-determined number of hours in order to eliminate sanding between coats. If you wait longer, you'll have to sand.

Except for these special cases, you should sand lightly between coats with 220 or 320 paper. Always sand parallel to the grain, and never sand if the varnish feels the least bit gummy or soft. Use a sanding block to avoid rounding off edges and

When coating recessed panels or doors, follow the numbered sequence illustrated here.

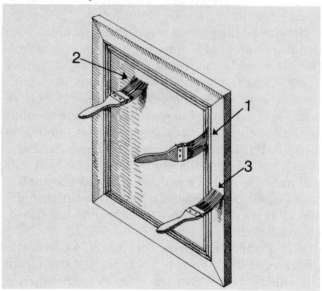

corners, and sand no more than necessary to dull the gloss and remove any dust specks, air bubbles, or other irregularities in the surface.

Dust is a perennial problem when varnishing, so no matter how careful you are, it is possible that your final coat will show a few dust specks on the surface. If you notice these while the varnish is still wet, the specks can be lifted off by using a finely tapered splinter of wood, or a round wooden toothpick with a pointed end. If you do this carefully and promptly, the wet varnish will flow together to fill in the tiny hollow that remains when the speck is removed.

Despite precautions, a final surface may sometimes feel slightly gritty because of dust that settles on the surface as it dries. If desired, you can remove these blemishes by rubbing and polishing the final coat with powdered pumice after the varnish has hardened for several days. This will give a truly professional-looking rubbed finish that will be satiny smooth, and as glossy or as dull as you like.

Though it's basically smoothness you're rubbing for, not luster, you can control the gloss by the amount of rubbing and polishing you do, and by the grade of abrasive that you use for the final rubbing.

Start by mixing a creamy paste of powdered pumice (sold in all paint stores) and a lightweight oil such as lemon oil or mineral oil. Fold a piece of felt into a convenient-sized pad, then pick up some of the pumice paste with this and spread it on over the surface. Press down with a moderate amount of pressure and start rubbing with long strokes parallel to the grain where possible. Overlap your strokes by at least half the width of the pad as you work your arm back and forth, but be careful to avoid bearing down hard along the edges or on corners of the piece to keep from cutting through the varnish.

Pick up the felt pad periodically to add more pumice paste as needed. If the paste shows signs of drying out, sprinkle a little more oil over the surface when necessary to maintain the original creamy consistency. After rubbing for several minutes in one place, examine the surface carefully by shining a light at an angle across a section that has been wiped clean with a separate piece of cloth. As an additional test, feel the surface, stroking lightly with your fingertips. You will know that you have rubbed long enough when the entire surface feels and looks perfectly smooth, and when it has a uniformly dull satin luster after the pumice paste has been wiped off.

At this point some people may prefer to leave their dull luster as is. However, in most cases additional rubbing with a still-finer abrasive—powdered rottenstone—is usually recommended.

Done properly, a final polishing with rottenstone will restore the gloss that the varnish had originally—either low-luster or high-shine, and in the latter case without that freshly wet look many people find objectionable.

Mix your rottenstone with oil, the same way you did with the powdered pumice. Now use another clean felt pad to pick up some rottenstone mixture and start rubbing, again with the grain, just the way you did with the pumice. Remember to periodically wipe a section clean and shine a light across it to determine when you have restored the amount of gloss you want.

If you want still more glow or gloss, finish by using a good-quality paste wax. However, if you decide to use wax, allow the varnish to harden for an extra three or four days before rubbing on the first coat of wax. Apply it sparingly and buff vigorously. Remember that a thin, hard coat of wax is more durable and actually provides better protection than a built-up heavy layer.

Shellac

Shellac is one of the oldest clear finishes around, and still coats some of the finest antiques, since it predates the invention of what we now call varnish. Actually, it is a spirit varnish made of a natural resin that comes from the lac bug, an insect native to India. The original flaky material is dissolved in denatured alcohol to form a sort of deep-orange or amber-brown material commonly known as "orange shellac." "White" or clear shellac is made by bleaching the material before dissolving it in alcohol.

Orange shellac can give darker woods a beautiful finish. It's sometimes used on mahogany and walnut to give them an aged look, or to highlight their natural coloring. It's sometimes even used on lighter woods, like knotty pine, to give them an "early American" look. You can also mix orange and white together to mellow or "age" some of the whiter woods.

Shellac is fast-drying and easy to work with, and it dries to a beautiful clear finish when properly used. But it is seldom used as final finish on furniture these days because it does have a number of real disadvantages.

For one thing, shellac discolors very quickly when any liquid is spilled on it—and it's completely dissolved by liquids that contain alcohol. It turns white when subjected to dampness, so unless it's heavily protected with paste wax, it's not a very practical finish on most pieces of furniture.

However, it is still excellent for use on decorative pieces that get very little wear—picture frames, for example—and its quick-drying characteristics can be valuable when something has to be finished in a hurry.

Unlike varnish, unused shellac deteriorates in time, just from aging in the can, so you can't keep quantities of it on hand for more than a few months. Most manufacturers recommend that shellac be stored no longer than about six months.

Some manufacturers date their cans, while others don't, so you are better off buying shellac in small cans only as you need it. If the can is not dated, and you have any reason to doubt its freshness, open the can and look at it. If it's very dark or gummy-looking, don't use it. As a further test, smear a little onto a piece of wood and let it dry. It should get tacky in 5 or 10 minutes and be completely dry in about 30 minutes.

Shellac almost always has to be thinned with denatured alcohol before you can use it on furniture. It is sold in various consistencies, known as "cuts." The most widely sold is 4-pound-cut, although some stores stock 3-pound-cut and 5-pound-cut shellac. The cut refers to the amount of shellac that has been dissolved in a gallon of alcohol. For example, 4-pound-cut means that 4 pounds of flake shellac have been dissolved in 1 gallon of alcohol. To reduce 4-pound-cut shellac to 2-pound-cut, for example, you would simply add 3 quarts of alcohol to a gallon of the 4-pound-cut shellac.

When shellac is used primarily as a sealer under varnish—for example, to keep a stain from "bleeding" through the finish—the shellac should be no heavier than about 1-pound-cut or 2-pound-cut. However, for building up a regular shellac finish, 3-pound-cut is usually preferred, although some experts would rather use 2-pound-cut and apply additional coats. Building up a finish with several thin coats, rather than one or two heavy ones, is how you get the deep clear luster that is characteristic of a fine shellac finish.

When building up a shellac finish, sanding lightly between coats and then removing all of the sanding dust with a tack rag is essential for a fine finish. Use progressively finer grits of sandpaper. Start with 120 after the first coat; 220 after the second coat; and 320 or 400 after the third coat. The final coat can be left as is and waxed, or it can be rubbed down with pumice and rottenstone just as you would a varnish finish (see section on varnishes).

Brushes and other tools that have been used in shellac are best cleaned in denatured alcohol, because this is the thinner for shellac (never turpentine or other paint thinners). Or you can save money by washing a shellac brush with ammonia and water, if the shellac is reasonably fresh.

French Polish Finish

In the days when shellac was *the* finish for fine furniture, one of the most beautiful—and durable—finishes was achieved by a method known as French polishing. It takes lots of hand rubbing—hours, and sometimes days, of work—but it's also highly practical, since it can withstand years of wear and exposure and can be easily touched up or renewed when necessary.

Of course, craftsmen in bygone days did not have today's varnishes and sealers that can give somewhat the same effect without all those hours of work, but some purists still feel that no modern finish can match the luster and beauty of a patiently applied French polish finish. Due to the amount of work involved, few craftsmen today still use this method, but for something really special, here's how:

1. If the wood has to be stained first, don't use a pigmented or oil-base stain. You must use only a powdered aniline-type dye stain that is mixed with water (see page 401), the only stain over which a French polish will "take." New, unstained wood is good, too.

2. Pour some 1-pound-cut shellac into a shallow bowl or pan, and fold a clean piece of lint-free cloth into a thick pad. Grasp this with your fingers, then dip the pad into the shellac and start wiping it onto the wood with light rapid strokes, working parallel to the grain if possible.

3. Keep dipping and wiping in this manner until the entire surface is covered, then wait for the first coat to dry hard (usually 15 to 30 minutes).

4. Apply a second coat in the same manner and again wait for this to dry, then sand lightly with very fine sandpaper (400).

5. Remove all sanding dust, then keep on applying additional coats, rubbing each one on quickly and adding coats until you have built up enough of a finish to see a slight sheen over the entire surface.

6. At this point add a few drops of boiled linseed oil to the shellac in the pan and then continue applying more coats by dipping the pad into the oil-and-shellac mixture and rubbing it on. Only this time, use a series of rotary or circular motions instead of rubbing lengthwise.

7. Keep dipping and rubbing, adding a little more linseed oil to the mixture from time to time, until you have built up the depth of finish and the luster or gloss desired. You'll know it when you see it.

You may find as rubbing progresses that you will have to rub harder and more vigorously to

For a French polish finish, wipe preliminary coats of shellac on with light, rapid strokes. Linseed oil is added after sheen starts to build up.

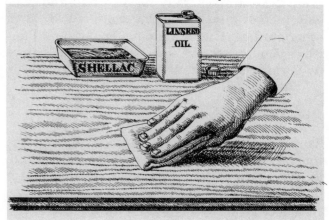

keep the pad from sticking to the surface. When this happens, add a little more shellac and alcohol to the mixture to keep it from piling up under the pad.

You can quit at any time and resume on the following day if you get tired, but when you do this, it's best to sand lightly before you get started again.

A little experimentation on scrap surfaces will give you an idea of how much oil, shellac, and alcohol you can use, although proportions really are not critical.

Lacquer

Lacquer has two advantages as a finish: It's very clear, and it's the quickest-drying of them all, which makes it very popular with commercial finishers. But most home craftsmen will find it the most difficult of all finishes to work with. Lacquers dry so fast that they're almost impossible to brush out, which is why the pros almost always spray them on.

Although spraying is much faster than brushing, few home craftsmen have the right type of spraying equipment for use with fast-setting lacquers. In addition, a considerable amount of experience is required to handle this coating properly. It must be sprayed on in many coats because it forms a thinner film than varnish or shellac, and because of the solvents used in lacquer it cannot be applied over varnish, paint, oil stain, and many other finishes.

There are a few lacquers on the market that have been mixed with special slow-drying solvents so that they can be applied by brush. However, these are generally hard to find and offer only the advantage of drying more quickly than other finishes. They still do not give as fine a finish as you can achieve with many of today's quality varnishes.

Penetrating Sealers

These are the easiest to use and among the toughest-wearing. They give a beautiful finish, especially if you want a casual, informal look—or prefer a "natural" finish.

Penetrating wood sealers, which are often referred to as "Danish oil" finishes, are made of synthetic resin oils and are designed to give the type of "oiled" finish that once could be achieved only by repeated rubbing with linseed oil.

Unlike linseed oil, an organic material, modern penetrating sealers do not oxidize or turn dark in time. Nor are they subject to fungus or mildew growth, also a problem with linseed oil. Best of all, they are far easier to maintain and a snap to repair—when necessary.

This type of finish is meant to take advantage of a wood's texture—no perfectly smooth or high luster, no built-up finish; when you touch a piece of furniture finished this way, you know you're feeling wood.

Penetrating finishes are often used on contemporary pieces made of open-grained hardwoods—oak, walnut, teak. What's more, with these woods, you're also eliminating a step for the glossier finish—applying paste wood filler. This type of finish is also perfect for today's "country" furniture, pieces beloved for their informal, almost no-finish look.

Unlike varnish and other surface coatings, penetrating sealers can be applied only over raw wood or wood that already has the same type of finish on it. It soaks into and bonds with the fibers of the wood to actually harden them so the finish is *inside* the wood and leaves no appreciable surface coating or film. Because of this, and because you wipe the excess off as each coat is applied, there is never a problem with brushmarks, and you virtually eliminate the problem of dust settling on the surface to mar the finished appearance.

Because there is no surface film, the finish left by a penetrating sealer has very little gloss. It can be buffed (with very fine steel wool) to a pleasant satin luster, and additional gloss can be obtained by waxing and buffing.

One advantage in not having a glossy coating is that there is no surface finish that can get scratched. The finish is inside the wood. (You can scratch the wood itself, of course.) Most spilled liquids will not harm the finish if wiped up with reasonable promptness, but even if they do, touching up is quite simple. All you have to do is rub additional sealer on with fine steel wool and then buff off the excess.

Penetrating resin sealers come in clear as well

as in various wood-tone shades. The colored sealers serve as stains that help to seal the wood in one application, although you can apply a clear sealer over them. Or you can use a regular wood stain first and then put two or three coats of sealer over it.

Generally speaking, penetrating sealers tend to darken wood more than varnish or shellac, but they will not obscure the grain or change the texture, so in most cases, people do not find the added depth of color objectionable.

You can apply these finishes by brush, or by wiping on with a rag. Application technique is relatively unimportant, since there is no need to worry about brushmarks or lap marks. All you have to do is make sure you apply sealer liberally and work it into the fibers of the wood. The idea is to make certain it penetrates as much as possible—which is why having surfaces horizontal makes the job much easier when this is practical.

Allow the first coat to penetrate for anywhere from 15 to 30 minutes, depending on the manufacturer's recommendations, then use a lint-free cloth to wipe all excess liquid off the surface. Wipe with long parallel strokes, using a moderate amount of pressure, and make sure all excess oil has been removed from the surface before you go any further.

After wiping the surface dry, allow the finish to harden for the recommended number of hours (usually from 4 to 24 hours, depending on the brand), then flow on a second coat and wipe off in the same manner.

Sanding between coats is generally not required, although some experts find that the finish will be smoother and more lustrous if you rub lightly with fine steel wool before the second coat of sealer is applied. This rubbing also helps to open the pores a bit more and thus enhances the penetrating qualities of the second coat.

As a rule, two coats are all that will be required. Tabletops, dresser tops, and other surfaces that can be expected to receive hard wear and more than average abuse should get a third coat.

After the last coat has dried hard, you can rub on a thin coat of paste wax for added protection. Buff vigorously with a soft cloth to achieve the luster desired.

Waxing is not essential, unless you want some luster and added protection. Just make sure you rub the wax on sparingly and buff vigorously after 10 to 15 minutes.

Colored Enamel Finishes

Although most people still think that all enamels dry to a high gloss, they actually come in a choice of finishes—high-gloss, semigloss, and satin. However, since there is no standardization of these definitions from one manufacturer to another, the only way you can be sure of the exact gloss is to see a dried sample of the actual paint, or test it yourself.

Bear in mind that the higher the gloss the more noticeable will be any irregularities or defects in the smoothness of the surface, so if you intend to use a glossy finish, take extra care with the sanding, patching, and filling before any paint is applied.

Gloss also shows dents, nicks, and scrapes more than the duller finishes, so you might want to consider this factor if you're choosing enamel for a child's room.

If you can't find a ready-mixed enamel in the exact color you want, you can start with a color that is close and then doctor this up with tinting colors that you can add yourself. However, most well-stocked dealers have paint-mixing systems with hundreds of different-colored chips, which they can match exactly by using factory-measured formulas. You can almost always find the color you want via one of these systems. Once you select a color, the dealer can mix it in a matter of minutes, then duplicate it at any time in the future *as long as you have a record of the color number*.

Like any other finish, enamel can be no smoother than the surface over which it is applied, so don't stint on the sanding and smoothing. If you are painting over an old finish, be sure you "feather out" rough edges where the old finish may have chipped off by sanding till smooth. Remove any of the old finish that shows signs of chipping or not adhering firmly, and when finished sanding be sure you remove all dust by wiping carefully with a tack rag.

As a rule, to achieve an even gloss and color at least two coats of enamel will be required. However, if you are applying the enamel over raw wood, or over a badly worn finish, an enamel undercoat will also be needed for the first coat. The two coats of enamel go on after this.

Enamel is supposedly ready for use when the can is opened, but as a practical matter some slight thinning will almost always be required as you work in order to maintain a good working consistency. If you are applying two coats, thin the first coat slightly (5 to 10 percent) and don't try to make it cover completely. The second coat will cover up any "thin" areas that remain.

Brushing techniques for enamel are similar to those used in brushing varnish (see pages 404–6). Use a good-quality brush with lots of soft bristles. Brushmarks and such are more noticeable in color than they are in a clear finish, so a good brush and patience are essential.

Like varnish, the enamel is flowed on with long strokes and with only a moderate amount of pressure. Never dip the bristles in by more than one-third their length, and whenever possible lay surfaces horizontal to help the finish flow out smoothly.

As a rule, it is best to paint across the narrower dimension of each panel first, then cross-stroke lightly with just the bristle tips to eliminate

Start brushing enamel on across shortest dimension first (top). **Then cross-stroke along length** (bottom). **Lift brush gradually at the end of the stroke by curving away from the surface without stopping forward motion.**

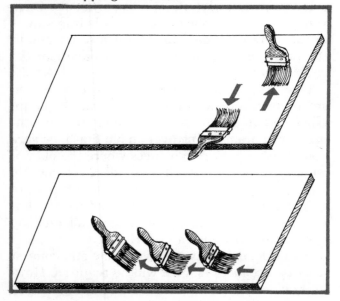

brushmarks and to smooth out uneven areas. As you work, keep checking for runs, sags, or drips, especially in the corners, and pick these up promptly with the tip of your brush to keep them from growing. However, once the paint starts to get tacky—thick and sticky—you won't be able to smooth out these irregularities, so just let them dry and then sand them out on the following day before the next coat of enamel is applied.

Sanding between coats is not always necessary between coats of a semigloss or low-luster enamel, but it is essential when putting one coat of high-gloss on top of another. Regardless of what the manufacturer's instructions say about drying time, always make sure each coat is completely hard before you try to sand it or start applying the next coat. If in doubt, test with a fingernail—the paint should be hard enough to resist easy indentation.

Then test-sand one spot; the paint should not gum up or rub off. If it does, the paint is not hard enough for sanding or recoating.

It is possible, by the way, to get the same fine, built-up look with enamel as it is with varnish. Follow the directions for building up and sanding three to four coats of varnish and rubbing down with pumice and rottenstone (page 407), and use either low-luster or high-gloss paint. Obviously, this is a fine finish, meant for a good piece that is designed to be painted.

Colored Lacquers

Colored lacquers dry much faster than enamels, which is why they are almost always applied by spraying. Professionals who have the proper type of spray equipment and are familiar with the techniques involved in working with these fast-drying finishes prefer them for that very reason. They can apply several coats in a single day. However, you have to have a fair amount of experience in order to get a really smooth finish.

Aside from its quicker-drying capabilities, lacquer really offers no advantage over enamel. Contrary to what many amateurs seem to think, you can get just as high a gloss with an enamel, and the finish is usually more resistant to chipping and abrasion, because enamels tend to be more resilient and less brittle.

Lacquers also contain powerful solvents,

which present more of an odor problem when working indoors. More important, perhaps, they generally cannot be applied over old enamel and other finishes, because the solvent in the lacquer will lift or soften the old finish.

Lacquers designed for brushing are available, but they are generally hard to find, and the color selection may be very limited. In addition, even though these lacquers have special solvents added to slow the drying, they are still harder than an enamel to brush out smoothly. And they still have all of the disadvantages of spray-type lacquers.

Antique or Glazed Finishes

This is one of the easiest of all finishes for the amateur to apply. It requires little skill, no stripping, and only enough sanding to make your surface smooth. Furthermore, you don't have to patch dents, gouges, and bruises, unless you really want to. This finish actually looks good with a few marks.

And for all this, it's an attractive, sometimes even beautiful, finish. It's the perfect way to rejuvenate "junk" furniture that still has some wear in it, and to give character and color to uninteresting pieces. It's also a way of rejuvenating a great old piece—even some fine furniture—with badly marred wood.

Although the terms "glazing" and "antiquing" are often used interchangeably, glazing is actually the process that is used to achieve an antique effect. It consists of a translucent or semi-opaque colored liquid that is applied over a previously painted surface and then partially wiped off. The end result is a two-tone effect in which the top color (the glazing color) partially covers and changes the effect of the base color.

The glazing process can actually be used to create several other finishes when a two-tone, color-on-color effect is desired—such as an imitation wood-grain effect or a "limed" or "pickled" finish. In the last two cases a light-colored glaze is applied over a darker-colored base coat. Glazing, however, is most often associated with the application of an antique finish.

Because of the popularity of this type of finish with do-it-yourselfers, many paint and hardware stores stock kits that contain everything needed to apply an antique or glazed finish. You'll find a can of semigloss base color, a can of glaze coat, an instruction sheet, and sometimes some assorted supplies such as a small paintbrush, a piece of cheesecloth, and possibly even a small piece of sandpaper.

While buying a kit of materials for an antique finish is convenient and often eliminates guesswork as to what the final effect will be (stores display samples of the finish you can expect), these kits do have their limitations. First of all, you will be paying more than you would if you bought the materials separately or mixed your own. Second, you will be limited to the colors offered. For example, the kit may show an olive-green background with a dark-brown (burnt umber) glaze, but you may want this same olive-green background with a more grayish (raw umber) glaze, or possibly with a glaze that has more red or maroon in it. Any of these variations, as well as an endless variety of different color combinations, are possible when you assemble or mix your own.

Applying an antique finish is basically a three-step process:

1. Paint the surface of your piece with the background color of your choice, and allow this to dry hard. The type of paint most frequently used for this background color—and the one that is easiest to glaze over—is a semigloss or satin-finish enamel.

2. After the base has dried hard, a colored glazing liquid, which you can buy ready-made or can mix yourself, is brushed on over the surface and then partially wiped off.

3. Although not essential on pieces that will get no handling, the finish is then protected with a clear coat of semigloss or low-luster varnish. This final coat of clear varnish is often omitted in the prepackaged kits, but it should be applied over any piece of furniture that gets normal handling. Otherwise the glaze coat will start to rub off prematurely.

The base coat of enamel can be applied by brush, painting pad, or spray. A perfect job is not necessary, but a reasonable amount of care should be exercised to avoid skips, sags, runs, and drip marks. You should sand the old surface a bit to get it reasonably smooth, and remove all wax, grease, and dirt by scrubbing with a deter-

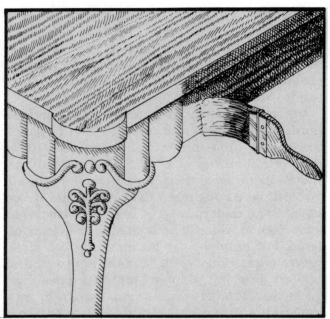

First step in applying an antique finish is painting on a base coat of satin-finish enamel to act as a background color.

gent, or by wiping down with a paint thinner. One coat will generally be adequate for this base coat, but if a radically different color is being applied—very light over very dark, for example—then you may require a second coat in order to ensure reasonably complete coverage.

Allow the base coat to dry until thoroughly hard (usually 24 hours). Even if the label says it dries in 4 hours, wait longer, because the process of rubbing the glaze on will soften paint that is not completely cured.

You can buy glazing liquid in ready-mixed colors in many paint stores, so if you can find the color you want, that is probably the simplest method. However, it is not very difficult to mix your own glaze.

To mix your own you can either buy an untinted glazing liquid, which some paint stores carry, or you can use a clear penetrating wood sealer as a glazing-liquid base. In either case you add color by mixing in regular tinting colors, or by adding small amounts of dark-colored enamel in various shades.

Since it is very hard to tell beforehand what effect the glazing color will have when it is rubbed on over the background color, some experimentation is essential. One trick that will save time is to paint the base coat onto several pieces of scrap wood while you are painting the actual piece of furniture. These scrap pieces will dry at the same time, so when you're ready to mix your glaze coat you can experiment on these scrap pieces first. This will not only help you decide on the color of the glaze coat, it will also help determine how much you want to wipe off and how hard you want to rub when wiping.

Since the glaze dries slowly, there is plenty of time to fool around with various wiping techniques. In fact, if you don't like the results you can always wipe the glaze off completely with paint thinner and then start all over again.

After the base coat of semigloss enamel has dried hard, start brushing the glaze coat on over one section of the furniture at a time. Smear it on liberally, using a brush or cloth, and don't miss any spots.

If you have coated some scrap pieces with the base color as mentioned above, try your glaze on one of these first. Depending on the type of glazing material used, and on the amount of color it contains, you may want to start wiping immediately, or you may find it better to wait a few minutes.

Wiping is most often done with a pad of cheesecloth or a piece of very soft, loose-weave cotton cloth. Experiment with the effects achieved by using the cloth while it's folded, as against using it while wadded into a loose ball. Other effects can be achieved by wiping with steel wool, with crumpled tissue paper, or with a coarse cloth such as burlap. For antique finishes, cheesecloth is by far the most popular method.

The final result is controlled by how much you wipe off and how hard you rub. The more you wipe off, the more the base coat will show through, so if your background color is white or off-white, more wiping will result in a lighter overall tone and less wiping will result in a darker tone. By the same token, if your background color is a dark color and your glaze is a light shade, then the reverse will be true. Bear in mind that the background color should generally be sharper or brighter than you think you want it to be, because the glaze color will ultimately dull or subdue it to some extent.

The final effect will vary with how you wipe the glaze off. It's probably the most important step in the whole process. The glaze should not be wiped off uniformly. Instead, allow more of the glaze coat to remain in the grooves and in the recesses, while rubbing more of it off on the high spots. On moldings, wipe parallel to the length of the molding and again wipe off more on the high spots and less in the grooves or recessed areas.

On flat surfaces such as doors or furniture tops, wipe off more of the glaze in the center of the panel and leave the panel darker around the edges and in the corners. This simulates the natural wear that a piece of old furniture would exhibit if the glaze had been worn off over the years.

Again, experiment with wiping techniques on some scrap pieces. In some cases wiping in a straight line is most appropriate, while in others the glaze will look better if wiped off with a circular or oval motion. Sometimes the most pleasing effect is achieved with little or no wiping and then stippling or patting lightly with cheesecloth.

Each wiping technique gives a different effect. If you don't like the results the first time you try, remember, you can always wipe the glaze off with

a rag moistened in paint thinner and then start all over again.

Another process that is often used to enhance the antique effect of a glazed finish is to spatter a little of the concentrated glazing color on after all wiping has been completed. The simplest way to do this is to use an old toothbrush. Dip the brush into the concentrated glazing color, then hold it a few inches away from the surface and flick the bristles with your thumb. This will spatter flecks of the concentrated color onto the freshly glazed surface. You can vary the size of the flecks by varying both the distance between the toothbrush and the surface and the speed with which you move the brush along.

After the glazing color has dried completely (wait at least 48 hours), apply a clear coat of varnish. Although a gloss varnish is sometimes used, most experts agree that a satin-finish or low-luster varnish is far more appropriate for a finish of this kind.

The varnish can be applied by brush or spray, and one coat is usually sufficient. However, tabletops, children's pieces, and other surfaces that get hard wear will stand up better if two coats are applied. Keeping the surface waxed is also a good idea to protect against spills and staining.

Imitation Wood-Grain Finishes

Sometimes you will want to refinish a piece of furniture or set of cabinets to make it look like a natural wood grain. The real wood underneath the paint may not be attractive enough to be worth stripping and finishing in the usual manner, or it may be so badly marred and mismatched that a "natural" wood finish is completely impractical. In such cases the same type of glazing process that is used for antiquing can often be used to achieve an imitation wood-grain effect. It's merely a matter of selecting the right glaze for the right background color, and then varying the technique used to wipe off and streak the glaze.

The background color you select as a base coat should be in a beige or brownish tone that is similar to the lightest part of the grain in the wood you want to imitate. For woods such as mahogany or maple, the background should have a slightly more reddish cast, while for oak or pine it

After base coat on piece for antiquing has dried thoroughly, a glaze coat is applied and then partially wiped off with cheesecloth. High spots are left lighter than grooves and recessed carvings for a natural, worn effect.

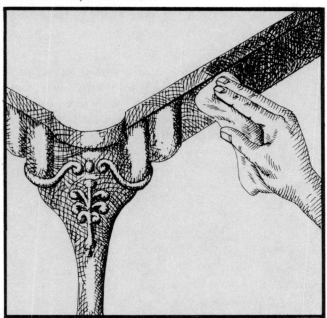

might have a creamier tone. Walnut is usually simulated by using a sand color or a light brown as a base.

The color of the glazing liquid will have to be quite a bit darker—something like the darkest streaks in the wood grain of the actual species being imitated. For example, you'll want a dark-brown glaze for walnut, while a medium-brown glaze will be more appropriate for pine or chestnut. For an oak grain the glaze should be more of a grayish or muddy brown. In each case, if you have painted a number of samples with the background color first, you will have pieces on which you can experiment until you achieve the color combination that looks right to you.

Actually, specific tones are not really critical in most cases, because all you want to achieve is the appearance of a wood grain—not necessarily to match a specific type or shade of wood. And as long as you don't place an imitation finish right next to a real piece of wood it's surprising how realistic the effect will be.

The most important step is the technique used in wiping off the glaze. The idea is to create streaks that will look like a natural wood grain. One popular method is to first wipe part of the glaze off with a coarse pad of steel wool dragged lightly along the surface. This will create a streaky effect without removing too much of the glaze color. As you finish each panel with the steel wool, go over it again by lightly dragging the tip of a dry paintbrush in the same direction over the same area. This will soften the coarse streaks left by the steel wool and will create a more natural-looking wood-grain effect.

Since no wood grain is ever perfectly straight, imitate a weaving pattern by twisting the brush slightly as you drag it over the surface, and by weaving it slowly from side to side as you move it lengthwise along the panel. Study a piece of natural wood grain to note how it has streaks that weave in and out and try to stroke your dry brush in such a way as to create this same appearance.

After you have achieved the effect you want, apply a protective coat of varnish to keep the finish from being rubbed off or damaged. You can use either a high-gloss or semigloss varnish for this purpose, but remember that the higher the gloss, the more it will show up irregularities and imperfections in the surface.

Gilding Techniques

Very often pieces of furniture with carved or molded edges will have these edges finished in gold. The traditional material used for applying a real gold finish is gold leaf, which is not a paint. As its name implies, gold leaf is exactly that—ultrathin leaves of 22-carat gold metal. These are

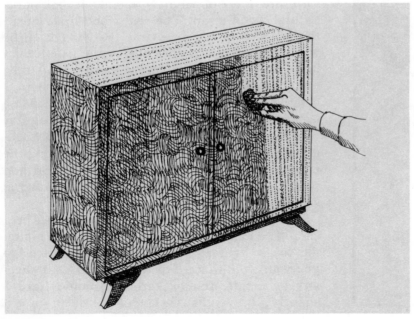

One way to create a wood-grain effect is to wipe the glaze color lightly with steel wool. Then use a dry brush to go over the wiped areas while still wet. Weave the brush slightly to heighten the effect.

Paste-type wax gilt gives a realistic gold-leaf effect in most cases, especially if applied over a base coat of artist's gold-leaf paint.

cemented to the surface with a special tacky varnish (called gold size) that is made for the purpose. The leaves of gold are so thin (four of them are equal to about one-thousandth of an inch in thickness) that they cannot actually be handled with the fingers. They would fall apart. They must be picked up with a special brush by using static electricity to make them cling (you run the brush through your hair to build up a static charge). There is also a type that has a special tissue-paper backing for handling. This permits you to press the gold leaf into place and then peel the tissue paper off.

Gold leaf is extremely expensive, and many dealers no longer stock it. This, plus the fact that it requires considerable skill to use and apply, makes it not very popular with home furniture finishers.

Fortunately, there are a number of synthetic materials that, while not as long-lasting as real gold leaf, will stand up for some time in normal use. Most art supply stores and many paint stores sell synthetic gold paints that are far superior to the old-fashioned gilt paints used years

ago. Better yet, these stores also sell paste-type, wax-base gilt finishes that are rubbed on much as you would shoe polish. These come in a variety of different colors or shades and build up to a beautiful gold luster if they are buffed after they have been rubbed on. You can also leave them as dull and as aged-looking as you like. They are easy to use and often look as good as the real thing.

One good method for achieving a lustrous gold finish is to use a combination of both of these materials. Start by priming the area to be gilded with orange shellac and allow this to dry for an hour or two. Then brush on a coat of artist's-quality gold-leaf paint, using a soft camel's-hair brush. Allow this gold to dry overnight, then highlight the finish by rubbing on a coat of paste-type wax gilt. Spread it on uniformly with a folded pad of cloth, and then buff lightly with a clean piece of cloth. When finished, the gold can be left as is, or it can be "antiqued" by wiping a glaze over the surface.

RESTORING AND REPAIRING EXISTING FINISHES

When an old piece of valued furniture starts to get dull and dingy-looking, or when it accumulates a lot of scratches, water marks, and other blemishes, most people feel that the only way to restore the piece is to strip it down and refinish it completely.

However, in a surprisingly high percentage of cases there is no need for going to this extreme. The piece of furniture can often be rejuvenated by simply repairing the damaged areas and then restoring the original luster to the finish with one of the techniques outlined in this chapter. Nicks and scratches can be patched or covered up, burn marks and water marks can be removed, and dull finishes can be brightened and restored with much less effort than would be required for a complete stripping and refinishing job.

The first step in any restoration job is cleaning the old surface in order to remove all of the old wax, polish, and oil, as well as the years of grime that may have accumulated on the surface. As a rule, the simplest way to clean wood furniture without damaging the finish is to wipe it down with a rag moistened with paint thinner. Since the thinner is inflammable, work in a well-ventilated room and make sure there are no open flames nearby. Although paint thinner will not harm most furniture finishes, it's best to play safe and try it on an inconspicuous corner or side first to see what effect, if any, it has on the finish.

Assuming that this test shows no harm to the actual finish, proceed with your cleaning job by dipping a folded cloth into the thinner, squeezing out most of the excess, and then rubbing vigorously over a small section at a time. Immediately wipe with a dry cloth to absorb or pick up all dissolved wax, polish, and grime, then continue wiping with thinner. Turn the rag frequently as it becomes soiled and change the thinner in the pan as it becomes very discolored. The idea behind all this is to pick up and remove the softened wax and dirt instead of merely spreading it around on the surface.

After being cleaned in this manner, the finish will almost always look dull and may even be slightly cloudy in places. If the finish is otherwise sound with no outstanding blemishes or other defects you may be able to restore it by simply applying one or two coats of a good-quality furniture polish or wax. Try one section as an experiment. Rub the wax or polish on sparingly, and then buff vigorously with a dry cloth. If this restores life to the finish, you can repeat the process on the entire piece.

Sometimes merely repolishing is not enough, because the old finish may be crazed, or so dull that simple polishing will not restore it. In these cases it is sometimes possible to rejuvenate the finish by a process often referred to as reamalgamation. This involves using a solvent to soften up and partially dissolve the old finish so that it flows together and forms a new film that is free of surface blemishes. However, to do this you have to know the kind of finish on the furniture. The technique works best with shellac and lacquer finishes; it is seldom effective on varnish finishes. However, most commercially finished furniture is not varnished—unless it was custom-made and finished by hand.

To test for a shellac finish, dip a rag into some denatured alcohol and rub on an inconspicuous corner. If the finish is shellac, the thinner will soften or dissolve it. If the finish is not shellac,

the alcohol will have little or no effect on it (other than perhaps to make it look cloudy or dull-looking).

To test for a lacquer finish, dip a rag in lacquer thinner and then rub one corner as just described above. If the finish is lacquer, the thinner will soften and dissolve it almost immediately. However, lacquer thinner will also break down a varnish finish—but the difference is that on varnish it will cause the finish to blister and wrinkle rather than merely softening it, and it will remove the finish entirely down to the bare wood.

To rejuvenate an old shellac finish with this reamalgamation technique, the simplest method is to rub denatured alcohol over a section at a time. Dip a pad of very fine (¾) steel wool into the alcohol and wipe this on in straight lines. Allow it to soak for about a minute, then wipe the same area lightly with a cloth that has also been dampened in alcohol. The idea is to soften the top layer of shellac without actually removing it so that it flows together to form a uniform film.

To use this technique on a lacquer finish that is cracked, checked, or cloudy, the same basic technique is followed, except that you use lacquer thinner instead of denatured alcohol. Some experts prefer to apply the thinner with a brush, rather than with fine steel wool, so experimenting with both techniques may be advisable to see which one works better for you. If you use a brush, spread the thinner on in straight lines parallel to the grain and then wipe immediately with a soft cloth moistened with additional lacquer thinner. Here again, the idea is to do all wiping lightly so that you don't remove the finish—you merely soften it and spread it around so that it flows out to form a fresh film.

After using either of these techniques to restore the finish, let it harden overnight and then build up the luster by using an oil-base furniture polish or a good grade of furniture wax.

Rx for Water Marks

One of the most frequent types of damage to an existing finish is a white ring that is left when a wet glass, dish, or similar container is left standing on the surface. Depending on how long the moisture was allowed to penetrate before it was wiped up, and depending on the shape of the container or spill, the white mark may be in the form of a definite ring, or it may consist merely of a series of spots or "blush marks" on the surface. As long as the spots are white, it means that the moisture did not penetrate all the way through the finish into the wood. This means there is a good chance that it can be removed without completely stripping off the old finish. If the water marks are dark it means that the moisture has penetrated completely through the finish and into the wood. The only way to correct a condition of this kind is to take off all of the old finish and then sand or bleach the dark marks out (see page 389).

If a white water mark on the surface has not penetrated much, it can sometimes be removed by rubbing with a rag that has been moistened with either denatured alcohol, turpentine, or camphorated oil. Try the alcohol first, then the camphorated oil, then the turpentine. If none of these works, then polishing with a very mild abrasive is the next step. Start by rubbing with one of the toothpastes that are advertised as having "extra brighteners" in them—these actually contain a very mild abrasive. Spread a little paste over the white mark and rub with your finger or with a small pad of cloth. If possible, try to rub parallel to the grain only. If the stain starts to lighten, keep rubbing until you have it all out.

If this fails, try a slightly coarser abrasive. Use some ordinary table salt with a little lemon oil or mineral oil. Sprinkle the salt on first, then dip a cloth into the oil and rub with this. If this seems to be working, then repeat with salt and vinegar, instead of salt and oil. (The vinegar acts as a mild bleach.)

If the stain still persists, then you'll have to use a paste made by mixing powdered rottenstone with lemon oil or mineral oil. This will remove the stain eventually, although a considerable amount of rubbing may be required. When you're done, the surface will be quite dull, but you can restore the luster by waxing or polishing in most cases. If much of the old finish has been removed, then a thin coat of varnish or shellac may be required, but try to avoid this, since blending in such a touchup is often quite difficult.

Repairing Scratches

Scratches and small nicks that are in the finish and don't go all the way through the wood can be repaired in one of three ways:

1. Touch up the scratch with a colored oil stain of the right shade, or with one of the various "scratch-removing" liquids that are widely sold in hardware and housewares stores. This will not fill in or remove the scratch, but it will color or

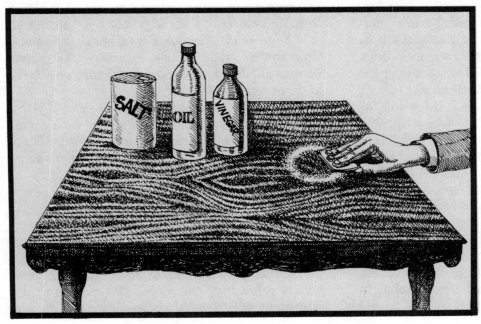

White rings on furniture can sometimes be removed by using salt mixed with oil or vinegar to polish them out.

camouflage it so that it becomes scarcely noticeable—particularly after you apply a polish or wax over the touchup.

2. If the scratch is a shallow one, you can often remove it by using the reamalgamation process (see page 418). A little solvent applied with an artist's pointed brush will cause the finish to dissolve at that point so that it flows together and the scratch becomes scarcely noticeable after it is polished or waxed.

3. Deeper scratches will have to be filled in and possibly colored in order to conceal them completely. The best material to use for this purpose is stick shellac. It comes in a range of different wood colors and is made specifically for patching wood finishes. Unfortunately, it is seldom stocked in local paint and hardware stores anymore, but you can buy shellac sticks from dealers that specialize in furniture-finishing supplies, or you can order them from mail-order houses that cater to home craftsmen. You can buy an assortment with enough colors to match any furniture finish, or you can blend two or more colors together to produce the exact shade needed.

To use a shellac stick for patching you'll need an alcohol lamp or similar source of smokeless heat. A cigarette lighter can also be used, but a candle flame is too smoky to be useful. A handy tool to use for applying the shellac is an artist's palette knife, because it has a thin flexible blade that is perfect for smoothing, although special spatulas are also available.

After selecting the shellac stick that most closely matches the color you need, start by heating the blade of the knife until it is quite warm. Hold the end of the shellac stick over the flame until it starts to melt, positioning it in such a way that any molten shellac that drips will fall onto the area to be patched if possible. If this is not practical, then heat the shellac till it starts to soften and scrape some off with the heated knifeblade. Use the warm blade to "butter" the shellac into and over the scratch so as to fill it completely. Actually it's better to build the patch up slightly higher than the surrounding surface and then reheat the knifeblade to scrape off the excess and make it level. If the shellac starts to cool while you're working it, heat the blade again, then stroke it over the hardened shellac to soften it.

To fill defects with a shellac stick, heat the stick with flame until it is soft enough to drip and can be smeared into the cavity with a heated knifeblade.

Instead of shellac sticks, there are also colored wax sticks that you can buy in most local paint and hardware stores. These wax sticks or pencils (some look like children's crayons, others look like wax-type marking pencils) are also available in a range of colors, and they can also be blended if necessary to achieve a specific shade.

The directions furnished with these usually state that all you need to do is rub them back and forth over the scratch until it fills in, but a much neater and smoother job will result if you use a heated spatula or knifeblade as described above for working with stick shellac. The heated blade will soften and partially melt the wax so it blends in more smoothly than is possible if you merely rub it on cold. Although wax sticks are easier than shellac sticks to use, wax is not as permanent as shellac, and the repair is more noticeable and not as clear looking.

After the scratch has been filled in with either one of these methods, touching up with a very thin coat of shellac and then waxing or polishing will help to preserve and further conceal the repair.

Repairing Burn Marks

Small burn marks or scorch marks, such as those caused by cigarettes and hot ashes, can usually be patched or repaired without need for completely refinishing the piece. The success of this treatment will depend to some extent on how

Scorched finish can be removed by scraping carefully with the point of a sharp knife held so the blade moves back and forth as shown by arrows.

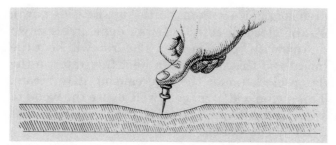

First step in repairing a dent in wood that has a finish on it is to prick holes with a pin or small tack.

large the burn mark is, and on whether or not the scorch mark is only in the finish or goes clear through into the wood itself.

If only the finish has been scorched, you should be able to rub the scorched material away by wrapping a small piece of very fine steel wool around one fingertip and then rubbing carefully with this till all the blackened residue is gone. If the scorch mark is deep and shows some blistering in the center, then a more drastic method will be required. Scrape back and forth carefully with a knifeblade held at right angles to the surface. Keep scraping until all of the blackened material has been removed. Then use a clean piece of steel wool to rub the spot smooth. Wipe all the dust away and examine the slight cavity that remains to see if the scraping has gone clear through the finish and down into the wood itself. If a good deal of finish still remains (even though it is dull) then you can probably restore the luster by simply waxing and polishing.

However, if you have scraped most of the finish away down to the bare wood, then you'll want to fill in and build up the slight cavity with several thin coats of varnish or shellac. Apply with a small artist's brush and allow each coat to dry before applying the next one. Use enough coats to build up the finish so that it matches the surrounding area, then polish with ⅘ steel wool that has been dipped into paste wax. Rubbing parallel to the grain will blend the patch in so that it's scarcely noticeable after you buff it.

Removing Dents

When wood is dented, it means the fibers at that point have been severely compressed. In many

cases you can restore the wood to its original shape by decompressing or swelling the fibers back to their normal size. The best way to do this is to use moisture and heat to create a mild steaming action. If the wood is unfinished, this is simple—the moisture can penetrate directly to the wood. However, if the wood is finished with varnish, shellac, lacquer, or a similar surface coating, then in order to make this steaming process work you will have to either remove the finish over that spot or puncture the existing finish with small pinholes that will allow moisture to penetrate. (These tiny holes will be easy to fill with dabs of varnish after the dented area has been repaired.)

Start by placing a wet cloth pad over the dent and then apply heat from a hot iron. The safest way to do this without damaging the surrounding

Place a small pad of wet cloth on top of pricked dent, position a metal bottle cap over this, and heat with iron. Steam may raise compressed wood fibers.

area is to place a metal bottle cap, flat side down, on the cloth directly over the dent. Press down on this with your hot iron. The iron will heat the metal and this will in turn heat the water in the damp cloth under the cap, causing it to steam. This steam will, if all goes well, cause the wood to swell back into its original shape so that the dent is no longer visible.

Although this technique is the most effective way of correcting small dents, it is apt to cause white spots or blushing of the finish because of the heat and moisture. If so, treat these as described on pages 418–19, then restore the luster by waxing or polishing. In some cases you may have to fill in or touch up with several finish coats of clear shellac or varnish before polishing in the usual manner.

How to Use Refinishing Liquids Without Refinishing

Often the entire finish on a fine piece of old furniture is so dull and worn-looking, or so covered with scratches and check marks, that it seems as though the only way to rejuvenate the piece is to strip it completely and then refinish from scratch. However, more often than not if the piece is basically sound and if the finish was originally a good one, then stripping may not be the ideal solution. Besides the fact that it is much more work, stripping may also take away a lot of the original patina of the wood and thus could change its appearance drastically.

When you have a problem of this kind there is another refinishing method that is often preferable. This calls for the use of a furniture refinishing liquid that is similar to—but not the same as—a regular paint and varnish remover. Made by several companies, and sold through paint, hardware, and housewares stores, these refinishing liquids contain strong solvents that will soften and dissolve most finishes. They remove a surface layer of the finish without taking all of it off down to the bare wood. In other words, the refinishing liquid takes off part of the surface coating and leaves a thin layer of old finish that is reconstituted into a fresh coating.

When dry, it is ready to accept a new coat of clear finish. This method is quicker and easier than complete stripping because it enables you to refinish a piece and restore most of its original color and tone without need for a lot of scraping, sanding, staining, or bleaching.

To use one of these refinishing liquids, you start by pouring a small amount into a shallow metal or glass pan. Dip a pad of very fine steel wool into this and then scrub it on over the surface with a series of circular motions (wear rubber gloves to protect your hands). After you have covered a small area (about 1 square foot), dip the steel-wool pad back into the liquid and squeeze it several times to flush it out. Then pick up more liquid and repeat the process on the next section.

Continue working in this manner until the entire piece has been scrubbed down, rinsing the steel wool repeatedly in the refinishing liquid. Use a fresh piece of steel wool as soon as the original one starts to shred or show signs of wear. When the liquid in the pan starts to thicken and get very dirty-looking, pour it into another container and add fresh liquid (the dirty liquid does not have to be discarded—you can allow the gummy residue to settle and then pour off the top portion to be saved for reuse).

After each panel or section has been scrubbed in this manner, go over it with a fresh pad of very fine steel wool and clean liquid—only this time

Refinishing liquid is scrubbed on with a pad of very fine steel wool in circular motions for the first application. The second application is in line with the grain if possible.

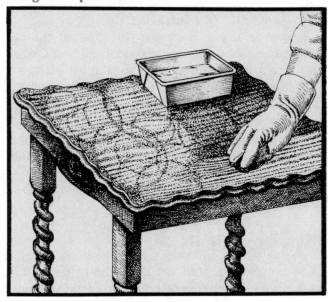

Most marble stains can be removed by applying a poultice of powdered chalk and solvent or bleach (left). **Cover mixture with plastic wrap to keep it wet overnight** (right).

rub in straight lines parallel to the grain in order to remove all of the swirl marks and circular streaks left by the original scrubbing. When finished, allow the wood to dry for about 30 minutes, then buff lightly with clean, dry steel wool (also very fine) to give the wood its final smoothing.

You're now ready to apply a fresh coat of clear new finish. You can use a regular varnish if you wish, but the most popular material to apply after this process (and the one recommended by the manufacturers of these various finishing liquids) is one or two coats of clear tung-oil-base wood sealer. This penetrating oil is rubbed on with a pad or cloth and allowed to soak on the surface for 15 to 30 minutes. Then the excess is buffed off with a piece of clean dry cloth. A second coat can be applied in the same manner on the following day.

CLEANING MARBLE

Although marble is a beautiful, rich-looking material that is also quite durable, it does need care, because it stains very easily and surprisingly enough is also quite porous. The best way to maintain it is to keep it clean by washing with a mild detergent when necessary, and by promptly wiping up spilled liquids or dropped foodstuffs. In addition, the surface must be kept well waxed at all times with a good paste wax.

When stains do occur and cannot be removed by ordinary washing, then the most effective method for removing them is to apply a poultice. This consists of a paste made by mixing powdered whiting or chalk dust (sold in most paint stores) with a solvent that is appropriate for that particular type of stain.

If the stain was caused by a greasy substance, then the poultice should be mixed by adding acetone to the powdered chalk until it forms a thick paste. Spread this on over the stain in a thick layer, then cover with a piece of plastic food wrap to keep the acetone from evaporating. Use strips of masking tape around the edges to hold the plastic down.

Allow this to remain in place overnight, then remove the poultice and rub the stained area vigorously with a dry cloth. Repeat if the stain has not been completely removed.

Stains that are caused by spilled beverages such as tea, coffee, soft drinks, fruit juices, and most other organic materials such as tobacco or flowers can also be removed with a poultice, but in this case you'll have to use a bleaching solution instead of a solvent. The most effective one is hydrogen peroxide hair bleach, which you can buy in most drugstores. Mix this with the whiting to form a thick paste and spread it on over the stain. Add a few drops of household ammonia to start the chemical reaction, then cover immediately with plastic. Allow it to remain overnight and then rub with a dry cloth to see if the stain has lightened considerably. If so, repeat once or twice as necessary. If the stain doesn't lighten very much after the first application, try a poultice with straight household ammonia to see if this is more effective.

The most difficult kind of stain to remove from marble is a rust stain—usually caused by allowing something metal to remain on the surface for some time while moisture is present. If this stain is relatively fresh and has not penetrated too deeply, you may be able to remove it by simply rubbing hard with a coarse, dry cloth. If the stain doesn't come off, then you'll have to try a poultice. Mix a liquid rust remover (sold in hardware stores) with the powdered whiting and allow to stand for several hours to see if this draws the stain out. Sometimes using a rust-remover poultice first, then following with another poultice containing a bleach, will do the trick when simple treatment with rust remover alone fails to remove the entire stain.

Polishing Marble

Many of the liquids and other substances that stain marble will also eat their way into and slightly etch the surface of the marble, leaving it dull or rough-looking. Also, after a poultice has been used to remove a stain the area will some-times come out dull or unfinished-looking and in need of polishing. For this a special polishing powder called tin oxide is used. You can buy it from many local marble dealers, and it is included in the kits that some department stores sell for cleaning and polishing marble.

To do the polishing job you first wet the surface of the marble with water, then sprinkle the powder liberally over the area. Fold a piece of cloth into a thick pad and then rub vigorously with this until the etch mark disappears and the surface luster is restored. Portable electric buffers can be used to speed the task if the entire surface must be polished, since a considerable amount of rubbing is required to do the job properly.

In extreme cases when home removal techniques fail, or when considerable polishing is required, it may be more practical to remove the marble top and take it to a professional marble dealer for polishing. He has the machines and materials needed to do this kind of work properly. Just remember that whether you do the job yourself or have it done professionally, the marble must be kept waxed with a good-quality white paste if you want to keep stains from causing additional problems in the future.

Index

abrasive paper, 37
acetic acid, 390–91
acoustical tiles, 137, 140
acrylic caulking compounds, 133
acrylonitrile butadiene styrene
  (ABS) pipes, 234–35
adapters, three-pronged, 202–3
adhesives, 52–55
  construction, 132
  masonry, 292, 293
  mastic, 135
  plastic laminate, 53, 54
  silicone rubber, 53–54, 137
  solvent-base, 54
  see also glues
aerosol-type spray cans, 183, 184
air conditioners, 279–82, 356
  energy-saving techniques for, 337,
    338, 339
  wall-mounted, 280–82
air-conditioning systems, 278–79
  filters for, 278–79
alarms:
  burglar, 361, 366–72
  fire, 361, 372–74
aliphic resin glues, 52–53, 391
Allen wrenches, 21
altitude gauges, 269, 271
aluminum oxide paper, 37, 384
amperes, 197
anchors, 47–51
  expansion, 48, 58
  hollow-wall, 47–49, 58
  masonry, 49–51
  plastic, 47–48
angle irons, 73
aniline stains, 400, 401, 402–3, 409
antique finishes, 383, 413–15
ants, flying, confused with termites,
  327
aquastats, 269
architects, 378
asbestos board, 33

asphalt, patching and sealing of,
  296–98
attics:
  exhaust fans in, 356–58
  insulation in, 338–39, 340–43, 345
auger bits, 29
augers, 251, 254, 255
awning windows, 99, 108

backsaws, 23, 75, 320, 321
ball-peen hammers, 14
basements:
  insulation in, 343–44
  leaks in, 298–304
bathtub faucets, 247–49
beams:
  collar, 70–72
  floor, 67
belt sanders, 37–38
bench planes, 26–27, 91
bits, drill:
  carbide-tipped masonry, 50, 312
  for hand drills, 29
  oversize, 32
  for power drills, 32, 33
  twist drill, 33
blacktop, patching and sealing of,
  296–98
blades, saw:
  abrasive-type cutoff, 33
  beveled edge of, 25, 26
  combination, 33
  hollow ground, 33, 63
  ripping, 33
bleaches, wood, 389–90
block planes, 26
blowers, heat, 265, 266
boilers, 269–74
  hot-water, 269–71
  steam, 272, 273–74
braces, carpenter's, 29–30
braces, joint, 73, 74

brackets:
  for shelves, 58
  for sliding doors, 94
brads, 43, 44
bricks, 294–96
brushes:
  paint, 161–64
  wire, 388–89
BTUs, 339, 356
bull floats, 290
bullnose treads, 154–55
burglar alarms, 361, 366–72
  perimeter, 366–67
  space, 366, 367–68
  spot, 366
  wireless perimeter, 366, 369–72
burning of blades, 25
butt chisels, 24
butyl rubber caulking, 324
BX cables, 202, 204

cabinets:
  hardware for, 55–58
  sliding doors in, 94–95
cables, electrical, 202, 204, 221–22
carbide-tipped masonry bits, 50, 312
carpets:
  door clearance for, 91, 352–53
  repair of, 157–58
cartridge fuses, 199–200, 201
casement windows, 99, 104–7
  crank mechanisms of, 106–7
  handle assembly of, 106
casing nails, 43–44
catches, cabinet, 57–58
caulking compounds, 53, 177, 291
  guns for, 322, 324, 325
  for gutters, 315–16
  types of, 133, 324
  use of, 133
C-clamps, 30, 31, 391
ceilings:
  fixtures in, 210–12

ceilings (*cont.*)
    painting of, 169–70
    suspended, 138–40
    tiled, 137–38
cement, 285–86
    asphalt, 304
    hydraulic, 300, 301, 304
    mixing of, 148, 285–86
    for patching, 291–92
    portland, 285, 295
ceramic tiles, 132–37
certificate of occupancy, 380
cesspools, 260–61
CFM (cubic-feet-per-minute rating), 357
chandeliers, 211
channel pliers, 17
"chicken ladders," 309
chimes, 217–21
chimneys, 277, 278
chisels, 24–26
    butt, 24
    cold, 14, 26, 50
    gouges, 24
    mushrooming of, 24
    sharpening of, 25
    use of, 24, 26
    wood, 24
chlordane, 328
chlorinated polyvinyl chloride (CPVC) pipes, 232–34
circuit breakers, 197, 199, 201
circuits, electrical, 199, 200
circular saws, 33–34, 35, 63
clamps, 30–31
    bar, 30–31, 391
    C-, 30, 31, 391
    hand screws, 31
    locking pliers as, 18
    spring, 30
    use of, 31, 391, 392
clapboard, 66, 178
claw hammers, 13, 14
CO/ALR switches and receptacles, 205
cold chisels, 14, 26, 50
collar beams, 70–72
compass saws, 23
composition board, 130, 131
concrete, 285, 286–92
    mixing of, 286–88
    patching of, 291–92, 293
    sidewalks, 288–91, 293
    striking off of, 289–90
    transit-mix, 287, 288
condensation:
    in walls, 345–47
    see also leaks; moisture

contractors, building, 375–80
    bids and estimates from, 377, 378, 379–80
    legal contracts for, 377–78, 379–80
    selection of, 378–79
coped joints, 23, 75–78
coping saws, 23
countersinking of nails and screws, 43, 46
CPVC (chlorinated polyvinyl chloride) pipes, 232–34
crawl spaces, insulation in, 343–44, 345, 347
cripple studs, 70, 119
crosscut saws, 22, 23
cubic-feet-per-minute (CFM) rating, 357
cyanoacrylates, 55

dado joints, 65, 73, 75
dampers, fireplace, 275, 276
"Danish oil" finishes, 410
darbies, 290
dehumidifiers, 298
"dikes," 17
dimmer switches, 206, 207
discharge registers, 266
"distress" marks, 396
doorbells, 217–21
doors, 79–95
    bifolding, 93–94
    binding of, 83–85
    for cabinets, 55–57, 94–95
    carpets and clearance of, 91, 352–53
    frames of, 70, 81
    garage, 329–33
    hanging of, 91–92
    hinges for, 81–85, 89–92
    locks for, 85, 86–89, 362–65
    mortises in, 55, 83, 84, 85
    painting of, 171
    planing of, 85–86
    sliding, 93–95
    sticking of, 81–83
    strike plates for, 86
    warped, 89–90
    weatherstripping of, 351–53
dowels, 14, 147, 391, 392
downspouts, 298, 314, 316
drains, 225, 251–54
    chemical cleaners for, 252, 253, 254
    rubber force cups for, 252–53, 254
drain tiles, 302, 303
drain-waste-vent (DWV) system, 225–27, 234
dressed lumber, 61
drill bits, *see* bits, drill

drills:
    hand, 28–30
    power, 28, 31–33
driveways, 293, 296–98
drop cloths, 168–69
drop matching of wallpaper, 191
drywall, 119–27
    cracks in, 124
    in patching of plaster walls, 128–30
    popped nails in, 123–24
    repairing holes in, 124–27
    taping seams in, 121–23
    working with, 119–21
ducts, insulation of, 347–48
DWV (drain-waste-vent system), 225–27, 234

edgers (disk-type sanders), 149–50, 151
electrical repairs, 195–222
    basic facts about, 197–99
    see also individual fixtures
electrician's pliers, 17
enamels, 168
    furniture finished with, 383, 411–12, 413
    types of, 168, 411
energy-saving techniques, 335–58
    for air-conditioners, 337, 338, 339
    for cooling devices, 354–58
    insulation, 337–48
    storm windows, 353–54
    weatherstripping, 99, 349–53
engineer's pliers, 17
epoxy adhesives, 53, 137, 296, 300, 301, 391
escutcheon plates, 88
expansion tanks, 269, 270–71
extension ladders, 38–40, 309
exterior house repairs, 317–34

fans, exhaust, 356–58
faucets, 240–51
    cartridge, 246–47
    compression-type, 240, 241–43, 249
    replacement of, 249–51
    rotating-ball, 245
    shower and tub, 247–49
    single-handle, 241, 245–47, 249
    spray attachments for, 248
    tipping-valve, 245–46
    two-handle, 243–45
    washerless, 240–41, 243–45
Federal Housing Administration, 372
fences, 333–34
files, 27–28
filters:
    for air-conditioning systems, 278–79

filters (*cont.*)
  for heating systems, 266
finishes:
  on floors, 143–47, 151–52
  on furniture, 381–424
  on plaster walls, 130
finishing nails, 43–44
fire alarms, 361, 372–74
fireplaces, 275–78
  smoking of, 276–78
fire stops, 70
fixtures:
  lighting, 210–12
  tile, 136–37
flakeboard, 33, 65–66, 67
flashing, roof, 310, 311, 312
flint paper, 37, 384
floats, wood, 290
floors, 143–53
  beams under, 67
  bridging strips for, 145
  care of, 153
  damaged boards in, 143–47
  finishing of, 143–47, 151–52
  insulation of, 338–39, 343
  parquet, 150
  repair of, 143–47
  sagging, 147–49
  sanding of, 149–51
  tiled, 155–57
floor sanders, 149–51
  disk-type, 149–50, 151
  drum-type, 149, 150–51
flues, fireplace, 275, 276, 278
fluorescent lights, 140, 215–17
flush tanks, 256–60
flux, soldering, 229
forced-flow tees, 267, 268
foundation walls, waterproofing of,
  302–4
framing out of walls, 66–72, 119, 343,
  344
framing squares, 19
French polishing, 409
furniture, 381–424
  antique finishes, 383, 413–15
  bleaches, 389–90
  burn marks on, 420–21
  chemical removers, 383, 386–89
  clear finishes, 405–17
  dents in, 421–22
  dowels, 391, 392
  enamels, 383, 411–12, 413
  gilding of, 416–17
  glazed finishes, 383, 413–15
  glues, 390–91, 393
  imitation wood-grain finishes,
    415–16

furniture (*cont.*)
  lacquers, 410, 412–13, 418
  linseed-oil finishes, 403, 409, 410
  marble, 423–24
  nails and screws, 393–94
  patching of, 396–97
  patina on, 383, 397
  penetrating sealers, 410–11
  polish finishes, 409–10
  refinishing liquids, 422–23
  repair of, 390–98, 417–23
  restoration of, 417–23
  sanding and scraping of, 384–86,
    397–98
  scratches on, 419–20
  sealing of, 400, 403
  shellac, 398, 408–9, 411, 418, 420
  stains, 383, 396, 399–405
  stripping of, 383–89, 422
  tack rags, 398, 399, 406
  types of finishes, 383, 386
  varnishes, 405–8, 410, 411, 418
  veneer, 394–96
  water marks, 418–19
furring strips, 130–31, 132
fuses, 197, 199–201

garage doors, 329–33
  adjustment of springs in, 331–33
garnet paper, 384
gauges, altitude, 269, 271
GFCIs (ground fault circuit interrupters), 204–6
gilding of furniture, 416–17
girders, roof, 74
glass:
  cutting of, 109
  safety, 110
  in windows, 99, 108–10
glazed finishes, 383, 413–15
glazier's points, 110
glazing compounds, 108, 177
glues, 52–55
  aliphic resin, 52–53, 391
  cement, 54
  epoxy, 53, 137, 296, 300, 301, 391
  instant, 54–55
  moisture-resistant, 53, 54, 55
  "one-drop," 54–55
  in refinished furniture, 390–91, 393
  resorcinol, 53
  white, 52–53
gold leaf, 416–17
gouges, 24
graphite, powdered, 88
grinding wheels, 25
ground fault circuit interrupters
  (GFCIs), 204–6

grounds, electrical, 199, 201–4, 208
grout, 133–34
gussets, plywood, 74
gutters, repair of, 178, 314–16
gypsum wallboard, *see* drywall

hacksaws, 23–24
hammers, 13–14
  ball-peen, 14
  claw, 13, 14
  impact, 26
  mallets, 14
hand drills, 28–30
  bits for, 29
  carpenter's braces, 29–30
  crank-operated, 29
  push-type, 29
  star, 50
hand sanders, 36–38, 385
  belt, 37–38
  disk, 36
  drills used as, 32, 36
  orbital, 37, 38
handsaws, 22–24
  backsaws, 23, 75, 320, 321
  compass, 23
  coping, 23
  crosscut, 22, 23
  cutting plywood with, 63
  hacksaws, 23–24
  keyhole, 23
  number of teeth in, 22, 24
  ripsaws, 22
hardboard, 65–66
  grades of, 65, 66
  panels, 130, 131
  perforated, 66
  tempered, 65–66
  working with, 67
hardware:
  for cabinets, 55–58
  for shelves, 58
hawks, masonry, 295, 296
header pieces, 67, 68
heaters, hot-water, 348, 349
heating systems, 264–79, 337
  filters for, 266
  fireplaces, 275–78
  forced-air, 265–67
  hot-water, 267–72
  steam, 272–74
  thermostats for, 269, 274–75
heat lamps, 108, 155, 238
hinges:
  for cabinets, 55–57
  for doors, 81–85, 89–92
  shims for, 82, 84, 85
hog bristle paintbrushes, 161–62

hollow ground saw blades, 33, 63
hollow-wall anchors, 47–49, 58
Home Remodelers Association, 378
house repairs, exterior, 317–34
humidifiers, 267
humidistats, 266
hydraulic cement, 300, 301, 304
hydrostatic pressure, 298
hyposulfite, 389

impact hammers, 26
insulation, 337–48
  in attics, 338–39, 340–43, 345
  in basements, 343–44
  batts and blankets of, 337, 340,
    342, 343
  in crawl spaces, 343–44, 345, 347
  of ducts, 347–48
  of floors, 338–39, 343
  foam panels, 344
  of hot-water heaters, 348, 349
  loose fill, 337, 338, 341
  of pipes, 237–38, 348, 349
  R-values for, 337, 338, 339, 341,
    348, 379
  vapor barriers for, 339, 340, 342
  ventilation and, 339, 345–47
  of walls, 342
insurance, liability, 380

jack planes, 26–27, 91
jack posts, telescoping, 147–49
jalousie windows, 99
jigsaws, 35–36
jointer planes, 26–27, 91
joints:
  braces for, 73, 74
  coped, 23, 75–78
  masonry, 295–96
  mitered, 23, 75, 78
  rabbet, 65, 67, 75, 108
  types of, 65, 72–75

keyhole saws, 23
"knee" walls, 70
knives:
  putty, 110, 127
  sharpening of, 25
knob-and-latch sets, 87

lacquers, 154, 162, 163
  furniture finished with, 410,
    412–13, 418
ladders, 38–40
  aluminum, 38
  extension, 38–40, 309
  grading of, 38
  step-, 38, 39
  use of, 38, 39–40

lamps, 212–15
leaks:
  in basements, 298–304
  in roofs, 307–8
levels, 19, 20
lights:
  indoor, 212–15
  fluorescent, 140, 215–17
  outdoor, 221
  timing devices for, 370, 371
lineman's pliers, 17
linseed-oil finishes, 403, 409, 410
locking pliers, 17–18
locks, 85, 86–89
  cylindrical, 87–88, 89, 92
  deadbolts for, 362–64
  for doors, 85, 86–89, 362–65
  latch bolts for, 86, 88
  misalignment of, 86–87
  mortised, 87, 89
  templates for, 88, 92
  tubular, 87, 88, 89, 92
  types of, 87–89, 361, 362–64
  for windows, 365–66
lumber, 61–62
  actual vs. nominal dimensions of, 61
  cutting of, 22, 33, 35, 36
  finishing of, 27, 61, 64, 66, 67
  grades of, 61–62
  panels, 130–32
  pressure-treated, 328, 333
  rotting of, 327, 328, 333–34
  splintering of, 26, 63–65

main, water, 225, 240
mallets, 14
marble, care of, 423–24
masking tape, 172
Masonite, 66
masonry, 294–96
  adhesives for, 292, 293
  anchors for, 49–51
  chisels for, 14, 26, 50
  drill bits for, 50, 312
  joints for, 294–96
  nails for, 43, 44–45, 49
  patching of, 291–92
  tuck pointing of, 285, 295
mastic adhesives, 135
MDO (Medium Density Overlaid)
  plywood, 63
measuring tools, 18–20
mechanic's pliers, 17
Medium Density Overlaid (MDO)
  plywood, 63
mesh, metal vs. plastic, 115
meters, electric, 198
mildew, 176

milled lumber, 61
mineral spirits, 163
mitered joints, 23, 75, 78
moisture:
  glues resistant to, 53, 54, 55
  paints and, 173, 179–80
  see also leaks
moldings, 26, 64, 132
  coping of, 23, 75–78
  mitering of, 23, 75, 78
  stop, 87, 90, 100, 101
  types of, 76
  working with, 75–78
Molly expansion anchors, 48
mortar, 285, 311
  joints, 294–96
mortises:
  cutting of, 24, 26
  in doors, 55, 83, 84, 85
muriatic acid, 261

nails, 43–44
  countersinking of, 43
  "dimpled," 120, 124
  driving of, 14
  masonry, 43, 44–45, 49
  popped, 123–24
  in refinished furniture, 393–94
  types of, 43–44, 72, 119
nail sets, 114
National Association of Home Builders, 378
National Sanitation Foundation
  (NSF), 232
needle-nose pliers, 17
nylon bristle paintbrushes, 162

occupancy, certificate of, 380
offset screwdrivers, 15–16
oilstones, 25
orbital sanders, 37, 38
outdoor painting, 173–82
  methods of, 178–79
  paints for, 173–75
  problems with, 179–82
  surface preparation for, 176–78
outlets, electrical, 171, 208–10,
  221–22
oxalic acid, 388

pads, painting, 161, 166–68
  "cutting in" with, 166–67
  types of, 166–67
  use of, 167, 170–71, 178
paintbrushes, 161–64
  bristles on, 161, 162
  choosing of, 161–63
  cleaning of, 163–64
  trimming with, 162, 169, 172–73

paintbrushes (*cont.*)
   use of, 171, 178
painting, 161–86
   of ceilings, 169–70
   of doors, 171
   outdoor, 173–82
   pads for, 161, 166–68
   rollers for, 161, 164–66
   spray, 182–86
   of walls, 170–71
   of windows, 171–73
paints, 161, 168, 174–75
   alkyd-base, 163, 166, 168, 169, 173, 174
   batch numbers for, 178
   enamel, 168, 383, 411–12, 413
   exterior, 173–75
   interior, 168
   latex, 160, 161, 162, 165, 168, 169, 173, 174
   moisture and, 173, 179–80
   oil-base, 163, 166, 168, 169, 173, 174, 175
   spray, 182–86
paneling, wood, 130–32
parquet floors, 150
particle board, 33, 65–66, 67
parting strips, 101, 102
patching:
   of carpets, 157–58
   of drywall, 124
   of furniture, 396–97
   of plaster, 127–30, 132
   of vinyl floor covering, 156–57
patina on furniture, 383, 397
patios, concrete, 288–91, 293
Pegboard, 66
pentachlorophenol, 328, 333
permits, building, 378
Phillips-head screws, 15, 45, 46
Phillips screwdrivers, 15, 16
pigtail electrical connectors, 205
pilot holes, drilling of, 28–29, 47
pipes, 227–35
   compression fittings for, 230–32
   copper, 228–32
   cracked, 239
   frozen, 237–40
   insulation of, 237–38, 348, 349
   sweating, 298
   threaded, 227–28
pipe wrenches, 21
planes, 26–27
   bench, 26–27, 91
   block, 26
   jack, 26–27, 91
   sharpening of, 25
   use of, 27, 91

plaster, patching of, 127–30, 132
plasterboard, *see* drywall
pliers, 16–18
   channel, 17
   diagonal cutting, 17
   lineman's, 17
   locking, 17–18
   needle-nose, 17
   slip-joint, 17
plier-wrenches, 17–18
plugs, electrical, 212–13
"plumber's friend," 252–53, 254
plumbing, 223–61
   cesspools, 260–61
   drains, 225, 251–54
   faucets, 240–51
   frozen pipes, 237–40
   noisy water lines, 235–37
   pipes and fittings, 227–35
   pliers for, 17
   septic tanks, 260–61
   toilets, 254–60
plumb lines, 67, 188–89
plungers, 252–53, 254
plywood, 55, 62–65
   grades of, 63
   panels, 130, 131
   working with, 63–65, 67
polybutylene (PB) pipes, 232–34
polyester filament paintbrushes, 162
polyethylene pipes, 232
polyurethane varnish, 152, 405, 407
polyvinyl acetate, 52
polyvinyl chloride (PVC) pipes, 234–35
pop rivets, 51
portland cement, 285, 295
power drills, 28, 31–33
   bits for, 32, 33
   reversing switches in, 33
   sanding attachment for, 32, 36
   screwdriver attachments for, 33
   variable-speed, 33
power saws, 33–36
   circular, 33–34, 35
   jigsaws, 35–36
   saber, 35–36, 63
   table, 63, 75
   use of, 35
pressure gauges, 269, 271
production paper, 37, 384
propane torches, 108, 155
pumice paste, 407–8
putty, wood, 64, 108, 410
   knives for, 110, 127
   use of, 396–97, 403–4

rabbet joints, 65, 67, 75, 108

radiators, 269
   bleeding of, 271–72
   cast-iron vs. convector, 269
rafter squares, 19
rasps, 27–28
reamalgamation of finishes, 418, 420
reaming out of holes, 28
receptacles, electrical, 205, 208
resorcinol glues, 53
ringed nails, 43, 44, 72, 119
ripsaws, 22
risers, stair, 153–54
rivet guns, 51–52
rollers, paint, 161, 164–66
   cleaning of, 165–66
   mohair-type, 164–65
   naps on, 164, 178
   use of, 165, 169–70, 171, 178
roofs, 305–16
   asphalt shingle, 308–10
   blistering of, 308, 312, 313
   drainage from, 298
   flashing on, 310, 311, 312
   flat, 312–14
   gutters, 178, 314–16
   leaks in, 307–8
   nails for, 43, 44
   roll material for, 307, 308, 312, 314
   slate, 311–12
   working on, 309
rottenstone paste, 408, 419
rotting of lumber, 327, 328, 333–34
rubber force cups, 252–53, 254
rulers, 18
rust stains, 178, 182
R-values for insulation, 337, 338, 339, 341, 348, 379

saber saws, 35–36, 63
sanders:
   floor, 149–51
   hand, 36–38, 385
sanding:
   of floors, 149–51
   of furniture, 384–86, 397–98
sanding blocks, 384, 398
sand mix, 285
sandpaper, 37, 384
sashes, window, 101–4
saw blades, *see* blades, saw
saws:
   hand, 22–24
   power, 33–36
scrapers, wood, 151, 385–86
screens, window, 115–16
screwdrivers, 15–16
   drills used as, 33
   flat-blade, 15, 16

screwdrivers (*cont.*)
jeweler's type, 15
offset, 15–16
Phillips, 15, 16
push-type, 16
screw-holding, 16
spiral ratchet, 16
"stubby," 15
use of, 16
screws, 45–46
countersinking of, 46
driving of, 47
in joints, 72
in refinished furniture, 393–94
types of, 15, 45–46
sealers, penetrating, 151, 400, 403
security, home, 359–74
burglary and break-ins, 361–72
smoke and fire alarms, 361, 372–74
septic tanks, 260–61
serrated nails, 72
shades, window, 111–13
shakes, 166, 175, 178
sheet metal, 14, 51
Sheetrock, *see* drywall
shellac, 67, 152, 162, 163
furniture finished with, 398, 408–9,
411, 418, 420
shelves, hardware for, 58
shims, 107
for hinges, 82, 84, 85
shingles:
house, 166, 175, 178, 321–22
roof, 307, 308–12
shower faucets, 247–49
sidewalks, concrete, 288–91, 293
siding, repair of, 66, 178, 319–21
silicon carbide paper, 37
silicone lubricants, 88, 95, 100, 107
silicone rubber adhesives, 53–54, 137
sized lumber, 61
Skotch fasteners, 73
slate roofs, 311–12
sliding doors, 93–95
slip-joint pliers, 17
smoke detectors, 372–74
ionization vs. photoelectric, 373
smoke shelves, 275, 276
snakes, plumber's, 251, 254, 255
sockets, lamp, 213–14
socket wrenches, 21
solar films and screens, 355, 356
soldering, sweat, 228–32
sole plates, 67, 68, 69
spackling compound, 64, 127, 128
spirit levels, 19, 20
splines, plastic, 110, 115, 116
spray painting, 182–86

spray painting (*cont.*)
equipment for, 182–84
techniques for, 184–86
squares, 18–19
stains, wood, 383, 396, 399–405
aniline, 400, 401, 402–3, 409
for shingles, 175
stairs, repair of, 153–55
Stanley Tools, 28
star drills, 50
steamers, wallpaper, 187
steel wool, 386, 397–98
stepladders, 38, 39
Stillson wrenches, 21
stop moldings, 87, 90, 100, 101
stucco, 285
patching of, 292–94
studs in partition walls, 66, 68, 69–70,
119
subflooring, repair of, 143, 144–47
subterranean termites, 326
sump pumps, 302
Surform tools, 28
switches, wall, 205, 206–7

tack rags, 398, 399, 406
tape:
for drywall seams, 121–23
masking, 172
templates, lock, 88, 92
termite problems, 324–29
treatment of, 327–29
Thermopane glass, 353
thermostats, 269, 274–75
threaded nails, 43, 44, 72, 119
tiles:
acoustical, 137, 140
ceiling, 137–38
ceramic, 132–37
floor, 155–57
timing devices for lights, 370, 371
tin oxide powder, 424
toggle bolts, 49, 58
toilets, 254–60
flush tanks for, 256–60
tools, 13–38
bargain vs. quality, 13
hand, 13–31
measuring and leveling, 18–20
power, 13, 31–38
selection of, 13
sharpening of, 25
Surform, 28
see also individual tools
transformers, 218–19, 220
traps, drain, 225, 251, 253
treads, stair, 153–55
trimmers, wallpaper, 191

trowels, 290, 295
trusses, roof, 74
try squares, 18–19
tubing, copper, 230–32
tubing cutters, 229, 230
tung-oil-base wood sealers, 423
turpentine, 163

UF cables, 221–22
unions, pipe, 228
urea formaldehyde, 53
USM corporation, 51
utility saw sets, 23

vapor barriers, 339, 340, 342
varnishes, 152, 175
furniture finished with, 405–8, 410,
411, 418
veneer, 63, 394–96
venetian blinds, 113–15
vents:
air, 180, 339, 345–47
waste, 225–27
vinyl floor covering, 156–57
voltmeters, 202, 209
volts, 197

wallboard, gypsum, *see* drywall
wallcoverings, 186–93
cutting and pasting of, 188–93
preparing walls for, 186–87
walls:
condensation in, 345–47
coverings for, 186–93
insulation of, 342
interior, 119–32
non-load-bearing, 70
painting of, 170–71
partition, 66–72, 119, 343, 344
plaster, 127–30, 132
water hammer, 235–37
water main, 225, 240
water-pump pliers, 17
water supply system, 225–27, 235–37
waxes, paste, 88, 153, 408, 418
weatherstripping, 99, 349–53
of doors, 351–53
of windows, 350–51
wells, dry, 298, 299
wet-or-dry sandpaper, 37
whetstones, 25
white glues, 52–53
windows, 97–116
awning, 99, 108
casement, 99, 104–7
double-hung, 99–104
glass panes in, 99, 108–10
glazing of, 108–10, 353

windows (*cont.*)
  jalousie, 99
  locks for, 365–66
  metal-frame, 110
  painting of, 171–73
  sashes of, 101–4
  screens for, 115–16
  shades for, 111–13
  sliding, 99, 107–8
  solar films and screens for, 355, 356
  sticking of, 99–101, 104–5
  storm, 99, 353–54

windows (*cont.*)
  venetian blinds for, 113–15
  weatherstripping of, 350–51
wire brushes, 388–89
wire cutters, 17
wire nails, 43, 44
wiring, aluminum vs. copper, 205
wood, woodworking, *see* lumber; *and specific tools*
wrenches, 20–22
  adjustable, 17, 20
  Allen, 21
  box-end, 20

wrenches (*cont.*)
  combination, 20–21
  fixed, 20
  open-end, 20
  pipe, 21
  plier-, 17–18
  socket, 21
  use of, 22
wythes, 278

zinc naphthenate, 328, 333
zoning, heat, 265, 269, 274